Authors of Their Own Lives

D1500875

Authors of Their Own Lives

Intellectual Autobiographies by Twenty American Sociologists

Edited and with an Introduction by
Bennett M. Berger

Essays by
Reinhard Bendix · Bennett M. Berger
Jessie Bernard · James S. Coleman
Donald R. Cressey · Cynthia Fuchs Epstein
John Gagnon · Herbert J. Gans · Nathan Glazer
Andrew M. Greeley · Joseph Gusfield
Dean MacCannell · Gary T. Marx
David Riesman · Barbara Rosenblum
Alice S. Rossi · Guenther Roth · Pepper Schwartz
Pierre L. van den Berghe · Dennis Wrong

UNIVERSITY OF CALIFORNIA PRESS
Berkeley · Los Angeles · Oxford

University of California Press
Berkeley and Los Angeles, California

University of California Press, Ltd.
Oxford, England

©1990 by
The Regents of the University of California

First Paperback Printing 1992

Library of Congress Cataloging-in-Publication Data

Authors of their own lives : intellectual autobiographies by twenty American
sociologists / edited and with an introduction by Bennett M. Berger.
   p. cm.
  Includes index.
  ISBN 0-520-06556-5
  1. Sociology—Biographical methods. 2. Sociologists—United
States—Biography. I. Berger, Bennett M.
HM24.S568 1990
301'.092'2—dc 19   89-5117
                                                        CIP

Printed in the United States of America
1 2 3 4 5 6 7 8 9

The paper used in this publication meets the minimum requirements of
American National Standard for Information Sciences—Permanence of
Paper for Printed Library Materials, ANSI Z39.48-1984. ⊗™

For Donald R. Cressey
and for Barbara Rosenblum,
neither of whom lived to see
this book in print. I doubt
that they ever met, but I think
they would have liked each other.
They were both tough and tender;
hard heads, soft hearts.

Contents

Contributors

Reinhard Bendix (1916–) is a former president of the American Sociological Association and emeritus professor at the University of California, Berkeley, where he served the departments of sociology and political science. Among his many books are *Work and Authority in Industry*, *Max Weber: An Intellectual Portrait*, *Embattled Reason*, and *Kings or People*.

Bennett M. Berger (1926–) is professor of sociology at the University of California, San Diego, and the author of *Working-Class Suburb*, *Looking for America*, and *The Survival of a Counterculture*.

Jessie Bernard (1903–) says she does not mind being called the doyenne of American sociology. She is the author or editor of literally scores of books on women, marriage, the family, and other subjects. Retired from her professorship but still as active as many sociologists half her age, she has had many honors bestowed on her. She lives in Washington, D.C.

James S. Coleman (1926–) is University Professor of Sociology at the University of Chicago. He has done distinguished work in a wide variety of sociological fields, from mathematical methods to rational choice theory. His many works include *The Adolescent Society*, *Union Democracy*, *Community Conflict*, *Introduction to Mathematical Sociology*, and *Longitudinal Data Analysis*.

Donald R. Cressey (1919–1987) was professor of sociology at the University of California, Santa Barbara, and the first dean of its College of

Letters and Science. The most important of his many studies in criminology are *Other People's Money* and *Theft of the Nation: The Structure and Operations of Organized Crime in America.*

Cynthia Fuchs Epstein (1933–) is professor of sociology at the Graduate Center of the City University of New York and a former president of the Eastern Sociological Society. Her research on women in the professions, business, and politics has produced such books as *Women in Law, Access to Power, Woman's Place,* and most recently *Deceptive Distinctions.*

John Gagnon (1931–) was the first sociologist on the staff of the Kinsey Institute for Sex Research, and he is presently professor of sociology at the State University of New York, Stony Brook. He has written extensively on sex (much of it with William Simon) in books like *Sexual Deviance, Sexual Conduct,* and *Human Sexualities.*

Herbert J. Gans (1927–) is Robert S. Lynd Professor of Sociology at Columbia University and a former president of the American Sociological Association. Trained both as a sociologist and a planner, his research interests include urban studies, ethnicity, and mass communications. He is the author of seven books, the most recent of which is *Middle American Individualism: The Future of Liberal Democracy.*

Nathan Glazer (1923–) is professor of education and sociology at Harvard University. He made his mark early as a co-author (with David Riesman and Reuel Denney) of *The Lonely Crowd,* and (with Daniel P. Moynihan) *Beyond the Melting Pot.* Among his other books are *American Judaism, The Social Basis of Communism, Remembering the Answers, Affirmative Discrimination,* and *Ethnic Dilemmas.*

Andrew M. Greeley (1928–) is professor of sociology at the University of Arizona, a research associate at the National Opinion Research Center, a priest of the Archdiocese of Chicago, and an author of best-selling novels. The most recent of his many sociological works is *Religious Indicators,* and among his many works of fiction are *God Game, The Final Planet, Angel Fire,* and *Love Song.*

Joseph Gusfield (1923–) is professor of sociology at the University of California, San Diego, and a former president of the Pacific Sociological Association and the Society for the Study of Social Problems. He has worked most extensively in the fields of alcohol studies and social movements. His first book, *Symbolic Crusade,* has become a classic. His most recent books are *The Culture of Public Problems* and (in *The Heritage of Sociology* series) *Kenneth Burke on Symbols and Society.*

Dean MacCannell (1940–) is professor of applied behavioral sciences at the University of California, Davis, and co-editor of *The American Journal of Semiotics.* He is the author of *The Tourist: A New Theory of the Leisure Class* and (with Juliet Flower MacCannell) *The Time of the Sign.*

Gary T. Marx (1938–) is professor of sociology at MIT in the Departments of Urban Studies and Humanities. *Protest and Prejudice* was his first book. His most recent is *Undercover: Police Surveillance in America.* In between, he has edited or co-edited several books and writes for a wide variety of scholarly journals and popular media. In 1989 he was named the American Sociological Association's Jensen Lecturer and he kayaked Idaho's River of No Return. He has returned.

David Riesman (1909–) is retired from the Henry Ford II professorship of the social sciences at Harvard University. Trained as a lawyer, he became a sociologist at the University of Chicago, where he taught for many years. He is the senior author of *The Lonely Crowd* and many other books on the sociology of education and on the character and culture of Americans.

Barbara Rosenblum (1943–1988) taught at Stanford University and in Vermont College's graduate program. She was the author of *Photographers at Work: A Sociology of Photographic Styles.* Before her untimely death she was working with a colleague on a book to be called *Cancer in Two Voices.*

Alice S. Rossi (1922–) is Harriet Martineau Professor of Sociology at the University of Massachusetts (Amherst) and former president of both the American Sociological Association and the Eastern Sociological Society. Her primary fields of study are family and kinship, sex and gender, and biosocial science. Among her major works are *Parenting and Offspring Development, Gender and the Life Course, Feminists in Politics,* and *Academic Women on the Move.*

Guenther Roth (1931–) is professor of sociology at Columbia University. He has written *The Social Democrats in Imperial Germany* and *Max Weber's Vision of History* (with Wolfgang Schluchter) and is editor and translator (with Klaus Wittich) of the three-volume *Economy and*

Society by Max Weber. He recently contributed a long introduction to a new edition of Marianne Weber's biography of Max Weber.

Pepper Schwartz (1945–) is professor of sociology and adjunct professor of psychiatry and behavioral sciences at the University of Washington, Seattle. Her writings include *American Couples* (with Philip Blumstein), *Women at Yale* (with Janet Lever), *Sexual Scripts* (with Judith Long Laws), and *Gender in Intimate Relationships* (with Barbara J. Risman).

Pierre L. van den Berghe (1933–) is professor of sociology and anthropology at the University of Washington, Seattle. His work on race, ethnicity, and sociobiology has taken him to Africa and Latin America. Among his many books are *South Africa: A Study in Conflict, Age and Sex in Human Societies, Human Family Systems,* and *The Ethnic Phenomenon.*

Dennis Wrong (1923–) is professor of sociology at New York University. He writes regularly for many general intellectual magazines and is the author of *Population and Society, Skeptical Sociology,* and *Power: Its Forms, Bases, and Uses.*

Introduction

It seems apt to preface what I have to say about autobiography and sociology by noting that my career as a sociologist can be understood as a series of misinterpretations. When I published my first book, *Working-Class Suburb*, I was quickly identified as an urban sociologist, invited to conferences on urban sociology, and often asked to contribute to symposia on it—although I had never had a course on the subject and although the book, and the research on which it was based, came out of my interest not in cities but in stereotypes of suburbia by intellectuals.

When my research interest turned toward youth and adolescence, some thought of me as a sociologist of education because the major institutional setting of youth was high schools and colleges. I was invited to speak to parent-teacher associations, provide advice to parents of troubled teenagers, and serve as a pundit on student rebellion by publications like the *New York Times Magazine*—although I had never had a course on the sociology of education and although my interest in youth had been stimulated by comparative and historical reading on age grading and by the popularity of the generation concept, also promoted by intellectuals and which I had first encountered in Karl Mannheim and José Ortega y Gasset.

When I began to study hippie communes and communal child-rearing, I found myself identified as a family sociologist. Although my attention to communes came out of my interest in deviant youth and the history of countercultures, I was invited to speak at the Groves Conference and other national organizations of family scholars. My work was represented in some of the standard texts and anthologies of family studies—although I had never had a course on the family and did not know its literature at all thoroughly.

Now, engaged for the past few years in a project to collect a group of essays in intellectual autobiography, I have noticed a tendency to impute to me a methodological interest in the use of life history data—an approach that goes back to the early days of Chicago sociology. Just recently I was asked by one of the editors of *Theory and Society* to contribute a piece on the use of life histories to the twentieth anniversary issue of that journal. I respectfully declined, informing him that my interest in autobiography had in fact partly developed out of my efforts to cope with some problems of bias in interpretive sociology, but mostly out of my efforts to teach graduate students how to read sociological theory to get a sense of the *presence* of the theorist in the text, learn to read between the lines, and hence more fully appreciate the meanings projected in them.

A series of misinterpretations, then. It has taken me far too many years to understand that what I have always been interested in was the *culture* of the groups to which I was attracted and the ways in which that culture was generated, sustained, and changed by the material circumstances of its group settings, the structure of whose accessible resources functioned as constraints and incentives on actors called on to justify or defend their efforts to do things to (or with) other actors in ways that usually produced palpable consequences, intended and not. I am, in short, an unrepentant generalist. Even when I passed fifty, to those who asked what kind of sociologist I was, I was still in the habit of replying frivolously that I was too young to specialize.

Now I have unambiguously arrived at the irreversible status of senior sociologist. One of the privileges of that arrival is to turn my attention to the group among whom I have spent my adult life as a professional; and in order to say something about the culture of sociology, studying the lives of sociologists (or what they say about their lives—which is not the same thing) seems a good place to start. When I became editor of *Contemporary Sociology*, I persuaded the university administration to fund two graduate students as half-time assistants for the journal. The pedagogic justification I offered was that over and above what they learned in classes or at the library, the students would learn as much sociology (if not more) just sitting around the office listening to my colleagues and me discuss which books were (and were not) worth reviewing or featuring, and which reviewers to select (and not to select) for which books. Sociological theory teaches that to learn about the culture of something is to learn about the thing itself.

All this, I admit, sounds rather defensive, and defensiveness is a quality not much admired in sociological writing—or any writing. Still, I hope I will be forgiven a certain defensiveness in introducing this book. It was obvious to me that asking sociologists to write about their lives constituted a substantial departure from the standard practices of academic writing, which constrain sociologists to keep themselves as decently or discreetly invisible as possible. Outside the entertainment pages, narcissism does not have good press, particularly in those fields whose "discipline" recognizes the logical irrelevance of the personal qualities of the author to the objective qualities of the work, and a radical separation between them.

One of the aims of this book is to narrow that gap—not to eliminate it entirely; the distinction, after all, is a sound and important one. That aim is to render the presence of the person in the work, the author in the authored, to the extent that the subject is capable of revealing it. I know that not everyone agrees about the wholesomeness of such a project. Different (and opposing) views about the autonomy of the text have been put forward, in the humanities, by the New Critics more than a generation ago and by the poststructuralists in the 1970s and 1980s, and in the social sciences by those committed to the propriety of impersonality in the genres of the monograph and the social-science journal article. Such views have always seemed to me of considerable interest in determining what is or is not appropriate, formally and aesthetically, to a given genre, but they should alert the skepticism of those of us who want to avoid the analytic dangers (there are several) of reifying cultural forms or taking them for granted. One good way of flexing the muscles of that skepticism is by inquiring into the conditions that generate, sustain, and transform those genres.

How, for example, did this book get off the ground? I was writing a long essay on the history of the relations between political and cultural radicalism when I got stuck and reread what I had written. I was appalled by how easily I could see through my own biases. Expecting that others would see through them as easily, I adopted the routine defense of responding to anticipated criticism. (Goffman and Bourdieu are masters of this device.) I started writing what I conceived as a preface to the main work, intending to cue my imagined readers to my own biases, their probable sources, and how I attempted to control or otherwise cope with them. Soon I had the makings of a short autobiographical essay about my own intellectual development.

It was only then that the first glimmering of the idea for this book came to me—that a collection of such essays by a variety of sociologists might be a valuable enterprise. Valuable how? For one thing it might help students to become sophisticated readers more quickly. As a teacher I had been recurrently frustrated by how long that process normally takes. I could remember, in my own student days, how easily I was persuaded by nearly every theorist I read, regardless of whether I was told that I could not be a Durkheimian and a Weberian at the same time, or a Tocquevillian and a Marxist. Read in isolation and without background, each important writer makes a persuasive case to an innocent student. Under normal conditions of study it can take years, even decades, to become attuned to the hidden agendas, the strategic omissions, the invisible antagonists, the metaphysical pathos (to use Gouldner's phrase, borrowed from Arthur Lovejoy) in a piece of sociological prose. Hence it can take years to become a critical reader, attentive not only to the objective historical contexts in which a writer writes but also to what Pierre Bourdieu calls the *habitus:* the experienced milieu whose more or less unreflectively internalized culture shapes the sensibility evident to a close reader in a piece of prose, and familiarity with which enables us to say of its author that we know, metaphorically speaking, where she's coming from, if not quite where she's going to.

But in addition, biographical information may tell us literally where a writer is coming from and thereby supply an added dimension for understanding texts. Raymond Aron comments that Comte did not think it necessary to leave his apartment during the revolution of 1848, so confident was he that his theorizing had predicted the important events occurring in the street. Frank Manuel's account of the lives of Saint-Simon and Comte (both of them textbook cases of deviance) made reading them a richer experience for me and humanizes them for students easily intimidated by the prospect of reading "classics" written by historically hallowed figures not easily imagined as flawed human beings. Weber asserts his "ethic of responsibility" with almost enough passion to make it an ethic of ultimate ends; the paradox of his passion for *detachment* is made salient and intriguing by that mysterious neurosis that interrupted his teaching career. These days many undergraduates have to be told that the rhetoric of Veblen's *Theory of the Leisure Class* is ironic; if they knew something of his life, or of Edwardian literary style, it would be easier for them to pick up on his ironies.

On the whole (despite some recent evidence to the contrary), contemporary sociologists are not very viable commercially as subjects for biographers. But autobiography, even allowing for some inevitable selectivity, distortions of retrospective reconstruction, posturing, and simple (or not so simple) misremembering of events, provides evidence of an author's self-image, which is seldom irrelevant to the sensibility evident in the text. This constitutes a response, if not exactly a solution, to the problem posed by Pierre Bourdieu who, by titling an essay of his "L'Illusion biographique" (1985), intended to suggest that life is messy but autobiography is linear and orderly, with a coherence imposed less by the facts of life than by the autobiographer's need to make sense of them. "Ideologists of their own lives" is Bourdieu's phrase describing what autobiographers do. (The phrase also provided the seed from which the title of this book grew.) Sociologists and their readers, however, often have especially good antennae for detecting ideology and are not easily deceived by it. Indeed, several of the autobiographers represented here are well aware of the problem and attempt to be reflexive about it.

Moreover, it is often possible for a careful reader to see meanings in events, accounts, and other information on a life course that the author who provides them may not see. Let me cite just two examples from the many in the essays contained here. Pierre van den Berghe describes at some length the generations of physicians and biologists in his family—particularly the influence of one of his grandfathers. But he never quite makes an explicit connection between his own mid-career turn toward sociobiology and his family's tradition, against which he regards himself as somewhat rebellious. David Riesman, from a patrician Philadelphia family, describes his mother's severe distinction between the "first rate" (great artists and perhaps a few great scientists) and the "second rate" and her aesthetic disdain for even those prestigious professionals who do the practical work of the world. But he does not explicitly connect this maternal aristocratism to his choice to devote the bulk of his teaching career to the general education of talented undergraduates at two elite universities rather than to the professional training of workaday attorneys as a professor of law, in which capacity he began his teaching career and which is usually regarded as more prestigious than teaching undergraduates.

Most sociologists, in fact, do not work in Thomas Kuhn's "normal science" style, immersed in the search for solutions to curious puzzles that the accumulating corpus of knowledge has left unsolved. Most of us pursue our ideas, formulate our hypotheses, and do our research in ways, and from sources, connected to what we care about and are moved by—which of course does not render the work any less objective. That is what Weber meant by *value relevance,* and what I mean by saying that most of us do not do alienated work—at least not most of the time. I hope that students will read this book because it provides access to contexts that can enhance their understanding of texts and their authors, and that journeymen academic sociologists themselves will encourage students to read it because professors have a stake in the early sophistication of their students as readers.

But imagine the worst. Suppose that the interest of readers turns out to be at least partly prurient; suppose that they have merely a gossipy interest in what eminent professor so-and-so "is really like"; suppose they are only looking for the inside dope to penetrate the passive voice and other façades of impersonality that dominate the prose of academics. Do these attitudes weaken the serious intent of the book? I think not. Perhaps a prurient interest is better than none. Gossip, after all, is talk (even malicious talk) about persons rather than issues, problems, or structures. To "bring man back in," as George Homans urged many years ago, may risk bringing gossip back in; and it is perhaps not inadvertent that Homans has published a full-length autobiography. To want to know, then, what professor so-and-so is really like may not be as banal as it seems at first. Knowing what he is really like can palpably affect a student's future. One of the major contributions of Jim Coleman's brilliant essay on his graduate-student days is his evocation of Paul Lazarsfeld, who was usually so full of ideas that he could not possibly pursue all of them systematically and was hence continually on the lookout to recruit or co-opt promising students and junior colleagues as collaborators.

The relevance of gossip and other inside dope is transparent in the spate of autobiography and memoir, especially, for example, among former presidential staff members, who recount private conversations and other events that take place in insulated offices and other inaccessible places and regarding which public records are not usually left—or if left, are marked "classified" and sometimes destroyed. Such information increases in importance as the discrepancies widen between what actually happens, what we know, what we may be officially informed of, and what we are free to say publicly. Of course we all know less than we need to know. But as receptacles of privileged information we also know more than the legitimate ways of expressing what we know can contain. And as scholars, I presume, we all have interests in seeing an increase in the number and variety of containers. Autobiography may be one of them.

But in addition to my hopes that this book will help create sophisticated readers more quickly and demonstrate the contextual relevance of autobiographical data to texts and careers, I hope that it will have influence on the future practice of sociologists. I do not mean merely the cliché of strengthening humanist (as against positivist) sociology; neither term is a favorite of mine. In my lexicon *humanist* refers to a certain moral and aesthetic quality of mind, whereas *positivist* refers to a particular epistemology (and perhaps its associated research methods). Whatever the tensions between them, I have never been persuaded that it was necessary to give up one for the other. Most sociologists will at least pay lip service to the idea that they are in fact part of the social reality they describe and analyze. When pressed, they will even admit that they may contribute to the construction of the realities their methods assume already exist "out there." But most do not *write* as if that were the case, except occasionally in prefaces, appendixes, or postscripts. In my last book I made some halting use of the autobiographical mode throughout the text—in effect attempting to take readers by the hand and bring them along with me to share some of the experience of doing field research. I told stories about what happened to me; about getting access to sites and data; about the interpersonal complexities that sometimes develop in long-term participant observation, and personal ambivalence about what to do next; about coping with resistance by respondents; and about thinking through the unanticipated problems of interpretation, then rethinking them as the research went along, all the while letting the reader in on the interior dialogues.

That more sociologists do not write candidly or well about their lives, work, and working lives is partly an expression of the hegemony that the rhetoric of impersonality exercises. It begins so early that most of my first-year graduate students in sociological theory have great difficulty complying with my request that before they undertake serious formal analysis they write five- or six-page weekly papers recording their immediate responses, associations, likes, dislikes, and so on, vis-à-vis the assigned reading. They simply do not believe me when I tell them that I want them to write on contemporary theory in their own natural voices (which I do to help them absorb serious theorizing into their own *routine* modes of thinking) rather than ape the language of the professional journals—thus requiring a cognitive blip in order to shift between spontaneous thinking and seminar talk or journal talk. The rhetoric of impersonality, I think, has been successful less for the bulk of reliable knowledge of social structure it has accumulated than for the powerful claim it in principle staked for sociology to the status of science, and hence to institutionalization in universities, and the considerable professional benefits that status carries with it.

Universities generally have difficulty accommodating in their academic curricula subject matters not clearly categorizable as arts or sciences, with their own accumulated "literatures." Journalism is a perennially disdained stepchild, often segregated in professional schools. The humanities are recurrently buffeted in one or the other direction. When the direction is toward arts, defenses of the humanities as the moral and aesthetic antennae of the nation become routine parts of the lecture repertoire of their senior spokespersons. When the direction is toward science, language, philosophy, history, and criticism turn toward "theory," and the rigor of one's logic or research design replaces substantive insight, discovery, or narrative grace as the major criterion of performance. Note William Irwin Thompson's prescient (and edgy) characterization of MIT's pride in its humanities program, where, as he puts it, "literature becomes linguistics."

Moreover, the rhetoric of academic impersonality has an elective affinity to the rhetoric of bureaucracies, in which most academics work. About fifty years ago there was a major shift in the social sciences in which most practitioners gave up talking to general intellectual audiences in favor of talking to each other in technical languages that excluded most nonprofessionals. In several respects that was a good bargain but some of its costs have been prolixity, unreadableness, and an obscurity not warranted by the complexity of what is talked about. *Oversimplification* is now a common term of reproach in academic discussions; everyone is against oversimplification. But there is no parallel term nearly as frequently used to describe the opposite phenomenon, which surely occurs as often, if not more so. Mystification, ethereality, and slovenly prose are probably less often subject to negative critical sanctions from within than oversimplification.

The autobiographical mode could be an effective antidote to some of this excessive professionalism. There seems to be something about the witnesslike character of the first-person singular (I was there; this is what I did; here is what happened—to me and to others) that transforms indifferent, obscure, or ethereal writers into good, or at least intelligible, ones. Social science has a potentially substantial audience, but we reach it so poorly in part because good social scientists often take foolish pride in their inaccessibility. We do not have to reach the nonprofessional audiences who care about our work because universities reward scholars for "technical" achievements and look with some skepticism on popular success. Nevertheless, each of the social sciences shelters a small crew of writers (seldom among the most prestigious in their disciplines) who have real audiences—writers who are read less because their readers need to keep up with the literature than because they believe that these writers have something important or compelling to say. I think there could be more such writers, and a book like this just might encourage their liberation from the impersonal language of bureaucracy. Whatever else it is, autobiography is personal, and I hope that sociology will become more accessible as its practitioners become less invisible. It might even help reduce our dependence on popularization—and our ritual complaints against it.

But in saying these things, which I know are contentious (and are surely not being said here for the first time), I can already hear some of the countercontentions before they are made, rebuttals even to contentions I have *not* made. Some readers will see a hidden agenda in my remarks, a code that derogates discretion and restraint. It will be assumed that I am making a raggedly veiled argument against professional detachment and hard-won criteria of scholarly accomplishment, and against objectivity, disinterestedness, elite standards, and academic asceticism. By contrast, imputed to me will be an effort to encourage narcissistic self-indulgence and "letting it all hang out"; for romanticism, against classicism; for Dionysus, against Apollo: "California sociology."

There may be a few kernels of truth in these contrasts, but I regard such polarities as banal, and I intend no such stark oppositions. They are in fact ideal types; real cases, of course, fall somewhere between them. Readers will note that despite my critical comments about academic impersonality, I have made them in the conventional academic style, and that dualism is as it should be. The essays contained here also cover a fairly wide range between these poles, and most of them show some oscillation between them.

Still, my project does contain latent cultural biases of the sort included in what Herbert Gans has described as taste cultures, and it seems likely that some readers, partisans of one taste culture, may be offended by the essays that represent another. Whenever questions of taste are raised (they are raised often by autobiography), one can be certain that important cultural issues are at stake—symbols and meanings necessarily taken for granted in order that discourse may be civilly conducted. Breaching them, therefore, is always potentially volatile, particularly among scholars, whose stately and impersonal modes of discourse are important conditions of the privileges accorded them as part of their academic freedom.

One early reader of the manuscript of this book, for example, seemed deeply offended by an essay whose author made an intimate sexual reference. One could almost feel the reader's recoil: "Do we *really* need to know that . . . ?" In fact there is relatively little intimate detail, private confession, or grievance expressed in these essays; not much talk about sex, spouses, or the adult family life of sociologists, particularly where traumatic or other painful experiences are involved. Those seeking titillation should look elsewhere.

But taste cultures are plural, even in the academy. Since the end of World War II there have been important changes in the composition of the American professoriat, and professorial sensibilities are now more diverse than they once were—partly an expression of some of the mobility stories told in this book. A second early reader of the manuscript, rather than being offended by intimate references and revelations, was instead bored by a few of the more statesmanly essays recounting the institutional events of a career. Tastes differ, and I dare say that the wide variety of essays in this book virtually guarantees that no single reader will like all of them unless he or she is capable of a huge Geertzian effort to appreciate "the native's point of view." As autobiographers, we are all natives.

Yet the importance of good taste was a major theme in the correspondence between me and Matilda Riley when she was planning the 1986 American Sociological Association meetings on "lives." This anticipated anxiety about taste is in one sense understandable because it is obvious that invoking the personal (as autobiography must) poses some threat to values taken for granted that are embedded in the stately rhetoric of academic discourse; and that rhetoric is usually experienced by its practitioners as self-evident good taste that needs no defending. But in another sense the anxiety is surprising because one of the major assets of microsociological research has been its demonstration that face-to-face interaction among real persons may have permanent relevance to the outcomes of macrosociological research, whose findings about patterns or structures are often presented as quantified covariation in operationalized indicators of abstract variables. The relevance, moreover, may be either supportive of the findings (by providing an account of how the macro covariations are "produced" in face-to-face interaction) or critical of them (by providing a validity-based critique of the misleading inferences made from them). As this book was taking shape, I was in fact cautioned by several friends and colleagues about the boundaries of good taste in autobiographical writing. I have duly noted those cautions. At the same time it seems appropriate to note that while prudence dictates *some* respect for extant canons of good taste, serious inquiry must not allow itself to be entirely governed by them. In fact, when sociological inquiry is seriously constrained by conventional wisdom, its typical practice has been to make the conventional wisdom problematic by questioning the assumptions on which it rests—in this case by implicitly asking what good taste reveals, what it obscures, and why—as Bourdieu has done explicitly and brilliantly in *Distinction.*

Class and ethnicity are (unsurprisingly for sociologists) salient themes in many of the essays in this book, and as both Gans and Bourdieu have shown, taste is closely correlated with them. Will anyone be offended if I say that the autobiographers represented here tend to write more personally, more intimately, if they come from poverty or are Jewish, and that the tendency is strengthened if they come from poverty *and* are Jewish? Is it absurd to say that John Gagnon writes like a Jew? He does in effect confess to being a philosemite—something I remember the anthropologist John Bennett writing about very poignantly in *Commentary* many years back, faced as he was with growing up in New York, where an intellectual's "natural" community was predominantly composed of Jews.

Exactly what the connections are, however, between class or ethnicity and tastes for the personal or impersonal, the intimate or the institutional, the blunt or the polite, may be very elusive. John Cuddihy provided a very complex (and controversial) explanation some years ago in his wonderfully titled *The Ordeal of Civility.* On the other hand, it may be nothing more complex than that the children of poor immigrants have little other than their personal, domestic, or neighborhood lives to talk about, whereas the wellborn, heirs to a greater variety of institutional embeddedness, develop a more stately understanding of their lives. In the essays by Dennis Wrong (son of the Canadian ambassador to Washington) and David Riesman readers will note the famous well-connected names and established institutions that form a natural backdrop to their early lives. There may have been some doubt about *what* they would achieve in their lives, but that they would achieve something significant appears not to have been in question. Patrician families seem often to hand down to their children a certain grace and easy confidence as valuable as their more material assets—although I understand that they probably hand down distinctive burdens as well.

For those starting near the bottom, it may be that rapid social mobility, with its sometimes sharp breaks in the experience of milieus, requires a self-conscious effort to integrate them and generates a more poignant and distressful mode of retrospective understanding than lives characterized by cultural stability, in which the procession from event to event is more continuous or regularized. Don Cressey's essay is preoccupied with poverty and class, with whether people are "classy," and there is an almost audible *whew!* as he concludes each episode of his narrative with an "I made it!" It was not clear that he would. Barbara Rosenblum's essay is a near model of the pain and sense of awkwardness (some of "the hidden injuries of class") as one moves up and away from the milieu of one's birth. It goes some distance to suggest why, in Bourdieu's terms, some people choose to remain in the habitus of their birthright despite the talent and opportunity to move up and out. By contrast, Gary Marx's mobility story would sound almost like that of a premature yuppie, were it not for the unusual candor and rue of his tale of early spectacular success that suddenly ends—or at least slows down. John Gagnon describes his family's descent from respectable poverty to "raggedy-ass poor," and the University of Chicago inadvertently appears as an all but unattainable Olympus, from within whose mists a mysterious promise of a better life beckons. A similar image appears in Joseph Gusfield's thoughtful essay, and Chicago's great university played this role for more than a few sociologists born poor. There are several archetypal stories of American social mobility in this book, and none of them is without its touches of poignance. But there are no self-congratulatory huffings and puffings about raising oneself up by the bootstraps. These are, after all, sociologists, who know more than a little not only about the power of social stratification but also about the role of historical structures of opportunity in the shaping of lives.

Nevertheless, lives are more complicated than social categories; too many variables intersect at a specific time and place in an individual's life to permit easy generalization about class or ethnicity. Cynthia Epstein and Pepper Schwartz, for example, each of them born to upper middle-class Jewish families, each of them accomplished sociologists and feminists, reveal themselves differently. Epstein is grave and reflective, very much the New York intellectual. Schwartz is pert, perky, scatological, and bright-eyed, still showing traces of the cheerleader she refuses to apologize for having been in high school and college. Reinhard Bendix and Guenther Roth, born to middle-class families in Germany, emigrated to the United States in their early adulthood. Both describe a gradual transformation of their interest in politics into an interest in political sociology. Yet Bendix titles his essay "How I Became an *American* Sociologist" (my emphasis), and he speaks and writes English with hardly a trace of the accent of his native language. Roth's German accent, by contrast, is apparently permanent, not only in his speech but also in the contours of his thought. Herbert Gans, from an assimilated German-Jewish family, left Germany at age twelve and not only confesses that he has no German culture in him but also acknowledges that he has become an expert on American popular culture. Dean MacCannell, American as apple pie, tries to answer the question of why a "French" intellectual (as he conceives himself) takes a doctorate in rural sociology and teaches at a university famous for its agricultural school. It would be hard to imagine two early lives more different than Barbara Rosenblum's and Dennis Wrong's. Yet each of them found in New York's bohemia of art and intellect a transitional shelter between what they had been and what they were yet to become. Rosenblum and Nathan Glazer share poverty, New York, and Jewishness as part of their backgrounds, yet Glazer's intellectual perspectives and career development have far more in common with Wrong and Riesman than with Rosenblum. Lives, as I said, are more complex than categories, and Alice Rossi's careful distinctions among period effects, cohort effects, and maturational effects, in an essay sometimes touching, sometimes subtle, sometimes brilliant, and sometimes all three together, may help explain some of that complexity.

Age is also a prominent consideration in many of the essays included here. Readers will notice that the authors in this book write much more revealingly about their childhood and adolescence than about their adult lives after starting their careers. Although there are exceptions (Coleman, Greeley), this tendency may be an obvious expression of the normal prudence expected of academics (indeed of most professionals) regarding their current career involvements. But something more comes from these pages: it is as if some latent consensus in our culture defines childhood and adolescence as *proper* focuses of retrospective reflection, whereas more recent periods of one's life represent practical accommodations to relatively congealed present circumstances, or a mere playing out of experience-shaping forces of much earlier origin (although Rossi's essay is surely an exception).

This book is full of memorable moments in each of its essays. If it does nothing else, it shows that, at our best, sociologists can write as well as any academic group. Guenther Roth tells us that he is still distressed to see people reclining on beaches and in parks because they remind him of the bodies lying in the streets of Darmstadt after a saturation bombing in World War II. Don Cressey worked part-time as a baker while he was in high school (a good craft, he thought, for a poor boy without prospects), and when he finally did go to college he was attracted to chemistry and was good in the lab because it was like baking: mixing the ingredients of a recipe—only very carefully. Pepper Schwartz tells of a female dean at Yale having to use the back stairs to attend a meeting because it was held at Mory's, which did not admit women. Pierre van den Berghe, born in the Congo, the son of a Belgian colonial, tells of a cousin who shot an African worker in the leg for malingering. Van den Berghe knows racism directly at its most virulent—in his blood, as it were—which may help account for his irritation with white Americans (who have only a superficial knowledge of racism) lecturing him about it. John Gagnon, on a long sit-up rail trip after his father's death, remembers the luxury of a shower in the sparkling bathroom of Chicago's Union Station, with its fluffy towels and hot water. Jessie Bernard tells us that she is reluctant to use not only a word processor but even an electric typewriter because she needs stiff keys to pound out her aggressions. Andrew Greeley outmarginalizes so-called marginal Jewish intellectuals by pointing to his own situation: he is distrusted by sociologists because he is a priest and by the Catholic church because he is a sociologist with an income of his own. He has his sweet revenge, though: in a self-sustaining cycle, his best-selling novels contain the knowledge he has gained about Catholic Americans through his National Opinion Research Center surveys, and the royalties from his novels fund further surveys and allowed him generously to endow a chair in religious studies at the University of Chicago, which, he tells us, accepted it with ill grace.

Although this book is far from unprecedented, the idea for it generated a lot of intrigued interest when I first talked about it with colleagues. It also generated a lot of skepticism: sociologists can't write; the first-person singular doesn't come naturally to them; sociologists don't have interesting lives; they won't be willing to talk about those very selves that their commitments to objectivity have routinely suppressed; even if they were willing to dredge up all that subjectivity, it would be bad PR for sociology, still not fully established as a legitimate objective science. Besides, who would be interested in the lives of a bunch of obscure academics—obscure at least by comparison with statesmen, military leaders, movie stars, literary figures, or tycoons?

Even before thinking the project through, I must have sent out more than fifty or sixty letters to a variety of sociologists (I did not think at all about sampling), asking if they would like to contribute to a volume of autobiographical essays. Only one of that original batch said no in a disdainful way ("not my cup of tea"). Several others also said no, but in an apologetic way (citing the usual range of reasons) that encouraged me to go forward with the project. Still others suggested that I use earlier autobiographical efforts they had made, or interviews conducted with them containing autobiographical material. But almost all were supportive, and some (like Jessie Bernard, Ed Shils, and Irving Horowitz) even took the trouble to provide me with references to earlier or similar efforts.

The selection of authors is in no way a careful sampling. After twenty-five years as a working sociologist I knew many of my colleagues, so I began with the networks I had. I asked myself who writes well, who is likely to be willing to write candidly about his or her life, who is likely to have had an interesting life to write candidly about. I only later decided that no life, really, is uninteresting, and that it takes a more or less deliberate failure of intelligence or sensibility to render one's life banal or otherwise boring. It was only later too that I wished I had sampled systematically so as to be able to claim more for the evidence contained here. Still, the essayists represent a fairly good distribution of age, from those in their forties just achieving national reputations to senior eminents in their seventies and eighties, like Jessie Bernard, David Riesman, and Reinhard Bendix. Included are several schools of thought, qualitative and quantitative sociologists, men and women, natives and foreign-born. Unfortunately there are no sociologists of color. Although several were asked, and some said yes, none delivered a manuscript.

As it turned out, too many manuscripts were delivered. Although they all contained valuable and interesting material, publishing all of them would have made a book too large to market effectively. The book was delayed while I struggled with the problem of whom and what to cut among authors I had solicited myself. I also repressed the problem, alternately waiting for a good fairy to eliminate it with a stroke of her wand (she never appeared) and evading it in Scarlett O'Hara fashion: I won't think about that today, I'll think about it tomorrow. After an unconscionable delay of almost two years, I did what I had to do, made the necessary cuts and unmade, I fear, a number of friendships.

I reveal such embarrassing facts less in a confessional spirit than as a historical footnote to one economic problem of book making with which I had no previous experience. Several colleagues have tried to reassure me that the book will be better shorter than longer (who was it that said, "If I had more time I would write less"?), and I am prepared to believe this; in spite of the constraints I feel that I must believe it. Nevertheless, I feel no constraint whatever in believing that this unexpectedly prolific outpouring of autobiography, flowing as it does from a group of academic sociologists for whom the first-person singular represents a radical departure from their normal modes of discourse, will help readers of sociology to see behind its sometimes formidable texts not authors, scholars, researchers, or professors, but persons, perhaps not unlike themselves.

PART I

Academic Men

CHAPTER ONE

Imagining the Real

Dennis Wrong

As one grows older, one is always surprised—and sometimes depressed—to realize the truth of "in my beginning is my end" and "in my end is my beginning." T. S. Eliot was, of course, thinking of personal identity in its deepest and fullest sense, but his words also apply to "merely" intellectual beginnings and ends, the more so when reading, writing, and thinking have from a fairly early age been central to one's self-definition.

I decided more or less consciously that I wanted to become an "intellectual" at a moment of abrupt and unwelcome transition in my life several months before my sixteenth birthday. After living two years in Geneva, Switzerland, where my father was Canadian delegate to the League of Nations, my parents sent me to board at a prominent preparatory school in Toronto. The school was not altogether strange to me, for I had been a boarder in its junior division the year before we moved to Europe after living in Washington, D.C., for most of my early life. Until now I had always identified myself entirely, indeed overeagerly, with my peers and had in fact been bitterly unhappy over the previous move to Europe. Twice my parents had dragged me, in a sulky and sullen mood, across the Atlantic. This time I was not only older but, feeling that my European sojourn had made me more refined and cosmopolitan than my schoolmates, I resisted making yet another readjustment to an environment I had not chosen.

We returned in the summer of 1939, and the coming of the war removed all possibility of my going back to Switzerland. It lessened my anger at my parents, but it made me, if anything, more inclined to idealize my years at school in Geneva and more determined than ever not to become a hearty, provincial, prep-school philistine. Since I laid claim to a personal relation to Europe, where the great events of the war were unfolding, I decided that I ought to be more fully informed about them. So I started to follow the world news and tacked maps of the battlefronts from the Sunday *New York Times* "Week in Review" section on the wall of my dormitory room, which my schoolmates regarded as a pretentious affectation.

I bought my first "serious" book, *Fallen Bastions,* by a British newspaper correspondent in Central Europe, to learn about the events preceding the war, especially the Munich crisis, which had the year before impinged on even our self-centered adolescent concerns at school in Geneva. The author, G. E. R. Gedye, passionately denounced the appeasement of Hitler and wrote favorably of "socialism." The leading Toronto bookstore—Britnell's, incredibly still there and looking much the same more than forty years later—carried other British Left Book Club publications; I bought a few and was quickly converted by a John Strachey pamphlet entitled *Why You Should Be a Socialist.* In the next year I read books, many of them British Pelicans that still sit on my shelf by Strachey, H. G. Wells, George Bernard Shaw, G. D. H. Cole, and Harold Laski on socialism, politics, and world affairs.

I also exchanged long, nostalgic letters with my closest Geneva friend, the late Stuart Schulberg, son of pioneer Hollywood movie magnate B. P. Schulberg and younger brother of the novelist Budd Schulberg, who later was for a long time the producer of the NBC "Today" show. I was astounded by his opposition to American entrance into the war, for at school we had all declaimed against the wickedness of Hitler. I wrote a letter to *Life* magazine denouncing the American isolationists—my first appearance in print—and Stuart wrote a letter disagreeing with me. His opinions, as I began to grasp, reflected those of the Communist party, to which he had been exposed through his brother, who had been a leading figure among the Hollywood Communists of the 1930s. Stuart had always been the older, dominant figure in our friendship, so I wavered in the direction of his views. I bought and read International Publishers' editions of the shorter writings of Marx, Engels, and Lenin, as well as *Capital,* managing to plough through at least the first (and most difficult!) chapters. The war maps on my wall were replaced by cut-out pictures of Marx, Lenin, and Trotsky, though some vague, intuitive wisdom kept me from including Stalin among them.

Never one to do things by halves, I offered my services—at the suggestion of a teacher who claimed to be a secret sympathizer—to the Canadian Communist party newspaper just before it and the party itself were banned, for Canada was at war and it was, of course, the period of the Stalin-Hitler pact. The editor, who was elected a few years later to the Ontario legislature after the Soviet Union had become our ally, asked me to proofread a huge manuscript, so I carried galleys of *The Socialist Sixth of the World* by Hewlett Johnson, the "Red Dean" of Canterbury, back to my dorm room. Even at my tender age, I found it hard to believe that there could possibly be a land of such milk and honey as the contemporary Soviet Union in the dean's description of it. Still, I rather cherish the memory of sitting in my room at Upper Canada College, identified by recent Canadian Marxist sociologists as the seedbed of the Canadian corporate elite, reading tracts for the soon to be outlawed Communist party.

I sometimes wonder if I am perhaps not the only person in the world who became a Communist sympathizer *after* the Stalin-Hitler pact and was disillusioned within a few weeks by the Soviet invasion of Finland. In my case, at least, the time at which I became politically conscious—which almost invariably meant adopting left-wing views—was undoubtedly crucial in shaping my later outlook. I began to read, even subscribe to, the *Nation,* the *New Republic,* and the *New Statesman,* which during the twenty-two months of the Soviet-German alliance were firmly anti-Stalinist, printing articles, often by former Communists, that were highly critical not only of Stalinism but even of Marxism. All these journals reverted to pro-Soviet apologetics and at times outright fellow traveling after Hitler invaded Russia, but I was immunized forever against the illusion that truth and virtue are always to be found on the left. I also picked up an occasional copy of the Trotskyist monthly, the *New International,* which provided crucial "anticipatory socialization" for my later encounter in New York with former or near Trotskyists associated with Dwight Macdonald's *Politics, Partisan Review, Commentary,* and, a bit later, *Dissent.* I continued to think of myself as at least a qualified Marxist and an ardent democratic socialist, generally sympathetic to the Canadian Commonwealth Federation, the Canadian party modeled on the British Labour party, in which I was later active as an undergraduate.

The political weeklies also contained cultural "back of the book" sections, which were resolutely highbrow, drawing their reviewers and authors from the most advanced Bloomsbury and Greenwich Village circles. Here I gleaned an idea of the proper preoccupations and values of the bona fide intellectual, a label that, as Daniel Bell has recently shown, scarcely predates this century and has today acquired a much looser, vaguer, and doubtless less "elitist" meaning than it used to have. I took up smoking cigarettes, cultivated less plebeian tastes in classical music, and plunged into modern literature. In the course of my two years at Upper Canada I read the poetry of Eliot, Auden, Spender, and Jeffers and the fiction of Hemingway, Fitzgerald, Dos Passos, Steinbeck, the early Joyce, Lawrence, Malraux, Romains, Silone, Isherwood, Saroyan, Thomas Wolfe, and Richard Wright. (I did not read the great Russians or the more "difficult" writers, except for some of the poets, until later.)

I decided, as many did in those days, that I wanted to be a writer. I wrote about a dozen sketches and short stories, very much in the vein of William Saroyan, most of them full of wide-eyed adolescent romanticism about the wonder and glory of it all. Several were printed in the school literary magazine and won me a prize on graduation for the best prose fiction. I also wrote political articles, especially in a short-lived school newspaper that I edited, exhorting my contemporaries to build a new, more just social order after the war and liberally quoting Marx, Lenin, Eugene V. Debs, Big Bill Haywood, and other left-wing luminaries.

I first encountered sociology in V. F. Calverton's 1937 Modern Library anthology. Calverton was hardly a sociologist or even an academic, but an independent, "premature" anti-Stalinist Marxist who included selections by, among others, Lao-tze, Augustine, Machiavelli, Locke, Darwin, Lenin, Hitler, Mussolini, Max Eastman, and Sidney Hook as well as such unambiguous sociologists as Spencer, Durkheim, Weber, and Cooley. When Robert Bierstedt revised the book more than twenty years later, he dropped many of the original choices, complaining that V. F. Calverton's "predilections" were "Marxian" and that he included too much "social philosophy." Accurate enough, but it occurs to me that my own sense of sociology may have been permanently formed—or, if you like, deformed —by Calverton's comprehensiveness. I would love to have possessed the wit and self-confidence, or perhaps the chutzpah, that led Daniel Bell as a fledgling graduate student to describe himself as a "specialist in generalizations" (though Dan says he spoke "without wit or irony"). I was, in any case, voted by my graduating class at Upper Canada the member "with the most opinions on the most subjects."

Although I acquired strong later interests, world politics and international relations, ideological politics centering on the left and Marxism, and literature have somehow stubbornly remained my bedrock intellectual concerns, perhaps helping to explain why I have never been able to embrace fully the identity of sociologist. Often enough I have tried to set aside and resist the claims of the first two—never, never, never those of the third! Politics was a kind of family heritage—obviously so in the case of international relations because my father was a diplomat and I lived for two years at an impressionable age in Geneva on the eve of the most terrible war in history. I thought of my radicalism as a rebellion against my family, Upper Canada College, and my class. But I grew up in Washington, D.C., and later spent much time there visiting my parents, who lived in Washington for a total of eighteen years in three separate periods from the 1920s to the 1950s. I lived more briefly in Ottawa but regularly visited my parents and my sister there and vacationed at a family summer cottage nearby for more than thirty years. Washington and Ottawa are notoriously one-industry towns dominated by the business of government and politics. I hardly needed to be instructed about the significance of the state, solemnly declared to be "relatively autonomous" by recent sociologists, having spent so much of my youth in capital cities as well as in the Geneva of the ill-fated League of Nations, where conflicts among states loomed so large.

I can't remember ever even contemplating going to any university other than the University of Toronto, though this may be only because with the war on, my choices were inevitably limited to Canada. My parents were both children of well-known Toronto professors. My mother's father, a classicist, had married the daughter of the second president of the university and had himself served as acting president and as principal of its largest college (the University of Toronto is a federation of publicly supported faculties and several small church-related colleges). My father's father had virtually created Canadian history as a serious field of scholarship, had founded the Department of History, and had written the textbooks on British and Canadian history used for many years in the Ontario high schools. My father had taught history at the university before joining the newly created Canadian foreign service. I did make a point of separating myself from my Upper Canada College classmates by entering the large nondenominational college, a third of whose students were Jewish. I had already acquired a kind of philosemitic outlook, for in Geneva most of my friends had been American Jews from New York or German Jews on the first leg of permanent migration from Nazi Germany. But there was an awful lot of anti-Semitism, at least of the genteel variety, in Toronto at that time.

During my freshman year I stumbled in my own reading on various mystical ideas, chiefly in the writings of Aldous Huxley and Henry Miller, and turned to philosophy in search of answers—to popularized accounts by C. E. M. Joad and even Will Durant, Schopenhauer, the essays of William James and Bertrand Russell, and some writings of Bergson, Dewey, and Whitehead. All of this reading knocked me for a loop because I wanted to think of myself as a hardheaded, atheistic scientific materialist. I didn't know what was happening to me and thought I might be having some kind of mystical experience or that I had been unlucky enough to hit on the ultimate secret, hidden from, or suppressed by, others, that nothing had any meaning. I babbled incoherently to a few people, including teachers and my father, and obtained a psychiatrist's certificate that I was suffering a nervous breakdown so as not to flunk out. In spite of doing little or no studying for my courses, I wrote and passed all my exams, achieving respectable grades.

I realize now that I was undergoing an acute anxiety attack. The discovery of so much that I didn't know and couldn't understand, of so many books that I hadn't read, overwhelmed me. I had never been any good at sports; I was not very successful with women, usually vainly pursuing popular, good-looking girls a bit older than me; and I had turned my back on wanting to be "one of the boys" in a passive, conforming spirit. My sense of personal worth depended totally on my intellectuality. I thought that I was nothing if I could not sound like the supersophisticated characters in Huxley's novels, or like Jallez and Jerphanion, the Parisian students of Jules Romains's endless "Men of Good Will" series of novels (utterly forgotten, it seems, today). Pathetic and juvenile, as I even half knew, but it was a long time before I fully recovered from this experience, which often recurred in milder forms for years afterward, usually at the beginning of the new academic year, and was the main cause of the writing block that I suffered in graduate school and for some time after.

The best students at Toronto enrolled in the honors program, requiring higher grades and an additional year of study to earn the degree. The program was designed as the opposite of Harvard's general-education curriculum, providing three years of fairly intensive specialized study in a particular field. I was tempted by a philosophy and English literature combination, but feared it after my "breakdown." Why did I choose sociology? Partly for no better reason than that my first girlfriend had chosen it, but also because it seemed relevant to my socialist beliefs and, the status of sociology being a lowly one, we were required to take courses in political science, economics, and philosophy as well as others chosen from an array that included history, psychology, and anthropology. My choice of sociology was also a rebellion against the family association with history. Several onetime colleagues of my father and grandfather even sought me out to try to dissuade me from wasting my time on such an unsound, newfangled, and disreputable pseudodiscipline.

Despite a small teaching staff, sociology was a popular honors subject, partly because an undergraduate degree in it entitled one to credit for a full year's work toward a degree in social work. This advantage attracted many women, who in my year outnumbered the four males by more than three to one. One of us was an older man who had already begun a career as a social worker, but the other two and I became close friends; with the addition of a few women, including several from the psychology program, with which we shared many courses, we formed a kind of nucleus of serious and interested students. In my senior year we were joined by a short, articulate young man named Erving Goffman. I had met him on a summer job for the government in Ottawa; on learning that he planned to resume his interrupted studies by coming to the University of Toronto to obtain the remaining degree credits he needed, I urged him to try sociology. (It may well be the only thing I am remembered for in future histories of sociology!)

Goffman stories are legion among those who knew him at all well, although mine go back farther than just about anyone else's. I shall confine myself to a few recollections about his intellectual outlook. The widespread notion that Erving was an inspired naïf, a novelist manqué with unusual powers of social observation, is utterly wrong. He already had an acute and far-ranging theoretical mind when I met him. He was much more intellectually advanced than the rest of us; I remember him rebuking us for reading textbooks and popularizations instead of tackling the originals. Once he defended Freud's emphasis on the body and the priority of infant experience against the more congenial neo-Freudian culturalists we all favored. His later antipathy to psychoanalysis is well known, but he created in me the first small twinge of doubt as to whether there was not perhaps more truth and profundity in the vision of the founder than in all the Erich Fromms, Karen Horneys, and Gordon Allports who were so ready to revise him. Erving had studied philosophy and had actually read in full Whitehead's *Process and Reality*. He argued in Whiteheadian language that reality should be conceived "along the lines on which it is naturally articulated," a rule he obviously followed in his later work.

All of us, including Erving, were most attracted by the cultural anthropology that strongly shaped the sociology we were taught. Its chief purveyor was the senior sociologist, C. W. M. Hart, an Australian anthropologist who had been a student of A. R. Radcliffe-Brown. Some of us also took anthropology courses from Reo Fortune, Margaret Mead's second husband, and in our senior year from a young anthropologist out of Chicago with whom we mixed a good deal socially. But Hart was the most inspiring of teachers and undoubtedly deserved major credit for the surprising number of Toronto students from this period who went on to become professional sociologists or anthropologists. He was a large, saturnine man, resembling depictions of Simon Legree. He had a reputation for being something of a reprobate; it was rumored that he had been banned for drunken brawling from several local taverns. This reputation, in conjunction with his witty mockery of conventional pieties in the classroom, led the Catholic college to forbid their students from studying sociology, and another denominational college to discourage theirs. Hart was a convinced functionalist. He gave us a year-long course (all Toronto courses ran for both semesters, with an exam at the end of the year) on Durkheim, especially *Le Suicide*, sections of which I translated since it was not yet available in English.

I missed the theory course offered by S. D. Clark, the other senior sociologist and later the dean of Canadian sociology, because he was on leave one year, but I first learned of the importance of Max Weber in his course on the development of Canada, in which he discussed religious movements. We thought of Clark as a historian rather than a sociologist, and unlike more recent students we were not very interested in Canada, whoring, rather, after universal generalizations. In many ways Clark was ahead of his time—not, as we thought, behind it—in his historicist conception of the atemporality of functionalist community studies. But he failed to enchant us with new vistas like those apparently opened up by functionalism and the study of culture and personality. In common with others at this time, my sense of the potentialities of sociology was strongly awakened by Erich Fromm's *Escape from Freedom*, which tried to synthesize three of my own major interests: an interpretation of fascism and the rise of Hitler, a version of psychoanalysis that was culturally relevant, and left-wing political sympathies.

Both Hart and Clark introduced us to Talcott Parsons's *Structure of Social Action,* and Parsons himself visited us for several public lectures.

I remember Goffman and me infuriating our classmates by asking him questions that gave him the impression that all present had read and understood his book as thoroughly as we had, with the result that his later remarks were over the heads of most of the audience. Robert Merton also came and gave us his famous discussion of manifest and latent functions. I was enthralled by his clarity and rigor after the rather fuzzy, organicist anthropological functionalism to which I had been exposed and decided then and there to do graduate work at Columbia instead of following the usual path of Canadian students to Chicago. To be sure, I was also excited by New York, where I had visited Geneva school friends several years before, and looked forward to the prospect of finding congenial literary and anti-Stalinist left political circles there.

In my senior year I read George Orwell and Arthur Koestler (including *Darkness at Noon* and his essay collection *The Yogi and the Commissar*) and discovered *Partisan Review*. I was fully aware that the political views I formed from these sources were far from popular in the university community. It was the last year of the war, and I could not know that in the passionate debate among intellectuals over communism and the Soviet Union that lay just ahead, the side I had chosen would be confirmed by world events before the end of the decade and was already attracting the most able and independent writers and thinkers. But the guest speaker at my graduating class banquet was a Soviet Embassy official resplendent in a Red Army uniform. (Less than a year later he was expelled from the country when it was revealed that he was the coordinator of Soviet espionage in Canada. Fifteen years later the same man became the first Soviet ambassador to Cuba after Anastas Mikoyan's famous visit had secured Fidel Castro's alignment with the Soviet bloc.) I was aware of the efforts of the Communists to penetrate the CCF, including the student CCF club of which I was president, and of their insistent demands for a new popular front. They were firmly resisted on grounds of principle by David Lewis, the CCF national secretary, later leader of the New Democratic Party, its successor party, and a former Rhodes scholar whom I knew and respected. When they failed, Communist candidates ran in several Toronto federal and provincial constituencies, in which I campaigned arduously for the CCF. Two of my teachers who were Americans took me aside and solemnly warned me to be sure in New York to shun the "profascist" followers of Trotsky and the Norman Thomas socialists. I silently resolved to do just the opposite and in due course acted accordingly.

Merton's lectures did not disappoint me, but my first year at Columbia (1945–46) was frustrating. I found that I already knew more sociology than most of my fellow students and, needing less time to study, was eager to explore the New York scene but could find no companions to join me. I retained a tendency to court unattainable women. Also, most of the students still adhered to the old pro-Soviet progressivism and were shocked at the idea that the Soviet Union was as totalitarian as Nazi Germany and that Soviet domination was a tragedy for the nations of Eastern Europe.

Years before, when I had first aspired to be an intellectual, I had been much impressed by the declaration of a character in André Malraux's *Man's Hope* that the way to "make the best of one's life" was "by converting as wide a range of experience as possible into conscious thought." (Still a pretty good definition of the intellectual's vocation, I think.) I was acutely conscious of the narrowness of my own experience and strongly regretted (I still do) not serving overseas in the war. So I jumped at the chance to work as a temporary seaman on a ship out of Montreal carrying a United Nations relief cargo to Europe. I enjoyed a proletarian-style Mediterranean cruise, stood the graveyard watch from midnight to four A.M., and caught at least a glimpse of the underside of postwar Europe when we docked for long stays in Venice and Trieste. Two summers later I repeated the experience, this time to the Baltic, docking at Gdynia, Hamburg, Rotterdam, and Antwerp. I was able to arrange to leave the ship and spent most of the summer in Paris, with shorter visits to Geneva, London, and Oxford. It turned out, alas, to be sixteen years before I again set foot in Europe, so these summers were much valued. I also cherish the memory of having worked and lived at close quarters—and played, on visits ashore in port—with a lively group of men from a working-class background quite different from my own. I have the impression that such an experience is less common among young people today than it was in my generation.

Back in New York, I fell in with a group of young literary bohemians in Greenwich Village. They were considerably more highbrow and self-consciously intellectual than the Beats who became famous a few years later. Essentially, they were a kind of junior auxiliary to the *Partisan Review,* toward which, though they were occasional contributors, their attitude was highly ambivalent. I was much influenced by this circle for nearly a decade. They were scornful of academic life and particularly contemptuous of sociology, which did not strengthen my own far from robust self-confidence. I felt guilty for lacking the nerve to emulate them by burning my bridges to an academic career, although I was also sensibly restrained by the unstable, *Luftmensch* traits I sensed in several of the group whom I knew best.

Thanks to Nathan Glazer, a fellow Columbia graduate student, I began to review books for the old Menshevik organ, the *New Leader,* and for *Commentary,* of which Nat was a junior editor and to which several of my literary friends were also contributors. My first two published articles, on family sociology and on demography, eventually appeared in the "Study of Man" section created by Nat, who was himself its most brilliant contributor. I wrote regularly for *Commentary* for more than twenty years until the early 1970s, when its editor, Norman Podhoretz, turned the journal in an increasingly strident and monolithic antileft direction, and I switched to *Dissent* as my major place of publication.

At Columbia I was inevitably drawn to C. Wright Mills, who was a link between the sociology faculty and the larger New York intellectual world. His conception of sociology was more to my taste than that favored by most of the Columbia department in this period of strenuous discipline building. Ten years later his *Sociological Imagination* was a book I would dearly love to have written myself—certainly my favorite of Mills's works, most of which I commented on in print at the time of their appearance, applauding their vigor and scope while criticizing the rhetorical radicalism that later made Mills a founder and hero of the New Left. As Irving Louis Horowitz has correctly stressed in his biography, there was more to Mills than his politics. His later work suffered, I think, from his rupture with the New York intellectuals and, more specifically, with his Columbia colleagues Merton, Richard Hofstadter, and Lionel Trilling (as reported by Horowitz).

I completed my course work and passed my written and oral comprehensives within two years but avoided writing any papers with the single exception of a long one, for Mills, on bureaucracy in the novels of Franz Kafka. I spent another two years in New York teaching part-time at New York University and fiddling with several abortive dissertation projects. Then I got married and took my first full-time teaching job at Princeton but was let go after a year. The experience was repeated the next year at the Newark branch of Rutgers University. The pay was low and the teaching hours long by today's standards. The main reason I lost both jobs was the shrinking enrollment caused by the small college-age cohorts born in the worst years of the Depression, but my confidence was shaken, and I still had not even settled on a dissertation topic. Partly to appease my parents' anxieties over my career vacillations, partly to show them that I was capable on their own terms, I twice took the examinations for the Canadian foreign service and was one of the dozen or so out of several hundred candidates who qualified on both occasions. But at the point of decision I drew back from the only serious alternative to an academic career that I have ever contemplated.

I was, however, much more influenced during those years than I then cared to admit by the world of my father. He was appointed the first Canadian ambassador to the United States and served for all but the opening eighteen months of the Truman administration, remaining in Washington for such a long time because old friends going back to the 1920s were now top State Department people, most notably Dean Acheson, the secretary of state. I visited my parents often, not only because the luxurious comforts of the embassy were welcome after drab graduate-student living conditions, but also to get the feel of official Washington and enjoy at least a worm's-eye view of history in the making. The succession of international crises and major decisions in the six years from the Truman Doctrine to the Korean peace settlement is surely unparalleled in American peacetime history. Canada, more than ever before or since, was involved in nearly all of them, and my father, always a tremendously hard worker, wore himself out. He died in his sixtieth year only seven months after finally leaving Washington.

In addition to what I had learned at second hand, I had chances to hear Acheson and other leading figures—among them Lester Pearson (often), Oliver Franks, Felix Frankfurter, Hubert Humphrey, and Christian Herter—discuss informally world (and also domestic) events. The decisions of those years were improvised under intense pressures, as is true, to be sure, of most political decisions. Acheson in 1969 entitled his memoirs *Present at the Creation,* but twenty years earlier neither he nor anyone else could have imagined that they were laying the foundations of an American foreign policy that is still in effect after nearly forty years. I learned enough to *know* that the attacks of the "nationalist" Republican right were mostly nonsense, as were the charges of American imperialism still heard at the time in my own liberal-left milieu and revived in the 1960s by the revisionist historians of the cold war. Realism about the cold war and foreign policy in general has perhaps more than anything else isolated me from the conventional pieties of academic liberalism.

I had one year of systematic education in the field of international relations. After losing my second teaching job, the opportunity came through my father to work as a research assistant to George F. Kennan on problems of American foreign policy at the Institute for Advanced

Study in Princeton. Few, if any, graduate programs could possibly have matched this experience. Most important, Kennan tried out his own developing ideas on his small staff. J. Robert Oppenheimer, then director of the institute, and several top Princeton professors often participated in our group discussions. Several State Department officials and foreign diplomats visited us, as did Isaiah Berlin and Hans Morgenthau. It was an unforgettable year.

Kennan used to say that diplomats differed from their fellow citizens because their careers required them to know sin. A slight exaggeration, perhaps, but one recalls that Machiavelli was one of the first professional diplomats. In any case, failure to understand the most elementary realities of relations among sovereign states is characteristic of Americans, American liberals, and American academics—in descending order of generality but ascending order of incomprehension, or so it often seems to me. Sociologists are probably the worst offenders, although Raymond Aron was an outstanding non-American exception. But despite the fact that Aron was Weber's heir on this as on other matters, his writings on international relations are not much honored, or even read, by American sociologists. Speak to a liberal academic about national interests, about the role of military force, or about necessary official relations with right-wing authoritarian governments and the response will be frowns and pained looks followed by a barrage of trendy clichés and a ringing declaration of principle morally condemning the whole wretched business. Since Vietnam a lofty and self-righteous isolationism has once again after half a century become the norm for many, if not most, American liberals.

My work for Kennan ended when President Truman unexpectedly appointed him ambassador to the Soviet Union. Seven years after having entered graduate school, I found myself unemployed, with a record of having been fired from—or, as Bob Bierstedt would prefer to say, non-reappointed to—two academic jobs, still with no dissertation even under way, and rumored to have left the field by working for Kennan. The time had come to fish or cut bait on the dissertation. Kennan had hired me to work on population problems, although I had merely taught one undergraduate course on the subject without ever having formally studied demography. But I had learned quite a bit and had overcome my block by writing reports for Kennan, one of which I had revised for publication in *Commentary*. Kingsley Davis had recently joined the Columbia faculty, and several friends were writing dissertations in demography under his direction. Davis gave me welcome encouragement, and, with some financial help from my father and a little part-time teaching, I was able to spend most of the next two years completing the first draft of a dissertation in demography.

With revisions yet to make, I returned to my old undergraduate department at the University of Toronto for a year of research on Canadian voting patterns. I was moving into political sociology as a research field, but I also managed to write a short introductory book on the study of population (which has gone through six editions and is still in print). The next year I joined the regular teaching staff. I was happy in Toronto, surrounded by old friends, but my wife, a New Yorker to the bone, was not. So after two years I reluctantly returned to the States, accepting a position at Brown University, where in time I was granted tenure.

Although I was past thirty, the five years at Brown through the quiet late 1950s were for me years of incubation. I became a father. My major ideas and areas of interest within sociology crystallized. Brown was developing a graduate program in demography, but many faculty members in the program knew so little else that I ended up teaching broad undergraduate courses in theory and social organization, with the result that I taught, thought, and wrote myself—the three have for me always been closely connected—right out of demography. I retain, however, much respect for that craftsmanlike discipline; a field whose basic subject matter is natural quantities, it never offended my sensibilities by artificial quantification or by forcing human reality into the mode of what Mills called "abstracted empiricism."

At Brown I buried myself in the growing literature on the Holocaust to the point where I sometimes not only thought it the most significant thing that had ever happened but the only significant thing. I also read Freud more widely and deeply, partly to accommodate students disappointed by a behavioristic psychology department and a quantitative sociology department. The article for which I am best known to sociologists, "The Oversocialized Conception of Man in Modern Sociology," was conceived and written at this time. I was powerfully affected by the utopian Freudian writings of Herbert Marcuse and, especially, Norman O. Brown some years in advance of the rise of the counterculture of the 1960s to which their vision contributed. Their influence on me was not only intellectual, for it played a part in the ending of my first marriage when I fell in love with a woman to whom I have now been happily married for nearly twenty years.

The crisis in my personal life took me back to New York as a member of the graduate faculty of the New School for Social Research. I became editor of the New School's social-science journal and learned much from having as colleagues the exiled German scholars who were still well represented on the faculty in the early 1960s. But financial problems, aggravated by alimony and child-support obligations, induced me to move in 1963 to New York University, where I have remained ever since except for short visiting and summer-session stints at various places, including interesting ones at the University of California at Berkeley, the University of Nevada-Reno, Trinity College in Connecticut, and Oxford. Our department at NYU has since the turmoil of the late 1960s been extraordinarily stable and harmonious; truly collegial relations among people of widely varying interests and backgrounds have prevailed there to an unusual degree. Although I live in Princeton, I have become, I suppose, a full-fledged New York intellectual, even serving on the editorial boards of *Dissent* and *Partisan Review*. Of course, New York intellectual life is not what it once was—what is?—and I often wryly remember Goethe's advice to be careful of what you wish for in your youth because you will get it in middle age.

Mills's definition of the sociological imagination as the understanding of "the intersection of history and biography within society" has always appealed to me, though not, as for Mills, because it makes possible the redefinition of "private troubles" as "public issues," thereby providing a rationale for political action. With age I have become not only more anti-ideological but more antitheoretical in general, and it now seems to me that historical knowledge is not just necessary but often sufficient to answer many of our most urgent questions. I remember my father arguing that sociology should only be a graduate subject studied after the acquisition of broad historical knowledge. That was also Sorokin's view when he was invited to head the first sociology department at Harvard, but he did not get his way. However, I am not prepared to capitulate completely to the shades of my father and those historians who long ago tried to dissuade me from studying sociology, for history as a discipline has since then enormously widened and deepened its concerns. To a considerable extent this expansion has been the result of enrichment by ideas, methods, and even subject matters— stratification, cultural *mentalités*, the family, demographic trends— taken over from sociology and anthropology. I was one of the first people to review at length Philippe Ariés's *Centuries of Childhood;* I suggested that because it deals with the lives of our own ancestors, archaic and distorted echoes of which still surround us, social history of its kind conveys more successfully to the reader than anthropological reports on primitive peoples both "the strangeness of time and change in the life of man and society" and, in Ariés's own words, "the tremor of life that he can feel in his own existence." But forty years ago we were right to be excited by the subjects sociologists studied. And this was a more important source of its appeal than the chimera of creating a social science modeled on the natural sciences that played so large a role in sociology's drive for disciplinary respectability.

"As we grow older the world becomes stranger, the pattern more complicated." T. S. Eliot was the poet of my generation, and some of his lines have become so much a part of me that I scarcely know when I am quoting. There is the strangeness of the sheer pastness of the past: anything out of the 1930s is for me bathed in a special light, a distant glow from the lost country of childhood. Not only is there the further strangeness of realizing that one's memories have become history, or the awareness of "a lifetime burning in every moment," but I find myself reaching back before my own life to find continuity in "not the lifetime of one man only / But of old stones that cannot be deciphered." Here, too, history and biography intersect. "People are always shouting they want to create a better future," writes Milan Kundera in *The Book of Laughter and Forgetting*. "It's not true. The future is an apathetic void of no interest to anyone. The past is full, eager to irritate us, provoke and insult, tempt us to destroy or repaint it. The only reason people want to be masters of the future is to change the past." Un-American, that, but so be it.

What I have come to value most in a sociologist is not theoretical reach, logical rigor, empirical exactitude, or moral passion but a palpable sense of reality. It is not a unitary trait, and it is more easily pointed to than described. My old classmate Erving Goffman had it, which is why his work will live. But it is not limited to accounts of microinteraction or everyday life. Raymond Aron had it too. Of the "classical" sociologists, it was preeminently possessed by Max Weber. When I first read Weber as a graduate student in the then new Gerth-Mills translations, my response was the same as that of Ernst Topitsch: "In the midst of this twilight atmosphere of insidious intellectual dishonesty, the work of Max Weber shed a flood of cold hard light. Anyone who has once been thunderstruck by contact with him can never see the world in the same light again."

If one lives long enough, one sees history—the sequence of events, not the discipline that studies them—disaggregate many things that once seemed indissolubly connected. At least that is true of life in the present century. Here are a few examples, fairly obvious ones no doubt. In contrast to forty or fifty years ago, protest against technological change and modernization comes today from intellectuals on the left rather than the right, although this may be further evidence that the left-right distinction itself is becoming obsolete. Who can believe any longer that the elimination of Victorian sexual repressions makes people more selfless, loving, and less acquisitive? The association between modernist cultural tastes and political radicalism, virtually the hallmark of an intellectual when I "decided" to become one, clearly no longer holds. To understand the world, one needs a feeling for the peculiarity and fragility of the present historical moment to avoid the fallacy of both eternalizing the present and exaggerating its novelty. No abstract theoretical model identifying relevant variables, nor the careful empirical charting of trends, can make up for the absence of such a sense of the present.

A keen awareness of the particularity of the historical moment, its precise location along the moving continuum of political and cultural events, was one of the most characteristic features of the New York intellectuals when I encountered them in the 1940s. Sometimes the striving for this awareness seemed labored, even ludicrous. I remember an intense, opinionated friend complaining after a woman had resisted his overtures that "women are taking the period badly." I thought this was a pretty classy way of easing the pain of sexual rejection, although even in those unenlightened days its unabashed male chauvinism seemed a bit raw. But this highly charged sense of the historical moment was not just a by-product of commitment to Marxism, for it reflected the truly apocalyptic events of the first half of the century. The theme of ceaseless change afflicting all of us with what has been called future shock has been rather overdone in recent decades. I sometimes like to argue that nothing really important has happened in the world since about 1950—nothing, that is, at all comparable to two world wars, the Russian Revolution, the Great Depression, the rise of fascism, the Stalinist terror, the Holocaust, the birth of new and powerful non-Western nations, the invention of nuclear weapons, and the beginnings of the cold war with the Soviet Union. A provocative exaggeration at best, at worst a half-truth. Despite the ever-changing surface, we still live in a world that assumed its present shape in the first half of the century. All epochs—or generations—may, as Ranke said, be equal in the sight of God, but not all of them are equally consequential in history.

Important as a sense of reality is to a sociologist, he or she is also subject to stringent additional intellectual requirements. For literature, however, the communication of a sense of reality through language is its very essence. I mean a sense of reality beyond the words on the page, the fashionable notions of structuralists and deconstructionists to the contrary notwithstanding. Because my intellectual generation had "literary sensibility," we had no need to develop the kinds of arcane and abstract theories of the primacy of the simple and concrete that have been so prominent in sociology since the antipositivist revolts of the 1960s.

I have never been to Dublin. I have sometimes been tempted to take one of those tours on or about June 16 to walk the streets that Leopold Bloom walked, peer at the façade of Number 10 Eccles Street, go out to the headland slope where Molly said yes, visit the Martello Tower, and perhaps even swim in the snotgreen sea. But I don't really need such a trip, for I can imagine well enough standing on the bridge over the Liffey where it flows into the harbor and listening to the water murmur, "And it's old and old it's sad and old it's said and weary I go back to you, my cold father, my cold and mad father, my cold mad feary father, till the near sight of the mere size of him, the moyles and moyles of it, moananoaning, makes me seasilt saltsick and I rush, my only, into your arms."

I was once in northern Mississippi for little more than an hour when driving east across the country alone. It was January; I was slowed up in Memphis by school buses delivering children to their homes, and when I crossed the state line a pale, late-afternoon sun shone on light snow. But everything looked as it should, and the air was full of voices—Sartoris voices and Snopes voices, the voices of Ike McAslin and Lucas Beauchamp, of Addie Bundren and Rosa Coldfield—but most of all doomed Compson voices—Benjy saying, or rather remembering since he could not speak, "Caddy smelled like trees"; Mrs. Compson whining, "It can't be simply to flout and hurt me. Whoever God is, he would not permit that. I'm a lady"; Quentin insisting, "I don't hate the South . . . *I don't hate it* he thought, panting in the cold air, the iron New England dark; *I don't, I don't! I don't hate it! I don't hate it!*" Clearest of all was the voice of Dilsey, walking home from the Negro church on Easter morning of 1928, tears rolling down her face, saying to her embarrassed daughter, "I've seed de first en de last. I seed de beginnin, and now I sees de endin." As I approached the next state line, I wondered how long I would have to live there before the voices would fade and it would become for me something more than Faulkner country. But the voices are not heard only in Mississippi. A few years ago a plaque was set in the wall of one of the bridges over the Charles between Cambridge and Boston commemorating the site where on June 2, 1910, Quentin Compson committed suicide by drowning himself in the river. But such an event never happened; Quentin Compson never existed, he is nothing but words on a page, the product of one man's fancy. The reality of the imagination and, inversely, the power to imagine the real lie at the root of all successful creations of the mind.

CHAPTER TWO

Becoming an Academic Man

David Riesman

I

My shift from law to an academic career in the social sciences, and sociology in particular, is perplexing to some people; it is a puzzle especially to my law colleagues, who regard their occupation as vastly superior to being a professor in a supposedly "soft" field teaching mere undergraduates. Some also have been bewildered by my ending up in a sociology department without passage through the ordinarily requisite Ph.D. program. That I became an academic, though, is not so surprising to those who know that my father, an exceptionally learned man, had been clinical professor of medicine and, later, of the history of medicine at the University of Pennsylvania; and that my mother had led her class at Bryn Mawr College and had won a European Fellowship at a time when it was still rare for women to go to college. Unlike many children of academic and intellectual parents, I was not openly rebellious, either at home or at school. Nevertheless, the picture of a young man following a parental bent would be a mistaken one. In fact, my father's example and the internalized verdict I accepted from my mother were perhaps the principal obstacles I overcame in becoming an academic man. And as my story will show, I followed a rather fortuitous, zigzagging path.

My father was born in Germany. His widowed mother brought him as a boy to Portsmouth, Ohio, where he worked in an uncle's store through his high-school years and then went to the University of Pennsylvania to study medicine, graduating in 1892. He had almost no money and lived with extreme frugality, as he continued to do out of dislike for ostentation when he won recognition as a diagnostician in internal medicine. In 1908, at age forty-two, he married Eleanor Fleisher, an elegant bluestocking, like himself of German Jewish background, of a family established in Philadelphia for three generations. He had a gift for clinical observation and immense conscientiousness. In medical education he became an admired teacher of interns and residents; he supported the more clinical focus of Pennsylvania as against the research preoccupations of Johns Hopkins and Harvard. He was sympathetic to the education of women as physicians and took an early interest in new forms of psychiatry. His concern with the societal aspects of medical care was evident in his last book, *Medicine in Modern Society* (1939), written at a time when I was old enough to help with editing and commentary. My father worked tirelessly. He would come for the summer to our cottage in Northeast Harbor, Maine, but to my mother's dismay would at times interrupt his vacation to look after an ill patient in the city.

He did not bring his medical problems home with him, even during the many years when his consulting office was on the ground floor of our four-story brownstone on Spruce Street (at the time known as Physicians' Row), near Rittenhouse Square. When being driven in his car, he would scribble notes on the yellow pad he had always with him, sometimes for a clinical paper or conference, sometimes for an essay such as "Irish Clinicians of the Eighteenth Century." My father was a bibliophile, and he had an amateur interest in astronomy. Cultivated Philadelphians enjoyed his company at the Franklin Inn Society. Occasionally he would entertain medical men from here or abroad at our house; I remember our Scottish maid saying to my mother during one such dinner that she should put on a waitress's uniform so she could listen to the splendid conversation!

But at the family dinner table, save on rare expansive occasions, my father's presence was more forbidding than inviting. Fastidious in manners, he was critical of mine. Moreover, if something came up in conversation, I would be sent for the encyclopedia to look up precise meanings or references, which I felt as a chore rather than an opportunity. When he and my mother were learning Italian to be able to read Dante in the original (already at home in Latin, Greek, French, and his native German), or studying the theory of relativity, I was avidly watching Philadelphia's two last-place baseball teams, the Phillies and the A's, and reading detective stories. But I also read some authors who were outside the Europe-centered orbit of my parents—almost everything by Mark Twain, sharing his deeply sardonic pessimistic side and not then put off by the brutality of *A Connecticut Yankee in King Arthur's Court*. I read Jack London and admired Rudyard Kipling.

Not surprisingly, my parents loved the opera and the Russian ballet, as did my younger brother (who followed my father into medicine and then disappointed him by becoming a surgeon) and also my musical younger sister, but I did not. However, I did regularly attend the Friday afternoon Philadelphia Symphony Orchestra concerts. At one of those concerts a dramatic event occurred, of the sort no longer likely when the patrons lack self-confidence and are afraid of appearing shocked. Leopold Stokowski played a symphony by a composer of whom I had not heard, Edgard Varèse; members of the audience started to shout in opposition, and a great many walked out. I found it thrilling. It was the first modern music I had heard, and I went on to look for more—a rare aesthetic area where my mother had not anticipated me.

One summer my brother, John Penrose Riesman, who was attending Bedales School in England, joined me in Grenoble for a bicycle trip down the Rhône valley to Marseilles and then west to Carcassonne. John knew the ground plans of the Gothic and Romanesque cathedrals, whereas only the Roman ruins had at that time much interest for me; indeed, for a time I actively disliked Gothic architecture. Often I would talk with museum guards or sextons in the cathedrals.

That I lacked the aesthetic tastes considered important in my family was probably less salient for me than my incompetence at the competitive sports valued at school. Only when I came to college could I find people as avid as I and yet of about my mediocre speed; I discovered squash and went on playing tennis, occasionally with Radcliffe "girls" (whom most of my classmates affected to scorn).

My father did things easily and deftly, whether mastering subjects or dealing with people; he was critical of me for my awkwardness, while he took for granted the fact that I did well at school academically. In contrast to my father's distance, my mother saw her older son as someone who shared her own style of intellectuality and what she also saw as its limitations. For her, intellectuality without creativity was sterile. Only the creative were "first-rate"; she was not, and by direct implication I too was not; hence I came to share the harsh judgment she passed on herself.[1]

There were some women in my mother's day who hoped to pursue both marriage and a career. More common was the acceptance of the verdict of M. Carey Thomas, president of Bryn Mawr, that "our failures only marry." Despite the encouragement of her teachers, my mother resigned herself after college to wait for callers from the small covey of eligible men, one of whom, a Philadelphia physician fifteen years her elder, had made a shy but persistent presence felt. My mother and her friends had discovered the excitement of books and ideas in college, and a few of these women did go on to pursue careers. But my mother's family had been very traditional, fearing that when she was awarded the European Fellowship to study in Europe, it would lead to spinsterhood, and did not encourage her. She herself was too self-mistrustful to embark on such an independent course.

She was indisputably an intellectual and later astonished my roommates and other friends, who envied me for having a mother with whom they could talk about Freud and Proust, D. H. Lawrence and Faulkner. For her, the only people who really counted in the world were the first-rate, the creative artists whom she early recognized and a few innovative scientists of such originality that they could be included in her pantheon. Correspondingly, in her romantic view the rest of worthwhile human activity served art as a kind of infrastructure or, as she would have put it, was merely second-rate.

Stricken in the 1920s with Parkinson's disease and later confined to a wheelchair, she could still lose herself in enthusiasm for Bach's B-minor Mass and Beethoven's late quartets, and she could enjoy the seascapes of Northeast Harbor and admire Florentine and French Impressionist painting—the latter in the extraordinary art collection of her and my father's friend, the acerbic collector and critic Albert C. Barnes. Most of the time her attitude toward life was relentlessly unillusioned. She hardly needed Oswald Spengler's *Decline of the West,* of which she was an early reader, to believe in his prognosis; she had already absorbed the views of Henry and Brooks Adams. But she added to those a particular curse, one which, pondering it in retrospect, may have served as a partial rationalization for the failure she felt at not pursuing the academic career toward which the award of the European Fellowship had pointed her. Descended from German Jews on both sides, whose businesses (silk, yarn, and banking) were now in the hands of those she called Russian Jews, she concluded that German Jews were a particularly doomed lot, too inhibited and uninventive to compete with the rambunctious, if crude, new immigration.

My parents were agnostic rationalists without religion. Being Jewish was not a theme discussed at home or elsewhere. It was certainly no asset to be Jewish, but neither did it make itself felt as a liability. For me a sense of Jews as in some respects different entered my consciousness most strongly when I went to Harvard Law School. For seven years at William Penn Charter School in Philadelphia I attended Friends Meeting every Fourth Day (Wednesday). I had a devout German Catholic governess to whom I was close. My mother arranged for a novelist friend of hers, Shirley Watkins, to read the Bible with the three Riesman children and the four children of my mother's Wellesley-educated sister. Although a few of my parents' acquaintances were observant Sephardic Jews, proud of their colonial American heritage—founders later, in opposition to Zionism, of the American Council for Judaism—my siblings and I had no familiarity with Judaism at all. My mother's brother had married a White Russian of the lesser nobility, an Orthodox Catholic. I married a Unitarian and became one; my brother married a nurse he met while serving as a doctor for the Grenfell Mission in Newfoundland and joined the Congregational church to which she belongs; my sister, still agnostic, married a Spanish Catholic.

II

My mother thought I was too young to attend Harvard College immediately after William Penn Charter School and suggested Exeter—perhaps to be followed by Antioch College; she admired Arthur Morgan, who had revived Antioch. I wanted to go on an educational cruise around the world. We compromised, and my mother found a school near Tucson, the now defunct Evans School. It was a dismal year. My principal pleasure and escape came from horseback trips in the mountains every weekend. A few of the students were semidelinquents who had been thrown out of schools like Saint Paul's, although I found in John Heinz II a good friend; he and I edited the humor magazine, where we used our sardonic energies against the lackluster masters and the largely indolent students. The English headmaster, Dr. Evans, taught Latin, but without the slightest interest in it.

At Harvard College I soon found myself for the first time in a place where I wanted to be. I actively went out for activities; I competed twice for acceptance onto the staff of the student newspaper, the *Crimson,* and, succeeding on the second try, made it my "club" for the next years. The *Crimson* not only legitimated my roaming curiosities concerning Harvard University but also focused my energies, and the severe criticisms we made of one another as writers and editors in the

"Comment Book" engendered a kind of competitive camaraderie and, at best, craftsmanship.

Mistakenly I thought my parents sensible when they encouraged me to study subjects at Harvard that could only be pursued in an academic setting, and that meant the natural sciences, for one could always read books. Thus I majored in biochemical sciences, making clear to curious friends on the *Crimson,* most of whom majored in English or another discipline of the humanities and had no heavy laboratory work, that the last thing I would ever be was a premed. Neither did the idea occur to me that I would ever become a professor. The science teaching I experienced, including that of James B. Conant, was routine until in my senior year I encountered Lawrence J. Henderson's magnificent course, focused on the physiology of blood.

But I did enjoy reading history, and as a sophomore I petitioned Arthur Schlesinger, Sr., for permission to take his course on American social history, open to juniors and seniors. It was a disappointment, for although Schlesinger was a fine person and an admired mentor of graduate students, he was a poor lecturer and did not seem to me to be a penetrating scholar. The following year I had a piece of good fortune in the visit of Charles Kingsley Webster from the University of Aberystwyth in Wales who gave a course in British diplomatic history in the era of Castlereagh and Canning. Webster had burrowed with ingenuity and thoroughness in the archival materials, and it was engrossing to be able to learn something in such fine-grained detail, including the British origins of the Monroe Doctrine—a relevant concern for me in the light of my already established misgivings concerning Manifest Destiny. I enjoyed a few conversations with Webster in his rooms in the Continental Hotel. I had "discovered" Webster, and I wandered about in the humanities, sometimes briefly auditing courses in literature favored by my friends. I shared their admiration for John Livingston Lowes but not their enthusiasm for George Lyman Kittredge's course on Shakespeare, which in my view was philosophical pedantry not made more palatable by his carefully cultivated eccentricities.

In my senior year, however, I had better luck and perhaps better judgment. Since I was writing an honors thesis (on a theoretical topic in biochemistry I have forgotten), I was permitted to reduce my course load to two rather than the standard four courses. In addition to Henderson's course, which entranced me (as did his book, *The Fitness of the Environment*), I opted for Irving Babbitt's course on romanticism. Babbitt's personality was not appealing to me, but I found his outlook bracing and attractive.[2] (Most students were uninvolved with Babbitt's

judgments. He displayed his erudition, and there was a students' betting
pool on the number of names he would drop each day; I sympathized
with Babbitt in the face of the philistines!) I wrote a long essay on an
extravagantly ambitious topic, "The Educational Theories of Goethe
and Rousseau." I did not read much secondary literature, and I pon-
dered *Émile* and other apposite writings of Rousseau as well as Goethe's
Conversations with Eckermann.

I appreciated Rousseau's originality, but not his vision. Well before I
encountered Irving Babbitt, I had gained a keen sense for the fragility of
civilization. Eight years old when the United States entered World War I,
which led to the internment of my governess's fiancé, a German merchant seaman, I was aware of the storm of hatred for "the Huns";
frankfurters became hot dogs; schools stopped teaching German. In the
1920s I read about the propaganda campaigns that helped bring the
United States into the war on the side of the Entente, whereas I concluded that had the United States sought to impose a peace in 1917, the
Germans would certainly have been willing, and the French might have
been forced, to accept a settlement. My sense of the volatility of public
opinion in a democracy and my misgivings concerning nationalism, in
the United States and among other potential combatants, have been
fairly constant in my outlook to this day.

III

I cannot recall how it was that I became a member of the Liberal Club,
but it was not out of an interest in politics. My involvement with the club
had to do with education, which was one of the interests I did share with
my parents, especially my mother, whose interest in Bryn Mawr College
was lifelong and who had an admiration for, and some acquaintance
with, John Dewey. As chairman of the Liberal Club speakers committee
during my sophomore year, I invited some venturesome college presidents to speak to our little group. The most memorable was Alexander
Meiklejohn, whose ouster as president of Amherst College had caused a
sensation and who had then founded the Experimental College of the
University of Wisconsin. Clarence Cook Little, the reform-minded president of the University of Michigan, came to speak; so did Hamilton Holt,
who had put Rollins College on the map. (Holt is admirably sketched by
John Andrew Rice, who left Rollins to found Black Mountain College, in
I Came Out of the Eighteenth Century, as well as in Martin Duberman's
fine book, *Black Mountain: An Exploration in Community.*)

Through my own interest and the default of other reporters and editors, I was able to make education at Harvard my beat on the *Crimson* (my fellow editors, notably Paul M. Sweezy, who easily beat me out for the presidency, prided themselves on their lively sports coverage). I "discovered" Henry A. Murray and his Psychological Clinic, devoting a full page to a story about his work—an unexpected visibility he regarded with a mixture of pleasure and unease. I gained a scoop on the iron lung that Dr. Philip Drinker, a friend of my father, developed at the Harvard Medical School. I prowled the law school, encountering, not for the last time, its pugnacious, spirited dean, Roscoe Pound. I ventured to the business school, then as later terra incognita to the Faculty of Arts and Sciences. I wrote an occasional column, "The Student Vagabond," about courses that seemed particularly interesting.

As a *Crimson* assistant managing editor the most difficult times came during reading period, when (unlike in the present lush days) there were hardly any advertisements and I had the responsibility for filling what seemed like acres of print, including writing editorials (a few of them attacking the Reserve Officers' Training Corps and the anti-German militarism of the war memorial murals in the Widener Library). I was an anxious perfectionist, and in slack news times I would wonder whether I would be the first editor in fifty years to end the night without a *Crimson* in press. I preferred to work on stories with a long lead time. My greatest excitement came in collaboration with Benjamin West Frazier III, who had been a Penn Charter classmate until sophomore year, when he had gone to St. Paul's School and from there to Harvard. He had come onto the *Crimson* as a photographer. Both of us were architecture buffs, and Ben, a concentrator in architectural sciences, was to go on to spend his life restoring old Hudson River valley houses. We discovered the incipient Harvard House Plan of President Lowell. Where Eliot House now stands was a gas station. We asked the manager when his lease was up, and made similar inquiries elsewhere in the area along the Charles River. Then we went to the offices of Coolidge, Shepley, Bullfinch, and Abbott, the Harvard architects, whose permanent hold on the university had not yet been moderated, and there saw mock-ups of the actual buildings. We learned from President A. Lawrence Lowell himself that land assembly was not yet complete, and withheld the story, exercising journalistic restraint in the interest of Harvard.

When it was permissible to break the story, I had developed an entire issue of the *Crimson* for a fall Saturday (for which the favorite journalistic assignment was the Yale game). I not only described the House Plan in detail, with its background in a Harvard Student Council report of 1926 as well as the Harkness gift, but also wholeheartedly supported the Plan. Among my friends I was alone in this judgment. Members of Final Clubs (Harvard's exclusive clubs for upperclassmen), whose mode of life Lowell intended to disturb, were of course opposed. So were others who had anticipated spending their senior year in the Yard—on such matters of tradition students then, as now, were conservative.

Even so, the two Houses that opened in the fall of my senior year were oversubscribed. My roommate, Alexander Langmuir (later one of the first persons to go directly from medical school into public health), and I were delighted to be selected for Dunster House and to find ourselves in a corner room overlooking the Charles. For us, living in Dunster House well illustrated Lowell's hope of close contact between tutors and undergraduates.[3]

IV

Living in a House dramatically changed the quality of life for me. Before my senior year, other than the historians I have mentioned, I had met no faculty members in the social sciences. Crane Brinton, the historian (later to write *The Anatomy of Revolution,* a book I admired), and Seymour Harris, the economist (with whom I was later to work, along with McGeorge Bundy, on a plan for a national self-liquidating student loan bank), were tutors in the House, as was Carl Joachim Friedrich of the Government Department. (I met Pitirim Sorokin only once, when I invited him to address a House colloquium; I still recall his opening comment that he was educating his son to shoot straight even before he taught him to think straight!) Entertained by tutors, Langmuir and I would in turn give tea parties for them, for fellow students, and for young women from Boston and occasionally Radcliffe.

What was truly decisive for me was meeting Friedrich, a nonresident tutor who had come to Harvard as part of a small group of German exchange students in the mid-1920s; he had not intended to stay, but at some point Professor Arthur Holcombe invited him into the Department of Government as an instructor. Friedrich was primarily responsible for my becoming an academic man. He had taken his doctorate at Heidelberg with Alfred Weber. At Dunster House he quickly had around him a circle of some of the most intelligent students. He was energetic and ambitious, of sanguine disposition, though capable of anger and contempt; he was a vigorous cello player. He was at home in French as well as general European art history (he later published *The Age of the Baroque*). He went on to a distinguished career in scholarship and public affairs in the United States and in post–World War II Germany. In due course I became one of his closest disciples. When I had become a student at Harvard Law School, we bought a rundown farm together near Brattleboro, Vermont. He introduced me to the European social sciences and to some American writers such as Thorstein Veblen. What was decisive for me, as I realize in retrospect, was that Friedrich was a magnetic and cultivated person, who not only was fond of me but also respected me as a potential intellectual colleague.

Had I lived in the Yard with most of my class, I would not have had this opportunity for easy intellectual commerce with faculty members and would have been less likely to encounter James Agee, then a junior, a haunted and engaging person, who was also in Dunster House. My interest in the Houses provided a few opportunities for conversation with President Lowell. (I quixotically sought to interest him in having Walter Gropius design one or another of the new Houses.) I was startled and found it clarifying to have Lowell dismiss my admiration for Henry Adams by saying that he was a whiner, full of self-pity. Lowell wanted Harvard, and particularly its law school, to turn out tough-minded leaders, potential statesmen, and also leaders of the bar—not aesthetes.

V

But my reasons for going to Harvard Law School had nothing to do with such ambitions. Like many people, particularly during my last two years, I had found a home in Cambridge and Boston more agreeable than my own home had been in Philadelphia.

Even if I had thought I had the capacity for the life of a scholar, I resembled my friends in not regarding our professors as leading lives we would want to follow. Since Harvard of that time had no rules for tenure, some of my teachers had been frustrated failed scholars, instructors in mid-life teaching affluent, uninvolved youngsters. When in Dunster House and elsewhere I met more interesting and sophisticated faculty members, I did not envisage them as models for myself. I had several classmates who were planning to enter Ph.D. programs, but they were not people with whose interests I could identify. One had an interest in forestry, worked for the Harvard Forest, and eventually got a Ph.D. in agricultural economics. Another, my school and college friend and classmate William Aydelotte, got a Ph.D. in history and was one of the pioneers in cliometrics. (He is the son of Frank Aydelotte, who had as president developed the honors program at Swarthmore College and who had impressed me as an almost ideal-typical Rhodes Scholar in his strength of purpose, his athletic prowess—when I knew him, at tennis— and his personal heartiness.)

I sought and did not get a Rhodes Scholarship myself (something I have not regretted since I dislike Oxford common room–style games-manship). However, a lot of my friends, and indeed about a hundred of my classmates, were going on to Harvard Law School. I recognized that intellectually I would probably find Yale Law School a more engaging locale. Yale already had a reputation for innovation and an effort to introduce the social sciences, chiefly economics. But since my primary purpose was to stay put, Harvard Law School was the obvious choice. Staying put, moreover, had the great advantage of allowing me to con-tinue my association with the magnetic Friedrich.

By my choice of roommates I took care to minimize what many of us who went from the amiable amateurism of the college to the fierce competitiveness of the law school experienced as culture shock. Having met Alexander Meiklejohn's son Donald, who was coming to Harvard as a graduate student in philosophy, I arranged to room with him. Another roommate was to be James Henry Rowe, Jr., a charming and ostentatiously indolent literary man, whose father was a judge in Butte, Montana; before coming to Harvard College he had spent a year at the Jesuit University of Santa Clara and astonished his classmates by arriv-ing from Butte with all the aplomb of one to the manor born. Rowe went on to become Oliver Wendell Holmes's last law clerk, an early energizer of the New Deal, and one of Franklin D. Roosevelt's "anony-mous assistants."

We lived at the Brattle Inn, along with several other lively would-be philosophers. I tried again what I had already done, which was to make something of Alfred North Whitehead's lectures. I could not get inter-ested in his discussion of Plato's *Timaeus* and Plato's imagery of the planets; the pleasure I had in the occasional Whitehead teas I attended could not be matched in the lecture room. In fact, my philosopher friends made me feel stupid; they seemed to play intellectual Ping-Pong, trading arguments back and forth, and this experience was one of the reinforce-ments I had of my parents' judgment on me. Philosophy seemed central to intellectual life. Only later did I discover philosophers—several of them European-born women (Suzanne Langer and Hannah Arendt)—whose work I could appreciate.

More interesting for me than the philosophers was Elton Mayo, who also lived in the Brattle Inn, where he and I, when we were having dinner together, were occasionally joined by Lawrence J. Henderson. I was fascinated by Mayo's work in the Fatigue Laboratory of the Harvard Business School, and it was through him, as I recall, that I learned about Lloyd Warner's research then under way in what became the Yankee City series of anthropological studies of Newburyport. Mayo took an interest in what he regarded as my naïveté about the world and what he saw as my obsessiveness. He told me about Pierre Janet's psychology both to interest me and to help me. Mayo's combination of physiological and social-psychological concerns was as remote from law school as I could have wished. Moreover, I felt that there was something mysterious about Mayo.[4]

VI

The atmosphere at the law school was rapacious, in contrast with the gentlemanly—and, in the eyes of Lowell and others, too leisurely—spirit I had experienced in the college. Fearful of failing on the one hand, and desperately eager to make the law review on the other, students formed into study groups, underlined their notes, and read and reread their cases. Virtually all casebooks at that time were prepared by the professors themselves and were unannotated selections of appellate opinions, from whose obiter dicta we were supposed to extract the holding—a figure-and-ground exercise many of us quickly learned. I enjoyed the cases for their details, though these were of course filtered through what the judges regarded as important.

But what the law school was about was teaching one, as the phrase went, to think like a lawyer. This adage primarily meant giving up sentimentality and naive notions of justice. I could appreciate, against the claims of distributive justice, the need for precedents and stability. It was periodically my common sense that was offended, as for example by some interpretations of the intricate rules of evidence, especially the hearsay rule, which frequently excluded evidence that was clearly relevant because the source could not be cross-examined in court. Also my common sense (but not that of anyone else I came across then or have come across since) was offended by the Fifth Amendment, for I did not think the democracies that had no such prohibition against self-incrimination were more oppressive or unjust than the United States, and I thought the amendment an overreaction to the fervent propaganda of the American Revolution that sought to portray the relatively mild British rule as archaically tyrannical. When legal rules led to what were clearly untoward outcomes, the legal system was upheld by most of my professors and ultimately by fellow students on the ground that allowing each side its day in court and its opportunities for argument would in the main lead to the discovery of the relevant facts, with the debate among opposing counsel eventuating in their correct interpretation. I found this debaters' outlook inadequate. But I was even less attracted to iconoclastic Thomas Reed Powell, who taught constitutional law in what was already known as the Yale realist style—an easy cynicism that saw judges manipulating precedents to arrive at decisions satisfying to their egos, their interests, or their whims; for Powell and his followers, it was enough to debunk the law.

I admired and came to know two of my first-year professors who were dramatically different from one another. Calvert Magruder, Jr., was an almost universally popular, cultivated, noncombative Marylander who taught torts and later became an eminent federal appeals court judge. The other, James Angell McLaughlin, taught property law; related to presidents of both the University of Michigan and Yale, he flouted courtesy and convention. He sometimes frightened students, like Professor Kingsfield in *The Paper Chase;* more often he offended them. Mischievous as well as sharing the then prevalent Bostonian snobbery toward Irish Catholics, he wore an orange tie on St. Patrick's Day and later changed his name from McLaughlin to MacLachlan.

As the academic year drew to a close, Rowe was convinced that he would flunk out, as allegedly a third of the students did. He had read French novels, spent much time at Smith College, slept late, and far more than I refused to adjust his Harvard College style to Harvard Law School routine. I decided that I would work hard in my second year in the hope of making the law review, and the way to do that was to have a roommate who was deeply involved in his legal studies. I found such a person in Donald Field, who had been on the *Crimson* and came from a legal family. We moved into the law school dormitory. I joined Lincoln's Inn, a semirefuge for the more socially acceptable law students, where some faculty were also members and where conversation at lunch was generally shop talk.

My sheltered youth gave me a desire to see how people lived under different conditions, an interest that had led me the previous summer to the Soviet Union; it was one motive for bits of settlement house work I did as an undergraduate under the auspices of Phillips Brooks House,

Harvard College's social-service center. It was through that center that I was taken on as an unpaid "wop" for a summer with a Grenfell Mission station at Northwest River in Labrador.[5] There I received a cable telling me that I must return at once to Cambridge to take up my duties on the law review, duties that began several weeks before the start of the fall term. I was incredulous. After an all too long and hazardous sailing cruise down the coast to Halifax, I left my three fellow sailors to bring the boat to Boston while I took the train so as not to be further delayed. I discovered that I not only was on the law review but also had led my class.

VII

Jim Rowe returned, having done a little better than just scrape by, his ingenuity and literary gifts coming to his aid. I regretted my decision to leave our Brattle Inn residence, and after a year with Donald Field returned there both for my third year of law school and for the fourth, postgraduate year to which those who had been anointed as Louis Brandeis's prospective law clerks were entitled.

I enjoyed the work of the law review. Even more than the *Crimson,* the law review was a diurnal affair. Few of the editors worried about their law school classes. It was heady to be able to edit one's own professors, or professors from elsewhere—I remember editing an article by the man I most admired in the law, Columbia's Karl Llewellyn. I should add concerning editing that it has helped me as a writer to have edited the work of others as well as to have been edited by the stringent standards of the law review. Sometimes these seemed silly standards, as when even a biblical proverb was said to require a citation. I was elected legislation editor, a position that took me out of the area of case law and into legislative draftsmanship and public policy. I took part, with fellow editors, in an assessment of the constitutionality of the early New Deal legislation, my assignment being Section 7a of the Wagner Act, whose constitutionality I defended and whose vague language was seized on by John L. Lewis and his cadres of organizers to encourage workers to join unions; the act was ultimately sustained by the Supreme Court.

A few of us debated the merits of Legal Realism, then in vogue at Yale Law School, which seemed to me to be simpleminded reductionism. But the mode of analysis of many of the Harvard Law faculty was not vastly superior, though it was more attractive because it did not seek to shock. It assumed that the task of judges, within the limits of precedent, was to balance interests. Decisions were admired that appeared appropriately to have balanced interests of contending parties and the larger groups they might be thought to represent. For example, decisions, even by the most strained reasoning, that found large corporations liable in suits for negligence and ignored the negligence of the presumably impecunious plaintiff were generally justified because they spread the risk of accidents, even though they did so in haphazard, nonactuarial ways that were of enormous benefit to the litigating bar and sometimes produced a windfall for the plaintiff. Law professors made no accompanying investigation into the real interests; assumptions were made of a generally liberal sort as to what was in whose interest, and the question was happily left at that. In fairness I should add that many of the law professors were men of exceptional integrity, fair-mindedness, and dedication as teachers and as the scholarly housekeepers of the law. Half a dozen became good friends during my law school years. Felix Frankfurter, to my surprise a pedantic teacher, was a frequent, lively host, quick to explode in outrage at local or national injustice, corruption, or stupidity, happy to introduce the young men he sponsored to each other and, where appropriate, to people in power.

VIII

Antitrust law as MacLachlan taught it was an exception, involving some understanding of economics and of industrial organization and combination. In my third year I had a one-term course with Ralph Baker, an older man who had come from the Harvard Business School. He devoted the entire course to a single utility rate case involving the utility's financial structure. I enjoyed that course more than any. (I realize, writing these reflections, that what I seem to have enjoyed was getting thoroughly into something reasonably complicated, whether British diplomatic history or the intricacies of utility rate regulation in a particular instance.) Most materials read in law school were appellate court opinions.

Though making the law review spared me from having to care a great deal about my courses and, beyond the necessary minimum to remain on the law review, my grades, I never became reconciled to the general atmosphere of the place. We were taught to the point of redundancy how to deal with case law, how to make and, presumably, win an argument. Some of my friends and teachers were remarkably intelligent; hardly any were reflective or had an interest in ideas beyond gamesmanship. I concluded that two years of law study was sufficient (with much to be said for a clinically oriented program whose time-consuming work with clients could occupy a full year or more). I showed my boredom with much of the program, more than perhaps I intended by writing one of my third-year examinations in rhymed verse.

IX

More important than law school was my growing closeness to Friedrich, who was a reflective person with interesting ideas and serious interests. He had originally looked forward to a career that would bridge Heidelberg and Harvard, much as Harold Laski had linked England and the United States in his transatlantic forays. But when Hitler came to power, Friedrich, who had feared that prospect, decided to become an American citizen. And what better way to become American than to buy a farm? In the depths of the Depression, Vermont farms were cheap. Many had been purchased with Federal Land Bank mortgages at very low interest. I had inherited some money from my grandmother and I put it into a farm Friedrich and I bought jointly. In my last law school years we would go up weekends, staying at a tourist home and spending our time clearing brush and working on the farmhouse itself, a sizable place that had been turned into a granary. And of course we would talk endlessly. Through him I met Gaetano Salvemini, a refugee from Mussolini's Italy, and Eugen Rosenstock-Huessy, a fascinating German refugee, and many others. (Friedrich and I were to work later on a project he founded and I directed for retraining refugee lawyers and jurists.) Friedrich encouraged the Busch family and Rudolf Serkin, also refugees from Germany, to relocate in Marlboro, near Brattleboro. We both enjoyed meeting Vermonters, whether gentlemen farmers or herdsmen, county agents or bankers. In *The New Belief in the Common Man* (1942) Friedrich expressed a faith in the capacity of ordinary Americans for self-government. That faith grew in part out of our experience with the Agricultural Extension Service and with self-reliant, competent dairy farmers in New England; it left out of account the slovenly farmers whose barns we visited, looking for cows to purchase. We were in agreement in our opposition to plebiscites and to proportional representation, were admirers of representative constitutional government, and were aware of virtues in the federal systems of both Australia and the United States.

Friedrich had wide academic interests, having written a book on

Althusius and having immersed himself in Roman law, early European history, and political philosophy. The study of public opinion was something of a side interest for him, but it was already close to my interests in contemporary events and history. I learned from him to do what I still do today, which is to look at the letter columns of a newspaper or journal as a way of getting a sense of opposing views. Later he was to bring Charles Siepmann over from the British Broadcasting Corporation, where he had been director of research, to introduce the study of mass communications for the first time at Harvard.[6]

Before me, every person who had preceded the Brandeis clerkship by a postgraduate year at Harvard Law School had received a doctorate in law. However, I had offended Dean Roscoe Pound by arranging for Karl Llewellyn to come up from Columbia for a talk billed as "What's Wrong with the Harvard Law School?" and by asking my faculty friend Zechariah Chafee, Jr. (who still suffered, despite his national distinction as a civil libertarian, from not having made law review), to talk in rebuttal. Pound first forbade us the use of a law school classroom but then relented. But he was also feuding with Frankfurter, and the combination of animosities led him to change the rules, so that the doctorate in law could no longer be given to anyone who came to the requisite year immediately after law school. To me it did not matter at all; the doctorate was useful to those planning to teach, especially in the nonelite law schools, or to any hoping for an academic career outside a law school. But since I had at the time no such aspirations, I did not contest the dean's ruling.

I did something else, however, which my friends considered reckless. Frankfurter had formed a strong dislike of Friedrich. He suspected this blond Teuton of being a secret sympathizer of the Nazis, and in addition I think he was jealous of Friedrich's influence over me. The person designated as the Brandeis clerk usually worked with Frankfurter on a thesis. But I intended to work with Friedrich; I held my ground, and Frankfurter, to his credit, said that though he distrusted Friedrich, I could work with him if that was my preference during this post–law school year.

X

My year with Brandeis at the Supreme Court did little to turn me toward an academic career and did even less for my self-esteem. I did not think I served the justice well. I worked only to try to improve, which I could rarely do, the opinions he had drafted; he had already arrived at his judgments. The "Brandeis brief" had been developed by him as an advocate, introducing evidence from the social sciences to sustain the reasonableness and hence the constitutionality of legislation. The very first case I worked on dispelled any illusion that Brandeis himself would be influenced by empirical data when in pursuit of the larger goal of creating precedents for federal judicial restraint. It was the "Oregon berry box" case (*Pacific States Box and Basket Company v. White*), in which Brandeis upheld for a unanimous court an Oregon statute concerning the shape and size of berry boxes. Assigned to write the opinion, Brandeis wanted to establish that the law fell under the state's power to protect the public interest and welfare. He sent me out to discover the actual reasons for the law. I soon found at the Department of Agriculture and the Interstate Commerce Commission that the law was designed to keep out berry boxes manufactured from redwoods in California (redwoods do not grow in Oregon); the law resulted in boxes less equipped for stacking in freight cars. To me, the law was an interference with interstate commerce. Brandeis thought in terms of a long-term strategy in which he wished to reduce centralized power, including the power of the federal courts to declare state legislation unconstitutional. In his building block of precedents he ignored the real story in order to uphold the state's authority, even though in principle he favored free trade and opposed monopolies. Other cases I worked on, such as the famous case upholding the Tennessee Valley Authority indirectly by denying the plaintiffs standing to sue (*Ashwander v. Tennessee Valley Authority*), involved only library work and not what was for me more exhilarating detective work and fieldwork.

I shared a house in Georgetown with a group of New Deal lawyers, including Rowe. One of my housemates was Thomas H. Eliot, several years my senior at college and law school, who helped draft and pilot the Social Security legislation through the Congress. Other young men from Columbia, Yale, and Harvard were exercising similar responsibilities. The brisk self-assurance of many of the young New Deal lawyers struck me as awesome in some cases but as disagreeable in others. I had already concluded that Harvard Law School and other national law schools cultivated a belief that outside of a patent, admiralty, or antitrust case, there was nothing one could not get up in a pretrial two weeks. If I lacked the self-confidence of others around me, I was growing in confidence that I might be able to understand events. For example, my early judgment that even unemployed Americans in the years of the Depression were basically conservative and would not become converts to socialism, let alone communism, was being borne out day by day. I sympathized with the strong Southern Agrarian streak in Brandeis, his distrust of centralized power, and his hope to use the states for small-scale, incremental experiments. However, I lacked the crusading spirit of Brandeis and many of his devotees.[7]

When I told Brandeis that I wanted to return to Boston, he sought to dissuade me, saying I had enough privilege and enough education; he advised instead that I go to Tupelo, Mississippi, and work there for the TVA and help develop Appalachia. I rejected his advice (as I had also rejected his harsh judgments against the English, based on the restriction of immigration to Palestine, and against the Germans, rather than simply the Nazis). Many notable lawyers and law professors had preceded me as Brandeis's clerk, and I compared myself unfavorably to them in terms of how I had served the justice; but as several Brandeis biographers have suggested, I also did not share the exalted view of Brandeis most of them held.

I was offered a position with the Securities and Exchange Commission but instead said to the lawyer who had hoped to recruit me that I wanted his help to get a job with a small Boston law firm, where I could learn my way in the law. He found me such a job with Lyne, Woodworth, and Evarts, a firm that defended Metropolitan Life and John Hancock in insurance cases and handled corporate reorganizations.

XI

Brandeis's law clerks were forbidden to marry. I had become engaged the previous summer to Evelyn Hastings Thompson. Evelyn's father was a professor at the Massachusetts Institute of Technology; her mother of an old Bostonian family. Evelyn followed her mother to Winsor School, a girls' school of high academic as well as social selectivity, and on graduation won the Nora Saltonstall Scholarship given by the Winsor School to study for a year in Paris. On her return she went to Bryn Mawr, where she majored in English, edited the *Lantern*, the college's literary magazine, and directed and acted in plays. When through a Boston classmate of hers I met her at a dance at Bryn Mawr in the spring of my last year at law school, I asked her what she planned to do on graduation; she replied that she wanted to put on Greek plays and act in them. That summer I looked her up in the course of a sailing cruise my brother had organized when we stopped off at our parents' home in Northeast Harbor. She was acting in a summer theater company in Bar Harbor. That fall I persuaded Evelyn to come to Washington, where she found a position as an editor of the consumer affairs magazine published by the Department of Agriculture. She had given up her dream of working in Greek drama and instead decided to turn to writing criticism and short stories. (Having done a great deal of editing in college, her gifts as a critic and editor have been of the greatest benefit to my own thought and writing.) We were married in Boston the next summer, in July 1936. I borrowed a car from a former law professor, Ralph Baker, and we took a trip out west to Seattle (this was before interstate highways), traversing some drought-ravaged and depressed areas in the farm states, as well as some magnificent country.

In the fall I began to work with Lyne, Woodworth, and Evarts. What I was looking for was an apprenticeship. I have already indicated that I regarded my legal education as too bookish and insufficiently clinical. Lyne, Woodworth, and Evarts handled more litigation than most corporate firms. Had I worked in Washington—or, indeed, for the TVA—I would have had as a young lawyer large responsibilities and a decent starting salary; in a private law firm I was only an adjunct at one hundred dollars a month, helping prepare trial briefs. But with a small private income I could afford to do it.

The few appellate cases I handled, involving relatively small amounts, did not give me a high opinion of the judges. In one case a man was receiving disability benefits under an insurance policy for "total and permanent disability." The insurance company had photographs of him actively playing tennis and golf in Florida, and on the basis of his recovery we appealed from a judgment against the company. The judge asked me, "How permanent is a permanent wave?" and went on to support the plaintiff's cause.

I found much of the work of a trial lawyer at once frustrating and strenuous. It was frustrating because I spent so much time waiting for a case to be called. It was exhausting during a trial to be always on the qui vive, at a time before discovery proceedings limited the surprises one might encounter; and when the courtroom day was done, I was busy preparing for the next day as well as trying to keep up with the regular flow of office work. Yet there was much novelty and hence interest in the actual trials, often in outlying towns like Salem or Quincy, in courtrooms far removed from the elevated discourse and the solemn and ceremonial quality of the United States Supreme Court.

The firm's trial lawyers, particularly a Mr. Murphy, for whom I largely worked and whom I liked, possessed a kind of combative idealism, a quixotic belief in justice, leading them to prefer fighting to settling cases of fraudulent claims against John Hancock or Metropolitan Life. By contrast, most of the large Boston firms settled such cases since the cost of defending them was more than the policy was worth and the defense seldom won. In a typical case a man would be told by his doctor that he had pericarditis; he would then with a zealous or perhaps corrupt insurance agent take out a policy with Metropolitan Life or John Hancock for his wife's benefit; shortly thereafter he would die of heart disease. Since he had said he was in good health in his application and the autopsy showed otherwise, the insurance company would refuse to pay and suit would be brought. In his summation to the jury, counsel for the plaintiff would read the Metropolitan Life's billion-dollar balance sheet and ask why the company was unwilling to help out the widow. It was a rare triumph for honest policyholders when suits based on egregious fraud were not successful. Fraud often was abetted at the trial by medical experts, such as a Harvard Medical School specialist who testified that myocarditis was no worse than a bad cold. At that time, and later when I worked in the New York County district attorney's office, I could observe the power of demagogic oratory on the part of solo lawyers virtually unrestrained by the rules of evidence I had learned in law school or anticipated in trial briefs. Conscientious but easily swayed juries had not yet been "educated" to award multimillion-dollar damages in accident, malpractice, and, quite recently, libel cases, but they were moving in that direction under the tutelage of a bar that Tocqueville had seen as a possible source of aristocratic restraint in a democracy.

I glimpsed high tragedy and low comedy in some of the trials. My superiors impressed me with the astuteness of their trial tactics, and I learned from them that the rules of evidence I had studied in law school were of little help in predicting the tactics of the plaintiffs' lawyers or the capriciousness of the judges. The office work generally was of greater intellectual interest, for example, grasping the details involved in the reorganization of the International Paper and Power Company.

Most of my evenings were free. I had time to attend sessions of a seminar Friedrich was giving and to keep in touch with the bright graduate students he was gathering around him, as well as with friends on the law school faculty. Evelyn and I also had time to make new friends in Boston, and we became particularly close to Mark DeWolfe Howe, Jr., a former law clerk for Oliver Wendell Holmes then also practicing in Boston, and to his actress wife Molly Howe, from the

Abbey Theatre in Dublin, who lived near us on Beacon Hill. This friendship turned out to make easier my decision on the next step in my career.

XII

By the luck that seems to have come my way at crucial times, the year in which I started work in Boston, 1936, marked the beginning of a new administration at the law school of the then private University of Buffalo. It had been a locally oriented school run by practitioners. Samuel Capen, president of the university, wanted to create a full-time, scholarly, national school. He turned to Francis Shea, a Harvard Law School graduate and former New Deal administrator in Puerto Rico. Dean Shea, a Frankfurter protégé, had recruited Louis Jaffe, who had preceded me as Brandeis's law clerk, and Ernest Brown, who had clerked for a federal appeals court judge; through Frankfurter's recommendation Howe and I were invited to join the group the following year. We encouraged one another to accept. When I told my friends on the Harvard Law faculty that I was planning to go to Buffalo, several of them warned me that I would ruin my career and added that if I wanted to teach law, they would try to find something for me at Harvard Law School. (They were wrong about the careers of all four of us; the other three—Jaffe, Brown, and Howe—became professors at Harvard Law School after World War II.) The fact that Buffalo was in no fashion a major law school made it more attractive to me because I would not be beginning my teaching in the highly competitive atmosphere of a national law school.

Moreover, for Evelyn and me the city of Buffalo had its own appeal. We were aware of our having been bounded by the northeastern "province" of the country, interrupted by transatlantic experience. Buffalo's primarily industrial character, with its large, not yet mobile Polish population, the whole city heavily Catholic, invited our restless curiosity.

XIII

The law school was in an old town house in downtown Buffalo, and the main campus was some distance away. The principal interest of my Harvard-trained colleagues was in the great subjects made central by the New Deal, constitutional law and the newly expanded fields of labor law and administrative law. The recruiting orbit of the school did not change with the replacement of most of the practitioner faculty by new full-time faculty. The students came from nearby and were mostly the first generation in their families to attend college. Some were disoriented by the high aspirations of the new faculty, which could not be matched by our influence in getting jobs in the New Deal agencies for even our ablest students in competition with the graduates of the major law schools. I was assigned two of the five first-year courses, criminal law (which I had not taken in law school) and property, and was glad to teach the staple subjects to the entering students. I would have preferred a chance to teach torts, for I had begun to develop an interest in the study of libel and slander, in the bearing of litigation over defamation on issues of public opinion and civil liberties. However, torts was in the hands of Philip Halpern, later a judge, a capable Buffalo practitioner who fitted in well with the newly recruited faculty. Teaching the property course, I used in addition to a standard casebook the advance sheets of the most recent New York State court opinions. When I had taught what I believed to be the law in New York State, I could briefly speculate concerning people's attachments to possessions—to what extent attachments to certain sorts of objects could be thought of as "natural" and other sorts as customary and particular.

This interest led indirectly to my first bit of empirical research, "Possession and the Law of Finders."[8] Traditionally the law is finders, keepers, unless the owner is known. I surveyed the policies of public-transit systems and department stores, as well as the practices of people themselves when they find something in a public place; many do turn it in to the lost-and-found department of a transit depot or store. They might, of course, believe they have a right to reclaim it if the owner does not, but few seem to act with this motive in mind. I did not conduct a survey of the general population but made sufficient inquiries to indicate that most people assumed that if they found something that had plainly been lost in, say, a store or a subway, they should turn it in to the lost-and-found department. The traditional case law did not support what was, in fact, common and desirable practice.

I realized that I greatly enjoyed teaching, always seeking to discover what my students might be learning, in contrast with what I thought I was presenting. I also took the more difficult and chancy road of eliciting discussion rather than calling on certain students to state a case and then on other students to say what was wrong with the exposition until I had elicited the "correct" response. Since a class based on discussion cannot be in the lecturer's control but depends on the students' motivation, preparation, and willingness (though not bombastic eagerness) to volunteer, I found then, as in all my teaching, that the discussion method often miscarried, leaving both students and instructor disappointed. I had to prepare questions that I hoped might provoke discussion, an effort that for me has never been free of anxiety. Focused as I was on what seemed requisite for the students, there could be only the most peripheral connection, if any, between my research and my teaching. The prospect that I might some day teach in a setting where there was less separation between my agenda for research, growing out of my intellectual interests, and what I was teaching did not occur to me.[9]

I was twenty-seven when we went to Buffalo, which did prove to be an interesting city. I soon became a member of the board of the Foreign Policy Association, gave a lecture to the Amalgamated Clothing Workers, and began my first teaching of social science at evening classes of the YWCA. I found friends at the university, notably Fritz Machlup, an evocative refugee economist; Walter Curt Behrendt, the city planner; and others in sociology, political science, history, and English. Evelyn and I met musicians, painters, and a poet, Reuel Denney, whom I was later to recruit as a colleague at the University of Chicago. Our efforts to explore the city did not extend to the Polish neighborhoods, which seemed to be isolated even from the other traditional Roman Catholic groups. At about this time I began an unorthodox psychoanalysis with Erich Fromm. I did so not because I thought I needed it—I did—but to please my mother, who wanted to be able to talk with me during the time she was an analysand of Karen Horney, who had recommended Fromm to her for me. Karen Horney had said of me that I was a rather resigned person, and this struck me as perceptive. On alternate weekends and when feasible, I would take the train or fly to New York and have two two-hour weekend sessions with Fromm before returning by train to be sure not to miss my Monday class.

When I went to see Fromm for the first time at his apartment on New York's West Side, I noticed a large shelf of the collected works of Marx and Engels. I assumed that a Marxist or Leninist would seek to propagandize me. When I had gone to the Soviet Union in the summer of 1931 with an Intourist group, some of whom were then in law school or graduate school or starting careers in journalism, there were fellow travelers among them who idealized whatever we were shown in the Soviet Union and derogated the United States. I had little use for either side of that seesaw.[10] Although several people I had known in college, for example Paul Sweezy, had later become Marxists, and several of the

New Deal lawyers I had met in Washington, notably Alger Hiss, had turned out to be Communists or close to the Communist party, none of my friends was even so much as a fellow traveler, and many of my law school friends, including Chafee and Howe, were vigilant civil libertarians. I had gotten this far in life with virtually no exposure to scholarly Marxists.

Fromm amusedly reassured me that he had no intention of converting me to Marxism. However, we often talked as if he were my teacher rather than my analyst. We discussed the study of society and the work on social character that he had done with Ernst Schachtel, whom I also met and admired, when Fromm was part of the Frankfurt group. Later, I was to attend seminars in New York for analysts in training, given by both Fromm and Harry Stack Sullivan at the William Alanson White Institute, and lectures by Schachtel and Fromm at the New School. While I resisted the efforts of my mother, with whom I stayed at her New York apartment, to draw me into intrapsychic inquiries, I was happy to talk with her concerning the larger social-psychological issues raised by both Horney and Fromm.

Fromm, who had, like Friedrich, a Ph.D. from Heidelberg, was widely read in history and biography. Like Friedrich also, he greatly assisted me in gaining confidence as well as enlarging the scope of my interest in the social sciences. Although he did not accept my criticism that his view of the United States and especially its middle classes was too monolithically and stereotypically negative, he did accept my criticism of his English prose and once encouraged me to redraft a chapter of *Man for Himself;* he thought my version perhaps improved, more nuanced, but characteristically decided to write "for himself."

If one recalls that my parents were Francophile and Italophile in culture and Anglophile in manner, then my interest in contemporary German—that is, Weimar—culture was a way of finding my own direction as distinct from theirs—a direction facilitated not only by Friedrich and Fromm but also by the many refugees I met through both those men and through my own concerns.[11]

XIV

Becoming a professor in a law school is not the same thing as becoming a professor in an academic discipline.[12] Competing directly with the profession, law schools pay higher salaries and give instant or virtual tenure to attract and retain young recruits. The law professors under whom I studied at Harvard Law School were categorizers of the law, organizing decisions for the purposes of teaching and, sometimes in proposed uniform codes, for the benefit of the profession and the country. Of course the major law schools housed researchers (as Harvard did Sheldon and Eleanor Glueck to study juvenile crime) and a handful of scholars who taught legal history, jurisprudence, and sometimes Roman law or contemporary foreign law. At Buffalo, in contrast with such recondite work, I taught a third-year seminar on the ordinances of the city of Buffalo. And I did what law professors do, which is to "keep up" with developments in the law by reading the advance sheets, that is, skimming through recent decisions in the areas of my teaching or research. But this harvest was not nourishing to me unless I was on the trail of a specific topic, such as the studies of defamation in comparative perspective to which I will come in a moment. Nonlawyers often have read the opinions of some of the virtuosos of literature and the law, such as Oliver Wendell Holmes, Jr., Benjamin Cardozo, Learned Hand, or Louis Brandeis. But most judges are journeymen who crib from the briefs of counsel, do not employ an annual crop of Harvard, Columbia, Michigan, or Yale clerks, and provide the case materials by which the professors in the major national law schools, who are brighter and better educated, can develop their not always endearing classroom sharpness. In comparison with the excitement I found in reading *Democracy in America* or *The Protestant Ethic and the Spirit of Capitalism*, the regular gruel of the law appeared thin. I could teach it in a sufficiently evocative way to relatively unsophisticated students who had to face the bar examination and the practice of law.

I shared many interests with my Buffalo Law School colleagues. But I differed from them and from the other law professors I came to know in several significant respects. I have mentioned my belief that the Fifth Amendment was a harmful archaism. (I had a similar view of several others.) I was opposed to the use of the First Amendment in what I thought to be a vigilante way to oppose aid to parochial and other church-related schools. Although I cared about intellectual freedom (as my later writings attest), that did not make me an automatic supporter of the agenda of the American Civil Liberties Union. Mark Howe was offended by my skepticism and, as a stoic, disapproved of my psychoanalysis. My colleagues and many other law professors found their involvement in New Deal reforms and the corresponding legal questions rejuvenating, but neither for pedagogic nor research purposes did I see superiority in the new subjects. I published an article, "Government

Service and the American Constitution," that developed some of the work I had done with Friedrich.[13] I wrote another article on a topic still germane—the question of legislative restriction on the freedom of Americans to travel abroad and fight in foreign armies, as some Americans were doing at that time in support of the Loyalists in Spain.[14] I wrote essay reviews of books such as Otto Kirchheimer's *Punishment and Social Structure* and Edwin Mims's offbeat *Majority of the People.*

After the intense work of learning to teach three courses, I cast about for a research topic that might relate my interests in public opinion to the law. Defamation, though in all countries a tort or civil wrong and in some still considered a crime, was not a major interest of professors of torts. What I wanted to understand in comparative perspective was themes in the scattered American case law concerning defamation, that is, libel (written) and slander (oral). The cases and comments on them indicated that in the United States not only politicians but also ordinary folk were supposed to be able to take it and, if need be, dish it out. Successful libel suits were uncommon. By contrast, in England, Austria, Argentina, and elsewhere slander and libel were deemed extremely serious in both criminal and civil proceedings. What did all this imply concerning American public opinion and attitudes toward individual privacy, publicity, and the press? In an earlier day in our history did different attitudes prevail, when someone might issue a challenge to a duel—at least against a social equal, perhaps especially in the South—in response to regarding himself as having been defamed? Along with Friedrich I had done some work for the Council for Democracy, a group combating fascist tendencies in the United States and Hitler and Mussolini abroad. I wondered whether the Jews, as a defamed group, might bring suits for libel, and I observed the use of libel suits by fascists to intimidate their critics in the press—much as Ariel Sharon, the former Israeli defense minister, recently attempted to do vis-à-vis *Time* magazine, and General William Westmoreland, no fascist but supported by the radical right, vis-à-vis CBS.

I recruited one of the refugee lawyers I had met, Lucie Krassa, as a research assistant and embarked on a comparative study eventually published in 1942 as "Democracy and Defamation."[15] In that work, and in a long essay, "Civil Liberties in a Period of Transition," I made use of cases as a social historian would, as clues to the temper of a country, region, or epoch. On the basis of such partially empirical grounding, I was prepared to speculate concerning the public policy that might permit freedom of opinion while exploring how the intimidation of opinion through defamation, as well as suits for defamation, might be prevented. I did not then, and do not now, believe that I found a "solution" to these again vexing problems, but at least I did not approach them on the basis of flat American contemporaneity.[16]

Among the law professors I knew, there was intense focus on the Supreme Court as it began to uphold, rather than interdict, New Deal legislation. The social-psychological and cross-cultural themes that interested me rarely had immediate focus in public policy through law. A handful of law professors, such as Willard Hurst, who taught legal history at the University of Wisconsin, and a cluster of the lively men at Columbia Law School could respond to my interest in the significance of defamation in an amiably tolerant way more characteristic of colleagueship among law professors than of that among comparably ambitious faculty members in arts and sciences. The people from whom I was learning, however, were primarily not in the law but in the social sciences. Robert and Helen Lynd's *Middletown* had attracted me during my student days, and I was delighted to meet them in New York and to begin to exchange ideas with them. I think it was through them that I met Paul Lazarsfeld and then Marie Jahoda. I also met Franz Neumann, a refugee political scientist and analyst of Nazism.

In 1940 I applied for a Guggenheim Fellowship to devote full time to this research; but I chose instead to accept a visiting fellowship for 1941–42 at Columbia Law School, which provided an office and potential universitywide colleagueship. New York also had the advantage of allowing more frequent analytic work and intellectual companionship with Erich Fromm.

Of the people Evelyn and I met in New York, Lionel and Diana Trilling were particularly important. Many of their interests overlapped with ours. They introduced us to their circles at Columbia and to editors and writers for *Partisan Review.* We met other writers, artists, and intellectuals through Dorothy Norman, founder and coeditor of *Twice a Year,* a journal devoted to the arts and civil liberties where an article of Evelyn's had been published. We met Selden Rodman, with whom I played tennis, mostly unsuccessfully; he edited the irreverent journal *Common Sense,* which supported the isolationists (as did my cousin Fred Rodell, one of the Legal Realists at Yale), fearing that America's involvement in the war might irretrievably destroy the country's liberties. Some of my colleagues at Columbia Law School (Karl Llewellyn, Herbert Wechsler, Paul Hays, and Walter Gellhorn) had broad intellectual and cultural interests in and beyond the law. I met Ruth Benedict and joined the ever-expanding circles around Margaret Mead.[17] Fromm and Helen Lynd were teaching at Sarah Lawrence, where a number of "New York intellectuals" taught part-time.

Friedrich had counseled me to pursue a Ph.D. in government. The financial constraints of a wife and three children aside, I never came to the point of seriously considering the idea. Moreover, as I got more deeply immersed in sociological questions and preferred to start with empirical data, the concerns with political theory of Friedrich and his disciples began to seem a bit abstract to me. In other words, I was in search of a mode of work more empirical—ethnographic, even—than government as it was then being taught could provide. If Robert and Helen Lynd had given me an opportunity to take part in a community study, I think I would have welcomed the chance. Innovative law deans at the University of Wisconsin, Ohio State University, and the University of Oregon offered me joint positions in law and political science. However, since my primary base would still have been in a law school while coping with a new intellectual challenge, I hesitated to commit myself and was inclined to return to Buffalo.

Soon, with American entry into the war, the Buffalo Law School prepared to close, and the question of returning there was rendered moot. I thought it likely that despite having three children, I would have to enter military service. (I also had some inclination to do so, and unsuccessfully sought commissions, knowing enough from others to fear the ordeals of basic training.)[18] Then by chance a Harvard Law School friend and classmate, Whitman Knapp, offered me a position as deputy assistant district attorney of New York County, working in the Appeals Bureau under Stanley Fuld, legendary for his erudition and his scrupulousness. It seemed like an interesting temporary job at that unsettling time, and wishing to remain in New York, I took it.

XV

My work was to read the records and write the briefs on appeal. Thomas Dewey had been the district attorney and had prosecuted a number of racketeers on evidence gained from wiretapping. A few were convicted, and I was one of a group writing the appellate briefs in an effort to sustain the convictions. The trial lawyers for the defense in criminal cases were mostly histrionic, objecting to practically everything presented by the prosecutor and then seeking to find flaws for appeal. The extravagantly permissive state lower-court judges allowed the defense to try to browbeat often reluctant prosecution witnesses and behave in ways that would be considered unprofessional in federal court. By a tacit agreement between party bosses and the bar associations, the elected judges, including those holding lucrative probate judgeships, were slotted in the lower courts on the basis of patronage, whereas the Court of Appeal, the court of last resort in New York State, though also elected, was allowed to become respectable and even distinguished; it had been Benjamin Cardozo's base and later was Fuld's. The latter was a perfectionist and insisted that we overprepare our briefs, no doubt boring the judges' clerks who had to read them since if a case from New Zealand was in any way apposite, we would be sure to cite it![19] The experience gave me a sense of the appeal of Wall Street and other metropolitan law firms whose predominantly corporate clients can afford (and are sometimes constrained by) the most carefully researched advice that hourly billing can buy.

XVI

I could have stayed in the Appeals Bureau, but after a few months I had pretty well exhausted the variety of cases and had many times rehearsed work not terribly different from that of the law review or clerkship in doing meticulous research and then writing a brief. When the United States entered the war, Friedrich undertook to direct the Civil Affairs School at Harvard to train administrators for a future occupation of Germany; no one doubted that the Nazis would in due course be defeated. Friedrich asked me to take part, but I declined. My knowledge of Germany was slim, and I questioned my competence to be of help in such a school.

As an alternative, I had the idea of seeking a commission in some branch of the armed forces where I might learn something about business. The services turned down my application since I lacked business experience, and plenty of lawyers were already available. Casting about for opportunities, I was introduced by a friend to James Webb, treasurer of the Sperry Gryoscope Company (later head of the National Aeronautics and Space Administration), who asked me to become his assistant. He wanted to assign me to labor relations, but I pointed out that as a professor I would be regarded as friendly to labor and would hence possibly be given undue trust by the United Auto Workers local. I preferred to work on problems not directly involving personnel. My expectation was that with some experience at Sperry, if I then were drafted, I could secure a commission where I would hope to be useful and also to learn something about organizational and business problems. Since I was not drafted but ended up as contract termination director after Webb left (to become a combat flier), I actually found myself dealing directly with the military for two and a half intense years.

Sperry was a small engineering firm of one thousand employees that had exploded to thirty-three thousand as a war contractor. The senior officers of the operating company were primarily engineers, patriotic and of high integrity. But with the enormous expansion much was out of their control. Sloppiness and waste occurred in the manufacturing process. Extramurally I confronted the familiar story of interservice rivalry. Intramurally some of my own effort was spent making clear to junior managers and workers on the shop floor (who thought that they were protecting Sperry against its naive and idealistic top officials) that the company could only lose, in reputation as well as through negotiation of profits later if materials were sequestered (this was not done for private gain) or contracts terminated with more than the considerable delays I had already explained to the military.[20] I found several capable people (chief among them Elizabeth Klintrup, a brilliant lawyer trained at the University of Wisconsin) to help me make the quick judgments on the basis of limited information that the tasks required. The deficit of competent people, and changes in procurement as emphasis shifted from the European to the Pacific theater, added to my responsibilities.[21]

I had to learn my way simultaneously among the military services (where I ran into the most difficulty with the shore Navy) and among the production control people and accountants in the company's Brooklyn and Long Island plants; I had no direct dealings with the hundreds of subcontractors whose contracts had to be canceled when Sperry's prime contracts were terminated. I worked hard under great pressure, with a kind of stubborn rationality. Negotiating a modus vivendi for settling Sperry's claims to recover for canceled contracts raised strategic and practical questions but not ones of intellectual substance; hence it surprised me that I was so intensely involved. It was, as I would remind myself, primarily only money (and occasionally matériel) that was involved, not people's fates—and the money itself, as already mentioned, was not Sperry's to keep but was subject to renegotiation. Sometimes anxious, sometimes exhilarated, and often both at once, I persevered in a way that I regarded as responsible both to the company and, in a microcosm, to the rational conduct of the war.

I had come to view the war as necessary, though after many hesitations and without believing (like the interventionists) that the end of the war would be wholly benign or (like my friends among the isolationists) that America would become fascist. In terms of the way the war was fought, my sympathies were with positions Dwight Macdonald took in *Politics:* I opposed the mass air raids on German and Japanese cities, which Sperry's products were helping make less inaccurate. At the time and since, I regarded the dropping of the atomic bomb on Hiroshima and, far more, on Nagasaki as the use of means wholly disproportionate, certainly vis-à-vis Japan, which could not directly threaten the United States. Moreover, I believed that the demand for Unconditional Surrender was wrong in principle and pragmatically, making it difficult for the emperor (always threatened by military fanatics) to negotiate a surrender that would keep him in place.[22]

XVII

With the war clearly ending, I had to consider what I would do next. In 1945 Helen Lynd and Esther Rauschenbush, two prominent leaders of Sarah Lawrence College, asked me if I would consider becoming its president. Shortly thereafter, the then president of Reed College approached me with a similar proposal. My interest in women's colleges, beginning, of course, with Bryn Mawr, had combined with an interest in educational innovation and led me to visit Bennington College while I was at Harvard; hence the attraction of the offer from Sarah Lawrence. I had great respect for a few coeducational colleges, notably for Reed. I have noted my admiration for presidents whose approach was experimental—for Frank Aydelotte of Swarthmore College, and for what President Lowell was seeking with the House Plan and other reforms at Harvard College. Academic administration is, however, still administration, and I had learned at Sperry that it did not fully engage me. More important, I recognized that I lacked some of the qualities I knew to be essential in a college president.[23] Academic administration would demand of me tireless energy almost certainly without the summer respites in Vermont working on our dairy farm. Moreover, I lack the equable, sanguine temper that an administrator, and especially a college president, needs. I can rarely assuage irritation and impatience with wit and good humor.[24] I could not imagine assuming the responsibility of leadership in the semiparticipatory milieu of an experimental college, so I declined these possibilities.

There was some talk that I might be invited to join the Yale Law

School faculty. But by this time I was thoroughly converted away from an engagement with the law that was never wholehearted. What I most wanted was colleagueship—colleagueship in teaching in a setting where I could educate myself more fully in the social sciences and, if possible, colleagueship in research—something the individualism of law school professors, comparable to that of professors in the humanities, did not provide.

At this point I had remarkably good fortune. I had gathered some of my work on public opinion and civil liberties together in a monograph, "Civil Liberties in a Period of Transition," which I had contributed to an annual series edited by Friedrich and Edward Mason and which was also available independently.[25] In the third-year social-science course in the College of the University of Chicago Edward Shils had gotten the staff to assign my essay. When he discovered that the author was still alive, unlike those of the social-science classics read in the course, he went to the administration of the College and proposed that I be recruited to the staff. Reuben Frodin, assistant dean of the College, had been editor in chief of the *University of Chicago Law Review* and had edited an article of mine in that capacity; he lent his support to Shils. I went out to the university to meet Shils and the other members of the staff of the course. I eagerly accepted the invitation to come as visiting assistant professor, confident that this opportunity was right and, had I thought it possible, the one I would have looked for.

I arrived in January 1946, alone, since no housing for my family was available (our farm in Vermont came in handy as a base during times of relocation). In my first several months emergency regulations forced hotel tenants to find a different location every five days or so; this anxiety of where I would spend the night added to all my pedagogical ones.[26] Although I had spent the previous summer immersed in my own crash course in sociology, beginning, as I recall with Comte and then some Durkheim, I had inadequate preparation for the course in which I would be teaching. I had two different reading lists to master simultaneously, one for the course that had begun regularly in the fall term, and another for an accelerated course for veterans who arrived on campus when I did, in the winter. Shils was welcoming as a sponsor and learned as a mentor. So in a different way was Milton Singer, who had a Ph.D. in philosophy and was beginning to reeducate himself as an anthropologist. Our staff and our coverage included political science and history. One member, Gerhard Meyer, a German refugee, was steeped in Weber and German philosophical thought. Familiar with psychoanalysis, Singer shared an interest in "culture and personality."[27] Economics was represented on the staff by Abram Harris, with some reading and lectures from Frank Knight; economic history was the province of Sylvia Thrupp. We met regularly for discussion of readings and assignments of the two lectures a week, which we took turns delivering, and were responsible for the separate sections, ranging from ten to thirty-five students with whom we discussed readings twice weekly.

The three-course social-science sequence at Chicago seemed to me extravagantly ambitious then, and even more so in retrospect. While experimental psychology lay at the boundary with the natural sciences, Piaget and psychoanalysis, and especially its cultural foundations and impact, were on the social science side; I gave four successive lectures on Freud in his cultural context.[28] I learned a great deal from lectures given in turn by my colleagues. I found pleasure in teaching undergraduates in the college's required curriculum, for every student was reading the same books, attending the same lectures, and becoming engaged, if erratically and sometimes even overzealously, with a curriculum that invited efforts at coherence.[29] I soon began to audit the graduate courses of Everett C. Hughes, who personally as well as professionally became my closest colleague.[30] I profited particularly from Hughes's course on field methods. Lloyd Warner, whose work I had known and admired earlier, was a member of the Sociology Department also, and we were soon involved in discussions concerning new directions in community studies. Having come with an interest in public opinion, I was grateful for the presence of the National Opinion Research Center and its director, Clyde Hart.[31] At Chicago, more than anywhere else, there was great overlap of intellectual and academic interests, nourished by the fact that the university is relatively small, not only in comparison with the major state university campuses, but also with its eminent private East Coast competitors or Stanford. Moreover, at that time virtually everyone on the faculty lived in the Hyde Park and Woodlawn areas, within easy walking and bicycling distance from the university. Stymied from influencing the academic departments in the graduate school, Robert Maynard Hutchins, the university's maverick president, encouraged the creation of interdisciplinary committees in social thought, human development, communications, and planning—the latter two short-lived; and the milieu allowed for relatively fluid grouping and regrouping among sanguine, energetic scholars.[32]

Much of the social-science program in the College consisted of what had been defined as Great Books and hence was compatible with Hutchins's distaste for what he regarded as merely empirical and transient. Yet the third-year social-science course, dubbed for short Soc 3, as well as the first- and second-year courses (Soc 1 and Soc 2), differed from a similar integrated program at St. John's College, Annapolis, Maryland, in including contemporary social, political, and juridical problems—otherwise, something as contemporary as my essay "Civil Liberties in a Period of Transition" could not have been made a required reading.[33]

My own attitude toward Hutchins was one of admiration tinctured with ambivalence. I believed then, and still believe, that he added greatly to the diversity and potential intensity of American higher education. Chicago's willingness to recruit students after the tenth and eleventh grades of high school still seems to me worth pursuing, while recognizing its hazards.[34] I admired the effort of the College under Hutchins to group disciplines into more comprehensive divisions and the refusal to allow student consumerism to dictate the curriculum.[35] Consequently, I supported Hutchins against his academic enemies in the graduate divisions and his political enemies elsewhere. His characteristic arrogance of the bright lawyer, coupled with wit and charm, made him an effective debater. One argument where he carried the day was a case of overreaching—his insistence that the College program be self-sufficient and sealed off from electives in the graduate divisions. When I came to the College, students had the option of taking two courses in one or another of the graduate divisions, which therefore retained the hope that they might acquire Ph.D. candidates who had become attached to a particular specialty as undergraduates. In his grand manner Hutchins despised specialists. When he, along with those I came to refer to as the "College patriots," added courses in history and philosophy to the College curriculum, thus closing off apertures for electives, I opposed the decision as a mistake—as indeed it turned out to be since the limited capital of goodwill the College had among the graduate divisions pretty much evaporated at this point. I also believed that students should be exposed to specialists as well as generalists as part of their general education—a judgment that Hutchins and his devotees easily dismissed. Another issue where we differed concerned my wish to increase the proportion of empirical work in the sequence in the social sciences. Hutchins considered such work trivial and ephemeral. Soc 2, though also drawing on the classics (Freud, Durkheim, Veblen, Marx, and Tocqueville), included materials with some empirical substance, for example, Piaget's *Moral Judgment of the Child* and Gunnar Myrdal's then recent *American Dilemma*. I decided to shift from Soc 3 to Soc 2 and persuaded Milton Singer and Gerhart Meyer to make the move along with me. Milton Singer was crucial in accepting the leadership of the expanded staff of Soc 2 and in retaining the breadth of intellectual horizons that informed the development of the course.

Milton Singer became the chairman of Soc 2 in 1946–47 and assigned to me the task of revising the course in cooperation with the other people teaching in it.[36] Among them, one of the most important, who left his mark on Soc 2, was Daniel Bell. Versed in the work of the great European theorists—Marx, Freud, Weber, and Durkheim—he also supported my effort to include unprocessed data that students and their mentors could interpret (for example, unprocessed field notes from community studies, or life histories, or the interviews gathered in a public-opinion survey). Robert Redfield, thoroughly interdisciplinary in spirit, became a part-time lecturer in the course.

Both Soc 2 and Soc 3 differed from Soc 1 and other College courses in the balance between discussion sections and formal lectures in Mandel Hall to the entire class. Some courses had three section meetings and one lecture a week. I found the section meetings so intense that two a week seemed just about right. And the number of lectures we had made it possible for specialists on the staff to exhibit their erudition to their colleagues as well as to students; if they sometimes spoke over the heads of many students, then the section leaders could help interpret what was said in later section meetings.[37]

The Chicago quarter system had advantages for faculty members. There was always a certain student attrition by the winter quarter, so that it was possible to teach (and do one's stint of lectures) during the fall quarter and take the winter and spring quarters off without imposing an excessive burden on the staff. Correspondingly, after teaching in the fall quarter in 1946, I was granted the next two quarters off to work on developing Soc 2 into what already existed of a course that would be termed "Culture and Personality," although still under the rubric "Soc 2."[38] The reading, consultation, and discussion involved in launching the revised Soc 2 gave me a splendid opportunity for learning as a teacher some of the things I would have learned had I been a graduate student in sociology at the University of Chicago at a time when the line between sociology and anthropology (united at the graduate level until the 1940s) was not sharply drawn.

XVIII

The intense demands of learning and teaching, of curriculum development and negotiation, of staff recruitment, and of service on the interdisciplinary committees all prevented me from embarking on research of
my own. By the nature of the interdisciplinary curriculum in the College, only a part of my research interests and disciplinary ties could be
embraced except by accident or at the periphery. For example, my interest in survey research and in the survey interview could only be brought
vicariously into the classroom. In my few spare moments I wrote several
articles that were extended essay reviews or drawn from addresses I was
invited to make. Only in occasional work with doctoral students who
had research interests congruent with mine was I able to combine research interests with my commitment to teaching.

I do not recall when I met Harold D. Lasswell, but I know I read his
work with excitement long before going to Chicago; he was the principal American-born political scientist who in the 1920s was using a
psychoanalytic approach to politics. I went to hear him lecture in downtown Chicago some months after my arrival, and when the lecture was
over, he suggested that we go across Michigan Avenue to the Art Institute. There he proceeded to delight me by his detailed and discriminat-
ing knowledge of painting. In person, more than in print, he was fascinating.[39] Lasswell was then a professor at Yale Law School. In 1947 the
interdisciplinary Committee on National Policy at Yale, composed
among others of Lasswell and his law school colleague Eugene V.
Rostow (whom I had met when I was a law professor as well as at their
summer place not far from us in Vermont) invited me to come to Yale to
do research on some aspect of national policy. There was no definite
assignment of what I was to investigate, but previous work had been in
economics, and there was some talk that I would focus on public opinion and mass communications. But I was to be free to proceed as I
liked—an awesome prospect, but one I saw as an opportunity. However, more immediately troubling was whether I could seize this occasion when I could give Chicago little advance notice. I did not have
tenure and was warned that a request for leave would make me seem
flighty, even disloyal to Hutchins's aims. But when I made clear that I
would teach the fall quarter, and do so for two successive years, the
arrangement went through with the support of Milton Singer and Dean
F. Champion Ward.

In his essay in this volume Nathan Glazer gives at once an acute and generous account of our collaboration on what became *The Lonely Crowd* and *Faces in the Crowd.* I had not met Glazer but had been reading his "Study of Man" columns in *Commentary*, with their cogent analysis of sociological work. I knew he had a connection of some sort with the Columbia Bureau of Applied Social Research, and having admired its director, Paul Lazarsfeld, since his days running the Office of Radio Research in Newark and then Princeton, that was a connection from which I thought I could learn. When I asked Glazer to join me in this research project, at first he was in doubt, but in the end he agreed to come part-time; Glazer's part-time, however, is worth more than time-and-a-half for most people! We began by examining interviews concerning political issues at the eastern office of the National Opinion Research Center. We were struck by the opinion-proneness of the respondents: that there were so few responses of "don't know" and that so many people had opinions on matters quite remote from them and often outside the orbit of even vicarious experience. Americans appeared to feel entitled to have opinions and almost embarrassed not to have any. My own continuing sense of the fragility of a democratic society helped lead Glazer and me to look at political apathy, including nonvoting, as not necessarily a bad thing; on the contrary, a wholly civic, mobilized population, expressing itself by referenda and similar direct measures, can be a risky departure from representative government.

Glazer had been working on the interviews done for C. Wright Mills that later went into *White Collar,* and we studied those interviews and made rough efforts to code them according to a dichotomy we first termed *conscience directed* and *other directed.*[40] Then we started to do interviews ourselves, borrowing what we thought might be projective questions here and there, adding our own, and then working painstakingly to interpret the answers as a gestalt in the mode illustrated in *Faces in the Crowd.* Reuel Denney contributed materials on popular culture. The effort to understand social character drew especially on the Fromm-Schachtel study of German workers. Glazer and I both profited from a seminar the Yale anthropologists were conducting to see whether or not culture and personality theorists, such as Ralph Linton, who chaired the seminar, and Erich Fromm, who came up from New York to participate, could interpret a culture on the basis of ethnographic accounts of the Truk Islands presented primarily by George Murdock and Ward Goodenough.

Rostow and Lasswell arranged for me to have a pleasant office on the top floor of the Yale Law School building, but I had virtually no contact with the school. The Yale committee that sponsored the work kept pressing me to make a report on it to Yale's social scientists, but knowing the tentativeness of our ideas, I was reluctant to do so. I recall that my audience, when I finally had to present material, was generally critical, with the economist Max Millikan being rather harsh—he had been, and remained afterward, personally friendly. Economists understandably dismissed our ideas as lacking in scientific rigor and probative value; some sociologists said we were simply translating into new terminology familiar concepts of gemeinschaft and gesellschaft. More derisively and imposingly, Joseph Schumpeter, whom I greatly admired, ridiculed my notions when I spoke at Harvard, declaring that I was trying to pull a heavy historical load with an oxcart. In the Department of Social Relations, M. Brewster Smith, Clyde Kluckhohn, and Talcott Parsons were interested and supportive. My rather limited Yale colleagueship came from John Dollard and other psychologists with anthropological connections and interests, from political scientists, and from historians—Yale at that time had no sociologists to speak of.

In the second preface to *The Lonely Crowd,* written in 1968–69 for the Yale paperback edition, I make clear how speculative and tentative an essay the work was intended to be. Friedrich had read it in manuscript and said that it was a difficult book, which he would use with graduate students, but it was too subtle to assign to undergraduates. We never anticipated the kinds of adolescent sophistication that would lead many to read the book while in high school. Moreover, since the themes of the book were confined to certain sectors of American life, we did not anticipate the following it continues to have. Although attacks on me by reviewers and essayists have never been particularly agreeable, attacks on the theses of the book itself, even when astringent, discovered few lacunae that Glazer and I had not already sensed. We saw the book as a contribution to an ongoing discussion shifting away from national character to the character of particular strata at a particular period—a less ambitious, but also perhaps more fugitive, focus than the nation as a whole.

XIX

In the fall of 1949 I returned to my position in the College at the University of Chicago, supplemented by membership on three graduate committees. One, which lasted only a short time, was the Committee on

Communications, which Bernard Berelson directed. I had already been a participant in the American Association for Public Opinion Research and a contributor to its journal, *Public Opinion Quarterly;* what I especially enjoyed in AAPOR was the inclusion of nonacademics— members of the professional survey organizations, on whose work I drew for understanding and for secondary analysis, and market researchers, who in my perhaps too vivid imagination generally know more about Americans in our "market segmentation" than do sociologists. I had informal ties with the Committee on Planning, from which I had recruited Martin Meyerson to teach in the College and then, with his wife Margy Meyerson, one of Everett Hughes's students, to work on a small community study in Vermont, which is briefly reported in *Faces in the Crowd.* From that committee I also recruited Staughton Lynd, who helped me analyze the sources of Thorstein Veblen's economic concepts for a small book I had agreed to write on Veblen.[41]

During my apprenticeship my most important graduate involvement was my membership in the Committee on Human Development, which included Lloyd Warner, Everett Hughes, Robert Havighurst, Allison Davis, Bernice Neugarten, and William Henry.[42] Plans were adumbrated to find a new locale for a community study, and I proposed that we look for a much larger community than the small and provincial Illinois town variously known as Jonesville and Elmtown—a community I defined as manageable in that one could gather forty influentials in a room and they could pretty much decide what was to be done. I recognized that no community was typical, not Granville Hicks's "small town" nor Lloyd Warner's Newburyport (Yankee City, later restudied by Stephan Thernstrom), nor the Lynds' Middletown (later restudied by Theodore Caplow and associates). Nevertheless, after I had briefly visited Springfield, Illinois, we concluded that with its one main "industry" of state government, it would not be a good locale, and Racine, Wisconsin, also with a single major industry, did not appear inviting either. At that time Homer Wadsworth, then director of the Kansas City, Missouri, Association of Trusts and Foundations, one of many organizations of pooled local charities, had set up Community Studies, Inc., to do social research in Kansas City. Havighurst, Hughes, Warner, and I considered Kansas City and connection with Community Studies as a practicable possibility. With the aid of the energetic Homer Wadsworth (formerly a Pittsburgh social worker and executive and now for many years doing similar work in Cleveland) it was possible to meet interested local elites who appeared to be the moving forces of the city.[43]

After I taught the fall term in Chicago in 1951, Evelyn and I moved to Kansas City, where I was hoping to learn how to conduct a community study with Martin Loeb and four graduate students in sociology (one of them, Warren Peterson, was working on a dissertation of great interest to me about Kansas City school teachers). I was a resident researcher from the supervising Committee on Human Development quartet, and Loeb was the director. The community study was framed around gerontological questions, but I wanted to go beyond those and also beyond the questions of social class that preoccupied Loeb and Richard Coleman, one of Lloyd Warner's students and his later collaborator.[44] For example, I was interested in the religious life of this predominantly Protestant community (so different from overwhelmingly Catholic Buffalo) but was unsuccessful in persuading Loeb and the others to spend their Sunday mornings visiting churches (discreetly of course) to understand, for example, the difference in liturgical practices, Sunday school, and sermons among the three Churches of Christ, one of which in an upper middle-class neighborhood had been built by Frank Lloyd Wright. In the hope of stimulating the group of colleagues, I made field notes of observations and interviews and circulated what I loosely termed "notes on this and that"; but neither Martin Loeb nor the graduate students reciprocated my efforts, and I found that I could neither lead nor follow a project that for a time floundered.[45] I had been made a pro tem member of the Department of Sociology, chaired by the genial and reflective Ernst Mannheim, at the University of Kansas City, then a private institution, and gave a course of evening lectures on sociology.

I also continued a mode of ad hoc inquiry into the varieties of higher education that was to develop into my own specialty in community studies, namely, the community of colleges and universities. I accepted invitations to speak at those types of academic institutions with which I was unfamiliar, and if the Midwest Sociological Society was holding its annual meeting at Indiana University, I would try to go a day ahead or stay a day after its conclusion to meet people at that splendid institution and learn more about its ecological niche in the state (for example, its relationship with Purdue), in the region, and in the country. I accepted invitations to visit sociologists at the University of Kansas, Kansas State University, and the University of Missouri at Columbia (where I briefly explored the limited legacies Veblen had left during his time there); in Kansas City I met Jesuits teaching at Rockhurst College, and educators experimenting with a modular program at Park College; I had earlier been interested in Stephens College, also in Columbia, Missouri, as an aspect of a continuing concern for women's education and the role of women's colleges in that education. These visits were exploratory, not systematic, but forerunners of later dedication to a kind of academic ethnography pursued in brief bouts of fieldwork of the sort Ray Rist once characterized as blitzkrieg ethnography.[46]

In 1954 Everett Hughes, as chairman of the Department of Sociology and with support from Morton Grodzins, then dean of the Division of the Social Sciences, persuaded the department to allow me to join it on a split appointment with the College. However, there was dissent from the demographers, notably from Philip Hauser. He insisted that I not be given the title professor of sociology but retain the one I already had as professor of the social sciences, and in the end that arrangement was agreed on.

But the enmity was a problem for graduate students who worked with Hughes and with me, as well as for nontenured colleagues, particularly Nelson Foote and Anselm Strauss, with whom I shared research projects and to whom I was personally and professionally close. Unrealistically, if understandably, translating acidulous comments by faculty members into actual proscriptions of what would pass muster, some able graduate students feared to write a dissertation without tables in it. Fears increased when Hauser, after a rough political campaign, was elected to the chairmanship in place of Hughes. I sometimes had the dismal experience of having as a doctoral candidate someone who had been a spirited undergraduate and watching that person become more timid and less original as time went by. Meanwhile, I had been engaged in cooperation with Hughes in recruiting members of a group who called themselves the Young Turks at the Bureau of Applied Social Research, of whom a modest and percipient account appears in James Coleman's contribution to this volume. Coleman himself came; we had adjoining offices in the Social Science Research Building, which is so constructed that secretaries do not act as buffers. Everett Hughes was on the other side of me, and communication was frequent among us. I recall my excitement in looking through high-school yearbooks with Coleman and pondering the reasons why in some schools an overlapping group of students not only occupied the elected offices but also edited the yearbook, played in the band, served as cheerleaders, and so on, whereas in other schools there was more of a division of labor. Elihu Katz came, and I brought in Rolf Meyersohn to be research director of the Center for the Study of Leisure, which I established with Ford Foundation support in 1955. Katz, Meyersohn, and I offered seminars on mass communication, among other things comparing academic with journalistic ethics in interviewing. Hughes and I traveled to Cambridge and were successful in persuading Peter and Alice Rossi to come to Chicago; they had formerly worked at the Bureau of Applied Social Research.

None of these people had tenure, and if the liveliness facilitated by their arrival was to be maintained, and the combativeness of the department contained, Hughes and I agreed that there needed to be a new, hence not previously involved, chairman. We went to New York to see if we could persuade Leonard Cottrell, Jr., then at the Russell Sage Foundation, to accept a position, if one could be worked out, at Chicago, where we had the strong support of the dean of the Social Science Division. He declined. We made other overtures, which of course had to be to persons of such distinction that there would be no question as to their academic legitimacy. None worked out. Concurrently, in the wake of Hutchins's departure, less autonomy was being granted to the College.

In the summer of 1954, I taught sociology in the Department of Social Relations at Harvard's Summer School. That fall McGeorge Bundy, the dean of the faculty of Arts and Sciences at Harvard, whom I had met and admired, asked me whether he could stop over to see me in Chicago as he would be on his way to Wisconsin; I responded that if he were coming with any thought of persuading me to leave Chicago for Harvard, he should not stop by, and he did not. The intellectual excitement of the University of Chicago outweighed the price it seemed to exact in terms of combative personal and professional relations.

Several years later, however, the balance began to tilt against Chicago, and I quietly began thinking about finding a more equable place. The California Institute of Technology was one place I considered. Cal Tech possessed able faculty in economics, history, anthropology, and psychology. I would have been happy to teach bright undergraduates who might be willing from time to time to relax narrow definitions of what is scientific and examine social life with disciplined subjectivity. Stanford was another possibility. However, when in 1957 Bundy again approached me, he persuaded me to come to a newly created chair where my principal responsibility would be to undergraduates. It was an additional attraction that I would be affiliated with the Department of Social Relations. Even so, I found it very hard to leave the University of Chicago, toward which I had developed intense institutional loyalty, almost a kind of patriotism. It was a wrench to leave colleagues with whom I had worked in teaching and in research, and the many friends

Evelyn and I had made and who urged me to stay. At Harvard I quickly managed to develop an interdisciplinary cadre to join me in teaching a large course, "American Character and Social Structure," in the General Education program.[47] Rather than returning to Dunster House, I took part in shaping Quincy House, which opened in 1959, a year after my arrival at Harvard, and which, with Henry Kissinger, H. Stuart Hughes, and others as associates, became the most politically engaged of the Houses.

One of the ironies of my shift of locale has been to observe that the University of Chicago survived the student-faculty protests of the late 1960s and early 1970s, and also more recent controversies over issues of race and gender, with its undergraduate curriculum unimpaired, its academic seriousness unquestioned. By moving to Harvard I did not escape departmental controversy! However, the small number of graduate students with whom I have worked and with whom, happily, I continue to work, though emeritus, have not been at risk. In 1976, I became in addition a member of the faculty of the Graduate School of Education. Some of the most mature and interesting graduate students with whom I have worked have come from that school.

Notes

I thank the following colleagues for their thoughtful reading of early and late drafts: Daniel Bell, Reinhard Bendix, Bennett Berger, James S. Coleman, Robert Gorham Davis, Lewis Dexter, Jo Freeman, Martha MacLeish Fuller, Herbert J. Gans, Howard Gardner, Nathan Glazer, Gerald Grant, Wendy Griswold, Joseph Gusfield, George Homans, Alicja Iwanska, Steven Klineberg, Michael Maccoby, Edward C. McDonagh, Barbara Norfleet, Charles H. Page, Evelyn Thompson Riesman, Michael Schudson, W. Richard Scott, Verne Stadtman, Jennings Wagoner, F. Champion Ward, Murray Wax, Steven Weiland, Robert S. Weiss, and Milton Yinger. I acknowledge financial support from Douglass Carmichael's grant to the Project on Technology, Work, and Character.

1. I have sketched my mother's outlook in some detail for a conference sponsored by *Daedalus* on woman in America. See "Two Generations," *Daedalus* 93(1964):72–97; reprinted in *The Woman in America*, ed. Robert J. Lifton (Boston: Houghton Mifflin, 1955).

2. Daniel Aaron, reviewing a biography of Babbitt, wrote, "Out of unchecked impulse came nationalism, imperialism, and tyranny. Babbitt thought that American democracy, given its dubious ideological antecedents and evangelical politics, was all too susceptible to cant." "The Hero of Humanism," review of *Irving Babbitt: An Intellectual Study*, by Thomas E. Nevin, *New Republic* 192, no. 24 (June 17, 1985): 36, 38. Harvard's aesthetes largely

ignored, or were repelled by, Babbit, and he himself was half proud to be an anachronism.

3. I have described the mise-en-scène in an essay, "Educational Reform at Harvard College: Meritocracy and Its Adversaries," in *Education and Politics at Harvard,* ed. Seymour Martin Lipset and David Riesman, prepared for the Carnegie Commission (New York: McGraw-Hill, 1975), pp. 281–392.

4. See Richard C. S. Trahair, *The Humanist Temper: The Life and Work of Elton Mayo* (New Brunswick, N.J.: Transaction Books, 1984).

5. The chain of mission stations established by Sir Wilfred Grenfell on the Labrador coast was designed to provide primarily medical services to the descendants of early British settlers who scraped meager livings from fishing. At inland Northwest River, where I was stationed, the "natives" booed and hissed Sir Wilfred when he came and lectured them on their failure to plant gardens to vary their diet, too much of which, in his view and in mine, was alcohol. I was not disillusioned by the indigenous population of Labrador (I saw hardly anything of the Indians, but I knew that they treated their dogs miserably and seemed immune to missionizing) because I had no expectations concerning them. But I was somewhat disillusioned by the medical missionaries. Our little group of "wops" lived all summer long on a diet of salmon fourteen times a week because the other stations, which had got provisions intended for us, refused to share, and it seemed to me that the generally Anglican station heads who were married sacrificed themselves and their families more than they could emotionally manage without engendering rancor. From these leaders I had expected too much.

6. One of Friedrich's students whom I already knew was Lewis Dexter. A student of public opinion and of the interview, Dexter had passed enough examinations to graduate from the University of Chicago in the record time of five quarters. After war began in Europe in 1939 Dexter became a member of the Foreign Broadcast Intelligence Service, monitoring broadcasts—a group that later formed the Office of War Information, and some of whose members entered the Office of Strategic Services. Almost immediately after Pearl Harbor, as perhaps my first serious political act, I went to Washington to work with others to try to prevent the deportation of Japanese-Americans on the West Coast. I worked closely with Dexter, and after 1945 we were periodic allies in the effort to control nuclear arsenals and to prevent their testing.

7. Unlike a number of my fellow sociologists who have written essays for this volume, I was not an early critic of the American social order. I did not know any Democrats, let alone Socialists or Communists, until I got to college. When in college, I worked briefly with boys' groups in several settlement houses. I did not identify with the youngsters I found very difficult to control.

When I met fellow travelers on my visit in the summer of 1931 to the Soviet Union, I regarded them as even more ignorant than I concerning the United States and gullible in the extreme concerning the Soviet Union. However, I was a pacifist. For fuller discussion, see "A Personal Memoir: My Political Journey," in *Conflict and Consensus: A Festschrift in Honor of Lewis A. Coser,* ed. Walter W. Powell and Richard Robbins (New York: Free Press, 1984) pp.

329–35. For a bibliography of my publications through 1978, see *On the Making of Americans: Essays in Honor of David Riesman*, ed. Herbert J. Gans, Nathan Glazer, Joseph R. Gusfield, and Christopher Jencks (Philadelphia: University of Pennsylvania Press, 1979), pp. 319–46.

8. *Harvard Law Review* 52 (1939): 1105–34.

9. For additional reflections on dilemmas of teaching and research, see David Riesman, "On Discovering and Teaching Sociology: A Memoir," prefatory chapter to *Annual Review of Sociology* 14 (1988): 1–24; and "Balancing Teaching and Writing," *Journal of the Harvard-Danforth Center on Teaching and Learning* 2 (January 1987): 10–16.

10. I had not harbored illusions about the Soviet Union before going there, but my experiences in the course of the summer (briefly described in the political memoir referred to above) led me to see that in a large, incipiently industrial society no amount of terror could create complete internalized belief and that at the margin there could even be disobedience. In the same year in which I sympathetically reviewed Hannah Arendt's *Origins of Totalitarianism* in *Commentary* (11 [1951]: 392–98), I also delivered a speech to the American Committee for Cultural Freedom, "Some Observations on the Limits of Totalitarian Power," in which I contended that totalitarian control was an unreachable ideal—a judgment that exposed me to attacks then and thereafter from often newly zealous anticommunists. The latter did not see the differences I saw between inefficient Stalinism and less efficient Nazism: both were evil; but it did not follow, as my adversaries contended, that both would forever remain unchangeable from inside. My address, first printed in *Antioch Review* 12 (1952): 155–68, also appears in my collections *Individualism Reconsidered and Other Essays* (Glencoe, Ill.: Free Press, 1954) and *Abundance for What? and Other Essays* (Garden City, N.Y.: Doubleday, 1964).

11. In David Riesman, "A Personal Memoir: My Political Journey," in *Conflict and Consensus: A Festschrift in Honor of Lewis A. Coser*, ed. Walter W. Powell and Richard Robbins (Glencoe, Ill.: Free Press, 1984), pp. 327–64, I indicate ways in which I worked earlier with Friedrich in helping German refugees from Hitler's Germany and in opposing fascist sympathizers in the United States, and later with Fromm and others in what seem now like quixotic efforts to establish a binational Palestinian-Jewish entity in Palestine, as well as my own civic concern about the dangers of a nuclear arms race and on behalf of a test ban.

12. I have described in an essay some considerable differences in culture between a law school and a school of arts and sciences. "Law and Sociology: Recruitment, Training, and Colleagueship," *Stanford Law Review* 9 (1957): 643–73. See also "Toward an Anthropological Science of Law and the Legal Profession," *University of Chicago Law Review* 19 (1951): 30–44; reprinted in *American Journal of Sociology* 57, no. 2 (1957): 121–35.

13. *University of Chicago Law Review* 7 (1940): 655–75.

14. "Legislative Restrictions on Foreign Enlistment and Travel," *Columbia Law Review* (1940) 40: 793–835.

15. "Democracy and Defamation: Control of Group Libel," *Columbia Law*

Review 42 (1942): 727–80; "Democracy and Defamation: Fair Game and Fair Comment I," ibid., pp. 1085–112; "Democracy and Defamation: Fair Game and Fair Comment II," ibid., pp. 1282–318.

16. I have returned to somewhat related problems recently in studying the impact of open-meeting or sunshine laws on searches for college and university presidents. Here it is the press that intimidates judges and institutions by forcing, as public-interest advocates also do, the opening of such searches to contemporaneous observation. For a case illustrating the way such insistence destroys academic autonomy while leading to subterfuge or what appears as subterfuge, see Judith Block McLaughlin and David Riesman, "The Shady Side of Sunshine," *Teachers College Record* 87, no. 4 (Summer 1986): 471–94.

17. A splendid sense of the capacity of Margaret Mead for mentorship and for connecting people with one another is presented in her daughter's biography of her parents: Mary Catherine Bateson, *With a Daughter's Eye* (New York: William Morrow, 1985). Years later Everett Hughes and I were to try to bring Margaret Mead, who never held a secure academic position, to the University of Chicago but could not overcome the professional disesteem in which she was held.

18. My pacifism had never been a matter of absolute principle but rather of skepticism concerning the justification for most wars in history, including all prior American ones. But the rise to power of Hitler changed my outlook as it did that of many others. I became a reluctant interventionist. See Riesman, "What's Wrong with the Interventionists?" *Common Sense* 10 (1941): 327–30. I regarded Hitler and his not insignificant ally Mussolini as an even greater threat to civilization, including the United States, than a war to defeat them. In recent years I have been an admirer of the work of Gene Sharp on the history and strategic uses of nonviolent sanctions. See my introduction to Gene Sharp, *Exploring Nonviolent Alternatives* (Boston: Porter Sargent, 1970).

Moreover, I became so caught up in the widespread hope for postwar internationalism that I was happy to accept an invitation from the American Law Institute to join a group of international lawyers, American and overseas, seeking to draw up a bill of human rights. See "An International Bill of Rights," *Proceedings of the American Law Institute* 20 (1943): 198–204. I had been skeptical about Woodrow Wilson's ideal of making the world "safe for democracy." In recent decades I have regarded the crusade for human rights for dissidents, especially Jewish refuseniks, in the Soviet Union as one of the chief weapons by which the American right has destroyed détente and as one of the chief factors preventing the achievement of a ban, or even a moratorium, on underground testing of nuclear weapons and enough of a rapprochement with the USSR as joint guardian of the planet to cooperate in limiting and policing the proliferation of nuclear arsenals to more, and more unstable, countries. See "Human Rights and Human Prospects," commencement address at Williams College, 1977; revised and reprinted as "The Danger of the Human Rights Campaign," in *Common Sense in U.S.-Soviet Relations*, ed. Carl Marcy (New York: W. W. Norton, 1978), pp. 49–55.

19. The national law schools, as Harvard had been for decades and Buffalo was becoming, and their law reviews—indeed in a sense all law reviews—

worked toward the "nationalization" of American case law developed from British common-law traditions, seeking, often unsuccessfully, uniformity across state boundaries. This breadth of reference enlivens American legal research, dividing the bar between the great private and governmental establishments and the solo practitioners attentive to local law and to the idiosyncracies of local judges.

20. In his marvelously vivacious autobiography George Homans describes his experience as a neophyte ensign commanding a small vessel in the Navy in World War II and an encounter with his chief boatswain's mate, who had picked up an unguarded coil of hawser and appropriated it, not as personal, but as ship's property. Homans forced him to return it, although the boatswain's mate could not comprehend why it was not "his positive duty to the ship to snap up, when he could, any such unconsidered trifles as spare gear that might at some time come in handy." Similarly, some Sperry employees might hoard scarce aluminum on behalf of the Navy even though it theoretically belonged to the Army Air Corps. See George Caspar Homans, *Coming to My Senses: The Autobiography of a Sociologist* (New Brunswick, N.J.: Transaction Books, 1984), p. 230.

Although I admired the probity of Sperry's engineering leadership, I was appalled by the arrogance of young officials who would insult a colonel just back from the European theater with ribbons for valor who wanted to know why Sperry could not shift production more readily; instead of being uncomfortable because they were not in uniform, these accountants and other semiprofessional Sperry officials would run up the flag of private enterprise in a company totally funded by the military. The self-abnegation of often modest officers may have been politically prudent in dealing with Sperry as a prime contractor, but it also conveyed to me how thoroughly they were indoctrinated in the subordination of the military to civilian control, a judgment later confirmed by my occasional visits to the National War College and the Air War College. Even the contravention of congressional authority in the 1980s by Admiral John Poindexter and Colonel Oliver North was in the service of higher civilian authority. I met no one remotely like General Douglas MacArthur.

21. The treasurer of the holding company, with offices in Rockefeller Center, would have had me fired instantly had he learned of the frankness with which I discussed Sperry's difficulties with the Army Air Corps officials who were our principal contracting officers. I had to explain why we could not shift production with the speed of Westinghouse or General Motors. Moreover, when he learned of pressures the services were putting on the plants, pressures for which I was a conduit, the treasurer's impulse, from which several times I had to restrain him, was to get on the phone with his friend, the secretary of the Navy, to chew him out for giving Sperry trouble. Such bypassing by Sperry's treasurer of the proper channels might, I contended, land Sperry in far deeper trouble—for example (as I occasionally emphasized in the plants), investigation by the Truman Committee, which at the very least could take away our cherished "E" for excellence. The treasurer may have thought that I was soft on the government, whereas in fact I was so firm that my immediate boss, an amiable Sperry vice president, upbraided me for refusing to bargain (as the law required)

with the Corps of Engineers, which had a minuscule portion of our contracts. I knew I could not give better terms to the Corps of Engineers than those I had negotiated with the Army Air Corps, for example, adjust the amount of our advertising expense included in overhead.

22. Vis-à-vis Nazi Germany, unconditional surrender was in part a concession to Stalin's fears of a separate anti-Soviet peace. But it also seemed to me to echo admiration for Ulysses S. Grant and his insistence on unconditional surrender in the Civil War, as well as reflect anti-German, apart from anti-Nazi, attitudes among key Roosevelt advisers. As Allen Dulles complained, this demand impeded the efforts of the German opposition to Hitler.

23. See, for example, my essays "Predicaments in the Career of the College President," *The State of the University: Authority and Change*, ed. Carlos E. Kruytbosch and Sheldon L. Messinger (Beverly Hills, Calif.: Sage, 1970), pp. 73–85; and "The College Presidency," *Educational Studies* 13, no. 3-4 (1982): 309–35. See also my introduction to Richard Berendzen, *Is My Armor Straight? The Life of a University President* (Bethesda, Md.: Adler and Adler, 1985).

24. I discuss some of my rather quixotic notions concerning the conduct of academics in "Some Personal Thoughts on the Academic Ethic," *Minerva* 21, nos. 2–3 (Summer-Autumn 1983): 265–84; revised in "Academic Colleagueship and Teaching," *Antioch Review* (1985): 401–22.

25. Ed. Carl J. Friedrich and Edward Mason, *Public Policy* 3:33–96 (published by John Wiley, New York, for Harvard Graduate School of Public Policy) 1942. See also "Equality and Social Structure," *Journal of Legal and Political Sociology* 1 (1942): 72–95. Marcus Cunliffe has written an essay, "Watersheds," *American Quarterly* 3 (1961), criticizing the self-importance of believing that one is living at a time of transition, or watershed, thus giving a spurious significance to one's own historical moment; it is a useful caution.

26. All sorts of makeshift housing, such as barracks, were in use at that time, and the returning veterans were scattered in digs all around the area. When in the first year I presided at a lecture by Milton Friedman in which he opposed rent control, the massed group of veterans booed him; I urged them to listen, reminding them that rent control would diminish the stock of housing.

27. Reinhard Bendix has also written about this era at Chicago; see his and Joseph Gusfield's contributions to this volume.

28. These lectures were later published in *Psychiatry* 13, no. 1 (1950): 1–16; ibid., no. 2 (1950): 167–87, 301–15, and are reprinted in *Individualism Reconsidered*. Although the published versions are of course more detailed and appropriately annotated, they give an indication of the expectations we held for our undergraduates, as well as the fact, which we jokingly recognized, that we lectured in part for one another. A critique of these lectures and of my approach to psychoanalysis and society appears in Steven Weiland, "Psychoanalysis, Rhetoric, and Social Science: David Riesman's Freud," presented at the biannual meeting of the American Studies Association, Philadelphia, Pa., November 5, 1983.

29. The infectious enthusiasm of the faculty, the fact that the students shared the identical program and did not question its legitimacy, and a college

culture that encouraged sharing ideas outside the classroom led to animated class discussions that could also be intimidating to the shy. In time I worked out ways to evoke response from the diffident without stifling the assertive students. See "My Education in Soc 2 and My Efforts to Adapt It in the Harvard Setting," in a forthcoming book about the course edited by John MacAloon on behalf of the University of Chicago.

30. On Hughes, see also Joseph Gusfield's essay in this volume, as well as my memorial address, "The Legacy of Everett Hughes," *Contemporary Sociology* 12, no. 5 (September 1983): 477–81.

31. When I took a leave of absence after the end of the fall term in 1947 to work on what became *The Lonely Crowd* and *Faces in the Crowd*, I began, along with Nathan Glazer, to read interviews, irrespective of topic, available at the eastern office of the National Opinion Research Center in New York City. Paul Sheatsley and Herbert Hyman helped us understand the interview and survey work. See David Riesman and Nathan Glazer, "Social Structure, Character Structure, and Opinion," *International Journal of Opinion and Attitude Research* 2 (1949): 512–27; and "The Meaning of Opinion," *Public Opinion Quarterly* 12 (1949): 633–48. See also the cogent discussion of *The Lonely Crowd* in historical perspective in Rupert Wilkinson, *The Pursuit of American Character* (New York: Harper & Row, 1988), pp. 16–19.

32. Some of those I met early were scientists, of whom the late Leo Szilard was one of the most notable; his Council for a Livable World, created in 1962 when he was dying of cancer, has had my admiration and support. One of the interests Edward Shils and I shared was in the *Bulletin of the Atomic Scientists* and the people who wrote for and edited it.

33. While the St. John's College program has included Tocqueville's *Democracy in America* and Marx's *The Communist Manifesto* and *Capital* and Freud and Keynes, resembling in this respect Soc 3, these works were not read in any historical context, but as parts of what the St. John's College tutors termed the great conversation. Soc 3 took for granted the importance of the historical context of the works read.

34. See Baird Whitlock, *Don't Hold Them Back: A Critique and Guide to New School-College Articulation Models* (Princeton: College Board, 1978), on how such a program worked at Simon's Rock College, now Simon's Rock Early College, administered by Bard College.

35. I do not share the contempt Hutchins had for students' interest in postbaccalaureate careers. However, believing as I do in the advantages of diversity among American colleges, I can be grateful both for the existence of the College of the University of Chicago and for institutions such as Carnegie-Mellon University, which are frankly and seriously professional. See David Riesman, "Professional Education and Liberal Education: A False Dichotomy," in *Preparation for Life? The Paradox of Education in the Late Twentieth Century*, ed. Joan Burstyn (London: Falmer Press, 1986).

36. The ever-expanding pool of students and the corresponding shortage of faculty, which had helped me receive my offer in the first place, made room for expansion of the Social Sciences staff of the College. That expansion of nontenured faculty was done with a facility that in retrospect is astonishing, in the light

of all the steps, including clearances for affirmative action, that one has to go through today to appoint an assistant professor. Whereas it may not be surprising that I had no difficulty in securing the appointment of my former law school roommate, Donald Meiklejohn, with his brilliant undergraduate record at Wisconsin and his Harvard Ph.D. in philosophy (he was then teaching at the University of Virginia), it is less easy today to grasp how I could persuade not only my colleagues but also the dean to invite Reuel Denney, a Dartmouth graduate and at the time a public high-school teacher, who had published a well-regarded book of poetry but had no Ph.D. and no scholarly record. Daniel Bell and, several years later, Lewis Coser joined the staff of Soc 2 and only thereafter went off to earn their doctorates at Columbia. Denney stayed on and became professor of the humanities in the College. See Michael Schuson, "The Intellectual History of Soc 2," in John MacAloon's forthcoming book. I would like to add here that I owe much of my knowledge of, and interest in, American popular culture to Denney's stimulation, some of it reflected also in *The Lonely Crowd*.

37. At one point Donald Meiklejohn, accepting his father's belief that lecturing was an antiquated idea and that only discussion with students in the Socratic mode was worthwhile, sought to reduce or eliminate the lectures and have three or four section meetings a week. I thought, as I have already indicated, that the idea was unwise pedagogically since the rhythm of lectures and sections had in my judgment worked well. Such a change would have meant an increase in the responsibility of each instructor, who would have to prepare three or four rather than two section meetings. I regarded many of the section meetings, conducted along Socratic lines ("What did Max Weber mean by this particular sentence?"), as a kind of Ping-Pong between a few bright students and the section leader. I thought it important that students be exposed to the full range of lecturers that the university offered rather than having their experience confined to the particular person in whose section they landed or to whose section they might shift. Happily for many of us on the Soc 2 staff, Meiklejohn's motion did not carry.

38. As part of the revision of Soc 2, we recruited another cultural anthropologist (Rosalie Hankey, later Rosalie Hankey Wax, who had done her fieldwork in the Japanese relocation camps) and added another sociologist with a historical slant (Helen Mims). Later we found a survey researcher (Mark Benney, who had done public-opinion surveys for the British government during World War II), a sociologist with an interest in leisure (Sebastian DeGrazia), and others; we already had a political scientist (Morton Grodzins).

I looked without success for an economist willing to join the staff. In methodological and perhaps conceptual terms, economics appears to have been the most advanced and, in student recruitment, the most attractive among the social sciences; the highly professionalized narrowness of some of even its most able practitioners may reflect this. (We found no one within our orbit who used the modes of thought of economics as do such Harvard colleagues and former colleagues as Thomas Schelling or Albert Hirschman.) Herbert Simon, in his Nobel Prize speech for the award in economics, emphasized the importance of studies of disaggregated economic phenomena in minute detail. Indeed Simon, with his wit and continuing interest in undergraduate education and his polymath probing and subtle curiosity, may be regarded as the ideal product of the University of Chicago in the 1940s. In my early years at Chicago I occasionally suggested to graduate students in economics that they take a leave of absence to do something akin to fieldwork by accepting a position, for example, as assistant comptroller in a small business; they would thus learn something about microeconomics in a direct way. Invariably their reaction was that aggregate statistics were more than adequate for the understanding of economic phenomena—and in any case, while they were in a company that would necessarily be dismissed as idiosyncratic, some disciple of Paul Samuelson would have published four articles in refereed economics journals! It was not a hazard that a bright, aspiring economist wished to take.

39. In her biography of Harry Stack Sullivan, Helen Swick Perry provides a subtle, unflattering portrait of Lasswell as gifted and vain—and something of a con man. See her *Psychiatrist of America: The Life of Harry Stack Sullivan* (Cambridge, Mass.: Belknap Press, 1982).

40. On my second leave of absence from the Soc 2 staff I arranged for Mills to take my place; he and his wife lived in our home, sharing it for that period with the Lewis and Rose Coser family. When I came back to the College, students told me how contemptuous Mills had been of some of the readings. He had begun his first class by planting his paratrooper boots on the seminar table and throwing *Patterns of Culture* across the room, saying in effect that he would be damned if he was going to waste time on some little tribes. No "New Men of Power," they!

41. *Thorstein Veblen: A Critical Interpretation* (New York: Scribner, 1953). See also "The Social and Psychological Setting of Veblen's Economic Theory," *Journal of Economic History* 13 (1953): 449–61; and "Veblen's System of Social Science," *Explorations* 2 (1954): 84–97. I came to regret my commitment to write about Veblen, for I judged that I had to read everything he had ever written and, less arduous since there was not an enormous amount of it, everything written about him in English. Veblen was in some respects an American provincial, having to deal with Marx but not with the great European thinkers who were his contemporaries. In his best works he coupled telling insights into the nature of work (for example, the "instinct" of craftsmanship), leisure, and the anthropology of war with brilliant and sardonic wit. They also display crankiness and great redundancy and include some interesting puzzles, such as the sudden desire of this reclusive scholar to engage in the crusade against Germany in the First World War by working for the United States government. A later book on Veblen, more sympathetic than mine and linking him to his European contemporaries, does not appear to me to solve these contradictions either; see John P. Diggins, *The Bard of Savagery* (New York: Seabury Press, 1978).

42. The study of aging was a particular interest of Neugarten and Henry, and I was peripherally involved in it. See David Riesman, "Some Clinical and Cultural Aspects of Aging," *American Journal of Sociology* 59 (1954): 379–83; and "A Career Drama in a Middle-Aged Farmer," *Bulletin of the Menninger Clinic* 19 (1955): 1–8.

43. In this exploratory period (1950–51) I came upon a phenomenon that still perplexes me. The local elites who were linked by their interest in commu-

nity development and improvement included the then editor of the *Kansas City Star*, a long established and influential newspaper. If there was a meeting to consider some exigent problem, be it the reconstruction of downtown or conditions in the public schools, the people who with near unanimity came to some conclusion did not believe the decision had actually occurred until it was legitimated by publication in the *Star*, though the *Star* editor had been among the consulting group. To put it in slightly comical terms, they did not know that they were the power elite until they read about themselves and the outcome of their consultation in the daily paper.

44. See David Riesman, "The Study of Kansas City: An Informal Overture," *University of Kansas City Review* 20 (1953): 15–22.

45. I later collected some of the notes bearing on religion, removed identifying details, and published them as "Some Informal Notes on American Churches and Sects," *Confluence* 4 (1955): 127–59.

46. For fuller discussion see David Riesman, "Ethical and Practical Dilemmas of Fieldwork in Academic Settings: A Personal Memoir," in *Qualitative and Quantitative Social Research: Papers in Honor of Paul F. Lazarfeld*, ed. Robert K. Merton, James Coleman, and Peter Rossi (New York: Free Press, 1978). The Kansas City connection had as one outcome the study of the University of Kansas Medical School, initiated by Everett Hughes, and later of campus cultures at the University of Kansas, in which I participated vicariously by reading the interviews and field notes. See Howard S. Becker, Blanche Geer, Everett C. Hughes, and Anselm Strauss, *Boys in White: Student Culture in Medical School* (Chicago: University of Chicago Press, 1961); and Howard S. Becker, Blanche Geer, and Everett C. Hughes, *Making the Grade: The Academic Side of College Life* (New York: Wiley, 1968).

47. Michael Maccoby, then a graduate student in the Department of Social Relations and secretary of the Faculty of Arts and Sciences, greatly helped in the staffing of the course. For a fuller account of the course and teaching at Harvard, see my "On Discovering and Teaching Sociology: A Memoir."

CHAPTER THREE

Columbia in the 1950s

James S. Coleman

Introduction

When at the age of twenty-five I left a job as a chemist at Eastman Kodak in Rochester, New York, and took on a new life, the transformation was nearly complete. Except for my wife (and other kin, who lived far away in the Midwest and South) I shed all prior associations. The resocialization I underwent at Columbia University from 1951 to 1955 was intense; after that resocialization, I was a different person, with different goals, headed in a different direction.

It could be put differently; my life can be divided into two parts: before I first entered Fayerweather Hall (the building in which sociology is housed at Columbia), and after Fayerweather. I could, then, write about before Fayerweather to give a sense of how the first twenty-five years led me there. But what went on in Fayerweather Hall and vicinity during this four-year period is of more general interest, for during those years Columbia's importance for sociology was at its peak. Thus, to write about them is to do more than give a view of the resocialization that shaped my direction as a sociologist. It is to tell something about an important part of the history of the discipline at Columbia in the early 1950s.

Recognizing this, I will concentrate in this essay on that four-year period, which generated the orientations I had when I left Columbia. I will approach this examination by abstracting, successively, five kinds of information from the concrete reality that was sociology at Columbia from 1951 to 1955. The first three are necessary to understand what was going on at Columbia in sociology. The fourth and fifth give additional information relevant to my own development.

1.   I will try to describe the social system of sociology at Columbia, the loci of power and authority, the distribution of attention, the status system, and the allocation of rewards.

2.   Analytically distinct from the social system are the personalities of certain Columbia professors, in particular Paul Lazarsfeld and Robert K. Merton. While much can be understood about sociology at Columbia by knowing the social structure, more is revealed by learning something about the modus operandi of its two principal figures, Lazarsfeld and Merton.

3.   But there was simultaneously a content to sociology at Columbia. To describe it constitutes a kind of history of ideas or sociology of knowledge to give an understanding of the relations, not between persons, but between ideas. It is this content, this interplay of ideas, that had special importance in shaping my (and others') work in subsequent years.

4.   Certain of the ideas current in the Columbia sociology department in the early 1950s were especially important for me; to understand my intellectual development at Columbia requires knowing something about them.

5.   Finally, I will try to describe my own trajectory through the social system of Columbia, entering as a neophyte and leaving as a professional sociologist.

To proceed in this way rather than more anecdotally and unsystematically may result in some redundancy and may even be less interesting. But I would not attempt such an enterprise without taking it as a *sociological* challenge, a challenge to describe and analyze the functioning of a social system.

The Social System of Columbia Sociology, 1951–55

In June 1951 I arrived at the steps of Fayerweather Hall to enroll in a course on the professions given by Everett C. Hughes, a summer visitor from the University of Chicago, and one on political sociology given by Seymour Martin Lipset, a Columbia graduate newly returned as an assistant professor. Those courses, my first in sociology, began to give me a sense of what the discipline was about. But it was not until fall that I got a sense of the social system of sociology at Columbia, for it was then that the department emerged from its summer hibernation. To a new student the social system of sociology at Columbia first appeared to be a planetary system with Robert K. Merton as the shining sun around which all revolved. The most intellectual of the graduate students from the hothouse that is New York City (who could brandish quotes from obscure authors whose very names were unknown to me, a chemical engineer from the provinces) thronged to Merton, crowding each lecture and hanging on each word. I followed at a respectful distance, entranced and enamored. Only slowly it became apparent that someone else was important as well, Paul Lazarsfeld, whose domain was not a lecture room in Fayerweather but the Bureau of Applied Social Research.

Much later it became evident that the system was in fact governed by a triumvirate. Robert S. Lynd was the hidden member. Robert MacIver, a major figure in the discipline, but by then retired, continued to have an office in the Department of Government but played no role in a sociology student's life. There were a number of others, but in the peculiar social system of Columbia sociology they seemed to matter little, or mattered only to those who themselves seemed to matter little: C. Wright Mills in the college, William Goode in general studies, Theodore Abel, William Casey (with his own brand of social theory, shared by no one else), Kingsley Davis, Bernhard Stern, and the young assistant professors, Lipset and Herbert Hyman. The list may be as startling to others as it is to me as I read over it, for it includes not only persons whose importance to the discipline has subsequently become great (Goode, Lipset, and Hyman), but also some whose importance even at the time was great (C. Wright Mills and Kingsley Davis).

The authority of each member of this triumvirate gained legitimacy from a different source. Merton's authority gained its legitimacy first from the students, through the extraordinary attraction of his lectures, and secondarily from the strength of his position in the discipline, which was recognized by the university administration. Lazarsfeld's arose also from students, but not primarily through his teaching in formal courses. It arose, rather, from the quantity of empirical research he generated and his leadership of the Bureau of Applied Social Research, which provided an institutional base for the research. But that base itself had only tenuous acceptance by the university. Such applied research as market research and communications research for radio networks, magazine publishers, and other business firms was an upstart activity with which traditional Columbia administrators were uneasy. Merton, by accepting, participating in, and sharing the governance of the bureau, was, it seemed, Lazarsfeld's protector, a shield against the university administration.

Lynd's rumored power was, from the students' point of view, the strangest of all because he held almost no interest for students and was not active in research. (I heard of his importance only indirectly, from Lipset, who was still close to graduate students in age and not far removed in status.) It seemed, according to students' second-hand information, to result entirely from the deference paid by Merton and Lazarsfeld to his views, thus deriving in the end from the bases of legitimacy that gave them their authority. (I attended a few lectures in a course of his one semester, but these were hortatory, more closely related to the style of the midwestern evangelists that were part of his background [and mine] than to that of a professor engaged in a search for knowledge. He preached his particular brand of homegrown leftism and had few student converts.)

It is relevant, in describing the concentration of power in this social system, to note the numbers of graduate students. If we had been fewer in number, there might have been less concentration. But in my year about one hundred graduate students were admitted. We were still part of the war-generated backlog, slowly making our way through the educational system. Indeed, for my first semester or so at Columbia I still had some GI bill benefits remaining. (The next year the incoming class was limited to fifty, and I congratulated myself on having entered when I did since I might not have made it after the limitation was imposed. I had applied also to Michigan and Harvard but was accepted only at Columbia.)

Certainly matters must have been more complex than this simple picture I have presented. Kingsley Davis (who left for Berkeley while I was at Columbia) had a smaller power base through a large Air Force contract which employed some students interested in demography. But his attractiveness was limited to the small set of demographically inclined students and was not spread throughout the student body, as was that of Merton and Lazarsfeld. He was outside the closed tripartite structure of power. (I took a course on the family from Davis but was unnerved by what I saw as his blunt manner. For example, in a draft of a term paper I used the growth in year-to-year variation in suicide rates to obtain a measure of the increasing interdependence [or common dependence on the same events] of apparently independent decisions of individuals. But I was afraid of a possibly caustic response to such a venturesome paper and instead submitted another, nonempirical paper, on which I received the comment, "A great deal of logic-chopping.")

To a student coming into Columbia, then, there were really only two persons at the apex, two persons whose attention one must try to get, two persons whose judgments mattered above all—Merton and Lazarsfeld. This concentration of attention was intensified by another fact as well: to the graduate student, there was no discipline of sociology outside Columbia. Instead we saw a self-confidence, a looking inward coupled with inattention to the outside. There was a sociological literature of some importance, a literature to which Merton especially directed our attention, but except for the work of Talcott Parsons, which Merton admitted to it, that literature was all written by Europeans no longer alive. The effective absence of a discipline west of the Hudson River was most strongly emphasized by the absence of interest in reading or publishing in the journals. Graduate students were not encouraged to read the professional journals; no self-respecting graduate student at Columbia entertained the thought of journal publication as a goal. To us, Lazarsfeld and Merton had no such interests (no matter that they did publish in the journals); the world of sociology was confined to Columbia. Graduate students followed suit, with no interest other than having a paper read by Merton or Lazarsfeld. Once *that* had occurred, there was little interest in having it read by others.

The interest of graduate students in gaining the attention of Merton and Lazarsfeld was strengthened by the imbalance in the supply of, and demand for, their attention. Appointments to see either during his office hours were made weeks in advance. The line outside Merton's door offered recurrent testimony to this imbalance. By contrast, a student could see and talk to other faculty, if not at will, at least with far less difficulty.

This small social system, with its abundance of eager and impatient graduate students, its periphery of young and also-ran faculty, and the concentration of attention on the two major figures in the department, had some special characteristics. One of them was the concentration of graduate-student prestige in only a few students. In my second year, at the Bureau's Christmas party, someone pointed out Maurice Stein, a figure whom I knew only by reputation—at the top of the heap a year earlier—who had returned to bask in his graduate-student glory. I stood in awe at the fringes and watched as he received homage.

But reputations were unstable and could rise or fall quickly on the basis of one piece of work liked or disliked by Merton or Lazarsfeld. Hanan Selvin, in a cohort ahead of me, and the reader of my paper in Merton's lecture course the first semester, was one of the few favored by both Lazarsfeld and Merton and had an especially high reputation. But once, when he produced something Lazarsfeld or Merton found wanting, his reputation plummeted, and his lustre disappeared for a time; he was never completely to regain his lofty position. And there were those who, though potentially very good, never caught the attention of either Lazarsfeld or Merton and remained among the mass of graduate students who would have to make their reputations, if at all, after they left Columbia.

Students who worked with faculty other than Merton and Lazarsfeld were less neglected, but their reputations never soared (nor plummeted) as did those of Merton and Lazarsfeld favorites. Martin Trow is a good example. He and I worked together with Lipset intensively in analyzing the data of the ITU (International Typographical Union) study, and he largely managed the project. He was a course assistant for Mills as well. But he never worked closely with Merton or Lazarsfeld. Even though as the *Union Democracy* manuscript progressed, it began to have an internal reputation as something of interest, Trow never gained the reputational heights while in graduate school. His reputation came only later. Lazarsfeld once asked me about Trow as we were riding in a taxi, near the end of my Columbia period, after a frenetic meeting characteristic of his style. He knew me and my work, and knew Lipset and his work, but wondered about Trow, whose years at Columbia had failed to give Lazarsfeld any sense of his abilities.

There was another phenomenon as well. A number of sociologists with high status in the system were neither graduate students nor faculty but were brought by Lazarsfeld, Merton, or Davis to work on one of the projects. They included Renee Fox, Herbert Menzel, Natalie Rogoff, Samuel Bloom, and Duncan Luce. For some of these young social scientists the postdoctoral years at Columbia played a central role in their careers.

During my stay at Columbia the social structure was undergoing a kind of change. Earlier Lazarsfeld's students and Merton's students had been more distinct and separate. Many of Lazarsfeld's, trained in audience and market research through his projects at the Bureau, had never written dissertations and were employed in the emergent market research industry in New York; few entered academic sociology. The stellar graduates had been students of Merton or Lynd. They were products of the prewar intellectual ferment that was largely Jewish, largely from New York high schools and City College. They had constituted the first postwar cohorts at Columbia; they included Lipset, Philip Selznick, Daniel Bell, Lewis Coser and Rose Coser, Suzanne Keller, and Peter Blau. Maurice Stein, who left Columbia as I arrived, was a remnant of those cohorts. There were rumors of others, such as Seymour Fiddle—mysterious, with an unbounded reputation but some incapacitating flaw. (He came in the night, it was said, to practice his magic in a course in general studies.)

Peter Rossi was of that crowd, but he was a Lazarsfeld student and reflected the beginnings of Lazarsfeld's move toward academic respectability. The succeeding cohorts, mine included, lacked the rich ideological, historical, and intellectual pre–graduate-school background possessed by those who had grown up in New York high schools in the late thirties. Hanan Selvin, who was my age but came to Columbia before me, was one of the earliest Lazarsfeld-Merton students, a coeditor of a reader in bureaucracy with Merton but writing his dissertation under Lazarsfeld. Patricia Kendall was another. What was happening about the time I arrived at Columbia was a merging of two streams of activity that had been rather distinct. Lazarsfeld was becoming more academic, Merton was becoming more quantitatively empirical. The Bureau provided the context and the facilities for Merton's shift, and its increasing acceptance by Columbia (it moved uptown to Columbia, at 117th Street, shortly before my arrival) provided the setting for Lazarsfeld's.

During my stay the Bureau became increasingly important to sociology at Columbia. There Lazarsfeld began the Behavioral Models Project with an Office of Naval Research grant, brought Duncan Luce from the Massachusetts Institute of Technology, enticed Theodore Anderson and Howard Raiffa from the Department of Mathematical Statistics at Columbia (Luce and Raiffa's *Games and Decisions* was born in this project). With the project they initiated an activity less stimulating, less frenetic, less innovative, but more like that of an academic research institute than the pickup projects in audience research that had built the bureau. Merton began the extensive and prestigious medical-school project with George Reader, Patricia Kendall, and Renee Fox. Kingsley Davis had his Air Force project in methodological research. Seminars involving graduate students and postdoctoral research associates were created around such projects as the medical-school project. In all these ways the Bureau was becoming respectable.

Much of this change took place shortly before I arrived. But the Bureau's importance to sociology at Columbia continued to grow during my stay. That growth can perhaps best be illustrated by a development that, though it was temporary and depended on particular persons, exemplified the change. It was the formation of what Lazarsfeld and Merton called "Charlie Glock's Young Turks" and what the members themselves called "the traditions group."

Around 1953 Lazarsfeld turned over directorship of the Bureau to Charles Glock and became less active in Bureau affairs. Glock was not a dynamic figure, but there were a number of restless people, all involved in one way or another in Bureau projects. I was working with Lipset and Trow on the ITU project and occasionally on one or more of Lazarsfeld's projects; Elihu Katz was working on the Decatur study (which produced *Personal Influence*), Herbert Menzel on concepts and indices, Lee Wiggins on Lazarsfeld's panel project, Philip Ennis on a popular-music project, and Rolf Meyerson on research in popular culture. Lazarsfeld had plucked William McPhee from a local polling organization in Denver to work with him and Bernard Berelson on the Elmira study (which produced *Voting*). We all needed research projects to support us, and without Lazarsfeld to generate the small-market research and mass-communications projects on which earlier cohorts of graduate students had thrived, we set out on our own, with McPhee as the popular leader and instigator. We held a weekly seminar, circulated memos to one another about potential projects in mass culture, uses and gratifications of the mass media, contextual analysis, and methodological issues in panel studies. We saw ourselves not as working in the established traditions of Bureau studies but as starting new traditions. Despite our declarations of independence (I once wrote a first draft of a manifesto for the group, and McPhee wrote a programmatic paper on research in mass dynamics), Lazarsfeld found this enterprise interesting, and once or twice he attended the seminar as an observer. His and Merton's interest in it, and the attention of others that that interest generated, increased for us the importance of our enterprise. We gained the confidence of our own ideas, the sense that we were initiators, sociologists inventing the future of sociology. For us, there was no sociology east of Morningside Drive nor west of Broadway; and the Lazarsfeld-Merton domain between these limits was showing signs of aging. We saw ourselves as successors with our own ideas (even though grounded in theirs).

The Power of Two Personalities

Though it was not quite proper to take Merton's course in theory as a beginning graduate student, I managed to do so in the fall of my first year. I found myself in a class of students from earlier cohorts; the classroom was completely full, with students sometimes sitting on the windowsills. Merton would enter and begin a kind of rhapsody. All were entranced. A few dared occasionally to ask questions. I did not.

What did Merton do? For all of us, he revealed a vision of sociology as a challenge to the intellect. He worked in detail through Durkheim's *Suicide,* showing the excitement of the problem and the methodical way Durkheim set about examining it. He demonstrated how Durkheim used the aggregate data that were available to examine deep questions about the psychic state of members of a social system—questions that could only be answered conclusively by disaggregated data but were turned this way and that until Durkheim had enough kinds of data to make firm inferences about the psychological states induced by social structure.

Merton's lectures were widely known. Nonsociologists from other parts of the city would steal into the room just to listen. Students, on meeting sociologists from other universities who knew him only through his writings, would smile condescendingly, armed with the secret knowledge that came only through presence at the lectures themselves. The word to describe his effect is one whose meaning he taught us, *charisma,* but that word is so loosely used that it fails to convey a sense of the almost electrical charge that pervaded those lectures.

Merton was excited by the publication in the fall of 1951 of Talcott Parsons's *Social System,* which he saw as the theoretical guide to the future of sociology. But when he set us to reading it, he demanded that we locate in the text every empirical generalization, every proposition, and every definition. In the end the enterprise—for me, at least—defeated the original goal, for I found definition after definition, with few empirical generalizations and few propositions that could be tested and confirmed or disconfirmed. Merton, by his demands that we analyze the text sentence by sentence, showed me that Parsons had designed a set of categories, a classification scheme, that might or might not be useful but could hardly be tested.

A part of Merton's impact lay in both the personal and professional distance he maintained and in the unreachable goal of sociological truth he held out. He brooked no compromise; his standards demanded perfection in what we did. A few of us formed a study group to discover together the precise meanings we fumbled for alone. He visited us once, and we were in awe, taking every comment as a command from above. We read, over and over, his essays in *Social Theory and Social Structure.* Merton held out to us a vision of a sociology that could understand society. That understanding, of which only the barest outlines had been discovered, lay in the future, and if we persevered, we might be part of that future. He captured us for sociology, even those who had come to sociology merely to be journeymen. He showed us that sociology could be—indeed, was—an intellectual challenge. We were affected by his singleness of purpose and his dedication to that challenge.

But it was important not to get too close. Some who attempted to work with Merton found themselves paralyzed by the incisiveness of his mind. One student reported in frustration that in writing a thesis for Merton, he felt a presence continuously perched on his shoulder, watching every sentence put down on paper, ready to pounce on the slightest fault.

I was not, during my time at Columbia, immobilized by this penetrating intelligence. In my third or fourth year I was a course assistant for him (not in the large theory course but in another), taking notes on his lectures, typing them up, and discussing them with him occasionally over lunch at the faculty club. On those occasions I continued to feel the awe of those first days, but he was perhaps more gentle with me, sensing my vulnerability. Once, as an outgrowth of Lazarsfeld's project on concepts and indices in the social sciences, I worked on a paper for him on the concept of social isolation and its use by social theorists. The paper was never completed in final form, and remained a learning exercise. Unlike Lazarsfeld's projects, for which a product was urgently needed to fill a specific niche, sometimes for a client, papers for Merton were finished for their own sake, or to complete a thesis, and the goal could stretch out into the indefinite future.

Much later, after I had left Columbia, I did feel the full thrust of Merton's critical intelligence. He and Robert Nisbet were gathering materials for *Contemporary Social Problems,* and had asked me to write a chapter on community disorganization. To gain the necessary state of mind to organize and develop the structure of the chapter, I went to the St. James Hotel at Mount Vernon Square in Baltimore (I was teaching at Johns Hopkins at the time) and isolated myself from the world for four days while I wrestled with the problem and finally developed an outline for the chapter. When I finally completed it some weeks later and felt satisfied with the result, I sent it to Merton and Nisbet for editorial comments and critique. The single-spaced, many-paged criticism I soon received from Merton devastated me—not merely because of the depth of his criticism but also because, agreeing with most of it, I felt that my shallowness of thought and weakness of documentation lay wholly exposed. I was ashamed of the manuscript, angry at myself, angry at Merton. I was unable to touch the manuscript, able only to write Nisbet (certainly not Merton) that I had to resign the task, that there was obviously nothing I could do to the manuscript to make it acceptable. But through nurturance, reassurance, and urging, Nisbet induced me to go back to the manuscript, deal with the criticisms as best I could, and send him the result. I did so, and the chapter became part of the book.

My first impression, that fall of 1951, that Merton was the center of Columbia's sociological universe was approximately correct, though I was to modify that impression later. It was Merton who defined sociology as a challenge worthy of the intellect, a pursuit at least equal to any other in the university. He created the intellectual tension that energized students in pursuit of the chalice of sociology.

Lazarsfeld, however, was no less important. I had originally applied to Columbia because of someone there named Lazarsfeld or Lasswell—I was not sure which—whose work I had read in a course in social psychology I was taking in evening school. (I had never taken a course in sociology and had never heard of Merton.) In the spring of 1952, my second semester at Columbia, Paul Lazarsfeld accosted me for the first time. I had been in a methods course of his, which was uneventful. The problem he raised with me was that there was a biophysicist from the University of Chicago, Nicolas Rashevsky, whom he had invited to give a lecture in a series on mathematical sociology the year before, and now, for the book Lazarsfeld was attempting to put together from the lecture series, Rashevsky had written up his lectures, in Lazarsfeld's opinion unintelligibly. He had asked Allen Birnbaum, a Ph.D. student in statistics, to write an intelligible exposition of Rashevsky but did not like what Birnbaum had done. Could I give it a try over the summer? We talked, he outlined what he wanted, and for the first time ever in the educational system I felt that someone had given me a responsible task to do. We met twice during the summer—once at a typical Lazarsfeld breakfast meeting in a hotel where he briefly alighted on his return from Europe—and I delivered the product he wanted at the end of the summer. Lazarsfeld's project was now complete—Rashevsky was exposited, and he could send the book to the publisher.

The incident is characteristic in one way especially: Lazarsfeld did not simply accept the paper of this distinguished mathematical biophysicist. It was unintelligible to him, and he wanted each of the papers in that book (which became *Mathematical Thinking in the Social Sciences*) to teach him something. Until it did so, he was not willing to publish Rashevsky's lectures. Indeed, in many respects one could characterize part of Columbia at the time—certainly in mathematical sociology and to a considerable extent in Lazarsfeld's other areas of interest—as a collection of people he had gathered around himself for the purpose of teaching him. His appetite for learning—and thus for people—was insatiable. He brought the economist William Baumol from Princeton to a seminar to teach him how differential equations could be adapted to study the dynamics of qualitative attributes—and then remained unsatisfied. He brought the philosopher Gustave Bergman from the Midwest to Hanover, New Hampshire, to teach him about intervening variables and then so pestered him with insistent questions that Bergman, a round little man, ended up rolling on the floor, flailing with arms and legs in helpless frustration. He brought Harold Kelly, John Thibaut, and Leon Festinger to Hanover to teach him about how Lewinian and other social psychologies constructed concepts. He brought William Vickrey from the other side of the Columbia campus to teach him how economists treat the concept of utility. He listened intently to his students—Lee Wiggins, Allen Barton, Elihu Katz, Hanan Selvin, William McPhee—whenever he thought he could learn from them. He invaded the statistics department and got Theodore Anderson to teach him about Markov chains. He brought Duncan Luce and Gerald Thompson to work on mathematical problems he could not solve. He brought Merrill Flood from Rand and, unawed by Flood's previous distinguished work, immediately found Flood uninteresting.

The attention of those in Lazarsfeld's orbit, unconcerned about the outside sociological world, was directed to problems. Each was concerned only with convincing Lazarsfeld that he had solved one of the problems that Lazarsfeld had set. Each of us after we left (and I write now only of those who did, for some found it exceedingly difficult to break away from the attractive forces that the combination of Merton and Lazarsfeld constituted, and some were institutionally affixed to Columbia) encountered what seemed at first a strange and far less exciting world outside. We found no one in the new environment who cared as Lazarsfeld did. If there was a sociological community out there, it seemed a distant and impersonal one. No one seemed as interested as he in solving problems, and certainly no one was as interested in the problems that anyone else might solve.

Despite all this, many of us around Lazarsfeld felt extreme frustration because at times the problems themselves appeared spurious or unimportant. Lazarsfeld was not satisfied to see his protégés and colleagues solve problems that others outside considered important but was only satisfied when a problem *he* considered important was solved—and solved in a way that made sense to him.

Toward the end of my time at Columbia, in 1954, I experienced this insistence. Lazarsfeld showed me a sheaf of extended quotations from various qualitative studies, mostly community studies, many from the Chicago school of Robert E. Park, such as *Black Metropolis* and *The Gold Coast and the Slum,* and some from an anthropological tradition. These quotations were examples of what Lazarsfeld called global indicators—indicators of some concept or property of the community or the neighborhood that could not be derived from individuals by aggregation. They had been gathered by members of a seminar that he and Patricia Kendall had led, and he wanted somehow to systematize them, to create a transmissible method out of what had been art. Lazarsfeld had a continuing interest in such global indicators, an interest that he describes in "Notes on the History of Concept Formation," one of the essays that appeared in his *Qualitative Analysis* (1972). It was this interest that led him to induce colleagues and students to examine work they would never otherwise have looked at. For example, with this sheaf of global indicators he directed me to read such diverse authors as Wilhelm Dilthey (on the characterization of a cultural system), Harold Guetzkow (on properties of a group), and Meyer Shapiro (on the use of art to characterize the style of a period).

In this case, as in many others, Lazarsfeld saw the person he put to work (and I was not the first with this problem) as an extension of himself. When the work I did failed to reflect his ideas, he argued with me at length over it. He could not be persuaded that the way I had done it was right; he did not want to see it published as I had conceived it, and I would not change my views. (I saw his distinctions as too mechanical, lacking in substance; he saw mine as blind to the methodological differences.) So he went ahead and with Herbert Menzel developed his own ideas further and published them in a paper that later became well known. I, some years later, published my long paper separately. This example could be duplicated, with minor variations, by many of Lazarsfeld's students. Before I arrived at Columbia, the "Decatur study" was one on which C. Wright Mills, as well as others, had been tried by Lazarsfeld and found wanting. Elihu Katz was set to work on it and it ended successfully, as *Personal Influence.*

The extent of this invasion of self that Lazarsfeld practiced was so great that many of those who had worked most closely with him (or, more properly put, whom he had pursued and captured) remained permanently hostile or ambivalent. For several years after the global-indicator affair I myself was angry. And when in 1978, two years after his death, I gave a warm and appreciative account of Lazarsfeld's work, several people who had been close to him mentioned how surprised they were that I could give such a positive and unambivalent account of this predatory man. Yet some of those same people were bereft when they left Columbia and were free of him.

Lazarsfeld's dual concern with people and with problems led to unlikely combinations, some of which foundered while others, perhaps equally unlikely at the outset, flourished. When he set C. Wright Mills to work on the problem of personal influence in Decatur, Illinois, this did not last long. Or when he began to work with pollster Lou Harris on a study of college faculty, this aborted. (Lazarsfeld completed the study with Wagner Thielens as *The Academic Mind.*) His work with Martin Lipset on a review of political behavior was somewhat more productive but rather short-lived. No one would have predicted that he and Ernest Nagel would manage a successful series of seminars in mathematical sociology, or that he and David Riesman would come as close together as they did—even so, remaining at arm's length—in the study of college faculties. And who could have guessed that his association with Merton would flower and become so important? That was Lazarsfeld's personal style: he could not stand to have a bright person, whom he respected, whether colleague or student, in the vicinity yet not working on problems he saw as significant. He used his own time, flattery, and attention; he used money, he used summers in Hanover, New Hampshire, he used projects at the Bureau; he used all the inducements at his command to draw others into his orbit. This was not charisma, which could properly describe the attraction to Merton. It was more nearly a matter of pursuit.

To bring this about was costly to Lazarsfeld. The tactics did not allow a posture of knowing more than he did. To engage the efforts of others on a problem, he had to declare his own defeat. But that he was willing to do. For him, getting the problem solved was most important (or perhaps getting another to work on his problem was most important); the fact that another might be the one to solve the problem was a sacrifice he was willing to make.

This unassuming aspect of Lazarsfeld combined with another attribute to make him a perfect complement to substantive sociologists. For Lazarsfeld had a difficult time understanding sociological theory. In some of his writings (the best sampling can be found in *Qualitative Analysis*) he exhibits his long-standing concern to understand action and his rich sense of the history of the theory of action. But substance that was more sociological came slowly to him.

The success of the Merton-Lazarsfeld seminars was this peculiar complementarity both in substance and in personality. Merton knew what Weber and others had written about bureaucracy, for example. He knew the theory. Lazarsfeld most explicitly did not know, and he asked questions. In part Lazarsfeld asked because he simply did not understand the substance. But in part he asked them because his desire for an answer outweighed any concern he might have had about being regarded as sociologically naive. In other cases the interaction was somewhat modified. Merton would lay out a substantive sociological analysis he himself had carried out, and then Lazarsfeld would pose the same or similar questions. In at least one case, having finally felt that he understood what the theorist meant, he attempted this understanding through formalization, in a joint paper with Merton.

This account of the personalities of Merton and Lazarsfeld does not do justice to the combination of the two and the impact of this combination on each of them and on those at Columbia. The difference in their personalities and the power of their personalities could have produced a standoff or an unending conflict. But each respected what the other could do, each deferred to the other in the other's realm of expertise, and perhaps each even yearned somewhat to have the other's talents. Whatever the complex character of this relation, its strength is what gave Columbia sociology *its* strength over the long period beginning in the 1940s and extending to the 1970s. Not surprisingly, its strength is what created such a vacuum in sociology at Columbia, a vacuum felt beyond the limits of that university once the combination was gone.

As has often been pointed out, at the same time Harvard had a counterpart to Paul Lazarsfeld in Samuel Stouffer, and to Robert Merton in Talcott Parsons. But there was never the joining of activities nor the joining of ideas between Parsons and Stouffer that occurred between Merton and Lazarsfeld.

The Content of Sociology at Columbia

In the early 1950s sociology was undergoing a change, and Columbia was on the forefront of that change. (I write this from the perspective of the present, not from my perspective as a graduate student at the time. Then, the Columbia sociology of 1951 was all I knew as sociology.) The watershed at Columbia came with the decline of Lynd and the arrival of Lazarsfeld. (It is perhaps ironic that Lynd brought Lazarsfeld to Columbia and then watched with some disfavor the transformation of the discipline that Lazarsfeld helped bring about.) Before this watershed, the unit for most empirical research in American sociology had been a community or an organization. The Lynds' study of Middletown is an example, as are Columbia Ph.D. dissertations of a slightly earlier period, such as Philip Selznick's *T.V.A. and the Grass Roots,* Martin Lipset's *Agrarian Socialism.* At the University of Chicago, W. Lloyd Warner's Yankee City series and A. B. Hollingshead's *Elmtown's Youth* were studies that, although they used the new methods of sample surveys, focused on the stratification system of a given community and thus continued the Chicago school's focus on communities or neighborhoods as the units of analysis.

But the four volumes in the *American Soldier* series by Samuel Stouffer's group during World War II provided a strong stimulus for change to a sociology based on sample surveys with the individual as the unit of analysis and individual behavior as the phenomenon under examination. That stimulus was amplified by the immensely influential *Continuities in Social Research: The American Soldier,* edited by Merton and Lazarsfeld. The Merton and Kitt essay on reference groups and the Lazarsfeld and Kendall essay on methods of elaboration in survey analysis, which covered both the substantive and methodological flanks of the new individualist movement in sociology, were the centerpieces of that volume.

Lazarsfeld's work in radio research, and mass-communications research more generally, was a major force for this new individualist direction at Columbia. The appointment at Columbia of Herbert Hyman, a social psychologist who had done work on reference groups, was another indicator of the change. Even the research that was close to traditional sociological concerns began to take the same form. Lazarsfeld's voting studies, Merton's study of the Kate Smith war bond appeal (*Mass Persuasion*), and Katz and Lazarsfeld's *Personal Influence* all took individual behavior or attitudes as the dependent variables to be explained; all were concerned with varying individual responses to a mass stimulus.

Other work at Columbia attempted to combine the new methods of quantitative survey analysis with studies of problems that involved the behavior of a social unit—a community or an organization. This work was in part due to Merton's influence always pulling Lazarsfeld toward sociological questions and in part due to the fact that the "community-study" period of sociological research had not completely passed. Even the two voting studies, precursors of national voting studies, were set in two communities, Elmira, New York, and Sandusky, Ohio, with the structured interviews supplemented by additional data on community organizations and the social relationships of the respondents. These attempts, reflecting a tension between the old problem and the new methods, met with variable success, though none was completely successful. In the voting studies the community data never came together with the interview data, and the problems studied remained those of individual voting behavior. In *Personal Influence,* set in Decatur, Illinois, snowball sampling led to greater success and to the concept of the two-step flow of communication. In Merton's medical-school project, questionnaire data from whole cohorts of medical students, rather than from samples, made possible the study of contextual influences on behavior, and the use of two medical schools rather than one allowed the study of school-level effects, though again on individual behavior. In the ITU study Lipset's focus on substantive problems of democratic theory at the system level led to an analysis that kept the behavior of the system at the forefront, but without fully integrating problems and methods. In all these ways sociology at Columbia in the 1950s contained a sizeable component of social psychology. In a large and steadily increasing fraction of the empirical research done at Columbia during the period, individual behavior was the phenomenon under study, not the behavior of a social system or any part of it beyond the individual.

Yet in large part this emphasis merely reflected the increasing individualism of society. In the 1940s Hollingshead had examined social stratification by studying Elmtown's youth, showing that the social position of the parent was transmitted to the child by way of the school. In the 1950s it no longer seemed sensible to study generational transmission of social stratification by studying Elmtowns; young people were changing their social positions, not within the stratification systems of these towns, but outside them by *leaving* their hometowns. Thus it became natural to study the individuals rather than the towns. Sociology at Columbia reflected that change and helped develop the methods and redefine the problems of sociology in such a way as to make the academic study of society congruent with new social reality. Much of what is today regarded as the mainstream of sociology constitutes the further development of that paradigm. Path analysis as a logical extension of the ideas of elaboration in the Lazarsfeld-Kendall paper, status attainment research with nationally representative samples as the replacement for the Yankee City and Elmtown community studies, and national election studies as the replacement for community-based samples all suggest the extent of change of the discipline as it mirrors changes in society.

The change that was occuring in the 1950s at Columbia can be described in another way. As the discipline embraced quantitative methods to study America's changing social structure, it retained the ability to study the effects of social structure on individual behavior (in part through methods of contextual and relational analysis that were being fashioned at Columbia). But it lost the capacity to reconstitute—still quantitatively—from individual actions the behavior of the social system composed of those individuals. What can be done discursively, in describing how the interplay of actions by individuals leads to system-level outcomes (say, in community decision making or organizational behavior or in the election of a president), remains largely beyond our quantitative grasp. This uneven development of quantitative methods has led to a concentration of quantitative empirical research on determinants of individual behavior, a shift from problems that occupied the discipline before the watershed I have described.

The Impact of These Ideas on Me

Because I came to Columbia with almost no background in any social science, the frame of reference imposed by sociology at Columbia was the only frame I had. I reflected, both in the methodological skills I developed and in the substantive problems I saw as important, the then current Columbia definition of sociology. But my development as a sociologist reflected more specifically the confluence of three streams of activity: the activities of Lazarsfeld, the activities of Merton, and the activities of Lipset. From Merton came not only the vision of sociology as a calling but also a focus on *sociological* determinants of individual behavior, following in the pattern of Durkheim, on whose analysis of social determinants of suicide (not *The Division of Labor* or *The Elementary Forms of Religious Life,* both of which had more a systemic, less individual, focus) Merton lavished attention in his lectures on theory.

Whether it was Merton's own orientation, the individualist direction of sociology at Columbia, or a positivist orientation I carried over from the physical sciences, midway through graduate school I concluded that Durkheim was engaged in one kind of endeavor and Weber in an altogether different one, and that I would choose Durkheim's path. I saw that path as the study of the force of social structure and social organization on the individuals embedded in that structure. Weber I thought of as engaged in the other side: the study of consequences of individuals' values, and the actions following from them, for social organization. Parsons I saw as trying to realize a Weberian program of theory construction and research, and although I felt it might have been done better by another, part of Parsons's problem seemed to lie in the Weberian starting point.

I have subsequently changed my orientation toward social theory to one more consistent with the Weberian program by taking purposive action as a starting point for social organization rather than social structure as a starting point for individual action. This problem, which can be described as the micro-to-macro problem, was not what I took away with me from Columbia. The Durkheimian orientation was far more compatible with the quantitative methods and the mathematical sociology I was learning there.

My orientation toward mathematical sociology came from Lazarsfeld via three channels, in addition to the Lazarsfeld-Nagel seminar and the evening university seminar on mathematics in the social sciences. First was the project he gave me of translating Rashevsky's mathematical biology for a sociological audience. Although this work (published in *Mathematical Thinking in the Social Sciences*) had little, if any, significance for the discipline, it was important for my development. Rashevsky was a mathematical biophysicist who had turned to sociological problems and had developed models of various social processes. What was important for me about Rashevsky's work was what was important later in Nagel's orientation and in some of the mathematical models we studied in the Lazarsfeld-Nagel seminar: it was mathematics dedicated to mirroring social *processes*. It was not just a compilation of statistical indices nor a static representation of structure (as was Lazarsfeld's latent structure analysis, a development that excited Lazarsfeld but left me cold). In this it was compatible with the applications of mathematics I knew from physics and physical chemistry and reinforced my belief that this mirroring of social processes was the most profitable application of mathematics in sociology. The orientation I found in Rashevsky, Nagel, and much of Herbert Simon's work (which influenced me while I was still in graduate school) is not one I have seen among users of mathematics in sociology whose background is in mathematics or statistics rather than the physical sciences or engineering. Nor did I find it in Lazarsfeld, whose preoccupation was with latent structure analysis and index construction.

The second channel was the Behavioral Models Project, for which I contracted to do a review and exposition of mathematics as applied to the study of small groups. In that work I learned about systems of nonlinear differential equations, beginning with Simon's modeling of Homans's propositions about small-group processes, and then discovering A. J. Lotka's work and Volterra's equations for predator-prey models—again a reinforcement of the process orientation I had found in Rashevsky. I also stuffed my head full of the work on random and nonrandom nets by Rashevsky's colleagues (Anatol Rapoport and others) at Chicago, which I applied to, and modified for, social networks. This work, however (which has recently been rediscovered by sociologists engaged in the study of social networks), attracted me far less than process modeling.

The third channel was Lazarsfeld's Panel Project, designed to develop methods for the analysis of panel data. The problem of panel analysis that Lazarsfeld posed was one I leaped on because it was hospitable to a model of a process; but his own solution to that problem involved index construction rather than construction of such a process model. It was the struggle to find a solution to this problem that led (with the aid of a suggestion from Richard Savage the year after I left Columbia) to the continuous-time stochastic process models that form the core (chapters 4–13) of my *Introduction to Mathematical Sociology* (1964) and to subsequent work in the same direction, as represented most recently in *Longitudinal Data Analysis* (1981). The compatibility of this direction of modeling with the substantive problems surrounding mass communications and mass behavior is not accidental, for those were the problems occupying Lazarsfeld as he formulated the problems of panel analysis.

Though Lipset was less important to the social system of Columbia sociology than Lazarsfeld or Merton, he was no less important than they to my development as a sociologist. Through a series of fortunate accidents I came in 1952 to be the third member (with Lipset and Trow) of the ITU research team. Lipset had started to plan the research as early as 1949, and it began as an organized research project in 1951. What was of central importance about the ITU study was the fact that it focused on a substantive macrosocial problem in political sociology (the social bases of political democracy) that had a rich history in sociological theory. Yet the research used quantitative data based on the new sample survey techniques to study the problem.

Macrosocial problems and sample survey techniques usually do not mix well in social research. How was Lipset able to bring about a successful mix? The answer, I believe, lies in the dominance of the problem over the data, a dominance buttressed both by the rich store of knowledge that Lipset had about the printers' union and by the fund of social and political theory bearing on the problem that he had at his fingertips. And as *Union Democracy* documents, the survey of New York printers was only one of a number of data sources, some of which (such as literature about printing unions and informant interviews with printers) Lipset had amassed before the survey project and some of which (such as observation of union meetings and chapel meetings, records of voting by locals in international elections, written material about union political issues gleaned from union publications) were obtained during the project itself. Although quantitative analyses of the survey data can be found throughout the book and indeed are central to the study, it was the *framework of ideas from social theory* that generated the analyses. Those ideas were, of course, modified by the results of the data analysis. For example, Lipset began with an idea of the importance of the occupational community for political participation in the union; but only in the analysis of the survey data did we discover the importance of certain formal clubs within the union for providing an organized base of opposition to the incumbents. Thus the initial ideas were richly developed, elaborated, and modified by the data. But the main point is that the framework of ideas was set by the macrosocial theory; the data analyses were forced to cope with those ideas, often partially testing a hypothesized macrosocial relation by testing the one or more implied micro-level processes necessary to generate it.

This data analysis, moving between theory such as that of the mass-society theorists and data that only indirectly bore on the theory, was far more important to the development of my data analysis skills than were any courses in research methods. It also led to orientations different from those I would have developed in such courses. One of these was a low level of interest in statistical inference (an orientation characteristic of Columbia sociology as a whole). The complexity of the linkage between, on the one hand, survey analysis involving relations between attributes of individuals and, on the other, the structure of macro-level relations they were designed to test made a prima facie case for ignoring standard tests and using other criteria to aid in drawing inferences about the social bases of political democracy.

Quite apart from these theoretical and methodological aspects, I found the ITU study appealing because it was consistent with, and reinforced my interest in, political pluralism, the social sources of political diversity, and the structural bases for opposition to an incumbent authority. It was partly these ideas that led to the proposal for a study of high schools that I tried to get funded when I was at the Bureau in early 1955 and finally pursued at the University of Chicago in 1957 (published in 1961 as *The Adolescent Society*). Treating the social system of adolescents in a high school as a partially closed social system, I wanted to study the effects of monolithic and pluralistic status systems on the behavior of adolescents, and to study the sources of these variations in status systems. (The proposal is included in an appendix in *The Adolescent Society*.) The theoretical aims of the study were never realized; *The Adolescent Society* was written largely for a lay audience and education professionals, with the theoretical work deferred to a later publication that never materialized. The contrast of *The Adolescent Society*, in which the theoretical aims did not dominate the data analysis, with *Union Democracy*, in which they did, is instructive, showing the ease with which the constraints of survey analysis can come to distort the original goals of the research.

Besides Merton, Lazarsfeld, and Lipset, others were also important to the development of my ideas. One was Ernest Nagel, both in his courses (logic, and the philosophy of science) that I audited and in the seminar with Lazarsfeld. Herbert Hyman, remarkably ingenious in using survey data to test social psychological ideas, was another. Others included statisticians, particularly Howard Raiffa and Theodore Anderson. Still another was a visitor, Harold Pfautz, who late in my Columbia career introduced me to some of the sociological classics I would otherwise have missed, including Adam Smith's *Theory of Moral Sentiments,* an extraordinary set of ideas about the self and society. (I had already been entranced by G. H. Mead's ideas, but I found Smith even more compelling.)

Quite apart from faculty, the set of fellow students and research associates at the Bureau was of considerable importance to each of us. It was, for example, in the traditions group seminars that the ideas about informal social structure and (as McPhee put it) the dynamics of masses began to emerge, ideas that strongly influenced my *Community Conflict*, the study that Herb Menzel, Elihu Katz, and I did (*Medical Innovation*) on diffusion of a new drug through the medical community, a paper on relational analysis that described ways of capturing the effects of informal social structure with survey-type data, and other methodological innovations, such as snowball sampling. These and others were the ideas that emerged four or five years downstream from the watershed that substituted mass communication and social psychology for community studies and social structure at Columbia. This orientation toward the study of behavior in loosely structured social systems is not all of sociology; but it was an important direction, and one that emerged not only from the combination of inputs we had received from the faculty and the research at Columbia but also from the further development of those ideas through our interaction.

This intellectual direction, which I had when I left Columbia, has not, of course, remained unchanged over the years. It has taken at least one abrupt turn, along with other, more minor ones. That, however, is another story, for which there is no space here.

My Traverse through Columbia

I came to Columbia resolving to give the educational system one last chance. It had failed, I felt, through high school and the several colleges I had attended. My teachers had been engaged in transmitting information, but none (except for two at Purdue) had been interested in me, in what I might do with the information they had imparted.

From nearly the beginning at Columbia I felt a difference. I sensed that some faculty members had a personal (that is, selfish) interest in some of their students. They seemed to be interested in those students in a way I had never felt since the ninth grade: their interest seemed tinged with the interest that parents have in their children. If asked to explain that now, I would say it is because, as children do for parents, graduate students help bring professors closer to immortality, extending their influence beyond their own life span. In the then large sociology department at Columbia this interest was in conflict with another, the faculty's desire to protect itself from graduate-student demands, so that for many of my fellow students graduate school did not have this special—perhaps essential—quality. For me, from nearly the beginning, it did.

I moved into an apartment at 111th Street and Broadway and sold my 1947 Chevrolet to a couple of Puerto Ricans, hoping they would not notice an ominous sound in the differential. I entered Columbia still a naive boy from Seven Mile, Ohio, and Herndon, Kentucky, with training as a chemical engineer and work experience as a chemist. I was not, however, in great awe of sociology. I had read enough by that time to have discovered that the density of ideas was not comparable to that in a book on physical chemistry. I wanted to progress rapidly, to skip background courses and proceed with the more advanced ones. As for statistics, I had had no courses but had read Quinn McNemar's statistical text over the summer so that I could enter the regular course on sociological statistics without preliminaries. But I decided after the first session to opt out of the course and take my statistics along with the statistics students in the mathematical statistics department. (It was the first of several courses I took in that department. My mathematical background from chemical engineering was strong enough to enable me to take courses in statistics that my sociology colleagues could not.)

As I have already indicated, Merton's theory course was riveting, a conversion experience for those of us eager for conversion. But my interest in coursework was largely confined to Merton's course and to the mathematical statistics courses. I did learn something about methods from Herbert Hyman and Charles Wright's research methods sequence. But with rare exceptions I have never found lecture courses particularly appealing as a medium for learning. Ernest Nagel's course in philosophy of science, which I sat in on, unregistered, was one such exception. The class always continued for ten or twenty minutes after its time with a group of students clustered around him, asking questions and arguing points. I stood on the periphery, verbally inadequate and unsure of myself, listening to the interchange and wanting to interrupt but remaining mute.

Seminars were another matter altogether. Some of the seminars were run by two faculty members, and the interchange was far more instructive than the lectures. In seminars we were induced to perform, to write and present papers, to show what we could do. The Lazarsfeld-Merton seminar in bureaucracy had both these components, as did the Lazarsfeld-Nagel seminar in mathematical sociology.

I sat in on a number of courses and seminars outside the department, stimulated by the extraordinary range of intellectual activity. One was Abram Kardiner's seminar, which I attended while I was reading his

Psychological Frontiers of Society; a second was Greenberg's course on linguistics; and a third was George Stigler's course in microeconomics. In an informal course on operations research I found an interesting mixture of statistics, mathematics, and an engineer's approach to problem solving. And I took a course in industrial engineering from Albert Rubenstein in which we engaged in a kind of sociology of formal organizations with an emphasis on patterns of communication.

So much for coursework. In my second semester I learned that Lipset and Trow were looking for interviewers for the ITU project, which was just going into the field. I applied for a job interviewing printers and was hired. I learned New York this way, riding the subways to the *World-Telegram,* the *Sun,* the *Times,* the *Herald Tribune,* the *Daily News,* the job shops, and printers' homes in Queens, Brooklyn, and the Bronx. I also learned interviewing. When the officials of the union were to be interviewed, Trow kept Joseph Greenblum and me on, and the three of us did those interviews. Then I helped in sending out mail questionnaires to get panel data on New York printers' voting preferences in the international union election.

That summer Lipset went to teach at the Free University in Berlin, and Trow went to help C. Wright Mills build a cabin on an island in one of the Great Lakes. The data were in, and they left me alone with it. At the end of the summer I had written up an analysis that I could show to them. Lipset read it, then asked me if I would like to be a coauthor of the book they were writing on the ITU. I said yes.

Thus began an enormously productive and instructive experience. We talked, wrote, tore each others' drafts apart and rewrote them. Lipset provided the intellectual framework and background for the study in the first chapters, and from there we shaped the analysis in extended discussions. Trow and I spent hours on the counter-sorters in the Fayerweather basement, pored over cross-tabulations together and separately, and in our extended arguments over data analysis, we taught each other. There were no long lines of students to curtail our interaction with Lipset. Nor was it all data analysis. We reread Michels, we read and argued over Mannheim, the mass-society theorists, Scheler, Emil Lederer, Hannah Arendt, and Selznick's *The Organizational Weapon.* I have coauthored books, but the interaction during the academic years 1952–53 and 1953–54 was unlike any other.

In the fall of 1953 Lazarsfeld asked me if I would work, for pay, on the panel project. I had to decide between that and continuing work without pay on the ITU project. I had a tuition fellowship and could manage without the extra money, so I said no and stayed with Lipset and Trow.

Lazarsfeld had three large projects, the Behavioral Models Project, the Panel Project, and the Concepts and Indices Project. In all three I was involved with Lazarsfeld but never was employed by him. Following the pattern of the Rashevsky paper, he paid me for products, not hours. One might say I worked as an independent contractor. It may have been this distance that made me less bitter at Lazarsfeld than those who had been closer. I stayed on the periphery of the Behavioral Models Project, never employed by it but attending seminars and, in the end, writing a report for the project on mathematical models of small groups. For the Concepts and Indices Project I wrote papers analyzing economists' use of concepts and analyzing economic indices (learning along the way more economics), and gained admission to the summer seminar at Dartmouth on concepts and indices. I was greatly interested in methods of panel analysis and wrote a paper attempting to extend those methods (which led some years later to my *Introduction to Mathematical Sociology*). That paper got me into another Dartmouth summer seminar, on methods of panel analysis. These summer seminars were extraordinarily important to my socialization in sociology, for I watched social scientists in action, debating points, arguing methods, developing ideas. I began to see myself on the same plane, emerging as a professional among professionals.

After two and a half years at Columbia I had reached an apex of status, prestige, and deference that I have never approached in my subsequent career. I then took my oral qualifying examination for admission to Ph.D. candidacy. I had prepared for the exam over the summer and had a rich and well-organized set of ideas and information about social theory and theorists. I remember the first question of the examination, a statistical question asked by Howard Raiffa, which I bungled miserably. I remember nothing else except that when it was over after two hours, I knew I had failed. I waited outside the examination room; Lipset summarized the examination when he came out and said to me, "If we all had not known before the exam that you would pass, you would have failed." The others were equally grim-faced as they left the examination room.

I trudged disconsolately down Amsterdam Avenue toward my 123rd Street apartment but was hailed by shouts from Sidney Morgenbesser and others from an office window across Amsterdam, a Bureau office I shared with Morgenbesser, with whom I was working on Lazarsfeld's Concepts and Indices Project. My friends had prepared a party in celebration of my passing my orals, but I had decided to skip it. They would not let me go home, though, despite my agony. So I went to the party and shared my troubles with my friends. Soon the members of my examination committee, including Merton, came over to wish me well and have a drink in what was a muted, but relieved, celebration. The incident was, I am sure, not forgotten (and may have been responsible for my not getting the job teaching Lee Wiggins's statistics course a year and a half later), but it was put aside and perhaps attributed to my general oral ineptitude. I went on to other things—the ITU analysis, my small-group monograph for the Behavioral Models Project, and my paper on properties of groups for the Concepts and Indices Project.

I finished my dissertation in the fall of 1954 and submitted it in December. The defense was in January. But matters were not so simple. Students did not finish so quickly at Columbia. Certainly if I had done my dissertation under Merton, I would not have finished then. No more likely would have been a quick completion under Lazarsfeld. Even under Lipset alone, matters would not have been so simple. But in the spring of 1954, I met with Merton, and he asked me about my dissertation plans. I said I didn't know; I had none. He asked why not the ITU study? Did I have chapters that were largely my own and formed a coherent whole? I said I thought they did. So, armed with this proposal from Merton, I went to Lipset and reported the discussion. He agreed to the dissertation. He might have done so anyway, or he might not have— for he was a young assistant professor, and the ITU study was his first major work after his own dissertation. Then a graduate student proposes to carve a dissertation out of a portion of it. Even though I was the principal author of the chapters I proposed to use, and even though many of the ideas in them were mine, they nevertheless had resulted from long discussions among the three of us and extended critiques from Trow and Lipset. Because they were intended from the start as potential chapters of the book rather than as chapters of my dissertation, Lipset gave them far more attention than dissertation chapters ordinarily receive.

The waters of Columbia were difficult to navigate, at least with any speed. It helped to have a sponsor interested in one's well-being. But it helped more to have two. Still more did it help to have three. Lazarsfeld was my mentor, but I did not do my dissertation under him and was not beholden to him. Lipset was the faculty member under whom I worked most continuously, but the structure of Columbia demanded that he be attentive to Merton's or Lazarsfeld's wishes. Merton was less close than either of the others to me but was ready and able to serve as my protector.

I finished my dissertation quickly in the fall of 1954, making the necessary modifications to form dissertation chapters from what had been book chapters and adding one analytical chapter for good measure. But I needed work that fall to support myself. I was finished with the department, and it was finished with me. The Bureau would be, if anything was to be, my home for the academic year 1954–55. Charles Glock rescued me by offering a monograph on community conflicts from the Twentieth Century Fund, a task someone else had botched. I worked on that project, producing *Community Conflict,* which the fund did not like very much but nevertheless was published by Jeremiah Kaplan's Free Press. (Of everything I have written, this small, awkwardly published monograph has probably sold the greatest number of copies.)

In the winter, in part as an outgrowth of the traditions seminar, a drug company, Pfizer, gave a grant to study the way doctors introduce new drugs into their practices. That project occupied me during the spring (though I wrote most of my portion of the report during one tense, and intense, week in which my wife and I were for other reasons not speaking). Meanwhile, it was not clear what I would do the next year. I had no job offers. Herbert Simon at Carnegie Tech had offered me a job the previous year, but Lazarsfeld had induced me to remain at Columbia. Now there was nothing. Lee Wiggins was to be gone (at the Center for Advanced Study in the Behavioral Sciences—its second year), and I hoped to teach his statistics course, a part-time job that would be enough for support. The department, however, decided I was not a sufficiently able teacher.

My time at Columbia was approaching an end. One day I stopped to see Lipset to discuss details of the *Union Democracy* manuscript, and he introduced me to his new research assistant, Immanuel Wallerstein. He was a bright, energetic, and self-confident member of a new cohort of graduate students. Through his eyes I saw myself no longer as a member of the elite among graduate students but as a former graduate student, outside that system, in limbo, Maurice Stein of 1955.

My destination for the next year was still unclear. I was preparing myself for another year at the Bureau, with hopes of getting funding for my new project, a study of adolescents in high schools. Then, at the beginning of the summer, I received an invitation from the Center for Advanced Study (occasioned by the last-minute defection of a more deserving scholar but also due in part to Lazarsfeld's and Merton's influence). Late that summer I set off for California with a two-week stop along the way at Carnegie Tech in Pittsburgh, at Herb Simon's invitation. (My wife and son had left earlier, stopping to visit her family in Indiana.) I packed the station wagon with all my belongings and stayed overnight at Philip Ennis's apartment on Ninety-sixth Street. The next morning I found my car plundered; the clothes I had left in the front seat were gone. I didn't much care. I was a journeyman sociologist, off to Pittsburgh and to the Center.

CHAPTER FOUR

My Life and Soft Times

Joseph Gusfield

There is a touch of chutzpah in autobiography, an arrogance that my life is a matter of such significance as to merit the reader's attention. My name may be known in seminars but it is hardly known in households. The self-analysis implied requires me to find some justification in a more universal rationale. I find it in Gerth and Mills's view of social psychology as the confluence of history and biography. An even more useful salve to my sensibilities has been supplied by Alvin Gouldner, who wrote that the perception of sociologists comes from two sources. One is empirical studies and theorizing—the role realities that the sociologist presents to the reader and freely acknowledges. The other, and often the more determinative, is the "personal realities" that the sociologist derives from his or her experiences. These are seldom acknowledged and are often half hidden from the writer as well.

My autobiography is a form of stock taking. It is also an exercise in finding the sources of the personal assumptions that have formed the temperament, the feelings, and the mythic and experienced bases from which theory, research, and conviction often spring. No life exists apart from history, from a time and a place. So too an autobiography that did not reflect the person "of this time, of that place" would mislead and misdirect. It is in this amalgam of person, place, and idea that I find my direction.

Kenneth Burke, whose work has had a great influence on me, writes of human beings as being "rotten with perfection." I understand him to mean the proclivity of people to invent typologies and then push them to their extremes—for example, for a sociologist to over-sociologize human action, for a Marxist to find capitalism everywhere, or for a Parsonian to see only system. Writing an autobiography induces that kind of perfection. It must lend a narrative quality to the events of a life, as if they had direction, purpose, and goal rather than being the result of accident, impulse, and drift. I have to be aware of who I am now when writing about who I was then. Let me make that discount at the beginning and set it aside, otherwise I might stop writing at this moment.

I write from a gazebo of time, looking backward at my life and discovering the present as future seen from the past. At sixty-five I am an aging sociologist living at the edge of America. Mexico is a half hour away, and the Pacific Ocean is down the street. It seems a fit location from which to write this musing account of a life that is probably duplicated in the accounts of many sociologists of my age.

Growing Up in the 1930s

Like many others of my generation, I came into academic life in a period of an expanding system of higher education in a prosperous economy. Growing up in Chicago in the 1930s I would not have expected that kind of future. In retrospect three facts of my childhood seem formative: Chicago, the Great Depression, and being Jewish in the 1930s.

The city of Chicago had, in the Prohibition and Al Capone years, gained an international reputation as a center of the underworld, the place Sandburg had called the "city of the big shoulders." And so it seemed to me—a place of continuing danger, where walking the streets was a daily adventure, and every stranger posed a threat. It was also a city of sharp ethnic lines, both territorial and social. The first question about anyone, of any age, was, What is he?—meaning, What is his nationality? This perception of the city was repeated in the University of Chicago's urban studies. Only later did I learn that Chicago's rigid ethnic boundaries probably represented an extreme among American cities. They extended to aspects of education as well. During my undergraduate days I became friendly with a fellow student, George De Vos (now professor of anthropology at the University of California, Berkeley). We were astonished to learn that we had been living for several years on opposite sides of a narrow street. He had gone to a Catholic parochial school, and I to public school, and we had not even been aware of each other.

The Depression was more than a bend in the business cycle. It was a cataclysmic destruction of belief in the special providence of America and a long period of deep anxiety and frustration. Many of us who went through it continue to feel that the structure of solid institutions is a facade, always liable to sudden and unexpected tremors that undermine the foundation.

Above all, growing up Jewish in the 1930s was more than a matter of what you were; it was the definitive statement of your place in history. The local ethnic conflicts kept anti-Semitism alive but they were always discounted, the disappearing reenactment of old-country relationships in a new environment. In my neighborhood on the Day of Atonement, Polish-American youth would throw stones at the windows of the synagogue and shout anti-Semitic slogans; Jewish youth would do the same but omit the slogans. (I have said often that I was beaten up by Polish hoods because I was Jewish and by Jewish hoods just for the fun of it.) The deeply serious happenings were overseas, in Germany. They colored our politics, our daily talk, and our sense of the security of being American.

The beginnings of what later became the Holocaust pushed me and many other Jews rapidly into both the Zionist movement and the left in politics in the late 1930s. Here too I learned the vagaries of trust in the stability of movements and organizations. I had been active in an effort to develop a branch of the American Student Union in my high school. The union was then an organization attempting to gain economic benefits for youth and college students. It was also committed to developing an anti-Hitler foreign policy and a consciousness of what was happening under fascism. I had invited the national secretary to a formational meeting. Between his acceptance and the meeting the Soviet Union had signed a nonaggression pact with Germany, and the union line changed to an attack on the war-mongering capitalist countries. I learned early that ideologies and political organizations are fickle lovers.

I suppose that in looking back and perfecting my narrative I could say that all those experiences create the aura of a world in which violence and discontinuity were palpable possibilities. They suggest a world in which rules are broken as much, if not more, than followed. I do not think that was my personal feeling about my own life, but it may well have shaped my sense of history as unpredictable and unmeasurable.

The War Years

The attack on Pearl Harbor was one of those moments when you realize that history and biography meet. Like most men in my generation, I was a soldier in World War II. In one way the war was not a turning point for me. I was an undergraduate at the University of Chicago when I entered the Army in April 1943. I was discharged on January 14, 1946 (a day of liberation I still celebrate), and returned three days later to the University of Chicago. But the experience of war and soldiering had a profound impact on how I viewed life. After almost forty years I still see the present historical period as the postwar world.

Perhaps my second day in the Army was a symbol of what was to come. A sergeant lined up the raw recruits and asked all those with some college education to fall out and walk across the yard picking up cigarette butts. "Now," he said to all the others, "I want the rest of you ignoramuses to watch these college kids and see how it's done." I did learn respect for raw intelligence that cuts across class and education. For a bookish and timid Jew from lower middle-class Chicago to live with Cajuns from rural Louisiana was an introduction to the similarities among Americans and among human beings that are not often as evident as the diversities.

I also learned the difference between front and back that distinguishes the sophisticate from the naive. I learned that the pious assistant to the chaplain, who spoke so fervently about the sweetness of his boss and about how much he missed his wife, was a busy whorehound who hated the woman he was forced to marry after he got her pregnant. I learned that he saw the chaplain as a naive man who could be played for gain by feigning a religious commitment. But I also learned that men who affect cowardice can act heroically, that people from whom you expect hostility can be helpful, and that though people can be worse than they seem, they are also sometimes better. What I was discovering, I think, was the appearance of a human quality outside the history and sociology that seem so often to be the constraining and shaping matter of our existence. Only later, in reflection, can it come to our consciousness in forms such as Dennis Wrong's "The Oversocialized Conception of Man."

The war helped create a certain indifference in me to ideologies and political programs that, except for the civil-rights movement of the 1960s, has remained a part of my political quiescence. Two events stick in my memory. One is like a classic movie scene: the first time I had to go through the pockets and wallet of a dead German soldier to identify him, I found a picture of his wife and child. It made me recognize that wars are fought against human beings, not against abstractions that can be hated.

A second event made me vividly realize the strange mix of good and evil that affects history. In the closing days of the European war the Germans had thrown old men and young boys into the front. After the surrender some members of the Schutzstaffel, or SS (the elite military unit of the Nazi party) continued to fight; some disguised themselves as members of the Wehrmacht (the regular German army). Wounded German prisoners were sent to our company, a medical unit attached to an infantry division, one level closer to the front than a MASH (mobile army surgical hospital). Because of my one year of college French, my smattering of Yiddish, and my sliver of German, I had, mirabile dictu, become the company interpreter. A German soldier was brought in who claimed to be in the Wehrmacht. Because he was in his late twenties I was skeptical and suspected he was an SS man in disguise. He spoke good English and said that he had sat out the war as a theology student but in the final days had been drafted (a story he later substantiated). I asked him if he had been in the SS (Schutzstaffel), for me and most Americans the embodiment of evil. "No," he replied, in an answer still with me. "I was not so idealistic."

The war was the supreme instance of William James's description of experience as "a big, buzzing, blooming confusion." For a soldier it was the experience of being a pawn in a chess game whose strategy and direction he could never make out. It began to seem to us, however, that the chess players were in the same fix; they could no more control the game than could we. Events were, as so often they are in politics and life, in command. The tragedy was the absence of true ideological or political content in the average soldier's commitment to the war—on both sides, as Edward Shils and Morris Janowitz's work on the Wehrmacht later displayed. Though Seymour Martin Lipset is probably correct that World War II was the only popular war the United States ever fought, the soldiers I knew understood little about Nazism and had no more than a vague devotion to patriotism and duty. I, of course, was different. As a Jew I had a strong feeling about the war, though it too was almost lost in the mix of human beings, death, destruction, and anarchy I encountered. That sense of fate, of the unknown, uncontrollable forces surrounding us, has never really left me. The root belief of the scientific endeavor, that the world is both knowable and malleable, has continued to seem to me a supreme delusion.

The University of Chicago

My decision to enter the University of Chicago on graduating from high school in 1941 was one of those turning points in my life when there was a fork in the road, and I took the right road. That I did so still seems mysterious to me. During my senior year in a Chicago high school I thought a great deal about going to college. It meant that I would be the first in my entire extended family to go to a full-time, four-year college. Neither of my two older brothers could afford that. Scholarships were rare in American higher education, although the University of Chicago was unique in granting scholarships to high-school graduates through competitive examinations. (I tried, but failed, to get one.) I lacked the money for anything but a free education where I could live at home and commute. I had a scholarship to a small college in Iowa and to a four-year "working-class" college in Chicago.

But I had set my heart on the University of Chicago, which I had visited as a high-school debater the year before. Both my uncles, whom I depended on for advice, cautioned prudence. Go to a junior college for two years, they said, or to Roosevelt College (later University), and transfer to the university later; save some money now. It was sound advice, and I knew it. In my senior year I read a collection of addresses by Robert Maynard Hutchins, then president of the University of Chicago and a major figure in higher education. I was impressed by the boldness and philosophical turn those papers displayed. Throwing caution and my uncles' advice in the ashcan, I decided to enter the University of Chicago. I had been working about thirty hours a week during the school year and more than full-time in summers and had saved one hundred dollars, enough to cover one-third of my annual tuition. I continued to work fifteen to twenty hours a week at the same supermarket as clerk and stock handler while going to college. With that income, as well as loans and scholarships, I was able to complete my first two years.

My sense that this was a formative decision well made must be tempered, however, by awareness of the common predilection to read history backward and find the oak tree in the acorn. O. Henry has a story, or stories, in which the hero finds himself at a crossroad and takes one of the four possible directions. The narrator follows him through each of the four choices and by each, through different experiences, he arrives at the same place. My fellow graduate student and later colleague Bernard Farber (now professor of sociology at Arizona State University and a leading figure in family studies) took another road: he did his undergraduate work at the Chicago college I rejected and has since had a career very similar to my own. But my undergraduate years nonetheless proved to be highly significant.

I entered the College of the University of Chicago in September 1941. Three months later the United States was at war. I lived at home and commuted about three hours a day to and from campus. Though I had friends at the university, I continued to find my social life among high-school friends in my neighborhood, and my work as a supermarket cashier took me to still another part of the city. Despite this fragmentation and the clear recognition that I would be a soldier in the near future, that period was perhaps among the richest intellectual times I have known. The university was the focal point of my existence, and although I was very much aware of the war, it was possible to lead a cloistered life in which Kant and Marx and John Dewey and Shakespeare were as much companions as they have been to others at other times and places. In several courses, I read all the assigned as well as the optional readings listed in the syllabi. As a commuter not engulfed by student norms, I learned only from a study group for the final examinations that such dedication was neither expected nor accepted. I had become a GDCR—goddamn curve raiser.

I regret not being able to convey the excitement of my freshman year and the intensity and exuberance of intellectual discovery. The University of Chicago seemed charged with an electric current that made every question a matter of analysis and argument, in which the intellectual exchange seemed to me to be as keen as possible. We all felt ourselves to be among the smartest and the brightest. Later many colleagues of mine would speak disappointedly of their undergraduate days, and I have felt very privileged to feel otherwise. I recall the intellectual rapture most vividly in an argument with a friend (now professor of mathematics at Purdue) after the final examination in the freshman social-science course. Returning home on the Chicago elevated train, we quarreled about the correct answer to an economics question. We were so carried away by our debate that we pulled down the window shade and drew supply-and-demand curves. Those years were definitive in establishing in me a love for disinterested intellectual play, still the best source, I think, of what we used to call scholarship and today call research.

I learned some other valuable lessons. One was that you don't have to be Jewish. Deep in my view of life was the unstated premise of supreme confidence in the capacity of poor Jews to overcome intellectual obstacles. Being lean and hungry as well as one of the people that had produced the Old Testament, the Talmud, and thinkers such as Einstein, Freud, and Marx, what couldn't I do? I soon became friendly with a group of fellow students who were Greek-Americans, and I learned that poor Greeks were also smart. I then learned that there were rich Jews who were smart and, again, that there were poor Gentiles and, to my amazement, even rich Gentiles who were smart. Many, if not most, of those students were smarter than I. I discovered the painful truths that leisure is more valuable to scholarship than hunger and that poverty does not breed either character or intellect.

Graduate Education and Intellectual Tension

Three days after leaving the Army I returned to student life, completing my college education in the first three-month quarter, almost as if the war had been only an intermission. I was twenty-two and felt that time was running out. My aim, developed in my sophomore year, was to take a master's degree in economics and a law degree and then to become what was known as a New Deal lawyer, working in government. By 1946 the years of study the plan involved seemed too long to wait before beginning "life," and I decided to enter the University of Chicago Law School.

In 1946 the law school students were largely veterans of the war. We were mostly anxious to find a life outside of history, to concentrate on career, marriage, and family—the private aspects of our lives. We felt that we had to make up for years lost in the war and had no time for the play of the mind. The mood of the campus, compared to that of my freshman year, was similarly privatized, though it retained the intellectual intensity I had known. The atmosphere was distinctly apolitical. Although there were great debates and intraorganizational struggles over the role of Communists in veterans organizations, the merits of T. S. Eliot or Thomas Aquinas could arouse more interest than could the coming elections.

After three years in the Army, the study of law was a replenishing change. The daily preparation and possible recitation (much like Professor Kingsfield's classes in the movie *The Paper Chase*) meant a rigid routine of disciplined study. Yet despite that routine and the standard curriculum, the law also possessed an intellectual, philosophical side that the faculty helped emerge from the pages of appellate court opinions. In discovering this side I was fortunate to have two excellent teachers—Edward Hirsch Levi (later chancellor of the university and still later attorney general of the United States under Gerald Ford), who taught jurisprudence, and Malcolm Sharp, whose course on contracts was one of the supreme educational experiences of my life. Sharp made his students see law as a meeting place of psychology, economics, sociology, ethics, and history, but that it was still Law. It had its own character as well.

But my undergraduate education was only completed formally. On my return to campus, my former college instructor in social science, Milton Singer (now professor emeritus of anthropology but then a recent Ph.D. in philosophy), had asked me to teach the sophomore social-science course for adults in the university extension division. College instruction after the war was a seller's market, and I was fortunate for an opportunity that today would go to an advanced graduate student. Teaching that course began to awaken in me the intellectual concerns that could be indulged only on the periphery of legal curricula, smuggled in by some scholarly teachers.

Whitman wrote that he was simmering and simmering until Emerson brought him to a boil. Teaching in the College did that for me. At the beginning of the following academic year I was asked to become a teaching assistant in the Social Sciences 2 course in the College. It has become a historic course, and the years I was associated with it have become legend. (Its fortieth anniversary was celebrated in 1984 with a symposium at the University of Chicago.) The teaching staff, about seventeen people, met each week to discuss the materials for lecture and discussion sessions. These meetings were less conferences about pedagogy than seminars about many scholarly matters, seminars marked by intense debate and rancor, pyrotechnical displays of ego and erudition, and great flashes of insight, wit, and critical analysis. The members of that staff have since found their merited niches in the academic pantheon—Daniel Bell, Lewis Coser, Rose Coser, Morton Grodzins, Abram Harris, Rosalie Hankey (Wax), Martin Meyerson, C. Wright Mills, Benjamin Nelson, Phillip Rieff, David Riesman, Milton Singer, Sylvia Thrupp, and Murray Wax.

Though the intensity of staff meetings was awesome to a timid and unsure assistant, they were nevertheless intellectual adventures that made law school seem confining. In the first quarter of the course we read Freud's *Civilization and Its Discontents,* Durkheim's *Division of Labor,* and Weber's *Protestant Ethic and the Spirit of Capitalism,* as well as works by Marx and Veblen. It was my first meeting with Durkheim or Weber. Weber's cultural analysis of the rise of capitalism was the most captivating book in social science that I had ever encountered, and it changed the way I viewed history and society. That year I also took a seminar on the sociology of law, which was taught in the law school by Max Rheinstein. We used as basic material Weber's *Law in Economy and Society,* which Rheinstein and Edward Shils had just translated. These experiences made me restless with a legal education that was becoming routine and constraining. (Ego compels me to say that I was a good law student; I even made the law review.) I decided to continue my education in some other area.

There is an image in my mind of a discussion about my future that took place under a tree on a quadrangle outside the law school with Milton Singer and Benjamin Nelson. Nelson felt that the Committee on Social Thought, one of several innovative interdisciplinary committees formed under Hutchins, was the logical place for me, but Singer felt that it was an unwise choice—a degree without a market. At one point I felt as if God and the devil were debating the disposition of my eternal soul. Whatever the merits of the debate, this time I chose prudence and entered the Department of Sociology.

I led a somewhat schizoid existence, between teaching in the College and being a graduate student in sociology. I have written at length elsewhere about the value of the tension produced by those two contrasting models (broad intellectual exploration and narrow disciplined research) of what doing social science should be. They were diverging paymasters, but I am convinced that the push and pull of each against the other has contributed to my thinking in later years.

The College and the graduate departments had completely separate faculties. The College faculty was junior in age and rank, with fewer Ph.D.'s and contemptuous of the specialization and narrowness of the departments. Its models of social science were those major works that had come to be regarded as classics—those of Marx, Freud, Mannheim, Weber, Schumpeter. These works gave readers a way of placing themselves in the historical stream of their times. They were "big" with significance and wide in scope. They provided the badge of the cultured, educated person; they formed a base for what the classicist James Redfield calls the objective of a liberal-arts education—the capacity for "good talk."

To me the Department of Sociology seemed a dull, narrow place in contrast to the intellectual excitement of the College. Its model of achievement was found in the famous Chicago series of observational studies, such as Harvey Zorbaugh's *Gold Coast and the Slum,* Walter Reckless's *Taxi Dance Hall,* and the then recently published *Street-Corner Society* by W. F. Whyte. Achievement meant completing a Ph.D. dissertation in imitation of the model. It meant becoming a craftsman, a sociologist. It seemed narrow and insignificant, a sop to the necessity of an academic degree for entry into academic life. Only later, in working on my thesis, did I come to appreciate the value of the craft and the necessity and joy of narrowness. Only later did I come to recognize the value to scholarship of the tension between these two different conceptions of social science.

Graduate Years

I entered the Department of Sociology at the University of Chicago in 1947 and received my degree in 1954, at the age of thirty-one. Though I left in 1950 to take a faculty position at Hobart and William Smith Colleges, I returned to Chicago every summer to teach in the College. I look on those years as important intellectually but even more important as the source of friendships that have continued throughout my life and have been of great significance to my scholarship as well.

As had been the case in law school, the sociology students were mostly veterans of the war, older than had been typical of graduate students and beginning to marry and have children. Unlike law school, however, in the sociology department there was a greater sense of intellectual and social play. We lived in the Hyde Park area near the university. Graduate-student life was a round of parties, study, and endlessly flamboyant talk. The faculty and classes were its accompaniment as well as its catalyst, but the talk was where the action was. Now, forty years later, it becomes romanticized in nostalgia, but it has long appeared to me as a period in life that I wished could have gone on longer and that I have often wished could return.

Strangely, it was a period without much concern for the future. We did not yet sense the expansion that was coming in higher education and in the economy. Like devout sectarians we felt that somehow God or the economy or the universities would provide. Living on the GI bill of rights and an instructor's salary, we scrimped but felt far from drowning. Since we were all in the same boat, the genteel poverty of graduate-student existence was no deficiency, and the GI bill kept us afloat. For myself, whatever the future held, it would not be the world of my father. A meat cutter, he had been buffeted by business cycles and the indignities of living on the edge of a statusless poverty.

I was especially drawn to the lectures of Herbert Blumer. He was perhaps the most theoretical and critical member of the faculty. His criticism of most sociological methods, however, made it difficult to think of a thesis that could meet his exacting standards. From Blumer and the reading in G. H. Mead I developed an interest in social psychology and chose self-conceptions as the subject of my master's thesis. As was the case with Ph.D. dissertations, the expectation was that the student would complete an empirical research project and not an exercise in theory or even history. After a course on the life history with Ernest Burgess I decided to study the self-conceptions of the aged among three generations of the same families. My reasoning was that if people develop new self-conceptions from the views of those around them, then the elderly would have a self-concept more like that of the young than would the middle-aged. Burgess served as chairman of my thesis committee; Albert Reiss, then an instructor, was also a member. The project was not exactly a fiasco, but I learned from it the subtleties of self-concept and the difficulties and limits of interview questionnaires. My original intention of developing the topic for a Ph.D. dissertation was discarded.

Despite my exposure to Blumer and my announced view of myself as a symbolic interactionist, my own early politics and my work in the College and the courses with Hughes and Warner had kept my vaguely structural and Marxian assumptions alive. When I left the University of Chicago in 1950, I had not yet found a dissertation topic. Blumer's work on collective behavior and social movements had interested me, and I had been struck by an account of the Women's Winter Crusades of 1873–74 in Park and Burgess's introductory sociology text. Social-movement theory was dominated by the model of the natural history. Weber's writing on the routinization of charisma and Michels's on the iron law of oligarchy had only recently been translated. The transformation of theories about collective behavior and social movements was in the air.

But there is more to the choice of a topic than the logic of theory. I was already interested in the temperance movement, and when I began to read more, I discovered things I had not known and that were hard to explain. This sense of anomaly seems to me the seed of good research.

Answering a question or solving a puzzle is still the model of what I am about in my work—that is, when I most like what I am doing. As I read about the temperance movement in America, I encountered agrarian radicalism for the first time and was astounded. I had always thought of political radicalism as something associated with an urban working class, and its ideology as brought to the United States by European immigrants. I thought that native and rural America was conservative and that the temperance movement and Prohibition were the programs of that conservatism. The discrepancy was a source of wonder. In the language of the 1960s, it "blew my mind," and I wanted to know how the movement had changed from its beginnings to what I assumed was its present conservatism. The effects of organization seemed to me to be a clue.

The final title of my dissertation was "The Woman's Christian Temperance Union: Change and Continuity in an Organized Interest Group." How did I get from there to *Symbolic Crusade: Status Politics and the American Temperance Movement?* I completed the dissertation in 1954; the book was first published in 1963. I could recount the theoretical and practical explanations for the transformation, but one element would be missing. I had fallen in love with the subject. Interviewing the members of the Women's Christian Temperance Union, or WCTU, gathering and analyzing WCTU journals and convention reports over seventy-five years of its history, and doing background reading in secondary sources, I had become fascinated by the history of the movement. There were good theoretical and practical justifications for studying it, but they would mask the joy and excitement of knowing a great deal about a subject, of trying to make sense out of what I knew, and of becoming an expert on something that interested me and, through my work, would come to interest others. In recent years historians have gone well beyond me in the study of temperance. I get much satisfaction seeing how my work has become both a stimulant to those studies and the foil against which most must measure their work and their arguments. In writing *Symbolic Crusade,* I was beginning to be wary of theory as a source of scholarship, to search for anomalies, and, above all, to see what Veblen called idle curiosity as a vital and prized part of being a scholar.

The Establishing Years

From 1950 to 1955 I taught sociology and social sciences at Hobart and William Smith Colleges in Geneva, New York. During that period I was the only sociologist in a college of about eight hundred students. (Pierre Bessaignet, now at the University of Nice, was the sole anthropologist in a two-person department.) Hobart and William Smith was an old Episcopalian college. After the war it had expanded from four hundred students and was widening its appeal from its original denominational base. It provided a good intellectual climate with a commitment to integrated social-sciences and humanities courses, modeled somewhat after the College courses at the University of Chicago. The faculty included a number of excellent scholars, many of whom later distinguished themselves elsewhere.

I had gone to Hobart and William Smith with some dread. Chinese entry into the Korean War had caused panic among young instructors in the College at Chicago. The reinstitution of an expanded draft seemed imminent. Instructors were warned they might not be rehired for the next year. Ithiel Pool visited friends at Chicago and told them he was also recruiting for Hobart and William Smith, where he had taught before going to MIT, where he spent the rest of his life. I applied, made a visit, and was hired largely on the strength of my experience in the College.

Hobart and William Smith proved to be a needed, pleasant, and fulfilling experience. For one thing, I learned about sociology. Being the only sociologist on the campus, I taught the gamut of courses from quantitative methods to marriage and family to public opinion. Through that experience I was up on the corpus of sociology for many years to come.

I grew up at Hobart and William Smith. It was my first encounter with a world of manners and tradition and a sense of established and secure authority. With the exception of my Army experience, it was the first time that I had lived in a gentile environment. At twenty-seven I had lived my civilian life mostly in one or another urban Jewish enclave. Neither the law school nor the sociology department at the University of Chicago had afforded a change. Some wit has perceptively described the University of Chicago in those days, and perhaps now as well, as a place where Protestant professors taught Jewish students Catholic philosophy.

Hobart and William Smith maintained, and perhaps still maintains, that mix of education and character training that colleges have provided in many societies. It was this educational approach that the University of Chicago (in Hutchins's speeches as well as in campus lore) so openly despised as anti-intellectual. As a young assistant professor, I, along with my wife, was pressed to chaperon fraternity parties, as the college guidelines demanded. The rules, manners, and poise of the students and the formality of dress contrasted starkly with the free and easy openness of the University of Chicago. There we had experienced a policy of treating all students as adults and eschewing the parental concerns of other campuses in the late 1940s.

My wife still talks about her surprise at the controls exercised by Hobart and William Smith and their continuity with the family life of many students. Chaperoning a dance one evening, she expressed amazement at the rule requiring women to be in the dormitory by 11 P.M., and midnight on Saturday. "Surely," she said to one young woman, "you don't have to be home by midnight in your own family?" The student replied that indeed she had; at home the curfew was 11 P.M. even on Saturday. For my wife, who was the only child of Russian-Jewish socialists and had grown up in the Socialist Workman's Circle and had gone to college at the University of Chicago, this was a strange world indeed.

Like many American colleges and universities, Hobart and William Smith had not only expanded considerably after World War II but was also in the process of absorbing new students into what was an old and traditional institution. The few Jews on the faculty were tokens in a new era, evidence of the tolerance and goodwill of an old Protestant institution. We were also exotic and thus sought after in a somewhat analogous fashion to the way blacks are today or to the way Hannah Arendt has described Disraeli's use of his Jewish origin as an admission ticket to British high society. But I came to admire a genuine tolerance and attraction that resonated with a New England tradition of fair play and civil liberties, cutting across political divisions of conservative, liberal, and radical.

Writing this sketch of my life, I came also to appreciate another facet of my experience in upstate New York that is bound up in its past. An image of Frankie Merson remains with me. She was professor of political science at Keuka College, a small women's college on Keuka Lake in upstate New York. Keuka College had a work-study curriculum long before Antioch College and was a Methodist school with a strong feminist mission. It was a vestige of the nineteenth century still existing in the twentieth-century world of postwar America. Professor Merson was the leading member of the Keuka WCTU, and she was one of my interview respondents. She had been a suffragette before 1920 and had been active in opposing the presidential candidacy of the Catholic and "wet" Al Smith. She had first come to my attention through a letter in the Geneva, New York, newspaper protesting the execution of the Rosenbergs. Such a strange mixture but not so strange in this piece of

America that had been the scene of many social movements and that one historian had called the burnt-over district.

The Illinois Years

Hobart was a part of the history of American colleges in its movement out from the circle of denomination into a wider world of American diversity. The faculty mirrored that polarity between cosmopolitan and local with which Alvin Gouldner, using Robert K. Merton's terms, described the loyalties and sources of aspiration of American college teachers. I had made use of my Hobart and William Smith years to write my doctoral dissertation. I had begun to feel comfortable in the small-college atmosphere, and that comfort made me uncomfortable. A colleague in another department explained why he left Hobart and William Smith. Only a few years older than I, he was introduced at an alumni meeting as "kindly old Professor Bartlett." I too began to sense the ivy growing around me and felt that if I stayed two or three more years I would lose the drive and stimulus that had come from a university environment. I would begin to feel comfortably at home and start absenting myself from national meetings for fear of meeting those who had been my fellow graduate students and who had lived up to their early promise of scholarship.

I wrote to Herbert Blumer, and he recommended me to the University of Illinois. I remained there from 1955 to 1969. Those were years of immense expansion in American higher education. The evolution of my own career paralleled the evolution of higher education in general, from institutions catering to a small minority of the American elite to mass institutions that absorbed the American middle class. In that process education became perceived as the sine qua non to mobility and the decent maintenance of already established family positions. In this respect the University of Illinois was caught on the same escalator as Hobart and William Smith, though at a different level. It had been a state university whose networks, both socially and occupationally, prepared students to return home to become the professionals of their local communities. As such it did not, except in football, compete with other universities, even the University of Chicago. They were in different intellectual and educational leagues. In the 1950s it was changing and had an eye on greater prestige in academia.

In the postwar world the large and comparatively wealthy state universities were intent on moving up. They became national universities as America was itself becoming a more national society. It was necessary for students to leave the local community, and even the Midwest, in search of jobs and family. The aspirations of administration and faculty were making even fraternity-sorority life and athletics subservient to the academic aspirations of the faculty. What David Riesman and Christopher Jencks later called the academic revolution was in full swing.

It was a period of expansion and security. For the junior faculty member in sociology it was a seller's market. Not much in the way of publication was needed to gain tenure. Sociology was still a new field, and with new universities springing up and old ones growing, new departments were being formed and old ones expanded. If a sociologist missed tenure at one school, there was another good job on the horizon. The welfare state was coming of age, and people were needed in what I call the troubled person's industries, such as criminology, social work, and clinical psychology. All this meant that college education was in; students were plentiful, and education was trusted to provide the necessary training. The expansion of higher education was also sold as a way of competing with Russian science and engineering. Scholars could ride in on the tails of the post-Sputnik rockets.

The Illinois years were ones of scholarship, teaching, and growth in family and friendships. The years at Hobart and William Smith had been the years of the cold war's beginnings, the McCarthy hearings, the Rosenberg and the Hiss cases, and the first Eisenhower-Stevenson election. The Illinois years were the years of the civil-rights movement. Provocative, disturbing, and flamboyant as they were, it was not until 1968 that the student movements of the 1960s became central to life on most American campuses. Even the Vietnam War does not, in my memory, override the importance and the emotional surge of the civil-rights movement. It set a tone and provided a model that opened the 1960s and gave it its motif.

In the early 1960s I felt that I was in a rut. I had been in school, in one form or another, since 1946. The world was changing in profound ways as new nations came into being, sometimes each week. I was not even sure that I wanted to continue in academic life. With a sabbatical due me, I thought of travel and decided to get out of Western civilization and see life in a developing and new nation. I chose India because I could teach and observe without learning a new language. I meant my year on a Fulbright fellowship to be an interlude. In some respects it was, but only in some.

India, 1962–81

I am writing this section the day following the assassination of Indira Gandhi, and India is unexpectedly and unusually prominent in the attention of the American public. In 1962, when I first visited India, it was a land almost invisible to Americans; it still is. I have been there four times now, for visits ranging from six weeks to nine months. I have taught for at least one term at three Indian universities and have lectured at many others. I have lived for periods from two weeks to five months in several major cities—Delhi, Patna, Bangalore, Calcutta. Though I have done some research and writing in connection with India, it has been peripheral to most of my work. And though some of my scholarship has been concerned with problems of national development, that too has been a minor theme. Most of my studies have been located in the United States.

Yet my experience in India has had a major personal and intellectual impact on me. I first came to India armed with the concepts of American social science. These, following a line from Durkheim through Parsons, were couched in the discourse of modernization with its clear movement from community to society, tradition to modernity, caste to class. India defied the efforts to be seen through such prisms. An aphorism I learned later, when living in Japan, puts the matter well. In India no one trusts the institutions to work because they know that socially organized life is fragile and will disintegrate. One acts to protect oneself and one's interests because social institutions cannot be trusted to sustain themselves. In Japan, there is the same sense of the fragility of social life but there is also the belief that if everyone works at it and helps sustain one another's roles, the social organization can be upheld. Americans are not worried about social organization being destroyed because they know that it will be replaced by a better one.

The culture shock that came from living in a provincial city in India was more than the usual experience of people going from one country to another. What accentuated it was the sense of illusion, that whatever was true today, or true at the level of public rules, or true of one region, was not necessarily a good guide to what might happen in the immediate setting. The intellectual shock was the realization that the concepts I had learned bore little relation to the observations I made. Community and society, tradition and modernity, caste and class, and democracy and autocracy were so far from ideal types that it was illusory to use them as contrasts in anymore than a literary, allusive sense. India was so big, so diverse, and had been a civilization so long that it humbled the casual visitor who expected a transformation to the American ideal within a decade.

But India did something else. It made me skeptical of much that I had learned in sociology and hence restored some freshness to my thinking. I found that economic man was not dead, that paradox was everywhere (the caste system adapted well to the egalitarianism of political democracy), and that tolerance of diversity was not a mark of Western modernity, nor were Westernization and traditional India as incompatible as I had believed. India was exotic—startlingly different and even frighteningly its own culture. It could not be understood or explained with the concepts in my bag. But if that was so for India, I realized how much it was also the case for America whenever I stopped to look without the blinders of theory. That skepticism toward conceptualization has not left me. Later periods of living in India, Japan, and England have substantiated it.

Pitirim Sorokin once wrote that probably the last thing a fish realizes is the fact that it lives in water. Only when taken out, gasping on the beach, does it recognize water. Like much of what I am writing about, the sense of one's culture as a tangible context forming the necessary basis for understanding is less a series of provable, logical ideas than a series of felt, believed, and acted-on assumptions. Our tacit knowledge sits on that bedrock. It is less ideology than myth.

California

Sometimes, half-facetiously, I say that I have lived in six cultures—general American, Jewish-American lower middle-class, Indian, Japanese, British, and southern Californian. Between 1965 and 1968 I was three times offered positions in southern California at campuses of the University of California, including my present one at UC San Diego. Each time I was tempted, and each time I drew back, in part out of a natural timidity about disturbing a comfortable life in Champaign-Urbana. But I also felt guilt and fear. The guilt came from having been a midwesterner most of my life. The Midwest is a section of American society that has a strong view of itself as having been passed over in American culture. Neither in climate nor in glamour can it compete against the claims of the East to cultural superiority or the attractions of the West and South in weather. In the 1960s it was clearly in decline economically as well. Any move to a place of such flamboyant hedonistic charms as sunshine and year-round bikinis carried a stigma of desertion.

There was also the fear that such charms would remove the press to work. This fear seems to me to have been compounded by a belief that academic work was like other occupations—not play but work, a means to an end, and that it required a whip rather than a steering wheel to keep us scholars at our "tasks." People in Champaign-Urbana would often praise the town by saying that since there was nothing much else to distract you, academics got a lot of work done, and created close friendships because sociability was so necessary.

When the University of California at San Diego again offered me the chance to start a sociology department in 1967, I accepted. I felt drawn by the climate and scenic beauty, as well as the opportunity to create a new department after my own vision. It would be a department that broke with the conventional quantitative bent of modern sociology and emphasized the central importance of observation and data collection. But the offer also held out the opportunity to begin a new intellectual life. I was growing aware of the great revisionist streams of philosophical and linguistic thought in Europe and the United States that were turning the academic world upside down. Noam Chomsky had lectured at Illinois in the late 1960s, and it made me aware of the revolution in thought coming from linguistics. While in Japan I had read Claude Lévi-Strauss's *The Savage Mind*. On my return to the United States in January 1968 I first heard of ethnomethodology and read Harold Garfinkel's *Studies in Ethnomethodology* and Jack D. Douglas's *The Social Meaning of Suicide*. These works displayed originality and yet also continuity with the "messages" of symbolic interactionists and social anthropologists that I had absorbed at Chicago with Blumer, Hughes, and Warner. They were all skeptical of the direction of mainstream sociology toward a scientific model that substituted instruments for a close relationship to subject matter. I had years of reading dissertations at Illinois in which sophisticated instruments and statistical analyses were applied to poor data, of coping with abstract concepts that came between the investigator and the matter being investigated—to say nothing of the poor reader.

Another, quite subsidiary push was that I hoped by moving to diminish the heavy load of what I called "paperwork." It was not only the committee meetings of department and university that caused me anguish but also the recurring mound of correspondence, including manuscripts to read, colleagues' work to evaluate, and journal articles to referee. Always my desk seemed overlayed by reminders of letters to answer, theses to read, and conferences to prepare for. They were continuing goads to my sense of responsibility and collegial duty. At UC San Diego I hoped—in vain, it proved—to manage these responsibilities better and to keep clear the center of my sociological life—teaching, observing, and writing.

On and Off the Wagon

The guilt and fear that troubled me in deciding to move to California were dissolved in the task of building a new department and a new campus. They were multiplied by the stress and storm of the student movements of the late 1960s and early 1970s at UC San Diego. Any idea that I had traded the hurly-burly of Illinois for the laid-back life of the West Coast was washed away quickly. These past fifteen years have been busy ones in all respects, professionally and otherwise.

Symbolic Crusade was published in 1963, and I turned away from alcohol and alcohol control as a subject. I wrote about India and development. With David Riesman and Zelda Gamson, I did an observational study of higher education. I conducted research in Japan and the United States with Ken'ichi Tominaga of Tokyo University. I wrote on social movements and produced a small book on the concept of community. But in 1971 San Diego County asked me to study sentencing and plea bargaining in the case of drinking-driving offenders, and I was back in the field of alcohol studies.

For the past twelve years, while I have continued to do other work, my focus has been the study of alcohol—alcohol and law, alcohol and knowledge, alcoholism and social movements, alcohol and the welfare state, alcohol control and class conflicts. Out of it has come the work of which I am proudest, *The Culture of Public Problems: Drinking-Driving and the Symbolic Order*. But I have been involved in a variety of other activities, including conferences and papers, review of research and the development of policy at the federal and county levels, and studies and observations at the local level. These activities have led me to audiences and arenas other than academic or sociological.

I like to say that alcohol has kept me honest. I mean by this statement that studying alcohol control has kept me in continuous touch with the nonacademic world. I also mean that study of a restricted body of materials acts as a brake to my disposition toward speculative isolation that lacks substantive existence. I see myself as a person who likes to develop ideas and explanations, essentially a spinner of tales. I need the bite of depth and complexity that a policy-oriented field of paradoxical and popularly accepted matters can provide. Alcohol has been a field through which I have been able to think through a variety of intellectual issues, to uncover alternative and diverse ways of looking at what others take for granted, as I have tried to do for drinking-driving. It has also given me an arena for bringing a diversity of perspectives and fields to bear. I would describe *The Culture of Public Problems* as a study in the sociologies of science, knowledge, and law. It draws on historical, literary, anthropological, and philosophical perspectives as well as field observations.

It is this quality of developing ideas on the grounds of a deep understanding of a narrow swath that I find particularly appealing and fun. It comes close to resolving the tension between the analytical generality and the empirical particularity that is, for me, the most useful and also the most difficult form of sociological scholarship. Over the years my distaste for abstract theory, for the gloss on gloss on gloss that fills so many sociological shelves, has increased. I have great respect for scholarship that has resulted from immersion into the detailed observation and study of substantive matter. If one thinks of sociology as a generalizing and scientific discipline, and history as more particularistic and humanistic, I have become drawn toward the historical pole among sociologists.

As part of this transformation, my felt assumptions about the fragility of social organization and the illusory character of much public presentation has deepened. My earlier title for *The Culture of Public Problems* was *The Illusions of Authority*. I wanted by that title to emphasize both the limited character of authority in modern society and the illusory quality of much that passes for knowledge and conventional wisdom in the topic of drinking-driving and in the general public and professional understandings of "the alcohol problem." I find the stuff of most public discussion, through the media or the political arenas, to be the maintenance of a facade, a theater of events rather than a reference point for understanding actions. I am writing this section on an election day. I will vote, but I have no great conviction about the importance of the choices. Not only am I skeptical about the assumed relation between political rhetoric and political acts, but I am also equally skeptical about the extent of governmental ability to affect social institutions, international relationships, or the day-to-day behavior of citizens in more than a peripheral manner. I feel a little like the woman I heard about who, when informed that Ronald Reagan slept through Cabinet meetings, said, "Despite that fact, I still won't vote for him."

The Now and Future Years

Writing this autobiography comes at a time of turning points for me. I am now well into my sixties and thinking seriously of retiring. For the next few years I will be engaged in a new intellectual turn—toward literary criticism, the history of ideas, and visual imagery—though in the study of social movements. But for some time I have been upset, frustrated, and angered by the busyness of my life. The mound of "paperwork" that disturbed me when I left the University of Illinois has grown into a mountain of matters that cannot be ignored without grave detriment to others and to my view of myself as a responsible person. I work part of most evenings and weekends. I have less time now for my painting than five years ago, although it has come to mean more to me. I have less time to read the mystery stories, novels, and biographies that I love. Even my teaching and writing suffer from things half done.

I have always been attracted by the Hindu view of life as ideally a series of *ashrama*s, or transformations over the life cycle, from the material to the spiritual, from family to self, from the profane to the holy, and from sexuality to celibacy (that one I never found attractive). The thought of being outside the swirl of institutional life is appealing to me. The idea of a life without a schedule of places to be at set times, without guilt for responsibilities not fulfilled or deadlines not met, and without the need to manufacture opinions seems an attractive utopia. I hear my wife's doubting refrain that I will be grossly unhappy when the phone calls stop, the letters and requests no longer appear, and nobody knows my name. Perhaps.

We live in a time when to be young is the aspiration of the aged. We must do what we can to keep ourselves young; to continue to be what we have been. So says popular wisdom, but I do not feel it. Let me proclaim my right, even my desire, to be old. I wish for the hedonism of the aged, the chance to shun responsibility and prudence. Let me live with only one deadline in front of me.

Afterword

I might have ended this sketch at this point, but in the act of writing, my image of myself and my times has undergone a transformation. I might have let stand the picture of a self-satisfied scholar, proud in his achievements, comfortable in his life, eager to expand his enjoyments. But this exercise in internal reflection has unexpectedly sharpened a lingering disquiet.

My generation of academics has been a privileged one. Perhaps that sense of having been privileged has caused my restiveness. I am struck by the self-indulgent tone of my account. My generation of scholars has had the luxury of absorbing work and public respect. At the same time academic life has provided us with much discretionary time and supported plentiful travel all over the world. For some time now it has given me more than a comfortable income. Teaching has been easy and enjoyable for me, though less so in recent years.

I watched the television reports of the last presidential election with an Olympian coolness toward the whole process. Skeptic that I am, I could not share the significance that others gave to it. The differences between parties and candidates were to me a dramatization, a symbolic action without much relation to events before or after. The supposed changes made by this or that administration appear to me overstated by friends and foes alike. The area in which government can act seems to me quite limited. The rhetorical bombast of the participants, even for tactical purposes, is more insulting to my intelligence than I can stand. Nor can I share the radical condemnation of the process: it too is grossly simplified and unbearably doctrinal.

Where does that leave me? I can identify with no one. After the elections I am neither happy nor sad. My only connection to them is that of the voyeur. I am not a part of my community, of the people around me—disconnected but not angered, not even alienated. Have I become Camus's Stranger?

The election is a microcosm, a metaphor that serves to locate a feeling. I have been aware of it, at the public level, as a part of the intellectual and scholarly culture of our time. But the other level, the level of personal restlessness, has been submerged. That feeling of being unconnected comes to my awareness more pointedly and poignantly as I write this autobiography.

It has seemed to me for some time that the intellectual and scholarly world of analysis and critical posture has moved us further and further from the communities of our time and place. It makes it difficult for us to lend ourselves to the missions, zeal, and emotional sensibilities with which others engage their worlds. When people outside my scholarly circles heatedly discuss public problems, I find I become the nay sayer. I am the skeptic who destroys the assumptions on which both sides of the argument base their conflict. Like a trained debater, I can always find something to be said for and against each side and can end up, as I recently titled a paper about the scholar of social problems, "Being on the Side."

The description is as applicable to others as to myself. My work in alcohol studies is a piece of that which characterizes the inner circle of serious scholars in the field. It is perhaps caught again by a title of a lecture I gave in New Mexico a year ago—"The Case for the Drinking Driver." We scholars are the critics of the lay people and professionals who work thinking they are making the world a better place. We undercut them with our skepticism and our knowledge.

That academic pride in, and love of, rational criticism to which I am clearly and fully committed is at the same time a disdain toward those who do not, or cannot, share it. In his history of American universities, *The Emergence of the American University,* Laurence Veysey writes of the nineteenth-century university as having offered the professor a haven somewhere between a business career and exile—neither monastery nor counting house. That very ambiguity of loyalties, Veysey argues, made an academic posture toward the society possible. We have in my generation tried to retain that quality of monastic retreat while reaping the rewards of the counting house.

My sense about the disconnectedness of academic life would not be so disquieting were it not for the other plane, the more personal one of emotion and feeling toward other people. There is a lack of selflessness in this account of my life, a lack that I find in most of my colleagues. I am amazed at people who perform acts of generosity and kindness that overwhelm me with their self-sacrifice. These are people who devote days of a busy life to help in hospitals, who adopt handicapped children, who give away sizable sums of money to aid a needy family, who leave their societies to work among the people in poor countries, and who minister to the sick. They give of themselves—their time, their income, their love—not for causes but for specific persons and in specific situations.

Selflessness is also a way of giving emotionally, of being attached to persons. We academics use our intellectuality to hide ourselves from each other. It cuts off the emotions of sympathetic feeling that might generate ties and commitments between persons rather than between colleagues. It gives our life and even our work a vision of a world of roles but not of persons. To be sure, I can display a record of public service on this board or that and charity to various causes. But I do not give time, and I do not give of my emotional self.

I have come to admire those whose work moves them to do something for others rather than to or about others. My wife is a social worker (a profession most sociologists look at with amusement and ambiguity) in a children's hospital. Watching her, the doctors, the nurses, and the volunteers work with cancer patients and their families makes me sense an accomplishment that I envy.

The universities are themselves a party to this pervading intellectual coolness. Still among the more decent institutions in this society, they have come to prize toughness in the struggle to raise the productivity (a word now common in academic circles) of the organization in the quest for prestige. The Nielsen-like ratings that infest present-day campus administration come to be the symbols of successful stewardship. We become ever more suspicious of decent motives of kindness and personal attachment lest human warmth interfere with organizational glory.

It is life lived at this microlevel, at the level called *communities,* that I miss in my account. Rereading it, I found myself appalled at its self-indulgence. In the very choice of how I would organize this autobiography I could not aim to touch the reader, to give of myself. Here too I had to hide behind the mask of role—the role of sociological analyst. Yet everywhere in the world I have been, in every class, culture, and country, I have learned that the elements that move and absorb our lives are those basic elements of human contact—our children, our parents, our families, our friendships, our communities, and our work. Birth, death, love, hate, lust, greed—they are the places in ourselves where we connect with others.

Such retrospection does not lead me to retract the sense of satisfaction I have with my life and my work. Only I wonder, like the character in that O. Henry story, what would it have meant to have chosen another road, to be writing another autobiography?

PART II

Doing It Their Own Way

CHAPTER FIVE

The Crooked Lines of God

Andrew M. Greeley

My life is not unique in that I am or think I am marginal. My impression, on the basis of a nonrandom sample of colleagues, is that virtually all sociologists think of themselves as marginal—a phenomenon that ought to be interesting to any psychiatrists specializing in treating sociologists. Nor is my sociological career unusual in that I am studying the phenomenon by which my marginality has emerged: the latter stages of the acculturation process of the Catholic immigrant group. Lots of us sociologists do that, though we do not always admit it.

If there is anything at all distinctive about my sociological efforts, it is that I write novels about that which I have studied sociologically. Moreover, the novels began as a test of a hypothesis in the sociology of religion: religion is fundamentally a matter of experiences, images, and stories, not of the acceptance of doctrinal propositions or the performance of ritual devotions or the honoring of ethical norms. Kenneth L. Prewitt, formerly director of the National Opinion Research Center and now president of the Social Science Research Council, summed it up with his usual flair for the epigram when he told me, "I'm not going to read any more of your monographs; all your sociology is in the fiction, which is far more palatable."

In May 1954 I was ordained a Catholic priest, something I had wanted to be since second grade, and I was sent two months later to one of the first college-educated Catholic parishes on the fringes of the city of Chicago. The theory in which we were trained in the seminary (if I can dignify with that term the assumptions around which the seminary experience was structured) implied that it was the role of the priest and the church to protect the religious faith of the uneducated Catholic immigrant working class. Until 1930, or even 1940, such a theory might have been valid. In the prosperity after the end of World War II the earlier Catholic immigrant groups (e.g., Irish) regained the beginnings of affluence they had lost in the Great Depression, and the later immigrant groups (Poles and Italians), benefiting from the GI bill (apparently the only groups in the society to benefit disproportionately from that legislation), also struggled to the borders of the upper middle class. The immigrant era for American Catholicism was over, though of course Catholic Hispanic immigrants would continue, and still continue, to keep alive the tradition. (How relevant the Hispanic immigrants are to the institutional church may be judged from the fact that the Archdiocese of Los Angeles does not count the more than one million local Hispanic Catholics among its members.)

The embourgeoisement of the children, grandchildren, and great-grandchildren of the immigrants was well under way. In the years between the end of the war and my ordination swarms of French clerical "religious sociologists" descended on Chicago and announced confidently, sometimes after only a week or two in the city, that with the breakup of the old national (foreign language–speaking) parishes and the movement of the offspring of the immigrants into the suburbs and into the middle class, American Catholicism would experience the same decline in religious observance that affected Catholicism on the European continent. For the "religious sociologists" it was not a matter that required empirical evidence. It was something obvious, inevitable, and fated.

However, at Christ the King Parish in the Beverly Hills district of Chicago, in the late 1950s, the empirical evidence overwhelmingly disconfirmed the French hypothesis. The new upper middle-class Catholicism was, if anything, more devout, more intense, and more eager than the Catholicism of the old neighborhoods. I was fascinated by what I was witnessing, and well aware that nothing I had learned in the seminary would equip me to understand these college-educated Catholics— especially the young people. The pastor did not trust me with the older laity of the parish, of whom he was very jealous, and he assigned me to work with the youth, doubtless figuring that I could do less harm there than anywhere else, especially because he did not mind losing them to me. So I began to devour the sociology books, pop and serious, concerned with social class, the affluent society, and the emergence of middle-class suburbs. One of the writers who most influenced me at that time was David Riesman, who years later became a close friend. Jim Carey, then a graduate student at the University of Chicago and now a professor at the University of Illinois at Chicago Circle, persuaded me to come over to the University of Chicago (an hour-and-twenty-minute streetcar ride— young priests were not permitted to own automobiles in those days—and several cultural eons away from Beverly) to meet with Professor Everett C. Hughes. Hughes listened eagerly to my description of Christ the King Parish and then pleaded with me to keep a record of my experiences. "Everything," he said, "has happened in and through the Catholic church, and as it becomes the church of the American middle class, everything is likely to happen to it and in it again." Although Hughes did not realize it, he had just prophesied the Second Vatican Council.

I began to write memos to myself on the implications for the Catholic church of this sudden and dramatic upward mobility of its laity, a movement that, more than a quarter of a century later, the leadership of the institutional church has yet to fully comprehend. Donald Thorman, a Catholic editor, heard me give a lecture on the subject and asked me to write an article for a Catholic magazine. Phillip Sharper, the senior editor of the Catholic publishing firm Sheed and Ward, read the article and asked me to write a book. Thus, with more courage than common sense, I violated the ecclesiastical taboo against priests, particularly young priests, setting word on paper and published my first book, *The Church in the Suburbs*, in 1958 at the infantile age, for a Catholic priest, of twenty-nine. The next year Alfred Gregory Meyer came to Chicago as archbishop, having been warned by priests in Milwaukee that one of the first things he should do in Chicago was to silence me, not necessarily because of what I had said but rather because I had the audacity to say it, or say anything. To this demand Meyer had replied characteristically, "No, I won't do that. It wouldn't be fair. I value what he does. I will encourage him."

Encourage me he did, and in the summer of 1960 he agreed to send me to graduate school in sociology at the University of Chicago while I continued as a full-time assistant pastor at Christ the King (to the chagrin and dismay of the pastor, who, being an obedient priest come what may, nonetheless went along with the cardinal's wishes). There could not have been a better time to appear on the campus of the University of Chicago if one were a Catholic priest. John F. Kennedy was running for the presidency, John XXIII was pope, and the Second Vatican Council had been convened: the winds of change were in the air. Meyer asked me whether I could stay in the parish and study at a local Catholic university, such as Loyola. I was delighted to stay in the parish, intractable pastor or no, because Christ the King was and is my first love as a priest. I responded, "Loyola or the University of Chicago."

"Oh, yes, that's right," Meyer said. "Chicago is closer, isn't it?"

And thus the long taboo against diocesan priests from Chicago attending the University of Chicago was smashed in the name of geographical convenience!

If I had gone to Loyola I suspect I might still be a graduate student there. But Phillip Hauser at the University of Chicago accepted me on the spot, and in the final week of September, during the fierce Kennedy-Nixon presidential campaign, I began my work as a graduate student in sociology, destined, I thought, to be a sociologist in service of the archdiocese and the church. My first course, open to both undergraduates and graduates, was in social psychology taught by James A. Davis and Elihu Katz at 8:30 in the morning to some hundred students. I was utterly at sea: six years out of the seminary, no experience of a secular university, or indeed of any university, wearing a Roman collar, and daunted by the apparent brilliance of the questions of the younger students with whom I was surrounded. How could I possibly survive, I wondered, in such brilliant competition?

The midterm examination required that we analyze Shakespeare's *Romeo and Juliet* in terms of the social psychology we had learned in the class. I took Friar Lawrence as my principal concern and explained in considerable detail how he acted as a "dissonance reducer" in the story. (I thought I understood what Jim and Elihu were saying; it was the students who scared me.) When the tests came back, I noticed with enormous relief that I had received an A. They are easy markers around here, I thought. Then Jim Davis put the distribution of grades on the blackboard: there were six A's. Ah ha, I thought, this place isn't going to be so bad after all.

After the class Jim offered me a job at the National Opinion Research Center. The diocese was paying for my graduate education, and as I already had a job, I declined. A few months later, urged on by Harrison White to finish my work as quickly as possible, I wandered over to NORC (in those days housed in a brick two-flat on Woodlawn Avenue) and asked Davis if he had any data from which I might write a dissertation. He did. There was a study in process of the career decisions of the June 1961 college graduates: would I be interested in analyzing the impact of religion on their career choice? In June 1961 I found myself at a tiny desk in the "bullpen" of NORC research assistants and started to work on my dissertation. Twenty-four years later my "temporary" and unpaid beginning at NORC continues.

When I asked Bill McManus, then superintendent of schools in the Archdiocese of Chicago and now bishop of Fort Wayne and South Bend, Indiana, if there was anything in which he thought I should be particularly interested in the project, he said, "Find out, for the love of heaven, why our kids don't go to graduate school!" At that time there was great concern among Catholics about the failures of "American Catholic intellectualism." Our young people, we were told, were very successful in the business world perhaps, but they were not becoming scientists or scholars. They were not pursuing arts and science academic careers or graduate-school education in preparation for such careers. None of the authors who wrote on the subject—Monsignor John Tracy Ellis, Professor Thomas O'Dea, and Professor John Donovan—seemed to think that it was unrealistic to expect immigrants who had been peasant farmers to immediately become scholars and scientists. Indeed the immigration factor was rarely, if ever, alluded to in their books. I expected to find confirmation of their hypotheses but also thought that among the young people whose families had been in the United States for several generations I would observe a tendency to go on to graduate school and pursue academic careers.

One Saturday morning that summer I stopped by NORC to collect the output from our project's IBM 101 counter-sorter (it actually printed raw frequencies). I did not even have to glance at the numbers on the sheet to realize that all the hypotheses explaining the lower graduate-school attendance of Catholics had collapsed: Jim Davis had written across the top of the paper, "It looks like Notre Dame beats Southern Methodist this year!"

Whatever had been true in the past was no longer the case. Catholics were indeed going to graduate school, and they were deciding on academic careers. I learned a lot from that experience:

1. Never trust a broad assertion that is not backed by empirical evidence.

2. Never expect cocktail-party liberals to abandon their conventional wisdom merely because you have empirical evidence to the contrary.

3. Never expect anti-Catholicism to yield easily to empirical evidence.

For over twenty years I fought this battle, first with Gerhard Lenski and James Trent and then with a host of other people, including Zena Blau. I think I have finally won the argument, though *Commonweal,* a Catholic magazine and one of my most bitter enemies, never really had the grace to admit I was right and they were wrong: there is no incompatibility between Catholicism—even and especially Catholic school attendance—and an academic career, academic productivity, academic excellence, and academic eminence.

Foolishly uncertain about how much time Meyer would give me to pursue my graduate work, I raced through the program at breakneck speed, holding what I still think may be the record for obtaining a doctorate from scratch at the University of Chicago—twenty months. Pete Rossi, the director of NORC, invited me to stay at NORC for two more years to work on a projected study of the effects of Catholic education, which would be the first national-sample study of American Catholics. (Later I learned that Rossi had attempted to obtain for me an appointment as an assistant professor in the sociology department of the university. He abandoned the attempt because of strong opposition. "I would no more permit that man in our department," a distinguished demographer said, "than I would a card-carrying Communist, and for the same reason." I do not think the man has changed his mind.)

Meyer at that time was busy with the Second Vatican Council and was not yet prepared to have me move into his house and teach him social science over the supper table, so he welcomed Rossi's idea and wrote a letter appointing me to NORC, a canonical appointment I still technically hold. In 1965, when Meyer died at the age of sixty-two and John Cody came to Chicago as archbishop, I suddenly found myself a marginal outcast. Archbishop Cody had no need for a sociologist, or indeed anyone else, to advise him, and he bitterly resented me for gaining attention in the newspapers and not depending on him for salary. (At the beginning of the parochial-school study Rossi insisted that I had to be paid so they could collect overhead from my salary. When I offered to give the money to the diocese, Meyer said, "Oh no, Father. I have enough responsibilities worrying about the money of the archdiocese. You should worry about the money you were paid.")

When I brought the galley sheets of *The Education of Catholic Americans* to Cody, by then a cardinal, he was totally uninterested in them. Who had sent me to graduate school? Who had given me permission to write? Who censored my books? How much money did I make? Did I still hear confessions? Did I realize that people said I wrote too much?

The same sort of people who had pleaded with Meyer to silence me had also pleaded with Cody. Meyer dismissed their envy; Cody accepted it. I was now an outsider in the diocese and the church, not because anything had changed in me, but because I had a different archbishop. I would later find out that most priests also resented someone with quality professional training in the social sciences, for such training violated the rules of amateurism and mediocrity—the notion that any priest can do anything—at the core of clerical culture. Morris Janowitz's joke that I was the company sociologist of the Catholic church could not have been more inaccurate. The Catholic church, as far as my archbishop and most of my fellow priests were concerned, did not want or need or approve of a company sociologist. Not only were my professional skills useless, but they were in fact dangerous as well—not because sociology was under suspicion but because a priest on the staff of the University of Chicago with an independent income was by definition suspicious in a clerical culture where the reward structure is extremely limited.

Thus my temporary assignment at NORC became permanent, and my dream of being a priest-sociologist in service of the church proved to be an illusion. I became, willy-nilly, a professional sociological scholar. In the twenty years since the fateful meeting with Cardinal Cody I have had three main sociological interests. First, the four studies my colleagues and I have done of Catholic education have provided solid time-series data on changes in the American Catholic church and the American Catholic population in the years since the Second Vatican Council. Second, in the seventies, principally working with William McCready and inspired by Daniel Patrick Moynihan and Nathan Glazer's *Beyond the Melting Pot*, I launched the first series of empirical studies of the survival of diverse ethnic subcultures in the United States. Third, through the years I have tried to reformulate some of the major questions in the sociology of religion, using the theoretical perspective originating in the work of Clifford Geertz on religion as a cultural system. My work in this area began with a study funded by the Henry Luce Foundation in 1972; it continued with a project funded by the Knights of Columbus in 1979 and finally with research funded from the ill-gotten royalties on my novels in the 1980s. Through this research I have fashioned a new theory of the sociology of religion, doing most of the work on that theory—which I think is my principal contribution to sociology—after I joined the faculty of the University of Arizona in 1979. In the process I have also done research on the sociology of the country club, the sociology of the paranormal (mystical and psychic experiences), and the sociology of papal elections.

One need only look over that list of interests and add to it the fact that I am, as one of my opponents at the University of Chicago remarked, "nothing but a loudmouthed Irish priest" (to which I replied, "And may they carve it on my gravestone!") to understand why my life has been colorful and interesting, filled with conflict and controversy and doomed almost from the beginning to marginality. Small wonder that in my native Chicago neither the church nor the university wanted me, or wants me.

Worse luck for them, says I.

I think my colleagues and I have established the academic excellence of Catholic schools, their importance to the work of the church (particularly in times of great religious change), and their enormous impact on minority students and disadvantaged students of every sort. American Catholicism, I have been able to document, has survived the traumas of the post–Vatican Council era remarkably well. In 1960, 15 percent of those who were born Catholic were no longer Catholics. By the middle 1980s that proportion had risen only to 18 percent. In the early 1960s approximately 68 percent of Catholics attended church weekly. Beginning in 1969—the year after the encyclical on birth control—church attendance fell precipitously, to 50 percent by 1975. (Protestant church attendance has remained unchanged in the United States since the late 1930s: 40 percent of Protestants attend every week.)

This decline stopped in 1975 as abruptly as it had started, and it seems to have been the result not of the Vatican Council but of anger at ecclesiastical authority because of the birth control encyclical. American Catholics, on the contrary, seem to have enthusiastically welcomed the changes of the Second Vatican Council. The most notable result of the council is that American Catholics now stay in the church on their own terms, making their own rules and following their own judgment as to when they will listen to their leadership. Thus, they reject the official teaching on birth control, premarital sex, abortion, and other related matters, although they oppose homosexuality, extramarital sex, and abortion on demand, in about the same proportions as do white American Protestants. Still they were notably affected by the letter of the American bishops on nuclear weapons in 1983. Before the letter 32 percent of Americans, Protestants and Catholics alike, thought that too much money was being spent on armaments. A year later, after the pastoral letter, the proportion of Catholics thinking that too much money was spent on arms rose to 54 percent. This finding is a classic example of what has come to be called do-it-yourself Catholicism. If Catholics happen to think that something the church leadership says is correct, then they enthusiastically accept it. If they happen to think that the leadership does not know what it is talking about, then they rather easily and cheerfully reject it.

Though the church did not pay for our research, and despite the fact that Catholic reviewers have routinely patronized it, there is little reason to doubt that there is more data on Catholics in the United States than on Catholics anywhere else in the world and that since no one has been able to refute or even dispute the NORC studies on Catholics and Catholic schools, they have become accepted as valid social knowledge in the United States. The Catholic leadership has never been able to forgive me for proving that the Catholic laity rejected the birth control decision (though Archbishop Bernardin, before he became the archbishop of Chicago, told me off the record that he could not sleep at night because of what "that goddamned encyclical is doing in my diocese"). And at the University of Chicago my fellow sociologists dismissed this work as uninteresting and unimportant and hence not worth considering when the issue was whether I belonged as a full-fledged member of the university community.

There is no point in this essay in rehearsing the story of my conflicts with the sociology department of the University of Chicago in any great detail. Briefly, in the late 1960s and early 1970s a number of other units in the university had recommended me for a regular faculty appointment. (I had been a professor with tenure at the University of Illinois at Chicago for two years and resigned to resume full-time work at NORC because I felt so much more comfortable there.) In each case certain members of the sociology department intrigued against the appointment at higher levels of the administration and defeated it. It is, as any reader of this essay knows, easier in the academy to prevent something than to accomplish it. I was convinced then, and am convinced now, that the reason for the opposition had nothing to do with the quality or quantity of my work but with the fact that I was a Catholic priest. I accuse the responsible people of anti-Catholic bigotry, and I accuse the university administration of cowardly caving in to such bigotry. Moreover, I accuse myself of gross stupidity for getting into the conflict in the first place. I should have been intelligent enough to stay out of it, knowing that there was no way to win.

Incidentally, my funding a chair at the University of Chicago in Catholic studies from the royalty income on my novels was not an attempt to get even with the university. As I said at the time the chair was announced, my only intention was to provide some kind of scholarly bridge between the academy and the church. If one wanted to do that in the city of Chicago, obviously the University of Chicago was the place to do it. I must say that the university's reaction to my funding the chair was singularly graceless. They accepted the money all right, rudely and churlishly, though they did not, like Cardinal Bernardin when he accepted a parallel grant to the seminary at Mundelein, act as though they were doing me a great favor. Once you are on the margins, you stay there.

In our research on ethnicity, my colleagues and I established that ethnic subcultures, distinctive styles of family behavior, religious belief, political activity, attitudes toward death, and especially drinking behavior persist from generation to generation despite education, the number of generations in America, the collapse of ethnic neighborhoods, and even ethnic intermarriage. (One Irish parent is enough to guarantee the survival of the Irish drinking subculture, for example.) Some people, most notably Orlando Patterson, have thought there was something chauvinistic and fascist about studying white ethnics (but not, oddly enough, black or Jewish ethnics). Scholarly research on ethnic diversity in the United States is now solidly established. The paradigms that McCready and I developed remain untouched. Patterson may think it is somehow uncivilized or irrational to be concerned about ethnic diversity, but those scholars and practitioners dealing with alcohol use and abuse are far more realistic. There are distinctive drinking subcultures with enormous durability that are passed on from generation to generation powerfully and unself-consciously. You do not have to think of yourself as Irish or participate in Irish ethnic customs or keep an Irish tricolor in your office to absorb the Irish drinking subculture, the Irish political subculture, the Irish family structure, or the Irish religious value system (a mixture of fatalism and hope).

In the process of studying ethnic subcultures we also established that the American Catholic groups had caught up with, and indeed in some cases passed, other groups in the society in income, education, and occupation. The Irish, for example, are now the best educated, the most affluent, and the most occupationally successful of the gentile ethnic groups in America, and the Italians are not far behind them. This finding, like my other findings about Catholics and the intellectual life, the rejection of the birth control encyclical, the acceptance of the Second

Vatican Council, the persistence of ethnic diversity, and the prevalence of incidents of psychic and mystical experiences in the United States (about a third of Americans have had intense ecstatic experiences of the sort described by William James, and these experiences correlate positively with psychological well-being; about two-thirds of Americans have had some kind of psychic experience) are widely unaccepted because they are profoundly unacceptable, either in the church or the academy or both. I started graduate school in 1960 believing, quite irrationally, that the Catholic church as an institution had a monopoly on both envy and dogmatism. I now realize that though envy is worse in the church than it is in the professoriat, it is still pretty bad in the professoriat, and that dogmatism, strong in the church, is equally powerful in the academy.

But the most important work, at least for my own life, that I have done as a sociologist has been on the religious imagination. This work has influenced my personal religious behavior, my philosophical and theological reflections, and my turning to poetry and fiction, thereby adding to roles I already had as priest, journalist, and sociologist another more controversial and extremely enjoyable role as storyteller.

The sociology of religion is one of the backwater subdisciplines in great part because religion has so little power as a predictor variable. It is acceptable to study religion as a dependent variable: how many people go to church, how many people believe in life after death, how many people believe the Bible is divinely inspired, and so on. But having obtained that information, the understanding of other social attitudes, institutions, and behaviors is not notably enhanced. Thus, in the mid-1980s analysis I have done of material in the NORC's General Social Survey correlating twelve social and political dependent variables (including attitudes toward government help for the poor, the death penalty, racial justice, and nuclear armament) shows that neither church attendance, nor intensity of religious affiliation, nor frequency of prayer, nor confidence in religious leadership correlate with political and social attitudes and behaviors. The founders of sociology, Émile Durkheim and Max Weber, were interested in religion. Religion is also something in which most Americans, if not most sociologists, are involved, but it does not seem to be of much sociological use.

Moreover, I have wondered through the years whether the reason for its lack of usefulness is that most sociologists of religion have been interested in the so-called secularization hypothesis—that is to say, in demonstrating that religion is no longer important and that religious involvement is declining. In a book called *Unsecular Man* (1972) I could find no support for the secularization hypothesis, and in *Religious Change in America* (1989), a book on religious social indicators published by Harvard University Press, I again could find no evidence for secularization. Sociologists have chosen as their units of measurement the kinds of religous behavior (such as church attendance) that might be expected to decline or fluctuate over time. Though many sociologists of religion would probably accept some form of Clifford Geertz's definition of religion as a culture system, value system, meaning system, and set of symbols that provide ultimate explanations of what life is about and patterns of behavior for living, they have rarely tried to measure such symbol systems in their research. Might it not be, I have asked myself, that if we could get adequate measures of religion as a culture system, as a system of symbols of ultimate meaning, we would have a more powerful predictor variable and win more respectability for religion as a sociological phenomenon?

While I was analyzing the data from my 1972 Henry Luce Foundation study, I was also recasting my own paradigms for religion, under the influence of the theological writings of David Tracy and John Shea, and working out this reformulation in a book called *The Mary Myth,* in which I approached the Catholic devotion to Mary, the mother of Jesus, from a sociological perspective. It was clear to me that Mary's function in Catholic Christianity had always been to represent the womanliness of God, the life-giving, nurturing, tender affection of God. Our theologians never quite said as much, but there was little doubt that the poetry, art, and music of Mary were designed to use her as a sacrament (manifestation) of God's womanly love. Many medieval Catholic theologians (most notably Saint Bernard and Saint Anselm), mystics, and spiritual writers were at ease with the image of God as mother (even a nursing mother). This ease seemed to me to be clearly linked to devotion to Mary. Later, in our study of young adults for the Knights of Columbus, we discovered that despite neglect from an ecumenically minded clerical elite the Mary image was strong, powerful, and benign among young Catholics—correlating well, for example, with sexual fulfillment in marriage and, as was not surprising by now, with the image of God as mother.

From these exercises in reflection and restructuring I developed a theory of the sociology of religion (articulated in *Religion: A Secular Theory*) that saw religion as the result of experiences of hope-renewal. These experiences are encoded in images that provide a template for life and hence are symbols, shared with others through stories, especially stories told in a storytelling community (church) of persons who share the same repertoire of images. Influenced in this theory formation by Shea and Tracy, by Geertz, Parsons, and Weber, and by Mircea Eliade, Rudolph Otto, and William James, I decided that religion was fundamentally and primarily an exercise of the creative imagination, the preconscious, the poetic faculty, the creative intuition, the agent intellect—call it what you will. Obviously, since we are reflecting creatures, it is necessary to reflect on religion and articulate it propositionally, philosophically, theologically, and catechetically; but such intellectual reflection, however essential, becomes arid and irrelevant when it is divorced from an awareness that the origins and raw power of religion lie in another dimension of the personality.

That conclusion was not particularly acceptable to most of my Catholic priest colleagues. It certainly could not be rejected as heretical, especially since I insisted that I was approaching religion purely from the sociological perspective and saying nothing about theological truth. But if it was not heretical, neither was it relevant, and in the years after the Second Vatican Council many Catholic clerics, especially the more influential ones, had pretty much abandoned religion in the sense I was using it and substituted for it social activism. I had no objection to social activism, but I thought of it as a consequence of religion and not as a substitute for it, as a result of religious faith instead of as a result of loss of nerve about the possibility of religious faith.

For such clergy nothing worthwhile could have happened in the history of Catholicism before 1963 and nothing could be more irrelevant, and hence useless, than to talk about the religious imagination. I had become an offense to them, not merely because I was drawing a professor's salary and had professional skills (through which I found that the laity were very critical of the quality of Sunday preaching); I was now a pariah all over again because I was talking nonsense. Of what possible use, as a Jesuit would ask in a book review in the 1980s, can the image of a Madonna's smile have in an era when the church has to be concerned about such life issues as abortion or nuclear warfare? I could demonstrate easily that those who were likely to have an image of God as mother were more concerned about nuclear war than those who did not have such an image; but for this particular Jesuit, as for most priests, I fear, empirical evidence mattered not in the slightest.

At the time I was developing this theory, I was influenced strongly by a major intellectual breakthrough in social research—the interactive data analysis techniques developed by my friend Norman Nie in the Statistical Package for the Social Sciences (Conversational Program: SCSS) package. Analyzing data with SCSS was like writing poetry: you could become locked in an affective relationship with the data and follow hunches and intuitions with ease. More important than the speed of SCSS was the instant turnaround that enabled the creative intuition to work in the analytic process.

Rossi and Davis had taught me that the purpose of data analysis was to tell a story. With SCSS the same creative dimensions of the personality used in writing fiction were unleashed in the struggle to find patterns of meaning in the data. Ever since I had read Michael Polanyi in graduate school, I was convinced that the distinction between art and science was deceptive and irrelevant. Data analysis was as much a craft as a science. With SCSS the craft could become art. Fiction and data analysis are both modes of storytelling, with a beginning, a middle, and an end, with plot, conflict, and resolution. Analyzing data prepared me to write fiction; writing fiction made me a more skilled data analyst.

As a result of my sociological reflection on Geertz, my theological reflection on Tracy and Shea, my work on *The Mary Myth,* and my preparation to write *Religion: A Secular Theory,* I came to two implicit, even preconscious, conclusions. The first was that I wanted to concentrate on my research on the religious imagination; the second was that I was going to try my hand at writing fiction. A lot of folks were talking about religion as story, but virtually no one was writing religious stories. If the theories were right, however, stories were the best way to communicate about religion, and the novel (and the screenplay) were the functional equivalents of the stained-glass window in our era. In January 1979, with one novel, *The Magic Cup,* about to be published (and disappear), I joined the faculty of the University of Arizona, and free from the burden of having to raise funds for our ethnic research center at NORC (where I continued to spend one semester a year), I had time to reflect on the issue of the religious imagination. With the success of my novels, beginning with *The Cardinal Sins,* I had funds from royalties to put into research on this subject. In a curious circle, my reflection on the religious imagination led to novel writing, and the novel writing in turn funded research on the religious imagination.

Thus far all of my novels have been situated in Chicago among the Irish Catholics of the community, continuing, I like to think, the work that James T. Farrell left off in his final book, *The Death of Nora Ryan* (which brings Farrell/Danny O'Neill/Ed Ryan to the mid-1940s). The novels, as I have said repeatedly, are theological tales, stories of God— comedies of grace focusing especially on the womanly tenderness of God. As Professor Ingrid Shafer has suggested in her research on my novels, each of them, in one way or another, is like *The Magic Cup,* a story of a quest for a holy grail, for the womanly affection of God as revealed through human lovers. They are also, however, portraits of the Chicago Irish in transition from the upper working class and lower middle class into the upper middle and lower upper class, and of the turbulence and traumas, the excitements, the disappointments, the enthusiasms, and the despairs of that transition, particularly since the Second Vatican Council. Hence Ken Pruitt's dictum that all my sociology is in my fiction.

In three different ways, then, my sociology has shaped my fiction. The context is the same as the context for my study of American Catholism. The subject matter is the result of my reflection and work on the religious imagination—the womanliness of God. And the impulse, finally, to set about storytelling grew out of my sociological theorizing about the nature of religion. Curiously—or perhaps not so curiously— whereas my colleagues in the priesthood have been furious at me for writing novels and even more furious at me for succeeding at it, my colleagues in sociology have seemed to be amused and even rather proud that one of theirs is able to tell stories and at the same time continue to teach and do research on sociological issues. They are even prepared to believe what my clerical colleagues will never believe, that it was my work in the sociology of religion that induced me to write stories of God.

I started out life wanting to be a priest. I continued my life in the priesthood wanting to be a sociologist to serve the church. I discovered the church did not need or want a sociologist and became a professional sociologist who was also a priest. Then my sociology persuaded me that the best way I could be a priest was by writing theological novels set in the same context and about the same subjects as my sociological research. Though this pilgrimage has scarcely won me any acceptance in the priesthood or from my own archdiocese, it has nonetheless made me a more effective priest for the vast number of readers (half of whom do not go to church regularly) who now constitute my parish and my congregation. As Pete Rossi would have said, there are many ironies in the fire.

In March 1984, the night before celebrating the publication of my most popular novel, *Lord of the Dance,* and my thirtieth anniversary in the priesthood, a functionary from Cardinal Bernardin's office came to visit me. If I wanted to be accepted back into the diocese (I was of course a priest in good standing, but he meant acknowledged as part of the diocese and not treated as a pariah who it is pretended does not exist), I would have to do public penance for all the harm caused by my novels. I protested that the research I had done on the readers of my novels indicated that they were by no means harmful. The functionary dismissed the research. The problem was not people who read my novels and benefited from them, he said; the problem was the "simple ordinary faithful" who had not read them but were shocked that I wrote them. (The "simple ordinary laity" are hard to find in any of the empirical research data but are a useful projection of the fears, anxieties, and worries of ecclesiastical bureaucrats.) If I apologized to them and promised them I would be sensitive to their needs in the future, then I would be welcomed back into the diocese and treated with honor, respect, and affection. "You have to crawl a little bit, Andy," he said.

As might well be imagined, I turned him down flat. Since they had not read my books, what earthly reason was there to think they would read my apology either? Besides, I was not going to abandon millions of people who, if the research evidence was to be believed, found religious benefit in my books, to placate a few people who had written nasty letters to the cardinal. I have been asked repeatedly whether I really think that Joseph Bernardin expected me to succumb to such ridiculous terms. Of course not. I think he knew full well I would not accept his terms, but he sent them to me so that he would be able to say to other bishops, the Vatican, the pronuncio, and the complaining priests and laity, I tried to reason with Andy and he wouldn't listen. The ability to give such a response was what Bernardin was really seeking. In fact, I think he would have been appalled if I had accepted his terms because then he would have had no idea what to do with me. Is this a coward's way out, or only an ecclesiastical diplomat's? Readers will have to judge for themselves.

The appointment to the University of Arizona was a complete surprise to me. I had often said that there were only four schools in the country that could lure me away from Chicago: the City University of New York, Harvard, Stanford, and Arizona—CUNY because of its distinguished chairs, Harvard because it is probably the best university in the world, and Stanford and Arizona because I loved the areas and because they both had become distinguished universities. However, when Philip Hammond, the chairman of Arizona's recruiting committee, and Stanley

Lieberson, the head of the sociology department, approached me, I did not think they were serious. The traumas in Chicago, both at the university and in the archdiocese, had through the years sufficiently eroded my self-esteem so that I did not think that a distinguished department like Arizona's could be interested in me. Moreover, I had heard that they were looking at three people for the vacant professorship and assumed, again I suppose as a result of my experience with sociologists at Chicago, that I was third on the list. But a trip to Arizona in January was always a pleasant experience, so I flew to Tucson and from the members of the department discovered that Stan Lieberson had been an ally through all my University of Chicago troubles, and we ate dinner at El Charro restaurant, which may be the best Mexican/American restaurant in all the world. There was indeed an offer. Lieberson and Paul Rosenblatt, then dean of arts and sciences at Arizona (and one of the best deans in America), were aware that my Chicago roots and my connection with the NORC would make it difficult for me to move to Tucson, so during Easter week in 1978, when I was taking my annual week off in Scottsdale, Lieberson called and proposed that we work out an offer on the phone. "No way," I told him. "I'm an Irish Catholic ethnic from Chicago. You and Paul are Jewish ethnics from Brooklyn. I'm going to come down and we're going to have tea and coffee and sweet rolls, we're going to work it all out and then shake hands." So we did, and I moved to Arizona for half the year and returned to the classroom. There I found to my astonishment that I was not merely a respected sociologist but, as far as the Arizona sociology department was concerned, a superstar. I am not prepared to place myself in that category, but having been treated like a pariah for a long, long time, I was perfectly prepared to accept the acclaim and attention, if not the title. Moreover, my new colleagues, especially Richard Curtis, Albert Bergesen, and Michael Hout, made me feel that however marginal I may be elsewhere, I am not in fact a marginal sociologist.

Adding the classroom experience in Tucson and the results of the Knights of Columbus study of young adults to my previous reflections on the religious imagination, I was finally ready to test my theories seriously against the empirical evidence. I devoted some of the money from my first sizable royalty check to paying for questions on the religious imagination in the NORC General Social Survey. After one year I was able to refine the questions so that a simple, easy to administer, four-item scale (four forced choices on a seven-point range: God is Father-Mother, Judge-Lover, Master-Spouse, or King-Friend) finally provided an effective measure of the religious imagination, which correlated significantly with political attitudes and behaviors, even when other measures were used to take into account the political, economic, social, religious, and life-style liberalism. People who scored high on measures of God as mother, lover, spouse, and friend, for example, were 15 percentage points more likely to vote against Ronald Reagan in the presidential elections of 1980 and 1984. Your story of God, in other words, is a paradigm of the story of your life.

My next scheme was to try to do research on the readers of my novels to learn whether the stories did affect their religious imaginations. I also hoped to gather evidence to refute the claim inside the Catholic community that the stories were pornographic and trashy, a threat to the church and the priesthood. Of the readers of *Ascent into Hell*, 68 percent said that the book enhanced their respect for the priesthood because it revealed the humanity of the priest, whereas only 6 percent said that it lowered their respect for the priesthood (the story was about a man who left the priesthood to marry a nun whom he had impregnated); only 11 percent thought that the novels were trashy or steamy, whereas 80 percent thought the sexual scenes were handled with delicacy and taste. There also emerged from this research (narcissism begins at home, as Stan Lieberson would have said!) the observation that the attraction of the books for readers seemed to be based on the intersection of three factors: the books made them think seriously about religious questions; they helped them to understand God's love; and they improved their understanding of the relationship between religion and sex. Therefore, I wondered, could reading one of my novels have an effect on the religious imagination of such readers? In fact, in five of eight indicators there were statistically significant differences indicating greater likelihood of thinking of God as mother, lover, spouse, or friend among readers who said the books helped them to understand the relationship between religion and sex and appreciate God's love for them.

Obviously, there were two possible explanations: one, the novel did indeed affect the religious imagination of readers; and two, those who had religious imaginations picturing a more intimate relationship with God were more likely after reading my books to say that they understood God's love better and also comprehended better the relationship between religion and sex. Either result was satisfactory to me from the viewpoint both of a sociological theorist and of a priest storyteller.

Finally, did the much publicized sexual interludes in the novels (which Cardinal Bernardin himself had admitted to me were tame compared to most modern novels) have an effect on the linkage between the story and the religious imagination? The correlation between, on the one hand, greater understanding of God's love and of religion and sex and, on the other, gracious images of God was specified in my final analytic exercise as existing entirely among those respondents who said they found the sexual interludes in the books compelling or sensitive. Far from being a scandal to the simple faithful, as my fellow priest contended, or trashy and steamy, as some of the hostile secular critics (mostly alienated Catholics) averred, the novels, including the sexual episodes in them, were just what I intended them to be—stories of grace appealing to the religious imagination of the readers and helping them to understand better the relationship between religion and sex and the depths of God's love. Based on the research, and on the thousands of letters I have received, I am confident that I have never done anything more priestly in my life than write those novels, which is precisely what my sociological theory has led me, with fingers crossed, to anticipate.

What next? More of the same, God She being willing.

I intend to continue to teach sociology and do sociological research, as well as to write stories and perhaps, again God She being willing, screenplays. And of course I continue to be a priest, wanted by the ecclesiastical institution or not. Mark Harris, in a cover profile of me for the *New York Times Magazine,* concludes by saying that after reading the letters I have received from readers, he does indeed believe that I am a priest and a parish priest. "His parish," he writes, "is in his mailbox."

As my friend from New York, Jim Miller, put it on the phone the other night, "Those so-and-sos at Chicago did you a favor. If they hadn't kicked you around, you never would be writing novels and you never would have the money to fund your own research or their chair." He meant the so-and-sos at the university, but the same thing could be said of the so-and-sos in the archdiocese. God, a French proverb tells us, draws straight with crooked lines. It is not a proposition that admits of empirical verification. (God thus far has not been at home to persistent NORC interviewers.) At this stage in my career, as a priest who is also a sociologist, journalist, and storyteller, I am no longer of any mind to question the crooked lines of God.

CHAPTER SIX

Looking for the Interstices

Bennett M. Berger

In the spring of 1982 I was invited to give a talk at the University of California, Los Angeles. When I asked (as I often do on such occasions), Why me? I was told that the students there were curious about how I had survived, flourished, and even prospered as a sociologist doing (in that old phrase) my own thing, relatively unconstrained by any one of the several schools of thought that compete for dominance in contemporary sociology. So I began to think about that.

Surprisingly, the thinking turned autobiographical—in the sense that C. Wright Mills meant when he spoke of the intersections of biography and history shaping the course of lives. I say "surprisingly" because the dominant norms of sociological practice discourage autobiographical thinking. In sociology, autobiography is usually regarded as risky, embarrassing, and tasteless for all sorts of familiar reasons (narcissism, subjectivity, and so on). We sociologists are taught to flee from the first-person singular, both for methodological reasons and as good scientific manners: "Art is I; science is we," says Claude Bernard. Yet, oddly, it is also a truism of the sociology of knowledge, as well as elementary sociology, that ideas are existentially based. It seems, therefore, to be sound sociological practice—even good academic manners—to try to put one's audiences in an optimally skeptical frame of mind by giving them all the evidence one can muster to *distrust* the ideas one is about to convey, instead of (or in addition to) laying out in advance all the methodological reasons they should be predisposed to trust the benignity of one's prudence, rigor, balance, integrity, and scholarly scrupulousness. With respect to the choice and formulation of theoretical questions, I see giving all the evidence one can muster as a conceptual (or prehypothetical) approximation of the empiricist's injunction that hypotheses be falsifiable.

Please regard the above as a bit of ideological spadework in defense of autobiography. But there are other, more familiar bits of ideology in its behalf. Even the conventional wisdom now asserts that knowing something about who a speaker (or writer) is contextualizes a discourse or a text and hence adds to it dimensions of meaning otherwise obscure or hidden. A printed page, for example, usually tells readers only what its author thinks he or she wants them to know, unless they are skilled at reading between the lines, which usually takes years of experience. Oral delivery adds dimensions of meaning, some of them unintentional, through the physical presence of the speaker and his or her accent, intonation, and body language. Autobiography adds a different dimension by equipping readers to make inferences from, and interpret, what a writer says; and it implicitly invites them to do so in a way that perhaps discounts what the writer says in terms of what the readers have learned about who he or she is. Nevertheless, even the most candid autobiographer projects distorted images, usually providing only selective information chosen to induce readers to make the inferences and interpretations he or she wants them to make. It is indeed a risky business. Still, I find it surprising that social scientists who chatter on abstractly about the importance of context (or who in fact do take the trouble to specify objective contexts) do not more frequently provide their audiences with specific autobiographical data, thereby enabling us to make more intelligent contextual inferences—as if we were all stupid enough not to make those inferences in any case.

I will practice what I preach and provide you with some data. I was born in Brooklyn and raised in the Bronx, in an immigrant Jewish family low enough in the lower middle class that its respectability was far from secure. Actually, we must have been pretty poor. I can remember the electricity being turned off in our apartment for nonpayment of bills, and I recall going to the grocery store when I was about ten and paying for my corn flakes with Depression relief stamps and feeling humiliated by the experience. It was not one of those Jewish families rich in Talmudic tradition and teeming with Tevyes or Workmen's Circle intellectuals. Although my mother, born here, managed to get herself an American high school education, my father's education ended before he was twelve, when he came to this country. I don't think he ever had a friend of his own—that is, someone who was not the husband of one of my mother's friends. He was a very primitive man, interested only in money because he never had enough of it, and was recurrently insulted and humiliated by those who had more. I observed some of these humiliations during a few of my teenage summers when I would help him carry some of the samples of fur trimmings for women's coats from his employer's factory in the fur district of Manhattan to the garment center ten blocks north where he would try to sell them to coat manufacturers. He liked to use big words (usually mispronounced) where little ones would do, and he particularly admired people who had reached "the pinochle of success." My sister-in-law once said to me, in awe rather than with malice, "you know, Bennett, your father has no redeeming virtues."

There were almost no books in our home. One of the few I remember was a Winston dictionary with several thumb-tabbed appendices from which I memorized such things as the twenty largest cities in the United States, the capitals of all the then forty-eight states, and the twenty longest rivers in the world. My brothers and I were typed early. My older brother was the smart one, I was the sensitive one, and my younger brother was the practical one with a good head for business. My older brother was in fact smart enough to graduate from high school before he was thirteen, but I was the first member of my family to get through college—although no one would have predicted it from my adolescence. My reading was limited to such books as The Hardy Boys series and *The Circus Comes to Town,* until I was around seventeen. I was barely a C student in high school, perhaps in part because I stuttered badly and rather than having to face the terror and humiliation of reciting in class, I frequently feigned ignorance. I did not begin to deal successfully with the stuttering until I was into my twenties, had left the parental household, and had a regular sex life. In the film version of *One Flew over the Cuckoo's Nest* there is a fragile young stutterer among the inmates of the mental hospital who spends a night in bed with a woman squirreled into the hospital exactly for that purpose. In the morning he emerges from the room beaming, and although the point was not telegraphed in any of the familiar Hollywood ways, I anticipated, when he opened his mouth to speak, that he would not stutter.

I do not mean to suggest it was a terrible adolescence; it was not. I had lots of friends, and I almost always had a good-looking girlfriend. I was a good dancer, and a fine athlete, often elected captain of my teams. The summer I was fifteen I hit a ninth-inning inside-the-park home run, with the bases loaded, in front of maybe a hundred people, including my mother, father, and girlfriend. Students of youth culture know that things like that are far more important to a kid than doing well in school.

Near the end of World War II, at eighteen, I was a private in the Marine Corps stationed on the island of Guam. When the fighting was over my company commander assigned me to administer an official Navy library that had just arrived by ship from San Francisco in several enormous wooden crates, which I can remember unpacking with a crowbar. (I do not know why I was so assigned; it could not have been my intelligence: this Jewish boy endured the shame of scoring higher on the Marine Corps' mechanical-aptitude test than on its general-intelligence test.) They gave me a rectangular frame building with double screen doors and shelves along the walls, and I spent much of the next year as a librarian. There was not much patronage at that jungle library, and I had nothing to do but sit there day after day, week after week, and read books, I who had hardly read any before. I read voraciously, without taste or system, anything that for any reason got my attention—classics, recent fiction, plays, history, current affairs. Doors leading out of the provinciality of my experience began to open, and that started me dreaming about getting educated when I became a civilian again. One more thing about that tropical library: they assigned me an associate, a black Marine from Harlem (we were both New Yorkers among the rednecks) who was a trumpet player, and before long we organized a band (I was a pop singer—it is common knowledge that stutterers do not stutter when they sing) that played in officers' clubs all over the island.

My first political experience came the summer before I went into the Marine Corps, when I got a job as a singing busboy at a resort hotel in the borscht belt owned by the grandmother of my girlfriend. About two weeks into the summer my fellow busboys delegated me to ask the old lady for a small raise in our wages. She fired me on the spot, calling me a communist and, worse than that, a traitor to her and her granddaughter. It had a happy ending, though, because I hitchhiked into the nearby Catskill mountain town where small theatrical agents from New York moved their offices in the summer, auditioned for a job as a singer at a better hotel, and got the job. I made more money and I did not have to bus tables.

My real introduction to politics came when I started Hunter College in the spring semester of 1947. A campus pol came up to me one day in the cafeteria and asked if I would like to be on the student council.

Sure, I said. Next thing I knew I was on their slate, and without lifting a finger I was elected. I thought it was fun, so in the fall I ran for reelection, this time campaigning hard. I lost by a fairly wide margin. I supposed I was a radical because most of my friends were, although at that time I was not certain what that meant. Some in my peer group were reputed to be "members of the party"; but my closest friends regarded them as mostly silly doctrinaires, and therefore I did too—especially when, after a literally sophomoric discussion of love, one of them told me he knew he was in love when he met a girl he "wanted to buck the system with."

I was reading a lot to compensate for the neglects of my athletic adolescence and to catch up with my friends, most of whom, it seemed to me, had been intellectuals at least since puberty. I denounced my college president as a cultured anti-Semite (I still think he was: in one of his books he had said that it was not difficult for him to understand why, for aesthetic reasons, a gentile would not want to marry one of the "daughters of Sarah") and participated in Henry Wallace's campaign for president in 1948, oblivious to charges that it was dominated by communists. I was still only vaguely cognizant of the differences between Stalinists and other parts of the left; I would have been more worldly had my literacy come only two or three years earlier.

My girlfriends contributed a lot to my education. They were always English majors (I was in political science), highly literary women who tended to mother me, seeing in me a diamond in the rough who could profit from the nurturance of their greater sophistication. I began to read poetry, and in my senior year I published my first real article, on W. H. Auden, in the college literary magazine.

The summer after my junior year in college I hitchhiked from New York to Berkeley to see a childhood friend (keeping a journal as I went). Berkeley was beautiful and summer-cool, and I had no wish to see a goodlier place. So I came back to become a graduate student, knowing absolutely nothing of what the University of California had to offer. It was as far from the Bronx and from home as I could get, and I had the instinct to sense that if I stayed, I would be sucked into the vortex of the family, not yet having the strength or vision to know what I wanted and hence ill equipped to resist what my parents wanted for me. Besides, I liked going to school, and I had become reasonably good at it. Since there was nothing else I wanted to do, I thought I would stick with it, although I do not remember considering an academic career then. I thought I was interested in studying political behavior, but at that time

Berkeley's rather traditional political-science department did not teach political behavior, and an adviser there sent me to the Department of Sociology and Social Institutions, as the sociology department was then called.

I sort of grew up with the Berkeley sociology department. (Some years ago when a magazine editor asked me for one of those brief bios that accompany an article I said that I was born and raised in New York City but grew up in California, to which I remained grateful.) When I arrived, the department had maybe a half-dozen sociologists, but they included Reinhard Bendix and Robert Nisbet, who encouraged me and from whom I learned a lot. During the years I was a graduate student there the faculty added Phillip Selznick, Herbert Blumer, Seymour Martin Lipset, Kingsley Davis, Leo Lowenthal, William Kornhauser, Nathan Glazer, Lewis Feuer, and, in my last year, young Erving Goffman and Neil Smelser. Others joined, too, and I could have lunch with these guys or drop in and chat without having to make an appointment three weeks in advance. For many of them their eminence was still ahead, so I was not intimidated by their not yet formidable names. There were several schools of thought, and a little bit of several of them rubbed off on my eclecticism.

During the six or seven years I was a graduate student at Berkeley, the university commanded only a part of my attention. The rest of it went to the demimonde of San Francisco and the bay area that came to be known as the "beat generation," through which I got to know people like Gary Snyder, Allen Ginsberg, Mike McClure, and the late Max Scherr, founder, editor, and publisher of the *Berkeley Barb*. I was a marginal part of that crowd, with one foot in the academy and one in bohemia. The sexual anarchy of my bohemian life scared me, I think, and in 1956 I got married (probably to escape from sex); in 1958 I got a Ph.D., and after a year of lecturing at Berkeley I went off to my first real job, an assistant professorship at the University of Illinois, Urbana, where I spent four happy and productive years learning the professor business.

But perhaps the happiest stroke of my continuing historical luck (the library on Guam, falling in with intellectuals at college, falling into Berkeley sociology at the start of its rise to eminence—that Millsian intersection of biography and history) was that I entered the job market at a very good time; even mediocre Ph.D.'s were getting good jobs. In retrospect it seems an unimaginable blessing that I never suffered a single day of assistant-professor anxiety. My senior colleagues at Urbana and the graduate students there quickly made it plain that they were glad to have this young turk from the newly eminent Berkeley department. My first book was well received; I published some articles and review essays, and after three years at Urbana I was promoted to tenure without even knowing that I was being considered for it. When I think of the recurrent ritual humiliations to which assistant professors are now periodically subjected in the system of faculty review at the University of California, I wonder why any intellectual of independent mind would seek an academic career; it is hard for me to imagine anyone getting through it without lasting wounds, deep bitterness, and a taste for revenge.

Despite the successful years at the University of Illinois, when the opportunity came to go back to northern California I grabbed it. I became chairman of the growing sociology department at the University of California, Davis, just as the free-speech movement and the student revolution were beginning down the road at Berkeley. But I was already in my mid-thirties by then, a married man with two small daughters and lots of grown-up responsibilities. In the privacy of my mind, though, I was still the perennial student, the perpetual kid, someone who had hardly done anything but go to school as a marginal outsider. Suddenly at Davis I was a boy imposter, recruiting faculty, playing the politics of FTEs (full-time equivalents), conferring with deans on weighty matters of medical schools and law schools, sitting on important committees judging the incompetence of research institute directors old enough to be my father. Few sociologists have anything good to say about chairing a department, but for me it was an important growing-up experience to be in administration, managing an academic unit and bearing responsibility for its operation and welfare.

Well, there are several pages' worth of autobiographical bits. What is it they contribute to a contextual understanding of my work and the way I go about it? Here is what I make of them: the fact that my family was poor and New York–provincial gave me my persistent identification with have-nots and my distrust and discomfort with men of power. But the humiliation I remember at the grocery store suggests I had aspirations toward middle-class respectability. That was my mother's influence, I think. She was the only woman of her generation in our extended kin group who spoke English without a Yiddish accent. That, along with the fact that she wrote a fine English script, gave her high prestige in our extended family, which compensated somewhat for the fact that her husband was never able to support her in the style she thought she deserved. She repeatedly would advise me to be cautious and discreet for the sake of my future, to wait until I was *somebody* before I opened my mouth too wide or too loud.

The stuttering, of course, was a continually painful embarrassment, and it was probably the beginning of my feelings of isolation and marginality. But it also gave me valuable early experience in coping with isolation and accommodating to it. Moreover, it made me hypersensitive to the rhythms of language. To evade blocking I had to rehearse silently and carefully what I wanted to say, choosing words and rhythmic structures that enabled me to get through a sentence without facing a crisis. To this day, when proofreading a manuscript back from a typist, I can immediately detect even the most minor error (for example, a misplaced comma) because the rhythms are not right.

That I was well coordinated and good at sports had, I think, two important consequences. It gave me confidence in my body, in my physical presence, which I consider valuable. Even more important, it gave me a sense of competence that is hard to fake. On the field and in the game, athletic competition is beautiful and moving because it provides one of the too few models where the criteria of performance are clearly central to the tasks at hand. It surely contrasts with intellectual life in that respect, and I think it helped give me my critical eye for sociological performance. I also learned a good bit about jazz phrasing from my friend the black trumpet player in the Marine Corps, and I think those rhythms are in my prose. Instead of using an outline, I hear chord progressions when I am writing well, as if I were soloing with rhythm support. Singing in public also gave me a sense of performance and some experience in overcoming fear.

That I almost certainly would never have gone to college had it not been for that library in the jungle made me sensitive to historical accident and skeptical of the determinisms claimed for macrohistorical variables unless I could see the way they operated in relatively intimate, close-up interaction. My experience in campus politics gave me a sense for the discrepancy between effort and reward and insulated me to some extent against the pieties of the Protestant ethic and the unfelt clichés of political speech—even political speech I agreed with—which are inauthentic *because* they are political, that is, uttered to win applause or other approval rather than communicate truth or feeling. (Almost all speech is to some extent political, of course, the present instance not excepted.)

The fact that I had a very late literacy made me feel that I had a lot of catching up to do. For many years my peers always seemed smarter, better educated, more sophisticated than I was. That I had to fake a lot under those conditions to maintain my face made me sensitive to the ways in which other people faked a lot to maintain theirs. I still feel more comfortable questioning the authority of authors and lecturers than I do authoring and lecturing myself.

Women have been very important in my life, and I have learned a great deal from them. I was part of a class of six hundred men fresh from World War II to enter a previously all-women's college with eight thousand female students and a heavily female faculty. In a sense I experienced being a member of a sexual minority. Some of the female faculty were hostile to us on the grounds that opportunities for female academics depended on the existence of women's colleges, which our presence threatened. I had my first sociology course from a woman; its subject was mainly women as a minority group. The women students, though, were happy to receive us men, two to four years older than they, battle-scarred and worldly-wise. I began to have a rewarding sex life. That I was athletic, intelligent, and eager, but unlettered, unsophisticated, and "rough," was looked on, I think, as romantic, even sexy, and I think that I was deeply strengthened, in obscure ways I still do not fully understand, to discover that attractive women frequently seemed to prefer me to other men whom I regarded as far more attractive than I was. I mention these matters for two reasons. First, when feminism came on strong around 1970, it was not a new experience for me; I had been significantly exposed to it more than twenty years earlier. Second, my favorable predisposition to feminism was strengthened by my gratitude to women not only for having played an important part in my education but also for having provided me with a good bit of security and ego support at a time when I needed both, to compensate for my amateurishness at intellectual life and help overcome the stuttering.

At Berkeley I finally got the education I was seeking. But unlike many graduate students, I was never anybody's boy or protégé. Reinhard Bendix was my main mentor, and I learned much from him, but unlike many of his other students I was never his research assistant, and I did not work in his style; hence I never had to get used to deferring to him. I learned a lot from Phil Selznick too, but he threw me out of his class once for sassing him, and I was not rehired as an assistant on one of his research projects after spending a year with it, doing my usual carping. Bill Kornhauser helped me with my dissertation, but we tangled over matters of form. Bill was a very formal assistant professor in the fifties (eventually liberated by the sixties) and I had to go over his head to Reinhard to get approval for my using the first-person singular. My dissertation itself did not arise out of the interests of any of the sociology faculty. It was another historical accident. I was looking for a job, and a business administration professor with a grant to study the Ford Motor Company was looking for a sociology graduate student to study the families of its workers. I got help from my committee with questionnaires and criticism of drafts of chapters, and financial support from the Institute of Industrial Relations, but I had almost no direct supervision in the research. I had to find the problem by myself, and the conception and execution of *Working-Class Suburb* were largely my own.

I do not mean to suggest that I was a deliberately recalcitrant or rebellious student, vain about my "independence" from influences. I was no more rebellious than the average anti-Parsonian in the fifties, and that was the mode at Berkeley then. Besides, I was in fact dependent on all sorts of things, like the goodwill of my teachers, assistantships, and (failing those) little jobs in bookstores on Telegraph Avenue and auditing courses for a commercial note-taking firm, which helped me learn to write concisely (as well as pick up a little economics and psychology) while putting bread on my table.

I was consistently ambivalent, with no milieu to which I wished to commit myself wholly. After a time I developed defenses against seeing that lack of thorough commitment as a vice or flaw (which armed me against those who later, in the sixties, continually urged "commitment" as if it were some unambiguously transcendent virtue). There was a lot about sociology that was intellectually timid and crushingly boring, but I stuck with it; there was a lot about bohemia I did not like, but I stuck with that too; there was a lot about New York intellectual life I wanted to distance myself from, but when invitations came to write for *Commentary, Dissent, The Public Interest, The Nation,* and the *New York Times,* the thousands of miles between them and me made it seem safe to do for a while. And there was a lot about marriage I did not like, but I was a scrupulously dutiful husband for what seemed like a millennium.

In fact, I actively sought discrepant, even contradictory, reference groups, eventually needing the contradictory reinforcements to counter or neutralize the claims that groups (occupation groups, families, ethnic groups, political parties, friendship networks) increasingly make on one's loyalty and identity. It was not the individualism of isolation or detachment I sought; conservative theories of mass society had persuaded me early that the unaffiliated person was not an individual but a cipher, all the more vulnerable to manipulation by centralized power. What I looked for was something closer to Georg Simmel's conception of the individual, who exists at the intersection of his or her group affiliations and (something Simmel did not emphasize) at a historically located biographical intersection.

The stuttering, I think, was the beginning of my search for the interstices. Being a Jew in the Marine Corps helped too; I had my first taste of anti-Semitism there. My late literacy made me feel like an imposter among intellectuals for a long time, which perhaps helps account for my greater respect for physical and sensual grace than intellectual sophistication. That I had been a jazz and pop singer and an athlete (and enjoyed both) made me marginal to those of my colleagues who would have thought it quaint in an academic. But having been an athlete and a singer also gave me my firm connection to, and taste for, popular culture and developed my ear for cliché: when watching television and bad movies I can often anticipate dialogue, annoying my family and friends by reciting a line before the character on the screen does.

The marginality and the historical out-of-jointness continued. I was an occasionally noisy radical in the silent, conservative fifties, but by the time the sixties rolled around I was already a successful young academic, too old to be a student radical but too young to be avuncular (which struck me then—and still does—as bad taste). By 1965 I wore orange jeans, began to let my hair grow long, and helped design the first (so far as I know) psychedelic poster to recruit graduate students to a university department. But I was also writing prudent and circumspect essays. The chancellor at Davis called me his hippie sociologist—and promoted me to full professor. There was something unsavory in that. By the mid-1970s, when the New Left had factioned away its communal solidarity, when the counterculture had declined into open and honest therapies, when men's barbers had become hairdressers, and when almost everybody agreed that the country was taking a sharp turn to the right, I was rereading Marx, discovering the neo-Marxists, and trying to find what was interesting in ethnomethodology and be seriously theoretical about the empirical study of culture and ideas. I began to conceive culture as a kind of communicable disease, carried on the backs of live bodies as they staggered through time—a disease I could not begin to understand unless I could identify the groups of sufferers that carried particular strains of it.

In retrospect, I think that my work has frequently defined itself *against* the dominant wisdom in my reference groups of intellectuals at particular times, thus reflecting my sense of marginality to them or, more accurately, my tendency to alternate between approach and withdrawal, involvement and detachment. In the fifties, when intellectuals were inveighing against the power of suburbia to transform its residents into mindless conformists, I showed that automobile assembly line workers liked suburban living and that it did not change them much, although, like my peers, *I* did not like suburbia. In the sixties, when there was a lot of concern with youth culture and the solidarity of generations, I tried to show that subcultures and countercultures were only tenuously connected with chronological age, a variable whose impact was often confounded by more powerful structural factors like ethnicity and class. I tried too to show that the concept of generations had a largely elite referent and that the rhetoric of generations was an ideological device deployable in the struggle to capture "the spirit of the age." In the seventies, when the conventional wisdom had it that the counterculture was dead, and communes passé, I spent several years, on and off, doing field research to discover how the counterculture survived in rural communes by adapting its ideology to the circumstances in which it had to live, thus maintaining the long adversary tradition for yet another generation to inherit. Throughout, my tendency toward involvement is represented by my attraction to topics of current cultural interest; but my tendency toward detachment is apparent in my always being less interested in the events or facts themselves (about suburban living; about youth, age, and cohort solidarity; about communes and countercultures) than in the ideas espoused about them and the cultural ambience in which the espousers moved.

Now that I have provided a selective answer to some of the relations between my life and my work, I want to turn right around and warn you to take nothing of what I have said at face value. Please do not misunderstand me; I have not told you any lies, at least not intentionally. But the account has been severely selective. I have not told you, for example, that along with the marginality goes a certain alienation, to which I am now fairly well accommodated. Still, I regret that expressions of ritual solidarity embarrass me and that I can hardly ever feel like a full participant in them. I am not a good conductor of ceremonies, which means that I am not good at domestic life. I think I would find it easier to be the head of a large corporation than the head of a family.

The facts are all true; the events recounted are not fictitious. But I have also imputed values and meanings to those facts and events, and in doing so I have done a job of ideological work, which is (far more often than not) adaptive or group-serving for collectivities and self-congratulatory for individuals. Not without some justice you could regard these pages as an effort at persuasion—even seduction. My colleague and friend Joe Gusfield might call it a rhetoric, a drama in which I have cast myself as Mr. Nice Guy, who raised himself up by his own bootstraps but never lost his identification with the underdog; the intellectual whose home runs proved he was no sissy; the fancy writer and talker still overcompensating for that stutter; the former ladies' man who affects gratitude but is really boasting. The modest late starter who had to hurry to catch up with, and pass, those who began with greater advantages is really gloating; the vaunted marginality or alternating in-and-outness is really no more than a sly and cynical gutlessness. And despite my mother's voice still at my shoulder counseling prudence, my disdain for the reward system that has so well rewarded me could turn out to be simple ingratitude or a more complex ambitiousness and pride that reaches beyond the academic reward system to a still more prestigious transcendence: hubris. By taking the role of the other, in this case a hostile other, I am trying to show that the autobiographical data I use in order to do self-congratulatory ideological work could well be used by a hostile ideological worker to cut me up. That is as it should be.

CHAPTER SEVEN

Working in Other Fields

Dean MacCannell

No one knows yet who will inhabit this shell [of industrial
capitalism] in the future: whether at the end of its
prodigious development there will be new prophets or a
vigorous renaissance of all thoughts and ideals or whether
finally, if none of this occurs, mechanism will produce only
petrification hidden under a kind of anxious importance.
According to this hypothesis, the prediction will become a
reality for the last men of this particular development of
culture. Specialists without spirit, libertines without heart,
this nothingness imagines itself to be elevated to a level of
humanity never before attained.

—*Max Weber,* Gesammelte Aufsatz zur
Wissenschaftlehre

It has been more than ten years since I left the sociology faculty at
Temple University for a research and teaching appointment at the University of California, Davis, College of Agriculture. I should be counted
among the lost generation of sociologists in the 1970s who work mainly
outside of the discipline. Like the man without a country, I sometimes
feel nostalgia for my old intellectual haunts. But there are other separations in my life deeper and more problematic than this one. Spatial and
institutional fragmentation is a fact of modern existence. The only question is how we handle it. Do we yield to the demands of this last
"development of culture" by narrowing our thoughts and feelings to fit
in to the fragments that are called business, government, education, and
the like? Or do we attempt, somehow, to change things, to create new
arrangements that can be inhabited by whole human beings?

I was born in Olympia, Washington, in 1940, the son of Earle H.
MacCannell and Helen Frances Meskimen MacCannell. My father and

mother were too young at the time of my birth (twenty-two and nineteen years old) to have begun their careers. They would both eventually finish college, attend graduate school, earn Ph.D. degrees, and become professors, my father going into sociology before me. But my birth and the birth of my brothers intervened, followed by World War II and a divorce, so that in the actual progression of events my father's first faculty appointment preceded mine by only ten years, and mine preceded my mother's by two.

Given the fact that my mother, my father, and my wife are all university professors, one might assume that I grew up in intellectual and bookish surroundings. Nothing would be further from the truth. I was born of two opposing American types and married yet another, and my entire life has been an exercise in synthesizing contradictions. My father's family is New England Yankee, MIT-educated, originally Boston-based professionals. My mother's family is militant working-class, ex-pioneer, Oklahoma oil field boilermakers and roughnecks, Depression migrants from the dust bowl to the Pacific Northwest. My wife's family is urban (Chicago and New York) European ethnic—Jewish and Italian entrepreneurs and professionals. The only major American experiences not in my background, or that of my children, are farming and oppression based on skin color, two topics that, interestingly, are among my current research concerns.

My father was drafted into the infantry in the late stages of World War II and remained with the occupational forces in Italy after the war, staying there until 1949. I lived with my mother and two brothers in enlisted men's base housing at Fort Lewis, Washington. My brothers and I were sent for visits, often long ones, with my uncles, aunts, and grandparents. My summers were spent with my paternal great-grandmother, Emily Amelia Hughes MacCannell. She was thin, passionate, sharp-witted, sharp-tongued, and very old. She made a habit of saying that I was her favorite among all her children, grandchildren, and great-grandchildren, a stance that provoked other members of my father's family. Her favoritism did not lead her to spoil me. On the contrary, she corrected each of my errors of grammar and etiquette on the spot and insisted that I read aloud at least an hour every evening and maintain regular habits of eating, sleeping, and dressing. Except for an early edition of *Uncle Tom's Cabin*, which I still own, she left me nothing material, but she prepared my heart to give and take unqualified love from another person. The value of this gift is incalculable since the alternative is madness.

I also spent many days and weekends with my maternal grandmother, Frances Meskimen, who was the only member of my family on both sides to own an automobile during the war and the immediate postwar years. She was the driver. My grandma Fran was also the first woman welder to enter the ship-building industry in World War II. She is featured in a news documentary from that era that still plays occasionally as filler on late-night television. She provided inspiration for a popular song, "Rosie the Riveter," and later was the subject of an oral-history project in the Women's Studies Program at the University of Washington. She was left-handed, as I am, so it fell to her to teach me to write in cursive. She was also a published poet, and she gave me a manuscript memoir, written in a clear and humorous style, in 1982 not long before she died.

I do not recall ever thinking like a child. My thought processes, as far back as I can remember, were substantially the same as they are today. This is a condition I share with my wife, Juliet Flower MacCannell: we both *feel* about seventeen years old. I recall my grandfather, Ross Meskimen, a tough, left-leaning union man, giving me my first lesson in critical theory when I was nine. We were walking together in downtown Tacoma when the air raid alert sirens were tested, as they were then once a week at noon.

"What's that?" I shouted.

"It's the atomic attack siren test," he answered, or something to that effect. (I remember the word *atomic* and that he pronounced *siren* "sigh-*reen*.")

"Why do we need it now that the war is over?" I asked.

"So the people who make sirens will have a market for their product," was his instant reply. There is no question in my mind that this childhood incident influenced the way I approached the nuclear question in my article "Baltimore in the Morning After."

My uncle and cousins on my mother's side to this day direct the crews that lift the high-voltage cables onto the towers at the points where the electrical grid crosses the Great Divide. They repair the damage to sawmills that results when a twenty-foot blade leaves its shaft at high speed and cuts its way through the other machinery. My brother William is a pioneer homesteader and frontier newspaper editor in Alaska, where he went to work as a dynamiter. Brother John is an Air Force systems analyst and weatherman but also a gifted builder. Of all the nephews and grandchildren, my maternal relatives refused to teach me their skills because they insisted that I should never have to work with my hands. But through them I came to regard writing as a form of handiwork, and I went with them to their jobs often enough as a child that, in spite of their efforts to shield me, I later discovered that I am a good pipe fitter and metal worker.

My mother's people did actively teach me never to cross a union picket line and, by example, instilled in me an attitude of fierce independence from authority. I do not believe that any of them ever stayed on a work site more than five minutes after forming the opinion that they were not receiving a fair wage, a fair hearing, or proper respect.

Growing up in this setting, I developed an attitude toward technology that remains with me even today: I feel I must know exactly how everything works. Probably no other quirk of my mind has led me to make so many mistakes. I have taken apart the carburetors of every automobile I have ever owned (including two exotic English sports cars) and have not, in every case, been able to fit them back together again. (I have only been a little luckier with Swiss watches, ignition systems, valve trains, hydraulic door openers, and submersible bilge pumps.) One night as a graduate student at Cornell I was working alone at two or three o'clock in the morning in the data processing lab when the equipment broke down in the middle of a calculation. I was impatient to see the results, so without hesitation I found tools and dismantled the old IBM 101 accounting machine that had failed. About an hour later, when dawn broke, I was surrounded by subassemblies, relays, nuts, wires, and machine screws. I had not found the problem, and in my exhaustion I had lost all sense of how to put the stuff back together beyond a crude, right-hemisphere gestalt not unlike science-fiction "machineyness." After agonizing over some moral and economic choices for a few minutes, I reassembled it as best I could and hung a sign on it saying OUT OF ORDER. It only took the repair person about an hour to fix it when the lab opened in the morning, but he complained more than once about that person who last had serviced the equipment.

Whereas I was able to absorb the values and competencies of my maternal relatives only partially, my mother positively rejected them, imagining academic life to be opposed to the life of a boilermaker, not an extension of it. When I was younger, I thought her position was in error; I still do, but I am softer in my criticism now. It could not have been easy for a little girl, who desired nothing more than to be feminine, to grow up in the Oklahoma oil fields in a family of men, with a mother who came home at night wearing filthy overalls and carrying a metal lunch box in one hand and her welding hood in the other.

Somehow, in this ragbag of defiant Americana, I learned to read before I went to school and quickly developed advanced taste in reading. When I was eight or nine, I read *All Quiet on the Western Front* and, soon after, an English translation of *Les Misérables.* I do not recall who gave me these books or why. On finishing *All Quiet,* I resolved never to go to war and to resist and oppose it with all my might throughout my life. My ship-building grandmother tried to dissuade me from my radical stand, but Grandpa Ross and my paternal grandmother, Alice MacCannell, supported my position. My pacifist convictions stayed with me until Vietnam, when I decided that armed struggle can be justified if it is necessary to secure self-determination and throw off the yoke of oppression. Thus my work in the antiwar movement coincided precisely with my first acceptance of war. I never changed my mind about *Les Misérables.* The figure of Inspector Javert attempting to elevate his bureaucratic heartlessness even above the events of the French Revolution still worries and haunts me.

In 1949 my father returned from Italy and entered the University of Washington as an undergraduate. We moved from military base housing to public housing and subsisted without supplementary income on the living allotment provided to students by the GI bill—$120 a month. Our poverty, and the poverty of the other people living in the project, was awful, and I made a silent vow never to go to college, as I judged the cost in human suffering to be too great.

At the university my father proved to be a gifted mathematician, carrying a double major in mathematics-statistics and sociology through the master's degrees, eventually doing a demographically oriented Ph.D. in sociology under the direction of Calvin Schmid in 1958. We were so poor that a research assistantship in the population laboratory brought relief. My mother was able to enroll, taking her undergraduate degree in "integrated studies," with emphasis on English. We all worked at diverse part-time jobs. By the time I was fourteen I was doing the summer gardening and winter furnace stoking for a far-flung network of middle-class households in the north end of Seattle. I started out working by the hour until my client and I could determine how much a particular service ordinarily cost. Then I cut the cost by 10 percent and switched to a piece rate so that I could work twice as fast and almost double my earnings. I built a system of regular after-school appointments on weekly and monthly schedules and was soon earning more than fifty dollars a week, which was more than my father's assistantship paid. In 1952 I spent my first hundred dollars on an English lightweight bicycle with gears. I was one of only two kids in Seattle with such a machine for about a year; the other was a Japanese paper boy named Art, known to me only because of his bike.

I vividly recall a conversation with my father from this period. We were discussing my social-studies class, in particular the unit on social conditions in urban slums. My father could tell from my comments that I was thinking of these slums as something quite remote, limited to East Coast cities, perhaps. "Step outside for a minute," he said, and I followed him. He gestured at our neighborhood. "You sounded as if you did not know about the slum. This is the slum."

By the time I was twelve I had been introduced to Stuart Dodd, R. E. L. Faris, George Lundberg, Otto Larsen, Norman Hayner, and the other pillars of the old University of Washington sociology department. In early spring of 1951 or 1952 my family was invited to visit with Lundberg at his summer home on Whidby Island in Puget Sound. It was during this visit that I received my first concrete lesson in sociological concept formation. The house had been sealed up for the winter, and Lundberg asked me to help him pry off a storm shutter. As the shutter came free, we uncovered fifteen or twenty ladybugs, which scrambled together rather than running in all directions when they were disturbed. Lundberg commented, "Hmm, I did not know them to be a socially organized species." Of course, until then I had not thought of animals, insects, or humans as possessing social organization. But there was a clarity of connection of concept and observation in the event that fixed social organization in my mind from that moment forward. Already I was aware of Lundberg's reputation as a leading social scientist, for there was a paperback copy of his *Can Science Save Us?* on my father's bookshelf. In those days it was the only paperback he had, except for several by Margaret Mead. I thought that any professor whose words were believed to be so important as to have been made available to a mass audience must be a genius, a serious ideologue, or both. Hence I was well primed to learn a first sociological principle from him.

In the early 1950s the families of the graduate students and faculty in the sociology department got together once a year for fun at the Alpha Kappa Delta picnic. I remember especially well playing baseball with Clarence Schrag. He was an excellent hitter in spite of having a wooden hand carved in the shape of a real hand and covered with a skin-toned leather glove. Bobby Faris told me that Schrag was the professor of crime and that his hand had been shot off in a prison break while he was doing research. I do not know if Faris had his facts right, but it was the sort of thing that made sociology interesting. (I had occasion to think of

Schrag's hand twenty years later when I was doing research in Holmesberg Prison in Philadelphia.) Bobby Faris was one year ahead of me in the same junior high school. Someone must have told him that he should act friendly toward me because he sought me out and introduced himself to me in the most singular way on the playground at recess. He walked up, placed himself squarely in front of me at about five paces, and flatly announced, "My name is Robert E. Lee Faris the Third, my father is the chair of the finest sociology department in the world, and I am a genius." Oddly enough, this statement did have the effect of putting me at ease with him, although it caused me, for a moment, to doubt my own father's good sense. When I reported this weird incident to my father, his response was, "It's all true." I was never close friends with the youngest Faris, but I would often accompany him home, or most of the way home, and warn him about traffic as he had the dangerous affectation of reading books while riding his bicycle. Some years later we were together again briefly at Cornell University as lecturers. His appointment was in mathematics, I believe. Just before he came to Cornell I met his famous father for coffee at the meetings of the American Sociological Association in Montreal, at his father's request. The older Faris told me that I was a sensible person and that I should check on Bobby occasionally after he arrived. He briefly dated our (Juliet Flower's and my) dear friend Leslie Burlingame, who is now a professor of history at Franklin and Marshall College, but no romantic interest developed, and that was the last I heard of him.

I was always sexually precocious and lascivious, and from age fourteen on I regarded every day's passage until I "did it" as a horrendous waste. I was so enormously frustrated that when it finally did happen, at sixteen, I actually lost my virginity twice in quick succession. The first time I thought I did it, I narrowly missed. (It was in the dark on rugged terrain—how is a boy to know?) The girl, a year older but as inexperienced as I, never let on until, on the occasion of our "second" time, I blurted out, "Hey, it didn't really happen last time." "I know," she said. "You were so happy I didn't have the heart to tell you." I could not then, nor can I now, say which of the two times was better. My girlfriend had a clear opinion on the matter, however.

While I was in high school, I determined absolutely that I would not go to college and that I would make a career as a builder and driver of racing cars. As with all my desires, I committed myself totally and absolutely to this goal. I worked for several dealerships in and near Seattle that had active racing programs, at first without pay. I became a good race strategist and was quick, especially in the rain, in small-displacement modified sports cars—Lotus 11, Porsche Spyder, Fiat Abarth Zagato, A. C. Bristol. On finishing high school I planned to go to Europe and apprentice myself to a major racing organization. Then, in 1957, my father took his first faculty position at San Diego State University (then only a college) and insisted that I join the family in southern California. The move threw me into a dangerous mental depression, from which I have the patient friendship of the great mountaineer Edward Douglas ("Bud") Bernard to thank for pulling me out. I barely finished high school and ran back to Seattle.

In late summer of 1958 a sociology conference was held in Seattle. My father came to the meetings and visited me at Scott Larson Motors, where I was working. He told me I should go to college. I agreed for a perverse reason. I had quite forgotten that I was in possession of a strong intellect, and I felt it would be easy for me to prove to him that I would fail. I tricked myself into thinking that if I made a good-faith effort in college, I could flunk out gracefully at the end of a semester, return to my racing, and not be bothered again after that. I figured the entire episode would be over in about six months and would cost next to nothing—tuition in the California State College system then was thirty-four dollars a semester, and books ran about twenty-five dollars, a small investment for a life of peace and prosperity in the automobile business.

Of course, that ill-conceived decision cost me a life of relative deprivation and turmoil, and the entire episode is not over yet. I earned high grades in college, much higher than in high school, and learned to enjoy taking mental risks based on intuition: for example, I predicted Fidel Castro's eventual victory on an essay exam in a political science course taught by a conservative professor. Two years later I transferred to Berkeley, and two years after that went on to graduate school at Cornell, supporting the effort with a patchwork of part-time jobs, fellowships, and assistantships. The part I loved most about my college coursework was the books I did *not* understand. I experienced a sensual thrill on first turning the pages of Bronislaw Malinowski's *Argonauts* and my statistics textbook, knowing that I did not understand what they meant but was going to find out. I still feel the same excitement today when I find an especially dense passage by Claude Lévi-Strauss, Noam Chomsky, Jacques Derrida, René Thom, or Charles Peirce. (I also love to read authors like Darwin, Marcel Mauss, Georg Simmel, and Mikhail Bakhtin who can represent complex ideas in clear and simple-seeming language and, in fact, base my own approach to writing more on this second principle than on "pleasure of the text.")

I studied anthropology instead of sociology at first only because I thought it unseemly to take courses with my father's departmental colleagues. When I transferred to the University of California, Berkeley (Bobby Faris's earlier assessment notwithstanding), I had a choice between what were then regarded as the finest sociology department and the finest anthropology department anywhere. I stayed with anthropology for the bachelor's degree for two reasons: First, it was richer than sociology because it focused on culture as well as social organization and was international in practice as well as theory, and second, it was technically more sociological than sociology—that is, it had not accepted psychological explanations of social phenomena to the extent that sociology had. Frank W. Young, who taught briefly at San Diego State before moving to the University of Pittsburgh and eventually to Cornell, made me read Durkheim's *Rules of Sociological Method,* and I took them completely to heart as only a sophomore can. When I read, "EXPLAIN A SOCIAL FACT WITH ANOTHER SOCIAL FACT," I could actually feel an old worldview deflate and sense a new direction for thought and beliefs. After such a manifestation, I thought, it was only a matter of time before we would clean up the last vestiges of psychological mystification and associated political beliefs in bourgeois individualism. That was because I had not yet learned Freud's concept of *resistance.*

The undergraduate avant-garde on the West Coast in the years 1958–60 was in a full-throttle skid. We would crowd into old cars and speed up the coast or deep into Mexico on a whim. The beat movement was at its crest, and it empowered many of us who were poor but smart to move in wider circles and into positions of leadership among our peers, positions formerly occupied by culturally middle-class, Junior Achiever types. We held ourselves intellectually accountable for much more than was asked in the framework of institutionalized education. If Marx, Freud, and Sartre were not taught in the classrooms, that made Marx, Freud, and Sartre all the more important to us. We got our true education, we thought, out of the old Cody's Books when it was still located on the north side of the Berkeley campus and Fred Cody still ran the register, ordered the books, knew us all by name, and hired us to do inventory when we did not have enough to eat.

My good friend and roommate in San Diego, and later on in Berkeley, where we went together, was Ronnie Wilson, a perpetually "returning" student ten years my senior. Wilson had been a child-prodigy classical pianist and was about to begin his professional career on the concert stage when he was drafted into the Korean War. He refused combat, so he was given the job of stringing communication wire to the front lines. I believe the experience of seeing men shot and flopping around in their death agony did something to this sensitive soul. In any event, he had an awful time concentrating on his studies and, of course, he refused absolutely to touch a piano. It was characteristic of the ironical quality of his life that he eventually played Carnegie Hall in New York, but as the drummer for the rock group Joy of Cooking.

When I left San Diego for Berkeley in the summer of 1960, I was not alone. An entire intelligentsia departed in a swarm that included Wilson, Tonia Aminoff, Linda Brown, David Crawford (brother of artist Richard Crawford), John Geyer (entering graduate school), Gilberto Leal, Gordon Madison (now an attorney in San Diego, I have been told), Gordon McLure, and others. Most of this group was unable to meet the rigorous Berkeley entrance requirements for transfer students. To the best of my knowledge, of those among us who were admitted, only Aminoff, Brown, and I completed Berkeley bachelor's degrees. In the summer of 1961 Tonia Aminoff and I were married at a judge's home in Oakland in defiance of understandable objections raised by her parents. But we were temperamentally incompatible, so we separated fourteen months later and divorced soon after that before leaving for different Eastern graduate schools.

At Berkeley I was friends with musician Peter Berg and Mike Rossman, an eventual free speech movement leader who was already showing promise as a fine writer and political analyst. Rossman and I talked a great deal about the coming revolution on campus and in the larger society, and out of sheer silliness we went bowling at least once a week. I earned my living then as manager of the new Berkeley Student Union building, and in that capacity I met Senator Barry Goldwater, Pete Seeger, Aldous Huxley, Sonny McGee, Dean Rusk, Soviet cosmonaut Yuri Gagarin, chair designer Charles Eames, and many other interesting people. I also was the first to authorize setting up tables in the student union for leftist student groups to distribute their information alongside the Marine Corps recruiting tables.

I arrived at Berkeley the week Alfred Kroeber died. The news came within hours after I first walked through the new Kroeber Hall thinking what an honor it was for a professor to have an office building named for him. Even though I loved to take the culture area courses in the Berkeley anthropology department, the curriculum was mainly stiff and theoretical, so I supplemented it with coursework in physics and art. Many years later, in 1976, Nelson Graburn would invite me to come and give a colloquium before the Berkeley anthropology department, and I admit to entering Kroeber Hall on that second occasion with exactly the same feeling of anxious anticipation as on the first. I also sat in the introductory sociology course that was taught by Erving Goffman and Herbert Blumer. There were about seven hundred students enrolled in the course, which met in the auditorium of Wheeler Hall. One day Goffman was lecturing on the essential asymmetry of face-to-face inter-action, and he summed up by saying that there are no occasions in which the interactants have equal status within the framework of the interaction. I spontaneously called out from near the back of the hall, "What about an introductory handshake between status equals?" Goffman stepped from behind the lectern and peered through the gloom of the huge auditorium: "Who said that?" I raised my hand and half stood up: "I did." "You'd better see me after class," he snapped and went back to lecturing.

After class he asked me to walk with him in the direction of Sather Gate. As we walked along, we had an interesting argument to which I contributed not a word. Goffman said, "You're right." Then he paused and seemed to be thinking hard about something. "No," he countered, "you're wrong." Pause. "No, you're right." After several such reversals he gave me an intense look of self-satisfaction and even some disdain and declared finally, "No. You are wrong." Then he turned and walked away without another word. We met face-to-face again three years later on Christmas afternoon at his sabbatical residence in Cambridge, Mas-sachusetts. He gave no indication then of recalling our first encounter.

I went to the Department of Rural Sociology at Cornell because it offered a strong applied and international program. Kennedy was presi-dent, and there were some indications in that brief moment between the Cuban missile crisis and the Vietnam War that the United States might develop sensible relations with the Third World. I thought there would be a shift in sociological theory and practice that would lead to the development of a new kind of sociology, truly international in scope, providing approaches to the problems of poverty, exploitation, oppres-sion, and false consciousness. I then thought that sociologists should be working in partnership with Third World nations, as well as with mar-ginal peoples in our own society, to create a research and intellectual base for leadership that would be neutral toward both Western capital-ism and Soviet Marxism. I was disgusted with the Soviet Union and the

United States for manipulating Third World peoples into positions of dependency and disadvantage, using force where there is resistance to intimidate the nonaligned—in the Dominican Republic, Bay of Pigs. I was disappointed in anthropology for its retreat from these problems, which developed in regions that included its traditional field sites. And I was equally disappointed in mainstream sociology departments for continuing to focus primarily on the Western urban-industrial proletariat, a class that was about to be superseded by an unprecedented increase in the level of exploitation of Third World labor. I could not understand how these social-science disciplines could fail to use the excellent tools they themselves had invented (especially demography and ethnography) to analyze the shifting base of their own domains.

As I applied to graduate school, I was concerned that the social and economic theories I had studied were not strong enough to explain what was happening in the world. I would eventually read with fascination Roland Barthes's description of the colonial African soldier saluting the French flag in "Myth Today" and see in these early structuralist texts the outlines of a new sociology. But structuralism had not yet developed "consciousness-for-itself," and though I was ready for it, I was also unaware of it. After Talcott Parsons tried it, I became convinced that no individual acting alone could complete the theoretical synthesis necessary to recenter sociology on the general conditions of social existence as they had evolved since 1867. But I thought that each student of society should attempt to *initiate* this recentering in our selection of research topics and approaches. For my part I wanted to find a program where I could study movements of national liberation, ethnic solidarity, rural poverty, and the adaptations of Western institutions as we attempt to extend our global dominance beyond our historical moment. I was not disappointed in my choice of rural sociology.

Cornell has a superior organization for its graduate education. As Ph.D. students we majored in one field and carried two minors, external to the major, which were potentially major fields in their own right. For example, a Ph.D. candidate in sociology might minor in history and economics. I majored in rural sociology and minored in research methods and anthropology. The comprehensive exams were given by a committee of the student's choosing composed of members of the graduate faculty from the major and minor fields. These exams were, by policy, not restricted to material covered in courses or reading lists. We had to go into the exams ready for anything the committee might ask us, so the preparation for the exam was an introduction to authentic scholarship.

Even though there were no requirements except passing the entrance, comprehensive, and thesis exams, all graduate students took certain courses as a matter of peer tradition. We all took Robin Williams's social-theory seminar this way. We read Parsons's *The Social System* aloud in class, line by line, with interpretations following every second or third sentence. Frank Young (my teacher at San Diego) gave the course on theories of development in University of Chicago style: What is the central thesis of this book? What is its theoretical orientation? In addition to doing coursework in my major and minor fields, I ranged widely, taking seminars in the history and philosophy of science, civil engineering, archeology, industrial and labor relations, and literary criticism. I made friends on the faculty and with other graduate students; many of them, including Henry Guerlac and Edward Morris, remained among my dearest friends for life.

Juliet Flower entered the graduate program in comparative literature at the beginning of my second year. We had many friends in common, including Barry Alpher, Donald Brown, Robert Maxwell, and Phillip Silverman in anthropology, Barbara Sirota in English, Alan Nagel in comparative literature, Leslie Burlingame in history, and Frances Dahlberg in sociology. I was powerfully attracted to Juliet, both physically and for her evident mental abilities and flawless character. We immediately began our collaboration, which continues to this day. I worked with her on a poem by Victor Hugo; she worked with me on the calculation of a tau rank-order correlation coefficient from Kendall's original paper. "If it is written even partially in words," she said, "we *can* understand it by reading." I was touched by such courage and innocence and proposed marriage. We were married in Lajas, Puerto Rico, on July 25, 1965, and from that moment I have loved her and our children as much as life itself.

I am not happy "making choices," a locution that is a code for fitting human life into bureaucratic and other institutional forms rather than vice versa. I thought there should never have to be a choice between, for example, science and humanism, Juliet's studies and my own, pure and applied sociology, or career and children. Instead of *either/or,* I always wanted *both/and,* not as a matter of indecision or greed but as a matter of commitment to wholeness and understanding. So after the original decision, the one all American males must make between sports and scholarship, I refused most other choices in my life, and I admit that this refusal has led today to some odd accommodations: airplane commuting, $300-a-month telephone bills, intimacy by appointment, too much high-speed driving, a life my colleague Paul Craig has labeled a masterpiece of organization. But by refusing the *either/or,* I have been able to continue to have fun, sometimes in excess. I have not always been able to "stay in line," however, and I am afraid that I sometimes irritate those who do.

At about the midpoint of my graduate studies at Cornell there was a closed conference at Johns Hopkins University, "The Languages of Criticism and the Sciences of Man: The Structuralist Controversy." It was attended by Roland Barthes, Jacques Lacan, Jacques Derrida, Paul de Man, and many others. I do not think it possible to overestimate the importance of this meeting even, or especially, for those of us who were not invited. I was attracted to structuralism because it proffered a totalizing comprehension of social life that matched my own personal predispositions. The structural explication of binary oppositions, as best exemplified in Roman Jakobson's linguistics or Claude Lévi-Strauss's study of myth, potentially lifts sociology out of its complicitous relationship with conventional morality and established social forms. By transcending and describing the oppositions that give order and meaning to language and life, structuralism was more than a way of doing social science. The structural enterprise paralleled the urgent need to reconstruct the integrity of the human self from the fragments of modern experience, not by looking backward or by assertion, as was occurring in the realms of religion and politics, but by careful scholarship and analysis. I would eventually find in the semiotic idea of the sign an original synthesis of *fact, idea,* and *interpretation,* the element from which all of social life is constructed. This idea of the sign would resolve for me some of the antinomies of modern sociology: the division between macro and micro studies, qualitative and quantitative methods, theory and application. But by the time that happened, I had already left the field.

The idea for a book on studying tourism came to me about halfway through my graduate studies when I was in southwestern Puerto Rico doing research on farm structure in some poor villages. I could not help wondering, What is the main form of North-South interaction, and what is really happening here of potential long-range importance? My attention would vacillate between the impoverished farmers in my sample and the glittering high-rise resort hotels on the beaches. My intuition was strong that some of the secrets of global intercultural relations and change lay locked up in a hidden connection between peasant agriculture and modern mass tourism. When I returned to Cornell, I proposed a study of Third World tourism as a dissertation topic, but my committee rejected it as too cumbersome. So, following my usual perverse practice when confronted with denial, I came up with a second proposal, as unwieldy as the first, to do a comparative structural analysis of social conditions in forty-eight states. I completed the data gathering, analysis, and writing in less than a year and won the Dissertation Award of the American Rural Sociological Society. Juliet and Goffman were angry with me for compromising on the dissertation topic. I was corresponding with Goffman, and we met when we could. He told me over lunch in a café near the University of Pennsylvania, "Any idiot can do an empirical dissertation. Back at Chicago, if we had someone who could do an empirical dissertation in less than a year, we wouldn't let them do it. We made them do ethnography and left the empirical stuff to the people who were actually challenged by it." I did not share Goffman's opinion that ethnography always and inevitably requires more rigor than research involving tests of hypotheses, nor did I argue the point with him. I think he was secretly pleased that I could do regression analysis.

Soon after my dissertation defense Juliet and I left for Europe. I was as excited to see Paris as anyone since Walter Benjamin, and I felt immediately at home there. I wrote a postcard to my friends at Cornell: "It is a great place to live but I would not want to visit here." In the United States I had real difficulty explaining my interest in rural sociology, often encountering virulent anti-intellectual stereotyping unfortunately even among my most intellectual acquaintances. "Rural sociology—what do you do, count cows? Ha ha." Not so among the French. My first Parisian cab driver said, "Rural sociology—*formidable.* Today there is nothing more exciting or important than trying to understand the Third World." My sentiment exactly.

Juliet studied with Derrida at the École Normale Supérieure, and I attended Lévi-Strauss's class on myth at the College de France in the afternoons after my French lessons at the Alliance Française in the mornings. Lévi-Strauss's lectures often exceeded my limited grasp of the language, but my difficulties were small compared to those of the blue-clad scholars from the People's Republic of China who sat to my right in the same row. It was in these courses, from Lévi-Strauss and Derrida, that we heard of semiotics for the first time as a living science, that is, as something other than a curiosity of intellectual history that pops up every three hundred years. Ironically, it was the French philosopher Derrida who introduced us to the writings of the American philosopher Charles Peirce, initiating our semiotic studies in earnest.

We left France at the end of the winter quarter and studied briefly in Zurich, but we hastily returned to Paris for the occupation of the Sorbonne and the events of May 1968. I can still give precise instructions on how, in the heat of fighting, to transform a street barricade from a defensive position into a serious offensive weapon. Some bittersweet images from that revolutionary moment (like the wall graffiti, "my alienation stops where your alienation begins") remain fixed in mind. The faculty delighted the assembled revolutionary students when, after hours of planning for the occupation of virtually every major institution in Paris from the stock exchange to the opera, the professors stood up and wearily announced that they would occupy their own offices. When the French government "forces of order" finally got the upper hand in the fighting and began their cleanup, Juliet and I made the grand tour of student-worker revolutions in Berlin, Bologna, and Istanbul. We tried to get into Czechoslovakia and Greece, where the most interesting fights were taking place, but we were denied entry. We were, however, welcomed as nonaligned American student hitchhikers in Yugoslavia as well as in Bulgaria, where we were provided friendly transit through some rural areas by a twenty-vehicle convoy of the Soviet army.

I thoroughly enjoyed my rides with Bulgarian truck drivers, who were able to give clear explanations of the difference between Eastern European socialism and Western capitalism, at least from their perspective. Yes, they owned their own trucks and carried loads for hire, establishing their own rates and routes. Their trucks cost them about five years of wages at a regular, unskilled job, and they had to pay in cash. Usually they lived at home with their mothers for about seven years while saving most of their wages to buy a truck. In short, as near as I could figure it, the main difference between socialism and capitalism, from the standpoint of a Bulgarian truck driver, was that under socialism mothers were used as a substitute for bank credit. I told them that the same was true for the underclasses in the United States.

According to an agreement worked out in advance, we returned from Europe in the summer of 1968 to my first postdoctoral academic appointment. I was senior research associate at the Cornell Center for International Studies and lecturer in rural sociology at a salary of twelve thousand dollars a year. Under the direction of William Foote Whyte, William Friedland, Frank Young, and Douglas Ashford (in the government department) I started the Macrosocial Accounting Project at Cornell, a data bank and methodology for measuring social conditions at the community level in Third World countries.

In the spring of 1969 the black students at Cornell armed themselves and occupied the student union building, issuing a series of demands for the establishment of an Afro-American studies program. The administration yielded to many of the demands, but the faculty refused to ratify the agreement between the black students and the administration. Immediately, virtually the entire student body sided with the black students and occupied several key campus buildings, closed the university, and threatened to burn it down unless the original agreement was ratified by the faculty. Although I was nominally on the staff, my sentiments were on the side of the students, and Juliet and I were with about eight thousand infuriated demonstrators in the gymnasium at the moment of the deadline when Professor Robert Asher of the anthropology department entered the hall and asked for "a few more hours." He told us that he had been with the faculty and that they were meeting continuously and were about to come to a decision he thought would be agreeable to the black students and their supporters. I knew Asher because he had been on my graduate committee, but few others did. He did not introduce himself, and he spoke for only about one minute; but his sincerity was evident, and there is no doubt in my mind that in that minute he prevented the certain torching of Cornell University. I do not know if Asher was acting on behalf of his colleagues or on his own. Either way, it took enormous courage to do what he did.

I was still "under thirty" and very restless. Juliet was finishing her Ph.D. It was highly unlikely that we could both find appropriate positions at Cornell, and no one should have to commute to or from Ithaca, New York. We agreed that if Juliet could find a faculty position in Boston or Philadelphia, I would quit Cornell and follow, even without prospects. Our reasoning was that she could begin her career, and I could write *The Tourist,* and that I might pursue postdoctoral studies in Boston with Noam Chomsky or in Philadelphia, my first choice, with Erving Goffman. And that is just the way it worked out. Almost. Juliet was appointed assistant professor of French at Haverford College, on the Philadelphia main line. So at the end of one year I quit Cornell, and we moved.

From my twelfth year on, the month of August 1969 has been the only time I was ever unemployed. I have quit several times and desired nothing more than to be unemployed, but have never been so honored. It also happens that during the month of my unemployment, while doing nothing, I made about five thousand dollars, a sum that is difficult for me to duplicate even in today's inflated currency. On September

3 or 4, I walked into the Temple University sociology department asking to teach a section of the introductory course for pocket money; I was offered, on the spot, an assistant professorship. When in a somewhat bewildered state I accepted, I was told that the university owed me two months back pay since technically I was hired as of July 1. This windfall, combined with six weeks of severance pay from Cornell (one month earned vacation plus two weeks of unused sick leave), made a goodly sum. Experience has convinced me that the reason I have little money is because I work so hard, and if I was only smart enough to stop working again, I would surely be rich. The richest people I have met do not work, and the poorest landless agricultural laborers are the hardest workers I know.

At Temple I eventually took over the required courses in graduate theory (classical and modern) from Roscoe Hinkle, who was about to return to Ohio State University. I taught these courses using close-reading methods I learned in literature seminars at Cornell. The students read theoretical texts by Durkheim, Simmel, Marx, Mead, and so on, usually four a semester, as well as selected secondary comments, reviews, and extended analyses of the original texts. Their assignment for each of the original thinkers was to show exactly how a particular secondary comment (of their own choosing) was in *error* in its evaluation or appraisal of the original text, using that text as evidence. The assignment worked at several levels, from simple misreadings and errors in accounting for facts to total failure on the part of the critic to understand the original theory. The students in all cases used this assignment to find the limits of their own critical abilities, learned basic theory seemingly by accident, covered much of the secondary literature, and developed considerable self-confidence in the process. The seminar often had more than fifty graduate students in it, drawn from all the social-science disciplines and professional schools on campus. Several students began or finished their Ph.D. work with me at Temple and went on to become professors: Grace Chao Ayang, Edward Armstrong, Janet Connolly, Glenn Jacobs, Patrick Nolan, and Deborah Schiffrin. In the early 1970s I taught a seminar in ethnomethodology and semiotics, the first such course given anywhere, I believe.

On arrival in Philadelphia I took Goffman's seminar in social organization at Penn, as planned, sitting in the course with my friend Robert Maxwell, also a postdoctoral student. In addition, I was hired by Paul Hare to work as senior research associate in the Haverford College Center for Peace Research, where I helped write training manuals for demonstration marshalls and wrote my monograph *A Dramaturgical Analysis of 146 Protest Demonstrations.* All this may sound like a fast and smooth beginning, but it was not. I was very fond of several of my junior colleagues at Temple, including Mark Hutter, Margaret Zahn, Patrick Luck, Richard Juliani, and Kenneth Reichstein, but I noticed right away that it was the less likable ones who were being advanced in the department. Where did I fit into this system, I wondered. Then, as soon as Juliet's departmental chairman at Haverford heard that I was to be employed, he fired her, effective at the end of her first year, commenting to me, "That is simply too much money for a young couple to have," and "I hear there may be something part-time for her at Beaver College." My reaction was irrational from an economic standpoint, but it satisfied my passions: I resigned my Temple appointment, also effective at the end of the first year. I still had not been able to begin writing *The Tourist,* and I had not yet developed a taste for dealing with the bureaucrats, weightless liberals, and small-time real-estate speculators who also happen to be faculty members and administrators in American universities.

Looking forward to freedom from institutional twaddle, we decided it was a great time to have a baby. So we finished what we thought was our first and last year as professors, methodically saving one of our paychecks each month, bought tickets on the SS *France* and moved to Paris. The war in Vietnam seemed as though it would never end, and we wanted our baby to have an option for non–United States citizenship. We were also concerned that we were among the "unindicted coconspirators" in the Harrisburg trial of the Berrigan brothers. The United States government had indicted the Berrigans and several other friends of ours for having "conspired to kidnap Henry Kissinger." Paris was the only place, we thought, to be unemployed and pregnant, inclined toward rural sociology and semiotics, and possibly fugitives.

Everything worked out as we had planned, except the unemployed part. Our son Daniel got his French citizenship in the American Hospital in Paris. I finished the first draft of *The Tourist* and gave speeches on guerrilla strategy at antiwar teach-ins. But immediately on my arrival I was contacted by the American College to teach their sociology courses. Their regular professor had suddenly fallen ill. I accepted.

When the U.S. and South Vietnamese armies attacked the Ho Chi Minh Trail and failed to stop the southward flow of supplies, I knew the war would soon end. I also knew that the United States government would take revenge on the universities by initiating an academic repression that would last at least a decade or until the coalition that had formed between intellectuals, Western social scientists, Third World peoples, and marginal domestic groups was broken. I felt directly and personally threatened and wanted desperately to return to the United States. I wanted a position in a strong, research-oriented agricultural university where I might monitor, up close, efforts to destroy recently hard-won knowledge about social and cultural development. I was even able to imagine in advance the precise form that the repression would take, namely, the redefinition of development in entirely business, economic, and technical terms, leaving out any serious consideration of culture or social consciousness except as constraints to be overcome. But at that moment there were no such academic positions to be found, certainly not for the generation of 1968. In fact, there were no jobs, period.

Then with uncannily accurate timing came a letter from Jack V. Buerkle, chairman of the sociology department at Temple. The letter explained that he and the dean had eventually decided to refuse to accept my resignation, that they had extended to me a one-year leave of absence without pay, and that they were expecting me to return and resume teaching the theory courses in September. There is something structurally peculiar about universities that makes traditional lines of authority something of a joke, and people who seek power within universities are often either deluded careerists or really serious political conservatives. But it has been my good fortune to serve under several department chairpersons and academic administrators who are also excellent and insightful, albeit low-key, human beings. Olaf Larsen at Cornell, Jack Buerkle at Temple, and Orville Thompson at Davis are among the best. I was, and am, genuinely grateful for Buerkle's help at that crucial moment. We returned to Philadelphia as requested.

The next four years were characterized by the usual academic combination of institutional success and personal poverty. I sent out my first papers for publication on my own: an empirical analysis of the causes of poverty (based on my dissertation) and a semiotically informed ethnographic report on an aspect of face-to-face interaction. *Economic Development and Cultural Change* sent back the usual petty and indecisive quasi-acceptance, but Thomas A. Sebeok, editor in chief of *Semiotica*, was unequivocal in his positive response. He made me want to publish and had an important effect on the form and direction of my writing that extends to this day. With fine teaching evaluations and acceptances coming in from *American Journal of Sociology, Human Organization,* and elsewhere, the annual renewal notes on my assistant professor's contract by the senior faculty were always unanimous. At the same time we were so poor that we could not afford to buy blankets for our bed or stay in hotels at professional meetings. My field notes were stacked in cardboard boxes around our apartment. We survived by my moonlighting at Rutgers against the expressed will of my dean at Temple and by contract research at Holmesburg Prison. The Law Enforcement Assistance Agency wanted to know why the inmates had stabbed the warden and assistant warden to death with sharpened screwdrivers. The inmates readily admitted their crime and said it was for political reasons and to dramatize their situation. Marge Zahn, Bob Kleiner, and I convinced the LEAA that an ethnographic report on living conditions might provide a more detailed understanding of the problem. So for a year, once or twice a week, I went unprotected into the prison population, including murderers and rapists, to feed my family. My situation was precisely that of all of the guards and most of the professional criminals in lockup: We all faced down each other to get a living. Actually, I was safer on my own than if I had enjoyed the protection of the guard. The custodial staff hated my presence, so I had to depend entirely on my friends among the inmates, which is the first thing both prisoners and ethnographers must learn in order to have a chance at survival.

In the course of my life I have driven across the United States from coast to coast a total of fourteen times, often taking about a month to make the trip, staying on back roads. Once, though, I drove from San Francisco to Ithaca, New York, in three days, unassisted. Most of those trips were made during the summers in the gas crisis years, 1971 to 1975. As soon as school was out in the spring, we would load our car full of books, field data, and notes, drive to Juliet's family home in the San Francisco Bay area, stay for the summer, and drive back to Philadelphia at the end of August, sometimes stopping at the national sociology meetings on the way. I began making observations for my current project on "American Mythologies" during those annual migrations. I am just now old enough to know what a slow worker I really am, that a project usually takes me about ten years from start to finish.

I did most of my writing in those years in Juliet's parents' garage on a table between the washing machine and the ironing board. Juliet's mother, Patricia Flower, was an extraordinary human being with acute insight into character, a gift she freely shared, getting herself into trouble with those among us nicely socialized to overlook all the little positive and negative details of thought and behavior. But I always looked forward to my conversations with her, and I miss them now. She was my best friend. The two traits I admire most are not often found together in the same person: critical insight that cuts to the heart, and love and acceptance of everything that is human. Patricia Flower had both those qualities in as great a measure as I have witnessed in anyone, although Goffman was a close second.

I pretend to no expertise when it comes to raising children. I fashioned a few crude principles at the beginning, focusing mainly on language, and held to them. We read to our children for at least an hour every night starting from when they were only a few months old. (And they still read, beg to read, for at least an hour every night, usually much longer.) I also made it my unwavering practice to discuss and explain everything with them from the moment of their birth, exactly as if they were an adult companion, even though that practice occasionally drew concerned stares from strangers in public places. And from the first utterance, we never let a mispronunciation or grammatical error go uncorrected. Interestingly, language is not something a very young child takes personally, and this model of precision and early adult competency extended itself easily and naturally into every other area of my children's lives (except, of course, sports). Today, at ages eleven and fourteen, Jason and Daniel are my traveling companions of first choice and my favorite conversation partners, as well as critical colleagues and the best audience around for a bawdy joke (and the best tellers). They have honored me with unforced respect, which far exceeds reasonable expectation, and from the moment of their conception have given me nothing but the greatest pleasure.

In 1973 and 1974 Goffman was sending my completed manuscript of *The Tourist* around to his contacts to help me find a publisher. I believe his effort was genuine, but he simply had no luck. Or, his contacts were enjoying rejecting my manuscript, something they might have wanted to do to Goffman himself but were afraid. After a year he gave it back to me, saying he was sorry but I was on my own. I got contract offers, including substantial cash advances, by return mail from both Schocken Books and the Johns Hopkins University Press. *The Tourist* remains in print to this day, selling as well now as in its first year, but only recently have sociologists begun to read it. In the first few years it seems to have been read mainly by architects, artists, and anthropologists, and it made many new friends for me in those fields. I was especially lucky to have met the great critic of modern architecture, Donald Appleyard, through *The Tourist* and to have many interesting and thoroughly enjoyable conversations with him before his untimely death in the early 1980s.

In the mid-1970s sociology seemed to be falling apart, mentally and physically. The University of Pennsylvania turned off the electricity at the Center for Urban Ethnography. I worried that if Goffman, William Labov, and Del Hymes could not keep their workshop open, who could? My closest ally among the senior faculty at Temple, Bruce Mayhew, resigned. One night Paul Hare dropped by. Recently divorced, he had a French friend with him and was as bright-eyed as a kid. He told me he was leaving for South Africa to head the sociology department at a university there. He took from his jacket pocket an associate professor's contract and a one-way ticket to Johannesburg, which he said were mine. All I had to do was sign them. I said something impolite like "You fucking maniac—what do I want to go to South Africa for?" Hare was dignified. "Because the war is over here. Because we need you. Because South Africa is where the next great revolution in human relations is going to take place. Because it is your chance to help make history." I did not even glance at Juliet as I handed Paul back his offer. My second son, Jason, was soon to be born, and I made one of those "choices." As it happened, that was my last chance to have a career in sociology.

For several years my friend Isao Fujimoto and a few others had been struggling with some success on the West Coast to bring human values into agricultural research at the University of California, Davis, and to establish a focus on food as well as commodities, on workers as well as machines, and on the needs of family farmers and rural ethnic groups as well as major agribusiness corporations. One day in 1974 Fujimoto called me up. "Could you come out and lend a hand?" I have always regarded Isao Fujimoto as one of America's living national treasures. "Certainly," I said. When I arrived, I found the Department of Applied Behavioral Sciences under Orville Thompson to be a structuralist's dream. It had a distinguished design group (now a separate department), a museum of Third World art, and subprograms in Asian American and Native American studies, as well as the community development group, of which Fujimoto and I were part.

Davis would eventually turn out to be an ideal setting for Juliet and me to write *The Time of the Sign*, a series of critical and theoretical essays designed for the social sciences and the humanities but without any specific disciplinary framework. Applied behavioral sciences was explicitly interdisciplinary, even antidisciplinary, in its original conception, and none of the discipline-based humanities or social-science departments had sufficient force or desire to co-opt our little semiotic revolution. We wanted to show that minds can exist outside of institutional categories and that many important questions in the social sciences and the humanities are not being asked from within the disciplines. In fact, a new life and career sprung forth from *The Time of the Sign,* as well as a new network of friends, including Thomas and Jean Sebeok, John Deely and Brooke Williams, Paul Bouissac, Paolo Fabbri, Umberto Eco, Jonathan Culler and Cynthia Chase, Nancy Armstrong and Leonard Tennenhaus, Louis Marin, Tony Wilden, Julia Palacios and Daniel Pedrero, Susan Buck Morss, and many others. In 1985 I was elected United States representative to the International Semiotic Studies Association. Juliet was called into a tenure position in comparative literature and English at the University of California, Irvine, where she teaches contemporary critical theory, something that was simply not possible at Davis. (Her thousand-mile-a-week commute actually brought enormous relief from the almost complete failure of her Davis colleagues to understand her work.) We are co–executive editors of the *American Journal of Semiotics.* Separated geographically we continue to collaborate. Ironically, after a ten-year hiatus, *The Time of the Sign* has begun to establish a link back to sociology, making new friends for us in that field, including Bennetta Jules-Rosette, Alain Cohen, Fred Davis, and Harold Garfinkel. (Of course, there were some friends in sociology who remained constant throughout, notably Erving Goffman and Bennett Berger.)

During most of this decade of intense semiotic activity that has carried us to many interesting parts of the world, I have served as chairman of graduate studies in community development at Davis. In this capacity I have honestly tried to create some new institutional arrangements for whole human beings. In its original conception, at Davis, community development meant research on material conditions and class relations, work, industry and agriculture, and the effect of all of these on community life. It meant communication and understanding (and failures of understanding) between ethnic groups at the community level. It meant understanding language, art, architecture, music, games, ceremony, and ritual, all that makes community life interesting, even possible. Finally, it meant advanced critical evaluation of larger social issues, nuclear technology and politics, gender relations, the environment, poverty, and inequality. In short, the program was originally designed around the production of knowledge that empowers people to create their own collective destiny. After we were able to recruit Marc Pilisuk from Berkeley, we had some of the best faculty available for these purposes.

I wrote Lévi-Strauss about the promise of the Department of Applied Behavioral Sciences at Davis shortly after my arrival in 1976. He wrote back saying that he was fascinated and he would certainly visit if he ever left France. Much to my surprise, he actually did visit in the winter of 1985 to receive an important honor from the university. We had a beer in the Davis faculty club. I told him about the design group, the museum, Indian art, studies of the structure of agriculture, ethnic groups, critical theory, and semiotics. What about them? The original pieces continue to exist, I explained, but, after the fashion of all institutional "progress," not together, not as a structural totality. Lévi-Strauss raised one eyebrow and looked down at the table.

CHAPTER EIGHT

From Socialism to Sociology

Nathan Glazer

A young scholar, Douglas Webb, has been at work for a few years on a book he proposes to title *From Socialism to Sociology*. I hope he does not mind me appropriating it for this memoir, for I am one of those—we seem to be legion—who has followed that trajectory. There are different variants of those of us who have managed the passage. I am tempted to construct one of those fourfold tables beloved of sociologists with the horizontal axis reading "strong or weak final commitment" and the vertical reading "strong or weak initial commitment." The upper left-hand box holds those who were solidly socialist and ended up solid sociologists. Three other possibilities exist, including the lower right-hand box containing those whose commitment to socialism was not as firm as it might have been—and whose commitment to sociology is not as firm as it might be.

Despite Saint Paul's injunction against those who blow neither hot nor cold, I feel I am best placed in that lower right-hand box. This is not to say I have no commitments, but they were not to socialism then, nor to sociology now. It is true that before college, during college, and after college I thought of myself as a socialist. But by 1947 I was no longer writing articles in which, directly or indirectly, I indicated such an affiliation. My transition from socialism to sociology occurred rapidly. My fourfold table does not include all crucial possibilities: there were those who were socialists before becoming sociologists and remained socialists after becoming sociologists. But in the mid- and late 1940s there was something about sociology—for those of us who were socialists and were becoming sociologists—that undermined faith.

Certainly, the kind of sociologist I became was affected by the kind of socialist I was. I was a socialist not by conversion but by descent. My father always voted for Norman Thomas for president. I recall—it must have been the 1936 election, when many New York socialists and social democrats were voting for Franklin D. Roosevelt, on the new American Labor party ticket, designed for such as they—becoming aware on election day that my father, a quiet man who did not try to convert anyone to anything, had voted for Norman Thomas. His children of voting age had voted for Roosevelt and the others naturally supported Roosevelt. (He had seven children, and I was the youngest.) But the term *socialist by descent* in New York City in the 1930s requires further definition: I was what would be called today a social democrat. Again, it was a matter of descent. My father, though mild, was strongly anticommunist. He was a member of the International Ladies Garment Workers Union and, after the fierce battle over control of the union in the 1920s, communists had as bad a reputation among ILGWU members as among middle Americans. Had he been a member of the Fur Workers Union, my politics by descent would very likely have been communist.

Undoubtedly other parts of my early political and cultural makeup must also be ascribed to family influences. My father was an observant Jew, but he read the *Forward,* not the *Morning Journal,* and did not like those who made too much of their orthodoxy. He expected his children to go to synagogue, as he did. Since he did not base his expectation on intellectual or theological grounds, there was no way of disputing him on those grounds, had we been of a mind to. To him it was simply what was done, without explanation or justification. His mildness extended to Zionism: ours was not a Zionist household, but neither was it anti-Zionist. He was content to send his children to a Hebrew school that taught Hebrew and displayed a map of Palestine, the Jewish national flag, and the Jewish National Fund collection box. He did not especially seek out a Yiddishist school, though that was the language he and my mother used at home and, I am sure, at work. I cannot recall him ever speaking English, though I think he could. In the clothing shops in which he worked, while there might be Italian and other workers, there were always enough Jewish workers, and Jewish foremen and owners, to make Yiddish a shop tongue. I do remember my mother speaking some English, however: I would go shopping with her, and not all the tradesmen were Jews.

I suspect that Jewish eclecticism was common in New York when I was growing up: socialist, but not too socialist; Orthodox, but not too Orthodox; friendly to Palestine, but not a Zionist; Yiddish-speaking, but not a Yiddishist. I was aware—who could not be?—of those who were more intense about‘some part of this mix and of those who were communists. Even in my father's *landsmanshaft*, a club or organization of people who came from the same town or village in Eastern Europe, there was at least one reader of the Jewish communist daily *Freiheit*. Our family culture rejected the extremes—an intense commitment to communism, Orthodoxy, freethinking, anarchism, Yiddish. Of all the Jewish variants of the day, the one for which I think my father had the most respect was Young Israel—the "modern" Orthodox youth organization that supported the creation of a Jewish state.

I speak of my father, not my mother, though she was by far the more vivid personality. She did not have strong views about anything outside the realm of proper personal and familial behavior. There she could be a terror. But when it came to all those variants of Jewish religion, politics, and culture into which the Jewish population of New York had splintered, she had no strong views except that, like my father, she opposed all excess and extremism.

In education, once again I think we were placed with that very large group, not written about much in memoirs and histories, in which the passion for education was muted. This meant we would get more education than our Italian neighbors, but we were not expected to go to college. My father's formal education was limited to a few years of religious school in Poland; he read Yiddish and the Hebrew prayer book. Both my parents wrote long letters in Yiddish to those they left behind in Poland.

We knew there were Jewish parents who were indifferent to education and showed their indifference by insisting that their children go to work, in the family store, or as errand boys, or doing whatever they could to bring in some cash. Poor as we were, there was no pressure to work while we were going to school. And I suspect my older brothers and sisters simply followed the norm for Jewish immigrant and second-generation children of their ages. My oldest brother went to work at twelve or thereabouts—but at that time graduation from high school was far from universal. The next two children, my older sisters, went to high school and took the commercial course. The next brother was the first over whose education there was family conflict: to go to a regular high school; my parents, thinking of our needs, insisted to his distress that he attend a trade school. Graduating during the Depression, he never worked at his trade.

The three youngest children all began college—my brother finished (and went beyond), and my sister left after a few years to go to work. I am enough of a sociologist to know that the fact that I was not put under any pressure to work or contribute to family expenses was simply because I was the youngest. I showed no sign of being the brightest; indeed, some evidence indicates that I was not. But I was able to pursue my education wherever it would take me. I do not recall my parents ever making a suggestion as to what I should become or do. My next oldest brother, the only other sibling who graduated from college, was my "manager," noting that I did well at school and figuring out what would be best for me.

I liked drawing. In another family someone might have suggested that I pursue a career based on that. But by the time I entered high school, it seemed clear—why, I do not know—I would do something with words, not in math, science, or the arts. The fact is role models were in scarce supply. I recall there was someone on our block who had become a high-school teacher. He was the object of universal admiration, as it was known to be very hard for Jews to become high-school teachers. It was believed they could not pass the oral examination because of their Jewish accent. But enough did: there were quite a few Jewish teachers in my high school, James Monroe, which we were told was the largest in the world—sixteen thousand students. Most of them attended "annexes," high-school classes in elementary-school and junior high-school buildings, and even when we got to the main buildings, we attended only a half-session, morning or afternoon. Classes were large, and it was not possible for teachers to pay much attention to us. We seemed often (perhaps more commonly in elementary school and junior high school) to be arranged by size, the smallest in the front and the largest, unfairly, doubling up in the back seats.

But the education must have been sound. For one thing, the curriculum was dictated by the requirements for entry into the city colleges, City, Hunter, Brooklyn, and Queens: three years of one language, two of another, four years of English, two and a half years of math, and similar amounts of history and science. One did have electives: most of my classmates added physics or trigonometry to their two or three years of math and science. In my senior year I took the course that made the deepest impression on me, fourth-year French, and found myself in a small class in which the first assignment was to read eighty pages of a detective story. (I had never before been asked to read more than three pages of French.) It certainly did wonders for my facility in reading, if nothing else.

The first glimmer of what was to end up as a career in sociology was neither an exceptional curiosity about the social world nor a bent arising from family culture. Rather, I realized that one should pursue one's best chances, and since I was not particularly good at math and science, and no one dreamed of a career in the arts, it had to be words. But what to do with words was not clear.

I entered City College in February 1940 (City in those days had two entering and graduating classes a year, keyed to the New York City public-school calendar) and majored in history. I liked history and had a good memory. But my academic life soon had to contend with another interest. I was persuaded by a fellow student to attend a meeting of Avukah, the student Zionist organization. I was not a Zionist but was willing to hear what there was to be said for Zionism. It was an accident that had a strong impact on the rest of my life. The speaker was Seymour Melman, a recent graduate of City College who had just spent a year in Palestine and was reporting on his experiences. Had Avukah been simply a Jewish organization, I doubt that it would have made much impact on me. But these were *socialist* Zionists. What is more, they were *intellectual* socialist Zionists and looked down on nonintellectual socialist Zionists.

Melman was a charismatic figure. (The author of many books, he is now a professor of industrial engineering at Columbia University. At the time there was no hint of what he might become—as was true of most of us.) What led me to speak to him after his lecture I do not know. But soon I was on the staff of *Avukah Student Action* (the organization's national newspaper) and had become a Zionist; indeed, before that was settled, I was named editor. No loyalty oaths were required to become a member of Avukah. We had a three-point program, presented in documents portentously titled "theses," and in theoretical pamphlets. The organization may have been Zionist but the culture was in most ways left sectarian. We were generally allied on campus issues with the anti-Stalinist left—the socialists and the Trotskyites.

The three points of our program were to build a "non-minority Jewish center in Palestine," to fight fascism, and to foster a democratic American Jewish community. This program represented a somewhat off-center Zionism. The term *non-minority* was meant to leave room for a binational state of Jews and Arabs. In those days we believed it possible for the two nations to share power, with neither being in the minority in a political or cultural sense. Our notion was that if both nations were guaranteed equal political rights, the Arab majority of Palestine would allow unrestricted Jewish immigration. At a time when Jews were being hunted down by the Nazis, when the doors of the United States and other Western countries were closed to Jewish refugees, and when Palestine itself had been closed to Jewish immigration by the British, unrestricted immigration was the minimal demand of every Zionist group, even one as eccentric as ours. In retrospect, our views were naive.

Avukah was a switching point on the road from socialism to sociology. At first it emphasized the socialism, of which I knew little until I became involved. But Avukah, following the pattern of other left sectarian organizations, had "study groups," in which we read not only Zionist classics but also socialist classics. Bukharin's *Historical Materialism* was particularly favored by some of our elders. But we were not Leninists. Though left, and critical of social democrats, the radical leaders of Avukah who tried to influence us were (Rosa) Luxemburgian—revolutionary, but against a directing central party and for education of the working masses. It was a very congenial bent. The only issues that called for action were Zionist ones; for the rest, education was sufficient. The doctrine hardly mattered, I am convinced. It is almost embarrassing to say we believed in revolution. The only way to relieve the embarrassment is to confess that we really did not.

What actually mattered to us was not our doctrines but the people we met and the things we read. For example, we read *Partisan Review* and *The New International,* in which Sidney Hook, James Burnham, and Dwight Macdonald then wrote. We often invited Macdonald to our summer camps, devoted to intensive "education." He had started the journal *Politics;* some members of our group attended the early meetings and some wrote for it. My predecessors at *Avukah Student Action* had been Chester Rapkin, then beginning a career as a housing economist that would lead him to Columbia and Princeton, and Harold Orlans, who studied anthropology at Yale while working in an insane asylum as a conscientious objector during World War II (he wrote brilliantly on the joint experience for *Politics*). Alfred J. Kahn, one of the three (very modestly paid) officers of Avukah, was to become a leading social worker and analyst of social policy; another, Meir Rabban, was to become, after some years in Palestine and Israel, a professor of psychology at Sarah Lawrence. It would be impossible to list all the members of Avukah who became professors. No one expected that they would become professors before the war.

As editor of *Avukah Student Action* one of my duties—as Chester Rapkin explained—was to liven up the pages with pictures and cartoons, and I could find them free at the *New Leader* by burrowing through a pile of cuts they received from unions and other sources. There I met Daniel Bell. An informal seminar took place every Friday afternoon at the *New Leader* office. I did not participate directly but listened as I looked for something we could use in *Avukah Student Action*. Seymour Martin Lipset, with whom for a while I took the subway to college, joined Avukah briefly. He told me about the gifted and learned new Marxist refugee, Lewis Coser.

Thus a second effect of Avukah was to introduce me to the New York intellectual milieu. I will not exaggerate my modest position: I went to more meetings than I can remember on what is living and what is dead in Marxism, and I heard Philip Selznick, then moving steadily toward sociology, speak brilliantly. Just what he said I no longer recall.

A third effect, as the names Bell, Selznick, and Lipset suggest, was to make sociology a possibility—not as a job (who dreamed of any job except a clerkship with the government?) but as a role definition. I recall I abandoned history for economics, economics for public administration, public administration for sociology, and graduated in January 1944 with a degree in sociology.

The inner core of Avukah believed in social science as the handmaiden of socialism and revolution. In our little study groups we learned about Erich Fromm's *Escape from Freedom* and about the interesting mix of the two scientific approaches, as we then thought of them, of psychoanalysis and Marxism being developed by the Frankfurt school, some of whose members had just arrived in the United States. Later, when Max Horkheimer was lecturing at Columbia, we all went religiously. After one or two lectures, he turned over the course to Leo Lowenthal. We were all deeply impressed by Lowenthal's range of learning. We read articles from the old *Zeitschrift für Sozialforschung*, aided by our German-reading members (young refugees), and from *Studies in Social Science and Philosophy*. We learned about Horkheimer, Lowenthal, Herbert Marcuse, Theodor Adorno, and Walter Benjamin before they became the objects of serious study, though we did not learn much about them—that may have been our failing. Having known them in their early years in America (of course, not Walter Benjamin; he, alas, never made it to the United States) colors our reading about the Frankfurt school now, when they have become legendary figures.

It was clear my bent toward social science owed more to nonacademic influences than to City College. I did not get to sociology until my third or fourth year. Though the sociology department had some able people, it did not influence me greatly. I remember other courses, in philosophy and psychology, better. These were the areas of strength at City College then, but I found that out too late.

I did learn one thing in the sociology department of City College, though. I learned about community studies and was fascinated by them. I wrote an honors paper on American community studies, and without ever having been to Chicago, I was converted to the Chicago style of ethnographic sociology. I knew very little about it, but I knew it was the kind of sociology I liked best.

By 1942, through Zelig Harris, one of the older people connected with Avukah and a gifted theoretical linguist, I had an opportunity to join a small wartime group at the University of Pennsylvania who were trained under Harris in what was then called descriptive linguistics. We were to specialize in various African languages and prepare teaching materials in case we were called on to teach them to soldiers. At that time I was in my third major at City College (public administration) with the vague thought it would help me get a government job. I leaped at the chance to work with Harris, and on something for which I would be paid (modestly). Harris believed that the only really difficult subjects were mathematics and theoretical physics and that anyone could learn linguistics and languages, in short order. He gave me two books, Edward Sapir's *Language* and Leonard Bloomfield's *Language,* and a few theoretical articles, and said, "Really, that's all there is. You won't have to spend much time on it [learning linguistics]." His was the arrogance of a supremely gifted mind. In time I was to be part of a team teaching Bengali; another team taught Moroccan Arabic. My own language, Swahili, was never called on. The fact that I was assigned Swahili indicated either that the American military was then very pessimistic (it is spoken in Tanzania and understood in the surrounding countries) or that Harris was particularly interested in it. Meanwhile I took courses in anthropology with A. Irving Hallowell and worked on a master's thesis on Swahili.

In the spring of 1944 I received a master's degree from the University of Pennsylvania and a fellowship to study there for a doctorate in anthropology. Hallowell took me aside and said it was not a sensible thing to do; there would be no jobs. (Whether he also thought, and said, that there would be no jobs for Jews, I do not recall; I had the impression later that that is one of the things he must have meant, but I may be wrong.) I regret taking his advice. I realized linguistics was not for me, but I found social anthropology very appealing.

And so I returned to New York to look for a job. One of the people one saw in those days when one was looking for a job was Daniel Bell. He told me that Max Horkheimer had been hired by the American Jewish Committee to do studies on anti-Semitism and was looking for an assistant. He tried me out, and I became his reader of American social-science literature. By the time he realized that was not what he wanted, I had found a job at another branch of the American Jewish Committee, the *Contemporary Jewish Record,* then being edited, surprisingly, by Clement Greenberg, the art critic of *Partisan Review.* He appreciated my modest connections with the intellectual left (after all, I had written for *Politics*) and the fact that I must have learned something about Judaism and Jewish life and politics while I was in Avukah. I knew less than he had hoped, but more than he himself knew. The future of the *Contemporary Jewish Record* was then being reviewed by a committee headed by Lionel Trilling, whom I did not know, and as a result of their proposals it was transformed into *Commentary,* under the editorship of Elliot Cohen, not long after I joined the staff.

I was twenty-two, I had a job, but I do not know what to call the "occupation" of a staff member of the new *Commentary* of 1945. I did not call myself a journalist because I did not go out on stories, except perhaps to cover a speech. Cohen, aware of my interest in sociology, suggested I write a column on the social sciences titled "The Study of Man." One reason it suited a Jewish magazine was that so much of the research of the time dealt with anti-Semitism, incipient fascist tendencies, and national character—why were the Germans that way, or the Japanese, or the Russians? Or, for that matter, the Americans? All this interested me enormously, and the column played a role for a while in the early postwar period in bringing the work of the social sciences, in particular sociology influenced by social psychology, to an audience that would not have known it.

Simultaneously I was taking courses at Columbia toward a Ph.D. in sociology, but my time horizon was extended indeed. In those days one could work toward a Ph.D. as a part-time student, taking most of one's courses at night. Robert Merton and Paul Lazarsfeld taught at night or in the late afternoon. The classes were large. I do not know how many of those taking courses really intended to become, or did become, sociologists. I received no support, but courses cost something like $12.50 a credit. The New School, where a galaxy of German refugees was teaching, was just as cheap. Since our friends often acted as ticket takers, we could sneak in and hear Erich Fromm and Meyer Schapiro free. Had I known of them, I would have tried to listen to Alfred Schutz, Albert Salomon, and Leo Strauss, all of whom I heard later but in individual lectures rather than courses.

I would not underestimate the education I received in sociology at Columbia University; the education I received at *Commentary* was, however, deeper and wider. At Columbia those two remarkable sociologists, Merton and Lazarsfeld, were presenting an exciting picture of the possibilities of sociology as a science. Merton's lectures brilliantly illuminated the nature of sociological thinking and sociological analysis; Lazarsfeld's were equally brilliant in demonstrating how the most subtle points of theoretical analysis could be tested through the analysis of quantitative data. C. Wright Mills lectured at that time in the college rather than in the graduate sociology department. But everyone went to hear him, and, from his own perspective, he also demonstrated the possibilities of a science of sociology. A few of us worked with him Saturday mornings at the old cavernous quarters of the Bureau of Applied Social Research on Fifty-ninth Street (where the New York City Convention Center now stands). Our task was to extract from long interviews, done by a previous class for the work that ultimately became *White Collar*, evidence in quantitative form for a large statement about what was happening to society.

Certainly I was as taken by these possibilities as anyone. For a while I was enthusiastic for sociology as a science. But by 1949 I had become doubtful. In that year I published a long essay in *Commentary*, " 'The American Soldier' as Science," reflecting those doubts. Man, I wrote, was part of history, not nature, and the uniformities we might discover, whatever their interest and importance for a given time, place, and issue, could never achieve the generalizing power of theory, hypothesis, and law in the natural sciences. *The American Soldier*, a series of books on which some of the leading sociologists of the time worked, made the greatest claim to establishing sociology as a social science or at least putting it on the road to becoming one. I argued that it was simply no more than a study of the American soldier in World War II: the generalizations that flowed from it and might be used in other settings were weak and thin, and the infinite variety of situations in which men were found in history ensured that result. What we learned would inevitably be bound by time and place. My efforts at generalization after that point were carefully restricted and narrow: situation, facts, and data were crucial for determining what was in fact true, and any large statements about society, culture, personality, capitalism, industrialism, social control, and so on I met with skepticism. It always seemed to me that whatever the large generalization, one would always have to comment, "It all depends."

Was it the counterpoint of *Commentary* versus Columbia sociology that led to this result? Very likely. I spent most of my time at the magazine, and only one day or so a week at Columbia. *Commentary* was then one of the best schools one could attend (as is probably true for all intellectual magazines). There was Elliot Cohen, once a brilliant student of English at Yale and a remarkably creative editor of the *Menorah Journal*, an excellent Jewish magazine in the 1920s and 1930s. He was a radical in the early 1930s, part of that group of New York intellectuals who founded *Partisan Review* and have since become the subjects of memoirs and research.

The staff was much younger, except for Clement Greenberg, still an editor of *Partisan Review* and becoming a major figure who explained and promoted the work of the then young New York school of painters. In his double life (one assumed *Commentary* provided him with the basic living that neither *Partisan Review* nor his art reviews in *The Nation* could) he represented good English style and a particular empathy (though I am not sure that is the right word to apply to his crusty personality) for the intellectual German refugees he had strongly favored during his tenure at the *Contemporary Jewish Record*. I learned more from the younger members of the staff, and the particular view of man and society that I have presented owed the most to Irving Kristol. Kristol had come out of the same radical group that had once included Phil Selznick and Marty Lipset, but he had, without any apparent guru, abandoned socialism and radicalism and was reading European philosophers and theologians. He brought to our environment a concrete, practical interest in politics and journalism. Other members of the ongoing shifting seminar that *Commentary* was in those days included Robert Warshow, a celebrated critic who died young, Martin Greenberg, Clement's younger brother, and of course the many authors who dropped in and talked. The pressure was remarkably low. There seemed to be time for work on the magazine, attendance at Columbia courses, my own writing, and even chess games beginning at lunch that sometimes lasted through a good part of the afternoon. The concrete education received at a magazine of high standards addressed to the general reader made us intolerant of nonsense or, even if it was not nonsense, anything that could not be made clear. This attitude was in some ways a help to me as a sociologist—we have a good deal of nonsense in our discipline (what academic discipline does not?). But it perhaps also led to an unwillingness to penetrate obscurity. Considering how much of what is, and has been, important in sociology is undoubtedly obscure, this unwillingness may have been a handicap to me.

In 1946 I went to the annual meeting of the American Sociological Association in Chicago to write a column on it for *Commentary*. There I saw Dan Bell, who had recently joined the staff of the social-science survey course at the University of Chicago, and I was taken with the idea of joining it myself. I was deeply impressed with the solid grounding in sociological classics the course gave. It is hard to realize that at the time the major works of Weber and Durkheim were not translated or in print in English, and special editions had to be prepared for these courses. Not long after, David Riesman passed through New York. As a member of the staff of the social-science course he was in a position to report back on my suitability. I did not go the University of Chicago: instead I took a leave from *Commentary* and worked with David Riesman on the project that became *The Lonely Crowd* and *Faces in the Crowd*. By the time *The Lonely Crowd* was published in 1950, it was clear to me that in addition to being a social commentator, an editor, and an expert on American Jews, I was also a sociologist.

It is true that my attendance at Columbia was erratic. Some years I took no courses; others, I returned to coursework with gusto. Whether I would ever get the doctorate was neither clear nor important to me. In 1955, at the invitation of Daniel Boorstin, I gave the Walgreen lectures on American Judaism at the University of Chicago. *American Judaism*, based on those lectures, was published the next year in his series on the history of American civilization. It might have served as my Ph.D. dissertation, but in a fit of bravado I decided I did not want to adapt it.

By that time I had left *Commentary* and was working as an editor at Anchor Books. Anchor Books was the brainchild of a recent graduate of Columbia, Jason Epstein, an editor who had wanted to start an American series of serious paperbacks modeled on the British Penguin series. In 1955 all American paperback series were for the mass market. It was Epstein's idea that there was or was going to be a market for paperback books in colleges. Among the first of the books he wanted to publish was *The Lonely Crowd*. It was, however, too long for his series, which required books short enough to keep prices down. It fell on me to cut *The Lonely Crowd* by about a quarter, a task I approached not only with an eye to reducing size but also to some modest restructuring for clarity. I do feel the resultant work was easier to read, and it was that abridged edition that was read by a million American students (sales reached that figure by the early 1970s).

I have been associated with David Riesman since, and for some years as a collaborator, for following *The Lonely Crowd* we published *Faces in the Crowd*. All along we produced joint articles sociological and political, including "The Intellectuals and the Discontented Classes," which first appeared in *Partisan Review* and then in *The New Radical Right* (1955), edited by Daniel Bell. This book was a collection of essays in response to McCarthyism, on which we held a somewhat middle position owing to our sense that intellectuals could not be entirely applauded for their distance from the experience and feelings of middle America. The article—and *The Lonely Crowd*—demonstrated David Riesman's remarkable ability to understand general currents in American culture even without spending much time experiencing them directly. He can from a few fragments imagine the rest—and most of the time get it right.

The nature of our collaboration, as of all collaborations, was distinctive. When we first met, I was still excited over learning something about how to analyze qualitative questionnaires with C. Wright Mills, and Riesman thought of me as possibly bringing the then newer techniques of social science to his intended study of apathy, the origin of *The Lonely Crowd*. And indeed, we did work with questionnaires of various selected groups and occasionally individuals either selected or found accidentally (many are in *Faces in the Crowd*). We also tried to develop ways of extracting meaning from them. But my role changed as we worked together. Influenced by the scientizing tendency of social science in those distant days, I tried to put Riesman's ideas, which were always intensely concrete, into some more general structure. He would take my bare, thin manuscripts and expand and embroider them, filling them with evocative details. These details often fought with the structure, and that clash is what many readers of *The Lonely Crowd* felt.

Collaboration with Riesman at Yale was an experience of living and working together, exchanging manuscripts for revision, expansion, and clarification (Riesman doing most of the elaboration, I attempting to introduce order). I believe, from conversations with Christopher Jencks, a later collaborator, that he too tried to bring order to the richness and variety of Riesman's insights. That often meant sacrificing a few of them. So many thoughts and observations in so many directions was not my style: my work alone is rather more bare and, I must confess, less original.

Collaborating with Riesman involved more than scholarly work: for him, as for me, analysis and action (at least some kinds of action) were never far apart. While we worked on *The Lonely Crowd,* Israel was being born. Riesman opposed a Jewish state, as did his mentor Erich Fromm, and as I did, from my own perspective. Riesman became involved in efforts to divert the steady march to the creation of such a state. I participated to some extent in those efforts. In retrospect, however, I believe the opposition did not fully grasp the power of the demands by the two ethnic groups, Jews and Arabs, for separate and independent states regardless of the costs—internal disorder and poverty in many Arab states, eternal conflict for Israel. I believe now that there was no alternative to statehood; Riesman's thinking has not proceeded in that direction.

On the danger of nuclear warfare we shared the same view, and this was one of the principal concerns of the Committees of Correspondence, which Riesman helped organize in the late 1950s and which I served for a while as editor of its newsletter. Riesman's path was from liberalism to sociology, rather than socialism to sociology; he was never a socialist. But he retained, as I did, a sense of sociology as more than a scientific discipline divorced from a life involved in political and social issues. Sociology is still for many socialists and sociologists the pursuit of politics through academic means, though it is today a far different politics, pursued with different means.

As a result of my work in abridging *The Lonely Crowd,* Jason Epstein asked me to join him at Anchor Books, and I left *Commentary.* My years at Anchor also served as an education: in an institution in which there were almost no Jews (the first time in my life I was in such an environment); in the strange divorce between commercial publishing and what I conceived of as the intellectual life, a divorce that it fell on Jason Epstein to overcome; in the incredibly dynamic quality of American business. For no sooner had the first dozen paperbacks come out at Anchor than we already had competitors—many of them. Unlike us, Penguin had had a clear run of some years because no one had thought to challenge it.

For some reason I did not think of myself as someone who would remain in magazine publishing when at *Commentary,* nor as someone who would remain in book publishing when at Anchor. The option of sociology was always available, and undoubtedly something in my temperament kept pushing me toward academic life.

In 1957 I joined the staff of the Communism in American Life project, funded by the Fund for the Republic (itself funded by the Ford Foundation), to write a book on the question of who became communists in the United States. Marty Lipset was originally supposed to do the book but decided not to and suggested I do it. It looked like a good idea, and I left Anchor. I thought that topic would fit the bill for a Ph.D. dissertation in sociology and submitted the published book, *The Social Basis of American Communism,* to Columbia University in 1962 to complete the requirements for the degree.

By that time I had already taught as a visitor at the University of California, Berkeley, at Bennington College, and at Smith College. I felt like a medieval journeyman, going from place to place with my tattered course outlines. But I had more or less defined my role as a sociologist. I taught race relations, or the sociology of ethnic groups, as well as urban sociology—I was, or felt myself to be, an heir to the University of Chicago tradition. I filled out my schedule with other courses—social change, nonquantitative research methods, and a variety of other topics. At Bennington I taught a course on women in developing societies. Over the years I thought of a number of projects in ethnicity or urbanism and finally ended up doing a study of the ethnic groups of New York City; this project became *Beyond the Melting Pot* (1963).

Beyond the Melting Pot was my second major effort in collaboration, but in this one I took the lead. It was not to be the end of my work with Daniel P. Moynihan, for afterward we considered, particularly after I relocated at Harvard in the late 1960s, conducting conferences and publishing multiauthor volumes on ethnicity as an international phenomenon. One such volume was published, *Ethnicity* (1975). I helped organize another conference on international dimensions of ethnicity and social policy, which has resulted in another book, edited with Ken Young, *Ethnic Pluralism and Public Policy* (1983). My original intention in *Beyond the Melting Pot* was to recruit a number of persons who had experience as members of an ethnic group and knew it from the inside to participate in a joint work I had outlined. Each section was intended to fit into an overall thesis about the character and meaning of ethnicity in New York and, by implication, in American society. At the time ethnicity was not a hot topic, and it was hard to find people I respected who were willing to collaborate within the framework I had designed. Moynihan was then at Syracuse University, after serving with Governor Averell Harriman. He had already written widely noted articles in *The Reporter,* then edited by Irving Kristol, particularly on the epidemic of slaughter on the highways, which made him an authority on automobile safety long before Ralph Nader. Kristol suggested Moynihan: it was clear on the basis of early meetings he could do just about any work, including an essay on the Irish of New York that was responsive to the framework I had set out. In the end he was the only person I recruited for *Beyond the Melting Pot.*

Working with Moynihan was entirely different from working with Riesman: Moynihan's prose is so elegant that I hesitate to touch it. Our collaborations have consisted of my writing what I have to say, and he writing what he has to say; then I knit the two together at the seams. Our styles are very different, and often we are saying somewhat different things, but the method has seemed to work, as in the long introduction to the second edition of *Beyond the Melting Pot* and the introduction to *Ethnicity.* Daniel Bell played a key role in the origins of *Beyond the Melting Pot,* because he suggested me to his friend James Wechsler of the *New York Post,* who was considering doing a series of articles on the ethnic groups of New York. The New York Post Foundation put up some money—a very modest sum. The foundation didn't like the first installments and cut off my funding, an action that may not have been legal. Whether the New York Post Foundation was a funding agency or a means of getting publishable copy for the *New York Post* was not clear to me. It also insisted, despite having withdrawn support, on sharing royalties. From its financial point of view the grant was one of the most productive it ever made.

I was not sure what I would do after *Beyond the Melting Pot.* From an academic journeyman spending a year teaching at one institution after another I had become a wandering semiacademic grantsman, collecting small grants to write one book after another. One possibility that attracted me strongly was to become an expert on Japan. During my year in Berkeley, 1961–62, I had become captivated by the Orient. Though China was closed, Japan was a possibility. I perhaps could learn Japanese and write about the one non-Western society that was becoming Westernized in some key respects (such as achieving technological competence). I would go to Japan, although to do what besides learning Japanese was not clear to me. I would tell my academic friends just to needle them; and without a definite project—except self-improvement!—I would go on my own money (I had some savings) rather than ask a foundation for a grant. My academic friends were shocked and prevailed on me not to do such a silly thing. One day when leaving Random House, where I was consulting for Jason Epstein—the publishing firm was then located in the wonderful brownstone Villard Houses that now form a forecourt for the Helmsley Palace—I decided to visit the Ford Foundation across Fifty-first Street. Doak Barnett was then working there. I told him that I wanted to go to Japan, and he asked me to write him a letter explaining what I planned to study. I did so, saying I wanted to learn about Tokyo by living in Tokyo, the way I had learned about New York by living in New York. How gloriously free and easy were the foundations in 1961! I was given a substantial grant and first-class airfare without having to trouble anyone for letters of recommendation, at a time when I held no academic position in the United States, and without having to arrange any academic affiliation in Japan.

My Japanese experience was too mixed to be summarized easily. After hard work I discovered that I would not, at thirty-nine or with my native talents, get very far in learning Japanese in the year I had available; instead, I decided to learn about Tokyo. I had some contacts and began writing about the city. I was able to publish articles, which I think still express a rather fresh sense of what makes cities work, in the *Japan Times* and in the Japanese periodical *Chuo Koron*. But it was clear I would never become an expert on Japan. I returned to the United States after one year with the strong feeling that I wanted to devote my attention to a country I could know well, as against one I could never know well, and get involved with something practical and useful to mankind. Washington, D.C., was then the seat of a wonderfully optimistic administration; Moynihan arranged for me to see a number of people, and since I now fancied myself an urban expert, I ended up in an undefined position in the Housing and Home Finance Agency (which later became the Department of Housing and Urban Development), then headed by the economist Robert Weaver. It was certainly one of the most exciting years of my life. The Peace Corps had started; major programs were being launched in the cities, with money from the Ford Foundation and the federal government, to deal with juvenile delinquency specifically and with poverty generally; the War on Poverty was being designed; and the model cities program would soon be under way. Since my job was poorly defined, I got involved in everything. But before the end of my first year Lewis Feuer, then teaching a huge (nine hundred students) social science integrated course at the University of California,

Berkeley, and finding it difficult to recruit fellow teachers in that period of ample support for academics, asked me to become a permanent member of the course staff. I had met Feuer originally through Irving Kristol, whose teacher he had been at City College. And so in 1963, at the age of forty, I became a sociologist by appointment and profession as well as through the content of my work, and I have remained one ever since.

What kind of sociologist? As a sociologist I have been more interested in specific issues than in the discipline of sociology itself, more in empirical subject matter than in theory, more in substance than in methodology. The issues, subjects, and substance have been drawn mostly from my experience. I wrote about Jews because I knew something about them and worked on a Jewish magazine. I wrote about American communists because having been a radical I had some experience of communism and felt I could understand why people become communists. I wrote about student radicalism in the 1960s and 1970s for similar reasons—and had so published *Remembering the Answers* (1970). I wrote about cities because I had always lived in New York (though by 1963 I could reckon a year in Berkeley, a year in Tokyo, and a year in Washington) and felt I knew about them; and I wrote about public policy because after my year in Washington and my subsequent involvement in various committees dealing with public policy I thought I understood that subject. I would not have dared on my own to tackle such a topic as the American character, as David Riesman did in *The Lonely Crowd*; but the one aspect of anthropology that truly interested me was the new culture and personality school of Ruth Benedict, Margaret Mead, Geoffrey Gorer, and others, and I felt fully committed to applying it to the United States. How to apply it was quite a problem: the culture-and-personality orientation has foundered on methodological issues, in part, but also because general confidence in social psychology and psychoanalysis has been deeply shaken.

Culture and personality is the only topic on which I have worked that I have fully abandoned. A book is often a hostage to the future. Even if one desires to get away from a subject, the investment of time and energy and commitments to speak or write on the subject lead, in the absence of a strong will, to reengagement with it. My involvement in ethnicity and race led into involvement in the policy issues they raised: and so *Affirmative Discrimination* (1975) and *Ethnic Dilemmas, 1964–1982* (1983). Though I have not written a book directly on urban issues, I have written many articles—and in the American context there is no way of making a sharp distinction between urban sociology and the sociology of race and ethnicity. Dealing with race, ethnicity, and urban issues, I was inevitably drawn into social policy, and much of my writing for the past fifteen years has dealt with issues in that field.

Clearly my experience has circumscribed the areas on which I feel I can write with any sense of confidence, and rarely does an article, essay, or book review of mine go beyond these bounds. I regret this narrowness. But with no base in either large theory or a generally applicable methodology, I do not feel I can deal effectively with a topic I cannot approach, at least in some measure, through experience—if not directly, then by analogy.

Plainly I am only in part a sociologist. I have also been an editor, for *Avukah Student Action,* the *Contemporary Jewish Record, Commentary,* and *The Public Interest* and at Anchor Books and Random House. The role of early connections is evident in my current editorial role with *The Public Interest,* founded by Irving Kristol and Daniel Bell while I was living in Berkeley. My succeeding Bell as coeditor reflected not only my own shift to policy concerns—a shift I date from the late 1950s and early 1960s but which was evident before—but also the shift of others, such as Kristol and Bell. Because I was, on the one hand, an editor and interpreter of ideas—not, I think, a popularizer—through my editorial roles and, on the other, interested in policy, sociology, which in its contemporary form has eschewed policy advice, was not fully congenial. Thus while I was a member of the sociology department at the University of California, my main job was the interpretive one of presenting the social sciences to non–social-science majors, and I cultivated connections with the Department of City Planning and the School of Social Work. As a member of the sociology department at Harvard my main job is in the Graduate School of Education—which is also something of a school of public policy and social issues. These mixed roles are in part a result of the mixed career I have followed and consequently of the opportunities that were offered to me; but they are in larger part a matter of taste. The skepticism about higher sociological theory that I first expressed as early as 1949 has not been modified by the history of sociology since then.

But sociology, I believe, was the only academic discipline that might have accommodated me and people like me. For a long time it was necessary to explain that sociology was not social work and not socialism. But for some of us who were involved with socialism, and who would never abandon concern with the practical issues of society that social work represented, sociology offered a spacious home. It was not necessary to vow fealty to any theory or methodology. An involvement with some key issues in the world, in which one abided by the normal canons of scholarship—read the literature, footnoted the facts, and examined the validity of one's ideas the best one could—was all that sociology demanded, at least of those who, through accidents of history, selected it as the discipline within which they would work. I hope that at the margin it will continue to offer this opportunity.

PART III

Mobility Stories

CHAPTER NINE

An Unlikely Story

John Gagnon

Naming the ways in which the events of an individual's life have influenced his or her works is necessarily a trickster's task. It requires a decision that, first, there is some work separate from the events of the life and, second, that the order of effect is from life to work. How much more interesting it might be if one asked how writing a certain article affected the way the author reared children or loved friends. Even as I submit to the usual autobiographical pretense that early life affects later life, that nonwork life affects the content of the work, I submit to the reader that we are conflating two temporary representations, the representation of a life and the representation of a body of works. Neither the events nor the works will be in this new representation what they were when experienced or produced.

This version will be full of denied absences and illusory presences, of voices strangled and ventriloquism practiced; it will add up to truths and fancies masquerading as each other. This creation of a plausible past must submit to at least two kinds of demands of the present, first to the contemporary selves that will recollect the past, and second to the present-day fashions of making autobiographical sense. When I think about my own past it seems to be a docudrama (perhaps a ficumentary, a doction, a faction) that I re-create, not quite on a daily basis but often enough, to produce a semblance of authorship for audiences of different weights and valences. There are, of course, certain epiphanies, episodes that when elaborated and condensed can be comfortably told to nearly everyone, including my self. But even these ritual professions provide only a fragile link between my recollections and the listing of works in my curriculum vitae.

Even when I reread in a current c.v. the small number of works attributed solely to Gagnon, I have no certain memory of having been the author of those texts. How much more suspect are the majority of citations listed as "... and Gagnon," "Gagnon and ...," or "..., ..., and Gagnon." Sometimes I recall the contexts in which I wrote or talked, and the colleagues who wrote or talked with me, but the ideas and the text into which they were made are strange to me. Although I am willing to take credit and salary for that portion of "it" or "them" that others believe I have done, the portion I believe I have done is somewhat different from the institutional estimates. Whatever my transient claims to *auctoritas* might have been, it is a sense of detachment that now dominates. I sometimes wish detachment would become indifference, but one must eat.

Lately I have, with some perverse comfort, begun to think of my life as an extended example of tourism. I no longer wish to be a successful native or even a virtuous traveler. I like better the figure with camera that has just stepped down from the bus to pause for a few moments in front of everyday façades crowded with tour guides, confectionery sellers, and postcard and souvenir hawkers, whose speeches and gestures and silences will only be fragmentarily understood.

My itinerary begins with conception. I traveled, while in the womb, from a Depression-gripped mining town in Arizona to be born in a dying mill town in Massachusetts. My mother was forty-three, but I was spared visible birth defects. She was a devout Roman Catholic for her entire life and came from hardworking and temperate Irish stock. She went to work in the braid shops when she was twelve. Mary Emma Murphy was married at age thirty to a French Canadian in a town where the Canucks were beginning to fall below the ambitious Portuguese in the ethnic morality play. My father had run away from home (and the cotton mills) when he was fifteen and had returned a decade later, an atheist and a Wobbly, after hoboing and hard-rock mining in Montana, Alaska, Colorado, and Arizona—or at least so the family legend went. I think I can attest to the mining, the atheism, and the anarchism, but not to the places.

In this divided house my mother forced a decision about my fate. I was to be *her* child, a child of the church, a child of Irish respectability, a printer or a post office worker—no atheism, no anarchism, no working in the mines. My father honored the bargain, though as I grew older he offered me a book or two that cast doubt on the morality of the robber barons and the mining industry. Secretly he may have been relieved by not having to bear the responsibility for my fate, but he never let on.

By the time I was four we were moving again, first to a Civilian Conservation Corps camp in Vermont and then, at the bottom of the Depression, back across the country to Bisbee, Arizona, the place of my conception. Goodbye to respectable poverty; hello, raggedy-ass poor. My mother changed my birthday to get me into school ahead of my class; I thought I was born on Columbus Day for at least another five years. Comic books, Flash Gordon, *Riders of the Purple Sage*, the Grand Ole Opry on the radio, *Life* magazine, heat lightning in the sky, barren ochre hillsides, mining slag heaps, pulled teeth, car sickness, eyeglasses, first communion, stations of the cross, nightmares. My sister went away to nurse's training at Hotel Dieu in El Paso; we took a bus to visit her when she graduated, and I saw *The Wizard of Oz*. My mother and I went to church; I skipped catechism, was afraid of the nuns and God, lied at confession, and played alone. My father read books and made speeches, and they ran us out of town.

We looked like Okies, and at the Yuma crossing into California the state police treated us like Okies. They said they were looking for prohibited fruit and vegetables that might be hiding the precursors of the dreaded Mediterranean fruit fly. So my father took the mattress off the roof of the Model A and emptied out all of the boxes and pillowcases and suitcases onto the ground. The cops fingered the cotton dresses and the denim work clothes and the worn bedding, but did not find what they were looking for. Welcome to the Garden of Eden.

Long Beach during World War II *was* paradise. The three of us lived in a one-room, wood-sided, canvas-roofed, army-style tent for two years and shared a one-room apartment after that. My parents slept on a Murphy bed, and I slept on the couch. I do not remember a primal scene. There was an antiaircraft battery stationed in front of the apartment building, between the boardwalk and the beach, until 1943. The night sky during the blackout was disturbingly full of stars. I learned how distant they were, and I was disturbed in a different way. I started school wearing short pants and was regularly chased home by redheaded Jimmy O'Reilly, whose father had taught him how to box. My father said I had to fight my own battles, so I took to skulking home by back alleys. My mother bought me long pants, but that did not make me brave. I liked a girl in the fifth grade and traded her mayonnaise-on-white-bread sandwiches for raw fish, but she was sent to a concentration camp in 1942.

In the center of town was one of Andrew Carnegie's libraries. By the middle of the war I had read my way though the children's section and was promoted upstairs to the adult books. I read without direction or discrimination; I was voracious, a cannibal of other lives. Sea stories, adventures, historical novels—I read *Beau Geste* and *Apartment in Athens* and *A Farewell to Arms* without raising my eyes from the continuous text. I thought *Moby Dick* was a book about whales and did not understand what the scarlet letter stood for. James Michener, Edna Ferber, Kathleen Winsor, Thomas B. Costain, Frank Yerby, Joseph Conrad, and Knut Hamsun had scribbled just for me. The library was a daily stop; it was safer than the alleys, and on each bookshelf there were places to hide. Books, particularly books that were not true, became (and remain) the most important source of knowledge in my life. Everything that has happened to me since then first became known to me through the scrim of text. I learned about tongue kissing when reading *Forever Amber* (a book they nearly did not let me take out) and about the thrill of looking up a girl's skirt from *Studs Lonigan,* a thrill I acquired without knowing what I was supposed to be looking at.

I caught the disease of science fiction while skipping catechism lessons for confirmation. There was a used-magazine shop in a bungalow down the street from the private home in which the priest met with those of us who did not go to parochial school. I began reading *World War One Air Aces* but quickly switched to *Astounding Science Fiction* and *Amazing Stories.* I spent lovely, guilty Saturday mornings leafing through the pulp pages, disappearing into the future while worrying whether my mother would find out that I did not know the justifications for the third commandment. The musty smell of decaying paper on shelves still evokes meditative quiet in me.

As my dependence on text grew, the grip of the church weakened. It was too demanding, too frightening, too singular. I was unable to treat religious praxis with the requisite balance of indifference and attachment, to view sinning and being forgiven as part of a cycle of casual pollution and easy purity. I took it all too seriously. The version of Catholic theology preached by the Irish primitives from the pulpit of Saint Anthony's offered no comfort, only terror. After a series of minor crises, visits to the Jesuits, and the like, my spirit left, but my body continued to go to mass with my mother until I left home. "There is no God," I said to Carlfred Broderick as we walked home from Benjamin Franklin Junior High School one sunny spring afternoon. I think I made some attempt at explaining why, and I think he was shocked. I was fourteen. I went to church until I was seventeen; I worried a bit about taking the wafer in my mouth without going to confession, but that passed. When I got to the University of Chicago, I read *A Portrait of the Artist as a Young Man* and discovered a more courageous ancestor.

My father died in the spring of my apostasy. A man in a green mackintosh came to the door at about four-thirty in the afternoon and asked where my mother was. He was the designated messenger, probably having been given the nasty job because he lived nearby: They don't have a phone, Charley, so you'll have to do it. Anyway it's on your way home. I told him that my mother was at work. We stood at the open door. When would she be home? I was not sure. We shuffled about for a moment or two. Then he told me that my father had died that day at work. He said he was sorry to have to bring the message, especially sorry to have to deliver it to a kid, but he couldn't wait around because he had to get home to his family and, well, he was sorry. I called the shipyard on a pay phone, hoping there had been a mistake, but they told me no mistake had been made. My mother came back an hour later, and I told her just like that. She shrieked "Oh my God" and immediately ran away to be comforted by a neighbor woman. I have always wondered why she did not doubt, even for an instant, the truth of what I said, and why she did not pause to comfort me.

My father's death settled the covert struggle over my religious, occupational, and political fate—no atheism, no mines, no anarchy. Long after my father died, my mother said to me that she was glad that she had outlived him because he was already thinking of returning to the mines. Indeed, he had taken some of their tiny savings to buy part of a gold mine with an old comrade from the Industrial Workers of the World. She had rescued the savings, and she thought she had rescued me.

At the same time his death was the most distal cause of my attending the University of Chicago. My mother faced the choice of whether we should continue to live in California or return to Fall River, Massachusetts, where her remaining family still lived. We journeyed north via San Francisco and Spokane and then east through Chicago and New York to Fall River. These were the closing moments of the age of the train. The summer of 1946 was for me a great numinous time, a preserve of fragments only one of which is relevant to this tale. On our way back from New York to California we had an extended stay in Chicago when the Golden State Limited was delayed ten hours. The day was full of touristic possibilities ready to be seized. First we took a luxurious shower in the white-tiled bathrooms of Union Station, sumptuous with soap, hot water, and fluffy towels, and then stepped outside to the Grey Line tour buses waiting in the August sun. Shall it be the north side of the city or the south side? The bus to the south side left first. We happily looked out the windows at train stations, black folks (who then lived in black belts), churches, and parks and then headed down the Midway Plaisance (oh World's Fair names!) toward Lake Michigan.

Our bus slowly rolled between Harper Library on the left ("The crowns on one tower and the bishops' hats on the other symbolize the separation of church and state," said the tour guide), Burton and Judson dormitories on the right. Again on the left we passed Rockefeller Chapel, Ida Noyes Hall, and the Laboratory School—fake late-Gothic stage sets. Though unlikely, it being the end of summer, perhaps William Ogburn and Ernest Burgess, and even Louis Wirth and Everett Hughes, may have been thinking sociological thoughts in their department offices at 1126 East Sixtieth Street at the very moment we rode past. But these were not names and thoughts that I would have conjured.

Perhaps it was the reverential tone of the tour guide, the hot shower, the freedom of being on the road again, going back to Eden, that made me say quite without premeditation—indeed, how could a poor fatherless child have meditated such a thing?—"I'm going to go to that university." My mother held her tongue but thought (as she told me later when I was testing my recollection of this story), Who the hakes [*heck*] does he think he is? It is fortunate for our continuing affections over the next four decades that she never let on whether she had found out. I do not know, but perhaps if we had taken the north-side tour first rather than second, I might have responded with equal passion to DePaul, Loyola, or Northwestern or pledged myself to becoming a Baha'i.

My desire to go to the University of Chicago remained only a wish that I invoked to defend myself when I was confronted by those who knew they were going to Reed, Berkeley, Stanford, USC, UCLA, or even Harvard. I secretly thought that I would go to Long Beach City College. Actually, I did not plan to go to college at all because I did not know the mechanics of going. Of course I had read novels in which people went to college, but they never said anything about how to write for catalogues or how to compose a convincing why-I-want-to-go-to-your-college-more-than-anything-else-in-the-world essay. I had never known anyone who had gone to college. That statement is not literally true; I had known many schoolteachers, but it never occurred to me that they had been licensed to teach what they taught by attending college. Our impoverishment both in money and, more important, in middle-class craft made all colleges, including the University of Chicago, seem as far away as the moon.

I was, however, rescued by a kindly man named Oakes, later registrar of the University of Chicago, who came to Long Beach Polytechnic High School on a recruiting visit. He told me how to apply to the university and may even have arranged to send me the application. Without that visit I would have gone to Long Beach City College. It perplexes me in retrospect why such a man was wandering around the United States in 1949 to recruit interested youth to the university (that is how we learned to call it, not the University of Chicago, or Chicago, just the university). Had the university put him on a train and aimed him west? Was he already in California for other reasons? It all seemed natural to me at the time. Was this not what all universities did? Much later I was told (perhaps falsely) that these recruiting efforts were part of an attempt to increase the national representation in the College. This I assume to be a code phrase for not having all of the undergraduate students—except the disappearing ex-GIs—be young Jews from Chicago and New York. I wonder sometimes who was left out when I was let in.

I went to the College of the University of Chicago as an innocent. I had not understood the plan of the university's president, Robert Maynard Hutchins (who now remembers the Hutchins plan?), nor that I was to be subjected to a week of examinations to "place" me in the course of study that would make me a liberally educated man. I recall being given a short story by Henry James and a paper on the theory of braids, both of which I was to read and on which I was to be examined in a few days. I did not understand either one. From these examinations I learned that it would take me two years to get a slightly tainted B.A. (True degrees take four years; time on task is education.) I was proud of getting the B.A. in two years until I realized that I was exactly where I should have been; the first two years of the College were meant for those who entered it after two years of high school. So much for precocity.

There was a second set of required examinations—the first complete physical I had ever been given. From these examinations I learned that I was defined epidemiologically as a wanderer. As a consequence of having lived four years in Massachusetts, one year in Vermont, five years in Arizona, and seven years in California, with asides to New York, my diseases could not have local origins. I rather liked the new label; it seemed a bit more promising than saying we moved because we were too poor to stay. I was also told my teeth were in bad shape, which was attributed to sweets but which I blamed on the welfare dentist whom I avoided because he did not use novocaine.

These were only the first of a long series of misunderstandings between the university and me, misunderstandings often of my making, to which the university remained generously indifferent until they became a bureaucratic irritant. Kindly deans then resolved them in my favor because they thought I had promise, but of such misunderstandings and forgivenesses are disorderly careers made.

My first term in the College was exquisite. I can still recall the syllabi and I still reread many of the assigned texts. I met up with culture and personality through Freud, Durkheim, Gunnar Myrdal, Allison Davis, and John Dollard. I cannot say that they made much sense to me on first reading, nor did a career in sociology suddenly seem a sensible option when I listened to David Riesman and Philip Rieff. More appealing to my tastes were works by Thucydides, Milton, Forster, Joyce, Austen, Dostoyevski, and Huxley—works of fancy that called for response more than analysis. From there on, it was mostly downhill; I was not in any way prepared to grasp and order the opportunity offered by the College and the university to make learning into a career. I did not know how, and so each idea came to me as sweetly and individually as a flower, and on occasion I would group a bunch of ideas into a bouquet. It was good to know, but knowing for what eluded me.

It took me five years to finish the two-year program of courses for the bachelor's degree, but not because I was idle. In retrospect I seemed to have been frightfully busy, but my life was evasive and tangential rather than centered in the academy. I cannot remember any deep intellectual experience with the faculty in that entire period—except with Edward Bastian, who remained kind even as I stumbled through a fine history preceptorial that he taught. He suggested I write about the Bloomsbury group and read Anatole France. He told me something I treasured as a compliment—that I had been born old in the soul.

During those five years I attended many classes, often at the introductory graduate level, but actually I was taking courses in Harper Library, middle-class practice, the city of Chicago, and Jewishness. My first job in Chicago was shelving books in the stacks of Harper Library. Shelve one, browse two. The quiet hours when I worked among the PN and PQ shelves were rather better than the doldrums of the Hs, though there were many pleasures in the DCs and GNs. The beginnings of middle-class craftiness and good manners I learned from young women, particularly two, whose families behaved with an uncommon generosity toward a young man who desperately wanted to please, did not know how to please, and hated himself for trying to be pleasing.

But it was the membrane between the university and the city that offered the most vivid possibilities. It was a stage for the most romantic, bohemian pretenses: drinking at the High Hat or Jimmy's; listening to jazz at the Cadillac and Crown Propeller lounges on Sixty-third Street, at the Beehive on Fifty-fifth Street, or at the Sutherland Lounge on South Parkway; and listening to folk music on Folkways record label, the local Young People's Socialist League singers, or at Big Bill and Moore's. I went to the movies without letup. There seemed to be projectors running in every rectangular room of the university as well as triple features at the Ken and the Kim on Sixty-third Street. And there was work that I did for pay on assembly lines and in machine shops, ice plants, and packing houses. The work kept reminding me of what I did not want to be, but I still did not know what I wanted to be. And it was the work that paid the rent.

If the University of Chicago had refused some Jewish applicant to accept me, a goy, it had, in an indirect sense, failed. For I was far more vulnerable to what appeared to me to be the coherent cultural claims of secular, cosmopolitan forms of Jewishness than theories of ethnoreligious origins might have predicted. In early adolescence I was already (if invisibly) detached from the religious feelings that are the core of Americanized Irish Catholicism, except perhaps the terrors of damnation. By the time I was fifteen even those fears came in infrequent surges, and finally they were replaced by an appreciation of the brute indifference of the physical world (nature signifying emptiness rather than an occasion for awe) and the thoughtful cruelties of humankind. I was also detached from my working-class world of intermittent poverty and intellectual mindlessness. As a somewhat cowardly and physically inept youth, the conventional working-class hierarchies of strength and sexual exploitation were outside my abilities even when they were relevant. At the same time I had no interest at all in Judaism, only in what I took to be a common marginality and a common interest in the book.

Being bookish took me to the university, and it was there that I first met a large number of people who were bookish beyond my dreams. They were nearly all Jews, part of that postwar release of Jews into the mainstream of life in the United States as the intensity of anti-Semitism in academic life began to fall. It was not that these young people were all intellectuals, indeed most were climbers in the bureaucracies and the professions or mere careerists of the book. However, they seemed to value, perhaps only for that moment and in that context, perhaps only for purposes of gossip and belonging, the only activities at which I had talent. Had there been a place for socially mobile infidels at the universities of Cairo or Baghdad in the great ages of Islamic life, I would have become a near-Arab.

I was unaware of Jews in any deep way before that time. I did not even know the universal Christian fact that the Jews had killed Jesus. I may have missed that point since I often daydreamed during mass. Even rumors of the whirlwind had passed me by in my provincial Eden, though the death march at Bataan and Wake Island were included in the attractions at the United Artists movie house. I may have fallen in love in the summer of 1949 with a girl about whom it was said that she, a Jew, had survived in German-occupied Poland by pretending to be a Christian. I am not sure anymore whether I was in love or even whether I should believe the story, but I like remembering that she looked like Ingrid Bergman.

I am carried back by this meditation further into my adolescence, to a time when I did not understand why Nathan Tucker could not play on Saturday. He would disappear above his father's tailor shop, where on every other day of the week sailors from the Navy would come to be fitted for their dress blues and buy their combat ribbons. It was the first stage of the ritual of "getting blued, screwed, and tattooed." After my father died, Nathan's father took us fishing in the Sierra Nevada mountains, where I did not catch a fish in a whole week. It was the only extended time I ever spent with Nathan's father. I never learned his first name, but it was of course a different time, and I would not have called him by it in any case.

During the period I knew Nathan he must have been bar mitzvahed, but I was not aware of that event even as a ceremony, nor was I aware that hundreds of thousands of children our same age were being murdered in Europe. Nathan and I quarreled violently on the handball court when we were fifteen; he hit me with the ball three times, I thought deliberately. I threw the ball at him and hit him, the only Jew I ever physically attacked, but I did not know then that he was a Jew. That quarrel seemed to end our friendship. Still I do not think that we would have been friends much longer, for he was not very bookish. It is out of the university context of Jewishness that I married a Jewish woman (by parentage, not religious training) and had two Jewish children (so identified by Mosaic, Nuremburg, and Soviet laws). I worry about them, as I do about my close friends, nearly all of whom are Jewish and nonreligious. I do not think the era of pogroms and holocaust is over. That worry, the circle of people I love, and bookishness comprise my Jewishness. In this peculiar union of Venn diagrams are represented the immediacy of terror and love and the distance found in the text and the library. What then to do or feel about Zionist colonization, land expropriation, orthodox theocracy, Menachem Begin and the Stern gang, the West Bank, Shatila and Sabra? Perhaps my Jewishness has nothing to do with those matters, but only perhaps. The world fashioned by history does not allow me to choose my connections. Zionist colonization came after pogroms, Israel after holocaust—one entwined in the other, as the Palestinian diaspora is another twist in the rope after the establishment of Israel. There is no place to stand at ease, happily convinced of the rightness of one's stand in the midst of competing injustice and misery.

I entered the graduate program in sociology at Chicago largely as the result of failure, drift, and misadventure. My vague occupational dreams in high school had been of the hard sciences, but an inept performance in calculus and a certain penchant for text deflected me from that path. Medicine was out early, a sort of nonchoice. It was my first encounter with the ungloved reality principle at the university:

PREMED ADVISER:	Do you have all A's in the sciences?
JG:	No.
PA:	Is your father a doctor?
JG:	No.
PA:	How much money do you have?
JG:	None.
PA:	Forget it.

Psychology was eliminated by two short interviews on a hot August day in 1952. I suspected that the first great love affair of my life was ending and hoped that if I could make an honest man of myself, she might think more positively of our sharing the future together. So I tried to get some vocational counseling as I slithered down the occupational aspiration scale. It is difficult to communicate the fusing of heat and smell of an August day in the Chicago of the 1950s. The sky was bleached milky white; the edges of real buildings quivered in the heat, whereas the edge between shadow and light was hard; the asphalt sucked at the soles of shoes. The wind blowing from the west was thick with mutant molecules. It carried the taint from the packing houses and tanneries and the heavy metals and complex organic waste from the vents of factories. The enamel finishes baked off the cars as they spewed lead, carbon, and sulfur out of their exhausts. Future cancers were in every breath.

In back of the University of Chicago Press building were some leftover World War II barracks, one of which housed rats and rat psychologists. On the second floor I found one of the healthiest men I had even seen. He was sitting quite composed at his desk, his brow not even damp, his shirt neatly pressed, his nose unoffended by the extraordinary stench of the place. Stretching away from us down the length of the barracks were what seemed to be hundreds of Skinner boxes in which rats were squeaking, pushing levers, eating rewards, and shitting through the grills into trays. The thousands of little clicks of the lever were being recorded by inked needles on endless loops of graph paper. There were a couple of animal tenders in white coats who seemed to be constantly engaged in filling the token dispensers with tiny pellets of food and wheeling out garbage pails full of tiny pellets of shit. The man told me that the future of psychology was now to be found in the intersect of physiology and learning, and he proposed a curriculum that sounded suspiciously like the premed program except that you did not get the golden handshake when you were done.

He asked if I minded whether he ate lunch while we talked. When I voiced no objection—indeed I encouraged him—he took out a bacon, lettuce, and tomato sandwich on white bread thickly smeared with mayonnaise. Each time he bit into it, a little mayonnaise pulsed up each of the grooves between his white, perfect front teeth. I thanked him for his time and bolted into the sunlight.

My second appointment was in a quasi-Victorian building across Fifty-eighth Street from the barracks where they kept the clinical psychologists. I climbed up four creaky flights of stairs until I reached a belfry office. The office was distinctly cooler and dimmer than the outside, and a small, dark man looked up from what he was reading to ask me what I wanted. I said I thought I might want to become a psychologist. Did I understand that many people became psychologists only to solve their personal problems? I knew enough Freud to nod appreciatively at this insight. Did I not think that it might be best to seek therapy, to set the mental record straight, so to speak, before making an occupational choice of this kind? I said that his idea had merit and thanked him and left. My suspicion that my lover might be planning to leave me for someone with better chances in life seemed sadly reasonable as I waited for the bus to take me to Continental Can for the afternoon shift.

I drifted around the university trying to avoid the fact that I had not passed the language course required for the B.A. It was also true that if I had passed the exam I would have had to give up a small scholarship that the university provided me and would have had to decide what to do when I grew up. So I sampled the graduate social sciences: a little anthropology, a disastrous sociology course from Everett Hughes, industrial relations, the history of trade unions, psychology, economic planning. Finally someone discovered that though I was still officially a student in the College, I had taken no courses in the College for a number of years and I was making no progress toward the degree. I was forbidden to register for further courses. I was still passing as a proletarian at the aircraft engine division of Ford Motor Company, and that job paid the rent. I was now also ready to marry, but we had agreed to do so only if I finally received a degree. Proletarians may be romantic, but only if they have the promise of becoming former proletarians. I passed the course, received a degree, and married—the alternative was the fantasy of learning to play flamenco guitar in a bar in Palma, Majorca. The meaning of the past does indeed come to meet one from the future.

I then began sliding down the academic funnel toward a graduate degree in sociology. I had already sampled the early-1950s Chicago department—Hughes, Anselm Strauss, Horton, Philip Hauser, and the young Otis Dudley Duncan—and then I took courses from the hybrid Columbia-Chicago department—Jim Coleman, Peter Blau, Peter Rossi, Elihu Katz, and (though they did not have the right ancestry, they did have the correct attitude) Goodman, Fred Strodbeck, and Jim Davis. These were busy years since by then I was working full-time at the Cook County Jail for the professor-sheriff Joseph Lohman. In a fit of sentimentality I even took courses from Clifford Shaw (does anyone remember *The Jackroller?*). There is no way neatly to summarize these years. I learned a great deal of sociology since I faithfully went to classes and did assignments. But no particular idea and certainly no intellectual posture of these teachers became mine. As I reread this passage it seems arrogant, but it is not meant to be. These scholars were interested in training people in the profession (and good training it was), and whatever other mental passions they had were hidden behind their extraordinary craft. I never met any of them outside of the classroom, nor could I call any of them a friend. The fact that they spoke and I listened made them seem much older than I, though they were not. I did not know well any of my contemporaries in graduate school, though I can trot out the names of the fairly large number who have become famous in the ways sociologists become famous. I knew Philips Cutright well for a time (our first marriages took place on consecutive days), and I knew Bill Simon better than most; we helped each other at exam time and in statistics but had no sense of a shared fate.

I do not know what I learned from working at the county jail. I was only twenty-three when I started and in time was third or fourth in administrative authority. When tear gas was fired to quell a disturbance, I was sometimes fifth or sixth, as Warden Johnson, Captain Makowski, and an Italian lieutenant took priority in those circumstances. I grasp for phrases that offer a glimpse of that place that was the center of my emotional life for three and a half years—sometimes it was biffo-bongo "Hill Street Blues" with real blood, sometimes a tragicomedy in the cloacal regions; it was always the heart of darkness. And it was also a job. The only remnants of those years are absurdist fables and the love I recollect having for a man named Hans Mattick. He was the assistant warden of the prison when I arrived, and what I learned from him are those banalities of spirit about which one is ashamed to speak in these modern times. My first wife thought I loved him more than I loved her. I protested against that view at the time partially because if it were true it seemed to be a betrayal of our marriage vows and partially because she insisted on labeling it latent homosexuality (psychiatric social work has its charms). I am now persuaded she was right on the love count, though I prefer, even now when such attachments are more generously regarded, the rhetoric of friendship. As a result of helping to manage this branch of the lower intestine of urban life, I had, by indecision, evolved into someone who was believed to know something about drugs, delinquency, crime, and prisons and who had passed the Ph.D. comprehensive examinations.

My career at the Institute for Sex Research began with a visit from Wardell Pomeroy, one of the coauthors of the original Kinsey reports. He was looking for someone trained in the social sciences who was knowledgeable about working-class and criminal populations (the lower social level, ISR people called them) and comfortable with the topic. Kinsey had been dead for two years, and the current team was completing the interviewing, data analysis, and writing for the publication of a major volume on sex offenders. I was more than a little ambivalent about the prospect of sex research (about which I had read only the selection on sexual behavior and social class in *Class, Status and Power*, edited by Reinhard

Bendix and Seymour Martin Lipset, 1953), and I was about as relaxed about the topic as any other upwardly mobile former Irish Catholic male. My own sexual life was as uninspired as it could be (I later discovered the hollowness of sexual inspiration), and whatever sexual history I had accumulated was largely from individual or joint follies. I was losing my job at the jail because of an Illinois law that forbade county sheriffs to succeed themselves in office, the justification of which was that if you could not enrich yourself in a single four-year term at the public trough, you did not deserve a second opportunity. No one else was offering me a job at the time, and to return to the university would have made me a degraded student again. My wife wanted to have a child, and there was always the rent.

I knew no more about the Kinsey reports than *Time* magazine was willing to tell. Actually, the first time I heard of them was in 1949 when I went out with the male troop who hung around on the boardwalk in front of our apartment building. We visited a homosexual man who lived in a flat in Seal Beach. He gave us beer and and told us about our mammalian homosexual heritage and that, according to Kinsey, one man in three had had sex with men. My compatriots had done some hustling, but I did not figure that out for nearly a decade. I had also heard Kinsey give a public lecture in Chicago just before his death, but I do not recall what he said; it must have been something about the conflict between culture, the law, and our mammalian heritage.

The first years of my career in sex research were pastoral. Blooming-ton, Indiana, where the institute was located, had peculiar powers of place, for it was a world without any distractions from the professional or the domestic. In those early years I learned a great deal about sex in various species, watched films of various species doing sexual things, wandered through the collections of erotica, even learned how to inter-view in the correct Kinsey fashion (for a description of this arcane skill see the section on interviewing in *Sexual Behavior in the Human Male*). It has occurred to me that if I outlive all of my colleagues of that period I may be the last person on earth to possess that knowledge in practice. I will be a living artifact waiting to be tapped for a marginal dissertation on the history of method. As I learned more about sex, I drifted away from sociology, though Alfred Lindesmith, Albert Cohen, and Sheldon Stryker served as my disciplinary anchors as well as my friends. Daily life was full of research and lawns and babies and faculty dinners and grant applica-tions and cocktail parties and local gossip and mortgages and swing sets and journal articles and backyard barbecues and rumors of tiny infidelities. The comforting rounds of young-faculty lives worked themselves out against the shaping purposes of university rhythms. We were allowed to be thoughtless because it had all been so well thought out before.

When I arrived at the Institute for Sex Research it was dying in the quiet way most institutions die, by reenacting its old routines. Indeed, the result of my first years there was a book that was the end of a tradition, the last of the great statistical life history studies of the varieties of sex offenders. *Sex Offenders* is of some use, even though it suffers from problems of sampling and analysis and, most devastatingly, from conceptual limitations. But for me it was a project with direction, a momentum that pulled me along. Whatever my doubts about the Kinsey tradition—the fictive nature of the sexual life history, its abstraction from individual experience, the transformation of pleasure into outlet, the fictions of the mammalian tradition—they were minor when weighted against the force of ongoing involvement. This is not a denial of my active participation in Kinsey work, only an attempt to place it at the intersection of three historical processes: the production of social-science texts, the production of a career, and, now, the production of a consideration of the same texts and career.

In the spring of 1964 William Simon drove through Bloomington as he traveled from Southern Illinois University, where he was teaching, to a COFO (Congress of Federated Organizations) meeting, a civil-rights movement training program at Miami University in Ohio. I was not in Bloomington then, but he stopped again when he returned west. We had seen each other a few times while he was still in Chicago, but only at the American Sociological Association meetings after he went to Southern Illinois. We had largely lost touch. For a variety of reasons he was on the job market, and for a variety of different reasons the institute was looking for a new staff member. It was a propitious pit stop, not least because a local restaurant offered us the curious delicacy "chocolate pie in season."

The institute was still winding down. Clyde Martin (one of the first of Kinsey's collaborators) had left in 1960; Wardell Pomeroy was thinking of leaving and finally left to go into private practice as a therapist in New York City in the mid-1960s. The full-time research staff would soon be down to two. Everyone was extraordinarily active, but most of the work was in the service of the collectivity and the past. The Kinsey ethos was to subordinate the individual to the goals of the collective (usually identified with Kinsey's). For example, until after William Simon and I left, no individual researcher received royalties for books or honoraria for speeches; all those moneys were contributed to the institute's own funds. The volume on sex offenders was a collective project conceived in the Kinsey era; it rested on interviews collected before 1960, and the analysis and writing of that book dominated our efforts until 1963. Research support for the institution at that time was a grant to transfer all of the original case histories (some seventeen thousand interviews) to punch cards. This coding operation required eliminating even the slightest chance of identifying subjects from the interview schedules as well as deciphering the arcane manner in which the interviews were originally coded. Even with a crew of a dozen coders the process took some three years to complete. The activities of the institute's library and archive bulked large in everyone's lives; new materials were constantly being added to the collection, and older materials needed cataloguing and preservation.

At the same time there was a constant stream of notables visiting Indiana University who wished to see the collections of erotica and be taken for a tour. The tour usually began with the mysteries of the interview schedule ("all items are memorized by the interviewer") and the fact that the key to connecting the name file and the interviews themselves was known only by memory to senior members of the staff ("they never travel on the same plane lest the code be lost forever"). The tour guide then opened selected green cabinets containing erotic examples of Peruvian burial pots, Japanese netsuke, and Chinese prints. The tour ended with slightly demoralized tourists looking at the spines of erotic books in the library. This was the second time I had been a tour guide; the first was at the county jail, where we took citizens' groups and various notables (Henry Fonda when he appeared in *Twelve Angry Men*, Nelson Algren after he had written *The Man with a Golden Arm*, a tough-looking general in the shah of Iran's army) around the prison to educate them about the need for prison reform. "In this institution," we would tell them, "we have city, state, and federal prisoners, men and women, adults and juveniles; we have a daily count of about two thousand prisoners in a building designed for thirteen hundred; all of the cells are six feet by four feet by nine feet, designed small to hold only one person, though we now have two people in more than half the cells in the institution; we turn over twenty thousand prisoners a year; 60 percent of the prisoners here have been sentenced, and sentences range from one day to five years; we have thirteen men sentenced to die—note the electric chair on your left."

In addition to the collective effort during this period, I wrote a number of unexceptional articles on sex offenders, victims of sex offenses, and sex and aging, primarily from archival data. I was committed to making the archives and library accessible to outside scholars since these represented enormous investments of time and energy that were virtually unused. The problem was to breach the barriers to the archives for outsiders, barriers that were created when the institute was in its initial phase of development. Can anyone today experience directly what it must have been like for Kinsey to wander through a 1940s and 1950s sexual underworld collecting erotica? To believe, and then to write, that masturbation, homosexuality, and oral sex were no crime? It was a world in which the nudist magazine, the striptease, and the stag night were the outer limits of the erotic. It was J. Edgar Hoover's world of the sex moron and sex pervert and of the Boy Scout manual's theory of masturbation. It was a world in which sex research was an academic offense. I was an adolescent in that world.

Beginning with these tours and with a certain amount of recruiting among friends a number of outside scholars worked on problems presented by the archives—although I needed to persuade my colleagues to make the archives available. Out of these efforts came Steven Marcus's *The Other Victorians* as well as Morse Peckham's *Art and Pornography* (probably the best theoretical treatment of erotica to date). I helped some graduate students do dissertations in a variety of areas, especially in literature and folklore. These efforts pleased me since they continued my connection to literature and the arts, if only from an underground perspective. And they allowed me to continue to acquire a varied supply of unconnected facts. I view them as having generally been a good thing, producing some of the few texts that give evidence of the peculiarities of my intellectual practice.

Bill Simon's arrival in June 1965 turned the focus of activity at the institute from inward to outward, from the archives and the past to new research and the disciplines (sociology, anthropology, etc.). I do not think that this shift would have happened without his coming to Indiana, at least not as dramatically. He was less respectful of the past than I was, better oriented toward conceptualizing problems in ways that were of interest to sociology. From his experience at the National Opinion Research Center he knew how to do survey research. We shared an interest in the work of Kenneth Burke and the softer side of the symbolic interactionist tradition (emphasis on *symbolic*) and a certain outsider status at Chicago, particularly as the sociology department grew more professional.

We collaborated daily from June 1965 to June 1968 and continued to work together, though with decreasing intensity, until August 1972. In the last months of 1965 we wrote three grant applications—one too many to have done them all well. I recollect some division of labor in the beginning: Bill supplied more of the disciplinary orientation, and I knew the substance of the research area. As we collaborated further, that difference grew less, and the balance and weight in contribution changed from project to project, paper to paper—indeed, from one period to another.

Each of the research projects was an attempt to bring the field of sexuality under the control of a sociological orientation. The novelty of what we did then was to lay a sociological claim to an aspect of social life that seemed determined by biology or psychology, but a claim that differed from Kingsley Davis's mechanical functionalism. The study of so-called normal psychosexual development in college students began with Erik Erikson and the crisis of the late 1960s among youth but finally turned into the ideas about the social elicitation and maintenance of sexual conduct that inform the opening chapter of *Sexual Conduct.* The research project on gay men (called homosexuals in those days) began with a distrust of etiological theories and a vision of sexual lives as determined by social factors. In the phrase *homosexual banker* our concern was with *banker* as much as with *homosexual.* Similarly, in our tiny study of lesbians we were interested in the effects of gender on sexuality. Ideas about scripting seem to be most visible in our early writing about pornography but grew slowly to have a more central place in our thinking, replacing Erving Goffman's dramaturgy with Burke's symbolic action.

In those three years the core of my and Bill Simon's joint work was effectively completed: two edited books, a large number of papers and presentations, and the volume *Sexual Conduct,* even though it was not published until 1973. It always strikes me as strange that all of this work was completed in a period that also contained so much political and personal chaos. The antiwar movement on campus was growing in intensity (I remember hearing students shouting "Napalm!" at Secretary of State Dean Rusk as he defended President Johnson's policy in Viet-nam). At Indiana the tension over issues of racism (then called discrimi-nation and prejudice) was chronic: in 1959 the barbers in the student union building would not cut the hair of black students; in 1968 black students threatened to block the running of the Little Five Hundred bicycle race, spring raison d'etre of the fraternities and sororities. Allen

Ginsberg and Peter Orlovsky came to campus and read poetry, to the pleasure of the students and the outrage of the governor, who declared, "No more cocksuckers on campus." The Fugs, a New York rock group composed of some serious intellectuals, stood outside the office building that housed the Institute for Sex Research and sang a hymn to the memory of Alfred Kinsey while attempting to levitate the structure itself.

I was not personally ready even for this modest success. I do not think that I had planned any speeches about how I had been done in by the mindless empiricists, thus explaining away my lack of productivity, but I surely was not ready to be a cheerful member of the profession. During this period my personal life became increasingly incoherent as the disordering opportunities presented by my life course were fulfilled and found unsatisfying. In a peculiar way as my desire for professional success had increased, and indeed such success had grown more likely, my contempt for the banality of my own desires flowered as well. As the Fugs's song went, "Love is not enough, fucking is not enough, nothing is enough."

By the spring of 1967 it was clear that the effort to pull the institute out of its inward-looking posture had split the organization. By the fall of that year it was also clear that Bill Simon and I would be on the job market and that the projects we had started would have to be reallocated. We took with us the college youth study, for which the field work had been completed, and left behind the study of the homosexual community that was nearly completed in Chicago. In June 1968 Bill left for the Institute for Juvenile Research in Chicago, and I went to the State University of New York, Stony Brook, as a lecturer in sociology. Lecturer? I have forgotten to mention that during the nine years that elapsed between my leaving Chicago and my going to Stony Brook I had not finished my dissertation. Why not? As the years went by and mild successes accumulated, the student role became simply too punishing to reassume. I could not face dealing with the faculty at Chicago, even though they were unfailingly nice in my sporadic attempts at finding a dissertation topic. Just walking on campus I could feel my IQ falling. It was that most paralyzing of afflictions: I had avoided a hurdle because I was afraid to fail; I then became so contemptuous of the hurdle and the hurdle holders that it was impossible for me to jump. This twenty-year gap between entering the University of Chicago and getting the Ph.D. made me expert on why graduate students should hang around and finish their degrees at all costs, but it also made me uncritical of those who do not. I am convinced as well that a disordered career such as mine was possible only in the era in which it occurred. There is now less forgiveness in the profession than there once was. Perhaps the question might be, Is a disordered career better than none at all?

I finished the dissertation after being at Stony Brook for one year. Kindly circumstances and Morris Janowitz allowed me to write a simple, but acceptable, five-variable, 180-page survey research document. Not quite Durkheim, but even at my advanced age the committee, composed of members of the third Department of Sociology at the University of Chicago I had attended, did not expect a classic. For the next four years Bill Simon and I continued to collaborate, but at a greater intellectual distance and less effectively. Each of us were caught in the daily circumstances of our lives, and our attention focused on the demands of the institutions in which we worked. We completed a number of papers from the study of college youth, wrote up our research on working-class young people, and finished a number of projects together, but the routine of collaboration was gone. Still, it had been a remarkable run. Its intellectual, professional, and emotional influence on my life I still feel directly and indirectly. We talk about collaborating again, now and then, and have even done so, in a set of four papers on scripting that are a substantial advance over the earlier work. It is not possible for me to separate what is mine from what is his. Even asking who authored what causes me pain that I want to avoid. I tend to look away, think of other things. Perhaps this experience is behind my deep distrust of the idea of *auctoritas* and authorship. Even writing about the time when we worked together seems invasive of his right to tell his version of the same events, in his own voice. Let me evade articulating my affection for him lest it require a false reciprocity from him.

Toward the end of this period I made a number of missteps. I became a dean and worked on projects in regional and environmental planning. Neither job came to much. The deaning gave me a higher salary. No publications resulted from the environmental work, but there were later benefits. In 1972–73 I was an overseas fellow at Churchill College, Cambridge, supported by a National Institute of Mental Health postdoctoral fellowship. It was a good year for me, but not for my children, who went to English schools, or for my first wife, who left her job to come to Europe.

After we returned to the United States, I went back to the sociology department to teach. I worked with two psychologists at Stony Brook on psychophysiological correlates of sexual response. I learned some psychology, but my sense was that they got more out of it than I did. I separated from my wife in 1975, and we got divorced in 1979. Also in 1975 I started to do some work in simulation and gaming, and that has now become a serious area of study for me. My kids grew up. I got older. I now live with my best friend, and I have two more Jewish children. I spent 1978 to 1980 at the School of Education at Harvard and the year 1983–84 teaching at the University of Essex. I reside in Princeton.

Why so cryptic about this recent period and so lush about the distant past? I think because the time since 1973 has been busy but indecisive. It has no recollective plausibility: the participants are still alive; the events are only events, not yet stories; even my texts of this time have no center. When I think about this period I have a strong sense of evasion and drift, but it is too soon for it to be adequately revised and protectively judged.

Will I do anything else interesting? It would be pretty to think so.

CHAPTER TEN

Learning and Living

Donald R. Cressey

My forty years as a faculty member have been spiced with delightful hours of teaching and research in criminology, which is the study of the process of making laws, breaking laws, and reacting to the breaking of laws. Over the years dozens of people have asked how I got into the professorial world and, more specifically, into my sociological speciality. I have repeatedly asserted that everything happened by accident. Few have accepted my assertions, and some have advanced theories of their own.

Anthropologists, psychologists, and especially sociologists have speculated aloud about events in my childhood that must have determined my choice of careers. Some of the sociologists, believing that I am an offspring of one of the two Paul Cresseys, cousins who each made a mark in sociology during the 1930s, decided that I simply followed in the footsteps of my father, as Robert E. L. Faris did. Not so. While attending the annual meetings of the American Sociological Association some years ago, I listened quietly while Paul F. Cressey told me that all the Cresseys are descended from a single indentured servant who came to America in colonial times. When he finished, I told him that my paternal grandfather was a poor Minnesota farmer who had been a poor English farmer before he emigrated.

Friends and acquaintances with a psychoanalytic bent, knowing that I have broken new ground in a couple of areas of criminology, have drooled in delight on learning that when I was a boy my maternal grandfather, Durkee Prentiss, was my idol and that in the 1890s he and my grandmother left Vermont to stake a claim for land in South Dakota. As teenaged newlyweds the pioneers lived for two years in a hut they built from virgin prairie sod. Then, close to starvation, they welcomed a letter from my grandfather's grandmother back in Milton, Vermont. She said she had a "fat pig and two sacks of flour" and that they were welcome to spend the winter with her. My mother was born the following summer, in 1898. She was soon bundled up and moved to a North Dakota farm where my grandfather was the hired man and my grandmother the hired "girl."

Those same Freudian friends, aware of my tough-guy demeanor, also have linked my interest in crime and criminals to the occupations my grandfather held. These include, in chronological order, saloon keeper, gun store owner, and small-town police chief. Similarly, deep Freudian significance has been attributed to the fact that I parted company with my father when I was about fourteen, shortly after he had been jailed in connection with a hit-and-run accident for driving while drunk. Because I have long been convinced that Freudian psychology is based on a misconception about the nature of personality, I have no more confidence in such explanations than I have in the analyses made by people who erroneously believed me to be the son (sometimes cousin or brother) of one of the famous Cresseys.

More fun, and thus more acceptable to me, have been diagnoses of what my real criminological objectives have been, coupled with armchair speculations about which of my childhood experiences set me on the path to such work. For example, undergraduates over the years have discerned that one of my criminological goals, subsidiary to the scientific one, has been to reduce the amount of pain and suffering in the world. Then, reasoning backward, some have guessed that my childhood must have been a painful one. There is a smattering of truth in these assertions. I doubt their significance, however, principally because I cannot convince myself that pain necessarily precedes humanitarianism. On the contrary, it seems to me that adults whose childhoods were painful are more likely than others to take pain and suffering as the natural lot of humankind.

The most thoughtful diagnosis and speculation of this type was made by Scott Greer when he was a graduate student and I was an assistant professor at the University of California, Los Angeles, in the 1950s. Scott, a poet and philosopher as well as a sociologist, decided that all sociological work is autobiographical. In coffee sessions and at beer busts he told fascinated audiences of graduate students and junior faculty members what each senior departmental faculty member was really doing professionally, and then he "revealed" how that work was just an unfolding of the person's life experiences. Some of his analyses were not flattering, so I will not recall them here. But more than once he also told me, and others, that I actually was dedicating my professional life to identifying the nature of honesty. Speculations about childhood moral and ethical conflicts followed as a matter of course.

There is an element of truth in these assertions too. Unlike Freudian speculations, they do not rest on hog-wild assumptions about mysterious, unconscious motivations. Still, I never have taken them to heart. It is true that my early sociological work, especially that on embezzlement, showed concern for the nature of honesty. I was convinced, and remain convinced, that most criminals perceive their dishonesty as something other than dishonesty, perhaps even as honor, duty, or an acceptable means of social control. But I never have been able to find any significant perceptions of this kind among my early childhood friends. Moreover, I have long known that I learned to distinguish sharply between honesty and dishonesty at a very early age.

From shortly after I was born, in 1919, until just after my thirteenth birthday my father manned the circuit panel switches at the Hoot Lake electric power plant, located about three miles from Fergus Falls, a small town in northwestern Minnesota. Our family was not rich, but we were not poor either. At Christmas I always asked for a toy, a new wagon or sled, a guitar, or a gun and usually got underwear, socks, and a new jacket or pair of overalls. I lived with my older brother, younger sister, and parents in a company house high on a cliff overlooking the generating plant. Except for the Dunlap family there were no neighbors within a mile. The seven Dunlap kids, all but one of them older than I, lived just down the hill. Their father was plant superintendent.

Some portion of this bunch of ten Cressey and Dunlap kids played together every day. We went to the same Presbyterian church on Sundays. When school was in session the five of us who were of grade-school age usually walked together down the narrow river valley leading to town and to the Jefferson School, about two miles away.

As we trudged along the dirt road on a crisp fall day near the beginning of my first year in school, I showed the gang a new pencil my mother had bought the previous day and which I was carrying like a jewel in the patent leather book bag slung over my shoulder. Someone asked about the price. My brother reported that the pencil had cost a penny and then bragged that my mother had bought five of them. Wells

Dunlap, who at age nine or ten was the oldest member of the group (I was the youngest), responded, "Shit, I can get them five for a steal." We giggled, snorted, and roared.

I tell the story to suggest that I knew the difference between honesty and dishonesty, or at least between stealing and not stealing, at the early age of six. Moreover, I never stole very much. So far as I know, neither did Wells or any other member of our bunch. I have never been arrested.

The honesty issue came up a few other times during my formative years. In every case I knew precisely what was honest and what was not. For example, when I was a second-grade student, our teacher staged a book-reading contest. At the end of the term, she said, a prize would be awarded to the pupil who had read the most books. The nature of the prize was a secret. Every Friday afternoon Miss Bratt would ask us to report the titles of the books we had read during the week. As we named our books, she made notes in a stenographer's memo pad. I won the prize handily. It was a book, and I still have it.

In the course of the contest I had to make a quick decision about the nature of honesty and dishonesty. I had no doubt about the difference. One Friday my list of books included *The Adventures of Robin Red Breast and Billie Blue Jay*. Miss Bratt queried me about the title, but I did not catch her intent. She made herself clear by asking, "That's two books, isn't it?" I knew it was only one book about two fine fellows, and I also knew that saying yes would be dishonest. I looked out the window. The teacher took my silence for assent and gave me credit for two books. I did not tell my mother or any of my friends I had cheated.

By the time I was in the sixth grade and about twelve years of age, my sense of what is honest and what is not had been honed to a sharp edge. As was customary in most of America at the time, no prayers were said in our school. On Tuesday afternoons, however, classes were dismissed so kids could go to the church of their choice for Tuesday school, which supplemented Sunday school. Further, school children were frequently warned about sin and especially about the sinful nature of intemperance—gluttony, smoking, and drinking—probably because Norwegian immigrants comprised most of the population of Fergus Falls.

At least once each year a Lutheran minister spoke to Jefferson School classes about the evils of drinking and smoking. We looked forward to his visits. He began by placing on the teacher's desk a small bowl of water in which two goldfish cruised back and forth. In the course of the preacher's talk, which I heard two or three times, he always moved from the perils of alcohol to the perils of tobacco. At the end he lit a cigarette with a big wooden kitchen match, took a puff, gagged dramatically, then blew the smoke through a straw (a *real* straw, not a cheap soda-fountain replica) into the goldfish bowl. After a few seconds, sometimes given over to furious stirrings of the water with a pencil, the goldfish died. We called the clergyman the goldfish killer.

During my sixth year in school the minister went too far. After killing the goldfish, he distributed printed forms for each student to sign. I read mine. I was being asked to promise that I never would drink or smoke. There was a shuffling of feet and a fluttering of paper as students signed the pledges and passed them to the front of the room. Only one student, me, held out. I lifted the hinged top of my desk a couple of inches and inserted the unsigned pledge. Our teacher, Miss Betts, saw me; I think the preacher did too. Neither said a word. The heat, I found out, was to be applied in private. The next day Miss Betts cornered me during recess. She had a mustache, and she spit little droplets when she talked. She asked if I were going to turn in the paper I had in my desk. I replied that I would give it to her but that I did not think I would sign it. I was not old enough to know about those things, I said; maybe when I grew up I would want to smoke or drink. She seemed to accept my reasoning.

A few days later, also at recess, Miss Betts singled me out again. I was afraid of her because when I was in the fifth grade (there was only one teacher for the fifth and sixth grades and one for the third and fourth) she had taken me to the teachers' lounge and hit me on the bottom with a piece of rubber hose. When I had reported to my mother that I got a licking because I had not heeded the teacher's warning to stop talking in the classroom, she had said I deserved it. Now, standing at the foot of the schoolhouse steps, Miss Betts asked if I had changed my mind about signing and returning the form. I had not. I did not want to lie, I said. She sighed, and I took that to mean I was off the hook. But that afternoon a lady from the Women's Christian Temperance Union telephoned my mother just to report, as I understood it, that I had not yet returned the signed pledge. In the questioning that followed, I confessed to my mother that I was the only one who had not signed the pledge, and I told her why. I asked her what I should do. She said she wanted to sleep on it. As I was leaving for school the next morning, she gave me a fat hug and then, as though it were an afterthought, advised me to do whatever I thought was right on "that pledge thing." I suppose she also called Miss Betts and asked her to lay off. For whatever reason there was no more heat. I never signed the pledge. I made it.

The advice my mother gave on the pledge was characteristic of her. Typically she encouraged me to make my own decisions. For example, when I announced to her that I wanted to attend Sunday school, she explained that if I elected to do so I would have to go way into town every Sunday morning, rain or shine, and that on some Sundays I would have to walk. Sunday school would be fun, she said, but it had its costs; I should not enroll unless I was dedicated. I chose to enroll.

Similarly, I once asked my mother to give me piano lessons. She was a fair pianist; as a girl she had for a short time accompanied silent movies with rousing piano tunes, and she often entertained me by describing war scenes while she played *The Stars and Stripes Forever.* ("Now the soldiers are marching to battle"; "Now the cannons are roaring and men are falling"; "Now survivors are limping home in their tattered uniforms.") In response to my request for lessons she told me she would gladly instruct me but only if I took piano playing seriously; I would have to practice regularly, skipping other things I enjoyed. She gave me a few days to think it over. I decided not to take lessons. It was a dumb decision, but it was mine, and it was all right with her. I expect that this training in decision making had a great deal to do with my later intolerance of sociological whiners, procrastinators, and fuzzy thinkers.

As I said, I am not a Freudian. When I dream about sex or power struggles, I do not do it in symbols. The real stuff is there. I therefore am confident that neither my early ability to make distinctions between what is honest and what is not, nor my early adoration of my pioneering and law-enforcing grandfather, had much to do with my becoming a professor, a sociologist, and a criminologist. A better hypothesis is that injustices I experienced as a boy are reflected in my criminological writings, some of which amount to pleas for a better quality of justice in America. If that is the case, it is not because the injustices triggered some Freudian mechanism such as projection, transference, sublimation, or rebellion. Instead, in my view, I simply learned early on that some people are unfair and then learned how to cope with this fact of life.

Miss Olson instructed the pupils in my first-grade class to take their new crayons from their desks and draw brown kites. We obeyed, and she collected our pictures. The next morning she returned all but one of the drawings to their creators. The one withheld was mine. She raised it high above her head for all the kids to see. "I asked you to draw a brown kite," she said, "but here's a boy who drew a green one." She dropped the paper on my desk. She seemed mad. The kids snickered, and I squirmed. At the time I did not know I was color-blind. I knew only that I was unjustly being ridiculed because I could not tell green from brown.

I learned two things from that experience. First, I sensed immediately that I had to make use of the reading skill my mother had developed in me before I started school. I noted that each crayon had its color printed on a wrapper. If I had only read the word *brown* on the brown crayon, I would have colored the kite correctly. My later kites (and grass, skies, trees, and animals) were properly colored because I carefully read the name of the color on each crayon's label before I got down to the job of doing art. When a crayon wore down so far that I could not read the name of its color, I gave it to my little sister. (Freudians should note that that incident may have been the source of my later resistance to so-called labeling theory.)

Second, I learned after considerable meditation that I was treated unjustly because Miss Olson had taken my unintentional deviance to be deliberate defiance. "I didn't do it on purpose," I told the Dunlap kids when they examined my green drawing as we walked home from school. I gave the picture to my mother but never told her it was the wrong color. In law school twenty years later I heard about strict liability laws. Jerome Hall, one of the giants I had as graduate-school mentors, demonstrated repeatedly that such laws are grossly unjust because under them people are punished for behavior they did not intend. One general rule of justice in our society, I subsequently noted, is that only deliberate deviance or negligence should have pain or suffering as its consequence. Conversely, deviance perceived as stemming from ignorance or some other condition beyond the control of the actor should not be punished; it should be corrected by education, including so-called therapy. Strict liability laws and procedures violate that rule, just as Miss Olson did.

A similar, but more severe, injustice was done to me in the second grade. Miss Bratt encouraged good grooming and hygiene. I thought I was in good shape because my father conditioned me to look after what he called the extremities—to keep my hair combed, my nails clean, and my shoes polished. But I had bad teeth. I had inherited a genetic defect from my grandmother and mother. My teeth, like theirs, had no enamel and were only little brown stubs. Miss Bratt did not know anything about hereditary defects. During a hygiene session she told the second-graders to look at Donald and see what had happened because he did not brush his teeth. I sank. I put my hand over my mouth as I usually did when I smiled, and as my mother and grandmother also did. Nobody laughed. Nobody questioned me. They just stared. Miss Bratt went on to give a lesson on brushing teeth. I did not tell my mother about the incident, but she heard about it from the mother of one of my classmates. She telephoned Miss Bratt and straightened her out, but the call did not undo the injustice done to me. I once again learned the hard way that unintentional deviance should be carefully separated from deviance due to badness or negligence.

Besides teaching me to read and to make my own decisions, my mother taught me not to hate people. Her position was that hate hurts the hater but has no affect on the hated. It was not until I was a sociologist that I discerned that she also taught me that attitudes of hate and forgiveness stem from assessments of intentionality. People who have experienced what they consider an injustice are likely to hate the person imposing the pain or suffering if they decide that the person acted deliberately. However, if the pain and suffering is perceived as having been imposed out of ignorance, the offended person is more likely to forgive than hate. The trick, according to my mother, is to recognize that most, if not all, injustices are unintentionally imposed. Miss Olson was forgiven by my mother and me because she did not know I was color-blind; Miss Bratt, because she did not have all the facts.

Hatred stemming from injustices leads to rebellion and even revolution. Forgiveness of injustices leads to tolerance and sometimes to attempts to effect personal and social change. I have usually opted for the latter, though a seemingly insignificant incident that occurred when I was about eight years old taught me both that people who are poor and ignorant are more likely than others to suffer injustices and that the recipients of injustices sometimes find it hard to differentiate deliberate from accidental oppression.

Through our cousin who lived in town my brother and I got a job peddling bills. The cousin worked for a Mr. Jacobson, who had contracted with the owners of the town's two moving-picture theaters to distribute notices of coming attractions. Each Saturday he hired three or four kids to do the work. They were paid fifty cents, a generous wage. Moreover, Mr. Jacobson was kind and considerate. He drove his Model T Ford out to our house and picked us up, then chauffeured us to various routes. When a carrier came to a sparsely settled locale, Mr. Jacobson was always there in his car to give him a lift between houses.

Before driving us home after one Saturday's work, Mr. Jacobson treated us. He took us to Nelson's Cafe (rhymes with *safe*) on Washington Avenue. We took seats at the counter. I got the stool next to Mr. Jacobson, perhaps because I was the youngest of the four boys who had worked that day. He told us to order what we wanted, but I somehow sensed that his offer was not to be taken literally. None of us had ever been in a restaurant before. There was a good deal of fumbling, stammering, shuffling, and removing of caps and coats. Finally, my brother asked the waitress for a hamburger, which cost a nickel. The rest of us, of course, followed suit. Mr. Jacobson waited patiently until all the kids' orders were in. Then he asked for a hot roast-beef sandwich with potatoes and gravy, a piece of apple pie, and a cup of coffee. Forty cents! I smelled both trickery and grave injustice. I knew that if he had ordered first I would have aped him. I concluded that he had not ordered first because he knew what I knew. As I chewed my dry hamburger with my little brown teeth, I further concluded that Mr. Jacobson was a bad man who had taken advantage of me because I was a dumb little kid. Riding in the back seat of his car on the way home, I changed my mind. After all, it was his treat; maybe he was just being polite when he asked us to order first. I forgave him.

A later incident had a different outcome. I clearly attributed a gross injustice to deliberate, intentional exploitation. My father was an alcoholic. Following an arrest for drunken driving in 1932, he lost his job at the power plant. The company house went with the job. By coincidence we moved to the upstairs rooms of a run-down house two doors down the street from Nelson's Cafe. There I encountered a case of deliberately imposed injustice. My father didn't tell me about it. He modeled it.

The Great Depression was in full swing. My dad could not find a job. We were desperate for food and for rent money, which came to perhaps ten dollars a month. My grandfather once paid the landlord forty dollars for back rent, but my father soon got behind again. Like other desperate men at the time, he decided to become a door-to-door peddler of soap, cosmetics, razor blades, or whatever. He needed money to buy some stock. He knew I had saved up $2.50 from the money I made as a paper boy, and he asked if he could borrow it. I went to the little room I shared with my brother and slipped the money from a secret hiding place under a pile of library books. Back in the tiny kitchen I handed him the two bills and five dimes. He cried. Because it was not the time to talk, he put his arm around my shoulders. Then I cried too.

That evening I stalked the people on Lincoln Avenue as usual, trying to get someone to buy a newspaper. I walked by the town's pool hall. My dad was a good straight-pool player, and when we lived in the country near the power plant, he often drove to town on Saturday afternoons to spend a few hours at this same pool parlor. Kids were not admitted, so I never saw him play. He told me, though, that he could not play for money; if there was as much as a nickel at stake, his game would go to pieces. When we moved to town, his former place of recreation became his hangout. That night I glanced through the plateglass window with POOL painted on it in shaded letters and saw him sitting at the counter. He was a fine singer, and he was at it. A crowd of deadbeats was listening. Through the open door I head his nice voice slurring the words to "The Old Spinning Wheel in the Parlor," which I had heard him sing a thousand times. Although Prohibition had not yet been repealed, it seemed obvious that he was boozing it up with my money. When I came home from school the next afternoon, he was sitting on a stool in the kitchen. I ignored him. I never told him what I had seen and heard at the pool room. I do not think he ever bought the gadgets he said he was going to sell door to door. He didn't repay the $2.50 and indeed never mentioned his debt. Neither did I. My reaction was to hate, not to forgive. It did not change when I later learned that alcoholics supposedly are sick, not evil.

Once we had moved to town, I had obviously become a poor kid— real poor. There was no welfare system in those days, and I went to work delivering the evening *Minneapolis Journal.* After completing my route, I sold papers on the street, mostly to traveling salesmen staying at the River Inn or the Kaddatz Hotel. On a good night I got rid of five or six, at a profit of two cents a paper. Before school I delivered the *Daily Reminder,* a mimeographed advertising sheet. Sunday mornings saw me carrying a ton of what we called the funny papers in a canvas bag slung over my shoulder. After I had delivered most of them I went door to door trying to sell the remainder at a profit of three cents a paper. I could not stand on a street corner and sell Sunday papers to people driving home from church because boys who were bigger and tougher than I "owned" the only two corners worth working. Besides doing all this newspaper work, I did odd jobs—shoveling snow, raking leaves, mowing lawns, pulling weeds, washing windows.

When we were evicted from the apartment near Nelson's Cafe because we could not pay the rent, we moved upstairs above Hansen's Harness Shop. My parents got divorced, and my dad became a squatter, living out by the river in a hut made of packing crates. I visited him once. Later he moved to Duluth, where he remarried. I visited him once there too.

As soon as my father moved out, my mother got a job as a maid, then as a helper at Ethel's Cafe. Ethel was one of her childhood friends. At the cafe the two of them did all the cooking, serving, and washing up. It is obvious to me now that Ethel gave mother the job because she knew we were going hungry. Before long our food was mostly leftovers from Ethel's, but my brother and I supplemented it with a purchase now and then. Also, in 1933 or 1934 my mother was allotted a bag of flour, some salt pork, and some other groceries by one of the budding New Deal relief agencies. I went to the basement of the post office and loaded the food into an old coaster wagon. The men distributing the stuff seemed contemptuous. One guy refused my plea for help in getting the heavy flour sack into the wagon. I felt like a beggar.

Most Sundays, after I had sold my papers, I bought a quart of ice cream and shared it with my sister. Because there was no refrigerator, we had to eat it all. Once or twice a week I went to Peterson's Meat Market and asked the high-school kid behind the tall glass counter for the cheapest respectable thing a person could buy at a butcher shop in those days—ten cents' worth of hamburger. When I entered the store one winter afternoon, three women and a man were standing in front of the counter waiting for the butcher to cut roasts or chops for them. Lawrence Olson, the kid, stood haughtily behind the counter with nothing to do but show off his butcher's cap. As I stepped toward the counter, he called out, "Ten cents' worth of hamburger, I suppose." I froze. In Fergus Falls in the 1930s poor people were thought of as sinners, lazy ne'er-do-wells who would not pull their weight, as my experiences while picking up the government dole of surplus flour and pork had demonstrated. Divorced women and their kids were considered moral lepers. Clearly, Olson's question was designed to let the other customers know that I was one of those degenerate deadbeats. But none of them looked up and stared, as I expected the crowd to do. I shuffled my overshoes in the sawdust on the floor, got my hamburger, and left.

As I entered my sophomore year in high school I gave up journalism and got an evening job working at Lunky Lundquist's Phillips 66 service station. Looking back, it was by far the best job I ever had in Fergus Falls, but I cannot recall how I got it. My associations at the station had a profound impact on my life. The proprietor was a young man whose father, a banker, had set him up in business. Another young man, Jake Smith, worked full-time for him. I thought of the two as old guys. From the banker's son I learned that it was important to have class, meaning that one should be a snappy dresser, speak well, smoke Chesterfields, be judicious, and know who is who in Fergus Falls. Jake Smith gave me a deep respect for knowledge.

I became convinced that Jake Smith knew everything. He gave me little lessons on physics, chemistry, and biology and helped me with algebra. He spoke German and knew a little Latin. He was forever telling me about prepositions and split infinitives. Equally important, he was screwing the seventh-grade English teacher, whom I considered wealthy because she owned a car.

I told my buddies about Jake, and the gas station soon became a hangout for my gang of high-school friends. On one cold winter afternoon four or five teenaged boys were lounging around the station with Jake, cracking jokes and showing off as usual. One complained, as high-school boys will, "There's nothing to do in this town." Jake listened quietly while the rest of us expressed our agreement, then responded by hurling an angry question at us: "What's the atomic weight of lead?" Nobody knew. He told me there was indeed something to do in Fergus Falls—go to the library and find the answer to his question. He kicked all the kids but me out of the station and said they could not return until they had the answer. I was exempt because I was going on duty in a half-hour, when Jake was due to be picked up by the English teacher. The boys, with others, returned after Jake had left. No one had learned the atomic weight of lead. The next afternoon we assembled in Jake's presence. Every boy had the answer, 207.19. Jake then wanted to know the weight of gold, silver, carbon, zinc, and even ruthenium. He did not care about gases.

I regret that neither Jake nor anyone else directed my reading. While I was still living in the country, the woman working in the children's reading room located in the basement of the Carnegie Library got special permission for me to borrow books from the regular library upstairs, where children under thirteen were forbidden. I became an exception, probably because the children's librarian grew weary of me. It was the same story every Saturday morning: after visiting my grandparents, who lived near the library, I lugged my heavy quota of twelve books to the desk, then asked for help in selecting a dozen books for the next week's reading. I was not asking for guidance; my problem was that I had trouble finding books in the children's section that I had not already read.

Moving up to the adult section was like moving into paradise. However, I now needed real guidance but was not wise enough to ask for it. I read randomly. I read classics without knowing it—I selected whatever looked like a good story. My voracious appetite for books continued for two or three years after we moved to town, but I cannot recall that in all that time I read one nonfiction book, including biography and history. Had Jake Smith or someone else set me on a course of reading, I might have turned out to be an intellectual rather than a scientist. By the time I reached my senior year in high school I was mostly reading magazines such as *Liberty, Saturday Evening Post,* and *Colliers'.* Being a sophisticated young man, with class, I also read each issue of *Esquire* from cover to cover.

Shortly after I started pumping gas at Lunky's, my mother left Ethel's for a job as cook at the City Cafe and Bakery. The steady work at fourteen dollars for a seven-day week of ten-hour days enabled her to settle us in the upstairs rooms of a small, ramshackle house in a rather classy part of town. The cafe and bakery were jointly owned by a sister and brother, but the two operations were independent. One afternoon a few months after my mother began working for the sister in the kitchen of the restaurant, I answered the brother's ad for a baker's helper. I got the job and went to work at once. I spent two hours cleaning huge baking trays and pans before walking down the street to my regular job at the service station. My mother was surprised to see me out back in the bakery, or pretended to be. Just before we moved from Hansen's Harness Shop, my brother, also by coincidence, had found a part-time job at the Park Region Bakery, the competitor down the street. Once he learned the trade, he gave up high school for a series of full-time jobs as a baker.

In my own bakery work I gradually advanced from clean-up boy to baker. My hourly pay did not increase correspondingly, but I did not complain. I was grateful, considering myself lucky to have a job and to be learning a trade. When school was in session, I cleaned pans after classes, bused dishes in the restaurant for my noon meal, and worked as a baker's helper on weekends. There were only two men to help—Lloyd Greenwood, who was the owner, and Ira Brown. On Fridays I started helping them at midnight and continued straight through until late Saturday afternoon when I finished up by cleaning the trays and pans. In those days small-town bakers worked outrageous hours during the hot Minnesota summer months when housewives did not care to fire up their ovens. During my last two high-school summer vacations every night was much like the school-year Friday nights and Saturdays. The long hours and the terrible heat from the coke-fired ovens did not make me hate my work. On the contrary, I loved it. In my eyes I was one of those picture-show heroes who meets adversity face to face and stares it down. Everyone who would listen heard me tell how hard I worked. Drudgery was honor. On top of that, I was learning to be a baker. Lloyd or Ira, sometimes both, taught me a new trick almost every night. Because there was little specialization in such a small shop, and because I was a fast learner, Lloyd was soon telling me, my mother, the cafe waitresses, and bakery visitors that I was a "good all-around man." For a seventeen-year-old adult, that was heady praise indeed. I had it made.

I am the first person on either side of my family to graduate from high school. So far as I know, not one of my four grandparents or their brothers and sisters went past the eighth grade. My parents' generation did a little better, but I believe that only two of them, my mother and her sister, got beyond common school, as the first eight grades were called. My cousins, like my sister and brother, dropped out after a year or two of high school.

Still I did not really believe in high school. The love of knowledge I acquired from Jake Smith had nothing to do with getting a high-school diploma. I attended, and graduated, because my friends did the same. I skipped school at two o'clock every afternoon of my senior year, as a matter of principle. I graduated near the bottom of my class, with less than a C average. I liked science and math, and I worked for C's in those two areas. The rest of the subjects did not have any relevance for me. By design I did not flunk any courses but settled for D's. My plan was to work in the bakery for the rest of my life, and I did work there full-time for two years after graduating.

There is contradiction here, for my attitudes were middle-class on most issues. Indeed, when I first read *The Protestant Ethic and the Spirit of Capitalism,* I thought Weber was describing me, my high-school friends, and their families. I desperately wanted to achieve and acquire, but I was going to fulfill that ambition by learning a trade, not by working for good high-school grades. Most of my friends had high aspirations too, but they saw academic achievement as the road to success. One close friend was valedictorian of his class, and two others were not far behind.

My poverty, though severe, was not like that experienced by present-day inner-city dwellers. Fergus Falls had what Oscar Lewis later named a culture of poverty, but I did not participate in it. As a teenager I associated primarily with middle-class kids I met at church, in Boy Scout and Sea Scout activities, and at meetings of the local chapter of the De Molays. The last two sources of friends overlapped the first. There were twenty-six churches for the sixteen hundred families in Fergus Falls, and church membership largely determined social activities. Unless next-door neighbors went to the same church, they ignored each other. Men who worked together but attended different churches sometimes associated socially, but even that relationship was unusual. Similarly, high-school students had few friends from churches other than their own. In the clubs and lodges, such as the Kiwanis, Elks, and De Molays, church membership had little importance; but they were an exception.

Like almost every other church in town, my Presbyterian church sponsored its own Boy Scout troop. At the age of twelve, boys who had gone to Sunday school together joined routinely. When I was fifteen I helped some of the older boys in our troop form a Sea Scout "ship." All but me were middle-class kids whose fathers were steadily employed or were in business for themselves. The "skipper" was a young lawyer who was soon to become mayor. Church members rich enough to own sailboats took us to their lake cottages for weekends of sailing.

De Molays are more or less junior Masons. At age fifteen a boy is eligible for membership if his father or some close relative is a Mason. In my case the relative was my grandfather. Admission was not automatic, however. A single member could veto an applicant. I was only a little worried on the night the group voted in secret on me. I was smart. I had class. I had several good De Molay friends who were Presbyterians and one or two who were not. I made it.

In De Molay activities I met mostly other Wasps: besides Presbyterians, there were Episcopalians, Methodists, and a few Baptists. In fact, it was a Methodist, one of my best buddies, who had encouraged me to join; his father was county superintendent of schools and a hunting and fishing companion of my grandfather. The religious beliefs of the town's four or five Catholic boys and one Jewish boy prohibited them from becoming members. Lutheran churchmen also frowned on the organization, thus discouraging the great majority of the town's boys from joining.

Our De Molay chapter had an ice-hockey team, and we regularly beat the hell out of the poor kids who had teams in the league. More important, the chapter staged three or four formal balls each year. These were significant social events for teenagers in the town. (The school board prohibited high-school dances because dancing, like smoking and drinking, was considered obscene.) Each De Molay was allowed to invite two or three nonmember male friends and their dates to each dance. At these affairs I met most of the sons and daughters of the town's elite, no matter what their religious affiliation. Even Catholic and Lutheran boys and girls attended. Some of these non-Presbyterians and non–De Molays became close friends. One became a Jake Smith guy, the name given by the high-school biology teacher to each of the boys who hung out at the Phillips 66 station.

One by one, most of my many friends went off to college. The two years I spent in the bakery after high school were lonely. I worked nights, when I supposed almost everyone I knew was having fun. I continued to play ice hockey, and I coached a peewee team. I became an assistant scoutmaster. I remained active in Christian Endeavor (a church group), and on Sundays I ushered in church. I took courses that enabled me to qualify as a Red Cross senior lifeguard and, later, a water safety instructor. I had swum, skated, hunted, fished, canoed, sailed, and ice-boated as a boy, but now I became passionate about these sports. I kept my membership in the De Molays and, after progressing through some lower chairs, was elected master councillor, the top dog. Then I made the big time by being elected junior councillor of all the De Molays in Minnesota. This statewide election, combined with the influence of the girl I was to marry, set me on the path to college and eventually a Ph.D. in sociology.

I became good-looking. I was now old enough to be fitted with full dentures. I saved up enough money to make a down payment toward the cost of the extractions and other dental surgery. Every afternoon for about six months I walked from my work at the bakery to the offices of a young man just out of dental school. He spent day after day pulling out pieces of my brown teeth, which were now rotten. When that job was done, he devoted his afternoons to taking a hammer and chisel and knocking pieces of bone off my upper jaw, which was deformed. Then he wired my lower jaw, which also was deformed, to the upper one. After each session I walked home and collapsed. I never failed to get up and go to work at midnight, however. I pretended that only the dentist and I knew about the work, though I discussed it with the bakers and discerned that my other friends knew what was going on. To reveal the pain would have been to show weakness and lack of class. Moreover, I convinced myself that the whole thing was being done for medical science, not just for myself. The dentist charged me practically nothing, saying he was performing the work as an experiment. With my permission he took pictures, which he showed at a dental convention and, he said, were to be published in a dental journal. Eventually I got the new teeth and adjusted to them. One of the girls I had dated in high school came home from college for spring vacation. I met her on a street corner. "Very becoming," she said. So far as I can recall, that was the only comment anyone ever made about what for me was a transformation.

Before long I met Elaine Smythe, the girl who was to become my wife. Her father was an agent for the Northern Pacific Railroad, and he was transferred to Fergus Falls when Elaine was a senior in high school. We met at an Easter sunrise service and soon fell madly in love. We dated steadily all summer, and when she went off to Macalester College in the fall, I gave her the agate ring my mother had given me when I graduated from high school. (My mother, as practical as she was wise, had convinced me that a "real" ring was a better investment than a class ring.) Elaine wrote to me two or three times a week, and almost every letter encouraged me to go to college too. When she came home for holidays, we spent most of our time with other friends home from college. Aside from my twelfth-grade senior English teacher, Rosalie Zien, Elaine was the first person to tell me I was too smart to spend my life in a bakery. I knew I was at least as clever as friends who were now attending college. The evidence was obvious: I had something none of them had—a steady job that paid good money.

The critical incident that sent me off to college was a tiff at the bakery. Lloyd, the boss and owner, had died, and his younger brother, Jimmy, had replaced him. Jimmy, like Lloyd, was a sportsman as well as a good and kindly person. Like Ira Brown, he took me hunting and fishing and let me borrow his car. Nevertheless, I did not have the respect for him that I had for Lloyd, perhaps because I believed that Lloyd was by far the classier of the two. The quarrel with Jimmy grew out of my earlier election as junior councillor for the Minnesota De Molays.

A meeting of state De Molay officers was to be held in St. Paul on a Saturday in February or March 1939. Although I knew very well that Friday nights and Saturdays were the busiest times in the bakery, I asked Jimmy for time off. He withheld his response until our work was done, when he told me he had carefully considered my request and that the answer was no. Any other day would be all right, he said, but there was just too much work to do on Friday nights and Saturdays. I blew up. "I'm going," I shouted. "And if I have to quit to go, I quit." I added, still yelling, that he had taken Friday nights off in the past, that Ira and I had made up for his absence by working harder, and that now he could do that for me. He flushed with what I think was surprise and embarrassment rather than anger.

I acted on the spur of the moment, but I was serious. I had no idea how I would earn a living if I quit my job at the bakery. Still, I seemed to realize that not attending the meeting was tantamount to declaring that I would never leave the baking business. Elaine had made me wonder if that was what I really wanted. The next night Jimmy and I barely spoke to each other. He followed me into the basement dressing room after work. Again he seemed embarrassed. He told me he had reconsidered and that I could have the time off after all. He ended up with a response to my earlier tirade. The gist of it was that he, as boss, was entitled to take a night or day off whenever he wished but that I did not have that option.

I attended the meeting. Jimmy's comments about his prerogatives gnawed at me. Before returning to work on Sunday night I made secret plans to quit the job as soon as possible. I began to consider college as an option. Despite my middle-class associates, I had always thought in terms of a working-class cliché: Learn a trade; they can't take that away from you. "They" were the powerful, and I was one of the masses. Now I saw my future in a related cliché: Get a good education; they can't take that away from you.

I decided to go to a town that had a college or university as well as bakeries. That way I could work nights, get a college education in the daytime, and "they" would not be able to deprive me of it. To decide on a major, I wrote to the Minnesota State Library for copies of interest and aptitude tests. The examinations told me what I already knew, namely, that I was a smart kid who liked mathematics and science. I picked chemistry, partly because of the bakery connection. A flour salesman had once told me about cereal chemistry, the vocation of people who do quality-control studies for flour mills. I wrote to the Pillsbury Mills in Minneapolis, saying I wanted to be a cereal chemist and asking where I should go to college. (I have a hunch that the salutation of my letter was "Dear Mr. Pillsbury.") Soon I received a letter advising me to attend the University of Minnesota, Kansas State University, or Iowa State University. I did not want to go to Minnesota because I had friends there and it seemed too big-time for me. I wrote to Kansas State and Iowa State for catalogues and literature. By coincidence the *Fergus Falls Daily Journal* soon carried a story about how a Kansas State track star had just broken a world record. I decided that Kansas, like Minnesota, was out of my league. That left Iowa State, in Ames.

In March I started putting my wages in the bank. In June I quit the bakery and took a job teaching swimming, rowing, and canoeing at a Boy Scout camp. In August I returned to the bakery for a month before setting out for Ames with $256.60 in my pocket. Once there, I found a cheap attic room, stowed my worldly goods in it, and walked down the street looking for a job. I found one within an hour—candling eggs in a grocery store. A week later I also got a part-time job in a bakery and another as a waiter for my evening meal plus tips. At Iowa State I was not at first eligible for a work-study program financed by the the National Youth Administration (NYA) because my high-school grades were too low. But at the end of the first quarter my college grades made me eligible for an NYA job at twenty-five cents an hour. I quit all except the bakery job and went to work in the psychology department, doing correlation coefficients on a hand-operated calculating machine. Then I transferred to genetics, where I inoculated mice with typhoid and also kept tab on mutant, tipped-winged drosophila. At the end of the first academic year, 1939–40, I went home with my $256.60 still in my hip pocket.

I never doubted that I could finish college. I knew my high-school grades didn't mean anything. Under what is now called an open-admissions policy Iowa State officials admitted anyone who had graduated from high school. Unlike current open-admissions programs, however, the Iowa State curriculum was tough. Half the members of my freshman class did not return after the Christmas holidays. Two-thirds did not return for the sophomore year. The policy was cruel but nevertheless democratic. Everybody got a chance. I made it.

By the beginning of my junior year I thought I could write. I was on the staff of the college literary magazine and had published a couple of short stories in it. I took a job as ghost writer for Agricultural Extension, giving up my bakery job, my NYA job, and also the room-and-board job I held during my sophomore year as live-in baby-sitter and handyman for a geology professor and his wife. Agricultural Extension was made up of a number of divisions, all headquartered in one old building. I started out by helping Robert Clark, who was in charge of the Iowa Rural Youth Division and, I think, had a Ph.D. in rural sociology. My principal task was to edit a monthly newsletter. The gimmick was that I wrote practically every word of every issue, including columns with various fictitious bylines. Word of this enterprise got around the building, and other division heads were soon giving me little writing assignments. I recall such articles as "How Rural Youth Can Prevent

Inflation," "How to Prevent Fire on the Farm," and "How to Raise Honeybees." I made seventy-five cents an hour, which was three times what NYA was paying and five times what the bakery was paying.

Academically I soon lost interest in chemistry. I liked theory but could not stand the laboratory work. The mixing and measuring resembled baking, so I was pretty good at it. But I now perceived bakery work as lacking in class, and that perception might have carried over to laboratory chemistry. My academic adviser, a botanist, told me that if I did not like the laboratory, I should get out of chemistry. In retrospect that was bad advice, but at the time it was reasonable because, after all, my declared interest was in cereal chemistry, a laboratory discipline. Further, I had no plans for graduate work, so I was destined to be a laboratory worker even if my interests shifted to another branch of chemistry. I changed to a major in geology, but the same adviser then convinced me that geologists' work lacked class too. He asked me to look ahead and visualize myself at work ten years down the road. Did I see myself sitting in a shack on an Oklahoma prairie waiting for an oil well to come in? I did not. I saw myself in an office job, though I had never had one. I started looking around for still another major.

Near the beginning of my junior year, as well, I met Bryce Ryan, one of four sociologists attached to the Department of Economics. (That department, I learned later, was clearly first-rate; it was headed by Theodore Schultz, who was to be awarded the Nobel Prize for his work on human capital.) I was introduced to Ryan by a mutual friend, a student, at a coffee session in the student union building. Much to my surprise he knew my name—he said he had read my stories in the literary magazine. I told him I was now trying to write the Great American Novel. He suggested that I might be able to improve my writing by taking a course in sociology and learning something about social relations. Until then I had scarcely heard of sociology.

I enrolled in Sociology 1A pretty much for laughs. Three times a week Ryan, who had just received his Ph.D. from Harvard, lectured an auditorium full of undergraduates on what I later learned was standard Harvard sociology: *culture, social structure,* and *function* came into my vocabulary. After lectures the students broke into small groups and met with a teaching assistant for discussion sessions. My TA was not very good, and the course was awful as a consequence. At mid-term all students took a common examination during one of the lecture periods. I made the best score. Better than that, Ryan came to my table at the student union and congratulated me. I told him that the key to my success was the fact that his lectures were similar to chemistry lectures, emphasizing bonds, links, valences, structures, and interactions. He was both pleased and impressed, and told me so. There were two consequences of such positive reinforcement. First, I became a smart ass: in subsequent discussion sections I told the TA on every possible occasion that he did not know what he was talking about. Second, I became addicted to sociology.

I changed my major. It did not seem like a radical change because to me sociology was like very complex chemistry—but without a mathematical base. Like Bryce Ryan, C. Arnold Anderson, then also an assistant professor at Iowa State, encouraged me to keep thinking along those lines. I still do. Neal Gross, by far the best graduate student then in the sociology department, took me under his wing and also had considerable influence on me. Among other things, he encouraged me to take courses in probability in the mathematics department. My professor was George W. Snedecor, a leader in the development of statistical methods for use in agricultural and biological experiments. I learned chi-square by studying litters of pigs and rabbits, and analysis of variance and multiple regression by studying the yields of millet fields, apple orchards, and plots of corn. Only when I became an assistant professor did I begin to lose my interest (and skill) in statistics.

When I switched from hard science to sociology I found myself with a lot of free time because there were no laboratories. Further, my work at Agricultural Extension did not require the physical energy that bakery work did. For the first time in my college career I had time to read and learn and to have fun while doing so. As I ran upstairs to the third floor of the chemistry building one afternoon, I remembered that when I was a freshman I had many times wearily pulled myself up the same staircase and, moreover, been amazed to see other students more or less skipping up the stairs. Being tired had been the norm, but now I was both energetic and exuberant.

College was no longer just a place to learn how to make a living. It is a bit corny, but I am convinced that Bryce Ryan hooked me on learning, just as Jake Smith had earlier hooked me on knowledge. To top that off, I borrowed four hundred dollars from Iowa State and moved into an apartment with three other seniors, two of whom also liked to play with ideas. The third student, a journalism major, often said he was just interested in reporting the facts; he is now the millionaire owner of a string of magazines. The rest of us eventually got Ph.D.'s—one in chemistry, one in psychology, and one in sociology.

Soon the military draft was instituted, to be followed by the attack on Pearl Harbor and America's entry into World War II. I wanted to get my degree before I went to war, so I took every sociology course in sight, hoping to beat the draft by graduating in March rather than June 1943. I soon ran out of courses. To obtain the number of sociology units needed for graduation, I took an independent-study course on crime and delinquency. My recollection is that I chose that subject because the range of choices was limited by a rule prohibiting independent-study courses on subjects covered in regular courses listed in the college catalogue. My supervisor was George Von Tungelen, a rural sociologist. He did not know any more about the sociology of crime than I did. At the end of the term he told me that my paper lacked focus and assigned it a B. Because I was making straight A's in my sociology courses, I was not pleased. But Von Tungelen was right. I still have the paper; it is awful. More important, however, the independent-study course introduced me to the work of Edwin H. Sutherland, who had recently completed his term as president of the American Sociological Society (now Association). I read *The Professional Thief* and the 1939 edition of *Principles of Criminology,* which contained the first version of Sutherland's differential association principle.

I made it. I graduated in March 1943 and went to war six weeks later. I spent the waiting period as a full-time research assistant to Ray E. Wakeley, a well-known rural sociologist and demographer and Iowa State's most prominent faculty member. I interviewed farmers in connection with a study of noneconomic factors in agricultural production. Previous studies had determined that rich Iowa farmers were not producing as much wartime food as they were capable of producing. It also had been learned that contrary to standard economic assumptions, offering farmers more money did not motivate them to change their behavior. My job was to find out how to get them to produce more. Wakeley arranged interviews for me. I heard him telephone a feed store owner and tell him about me, "He's young, but he's got a good head on him." I liked that. Conducting this simple investigation and writing up the results convinced me that I was a research sociologist and that sociological research was both easy and fun.

Most of the farmers agreed that they were not producing up to capacity. They said the reason was that their machinery had broken down and replacement parts were not available. When I suggested to some that they form machinery cooperatives with their neighbors, they denounced me as a communist. In the report I wrote for Wakeley I nevertheless advocated more cooperatives. Then I made two proposals. It pleases me to recall that one was for positive reinforcement, one for negative reinforcement, though I did not meet B. F. Skinner until I was a graduate student and did not become a behaviorist until I was well into my career as a sociologist. Positively, I proposed that a federal agency start giving farmers medals for producing. Executives of well-managed factories producing war goods were awarded E banners (for *efficiency*) to fly from company flagpoles. My suggestion was that a similar symbol be awarded to efficient farmers. (The theme of one issue of my Agricultural Extension newsletter had been "Food Will Win the War and Write the Peace.") Negatively, I proposed that vigilantes splash yellow paint on the houses of farmers who had deliberately chosen to be slackers.

Two or three months after I gave Wakeley my report on the project I was sitting on my bunk in an Army Air Corps barracks at Buckley Field in Colorado. Mail call brought a copy of the *Iowa Farm Economist*. There was no accompanying letter. Puzzled, I flipped the pages. In the middle of the journal was a glorious version of my first sociology article. What was missing was my name: the report had been edited and then published under Wakeley's. I did not feel exploited, for it had been clear from the beginning that my report was the boss's property. I proudly showed the magazine to my fellow soldiers. They were so impressed that I joined the American Sociological Society and asked my mother to forward my copies of the *American Sociological Review* to my various military addresses. The first issue arrived when I was attending the Air Corps' Engineering and Operations School at Colorado State Teacher's College in Greeley; I carried it under my arm as I walked from class to class, and I made sure that all the instructors saw it on my desk. I doubt that the *Iowa Farm Economist* article had any influence in Washington. Nevertheless, by the end of the war the government was awarding agricultural E banners to patriotic farmers. I have been suspicious of neoclassical economic theory ever since.

After I had completed my first year of military service, most of it in India, Congress passed the GI bill. Bryce Ryan wrote to me almost immediately. The essence of his message was that the bill made it possible for me to do graduate work in sociology and that I ought to plan to do so as soon as the war was over. I deeply appreciated his interest, but the message seemed irrelevant at the time. I was busy helping B-29 aircrews bomb Japan from India and China.

After the marines and infantry captured the Marianas Islands, my outfit moved to Tinian and bombed Japan from there. Another year went by. Then a B-29 squadron on our island dropped the atomic bomb. Suddenly the war was over. I was still alive. I had made it.

During the four months my squadron waited for a ship to take us home, I necessarily thought about what I was going to do as a civilian. Two past events became highly significant. First, I recalled Bryce Ryan's letter encouraging me to do graduate work in sociology under the GI bill. Second, I recalled the name of Edwin H. Sutherland from the independent-study criminology course. In a short V-mail letter to Sutherland I said little except that I would like to do graduate work with him at Indiana. I described my undergraduate record and then cheekily asked for a teaching assistantship, saying that I had married before going overseas and that the GI bill would not pay enough to support us. I enclosed no transcripts of grades, no letters of recommendation, no Graduate Record Examination scores. Sutherland fired a note back to Tinian. He said that he would be delighted to have me as a graduate student, that I had been admitted to Indiana University, that he had reserved a teaching assistantship for me, and that I could come to Bloomington and start work whenever I got out of the Army. It was that simple.

I was discharged in San Francisco, where my wife was working as a medical technologist, in December 1945. Three weeks later I enrolled in the second-semester courses at Bloomington and started working as Sutherland's teaching assistant. (Later I became his research assistant and in that capacity helped him wind up the research for his book *White Collar Crime*.) I was extremely insecure, which was unusual for me. I had done nothing but grunt for three years. Worse, I did not know any sociology. Sutherland, fortunately, was the gentlest man I had ever known. He was very supportive, as were August De B. Hollingshead, Alfred R. Lindesmith, John Mueller, Mary Bess Owen, and others on the faculty. Karl Schuessler, then an advanced graduate student who had returned from the war to write his dissertation, was the person most aware of my insecurity. Besides teaching me sociological methods during long coffee sessions at Tom's Grill, he kept telling me to relax, take it easy, and not try to learn everything in two weeks.

In April I found the confidence and security I was lacking. At the meetings of the Midwestern Sociological Association in Columbus, Ohio, I heard Paul Hatt read a paper on how difficult it was for a veteran to adjust, not to civilian life in general, but to the host of incompetent people passing themselves off as sociologists. Even though I did not know enough about sociology or sociologists to make an intelligent decision about Hatt's attack, I endorsed it with enthusiasm. Then I heard a terrible paper on housing in Cleveland, whose punch line was "Why, in many houses the rats run in and out freely." The paper changed my life. If such crap was sociology, I concluded, then I was surely capable of becoming a competent sociologist. I thought I had it made. I was right. I made it.

CHAPTER ELEVEN

Reflections on Academic Success and Failure

Making It, Forsaking It, Reshaping It

Gary T. Marx

> When I came West with the wagon, I was a young man
> with expectations of something, I don't know what, I
> tarpainted my name on a big rock by the Missouri trailside.
> But in time my expectations wore away with the weather,
> like my name had from that rock, and I learned it was
> enough to stay alive.
>
> —*E. L. Doctorow,* Welcome to Hard Times

My attitudes toward work and life were shaped by an unusual early career pattern—success beyond my wildest expectations, followed by unexpected failure. Given the formative power of that experience, I will restrict my attention to only one of the many topics that an article on work and life might treat: occupational success and failure.[1]

Academic work is publicly and correctly viewed as having a sacred quality involving the pursuit and transmission of truth. But it also involves a job or career carried out in a competitive milieu where the usual human virtues and vices are never far from the surface.[2] I will try to shed some light on this secular side of the profession and to offer some practical advice. I first describe my experiences, then discuss seven characteristics of success and some practical conclusions I have drawn. Although the themes are universal, I have written with two groups in mind: persons beginning their career, and those at mid-career sorting it all out—the former because I wish someone had told me these things when I was starting out, and the latter because they may believe them.

Life Could Be a Dream

In 1970 there could not have been many sociologists just three years beyond the Ph.D. who were as professionally satisfied and optimistic as I was. The promise of the popular 1950s rhythm-and-blues song "Sh-boom" that "life could be a dream" had come true. Immigrants, gold miners, and aspiring actors might head West, but as an ambitious academic born on a farm in central California I had headed east to where I thought the real action was—Cambridge, Massachusetts.

I had a job at Harvard with a higher salary and a longer contract (negotiated under threat of deserting to another Ivy League school) than the other assistant professors in the Department of Social Relations. I taught only one course and had a mammoth corner office, where I was protected from intruders by my own secretary in an outer office.

My book *Protest and Prejudice* had sold fifteen thousand copies and had been translated into Japanese. Various chapters had been reprinted in more than twenty books. The major newspapers, magazines, and radio and television media gave good coverage to research I had done on the civil-rights movement, civil disorders, and community police patrols. From my experience in presenting papers at the annual meetings of the American Sociological Association I assumed that it was not unusual to receive more than 150 requests for preprints of a timely paper.[3]

After receiving my Ph.D. from the University of California, I had barely settled into Cambridge and got over jet lag in September 1967 when I received an invitation to join the staff of the National Advisory Commission on Civil Disorders. Barely a year before, in beard and sandals, I had been sitting in smoke-filled cafés on Telegraph Avenue in Berkeley, listening to folk music and talking about the machinations of the power elite, plotting coups and bemoaning the sad role of co-opted American intellectuals. At Harvard I became a regular on the Boston-Washington shuttle and dressed in a three-piece suit. I eagerly rejected Thoreau's advice, "Beware of all enterprises that require new clothes." Ignoring the sarcasm, I chose instead to follow Bob Dylan's advice, "Get dressed, get blessed. Try to be a success."

A student-published course evaluation booklet (*The Harvard Confi-Guide*), known for its biting critiques, praised my courses: "Marx ranks among the best lecturers in the University. . . . If you don't take the course, at least sit in on some of the lectures." I was fortunate to encounter an unusually bright, well-read, socially conscious group of graduate and undergraduate students, some of whom are now major figures in American sociology. We were on the same side of the generation gap and shared intellectual interests, a desire to see research aid social change, and a quest for professional status. Training students and involving them in research was deeply fulfilling. (It also allowed me to get more work done.)

I received several prestigious fellowships that enabled me to take leaves of absence. My name was added to the list of those under consideration to be invited for a year in residence at several think tanks. Consultation and research money was falling into my lap. CBS-TV needed a consultant for a series on urban areas. ABC-TV wanted a commentator on the Kerner Commission report. *Encyclopedia Britannica* wanted an article on riots. The Joint Center for Urban Studies of MIT and Harvard offered summer salaries. Unsolicited, funding sources such as the Urban Institute and Law Enforcement Assistance Administration offered me money for research; all they required from me was a letter of a few pages, and I would receive a grant.

At a relatively young age I was fortunate to have the chance to serve on the editorial boards of several major journals and was elected to the Council of the American Sociological Association, enjoying the company of senior colleagues old enough to be my parents and even grandparents. The mail routinely brought inquiries about positions elsewhere, along with requests to write books, articles, and reviews for both academic and popular publications, serve on editorial and other boards, participate in symposia, and give lectures and deliver papers at an array of academic meetings both in the United States and abroad. The invitations removed from me the anxiety and risk many of my peers experienced as they sought professional attention. I was not conducting research with only a hope that someday, somehow, the results would be published. Instead, I could adopt the more cost-effective and safe technique of filling orders on hand. Since invitations were usually general, I had the freedom to write on whatever I wanted.

It seemed to be a seller's market. In one of those nasty social principles wherein the rich got richer, each invited article or presentation triggered new invitations in an almost geometric expansion. Each article was an investment that earned interest. My problem was not having the goods rejected but finding it impossible to keep enough in stock. The certainty of publication probably encouraged me to produce more than I otherwise might have and perhaps to let it go to press earlier. It also may have meant a freer, more interpretive writing and research style because I did not have to conform to the expectations of an editorial board or reviewers committed to a narrow notion of sociological research.[4] Since esteemed members of my profession were offering these invitations, my self-confidence increased and I came to believe that I had important things to say. Perhaps a positive labeling effect was at work.

I brushed up against a busy world of movers and shakers, elites, and academic gatekeepers. Editors, reporters, lawyers, and heads of social-research consulting firms asked me to dine at expensive restaurants and private clubs or tendered invitations to cocktail parties. Often they asked me for my opinion or help on topics I knew nothing about. I negotiated a contract to do a race-relations textbook with a colleague for what seemed in 1970 to be an unprecedented sum, far greater than my annual salary. I had lunch with Vice President Humphrey and dinner with several Cabinet secretaries. I attended briefing lunches and dinners with other real and aspiring political leaders. I was approached by a former (or so he claimed) CIA agent still working for the government but in some other capacity. He had read *Protest and Prejudice* and wanted to talk about the student movement. I eagerly responded to a request to join a group of academics helping Robert F. Kennedy's 1968 presidential campaign and drafted a position paper.

This bountiful professional harvest spilled over into private life. We lived in a university-owned apartment in the heart of Cambridge in a former botanical garden. We were invited to large, somewhat formal dinner parties attended by celebrated American intellectuals in eighteenth-century homes. Our son was the only nonconnected four-year-old accepted into Shady Lane, a wonderful Cambridge school founded by William James and John Dewey. We bought an expensive foreign car and land on Martha's Vineyard. Plans for the summer home were drawn up. I developed a taste for sherry and even pretended to enjoy playing squash.

I had moved from being an unknown graduate student at a state university in the outback to what seemed to be the core of American academic and political life.[5] George Homans, Alex Inkeles, Seymour Martin Lipset, Talcott Parsons, and David Riesman were all down the hallway from my office. It was the same hallway that not long before had been graced by Pitirim Sorokin, Gordon Allport, and Clyde Kluckhohn, located in a building named after still another illustrious predecessor, William James. The periphery of the Kennedy circle of advisers from Harvard beckoned. One of my mentors, Daniel P. Moynihan, had moved on to a job in the White House.

I would eagerly return to my office (after an afternoon or day away) in the hope of finding several neatly written pink phone messages requesting that I return a New York or Washington call. Those little pink notes were lifelines, unobtrusive symbolic indicators bearing evidence of a career in motion. The higher reaches of sociology and perhaps even American intellectual life, public service, the mass media, and a patrician life-style all seemed to be beckoning. This was heady stuff for a person whose highest aspiration a decade before had been to write a master's thesis that would receive one scholarly citation[6] and who kept the following lines from jazz-blues singer Mose Allison in his top drawer:

> I made my entrance on the Greyhound bus
> I don't intend to cause a fuss
> If you like my style, that's fine with me
> But if you don't, just let me be
>   I got some kids,
> I got a wife
> I'm just trying to swing my way through life

As a student of American society I knew all about blocked mobility aspirations. But my situation was the reverse (or so it seemed during those glorious years of ascent). I had not been denied anything I felt entitled to. Instead I sometimes felt I had received things I did not deserve. In three short years, from 1967 to 1970, I had already achieved far more than I ever intended or expected.

In the warm glow of solidarity offered by elites who validate each other's status through self-fulfilling effects, it was easy to believe that what I was doing was important and that my success was meaningful and appropriate and could only increase. True, I knew that the chances of someone who had not received at least one degree from Harvard getting tenure were very slim.[7] But I was too busy to think much about tenure in those early years. Besides, there was always the exception, and wasn't I on the fast track (as the list of achievements I also kept tucked away in the top drawer of my desk indicated)? Clearly sociology offered a great career if you had the right stuff. Who knows where it might lead?—an endowed chair, a deanship, a presidential appointment, honorary degrees, plenary addresses, editorships, more foreign translations, directorship of a research center, perhaps a best-selling novel and even a movie career. Was life ever so sweet for a young academic? Could a surfer from California disguised in academic clothing find happiness in an eastern elite academic setting? Did the rising sun have to set?

My academic knowledge of stratification and fashion should have told me that the dream could not last. That realization was not as sudden as when my chance for all-city high-school track medals was dashed when I broke an ankle just before the big meet in the Los Angeles Coliseum. There was no single calamitous incident. But gradually the sweet smell of success turned slightly rancid. As traditional achievements became less satisfying and little failures accumulated, stalagmites of disillusionment, anger, and confusion built up over several years.[8] What I had naively assumed to be the natural order of things turned out to be but a passing phase conditioned by historical factors and luck.

After the Fall

In 1972 someone even younger than me, and with (at the time) a less impressive teaching and publication record, was suddenly given tenure in sociology. I had to give up my big office as a result. My book went out of print. A race-relations reader I edited did not sell well enough to recoup the advance. The race-relations text was never written. A partially written introductory text done with several colleagues, and which was supposed to make us comfortable and even rich, was rejected by the publisher. A number of editors I knew lost or changed jobs. After more than a decade of receiving everything I applied for, a grant application was rejected, and then another. The Republicans had taken over Washington. Whites writing about minority groups and favoring integration came under increased attack from segments of the left and the right. Liberal approaches to social issues became less fashionable. Advertisements made up an increased proportion of my mail. The reporters stopped calling. The pink phone messages were mostly from the library about overdue books and reminders to bring home a quart of milk and some bananas.

When my two most supportive senior colleagues and mentors left Harvard for Stanford, I realized that it was time to look further afield for work. Yet by 1972 the job offers had become fewer. A long-promised job in the University of California system turned out not to be there when I finally wanted it. A promised year at the Russell Sage Foundation suddenly fell through. I had several years left on my Harvard contract in 1973, but in an anticipatory version of you-can't-fire-me-I-quit, I left Harvard for an associate professorship at MIT. Although certainly a good move in a market that was starting to tighten up, it was not the move to full professor that I naturally assumed would be my right should I leave Harvard.

My son made some great ashtrays in his progressive private school, but my wife and I came to have doubts about its permissive learning environment. Leaving Harvard meant giving up our ideal Cambridge apartment in our ideal academic ghetto and moving to a faceless suburb with affordable housing and neighbors whose politics, life-styles, and landscaping were far from what we had become accustomed to. The engine block in our foreign car cracked. A forest fire burned our land on Martha's Vineyard and exposed its proximity to the Edgartown dump. We sold the land.

I now had to confront ghosts that had lain dormant during the past decade of continuous graduate school and professional success. My need for achievement had been well served in those early years. I was able to leverage the success I found against inner demons always ready to tell me that I was not worth much.

Of course the need to display occupational merit badges is part of the American achievement ethos. But I was also responding to childhood experiences with a father who, whatever his virtues, was difficult to please. His own needs were such that he made me feel very inferior.[9] As a result I had a strong need to prove myself. Seeking the external symbols of success was a way to demonstrate to the world and myself that the inner doubts I harbored were mistaken. Like Max Weber's Puritans looking for a sign of redemption through their worldly striving, I looked for evidence of my competence through competitive efforts—in high school through athletics, speech contests, student government, and stylish conspicuous consumption,[10] and later in graduate school and beyond by applying for grants and submitting papers for publication.[11]

My experience in those early years had supported a simple, adolescent, Nietzschean (and probably male) view in which the world could be neatly divided into winners and losers, leaders and led, those in the inner circle and those outside it. Of course, depending on the arena, one might be in or out. But many of my youthful memories revolve around a desperate need to be in that circle. Good taste required not openly acknowledging the intensity of the drive or that sweet, smug feeling that success made possible. But the quiet, invidious feelings achievement permitted were terribly important. Through grit, determination, hard work, and luck I had done a good job of showing the world where I stood—at least up to the early 1970s.[12]

Then things changed. The appropriate tragic model was not the Greek hero destroyed by his own virtues, but the Biblical hero Job brought down by random external forces. I was the same person doing what I had always done (and probably even doing it better), and yet things were not working as they had before. I had jumped through what I thought were the appropriate burning hoops, but the cheers were now muffled.[13] I had worked very hard to reach the brass ring, but it was always just out of reach. I had constructed a positive self-image based on possessing a nice suit of clothes, but they now were in danger of becoming outmoded and even being repossessed. I was suddenly vulnerable in a way I had not been before. What is more, the achievements that had given me so much pleasure in the past seemed less fulfilling on repetition.

Not even old enough for a real mid-life crisis, I went through a period of reassessment and asked all the familiar questions: What did it all add up to? Was it worth it? Why keep playing the same old game if the connection between merit, hard work, and reward was not assured or if the reward was not all that great to begin with? What were my goals? Who was I, after losing some of the formal trappings of success? What was important? Was there life after Harvard and the bountiful harvest of my first decade in sociology? My answers were hardly original, but they worked for me.

I came to terms with both winning and losing and was better able, as Kipling advised, to "meet with Triumph and Disaster and treat these two imposters just the same." I developed a perspective that made both failure and success easier to understand and accept. A part of this perspective is awareness of a Woody Allen paradox wherein when we do not have what we want, we are unhappy, but should we get it, it turns out not to be enough.[14]

Seven Characteristics of Success

While success is nice to have, it is not all it is cracked up to be:

1. *It does not last.* Mark Twain said, "One can live for two months on a good compliment." Depending on one's psyche two hours or two weeks might also apply. But as a character in a Neil Simon play observes, "Nothing recedes like success." With appalling regularity, there is always a later edition of a journal or newspaper telling someone else's story. Books go out of print and journal articles cease to be read. The

pages rapidly yellow and are forgotten. People ask what you are doing *now*. Colleagues who know what you have done retire, and they are replaced by younger persons unaware of your contributions. To make matters worse, unlike the natural sciences, sociology is not very cumulative. Whatever social wheel you discover may be rediscovered a few years later by someone at another school or in another discipline unaware of what you have done (or at least not acknowledging it in a footnote). The Romans were wise to have servants march next to victorious generals in parades and whisper in their ears, "Fame is a passing phenomenon."

2. *You can never be successful enough (at least in your own eyes). No matter how good you are, there is always someone better.* Whatever you did, you could always have done it better and done more, or done it earlier. You never were as important or well known as you thought you were. Even the truly famous are not exempt.[15] What is worse, you never really get there. As Durkheim observed, in a rapidly transforming society you can never achieve enough success. When what is at stake is something as open-ended as reputation, productivity, impact, or accumulation, there is no clear limit. With each higher level of achievement the definition of success changes such that it is forever out of reach. By contrast, failure more often seems limited and finite: you know when you have hit the wall.

3. *The more success you have, the harder it becomes to reach the next level of achievement.* As one moves from getting accepted to graduate school, to getting a Ph.D., to getting a teaching job, to getting tenure and national awards and distinction, the competition gets stiffer, the number of slots declines, and the price of success increases. With each level of achievement the field is narrowed. Once a certain level is reached, there is little variation among participants. Everyone is qualified and hardworking, and there are fewer rewards.

4. *There is a diminishing-returns effect.* National Basketball Association star Larry Bird captured it in his comment on receiving the Most Valuable Player Award a second time: "It's funny because when you're a kid you can't wait to get those trophies. You get 'em home and shine 'em up. Now I forget all about 'em. I got one last year that I left in a friend's truck for a whole year before he reminded me of it."[16] The satisfaction from external rewards is not as great the second or third time around, whether it be delivering or publishing a paper, writing a book, or getting a grant. Part of the reason may be just the diminution of passion that

comes with aging. But repetition does not have the same kick. The sense of curiosity and expectation that accompanies the initial pursuit of rewards weakens once they have been achieved. It has become clear to me that a meaningful life cannot be constructed out of repetitively doing things to please an impersonal public.

5. *Success may have costly and unintended side effects (apart from the price initially paid to achieve it).* There are the obvious dangers of hubris and taking yourself too seriously and the bottomless-pit (or perhaps ceilingless-roof) quality of success. Less obvious is the paradox that success brings less time to do the very thing for which you are now being recognized. In an academic setting increased achievement is associated with increased responsibility. Being well known brings good-citizenship requests to review articles and books, write letters of recommendation, and serve on committees. Although such invitations are symbolic of success and can be directly or indirectly marshaled to obtain still more success, they can seriously undermine productivity. A virtue of obscurity is greater control over your time and greater privacy.

Public visibility may bring requests for more information about your research, job offers, and speaking, consulting, and research invitations. But being quoted or reviewed in the print media or seen on television may also bring appeals from job seekers, salespersons, and charities and requests for free advice or help on topics you know little about. When your topic is controversial, as mine on race, civil disorders, secret police, and surveillance tended to be, you are also likely to get bizarre missives including hate mail and threats, incomprehensible letters from very crazy people, and be besieged by persons seeking to recruit you to propagate strange ideas and schemes.

6. *The correlation between ability, or merit, and success is far from perfect.* This is of course a central sociological message. Factors beyond merit that may bear on the distribution of rewards include the makeup of the selection committee, what it had done the previous year, timing, the characteristics of the applicant pool, and intellectual, ideological, or personal biases. Even when the selection process is fair, rejections are often more a comment on the scarcity of rewards than on the incompetence of applicants. The major factors here are surely organizational. But the structure and ambiguity of reward situations also make it possible to mask the role sometimes played by corruption.

With age and experience you come to feel comfortable judging, and even sometimes doubting the judges.[17] There are enough questionable cases involving tenure and promotion, the awarding of grants, and the acceptance of materials for publication to make clear the role of non-achievement criteria in social reward. Cynical awareness of this state of affairs need not make you throw in the towel or become corrupt, but it may mean slowing down, putting less emphasis on outcomes, and becoming more philosophical about failure and success. This awareness can take some of the sting out of defeat. It also ought to take some of the pride out of victory.[18]

7. *There is no reason to expect that what you do next will be better, by your own standards, than what you have done in the past or will necessarily bring equivalent or greater recognition and reward.* In graduate school and the early professional years this may not be true. You start with little, so each achievement is a milestone and more rewarding than the last. Yet this training effect is short-lived. Career satisfaction in academia and the quality and quantity of productivity are not linear, in spite of the rhetoric of cultural optimism and metaphors of growth. Academics are not like professional athletes, many of whom gradually peak over a period of three to six years and then fall off. For the minority of Ph.D.'s who continue to do research after receiving their degrees, the average pattern for both the quality of their work and the recognition it receives is probably jagged.[19] There may be periods of intense creativity and productivity, followed by periods of reading, pursuing unrelated interests, or laying the ground for the next period of activity. Fallow periods, if that be the right term, are nothing to worry about (at least if you have tenure). As in agriculture, they may even be functional.

Practical Lessons

Three broad practical lessons follow from these perspectives on success and failure: (1) value the process of creating as an end itself; (2) develop new professional goals; (3) do not make your career your life.

Turning to the first, it is necessary to value the process of creating. Work has to be fun and interesting in its own right, apart from any external rewards once it is finished. Harry Chapin caught this idea when he sang:

> Getting off this dirty bus
> one thing I understood.
> It's got to be the going
> not the getting there that's good.

In graduate school I was impressed by Erich Fromm's argument to live life such that you did everything as an end in itself and not as a means. At the time I saw this directive in terms of interpersonal relations. It never occurred to me that the argument had local occupational application. But I now see that once you have tenure, if you do not enjoy the research or writing (apart from whatever payoff the finished product might bring), then it is not worth doing. I came to realize that I got pleasure from finding partial answers to questions I wondered about, turning a clever phrase, ordering a set of ideas, and seeing connections between apparently unrelated phenomena. In a competitive world of uncertain and perhaps unsatisfying reward there is much to be said for valuing the process of production as an end in itself.[20]

The focus on process and becoming can mean less concern over the quantity of work produced and fewer comparisons to colleagues. It can protect against judging yourself by some quantitative standard wherein whatever you do next has to be more and better than what you did earlier and bring greater rewards. If for personal satisfaction what matters is enjoying your work, then it does not much matter how many publications that work eventually leads to, or how quickly, or even in which places it gets published. I am not particularly troubled that some of my work may never be published, or may be published a decade after its completion, or may bounce down the prestige hierarchy of journals before finding a resting place. This attitude contrasts markedly with the rational cost-benefit calculation and the intensity and snobbishness about publication I felt as a young academic. What matters most is a sense of engagement with your work and of movement. I do not deny that the need for social recognition can be congruent with, and even conducive to, the advancement of knowledge or that there is pleasure in seeing an article or book in print—producers need markets for validation and feedback. But that is not enough to sustain research activity, particularly after a professional reputation is established.

A second conclusion involves the need to develop new professional goals because of the diminishing-returns effect and the increasing difficulty of climbing ever higher. I broadened my professional and personal goals (described in the next section). In the case of the former, I expanded my intellectual repertoire. You are likely to discover early in your career that you quickly master contemporary sociological research knowledge regarding your topic (or if not, at least get bored with it). Occasionally there will be some highly informative, useful, or fresh empirical findings, concepts, theoretical approaches, or methods, but not often. Although by and large it is not true that sociology consists of "findings of the obvious by the devious" (as an Alison Lurie character suggests), there is not much new under the sun after you have been out in it for a while.[21]

I sustained intellectual interest by developing new substantive areas of interest, turning to comparative research and to other disciplines, investigating new sources of data and methods, and taking up consulting. My initial interest was in race and ethnic relations, part of a more general interest in stratification. Partly as a result of being a white studying blacks in an age of black power, but more out of the fatigue I have described, I shifted from race-relations research to questions combining my interest in race and ethnic issues with an interest in collective behavior and, later, deviance and social control. I now see the latter giving way to an interest in questions concerning technology and society. Such moves are gradual and not very rational. You cannot predict your intellectual trajectory by what you are concerned with in graduate school. But I would venture that unless you change and expand, it is easy to get turned off to intellectual inquiry.

Variety can come from studying in some other country what you have studied here. It is fun, and there are solid intellectual grounds for doing it. I went to India to study race relations. I went to France and England to study police. I hope to go to Scandinavia to study computer systems. Beyond the new intellectual horizons travel presents, it offers a new set of colleagues and new bodies of literature and outlets for publication. Whatever knowledge may be gained, I get a strange pleasure from struggling to read the French journal I receive.

Variety can also come from learning what other disciplines have to say about your topic. One consequence of having spent more than a decade in a planning department that is problem-centered rather than discipline-centered is a continual reminder of the variety of perspectives, methods, and data sources needed to understand a phenomenon. In this sense discipline-based professional education, with its insular, self-aggrandizing, and often imperialistic tendencies, does an intellectual disservice.

Although I always start with sociological questions, they are no longer enough. Over the years they have been supplemented by a series of questions from psychology, political science, economics, history, law, and ethics. What is more, for the research that touches on public issues I have added a broad normative question: given what I have learned from my research, where do I stand on a policy issue, and what would I recommend? In graduate school, still reeling from the conservatism of the 1950s and the thrust to make sociology a science, such issues were ignored or seen as disreputable.

I have also broadened my definition of data and of what I feel comfortable working with. For both my M.A. thesis on Father Coughlin and my Ph.D. dissertation on the civil-rights movement I used standard survey research data. I continued to conduct survey research for several years after getting the Ph.D., but now rarely do. Instead, I have made increased use of observational, historical, and literary materials. My book *Undercover* has a historical chapter. In my work on forms of interdependence between rule breakers and rule enforcers I am analyzing novels and film. In my work on social movements I am investigating the role of art and songs in mobilizing people. My work on electronic surveillance methods for discovering violations deals directly with ethics. This broadening I advocate may not endear you to those with highly specialized disciplinary concerns who have their hands on the reward levers of your profession. But it is likely to enhance the quality of the intellectual product. The sense of growth and development it offers feels good and helps keep one fresh.

What I have described represents diversification rather than displacement. I have expanded the questions I am concerned with, the kinds of evidence I see as data, the places I look for them, and the methods I use. The movement between questions, data, methods, and location has not been linear. Instead it has, to a degree, been cyclical. I think that characteristic is another key to staying motivated. It is easy and fun to come back to a topic after having been away for a while. New materials will have appeared, and the experiences you have had in the interim may cause you to see what was once familiar in a new way. There is some salvation in moving back and forth between qualitative and quantitative, domestic and international, contemporary and historical, basic and applied questions and the various social-science disciplines.

This diversity also makes it easier to have a few irons always in the fire. If nothing more, it gives one a modest reason to go to work: to check out the mail. Beyond statistically improving your chances of success, having submitted multiple articles, proposals, and grant applications can serve as a kind of safety net for the imagination. When a rejection comes, you have the hope that the other things still out will meet with a happier fate. Of course, there is the risk of a harder fall if they all end up being rejected. However, with enough nets and fishing lines out, that need never occur. The future has an open-ended quality that can be wonderfully conducive to optimism. I also guard against demoralization from rejection by typing out two letters whenever I submit an article. The first is to the journal to which I am submitting the article, and the second (undated) is to the next place I will send the article if it is rejected. I would not deny, though, that there is also wisdom in knowing when to fold, as well as when to hold.

Another professional goal that I actively pursued for a while (but am now ambivalent about) involved earning extra income through consulting and textbook writing. Earning money did not become an obsession, but I stopped seeing it as necessarily an unworthy goal. It was what I did to earn it, I thought, that merited moral evaluation, not the goal per se.

If making all the right academic moves did not insure success or satisfaction, why not use the same skills and credentials to get rich? The payoff was likely to be more certain and immediate, and the standard required was less demanding. Given disillusionment and fatigue with academic amateurism, it was easy to rationalize spending more time playing for pay instead of for honor, footnotes, and the acclaim of adolescents.[22] However, as will be noted, this emphasis is not without problems if you remain committed to academic values.

A reassessment of the bourgeois life began with my move from Berkeley to Cambridge. My senior colleagues were living well, and well beyond their academic salaries. Spacious, elegantly restored historic homes with cleaning services, travel to exotic places in the winter and vacation homes in the summer, camp and enriched education for children, gourmet foods and foreign sports cars were not available to persons who gave all their royalties to political causes (as I had originally planned to do) or who only did social research gratis on behalf of causes they believed in. This shift in emphasis began symbolically with my gradual acceptance of, and eventual belief in, the usefulness of an electric can opener. We received one as a wedding present in the 1960s, and it stayed in its unopened box for many years. For reasons I cannot clearly recall, at the time it seemed to epitomize all that was wrong with our society. Brick-and-board book shelves were replaced by real book shelves. A new sofa eliminated the need for a draped Mexican serape to disguise the sorry state of the sagging couch beneath it. We came to view paying someone to clean the house as salvation rather than exploitation.

While it was nice to have the extra income, earning outside money was not all that great either. It got boring, and I did not like the feeling of being a sociologist for sale: have ideas and methods, will travel. I was not comfortable with the salesmanship that pleasing and finding clients seemed to require. After all, I had chosen an academic life rather than the commercial life of my ancestors precisely to avoid the need to pander to customers. The pressures to meet deadlines were much greater than in the university. I felt the consulting reports I wrote were generally unappreciated and unread, except for the oversimplified and watered-down "executive summaries" with which they had to begin.

There were also role conflicts. The norms of scholarship sometimes conflicted with the interests of my employer. The substitution of market and political criteria for those of truth and intellectual rigor troubled me. It was alienating to be told what research to do and to have business persons and bureaucrats place conditions on intellectual inquiry. I did not like the lack of editorial and distributional control over what was produced.

I encountered bad faith on the part of employers. Thus, in an evaluation of a community-oriented criminal-justice project I pointed out how innovative and important the program was, while also honestly documenting problems and ways of overcoming them. Imagine my surprise when the research document was not used to improve the program but to kill it. It became clear that the hiring agency viewed research as a tool to pursue a course of action that had been decided before the research was undertaken. In another example a well-established consulting firm hired me to write a proposal for a large grant and promised me a major role in it. The grant was funded, although all I received was an invitation to serve on the advisory panel of the study.

I felt uncomfortable with the pressures and temptations to dilute work, cut corners, treat issues superficially, and delegate tasks I was hired to do to much lower-paid graduate students. These could be rationalized since consulting standards were generally lower than those of academic peer review. The goal was to maximize income rather than obtain a high level of craftsmanship, which in most cases would not have been recognized or appreciated.

I emphasized earning extra income for about five years. I met with some modest financial success and learned some things about government programs, textbook writing, and social science as business. It was a nice break from my early years but clearly could not sustain me. I gradually moved back to a predominant focus on academic work and caught a second wind. I still appreciate the benefits of doing sociology in applied and remunerative settings, and I have not given up such activities entirely—they can keep you fresh, involved, and informed and be a source of research data and a way to influence policy and shape debate.

It is refreshing to meet people who actually do things rather than merely talk about what others do. Yet if you are fortunate enough to have a job in an academic setting, it seems foolish not to take advantage of the freedom for intellectual inquiry it offers.

The third practical conclusion I reached was that your career cannot (or should not) be your entire life. Not only did I question the payoff from occupational success beyond a certain point, but I also saw the price that excessive devotion to a career could extract from personal and family life. The prospect of being a narrow, one-dimensional person with a good chance of having family trouble and an early heart attack was unappealing, even if there had been greater certainty in the hard work-success-happiness connection.

In the initial years after moving from Harvard to MIT I left several projects undone for lack of funding and graduate students. A bit weary and cynical about the single-minded pursuit of academic achievement, I devoted more time to highly personal, noncompetitive activities over which I had more control. I spent more and better time with my family, rebuilt a dilapidated Victorian house, learned to play the guitar, read novels, kayaked wild rivers, and worked on a family history project. Watching "Sesame Street" with a young companion, plastering and painting walls, scrutinizing the 1840 Detroit census for information about a great-grandfather, struggling with an out-of-tune guitar, and catching up on a decade's worth of unread novels were far removed from the usual academic obsessions and compulsions.

The respite from an unrelenting focus on academic work gave me great pleasure. Concrete activities provided immediate rewards. Ascriptive rather than achievement criteria were present. There were no risks and no concern over whether distant judges would find me wanting. These activities belonged to me in some very basic sense. They could not be taken away or withheld by editorial or academic gatekeepers. My family history, for example, was simply waiting to be discovered. The work was intensely personal and involved no deadlines or evaluations.

Yet as with exclusively playing the monastic academic game or going commercial, focusing primarily on quality of life also has its limits. It is not much fun to paint the same room a second time. Small children quickly become adolescents who do not want to go on family outings with you. You can trace back family history only so far.

After five years of spending considerable time on other things, I returned to the conventional academic activities of applying for grants, writing journal articles, and presenting papers. I was fortunate to find and help develop a broad topic involving social control, deception, and technology that has sustained me for more than a decade. I find issues of surveillance and society and the revelation and concealment of information endlessly fascinating. The topic has implications for social theory and social change. It is of interest to academic, practitioner, and general audiences, and I have not had trouble obtaining resources to investigate it. Through working with congressonal committees, federal agencies, public interest groups, and the media, the research has also had some modest impact on shaping national debate and on public policy.[23] But I have not pursued this project with the same single-mindedness or desire for professional success of the early years. My life has become more balanced.

There are some issues that I have not resolved. One concerns feelings of being underutilized and underappreciated,[24] which comes with being the only academic sociologist in an interdisciplinary department of urban studies and planning at a technology institute.[25] To be sure, in other ways my department and MIT have offered a superb home. There are advantages to being left alone in an environment where no one is like yourself. But it leaves a vague sense of loss.[26] The part of academic life that I have found most satisfying is mentoring and working with younger colleagues and students on research. I would have learned and published more and done less self-questioning had I had the steady flow of students and the day-to-day validation and chance to contribute that large graduate sociology programs offer. It does not feel right to offer a new class or hold office hours and have few or no students appear. What kind of a professor are you if no one seems interested in what you profess?

Another unresolved issue is what to do with the anger I still feel toward certain persons who have treated me unfairly or simply wounded my pride. These actions were in discretionary contexts where what I believe to be the ideological and personal motives could easily be masked. On any broad scale such events were minor and are now long gone. Intellectually I know that to dwell on the past is unproductive and I may even be wrong in attributing personal and political moves to some of the rejections, but the feelings remain. Life is too short to waste time on replaying the past, and the evidence indicating unfairness is rarely unequivocal.

But in general I have ceased being so self-reflective. The issues about work, life, and identity that had troubled me became less important. I realized I was caught in the paradoxes of achievement and its discontents. I became more accepting of dilemmas and tensions that had once consumed enormous amounts of emotional energy. Instead of viewing these as problems to be solved and choices to be made, I was better able to accept personal and professional contradictions and multiple motives as the order of things and, in Robert Merton's words, to appreciate the "functional value of the tension between polarities."[27] Sometimes I would be drawn to one end of a continuum and at the other times to its opposite. Sometimes I would try to combine them in my writing or bridge them in my political work.

I also realized that I wanted a number of things that could not be had to the fullest extent or necessarily all at the same time. I compromised and settled for less of any one in order to have some of each.[28] Instead of worrying about what I "really" was and what I valued most, I saw that I was probably more marginal than most people. I came to value being something of an invisible person and social chameleon, able to fit into, and move in and out of, different worlds. This quality may be part of my intellectual interest in deception, passing, and infiltration.

I am both the intensely driven, hardworking, competitive, ambitious person (like those I encountered early in my career) and the laid-back bohemian surfer of my California days; the intellectual interested in ideas for their own sake and one of the progeny of Karl Marx and C. Wright Mills who wanted to see ideas linked to change (perhaps a committed spectator, as Raymond Aron termed it); the quantitative and systematic sociologist and the journalist seeking to describe in language that people could understand what Robert Park called the big story; the scholar and the handyman; the athletic, river-running, beer-drinking, former fraternity man who could admit to still having some neanderthal-like macho attitudes and feelings and the righteous carrier of a new gender morality; a Jew with German and Eastern European roots and a secular American at home on both coasts (and in northern as well as southern California); the pin-striped suiter who could easily pass among elites and yet announce when the emperor was scantily clad or naked—but always with civility and in the King's English. And, as Lévi-Strauss notes, sociological inquiry can be enhanced by the skill of distantiation.

A cynic might suggest that the cautionary wisdom I have offered about success be viewed skeptically, as sour grapes. Are my new goals just compromises made out of necessity or, with appropriate professional socialization, is it possible to start a career with them? If my career trajectory had continued upward at its original pace, and had there been no fall, would I still have reached the same conclusions?[29] I certainly would not have thought as much about these issues, and the emphasis might be somewhat different. But since the fall I described was temporary, I am confident that my advice is sound and represents more than the idiosyncracies of my personal situation. It is based on two decades of successes and failures, and not only those in the beginning.

Unlike the Doctorow character quoted in the epigraph to this essay, I came East rather than West as a young man, and my expectations did not really wear away. However, they did change, and I was able to put them in perspective. Human existence is dominated by vast contingent forces that we gamely try to channel and control. That we sometimes succeed should no more lull us into thinking we can continually pull it off than should failure lead us to stop trying.

It was once said of Willie Nelson that he wrote songs out of love but was not above accepting the money. Nor am I above accepting professional recognition should it come. Yet I have become more concerned with process and learned more about how to deal with outcomes, whatever they are. I have become less troubled by rejection and also less thrilled by success. I have sought a more balanced life.

The Greeks gave their Olympic champions laurel wreaths as an ironic reminder that victory could be hollow. In Greek mythology Apollo pursues the nymph Daphne. She flees, and he runs after her. Abhorring the thought of marriage she prays to her father to save her by changing the form that has so attracted Apollo. Just as Apollo is upon her she is changed into a laurel tree. Is it a sign of modernity and a cause of its malaise that we offer our Olympic heroes gold instead?

Notes

I am grateful to my wife, Phyllis Rakita Marx, who has patiently and lovingly helped me sort out these issues, and for further critical comments and suggestions I wish to thank Jerry Aumente, Judith Auerbach, Murray Davis, Rosabeth Kanter, John McCarthy, Nancy Reichman, Zick Rubin, Susan Silbey, Barry Stein, Mike Useem, John Van Maanen, Chuck Wexler, and Jim Wood.

1. Among other themes I would like to pursue at some point are the experience of being at Berkeley in the 1960s; the move from the West Coast to the East Coast; family life, parenting, and professional ambitions; teaching; the selection of research topics; the uses of sociology and the role of moral commitment in sustaining research; the method (and challenge) of writing critical yet scientifically grounded essays. I have dealt a bit with the first theme in "Role Models and Role Distance: A Remembrance of Erving Goffman," *Theory and Society* 13 (1984), and the last two in the introduction to *Muckraking Sociology* (New Brunswick, N.J.: Transaction Books, 1972).

2. This seems to be particularly true for a discipline such as sociology that specializes in the study of stratification and in which there is only limited consensus about what constitutes good work. One observer even suggests that academic fauna can be ordered according to the degree of concern shown toward the outward presentation of self. Variation is inversely related to a discipline's certainty of results: "Thus at one end of the spectrum occupied by sociologists and professors of literature, where there is uncertainty as to how to discover the facts, the nature of the facts to be discovered, and whether indeed there are any facts at all, all attention is focused on one's peers, whose regard is the sole criterion for professional success. Great pains are taken in the development of the impressive persona. . . . At the other end, where, as the mathematicians themselves are fond of pointing out, 'a proof is a proof,' no concern need be given to making oneself acceptable to others; and as a rule none whatsoever is given." Rebecca Goldstein, *The Mind-Body Problem* (New York: Norton, 1983), p. 202.

3. Only later, when I gave what I thought was an equally timely paper and received only a handful of requests, did I realize that on average 150 might be more appropriate as a lifetime total.

4. This more interpretive, discursive, sensitizing style inspired by authors such as David Riesman, Erving Goffman, Herbert Gans, and Howard Becker was later to get me into trouble when I had to take greater initiative in submitting articles and applying for grants. Ground rules different from the ones pertaining to the invited contribution were in force. In assessing my mounting collection of failures in the early 1970s, I learned that as a humble petitioner, rather than an invited guest, one had to conform more rigidly to the conventional academic rules. Moreover, at that time quantitative methods as ends in themselves were ascendant.

5. I am reporting the elitist views encountered at Harvard. The University of California, though not an Ivy League school, was certainly an institution of enormous distinction.

The consequences of being around highly successful people who work very hard and see themselves as among the chosen are mixed. On the one hand, they become role models and you mimic them. You get more done than most people, and their sponsorship and advice help your career. On the other hand, you have doubts about whether you could ever do anything as impressive as they have done and (even if you could) whether you wish to pay the price that such success may require.

6. With success came ever greater aspirations. My modest goals as a young professional were closely linked to what I thought I could accomplish. This was no doubt a self-protective device. I had not yet learned to shoot for the moon with the hope that if you miss, you might still grab a few stars. I think the willingness to take risks and face failure are as (or more) important a determinant of academic success as native ability.

7. Even with a degree from Harvard, the odds were still against tenure, as the cases of prize-winning sociologists Theda Skocpol and Paul Starr indicate.

8. In retrospect I now see that this pattern was more a leveling off than a fall, but that was not how it felt at the time. What had been unusual (and more

worthy of explanation) was the degree and consistency of the early success, not the far more common pattern of intermingled success and failure that followed.

There are of course variants of falls. Some are easier to deal with than others. However poignantly felt, mine was gradual and partial. I had lots of time for hedging bets, putting out safety nets, and devising alternatives. That kind of fall is easier to respond to than one that is swift, total, and unexpected. The latter is the case with the assistant professor who had planned a large celebration and whose oh-so-sure department head had sent him a case of champagne the night before the faculty voted to deny him tenure.

9. Two examples will suffice. An account I heard too many times was that when my mother would push me in the baby carriage accompanied by our handsome collie, people would stop her and say, What a beautiful dog. A corresponding family tale stressed my father's resemblance to Rudolph Valentino.

10. To wit a "real sharp," chopped and lowered 1949 Pontiac convertible with duo carburetors, chrome pipes, and dice hanging from the rearview mirror and what used to be called "real cool threads"—a powder-blue one-button-roll zoot suit with enormous shoulder pads. The car did get attention, but to my chagrin it was never chosen by the school newspaper as "heap of the week."

11. The first three years of my undergraduate career were an exception to the pattern of success in high school and my first decade in sociology: I looked but did not find much. This lack of success partly was due to a demanding outside job, but also to the confusion and dissipation of youth in southern California (in the surfing film *Big Wednesday* a girl from Chicago, recently moved to California, observes, "Back home, being young is something you do until you grow up. Here, well, it's everything.") I was surprised when after a series of aptitude and vocational tests at UCLA in my senior year I was told by the psychologist that I could be a professor if I wanted to. An expert had passed on my qualifications and given me permission to go on and become a professor.

12. In high school I had an experience that should have taught me something about the pitfalls of narcissism and hubris. There is a Fats Domino song with the lines "I'm gonna be a wheel someday, I'm gonna be somebody." I can still recall the excitement I felt working as a box boy in the King Cole Market on Los Feliz Boulevard in Glendale, California, when I saw a vegetable box with the label "Big Wheel Produce" on it. It was the perfect thing for a self-fancied big wheel to hang on his bedroom wall. I deserted my assigned duties and proceeded to cut out the label. When the knife slipped and cut deep into my index finger, I knew there was a God and that he or she had caught me. Not only was I guilty of hubris, but on company time. The scar is still there. As in Pinocchio, *mutatis mutandis,* it sometimes itches when I get too carried away by achievement fantasies.

13. Of course there is always ambiguity about, and a gap between, theory and practice with respect to the rules that govern the awarding of tenure, receipt of awards, or acceptance of an article for publication. See, for example, John Van Maanen's consideration of types of rules surrounding career games, "Career Games: Organizational Rules of Play," in *Work, Family, Career,* ed. C. Brooklyn Derr (New York: Praeger, 1980), pp. 111–143.

14. George Bernard Shaw observed in *Man and Superman,* "There are two

tragedies in life. One is not to get your heart's desire. The other is to get it." In some ways our culture does a better job of preparing us to cope with failure than with success.

15. Paul Newman received the following letter complimenting him on his spaghetti sauce: "My girlfriend mentioned that you were a movie star, and I would be interested to know what you've made. If you act as well as you cook, your movies would be worth watching. Are any of your movies in VCR?" *New York Times Magazine,* Sept. 31, 1986.

An academic career is strewn with humbling little reminders that bring you back down to earth. For example, several times I have eagerly turned from a book's index to the pages where G. Marx was referenced only to find that the reference was to Groucho or discover that as a result of typographical errors I was given credit for Karl Marx's ideas. I well recall the smug feeling I had when I received a call from the president of a midwestern school telling me I had been the unanimous choice of their faculty to deliver a prestigious lecture. Since a recent publication was receiving considerable attention, it seemed only fitting. Yet it soon became apparent that the invitation was for my esteemed MIT colleague Leo Marx.

16. *Boston Globe,* June 4, 1985.

17. Beyond an occasional case of corruption the questioning of judges' decisions is aided by the lack of consensus among sociologists about what quality is (beyond the extremes) and how quality in different areas (qualitative–quantitative, comparative–domestic, contemporary–historical, theoretical–empirical) ought to be weighed. Every way of seeing is also a way of not seeing. Among my collection of diametrically opposed responses for the same research proposals and articles I have submitted are the following: "This is the best article I have ever reviewed for this journal—an absolutely outstanding contribution" versus "This tiresome review of things everyone knows does not merit publication here"; "An extraordinarily important project . . . absolutely indispensable. I urge strongly and without reservation that this request for support be approved" versus "This study offers little that would improve the infrastructure of science. Do not fund it."

18. It is comforting to think that when we fail the causes are structural and the system is unfair and when we succeed the causes are personal effort and the system fair. My naïveté and ego needs in the early period of my career probably led me to overemphasize the latter. That some of my success had little to do with merit per se was something to which I gave little thought. To be sure, I had worked hard and done respectable work. But there were a lot of things going for me that I had no control over. As research in the last decade has made clear, there is a sense in which demography (and timing) is destiny. In the case of my first job at Harvard one of my Berkeley mentors was then teaching there, and another held in very high regard had left not long before my arrival. I thus had a strong push from the outside and pull from the inside. What is more, the year I went on the job market Harvard had three openings at the assistant-professor level. Berkeley as an institution for training sociologists was at its height, and its graduate students were then very competitive on the job market. I had done my thesis on the civil-rights movement and specialized in race relations, topics

much in demand. The macro factors that aided my success in the 1960s ceased doing so in the politically more conservative period that followed.

19. As paragraph 6 suggests, these patterns can be independent. For quantity, a major pattern is flat. Some people hit their stride early and stay with it, producing about the same amount of work each year of their career.

20. As a graduate student one of the most important things I learned from Erving Goffman was that you had to click with your topic and really care about it or else you were in the wrong business. He implied it would happen early—it either grabbed you, or it did not. Since that was a time of many job offers for each applicant, rather than the reverse, this advice needs to be qualified.

21. This partly explains the exhaustion with reading journals as one ages (though an additional factor is an expansion in the number of journals). Although I would not go as far as a colleague who said he could not think of a worse way to spend an afternoon than to read the *American Sociological Review,* the moral imperative I felt as a graduate student to read it from cover to cover is long gone. The imperative has been diluted to reading the table of contents and occasionally marking an article to read later. I took this step with some of the same trepidation my grandmother reported when she made the decision to ignore kosher restrictions regarding the mixing of meat and dairy dishes and waited for God to strike her down. In neither case did harm befall us.

22. To be sure, in my early years there had been extra income, but I had not actively sought it out. I also felt a little uncomfortable being paid for work I would have gladly done for free.

Although I did not neglect my students, I must admit to an increased curiosity about those teachers whose moral (or immoral) code permitted them to devote an absolute minimum of time to teaching. Examples include the professor who required students who wanted to see him to make an appointment by calling a phone number that was rarely answered; the professor who did not have his name on his office door; the professor whose lectures consisted of reading from someone else's book; the professor who always came late to the first class meeting, did not have a syllabus, and was vague about just what the course would comprise (other than a heavy load of exams and term papers); and the professor who offered political (antielitist) and pedagogic (students should learn from each other) justifications for never preparing for class and never lecturing.

23. The research is reported in *Undercover: Police Surveillance in America* (Berkeley: University of California Press, 1988) and *Windows into the Soul: Surveillance and Society in an Age of High Technology* (forthcoming).

24. More broadly, such feelings seem to characterize American social scientists and humanists relative to scientists and engineers in academic settings, and academics relative to persons in applied settings.

25. It appears that sociology is increasingly being practiced outside traditional departments, whether in various interdisciplinary-studies programs or in applied contexts in professional schools. This goes beyond seeking new audiences; it is a matter of economic survival. In most of these settings one sociologist is fine but two is too many.

26. Though to a degree this sense of loss is also my fault. I did not try to

construct a more satisfying campus life or sell sociology. Instead I kept a low profile to maximize the time available for research.

27. Robert K. Merton, *Sociological Ambivalence and Other Essays* (New York: Free Press, 1977), p. 63.

28. William Butler Yeats ignored an alternative when he wrote, "The intellect of man is forced to choose. Perfection of the life, or of the work." One can opt for doing each as well as possible, but coming short of what might be accomplished by pursuing only one.

29. A related question is whether I could have reached these conclusions without experiencing the success with which I became disillusioned.

CHAPTER TWELVE

Becoming an Arty Sociologist

Barbara Rosenblum

Little did I know that the form my adolescent rebellion took in 1958 both crystallized and foreshadowed the themes that would dominate my sociology and my life. Teenagers do strange things in adolescence: some overconform, some become exaggerations of a superstar, some become football players or cheerleaders. I became arty. Every Friday afternoon I would take the forty-five-minute train ride from Brooklyn into Greenwich Village in Manhattan, go to the Cafe Rienzi, order that foultasting coffee called espresso with the intense hope that someday I would like it, and read translations of Baudelaire and Rimbaud. After all, wasn't I going to major in comparative literature when I eventually went to college? On my napkin I would practice spelling *existentialism*, a word I was just learning. I read novels that were deep and meaningful. At home I practiced the guitar and sang folk songs, memorizing lyrics about social justice and black blues. I wrote poetry in the style of Allen Ginsberg. And, of course, there was jazz, the most vibrant, robust, alive form of music I had ever heard. I saw movies that made me suffer. I used the word *absurd* about a hundred times a day. More absurd was that I wore black beatnik clothes and looked like a teenage jerk. But arty and cultured I did in fact become. Later on, my field became the sociology of art and culture, and I became arty and cultured with a vengeance.

Becoming cultured, for me, had two essential ingredients. First, it was not enough to learn about one field, such as music, read about it, study it, and become one of the cognoscenti; that would be too simple. Rather, to be cultured meant becoming a generalist, knowing all the arts. I had to learn about music, theater, literature, film, poetry, photography, and painting. I was driven into a kind of hypervigilance in which I had to know what was going on where, who was performing what, and what the New York critics said about it. Reading newspapers, especially the critical reviews, became my daily devotional study. No day passed when I did not submit myself to the process of taste formation and aesthetic discrimination. I had to know everything. I had to take courses in everything as well—music theory, Elizabethan drama and poetry, American cinema. The cultural landscape was there for me to gobble up and for no other reason. The notion of a single major in college seemed ludicrous to me. Wasn't everything connected to everything else? The artificial intellectual boundaries of majors or disciplines, I knew, were merely organizational conveniences for the creation of subdivisions for financial allocation and control of personnel. I was an intellectual. I was a generalist. I was cultured.

I embraced everything that was new and radical. I became a neophile. The avant-garde became my avant-god. For example, it wasn't enough for me to like the standard string quartets, though most enthusiasts felt a smug, often secret aesthetic superiority that distinguished them from lovers of the symphony. They could take joy in their selection of the most elite form of composition as their favorite kind of music. But I was compelled to learn to like the jarring and dissonant sounds of Bartók's dark and disturbing quartets. And then Bartók became insufficient for my psychological need to embrace the new. I sought out Berg and Webern, Henze and Stockhausen, Berio and Babbitt, Subotnik and Rochberg. I studied their compositions in the same intense way that I was learning angst-ridden modern literature and the names and styles of all the New York painters.

My sociology is dominated by the same themes. I became a generalist devoted to the sociology of knowledge, art, and culture. What other category could be large enough or more sanguine for one's needs? It was perfect—sociology at its most general, encompassing the entire world. But the second theme, embracing the new, also filtered into my sociology. I felt a need to know what was going on at the edge of social thought. I studied the latest in French and British social analysis and became knowledgeable in the work of Louis Althusser and Michel Foucault. My sociology was on the edge, too, when in 1970 I chose to study the organizational determinants of photographic aesthetics, long before the sociology of art became the relatively legitimate field it now is.

One day, when I felt superior enough and sufficiently protected against my own insecurity to relax a bit, I found myself crying over the heart-wrenching themes in those damned Russian symphonies my father played when I was a child. Was I running away from Tchaikovsky all the time, from my own sentimentality, my own class background, where I frequently heard the Russian symphonies, with their grand, sweeping-across-the-steppes-of-Russia themes?

My mother was one of seven children, only two of whom survived World War II. She got out of Europe in 1929, avoiding bodily harm and probable death. When she was very young, she lived in a small Jewish ghetto, a farming town in rural Poland. Later, when I read Jerzy Kosinski's *The Painted Bird*, I was not horrified by the brutal ignorance and religious superstitions of rural Polish peasants, which I had been told about by my mother. As a child she worked instead of going to school and hence never learned to read or write properly. My father, however, was a city boy, was literate, had a bicycle, and wore shoes. He too left Poland before the war, in the 1930s. They met in America, first spoke to each other in Polish, and went to night school to learn English and study the Constitution. The combination of Polish, Yiddish, and English was the first linguistic music I ever heard.

When he arrived in the United States, my father had a marketable skill: he could cut hair. In Warsaw he had worked as a barber since the age of eleven. He too had strange stories to tell, of bleeding customers with leeches and applying heated cups to the chest to relieve congestion. When I heard my parents speak of Europe, I never saw in my mind any version of the photographs I would see many years later—pictures of gentlemen in the street, walking in long black coats and beards, engaging in the routine work of peddling or selling while retaining a pious demeanor. Rather, my father's stories created visions of dark medieval towns with sickly flagellants running to escape the plague.

But when he came to the United States, he thought he might do something other than barbering, so he tried new jobs. It was the Depression, and work was not easy to get. For a while he worked in a shoe factory but lost his job when he participated in the unionization of the factory and a subsequent strike. Leftist sympathy with working people is something I grew up with; to this day it is in my bones, as it was in his. When American industries began to produce for the war in Europe, my father found work in the Brooklyn navy yard as a ship fitter, a job he kept until he was drafted in 1943.

During her first years in America my mother did not read or write well; consequently, she worked as a live-in housekeeper and later, when her English improved, as a governess. When the family that employed her was hit by the Depression and had to fire her, she next found work in a small factory shop sewing buttons on dresses. After that, she worked as an alterations seamstress for a department store in Brooklyn.

My father's military salary was the last solid, steady, and predictable wages that our family would see for the next twenty years. When he returned from army service, the barber-shop partnership he had formed dissolved and he was without steady work for a year. He free-lanced as a barber while looking for regular work. On borrowed money he bought one-fifth of a partnership in a tiny New York–style luncheonette, where racing forms, newspapers, magazines, comics, cigarettes, chocolate egg creams, and cherry lime rickeys were sold and fresh sodas made from syrup and fizzing seltzer streaming from spigots. I worked in his store from the age of ten. My father's mastery of numbers always impressed me. He could add up a column of numbers written down the side of a brown paper bag in no time flat, faster than any other person I knew.

We were very poor. We lived in low-income city housing in predominantly white-ethnic and black neighborhoods. I wore hand-me-downs except for one skirt and white blouse I was required to wear every Thursday for school assembly. The menu in our house was different from that in my friends': I thought that the category *meat* consisted of cow organs—lungs, pancreas, heart—and chicken feet. I did not taste steak until I was ten years old.

Being a poor kid in a city housing project and having immigrant parents was no fun. When my parents fought, it was always about money. From an early age I knew I had to earn money as quickly as possible, to work as soon as I was able, and to help my family in any way I could. Any thought of college was remote—it was not even a word I heard while growing up.

Being poor meant waiting—waiting in long lines in health department clinics, waiting hours to hear a bureaucratic voice call one's number on a loudspeaker, waiting for a social worker or eyeglasses or somebody or something. Being poor meant having one's finances investigated constantly, sometimes for seemingly insignificant and arbitrary reasons. In those days social workers were not as sensitive to matters of privacy as they are (or are told to be) now. Then a civil servant's primary duty was the assiduous detection of cheaters. My father's tax forms were examined every year to see if we were still eligible for the privilege of living in low-income housing projects. When my parents wanted to move from one housing project to another in a better neighborhood closer to where my father worked, they were endlessly interrogated about their finances, having to admit time and again in the inquisitional ritual that they were economic failures. When I was sent to summer camp, my family's financial records were scrutinized carefully. We were poor, yes, but were we poor enough to qualify me for summer camp at a cost of one dollar? Yes, we were poor enough.

Being the child of immigrant parents also meant I felt like an outsider, not only because we were poor but also because my parents and I were different. Our ways, habits, talk, and rhythms seemed strange and bizarre. I lived in an un-American house, which my young mind linked with the congressional committee on un-American activities when people began to associate Jews with stolen atomic secrets, spies, and dangerous foreigners. The first comparison and difference was linguistic: we were other. To my unschooled ears the language spoken by my parents' friends, despite their Brooklyn drawl, sounded like the King's English. My parents sounded like foreigners.

My father's luncheonette became the locus of my education. From the comic books, newspapers, and magazines he sold, I learned to read. There was a bar and grill next to my father's store, and the waitresses and neighborhood prostitutes congregated there and often came into the store. I learned about the race track, horses, violence, protection, personal threats, and kissing from the young hoods who hung around there.

In the 1950s my parents' cousins and distant relatives began coming in droves to the United States. I remember being introduced to vast numbers of new people to whom I was bonded by blood but little else. Some of my mother's relatives were Chasidic Jews. The men had long hair, and the women wore wigs over their short-cropped hair. They were animated, hummed to themselves, and laughed a lot, and when they smiled, they showed a mouthful of gold front teeth. They all had tattooed numbers on their forearms and some, I would later see, had scars on their bodies from having been experimented on by Nazi physicians. They seemed to come by the hundreds: ragpickers, junk men, diamond dealers, watch repairmen, salesmen. They passed through my life bringing the names of the dead and stories of the living to my parents. Relatives came and went: I would meet someone and next thing I heard, somebody had moved to Israel and another went to Montreal, probably to become a character in a Mordechai Richler novel—maybe even Duddy Kravitz.

When I entered high school, I was placed into an accelerated program called the Honors Program, which was the first time I was formally separated from my neighborhood friends. I found myself among bright kids from middle-class neighborhoods that the school district also encompassed. Although my own neighborhood was largely working-class ethnic and black, the Honors Program had few students from these backgrounds. For the first time I met Protestants who were not black, working-class ethnics who were not Italian and whose fathers were not in the garbage business, and middle-class Jews whose fathers were physicians and accountants. No question about it: they were different, and I felt different from them. But being in the Honors Program was an opening and a separation. My friends took secretarial courses; they studied typing, stenography, and bookkeeping. I took college-preparatory courses and hated it. The work itself was not difficult but being differentiated and separated into formal programs drove a wedge between me and my friends.

I did not want to be a secretary; summer employment in an office during high school taught me that. And I knew I did not want to be a postal clerk, my father's ambition for me. He wanted me to work for steady wages, have job security, and be employed by the government. And I really did not want to go to college. I knew I wanted to be arty, and I knew that college would bring me closer to that goal than anything else; so I went.

As I began to grow accustomed to the idea of myself as a girl who would go to college, I began to practice talking about things I was learning in school. When I would do so or use a word I had recently learned, I would be accused by my neighborhood friends of being phony and putting on airs. After high-school graduation my friends went to work, and I began Brooklyn College. The women worked as secretaries or bookkeepers in Manhattan and began taking business courses in night school at the college. Within a year or so, some dropped out of night school, got better jobs, married, and moved to Queens. The men went to work for their uncles' construction companies and drove trucks filled with concrete and garbage.

I started college immediately after high school and was one of a group of seventy-five kids from the housing projects whose grades were good enough to be accepted into day college rather than on probationary status into evening classes. When I entered Brooklyn College, I parted company with my neighborhood friends; but at the same time I could not relate too well to my new fellow students. They looked like they came from another planet or tribe, wearing funny gold chains with totemic representations called charms. The men wore penny loafers and ties and looked crisp. The wŏmen looked prim, proper, and pinned. I wore black beatnik clothes and already knew about Thelonious Monk, marijuana, the Mafia, illegitimate children, contract murders, bars in Greenwich Village, homosexuality, interracial couples, heroin, and French existentialist novels. Brooklyn College seemed like a monster movie starring live Barbie and Ken dolls. It was a world I did not fit into, a world I did not feel comfortable in. After a year I dropped out.

I was caught: I could not go to college and move up because I felt so terrified and uncomfortable with class differences, but it was impossible to move back down. My own solution was to embrace an arty life-style permanently, a move that in our society signifies class exemption and arrogates to itself privilege through difference, rebellion, and nonconformity in the service of higher values; through otherness.

For the next six years I lived in the Village. I studied classical guitar, took music theory, philosophy, and literature courses, and held a variety of jobs, which for the last four years were in the music business. My lovers were as unconventional as I was: musicians or artists, they were all soulful, misunderstood, brilliantly talented, and unspeakably poor.

The music business was the perfect solution for my dilemma. I loved the music, the people, the recording sessions, the free concerts, the payola lunches, and reading *Cashbox, Variety,* and *Billboard.* There was one problem: as a woman, I was doing the secretarial work I disliked, and there was little opportunity for me to do creative work. Women were not writers or producers and had none of the jobs I might have considered moving into. The work itself was becoming boring. At the same time New York became a center of civic energy. It was the time of John F. Kennedy, and I got caught up in what I could do for my country or my city and became involved in political action at the local level, organizing rent strikes and neighborhood improvement campaigns. After a six-year leave of absence I returned to school for a credential as a city planner. Now school was important because I had a vocational goal: to work in a municipal agency in New York specializing in problems of transportation. I had grown to hate subways and city housing projects: both had made me—and thousands of others—feel demoralized, hopeless, and poor. I wanted to do something about them.

When I returned to college in 1967, there was energy, there were causes, there was a war that people hated. The Barbie-and-Ken era was over. Students looked beautiful in their hippie clothes, and things mattered to them in a different way. I took sociology courses as part of my city planning program. I did not expect to fall in love with sociology, but I did, and then graduate school seemed like the next place to go. So I went.

At Northwestern University near Chicago I met blond people, one of many types of people I had never met before. They looked, spoke, and acted very differently from New Yorkers. They hardly understood my New York put-on jokes. But I had to learn their behavioral code to make it in their world, so I did.

When it was time to choose a dissertation topic, I decided to study photographers and the organization of labor as a partial determinant of photographic aesthetics. That was an important decision for me and, again, crystallized the arty theme in my life. Up until that time I had studied suicide prevention centers, psychiatric intake procedures at a hospital, and an agency dealing with child abuse and neglect in Chicago. I had planned to expand one of these topics into a dissertation since they were in keeping with the ideology of service to others, a strong sense I retained from my activist days. But I did not want to study these areas any more: the pain was much too great, and I could see that my days of doing field work filled me with rage and despair. Moreover, my passion for social change and service to others was finding expression in the antiwar movement. I decided to study something that was interesting, fun, and would be just enough on the edge of my bohemianism to be psychologically comfortable for me.

My years doing field work with photographers were, without exaggeration, some of the happiest of my life. How terrific to have a fellowship and take photography courses at the Pratt Institute in New York and later at the San Francisco Art Institute while interviewing and observing some of the most interesting people I had ever met! I was, in a manner of speaking, a state-supported arty type. The field work ended, and reality intruded: it became time to write the dissertation and get a job.

Having an arty countenance may have been necessary for my psychological equilibrium at the time, but it did not prove useful as a basis for social skills in the academic world. There was much more to university life than doing interesting studies and being an intellectual. My first lesson came during my first week at Stanford University as an assistant professor. One of my colleagues took me aside and suggested, "You aren't working in the university to be an intellectual. You have to start immediately getting grants and supporting graduate students. That's your first priority."

One of the detrimental consequences of my bohemianism was my lack of experience in socially strategic behaviors, academic financial matters, and other ephemeral, but essential, qualities of academic life. Such practices as the one my colleague suggested came as an abrupt surprise to me. I had just spent several years as a graduate student during the heyday of sociology in America, the golden years when government money and support flowed from Washington. Who would have thought that my first priority as a young assistant professor would be to bring in money to the department? Such a notion, I ruefully admit now, stemmed from my naive attitude about the mixture of money and ideas, the sacred and the profane. But with this incident my initiation into the realities of university life began, and I gradually came to understand the altered priorities of professional life. With it too came the discovery that my devotion to being cultured was irrelevant in my new setting. I thought I had spent my life acquiring the culture that would unlock a world to me, and I was wrong. There was much more to the bureaucratic culture than I had ever realized. My accommodation to it came a few years later, after exposure to the culture of the university, and I did finally master the strategic behaviors and other skills requisite for bureaucratic survival.

I began to search into the nature of social class in a way that was eye-opening for me. Of course, like any good sociologist, I knew the basic issues and debates in social stratification. In general, from reading sociological studies of class I imagined the class system as stratigraphic, that is, consisting of fixed strata. It was a solid image with clear demarcations, allowing members of a society to locate themselves in a spatial framework. It was also a ladder-of-success image. But these everyday images and sociological conceptions of social class were remote and lifeless to me, inapplicable to my own experience. These models did not illuminate my personal confrontation with class-mobile situations. I was experiencing, on a social-psychological level, some invisible aspects of class that I had never read about. The keen observation that the personal is political, which became a slogan of the women's movement, became an insight that I could apply first to my own experience and then to the social world. The personal is social. I began to ponder my own history, and out of this personal examination came a richer and much deeper understanding of social class.

I thought that all I had to do was move up educationally and the rest would happen automatically. And didn't I have a head start, being super cultured? Education in and of itself was a guarantee that opportunities would be open to me, but as I later found out, it was no guarantee that I would also acquire the other skills to fit in. What was missing from this picture was my deeper appreciation of the tight grip that social origins exert despite high educational attainment. Although my conceptual skills and my educational credentials bought me admission, I simply did not yet have the requisite social skills, political savvy, and interpersonal sophistication to move in this social world. And I am sure to this day that had my social background been more middle-class, the acquisition of such bureaucratic orientation would have been second nature.

Class works in psychological ways, keeping people in their appropriate substrata. Class works by making movement across strata psychologically uncomfortable, even painful and, for some, intolerable. Earlier I mentioned that when I began using big words in my circle of high-school friends, I was ostracized. That process operates all the time. Class works by making people feel marginal when approaching class or status boundaries. Social markers, like signs on the highway, are always telling people, Stop! You are going the wrong way. Social life is filled with such markers.

Sociologists now pay attention to class markers and look at things like etiquette, social manners, dress, demeanor, taste, self-assurance in personal comportment, understatement, and so on as key concerns in the understanding of social class. Norbert Elias's work on the social evolution of manners is now being read in America and is enlarging the scope of the study of social class by looking at aspects of class-based social sensibilities. In their study *The Hidden Injuries of Class* Richard Sennett and Jonathan Cobb grasped the fundamental idea that class operates on a psychological level, and they attempted to document it. Theirs was a first look at the phenomenon, and since that time sociological sensitivities to subtle determinative aspects of social class have increased only slightly. But with Pierre Bourdieu's work on the influence of social origins and educational level on taste formation, an important avenue to this problem may now open up.

What makes class fascinating to me is the subjective side of social mobility, which takes the form of stories people tell about their own upward social mobility.[1] Everybody has a story, and most people will recall occasions and situations when they felt out of place and counterfeit. Most people have experienced interclass movement in a subjectively meaningful, painfully real way. Class is not merely some set of income and educational categories that sociologists fill with demographic figures and distributions. Class works by making people feel fraudulent, like they are "passing." Despite knowing about the best cuisine and fine wine, many people still feel like lower-class frauds, as if they contained dual class identities; indeed, they often do. They speak of experiencing themselves as having a veneer and never can predict when and how they will inadvertently disclose their class origins. They tell stories about their awkwardness at dinner parties, the instant recognition that their clothes were inappropriate and that even as their words left their mouths, they knew they were saying the wrong thing for the occasion. Class works by reminding people that they do not belong and by making them feel ashamed of even trying to get in.

There are still many stories to be told. Nothing is as powerful as a personal history, especially contemporary histories. My friend Eleanor tells how she learned to say thank you at the late age of twenty-five. Now living in an exclusive part of Westchester County, New York, she grew up on the Lower East Side of Manhattan. During World War II and after, with tin can in hand, she begged for money to send to the children of Israel. After every coin was dropped in the can, Eleanor said thank you. She did not know that the phrase *thank you* was an ordinary part of good manners, not the automatic reflex to a coin being dropped. Like most people I have talked with, Eleanor remembers the moments of class awakening most vividly in connection with table manners. She never knew how to set a table properly because in her home, as in many other working-class homes, families did not eat together. Everyone was on a different schedule and just grabbed a knife and fork and dumped food on a plate from the big pot sitting on the stove. After she married and began to entertain other couples, she served the same way, expecting her guests to take a knife, fork, and spoon and help themselves.

Those poignant stories illustrate the inescapability of class considerations and indicate the vanity of my intense desire to deny the realities of my working-class background by striking a highly cultured, bohemian pose. As I look back, I see that I did not integrate my cultural tastes because my social background did not prepare me to do so. My cultural side, as serious as it was, was like a graft: some of it took, and some of it did not.

My own story is an example of the way in which I have come to include a richer understanding of social class in everything that I study. These concerns are reflected in work that I continue to do. I have just finished investigating the problem of the alienation of the artist, taking a close look at marketplace conditions that become structural sources of alienation for artists, a population usually thought to have enormous control over the production process. Before that, I examined the effects of the art market on the strategic attempts of artists to gain fame and recognition through means that increase their social visibility. Another project I am working on concerns the social history of bathing practices, a theme not unrelated to stratification and cultural practices. An examination of the floor plans of bathhouses built in Britain during the height of the public bathing and hygiene movement shows that two and sometimes three sections were created, each for separate but equal bathing by the different social classes. I have a passionate personal interest in these intellectual problems and have found a way to integrate all the parts of myself—emotional, intellectual, cultural, and historical—in all the work I do.

Note

1. The strongest documentation of the subjective side of upward social mobility and its impact can be found in autobiography. Norman Podhoretz's *Making It* is a well-known example and details his rise from poverty to become editor of *Commentary*. Richard Rodriguez, a Chicano who went to Harvard, has told his story in an interesting autobiography entitled *Hunger of Memory*. After his transformation from a migrant farmer's son whose first language was Spanish into an Ivy League literature scholar, Rodriguez found himself turning down a variety of offers from prestigious universities because he refused to be somebody's token Chicano. Now he works alone, writing books with occasionally painful passages about his ethnic and class background and trying to make sense out of what has happened to him. For him, as for me, educational attainment alone, though it is the life-rope that lifted us out of the ghetto, can never deliver on its promise to feel comfortable about fitting into the dominant, legitimate American culture.

Another moving and powerful autobiography is about two black brothers, John and Robert Wideman. Both grew up in Pittsburgh, and John's story, *Brothers and Keepers* (1984), is almost archetypal in its content and structure, reminiscent of the movies about two Irish brothers, one of whom becomes a priest or a cop and the other a criminal. The autobiography documents the thoughts of a man whose privilege in the white world was granted on the basis of his gifts as a novelist, writer of short stories, and professor. His brother was caught in the criminal traffic of the brutal dope-dealing street world of the ghetto and did not escape it. As a consequence of a series of errors, he murdered someone and is now serving a life sentence in prison. John describes the repercussions of these events on his own life, reflecting on the circumstances that created the differences between their worlds. He brings to his story what W. E. B. DuBois called double consciousness, the ability to discover profound truths about both worlds, by viewing those worlds from within the hazy space between them.

American literature, especially novels written in the early part of this century, is filled with stories of upward mobility and its effects. Edith Wharton's *The House of Mirth*, Sinclair Lewis's *Dodsworth*, and F. Scott Fitzgerald's *The Great Gatsby* are all strong examples. The master of this genre is Theodore Dreiser, whose *Sister Carrie* and *An American Tragedy* tell powerful parables about the insidious and often pernicious subtle effects of upward social mobility.

PART IV

Three Generations of Women Sociologists

CHAPTER THIRTEEN

Seasons of a Woman's Life

Alice S. Rossi

Dedicated to S. W. S. with admiration and affection

An autobiographical essay provides an opportunity to link an early love of mine for writing and biography with contemporary intellectual concern for adult development. My years as a graduate student at Columbia University overlapped with the tenure of C. Wright Mills, and from exposure to his thinking I carried forward the view that sociology is properly located at the intersection of biography and history. Mills's views, however, were little more than a perspective on the discipline, not a theoretical framework. It has only been with the emergence of life-span development theory in psychology and age stratification and the life-course perspective in sociology that a more rigorous framework has become available within which to sift out the relative contributions of cohort membership, historical or period effects, and maturational change to an understanding of individual lives and the process of social change. Hence it is to both sharing a personal biography and demonstrating a theoretical perspective that this essay is dedicated.

The phrase *love and work* is commonly taken to refer to personal family life and public occupational life. This was clearly Freud's meaning when he referred to *lieben und arbeiten* as the chief ingredients of a full life. Sociological tradition has similarly distinguished between the family and the economy as major social institutions serving the core functions of reproduction and production to assure species and societal maintenance and survival.

To link love to family, and work to the economy, is to reinforce the conception common to the social sciences that family life is the expressive setting for deep feelings and strong emotions, while work life is the instrumental setting for rational thought or physical labor. In this essay I will depart from such traditional usage to share a hard-earned insight from personal experience and intellectual efforts to understand adult development: *how much work there is in loving, and how much love there is in working.* In contemporary society it is in the family setting that we engage in hard physical labor, long hours of work, and considerable rational thought about how best to spend time and money, rear children, and relate to spouses. And for many people it is their work setting that triggers their most intense positive and negative feelings and commitments. I will use love, then, as a metaphor for caring, including the pain, joy, anger, and lust that motivate us, however skillful we are at disguising these limbic components of our behavior. And I will speak of work as a metaphor for efforts toward goal attainment in any sphere of life.

This is also a self-reflective essay, meaning that I will use my own life as a data base to demonstrate a sociological analysis of self in time and place. The theoretical framework is that of life-span development, and the goal is to demonstrate its utility in distinguishing the relative contributions of cohort membership and historical or period effects from the influences rooted in biosocial processes of maturation and aging.

To provide the biographic data for such an analysis, I will use the technique of life-stage vignettes, five developmental phases for the six decades of my life: birth and childhood, puberty and adolescence, early adulthood, the middle years, and a preview of old age. Following the vignettes I will go back over the biographic data to discuss the specific respects in which my experience and values have been shaped by cohort membership, historical events, and the experiences of growing up and growing old.

Birth and Childhood

I was born where I was conceived, in my parents' bed in a top-floor apartment of a brownstone town house on a one-block-long street, Alice Court. The place was Brooklyn; the time, 1922. Those four floors housed three layers of maternal kin who peopled my early childhood: a German-Lutheran immigrant grandfather and one aunt on the street floor, two unmarried aunts on the second floor, my parents and me and an unmarried uncle on the third floor. The Schaerrs and the Winklers shared the big kitchen and dining room on the half-submerged first floor for communal evening meals prepared by my mother and aunts.

I was made to feel special in that household as the first child, first grandchild, and first niece. There was little communication between the sexes or the two older generations, however, and the only warm alliance was among the four sisters. Whatever merriment or exchange of intimacy took place was within that foursome or between me and one of the adults when they, each in turn, took me into their separate, secret worlds. Let me sketch my people for you:

My grandfather was a quiet, somber man, a socialist of a homespun variety who spent most of his life as a stonemason and carpenter on the construction of an Episcopal church in Manhattan, which to this day has not been completed. Stern with his daughters and son, he was easy and loving with me, sharing German folklore, his love of craft, and his dream of the cathedral-to-be. Like many socialists in Europe, and unlike their American counterparts, he happily blended his political and religious visions of the good society.

My Uncle Ted, gassed in World War I, was the wheezing, asthmatic occupant of a tiny bedroom across the hall from mine. A telephone lineman by day and a violinist in the Brooklyn Symphony by night, he let me peep beneath his silent persona to share his love of sound on strings and his love of the sea.

My Aunt Minna was no longer considered marriageable by herself or the family once she passed her twenty-eighth birthday. She kept the books and supervised a factory floor in a bookbindery and devoured gothic novels. She read me passages, taught me to read, and assured me a library card was a magical key to worlds beyond my imagining. She was even capable of fibbing to my mother, taking me off to see not a children's movie but a sexy one—*Red Dust,* with Jean Harlow—and then telling my mother she got the dates mixed up.

My Aunt Martha was lively and gay, in love with a garage mechanic from New Jersey. I loved to watch her primp before her mirror on nights she saw her Charlie. On rare occasions I was permitted to go with them on daytime dates. No delight exceeded those excursions. I sat in the rumble seat of Charlie's Ford watching them exchange glances and listening to their high-pitched laughter, or accompanied them on walks on the boardwalk at Coney Island or Jones Beach, feeling the current running between them through me as each held one of my hands; they gave pleasure squeezes I happily passed on from one to the other when something struck them as funny, which seemed to happen with great regularity.

The oldest of the sisters, my Aunt Anna, was scrappy and bossy, with a precarious hold on the affections of her sisters and myself. She was the chief housekeeper and cook until her marriage. In that household, headed by my widowed maternal grandfather, it was the daughers who took over the duties of their mother after her early death at forty, whereas in the household headed by my widowed paternal grandmother she herself assumed the breadwinner role by taking in four boarders, doing their laundry, and cooking meals for them as well as the three sons and a daughter still at home.

My father was quiet, strong, and moody, an experimental machinist inordinately proud of his machines and his skill in creating equipment for scientists at the Rockefeller Institute in Manhattan. His great gift to me was a belief that I could do or be anything I set my mind to, and he defended me against family scoffing when at six I wished to be a chemist, at fourteen a poet, and at twenty-two a sociologist.

My shy and yielding mother, the hub of my world, was in perpetual fear of displeasing either her father or her husband, but for me she radiated warmth and the pleasure she took in food, fabric, and flowers, a triad of cooking, sewing, and gardening that has been a common ground between us for more than fifty years.

Except through me as a go-between, my people had little to do with our neighbors, of whom more were Catholic than Protestant, more Irish and Italian than German. My first playmates were Irish Catholic girls. We screamed in terror when our fathers had a fist fight during the Al Smith presidential campaign in 1928, then followed suit the next day with a fight of our own for reasons we could not fathom. School was an ancient, overcrowded, red brick building, most of whose students came either from a black ghetto or an enormous orphan asylum a block from the school, a frightening place with jagged glass in the cement top of its brick walls. My first friend at school was a black girl I was made to share a seat and desk with as punishment for misbehavior in first grade. (If blacks misbehaved they were made to stand in a corner, whereas whites were made to sit with blacks.) We both knew neither of us would be welcome in the home of the other, but we walked to the corner of each other's block many times to glimpse the place that held the good friend and to prolong our endless talk.

I did not know it for a long time, but I have drawn deeply from that early world of kin and the ethnic and racial diversity of my neighborhood. And I learned early how different men and women were when alone or in mixed company. By day my aunts and my mother seemed lighthearted and merry, lingering over lunch, laughing with the canaries in the sunlight, sharing their hopes and woes. By night they turned into shadowy figures serving the food and giving silent assent to all that the men said. My grandfather and father ruled the big table under its apples-and-pears Tiffany lamp, snapped commands, showed no pleasure, and gave no thanks. Yet these were the men who shared, when alone with me, their love of texture—of wood, marble, metal, pansies. When I carried an observation from one side of the gender barrier to the other, the grown-ups stared at me in disbelief: "Your grandfather couldn't have said that!" my aunt would pronounce firmly; "Your mother really didn't say that!" said my grandfather equally firmly. They all concluded, with sad shakes of the head, "Alice has a vivid imagination." So in time I learned to keep things to myself.

But that world did not last. In 1930 it collapsed around us. My best friend's father committed suicide, my uncle was laid off, and my father could hardly make his payroll. The men scowled and withdrew into silence and drink. The women frowned and cried. The grim decade of the Depression had begun. We moved away to where no canaries sang, no aunts or grandfather brightened my days, and my childhood ended— at eight.

Puberty and Adolescence

The deeper the family slipped into hard times, the more my father drank and the less we had to eat. My mother skipped lunches and became a janitor in a four-family building, shoveling coal into a greedy furnace and lugging a dozen cans of ashes up treacherous stone steps twice a week. She sewed lovely things for a rich doctor's wife and her friends. Men did not have enough work, and women had too much work. As a girl and an oldest child (by now with a younger brother and sister) I was swept into my mother's work. When not in school, hours were given to scrubbing clothes and floors, ironing, and doing household shopping. Shopping meant a five-mile walk each week to scattered stores with low prices: the butcher, the dairy, the German pork store, the bakery for day-old bread, and, once in a while, the Nabisco factory for broken crackers at bargain prices.

The one advantage of our numerous household moves was the schools I attended. Declining neighborhoods from which many had fled even before the Depression meant lower rent for our apartments but also schools with small classes, and teachers who poured their talents and hopes into fewer students. In another era some of my grade-school and high-school teachers would have been college teachers, so I was the beneficiary of their considerable knowledge and fallen hopes. As a proud possessor of that magic key, a library card, a highlight of my week was a two-mile skate to the nearest library. I devoured my weekly ration of five books as my aunt had done before me, in hours stolen from the night. In my case a book, my head, and a night lamp were huddled under a heavy flannel bathrobe to hide my reading from the disapproving eyes of my mother. It was years before I understood the fear of losing her daughter that lurked beneath my mother's suspicion of what she called my "reading and scribbling."

I reached my present height at twelve, towering over my classmates, the last in line marching into gym or auditorium, defensively tough, secretly tender. My dream of public stardom was doomed by a tendency to blush, so I was the behind-the-scenes producer and director of plays, and later the playwright as well. My sixth-grade triumph was a production of *Alice in Wonderland,* complete with crepe-paper costumes I made for all fifteen characters. My only terror when the play was put on in half a dozen schools in the borough was having to come on stage to take a bow after the performance. But beneath all that local limelight I was frustrated, a never-to-be star of the show, like Lewis Carroll's Alice.

In high school I found wider scope and at least some souls who shared my passions. I edited the newspaper, served in the student senate, was president of the poetry club, and dared to dream of college. Summers were spent in my aunt's bookbindery at a wage of twelve dollars for a forty-eight-hour week. Innocent dreamer that he was, my father assured me I could attend any college of my choice. "What's the best one?" he asked. Not knowing, but remembering a novel with a college setting, I promptly said "Vassar College." It took very little inquiry about cost to land me in tuition-free Brooklyn College, not Vassar.

I entered college a literature major but quickly shifted to sociology after one semester with Louis Schneider as my teacher. An incipient rationalist, I checked out this shift in major by taking the Strong Interest Inventory Test. The college counselor told me I scored exceptionally well on both art and science. In some puzzlement he concluded, "Well, maybe a social science is a good middle-of-the-road compromise!" And so it has been, though if the truth be known, I hungered to be an artist and a scientist. As well as a sociologist, of course.

My late development provided a psychosexual moratorium in adolescence, during which studies, athletics, and same-sex friendships filled my days. But when it came, the moist fire of sex threatened to overturn my intellectual interests and would have done so had I not moved in a radical student subculture that espoused some measure of equality between the sexes. Even so, I made fearful mistakes. After a tragic first affair that ended with my lover's death in a car accident, I remet and married a former economics teacher twelve years my senior. Adolescence ended with a premature marriage at nineteen.

Early Adulthood

War was declared against Japan and Germany a few weeks before the marriage, and by the spring of 1942 I withdrew from college and spent several years as an army wife largely in southern towns—Anniston, Columbia, Raleigh, Jackson—and then in Washington, D.C., and Trenton, New Jersey. My first trip South was to Anniston, Alabama, where, with my head full of antebellum novels, I expected to find women in dainty dimity and white gloves and carrying ruffled parasols. It was a culture shock to find my first landlady in black satin, highly rouged, a cigarette in the corner of her mouth, on her way to her job as an "entertainer," as she put it. I was a civilian replacement first at an airbase and then at a prisoner-of-war camp, and a child tender in a municipal day-care center for factory women's children in Jackson, Mississippi. I sold fabric by the yard to poor whites in Alabama and worked for Soviet engineers in Washington, processing lend-lease shipments of petroleum products to the Soviet front. I even delivered a black baby in South Carolina, when I volunteered to find out why my landlady's "girl" did not show up for work and found her alone in advanced labor.

After the war I returned to finish college and moved on to graduate study at Columbia University. Though I did not define it as work at the time, I also spent two painful years trying to salvage a marriage and then adjust to its failure. After several foolish affairs I finally grew up secure enough to form a new and good marriage, at twenty-nine, to a man my own age. This has been a lasting love, with sparks in the mind, shared tastes of palate and politics, a spicy difference in intellectual flair, a mutual love of hard physical work—a heady brew still potent after thirty-five years. With a degree behind me, I also tasted the pleasure of being paid for what I wanted to do anyway—work with books and ideas and typewriter. Still under the influence of the manual-work ethic from my Lutheran kin, I was dismayed while on a first professional job to calculate what I cost my employer by dividing the number of pages I wrote in a year (600) into my annual salary. The cost per page was so high, in my judgment then, for doing something that yielded so much intrinsic reward that I was convinced my boss Alex Inkeles must have considered me a poor investment.

But the joy of that work paled beside the miracle of birth and the powerful bond of flesh and heart that came with parenthood. Always greedy for experience, I had three births in four years in my middle to late thirties. With the love came the work of parenting, the unrelenting hours that squeezed out thought and spirit, all made particularly taxing because of the superwoman standards I imposed on myself: perfect wife, mother, hostess, gardener, and college teacher, all held together by a fragile scaffold of nursery schools, housekeeper, luck, and physical strength. The price I paid was insomnia and neuritis misdiagnosed as arthritis, and the cure was giving up part-time teaching and taking on a full-time research appointment.

The Middle Years

At forty we fell in love with a house in Kenwood, a neighborhood just north of the University of Chicago. It was huge, ugly, Victorian, but beautiful in our eyes: a dream of grace and space come true. It prompted the purchase of a floating blue chiffon gown for a housewarming party and dreams of children's weddings within its spacious rooms. But that Victorian shell held five complex, changing creatures within it: an anxious, overextended research administrator; a harassed, torn, and puzzled woman; and three small people struggling for room in our lives while flexing and testing who they were.

I also underwent the painful experience of being fired by an anthropologist when he saw a good thing in a study I had designed and fielded. Since his title under the grant was as principal investigator and I only a research associate on the payroll, the dean told me the anthropologist was "valuable university property," whereas I was expendable. It was my first consciously defined experience with sex discrimination, and it began a slow burn that gathered momentum and was gradually transmuted into my first feminist publication (Rossi 1964). I spent a year on that essay, with blisters on my mind from the struggle to unlearn the functionalist theory I had swallowed whole during my graduate training in sociology and to distill and transcend my personal experiences. The six-draft germination of that essay was a far more painful birthing than the three natural childbirths that preceded it, and its publication in 1964 was a turning point in my personal, political, and professional life.

I withstood the pressure against political activity from my academic colleagues by plunging into abortion law reform in Illinois in the early 1960s and helping to found the National Organization for Women (NOW) and Sociologists for Women in Society (SWS) in 1970. I took special pleasure in following in John Dewey's footsteps as national chair of the reactivated American Association of University Professors (AAUP) committee on the status of women in academe. Professionally I shifted from such topics as voting behavior, intergroup relations, the sociology of occupations, and the Soviet social system to the study of gender roles, family structure, academic women, and social movements. I indulged my love of biography and history for two years while working on *The Feminist Papers* (Rossi 1973). Politics and research were also a stimulating combination in editing the Russell Sage Foundation volume on *Academic Women on the Move* (Rossi and Calderwood 1973) and writing *Feminists in Politics* (Rossi 1982), a quantitative panel analysis of the first national women's conference.

Along the way, following a wrenching move from the Kenwood home we loved to a Baltimore home I disliked, I shifted from the uncertainty of research appointments on soft money at Johns Hopkins University to the challenge and security of teaching women at Goucher College. I look back now with a mixture of self-admiration and horror at the pace of those years in the early 1970s: teaching seven courses a year while chairing a department; lectures and political obligations that had me in a plane thirty-two times one year; and two books in process. In addition to these political and professional commitments, we were coping with pubescent and adolescent children, then experimenting with vegetarianism, hippie culture, sex, and an alternative school, and I was trying to cope with the erratic mood swings of an early menopause. Winding-up adolescents and winding-down parents make for domestic sparks. It was this personal insight that led to a study of parenting and aging in the middle years, in which I tried to explore what difference a mother's age made for her relationship to an adolescent child (Rossi 1980a, 1980b).

I learned a bitter lesson in those years: it is far easier for a woman to add to her level of participation in parenting and domestic management than to reduce the level of participation that has been in place for a long time. In retrospect it seems a miracle that the children and the marriage survived those years intact. Had we still been riding the crest of youthful narcissism, that fragile family might have collapsed and fragmented. At twenty-five we are immortal, and impulses are apt to burst their containment. At forty-five caring is more likely to mean a restraint on impulse, and a hard working-through of an impasse in a relationship of long standing.

So it was, and so it is. In the calmer waters of one's sixties, time is telescoped and life in and for itself more precious than ever before: each day to be savored, from work at a desk or lectern, to time snatched for gardening or sewing, to pasta and Soave at day's end. For city-bred people like me, living in a small town in western Massachusetts is a source of daily wonder: after fifteen years, I am still startled to see a setting sun slip below a mountain ridge from my study window.

Looking Ahead

Now, well past the meridian of life even with greatly extended life spans, I feel no impulse to rest or retire. I have an image of a retired self that is outrageously eccentric: a figure in a purple cape with a walking cane. But at the moment I continue to struggle with the question, How have I managed to come this far on life's path and still be so far from the achievements I dreamed possible at thirty? There are half a dozen studies I wish to do and at least three books I want to write.

But I also want to have time and space to indulge two other passions, one new and one old. The new one is watercolor painting, begun in 1980. I want to capture the essence of New England rocks, shells, and flowers as Georgia O'Keeffe caught the essence of the desert Southwest in bones. The old passion is clothes design and sewing: for the past several years I have made children's clothes, tailored silk blouses, and placemat sets under my own label for sale in a local boutique.

My dream of the good life after retirement is not stopping work but letting the day structure what the work will be: separating an iris clump, drafting a paper, exploring an image in watercolors, discussing a new idea with Peter, testing it on the computer terminal, making a crème caramelle. To borrow a lovely phrase from May Sarton, I shall strive for a life in which "the day shapes the work, and not my work, the day."

This ends the five vignettes. Much has been left out, of course: my paternal kin, my brother and sister, my friends in adolescence and adulthood, teachers and peers who were important mentors. But I think I have touched on the central facts of early family, marriage, and parenting and the broad contours of career and political involvement, and I have tried to be honest in communicating the passion and pain along the way.

But enough of biographic profiles. What can we do with these data from a sociological perspective? What elements of this life reflect the time and place in which it was lived? What are its unique, what its common, features? A life-span perspective will help us distinguish between the effects of maturation, cohort, and historical period (Baltes and Schaie 1973; Bengston and Troll 1978; Neugarten and Hagestad 1976). It also moves away from the psychological premise that humans are essentially formed by the time they reach the age of ten or so. Instead it makes two important assumptions: (1) social structural characteristics of early family life are more predictive of adult personality and values than the psychodynamics within the triad of mother, father, and child; and (2) development is a continuous process at all stages of life, subject to change from the impact of historical events and the institutions that hold us in their grip during our adult years (Brim and Kagan 1980; Riley 1979). I will try now to tease out the major elements of cohort, period, and maturational effects from the descriptive biographic vignettes.

Cohort Characteristics

A great deal is known about the cohort I belong to—the birth cohort of the 1920s—as a consequence of several longitudinal studies begun with child subjects during that decade. Best known in sociological circles is Glen Elder's *Children of the Great Depression* (1974). Other cross-sectional studies on middle-aged adults in the 1970s are also based on research subjects from my cohort (Gould 1978; Levinson 1978; Lowenthal et al. 1975; Rubin 1979; Sheehy 1977; Rossi 1980a, 1980b). Such studies, however, were either of subjects living on the West Coast (Elder, Gould, Lowenthal et al., Rubin) or of men (Levinson). None were conducted on East Coast families like the one I grew up in. Hence there is no hint in most of these studies of grandparents, aunts, and uncles of the subjects who grew up in the 1920s and 1930s. The chances are that these relatives were somewhere in the Midwest or East rather than the West.

Yet the fact of having spent the first eight years of my life in an extended-family household had important consequences. I was a third-generation child in a lineage that emigrated to the United States in the late nineteenth century. Grandparents, aunts, and uncles were colorful, important figures in my life, as they were in the lives of others of my cohort in eastern cities; if not living together, they were often close by in ethnic neighborhoods. As Hansen noted long ago (Hansen 1952), grandchildren often wish to know what their parents want to forget about their ethnic and national origins. Neither of my parents could understand my fascination with stories my grandparents told about their childhood in Germany and the adventure of emigrating to the United States. At my urging, my grandmother told the story of her crossing the Atlantic several dozen times, until the image of her red-cheeked, blonde-braided, seventeen-year-old self, organizing dances for sailors and young girls in steerage (ever the managerial type!), became as sharply etched in memory as any childhood experience of my own.

A household of three adult men and four adult women for a first child, grandchild, and niece also had important consequences: my affection was diffused among them, not concentrated just on two parents. Predictably I was a very adult-oriented child, but my image of the adult I could become had an openness to it because of the sharp differences among the women and men who provided daily models: my mother's disapproval of reading was countered by my aunt's love of books; my grandfather's objection to his son's "fiddling" was countered by his unique emotional accessibility to me. With all those loving adults around me, I felt no rivalry when my brother was born when I was three, though I did when my sister was born when I was eight, for by the time of her birth the number of adults in my daily world had shrunk from seven to two.

A child in an isolated nuclear household cannot observe male-female relationships in the courting and honeymoon stage of a marriage, whereas I had exposure to the very positive image of my aunt's courtship. I also saw meaning in the lives of unmarried adults, and I had the opportunity to observe same-sex adult relationships at close range. Of special importance was the daily exposure to the four sisters' alliance, the key solidary force in the household. A superficial observer of my extended family might see a patriarchy with repressed and exploited women, but I knew in my bones the power of sisterhood as a kinship, not a political, phenomenon. There was no doubt some repressed anger in the women, and indeed my mother has been happier as a widow for the past twenty years than she was for most of her life as a wife, but I am speaking here of a child's experience. I also knew the tender underside of patriarchal males, the passion and pride in craft, and the love for a girl child beneath their barked commands to wife, daughters, and sisters. Clearly I was the recipient of a superdose of love and trust during those early stages of life.

There is also an androgynous quality to the manner in which a firstborn child is treated, perhaps particularly a firstborn girl. Few limits were imposed on me because of my sex, as they were on my younger brother and sister. No one said I could not learn to use tools or play a violin or move out into the world beyond the house and neighborhood. I was sent to shop at a neighborhood store at three, clutching a penciled note over the coin to give the grocer. At five I was taught to use a saw and hammer by my grandfather, along with a knife and needle by my aunts and mother.

The most lasting influence of that early household, and a mark perhaps of my cohort, was the work ethic it lived and breathed. If it is worth doing at all, it is worth doing well; If you start something, you finish it—those sayings were drilled into me as family homilies. Mine was a secular family that attended church only for marriages, christenings, and funerals, and the household god was labor. To learn to sew at the age of four, my mother gave me a square yard of muslin with two dozen rows of different sewing and embroidery stitches down one side, each two inches long, rows I was required to complete over the remaining thirty-four inches to master the stitches. Praise was given only for a job done with exceptional skill, not for any ordinary performance, and never if it was not done in the expected time, for dawdling was taboo. I still have difficulty giving praise to my students except under similar circumstances of exceptional performance in a reasonable period of time.

Another value I internalized was the importance of women's work. Few of the homes in my kin network would have survived without the labor of the women. One simply could not afford to waste or spoil food, scorch a shirt, or discard a torn sheet. It was my mother's strength and capacity for hard work that kept my own family intact through the Depression, as my widowed grandmother had kept her sons away from poolrooms and saloons, while the older men in the family and neighborhood were apt to crumble under economic pressure into quarrels and drink. Years later it was with a shock of recognition that I read Harriet Martineau's 1837 judgment that American women were soft under affluence but showed their strength under adversity (Martineau 1837). This observation was clearly applicable to the Depression, as it is today to so many impoverished black communities. It did not take a feminist awakening for me to acquire pride in women's strength and abilities.

Period Effects

Three major historical events were of profound influence in my life: the Depression of the 1930s, World War II, and the renascence of the feminist movement in the 1960s.

Much has been written on the impact of the Depression on families and individuals. Indeed, there is renewed interest in the topic because of the structural unemployment facing the nation in the 1980s and the financial stress that is growing in the international economy. Reference-group theory applied to intergenerational relations is of particular help in illuminating this impact. My immigrant grandparents had little sympathy for the dashed hopes their children experienced under the weight of the Depression, for they had known far harsher poverty in Europe, compared to which any American experience seemed very mild.

In addition, immigrants are self-selected from their national stock and families, spunky enough to leave a known world for an unknown one. Their children were more diverse, including the timid along with the bold. My second-generation parents never fully recovered either economically or psychologically from the Depression years, and their achievements fell far short of their youthful dreams. By comparison, my generation came to adulthood with more education and entered an expanding, affluent economy, so we could more easily fulfill our aspirations and exceed those held for us by our parents. I worry that my students in the 1980s may face the dashed hopes that marked my parents' generation.

The concept of relative expectations also illuminates my father's confidence that I could become anything I wished to be. In fact, I did not gain this insight until writing this essay: what I experienced as great confidence in me as a young person requires the qualification that my father's message reflected the narrow horizon of choice he could even imagine for me. He harbored no hopes of my becoming a senator or a professor. His conception of a chemist was a laboratory technician or bench chemist; of a poet, someone who scribbles in her spare time; of a sociologist, someone who belabors the obvious. Under the influence of my teachers and mentors my range of choice exceeded anything in my father's imagining. Had I become a white-collar bookkeeper, his paternal expectations would have been well confirmed.

The impact of growing up in the Depression is a continuing mark on my generation. We are survivors who delight in possessions, gluttonous consumers of mail-order catalogs. I still find the best device to cope with anxiety and depression is a shopping spree—hats in my twenties, plants in my sixties. By contrast, my own adult children travel light and rely on jogging, sleep, and loud rock to cope with stress.

The second historical event of great influence was World War II, which shook me out of a New Yorker's parochialism, deepened my appreciation for regional differences, and provided a range of job experiences more profound in their impact than any reading of the sociological literature on occupations and social class. Living in rented rooms in a dozen southern homes gave me intimate access to family and race relations. I was astonished by the extent to which a gracious life-style penetrated down to lower class levels more than was possible in the North, facilitated by an underclass of poorly paid blacks. I was amazed that the husband who returned home for lunch served on linen and china, with a tinkling silver bell to summon the next course, was a hat salesman in a local department store. In other homes I was witness to the same female alliance I knew from my aunts, only in interracial, mixed-age sets of women and children. Stories and shared intimacies flew back and forth in one Mississippi household, where my landlady insisted that all the women and children, black and white, gather on a big bed in an inner room, where she assured us we were protected against lightning bolts that might otherwise strike us. The rainy season reinforced female and, to some degree, interracial solidarity and furthered the oral transmission of legends.

Years before any murmur of a civil-rights movement, I was impressed by the quality and content of interracial relationships among women. One upper-class woman I befriended in South Carolina, for example, used her wealth to run a summer school on an island off the coast for promising black youth secretly referred to her by black teachers in her county. I left the South chastened by my human encounters there, freed of many northern stereotypes of the South and southerners.

I have almost left out one important additional impact of World War II, perhaps because it involved such pain: the replacement of pride in my German heritage with shame. Just before the war, I had battled, to the point of leaving home, my father's views toward Hitler's Germany. And it was thirty-five years before I felt up to crossing the border into Germany on European trips. Ethnic orphan that I was, I adopted my husband's ethnicity as my own. This was no hardship, for Italy is one of the loveliest lands in the world, and I have never had complaints from guests about my basically north Italian cuisine.

The third historical event of great impact was the renascence of feminism in the 1960s. In retrospect I think some of the androgynous roots of my childhood, hidden behind a facade of traditional patriarchy, influenced many choices I made in early adulthood. Combined with involvement in a radical student culture during college years, my choice of profession and my persistence in working at it while rearing children made me a marginal person in the cohort of women to which I belonged. I was what Vern Bengtson calls a forerunner in my generation. My unmarried aunts, women teachers, and the women writers I loved were important models supporting my own marginal choices. My experience of sex discrimination at the University of Chicago pointed up a long predisposition to feminism.

Historical or period effects differ in their impact depending on the age at which they are experienced. That the feminist renascence was begun by employed middle-aged women like myself reflects our experience as women with permanent attachments to the labor force who found barriers to promotion or who received lower pay than men doing comparable work. Hence our political efforts were on improving the educational and occupational opportunities for women. Our personal lives had jelled by that point, so it was left for younger feminists to call for change in private, sexual, and family life.

This point was first brought home to me by the different reactions of older and younger women to my early feminist publications in the mid-1960s. The bitter, angry letters I received were from women over fifty, whose response centered on their lost chances. As one woman put it, "Had anyone written as you do when I was twenty, I would have had two, not six children, and I would not have given up my desire to be a lawyer." By contrast, women in their twenties and thirties said such things as "I've decided to postpone getting married, and will finish college first"; "I'm going back to school instead of having another child"; and "I think I have the courage now to face the fact that my marriage has been dead for years."

Later I found this same age difference in an analysis of the political issues on which delegates to the first national women's conference had been active (Rossi 1982). Younger delegates seemed to leave gender issues of educational and job opportunities to the by now older branch of feminist organizations. The younger delegates' energies were invested in sex issues like women's health care, rape, and spouse abuse. The unifying commitment of both young and old delegates was to increase representation of women in politics so that they can make the laws, not court the votes of men. Their joint efforts have contributed to the growing gender gap in voting behavior and position on political issues in the 1980s. In the coming decade I predict a great increase in the proportion of women holding public office (Rossi 1983).

Maturational Effects

I have left for last a cluster of changes that may be true maturational effects. These changes are an inherent function of the process of growing up and growing old that can speak equally to people of all ages—hopefully with an echo of recognition for readers my age, and with a note of prescience for those younger.

One key maturational change is an altered perspective on time. In youth and early adulthood one rarely thinks of time running out. Psychologically time feels limitless, so if you take one option rather than another, you can expect one day to also experience the postponed option if you still wish it. With age, one begins to rely on a time calculus: if I do X, will I ever get to do Y? If I write a book on kinship, will I ever get to do one on the sibling relationship? Will this be the last time I see Venice or Taormina? As Neugarten suggests, a shift in time perspective occurs when one passes the meridian of life, from viewing life as years since birth to viewing it as years left to live (Neugarten 1968).

Closely related to this shift in time perspective is an altered sense of one's body. Health and stamina are no longer taken for granted; they become things to work at. The sociological concepts of achievement and ascription apply here, at least in a figurative sense. In youth, one's body is an ascribed fact, a healthy instrument one does not hesitate to challenge, push to extremity, and overindulge without fear of the consequences. From middle age that body becomes an achieved fact—an instrument to listen to, tune up, pamper, and, if need be, transcend. An unusual ache or stiff back may be a harbinger of some chronic disability rather than something that will surely pass. These experiences trigger a more cautious use of energy and a reduction of the excesses of food, drink, and exercise that characterized youth. In a sense they are small rehearsals for the acceptance of the loss of close intimates—parents, spouse, and friends—and of our own death.

Overview

The stress on cohort membership and the influence of historical events is congenial to most sociologists since they illustrate both the potential for change in adulthood and the influence of social factors on personal values and personality. We sociologists like to think that we are what we do, that is, that we are molded by social situations and the institutional webs that enmesh us (or at least that enmesh our respondents, if not the free-agent, rational beings that sociologists consider themselves to be). There is certainly ample evidence of the marks left on me as a member of the 1920s birth cohort and of the particular historical events that impinged on my life at certain critical stages.

By contrast, before the mid-1970s most psychologists were committed to the view that early childhood is a critical period of development that leaves indelible marks on people for the rest of their lives. Clearly parents exert influence over their children in the years from birth well into adolescence. As key socializers of the child, parents are central transmitters of values, skills, and expectations. The picture becomes murky when parental influence is traced in the adult years of the children. An extensive review of parent-child pairs by Lilian Troll and Vern Bengtson (1979), covering a wide range of studies including political opinions, voting behavior, religious beliefs, and life-style preferences, showed only modest correlations between parents and adult children. But affective solidarity between parents and adult children was not impaired by discrepancies between them in politics, religion, or life-style. Such findings refute most of the theories that have been brought to bear on child socialization (whether psychoanalytic theory, symbolic-interaction theory, learning theory, balance theory, or exchange theory), all of which assume that the stronger, closer, and more attractive the bond of a child to a parent, the more similar the behavior, attitudes, and values of the child will be to the parent. It may well be the case that in all social relations *except* the parent-child relationship such discrepancies would lead to an attenuation of affectionate bonds. The uniqueness of the parent-child bond may lie precisely in the simple fact of genetic relatedness: *my son the criminal* may be embraced along with *my son the doctor,* and parents remain salient to our sense of ourselves even after their deaths. Despite the considerable social mobility from my family of origin, and wide differences in politics and religion between myself and either of my parents as a consequence of cohort and historical influences, they have remained central to my affective and social life.

As I have grown older, my relationship to my mother has, if anything, intensified further. I suspect one reason for this change is coming to grips in more direct terms with mortality. Our ties to parents may weaken during adolescence and early adulthood, but toward the end of life, these bonds take on a renewed emotional salience similar in intensity to the attachment we experienced at the beginning of life.

Such thinking does not sit well with sociologists since they tend to prefer upbeat perspectives on life rather than a bittersweet one with hints of deeper levels of human relationships rooted in genetic linkages between people. In recent years developmental psychologists have also come to stress a self-generating conception of adulthood—the self as an active agent determining the direction a life will take (Brim and Kagan 1980)—much as the majority of youthful feminists do. Developmental change is the "in" concept, whereas stability has become a concept on the wane. This view is certainly supported by sociological work on occupational success among subjects under forty-five years of age. The consistent finding from status attainment research is that parental class and parental encouragement affect the final educational attainment of the child but do not extend to the occupational success of children by the time they are in their thirties. Dennis Hogan (1981) has been critical of status attainment studies on precisely the grounds that they neglect contemporary pressures that replace or supplement early family and school influences, pressures like those rooted in different labor markets, occupations, or firms with different promotion rates, or variation in family size and economic circumstances impinging on adults in the families they form.

For most people the decades of their twenties and thirties are marked by several simultaneous, powerful transitions that seem to produce changes from earlier periods of life in one's family of origin. But one publication from the Oakland and Berkeley, California, growth studies poses a serious challenge to the assumption that change is the constant in adulthood and that there are radical and irrevocable breaks from earlier years. Dorothy Eichorn and her associates (1981) report a sleeper effect when adolescent characteristics are related to early versus middle adulthood. That is, there were very low or insignificant correlations between adolescent and early-adult personality characteristics, but adolescent characteristics did correlate significantly with characteristics in late middle age. It is tempting to interpret this to mean that, all other things equal, from mid-life on, we become more like we were in our youthful years than we were through the years of early adulthood, when the press of job and family often required us to act "out of character."

For men in early adulthood, role obligations involve the suppression of their tender, feminine side, and for women, their agentic, masculine side. Consistent with the Eichorn findings on middle age, a number of studies suggest a reversal in sex-role characteristics in later life (Gutmann 1968, 1969, 1975; Lowenthal et al. 1975; Neugarten and Gutmann 1968). With increasing age, older men become more nurturing and older women become more assertive. Perhaps that is why I experienced a different man in my grandfather than his children had known, and why many mothers-in-law are often considered intrusive and opinionated. Years ago I thought this contrast between a parent-child relationship and a grandparent-grandchild relationship reflected the fact that parents must exercise discipline and authority over children, whereas grandparents are released from this role demand and are free to indulge pure pleasure in, and affection for, their grandchildren. But it could also have to do with maturational change since grandparents are typically over fifty, whereas parents are in their twenties and thirties. Moreover, I have observed the beginning of this sex role reversal in my husband and myself. Years ago he was a dominant, assertive man who suppressed the tender side of himself, but that tender side is revealed more each year, while I feel much more freedom to be dominant and assertive than ever before in my life. This interesting shift shows itself in all our social roles, as parents, spouses, teachers, and organizational officers.

And so at sixty-seven I feel closer to the Alice of thirteen than to the Alice of twenty or thirty. I like this new-old Alice better too. Does anyone know of a play calling for a woman character with a purple cape and a walking cane? I feel old enough, and young enough, finally to take center stage.

Note

This is an edited version of a pamphlet privately published in 1983 by Hamilton Newell, Inc., Amherst, Massachusetts, and distributed by Sociologists for Women in Society.

References

Baltes, P. B., and K. W. Schaie. 1973. *Life-span developmental psychology: Personality and socialization.* New York: Academic Press.

Bengtson, V., and L. Troll. 1978. Youth and their parents: Feedback and intergenerational influence in socialization. In R. M. Lerner and G. B. Spanier, eds., *Child influences on marital and family interaction*. New York: Academic Press.

Brim, O. G., Jr., and J. Kagan, eds. 1980. *Constancy and change in human development*. Cambridge, Mass.: Harvard University Press.

Eichorn, D. H., J. A. Clausen, N. Haan, M. P. Honzik, and P. H. Mussen, eds. 1981. *Present and past in middle life*. New York: Academic Press.

Elder, G. 1974. *Children of the Great Depression*. Chicago: University of Chicago Press.

Gould, R. L. 1978. *Transformations: Growth and change in adult life*. New York: Simon and Schuster.

Gutmann, D. 1968. An exploration of ego configurations in middle and later life. In B. L. Neugarten, ed.,*Middle age and aging*. Chicago: University of Chicago Press.

———. 1969. *The country of old men: Cross-cultural studies in the psychology of later life*. Occasional Papers in Gerontology, no. 5. University of Michigan: Institute of Gerontology.

———. 1975. Parenthood: A key to the comparative study of the life cycle. In N. Datan and L. H. Ginsberg, eds., *Life-span development and behavior: Normative life crises*. New York: Academic Press.

Hansen, M. O. 1952. The third generation in America. *Commentary* 14 (5): 492–500.

Hogan, D. P. 1981. *Transitions and social change: The early lives of American men*. New York: Academic Press.

Levinson, D. J. 1978. The seasons of a man's life. New York: Knopf.

Lowenthal, M. F., M. Thurnher, and D. Chiriboga. 1975. *Four stages of life*. San Francisco: Jossey-Bass.

Martineau, H. 1837. *Society in America*. London: Saunders and Otley.

Neugarten, B. L. 1968. The awareness of middle age. In B. L. Neugarten, ed., *Middle age and aging*. Chicago: University of Chicago Press.

Neugarten, B. L., and D. Gutmann. 1968. Age-sex roles and personality in middle age: A thematic apperception study. In B. L. Neugarten, ed., *Middle age and aging*. Chicago: University of Chicago Press.

Neugarten, B. L., and G. O. Hagestad. 1976. Age and the life course. In R. H. Binstock and E. Shanas, eds., *Handbook of aging and the social sciences*. New York: Van Nostrand Reinhold.

Riley, M. W., ed. 1979. *Aging from birth to death: Interdisciplinary perspectives*. Boulder, Colo.: Westview Press.

Rossi, A. S. 1964. Equality between the sexes: An immodest proposal. *Daedalus* 93(2): 607–652.

———. 1973. *The feminist papers: From Adams to de Beauvoir*. New York: Columbia University Press.

———. 1980a. Aging and parenthood in the middle years. In P. B. Baltes and O. G. Brim, Jr., eds., *Life-span development and behavior*, vol. 3. New York: Academic Press.

———. 1980b. Life-span theories and women's lives. *Signs: Journal of Women in Culture and Society* 6 (1):4–32.

————. 1982. *Feminists in politics: A panel analysis of the first national women's conference.* New York: Academic Press.

————. 1983. Beyond the gender gap: Women's bid for political power. *Social Science Quarterly* 64(4):718–773.

Rossi, A. S., and A. Calderwood, eds. 1973. *Academic women on the move.* New York: Russell Sage Foundation.

Rubin, L. B. 1979. *Women of a certain age: The midlife search for self.* New York: Harper and Row.

Sheehy, G. 1977. *Passages: Predictable crises of adult life.* New York: Dutton.

Troll, L., and V. Bengtson. 1979. Generations in the family. In W. R. Burr, R. Hill, F. I. Nye, and I. L. Reiss, eds., *Contemporary theories about the family.* Vol. 1, *Research-based theories.* New York: Free Press.

CHAPTER FOURTEEN

A Woman's
Twentieth Century

Jessie Bernard

I am a born writer. I began my writing career more than seventy-five years ago when I was in the third grade at Horace Mann School in Minneapolis, Minnesota. The novel I began that year was never finished. I didn't have enough time. So I didn't become a published author until the next year when one of the weekly pieces schoolchildren throughout the city wrote for the *Journal Junior*—part of the Sunday edition of the *Minneapolis Journal*—appeared over my name. The best pieces won prizes— beautiful framed pictures—for their authors' schools. All told, in addition to publishing numerous pieces, I won two such accolades and, with my chum Mona Emslie, carried them around the school from room to room to receive the recognition due such achievement.[1] My one and only dramatic success was the script for a playlet based on Beowulf for tenth-grade English at Central High.

But I kept on writing. At the University of Minnesota I majored in English and wrote stories, essays, and novels on assignment. It was not until I was a junior, though, that I discovered my true genre. One of my English professors suggested that I take a course or two with Professor Bernard in the sociology department. I did. I didn't realize until later that I was going to get hooked, that sociology was to be my genre. In fact, I was still writing novels a decade later in a seminar at Washington University.[2] But my fate was sealed. There was no way I could escape it. I was doomed to a life at the typewriter—even worse, a compulsory life at the typewriter.[3] And the words were to be not literature but sociology. I am not discounting the part played in this switch by an engaging teacher. But neither can I deny the fascination of the subject matter itself.

It was, of course, a long time before I recognized why sociology was so fascinating to me, how much history I was myself a product of and participant in. I had lived all my life in the swirls and eddies of numerous historical currents. The paternal grandfather of my three children—born in 1941, 1945, and 1950—fought in the Civil War. He and his family were part of one of the great treks in United States history in the 1880s, from Kentucky and Tennessee to Texas. Their maternal grandparents, my parents, were part of a different kind of trek in the 1880s, from Romania—either Moldavia or Transylvania, I'm not sure which—to the United States. The 1890 U.S. Census books have been destroyed, so the first official recognition of their existence in this country is in the 1900 volume. And there they are, Bettsey, my own grandmother; Bessie, my mother; and David, my father.

Historians tell us that the twentieth century did not really begin until World War I. That means, for all intents and purposes, that I was reared in the nineteenth century, that I was enveloped in its optimism, its belief in progress, its can-do mind-set, its unquestioning belief in science and scientists, its confidence in human ability to solve societal problems, its innocence. It was a time of getting used to the idea that the old Western frontier was passing. It was the Progressive Era.

I was reared in Republican territory. The first newspaper story I ever read was about Teddy Roosevelt, a hero of mythic stature. I was born only thirteen years after Frederick Turner had told us that the era of the frontier was over, in a city not too far from what had been authentic frontier only a few years earlier. My mother's cousin Mendel and his wife had homesteaded there, in North Dakota, for several years. Mendel: student, scholar, gentleman with pince-nez glasses. How come, I now wonder, he hadn't known about drought and locusts and grasshoppers? He learned soon enough and returned to Minneapolis.[4]

It was a time when immigration was a major issue, a time of belief in the melting pot, and of learning how to deal with the great tides inundating—or, as some said, hordes invading—our shores.[5] In Minneapolis many of them were Scandinavian. My neighbors had names like Johnson, Peterson, Olson, Hanson. But there were Wasp names among them too: Waite, Emslie, Strand, Cormier. The woman with the long gray curls hanging down her back who came every week to clean our house was Mrs. Proven, and she took our laundry home to be done by her mother, Mrs. Brandon. Both were New Englanders and members of the most elite church in town. There were two black families in my neighborhood, and in both of them the mother was white. In my class at Horace Mann School there were two black girls: Frances, who was sweet and quiet, and Lucy, who was angry and resentful. There was an old man, Mr. Peebles, born a little more than half a century earlier, who sat in the sun at the carpenter's shop down the street.

The city was run by the New Englanders who had come in the nineteenth century to establish the flour mills, operate the banks, manage the wheat market, and run the railroads—and the public schools. I sometimes say, in fact, that I went to a New England academy. In my high school you could take four years of Latin and, if you wanted, Greek too. You could take four years of science and three of mathematics, as well as French and Spanish—though not, I must add, German during the years I was there. At that time, every trace of German history or culture was eliminated from the curriculum.[6]

In addition to the classic New England curriculum was the cadre of teachers, most of them women, and women of a special kind, stamped with a New England brand. The great American poets and novelists were naturally the New England writers. In United States history the preeminent figure was Alexander Hamilton. It was years before I realized that Thomas Jefferson was much the greater man of the two, and that George Washington was, of course, even greater. And that midwesterner, Abraham Lincoln, towered over all of them.

My great women teachers in high school were suffragists. They transmitted the feminist message. One of them, Mrs. Gray, my English teacher, told the story of the gentle lady who invited a gentleman to have tea with her. In the course of the afternoon the conversation turned to the suffrage movement. "How absurd," the gentleman said. "Think of your cook voting." To which she replied sweetly, "Yes, I often do. You see, he does." I had great women teachers in college, too. There was Anna Helmholtz Phelan, a statuesque Athene, who overwhelmed by her presence as much as by her learning. And Marjorie Nicholson, whom we lost to Columbia University. And Alice Felt Tylor, who taught sections in United States history but could never secure a regular appointment, despite her published work, because of the nepotism rule that precluded it for her as the wife of a professor in the department. And then there was Dr. Martin, who left for Smith College because as a woman she had achieved as much as she could professionally. It is not surprising to me now that a young woman with a background like mine would, with a little encouragement, become a sociologist.

The class position of my family was equivocal. My father had been a butter-and-eggs man who worked for his brother, the first in the "immigration chain," delivering—literally—butter and eggs to his brother's customers.[7] By the time I was born a decade or so later, he was running a haberdashery on Washington Avenue and hiring another brother, the last in the immigration chain. A few years later he was buying up bankrupt stores in small towns in Wisconsin, Montana, and the Dakotas, running sales to dispose of their inventories. If he had such a sale going on in the summer we children sometimes joined him for vacations. The pleasantest places were in Wisconsin. I suppose by definition he was a middle-class entrepreneur, a risk taker who knew how to assess an inventory of goods and make a suitable bid for it. Sometimes he made mistakes—bid too much or misjudged the town's taste—and lost money. But overall he seemed fairly successful. It was strenuous, though, and it meant separation from us; as soon as he felt he could afford to, he gave it up and invested in Minneapolis real estate instead.

As soon as my mother, who had been brought to this country by her mother, had completed what education she was to have, she went to work in the garment industry in New York City. She remembered those years with considerable pleasure, sometimes singing to herself the songs that were popular at the time. Her mother had willingly allowed her to march in the suffrage parades of the day but never, never, to take part in any union-organizing activity that might threaten her job. And she was an obedient daughter.

I don't think my own class attitudes were influenced by either my father's "capitalist" background or my mother's experience as part of the "toiling masses." They were, however, influenced by the radical friends my older sister brought home from the University of Minnesota from time to time. Hidden in a corner, I listened and became caught up in their lively political discussions. They were ardent socialists. The name Eugene V. Debs came up often. They were persuasive—there was no one opposing them in those discussions—and I never doubted the validity of their arguments. One of them, the brother of one of my sister's best friends who was studying law, became a national labor leader; another of the young men became an international award-winning medical researcher; another a run-of-the-mine lawyer. The women became teachers. To this day my automatic response to, say, a labor-management issue tends to be a management one; my considered response is usually a labor one.

No one in my childhood or girlhood seemed to fear socialism. I don't think I ever made a connection between my father's small-business capitalism and the bogey of my sister's friends. As an undergraduate I sometimes attended meetings of the Seekers, a communist group on campus whose faculty mentor was a sociologist named L. L. Bernard.[8] The city itself was more concerned about the Farmer-Labor party.

I entered college at sixteen in January 1920. By that time World War I had been over a little more than a year, and the twentieth century was well on its way. Women had already been making themselves felt by doing important work like establishing government agencies, running the Children's Bureau and the Women's Bureau, transforming the Poor Laws, exploring new kinds of services for new urbanites, and designing a modern welfare state for the New Deal a decade later. They were to achieve suffrage that year. Now young women were demanding even more—the right to smoke, drink, wear short skirts, dance sexy dances, even appropriate Freud, and in general thumb their noses at the now-jettisoned nineteenth-century standards of ladylike behavior.

Women's clothes had changed—not only outer garments but under-clothes as well. The year before I came to campus there had been a "corsetless coed" movement, and women were now wearing garter belts to keep their stockings up or just rolling them below the knee. Brassieres had already replaced beribboned camisoles or corset covers. Women were freer in their behavior. They walked differently.

The men returning from the war did not know what to make of all this. They did not understand this postwar generation. They misread our bobbed hair, rolled stockings, short skirts, and uncorseted bodies. They had gone to war at the tail end of the nineteenth century and returned in the twentieth. They had never known twentieth-century women before the war. They were not ready for them after the war.[9]

My generation is remembered as a Charleston-dancing, Prohibition-defying, sex-indulging young people roaring through the twenties in reaction to the end of the trauma of war. I do not remember the 1920s that way. True, we did go to private rooms at hotel parties for wine. But we were quiet, well behaved, low-key. The men wanted us to be safe, and they protected us. If anyone had annoyed us by unwelcome advances he would have been stopped. When I had to be on campus especially early for a college event, I sometimes spent the night in my date Mark's bed in an apartment he shared with a classmate and his wife. Mark never once so much as hinted at the possibility of sharing the bed with me. I never went to a "blind pig."[10] I did not dance the Charleston, though I did dance cheek to cheek, but so innocently that my brother and I were once asked to leave the floor of a dance hall for such impropriety.

Sociology had just barely achieved academic respectability and legitimacy as a member of the community of science when I was introduced to it in the early 1920s. At Yale, W. G. Sumner, ostensibly an economist, was teaching Republican doctrine to undergraduates but also assembling a great store of historical and anthropological materials for his course on the science of society, published in a book, *Folkways,* still fascinating almost eighty years later. Race was attracting a lot of attention. It was all that Franz Boas at Columbia could do to defuse the racism that tainted immigration policy. At the University of Chicago Robert Park was turning the city of Chicago into a laboratory for the study of urban life. Theories of progress were still being taught at my alma mater, Minnesota. There was a lot for this discipline to tend to, and I soon wanted to be part of it.

Professor Bernard always had a lot of groupies around him as well as radicals. Incredible as it seems in the 1980s, communist groups were not forbidden or negatively sanctioned on that midwestern campus in the 1920s. When the Seekers asked Professor Bernard to be their faculty adviser, he accepted. It seemed a matter of course. He took social criticism seriously, holding it to be an important part of his function as a sociologist.[11]

Mate selection was once a major research interest among family sociologists, and they produced a sizable store of data. But there remain a lot of subtleties that might well fall between the cracks of all the variables. I was courted by the most eligible man in the social circles I moved in. It was precisely his social eligibility that made it ultimately impossible for me to marry him. When I heard about his family's lifestyle, their comings and goings, I drooped. I was intimidated by the homes his family and relatives lived in, by the kind of social life they engaged in, by the clothes they wore and how they wore them, by the style they entertained in. His wife would have a kind of life I could never successfully, or at least happily, live. She would have to run a certain kind of household, with elegance, dress a certain kind of way, with flair,[12] entertain in a certain mode, with sophistication. I had no stomach for that way of living, no talents or skills for it. Just as Jo in *Little Women* knew that she could not marry Laurie, I knew I could not marry him. I ended up by marrying my professor, L. L. Bernard.

I was twenty-two years old. I had my second degree and was working toward my third. I had been elected to Phi Beta Kappa and Sigma Xi. I had presented my master's thesis, which had already won a local prize, to the American Sociological Society. I had lived in a warm, safe world, free to roam but protected on all sides. I had read a lot of books and taken a lot of courses. I was massively ignorant. I was vulnerable. What I had seen ahead of me was a pleasant career as Professor Bernard's research assistant. He was an enchanting man to work with and for. As my mentor he had shaped my mentality. I saw the world through his eyes. But I had not seen marriage to him in the cards. I had not been looking closely enough.

The marriage lasted till death did us part, just over twenty-four years—if it could be called the same marriage over all that time. It was at first an apprentice-master relationship. It was to end as a collegial one.[13]

A few years ago I was introduced to an audience as the venerable Jessie Bernard. My reply was so witty that I repeat it every chance I get. "I suppose," I said, "that when one ceases to be venereal she becomes venerable." Not too long after that I was introduced by a former student to another audience. He said I was childlike, no offense intended. I had no witty answer this time. I agreed. I am childlike, no offense taken.

I can only account for my being childlike by the kind of atmosphere I grew up in, was, in fact, born into. Eric Erikson—of whom I am not a disciple—tells us that infancy is a time when trust is established in the child. I never had any occasion to mistrust anyone or anything. I assumed, took for granted, accepted without question, that I would always be taken care of, that the world was a friendly place. When I lost my rubber in the mud coming home from kindergarten, I knew my mother would fetch it when I told her where it was. When, at five, I got all but buried in the snow on my way home from school, I knew I would be found; no cause for alarm. There were close calls from time to time, to be sure. I sat on the front steps evening after evening waiting for my father to bring home the doll I wanted so much, and when the doll never showed up there I began to have doubts. I broke into tears. When he learned about the doll, of course it appeared. I had taken it for granted that because I wanted it so much surely he could see that I did. Although my relations with my indulgent father were wonderful, those with my mother were more profound. Many years later when I had occasions to cry into my pillow it was my mother I called for, not my adoring father.

There were occasionally other crises of trust. There was the one when the house was filled with excitement as my older brother and sister were preparing for a visit to Mendel's farm in North Dakota. I assumed that I would be going too. I was four. At train departure time all nonpassengers were told to leave the coach. Not until my father gathered me in his arms to take me off did it dawn on me—much to my dismay—that I was not to go. An ice-cream cone hardly provided enough balm that time. There were other such occasions but never any serious enough to pierce the cocoon of absolute faith. That kind of faith is a kind of grace—a gift. But it also had its cost. A great many useful skills—"street smarts"—were unattainable. Still, without trust, one of those game-theory prisoners loses his life.

Perhaps such childlike trust should be classified in adults not as a gift but as a kind of deficit, like, for example, lack of musical pitch, or inability to repeat a dance step after simply being told how to do it, or to follow a who-done-it and understand its resolution. When my children and I used to watch Perry Mason on television they had to explain Mason's last-minute solutions, how he had used the clue. They did not have my childlike trust. They were products of a different historical moment and a different family experience.[14]

In 1958 we were told that "women scholars are not taken seriously and cannot look forward to a normal professional career" (Caplow and McGee 1958, 226). Fifteen years later, in 1973, Eleanor Sheldon told us that in those years "activist women . . . succeeded in putting the disabilities suffered by women in academia as a class high on the national list of social injustices in need of rectification" (Rossi and Calderwood 1973, ix).

I entered academia professionally in 1940, fairly well along in my career. Family had not been a major sociological interest of mine; the department at Minnesota had not played it up. Broken families, homeless men, and illegitimacy were dealt with in courses in the social work curriculum under Mrs. Mudgett at one end of the corridor; "the" family, on a quite different wavelength, came under sociology at the other. Robert Merton said in 1972 that "the handful of women sociologists were expected to study problems of women, principally as these related to marriage and the family" (1972, 13). I was a little late in recognizing this expectation. But, sure enough, just as Merton had said, when I became a college teacher—at Lindenwood College—the family became my beat. It was taken for granted that it would. My earlier work on success in marriage had been part of my absorption in measurement, not a leaning toward the study of marriage qua marriage. Not that I objected in any way. I began at once to delve into the literature and two years later published *American Family Behavior* (1942).[15] It was well received but, alas, became a casualty of World War II. The plates were melted down for war material, and the book was not reissued until some thirty years later.

Although a dedicated sociologist, I proved to be an undisciplined one. I did not take easily to the restriction of discipline boundaries. I enjoyed excursions into outside territory. I have been the prototypical marginal man. Although I became identified with the sociology of marriage and family, I have been equally concerned with the sociology of knowledge, especially of science, and of course with its history. Outside of my discipline I have enjoyed community with psychologists, historians, anthropologists, home economists, even—at some remove—mathematicians.

As a Comtean positivist, I believed, as the positive philosophy taught, that mathematics was the queen of all the sciences, including sociology. True, the only practicable way of using it was in the form of statistics, a subject not yet wholly at home in sociology departments when I was a graduate student. F. S. Chapin had been reduced to assigning a textbook in biostatistics in his graduate course on social trends.

World War I had enormously stimulated growth in measuring instruments.[16] I was in the audience when L. L. Thurstone told us that even attitudes could be measured (1929). Years later there were instruments for measuring anything one could think of. In the early 1930s at Washington University I came in contact with a "measurement freak" in the psychology department. He was a compulsive measurer and I caught the fever. I wanted to measure everything. It became a mania. Just point me to it and I was off and running to measure it,[17] at least to count until measuring instruments became available.

At midcentury I was enormously atttracted to the game theorists. They seemed to be the wittiest among all the social science communities. They wrote with a sense of humor. The games they concocted for their players were fascinating. They were mean people. They were always trying to do one another in. And sometimes, as among those notorious prisoners, they were deadlocked, even with their fate depending on trust in one another. I was, nevertheless, attracted to the theory and tried to apply it to marriage and family, first in a chapter of the Harold Christiansen *Handbook on Marriage and Family* and then to the relations between the sexes in *The Sex Game*. I was invited to participate in a conference of game theorists—they turned out to be kind, friendly, hospitable even to this untutored outsider who so obviously did not know what they were talking about. I carried on a minor correspondence with several of their stars and audited a faculty seminar on my own campus on the subject, but I knew I was far beyond my depth. There was no way I could ever begin to keep up in that fast lane.[18]

In the early 1970s I was invited to participate in a conference entitled *Successful Women in the Sciences.* I replied that I would be glad to participate but not under the title then planned; it was too elitist. "I find myself," I wrote, "somehow or other turned off by the aura of elitism." It was too much like the then-current cliché of Queen Bees: "I made it. Why can't you?" The conference changed the title to *Women and Success,* but still I did not participate. When the book of conference proceedings was published I was charged, along with others, with being a pathetic example of women's fear of success.

Several women who were invited to participate objected to the idea of having a conference dedicated totally to the subject of "successful women." "The idea of 'success' was objectionable to some women. . . . The reluctance of these women to be considered successful was a pathetic revelation. As Matina Horner points out . . . women are basically afraid of success. In a woman . . . success is considered deviant behavior" (Kundsin 1973,11). That comment stimulated a lot of questions in my mind. "Pathetic" was, like beauty, in the eyes of the beholder, and there was nothing I could do about that.[19] But "fear of success"?

What was success? How did one measure it? Kundsin herself defined success in the context of her conference as "the ability to function in a chosen profession with some measure of peer recognition" (9). I think I passed that test.[20] Jo Ann Gardner, an outstanding feminist, defined success in terms of "whether or not people get to do what they perceive as their work." I know I passed that test.[21] My Oxford Dictionary was not very helpful. The first two of five definitions are archaic, and the third, dating from 1586, is "the prosperous achievement of something attempted; the attainment of an object according to one's desire, now often with particular reference to the attainment of wealth or position." I think I passed. I am hesitant because of the use of the words *attempted* and *according to one's desire.* They imply that I set up objectives or goals—wealth or position—and then hewed to the line. I am well aware that I may be fooling myself, that the "me" others see is not the person "I" see. But it seems to me that what really drove me was the need to write, to research, to report, to tell myself what I saw, felt, and lived. A great many of the accoutrements of success were bestowed on me.[22] If they had not been, would I still have been so driven? I don't know.

If I had not been so pathetically fearful of success how much more successful would I have been? What fear prevented me from doing what would have made me successful? It was, I finally concluded, not fear of success but fear—like Lord Acton's—of power that kept me from (the dictionary-defined) fear of success—power in my own or in anyone's hands. I did not want to be powerful. I didn't even want to be in charge. I didn't want to be boss-woman. I didn't want to be top banana. Leadership, OK. It did not imply coercion. Accolades like Eminence Grise I devour. Doyenne is fine. Elder Stateswoman, great. This was the kind of success I lapped up. All these honorific tributes were bestowed on me even before I achieved venerability. Only good sense and a sense of humor have saved me from being reduced to a cult figure, for which I am grateful.

In a less academic context the expression "use it or lose it" has more general application. It holds also for status. Unless one hews to the line of prescribed high-status behavior one falls back. One has not only to look the part—which I never did—but also to act the part. At one time or another, for example, I have served as mentor to a number of men and women; all were properly appreciative, rewarding me with kudos for my—relative to them at the time—higher professional status. Then their own careers flourished, and soon they were patronizing me. I neither looked nor acted the part of a high-status professional. (I had, I was once told, a "gee whiz" aura about me.) One woman, commenting on my insistence on running with the pack instead of at least playing the part of star, once said, in effect: "Go sit down and be a matriarch." Why did I insist on continuing to do sociology? If this was fear of success, I have been guilty of harboring it.

I have experienced a number of epiphanies in my life. Only two are relevant to my career as a sociologist. Both had to do with the sociology of knowledge, one related to the Nazi degradation of science and the other to the feminist augmentation of it.

In the 1940s half a dozen articles—on power, science, conflict—issued from my typewriter. They did not add up to an integrated treatise, but they did cohere; they elaborated a consistent theme. From one perspective or another they portrayed a mind if not in anguish at least in a state of serious malaise. If I had waited to write them all together they might have constituted a book on the nature of science and of scientists and on the uses to which science is put—or, rather, on the loss of my nineteenth-century heritage of faith in science. It was a troubled time in which, almost day by day, I was learning about the underside of science and the vulnerability of scientists. It was a decade of growing disillusionment with science, scientists, and the uses to which science can be put.[23]

In my part of *Origins of American Sociology* (1942) I had traced the burgeoning belief in science as the means, in effect, of social salvation, as exhibited in the American Social Science Movement, which was characterized by a worship of science. I had paid tribute to the "monumental dream" of a society based on science. I had been dazzled by the idea of a science in the service of human betterment. I "believed" in it. I had organized my intellectual life around it. It served as a sort of religion, an integrating force, in my life. I had a great deal invested in it.

In the first decades of this century it had been easy, as part of the nineteenth-century optimism, to accept that century's idea of scientists as ethical men, as, in fact, the heroes they were depicted as being in biographies and fiction. True, there did surface, from time to time, examples of the fragility of the ideals of science. There were researchers who violated its canons, who manipulated their data, falsified results. But the sanctions imposed by peers were so severe in such cases that at least in one, that of Paul Kammerer, exposure precipitated suicide.

The first world-class example of the contamination of science by ideology that I knew about was the notorious case in the USSR in which Lysenko had to design his research to prove the ascendancy of environment over genes in plant and animal experiments. The disastrous results in time supplied a corrective.[24]

A decade after I had paid tribute to the nineteenth-century's "monumental dream" of science in the service of humankind, disillusioned, I was writing: "The scientist is the key man in control of the greatest power in the world today, the power of science. Men who want to control that power are not going to permit the scientist to remain aloof. Nor are scientists in a position to withstand them." What happened in those ten years? It is hard to trace one's intellectual tracks. But, for one thing, we had by then begun, little by little, to learn the story of science in Germany in the 1930s and of the behavior of scientists. In my parochial naïveté I had not known that my nineteenth-century image of the scientist was, in effect, a parody—or rather a burlesque—of what had actually been going on there. I hadn't noticed the scientists' feet of clay.

It was to take us a long time to learn what had been going on in the scientific community in Germany in the 1930s.[25] There even the cynosure of all the sciences, the science in the most strategic position to protect its mores—physics itself—was being politicized. Some, including two Nobel laureates, had—horrible dicta—propounded proper

"Aryan" physics, which was based on observation and experimentation, and fought "Jewish" physics, which was too mathematical and theoretical. The Nazi "dismissal policy" in the universities was soon to correct the overrepresentation of such non-Aryan "deviationism." Why had their fellow Aryan scientists permitted this drain on their talent resources? Why had they not resisted the dismissal of these "non-Aryan" scientists? Why had so many of them chosen "prudential acquiescence," "inner emigration"?[26] "The foremost concern of the physics community during the Nazi years was the protection of their autonomy against political encroachment." Why did they not see that acceptance of the dismissal policy was, actually, acceptance of such political encroachment? Why did "the ethically correct course of action . . . [seem to be to] learn to be silent without exploding?" (Beyerchen 1981, 207). Beyerchen comments that it was "not that scientists were political cowards, but that they did not know how to be political heroes."[27]

There may have been extenuating circumstances. The dismissal policy was implemented by way of what conflict theorists have called "salami tactics," small incremental steps.[28] There seemed to be no point big enough to take a stand on. There seemed to be no moment to say, no more. If we accepted the dismissal last week, why fight this new one now?

Would the ideal-typical scientists whose roles had evolved in the nineteenth century have known how to be political heroes? Would I have? The question has troubled me. How, I have sometimes asked myself, would I have acted in Hitler's Germany? This is a hard question to wrestle with. As a scientist would I have gone along with the other physicists on the dismissal policy? Would I have seen such a policy primarily as a denial of the autonomy of my community or as an injustice to my colleagues? Would I have been solicitous of the "non-Aryan" physicists and helped them, or would I have been glad to get rid of their competition? Would I have warned mainly on the grounds of the impact on the prized reputation of German science, or would I have argued on the basis of principles of human justice? As a run-of-the-mill German, would I, in mortal fear, have turned away from my "non-Aryan" colleagues, as some did, even denounced them, or would I have protected them? Would I have actively dissented from Nazi policies, joined the underground? As a Jew would I have groveled and tried to prove myself more Nazi than Hitler himself, or insisted that it was all just a transitory aberration and would soon be over? Or would I have been somebody's "pet" or "exception" Jew, protected from danger? Would I have accepted such protection, with all the psychic and ethical costs involved? I am never comfortable with any answer, nor at all sure that I could have passed on my own standards of ethical behavior.[29]

It was not, of course, these "Aryan" physicists themselves who were to perpetrate the Holocaust of the 1940s. That could not be laid at their door. But the mentality that could accept the dismissal policy—as drastic for their scientific colleagues as the expropriation of more material treasures was among less distinguished "non-Aryans"—thus stamping it with an anti-Jewish ideology, cannot be held wholly innocent of complicity either.

The violation of the canons of science, the imposition of the Star of David on Jews, the discriminatory laws—these we were just beginning to learn about in the 1930s. We began to hear also about the Nazi use of human subjects in medical and pharmaceutical research, of race tests based on skin and hair and eye color in an effort to "Germanize" their population. There were also reports of breeding retreats where unmarried Nordic women were invited to come to have their Nordic babies. The old nineteenth-century chimera of eugenics was once more becoming visible. There were stories of euthanasia of the old and unfit. But not yet about the Final Solution.

Our ignorance was not fortuitous. It was, in fact, performing well the intended function of ignorance. The Nazis had been understandably secretive about their policy of extermination. They had gone to great lengths to keep it as hidden as possible or at least as inconspicuous as possible, even to the prospective victims themselves. If the function of ignorance was so well performed, it is understandable that the rest of the world knew so little.

Information about the crematoria percolated only slowly by way of the mass media.[30] It came in bits and pieces, an item here, an item there, often in formal reports not easy to understand without context. My own writing had not been influenced by it at all. Until now it had been only the intellectual significance of Nazism for science that had had an impact on me. But subliminally it all must have been adding up in my mind. For, suddenly, it began to fall into place. I remember the very moment when it happened. I was in the university library reading an article on the psychology of the extermination camp. I had in my own professional training read countless books on prisons, prisoners, war. But nothing prepared me for this. Was it scientific? real? accurate? I was competely at sea. I could not handle it. There was nothing in my experience or reading that gave me an intellectual preparation for it.

There have been other holocausts in human history. The destruction of whole cities was not uncommon in Old Testament times. The Armenians still remember the massacre more than half a century ago, as do the Ukrainians the starvation visited on them by Stalin's agricultural policies. But there has never been, as here, a demonstration, coldly and scientifically carried out by civilian bureaucrats, that reduced the human being to less than zero.

By the end of the decade the intrinsic ethics in science had become indisputably clear to me. The argument of its value-free nature was untenable. It was still strongly urged by some, including George Lundberg, an outstanding representative of the positivist position in sociology. He had been a fellow graduate student at Minnesota. He retained his firm belief in the value-free position. In 1949 I published a letter to the *American Sociological Review* in which I noted my misgivings that he was overselling science in his book *Can Science Save Us?* (1947). It seemed to me he had oversimplified many of the ethical implications inherent in the application of science to social life. He hoped for the time when science would be used for what the "masses of men" wanted as determined by polling. These "masses" were to articulate the ends to the achievement of which science would be applied. I did not complicate the point I was trying to make by challenging the value of polling the masses of men as a way of determining the values to use as guides for the application of science. Our Constitution had the basic function of protecting us from guidelines so susceptible to antisocial ends. And, fortunately, such protection was safely beyond Lundberg's suggested polling of the public, which—several studies had already shown—did not always accept some of the ends, like freedom of speech or press, that the Constitution protected.

Science was, of course, indispensable; in that I concurred. But more was needed. Lundberg had said that "any scientific statement ('if the spark, etc. . . . then the explosion') contains no . . . implicit ethical conclusion because the culture (or other conditions) to which scientific statements are relative are always explicitly and conditionally stated." In my letter, I replied:

> The ethical implications are present because the conditions necessary to produce the given result constitute, in effect, a prescription which may become an imperative for action. "If the spark, etc. . . . . then the explosion" can also be stated technically: "to set off the explosion, apply a spark." The implicitly ethical formulation would be: "If you want to set off the explosion, apply a spark." The sequence is thus: a pure-science statement of

antecedents and consequences; a technical or engineering statement of the necessary antecedents to produce the given consequences; an ethical statement ordering the antecedent behavior in order to achieve the consequences. When the element of will is introduced, "if you want to get such and such a result, do thus and so," the pure-science contingency statement has become transformed into an ethical statement.

As I have sat here reviewing the intellectual trauma of that difficult time I am struck with its relevance some forty years later. In the 1940s the great scientific ogre was the atomic bomb. And as some of the scientists who had thought it through and solved the theoretical problems came to be filled with guilt, they organized to prevent its ever being used again. And later, with the discovery of the double helix and the burgeoning advances in medical knowledge and technologies, all the old ethical problems vis-à-vis the uses of science multiplied almost endlessly. The term *algeny* was invented as the biological counterpart to *alchemy*. Like the alchemists, the algenists were urged to be careful in the uses made of their knowledge of genes and their skills in applying it. And I am still, personally, struggling, like many others, with both the politics and the ethics of science, including my own.

Not the least of the traumas I experienced regarding my own disillusionment with science and scientists was having to recognize the painful traumas LLB was also experiencing. There was no way, as he himself had recognized, that science could be prevented from being used perversely. I never discussed the matter with him. And by the end of the 1940s he was already a spent man, too ill to care. This brilliant man, this galvanizing teacher, this idealist, was dying.

After the dark night of the 1940s and 1950s the renaissance of feminism in the 1960s was like a burst of beautiful lights that illuminated the scene and brought with it a spreading warmth. The turbulent 1960s reached me first through my daughter—a freshman at Sarah Lawrence—who, along with her peers across the country, was becoming angry at the anticommunist activities of the House Un-American Activities Committee (HUAC) while researching it for a college term paper. For all intents and purposes she might herself have been one of those protesting Berkeley students. To me it seemed quite far away. And anyway California students seemed always to be involved in something or other avant garde. But this time I had to catch up. The movement was spreading beyond civil rights. There was all this talk about drop-outs, hippies, and, most ominously, drugs. Presently it was necessary for me to face the issues in my own household.

Thus at the same time that I was tangling with the military to prove the authenticity of my son's conscientious-objector status, my living room floor was sometimes lined wall to wall with youngsters from school he had brought to Washington for antiwar demonstrations. The issues of peace and civil rights were bringing conflict and challenge to our very doorsteps. Nor was I exempted. I was myself participating in the early activities of the Women-Strike-for-Peace movement. It seemed little enough.

Toward the end of that tumultuous decade I became aware of an amazing underground network press, of articles and papers mimeographed, stenciled, sometimes printed—from Boston, New York, Washington, Chicago, Memphis, Berkeley—which were circulating among women and carrying astounding contents: reports of feminist meetings, of feminist ideologies, of feminist arguments.[31] This was obviously something that as a sociologist I had to know more about. It wasn't going to be easy. The women I approached were not hospitable. I finally managed to get an invitation to a meeting. This is how I later reported on my first lesson:

> Early in 1968 I became exposed to the Women's Liberation Movement in the underground press. My first reaction was purely academic; I saw it primarily as something interesting to study, as something I had a professional obligation to observe. When, after considerable effort on my part, I received an invitation to a consciousness-raising session, one of the young women there said that I "threatened" her. Sitting quietly on the floor in their midst, showing, so far as I knew, no disapproval at all, my academic objectivity, my lack of involvement, my impersonality, was giving off bad vibrations. This incident gave me something to think about, including my stance vis-à-vis research and also my discipline.

A few years later all the excitement generated by this movement began to surface in the established press, and the cauldron of ideas, theories, and insights bubbled throughout our society. The power of sisterhood was beginning to emerge.

Although I had intended originally to watch the new movement primarily as a research concern, like so many others who came to scoff I remained if not to pray at least to ponder. It proved to be the first rumbling of a resurgence of feminism. It gave us the concept of sexism that rendered a whole sociological universe visible. Like the term "racism," which we had not felt a need for until the 1960s, when it first got into the dictionaries—because until then such concepts as prejudice and race hatred had seemed adequate for the analytic job—so also with sexism: we now needed it to help us first to see and then to analyze sociological phenomena we had not bothered to analyze before.

The feminism I had been reared in had subsided after 1920 and been all but wiped out by the feminine mystique in the 1950s. I was myself among the mothers of the baby-boom babies associated with that mystique.[32] My initial response to this renaissance of feminism was not, however, as a member of that cohort, but as a sociologist.

"Your feminism is too cerebral," I was once told. I could see what my accuser meant. For although I was, to borrow from the Friends' vocabulary, a "convinced" sociologist, I was also, to use the conservative Christian terminology, a "born-again" feminist. Not, that is, a knee-jerk or gut feminist. I was—I believe—convinced by its logic and persuaded by its ethos. It made sense to me even on the basis of male criteria. That it conformed to the values I believed in was icing on the cake. I had been so far from being a born feminist that I had to be alerted to sexism. I had to be told when I had been insulted.[33] I learned even to laugh about it.

What passion I came to invest in feminism was aimed at its relevance for the sociology of knowledge. I could understand how it had happened that practically all human knowledge had been achieved by men, that it dealt with problems they were interested in, that it was from their perspective. I had to accept that. But the male bias did not have to be perpetuated. I wanted the discipline of sociology to be as good as it could be by any standard. Ignorance or rejection of the growing corpus of feminist research relevant for sociological analyses was detrimental to the discipline. I became dedicated to the incorporation into the corpus of human knowledge of the insights and data contributed by this scholarship.

Not that I eschewed activism to achieve a wide gamut of specific, practical, immediate changes that justice called for (from potable water, to occupational training, to simple industrial technologies, to health care in the third world, to affirmative action, to equal pay for work of equivalent value, and to women's control over their own bodies in the developed countries) but that I thought the most useful form of activism for me was investment in the spreading of the feminist message—in writing.

My feminist activist writing has taken the form not only of sociological writing but also of letters on behalf of women in academic jeopardy, on behalf of promotion and tenure. And, of course, in writing checks. There have also been marches, demonstrations, meetings, and fundraising events.

I am as undisciplined a feminist as I am a sociologist. I mind being restricted to any one ideological position. I have been called Marxist by dedicated feminists, and it has been intended as a compliment. By others I have been called non- or even anti-Marxist, and it too has been intended as a compliment. Or, sometimes, in either case, a hostile criticism. If either charge is true, it is coincidental. My preferred stance is non- or multi- or omni-ideological. I find it oppressive to hew too consistently to only one line. I seem to be unable to catch the delicate nuances that require one to reject all of any particular canon in order to accept any part of another—even opposite—canon. I find myself comfortably accommodative of parts of many ideologies.[34] If one accepts the assumptions on which the premises are based, most ideologies can make a good case. So, although I have learned a great deal from feminists of many stripes I am not a member in good standing of any of the groups that have been distinguished—radical, Marxist, socialist, psychoanalytic, whatever. Most seem fruitful, some sterile.

Whatever form feminist activism takes, it seeks structural changes in the institutions of a society—laws, court decisions, contracts, guidelines, regulations, administrative orders, and the like. Some forms seek change in the "minds and hearts" as expressed in the manners and morals of a society, in the sexist humor that puts women down, in the insulting expressions, in the ignorance of female sexuality, in the refusal to take the ideas of women seriously, in the implication of male superiority, and the like. Blatant discrimination, exploitation, and oppression can be dealt with by formal political means. Subtler forms call for additional and different remedies.

I am finding, in brief, that although my professional feminism tends to be cerebral as charged—dedicated to the improvement of my discipline— my personal feminism is more than merely an intellectual preoccupation. Like a great and increasing number of men, I believe that the contribution of the female world to the making of policy everywhere is long overdue. I find myself "believing" in feminism as I once did in the nature of science—and hoping that it will not suffer the same fate. I find myself hurt when the female world falls short of what I conceive of as its potential. I find I have a vested interest that it find its own way and not become merely a reflection of the male world.

In the last few years my interests have turned in the direction of the female world seen from a global perspective. As a participant in an increasing number of international meetings of women from all over the world and as a member of international feminist networks and as an eager acolyte in a burgeoning cadre of women researchers learning and teaching about the lives of women everywhere, I continue to find myself—at eighty-six—doing sociology with sustained excitement and verve. Everyone should be so lucky.

Notes

1. Several years ago I wrote to ask if the pictures were still hanging on the walls of Horace Mann School. The building had been demolished some years earlier. I tried to trace the stories in the Sunday editions of the *Minneapolis Journal* between 1910 and 1915 but became impatient and gave up. Sic transit gloria. Those were the first accolades I ever received. The more recent ones are far less exciting. In fact, it seems to me that increasingly they tend to be tributes to my longevity rather than to anything I write.

2. Mine was the only novel the professor had ever seen completed by a member of that seminar as long as he had been teaching it. A psychologist friend of mine once commented that I had enormous "consummatory" drive. That I cannot deny. I have to finish it, whatever it happens to be. Perhaps the consequence of having been taught as a child always to clear my plate? Even a plate of professional chores?

3. And not even a modern typewriter. I don't know how many manual typewriters I have worn out. My friends have implored me for years to get at least an electric typewriter. No way. That would be too easy. Typing is more than transferring thought to paper. It is, for me, an act of aggression. I pound the keys to get rid of my aggressions. I owe my reputation for nonaggression to the keys I batter mercilessly instead of the people who make me mad. George Lundberg once called me "Christlike," which was not a compliment in his vocabulary. Now I am fighting all my friends who insist I must have at least a word processor. Again, no way. Writing is not for me a matter of processing words. Words are very real entities for me, not, of course, human, but certainly having personalities. I enjoy browsing through my Historical Oxford Dictionary when I have time. Sometimes I strike a gem which starts me off on a train of thought that sooner or later may find a home in something I write.

4. A cousin of my father, M. E. Ravage, was a popular writer on immigrant topics in the second decade of the century. Among his books were *An American in the Making* and *A Sentimental Journey*.

5. Many years later the nature of the ambience of my childhood became clear to me. In the early 1930s I was invited to spend a summer as the guest of E. A. Ross in order to do research for a biography of him I was to write. I interviewed him daily, went through a lot of his files, learned how he organized his data, became fascinated by him, but never wrote the book. He wrote it— *Seventy Years of It*—himself. I couldn't have written it, in any event, but preparing to was an illuminating learning experience for me, however equivocal. He gave me insight about the ambience of my own childhood. He was a Midwesterner and so was I. I could recognize the common background we shared. I

could see the mentality of the Progressive Era that he so archetypically represented, even embodied. I could understand it was the prevailing mentality of my own childhood. But there was also his Waspism, his anti-immigrant attitude, his view of immigrants as an invading horde. I had been taught by teachers of a different stripe. One of them was Professor Jenks, who, I learned many years later, was important in the Americanization movement of the second decade of the century. He was appointed by the president in 1907 to serve on a Federal Immigration Commission set up by Congress "to make full inquiry, examination and investigation . . . into the subject of immigration." In 1919, the Minnesota legislature passed an Americanization Aid Law and appropriated $25,000 to maintain active cooperation with the University of Minnesota for an Americanization training program "under the capable guidance of Professor A. E. Jenks." My sister invited him to our home from time to time and for all I know we may have appeared somewhere or other in his memoranda or reports to congressional committees. I never realized that I had been part—however remote—of a movement that "takes its place, alongside those other great crusades of the past, abolitionism, woman's suffrage, civil service reform, and universal education" (Edward George Hartmann, *The Movement to Americanize the Immigrant* [New York: Columbia University Press, 1948], 273).

My family had come to the United States a little too early to be part of the "Americanization" movement, as had the families of my Norwegian friends. But neither they nor I knew of the general harassment of immigrants said to be common in Minnesota, Wisconsin, Iowa, and North and South Dakota before World War I. Norwegian-Americans had long debated the virtues of assimilation versus retaining the ways of the old country. When war broke out in Europe, Norwegian-Americans, like most immigrants, leaned toward assimilation and Americanization, but between the wars many tried to revive interest in traditional life. Nevertheless, ethnicity faded in the immigrants' children and grandchildren, who grew up as Americans. I later learned what a common pattern this was among ethnic groups, and I noted a point in curricula development when courses on the problems of immigration became courses on ethnic groups.

6. The emotion triggered by that intellectual vandalism has remained with me ever since. I finally did learn enough German to pass the required doctoral examination, but it has always remained difficult, and I have been blocked from reading German sociology in the original. I once had to resort to a Spanish translation of something by Simmel that had not yet appeared in English.

7. An "immigrant chain" was literally a succession of family members who came to the United States either one by one or as family members. Usually it was the oldest member who came first to earn enough—and learn enough—to pay for the expected family members next in line. The concept of an immigration chain may have been a contribution to the language by my own professor—A. E. Jenks q.v.—at the University of Minnesota and a high official in the Immigration Commission of 1907. It strikes me now that the concept was completely lost from the sociological vocabulary when the phenomenon itself no longer existed.

8. Many years later, as authors of *The Origins of American Sociology*, we were called "stooges of capitalism" in a Soviet review of the book.

9. This is how William Kephart described this period in 1961: "As women achieved legal and economic equality with men there was a tendency to do other things that men did. . . . After World War I the dam burst with a vengeance. . . . Much to the dismay of the older generation, young ladies began to smoke, drink, use a male vocabulary, listen to risqué jokes. . . . It was almost unavoidable that women's fashions would change. . . . Necklines became lower, sleeves and hemlines shortened. . . . Make-up became a self-styled art, with lipstick, powder, rouge, eye shadow and mascara, perfume, face creams, and nail polish the outward symbols of the new femininity. Hair-styling and hair-coloring became national fetishes, and local female headquarters often came to be centered in the Beauty Shop."

10. A "blind pig" was a secret or police-protected night club or bar where your phony credentials were examined as safe from the "blind" police—themselves well paid for their blindness—before you were allowed to enter.

11. In his teaching he ran, in effect, a school for subversion, almost by design. He did not call it that, but he felt it to be part of his role to challenge the status quo, to get students to see it as a human creation. He called the Jewish ban on intermarriage an "ethnocentric taboo." Young Jewish students brought their praying shawls to the department museum as gifts. Some seminary students came asking how they could incorporate what they were learning in their sermons. Others protested, charging him with attacking religion.

12. I was aware even then of my lack of flair in clothes, and in time I gave up the effort to be anything more than inconspicuously dressed. Many years later when a newspaper reporter described me in a story as "dowdy," however, I was hurt until she called to apologize, explaining that she had written "doughty," not "dowdy." Since "doughty" means formidable as well as capable, virtuous, and valiant, I wasn't altogether appeased.

13. It was a very creative and complex relationship. He insisted I get a doctorate and that I work and achieve, and I worked on his research with him for many years. He was a very unusual man—a poet, and a very charming person. He cooked better than I and he sewed on the sewing machine better too.

14. The real test of my faith was to come later, when I learned of the violation of the ethos of science, described later.

15. A number of current preoccupations appear in that book, including an analysis of housework that deals with such items as homemakers' fatigue (494–99), now called overload, for example; isolation (534–35); housework as an occupation and the asynchrony of its time schedule (535–36); as well as marriage trauma (470–71). After the book was already in galleys I removed a discussion of female orgasm, the nature of which was just then becoming an issue among (mainly male) researchers. The reason for not including it was not theoretical but wholly practical. Most of the women students had never even heard the word *orgasm,* and I did not want to take the time from this course to teach that time-consuming material. I suggested that the physical education courses take that chore on. I am not at all pleased with that cop-out. Later came books on American family behavior, on the future of marriage, on remarriage, and on marriage and family among black Americans, together with a host of

family- and marriage-related articles and papers for encyclopedias, anthologies, and the like.

16. There were already enormous publishers' catalogs listing the dozens of instruments becoming available, and if there wasn't one yet available for what you wanted to measure there was a standard procedure for creating one.

17. I had revealed this propensity for measurement in my master's thesis on a theme I got from E. A. Ross, namely, that customs tend to change more readily than traditions, in which I devised a laughably simplistic and unsophisticated method for measuring change. But by the early 1930s I was going full force, measuring the distribution of success in marriage, some factors in success in marriages, remarriage, neighborhood behavior—of adolescent boys, of women—anything. In *American Family Behavior* I measured the success of families in carrying out their several functions (reproduction, socialization, protective, affectional, institutionalization, and even—love). (I resist using an exclamation point here.)

18. At Penn State I took a course with Sidney Siegel on nonparametric measurement and managed to struggle through. But I knew I was way beyond my depth when in a faculty seminar in the mathematics department one of the men put an equation on the board that traversed two walls of the classroom. Everyone followed him admiringly. Then, after several minutes, one member of the class raised his hand and pointed to one particular point in the long equation. The others studied it a moment, and then, without a word being said by any one, they all nodded their heads in agreement. There was a defect in the argument. Not a word was needed. This was clearly a kind of communication I could *never* master. However much the Comtean love affair with the queen of the sciences might intrigue me, I knew she was forever beyond my reach.

19. "Pathetic" may have referred to my being "childlike." I did not look the part.

20. Linda Thompson, a biographer, tells me, for what it is worth, that citations of my work are among the most numerous. I discount this somewhat because with so many decades of publication, it is sometimes difficult to avoid citing me.

21. Passing was not a reward of talent or ability but a matter of luck. During a sabbatical in Europe in 1953 I had seen the IBM THINK signs everywhere, even in the back ways, and at home I watched Pennstac—one of the first computers, in the days when they all had names of their own and covered what looked like acres of space—pioneering the wave of the future. I bought IBM stock. I sold it too soon but not until it had made it possible for me to leave academia to do my own work unfettered by academic restrictions, psychological as well as bureaucratic.

22. I was offered every office my profession could offer. All kinds of honors and awards were bestowed on me. I even declined nomination for the office of president of two prestigious professional organizations—not, I must admit, without a feeling of guilt for not being willing to assume responsibility for the performance of important professional functions. I was also twice nominated, I am amused to report, for one nonprofessional honor, which, however, I was not

awarded either time. It was the *Ladies' Home Journal* "Woman-of-the-Year" award in my area. I don't remember what area it was. Or who won it.

23. It was not coincidental that this was also the decade of the first atomic bomb and of the Holocaust. My second child was born a few weeks before the first atomic bombs exploded over Hiroshima and Nagasaki.

24. I found it amusing to note the difficulties the USSR was having in finding an ideological rationale for their change vis-à-vis statistics. "In the 1930s they [Soviet ideologues] believed that since statistics dealt with chance it would of necessity die out in a socialist society where chance would not be allowed to operate. By the 1950s they concluded that they had been wrong. They needed statistics. But they were still stumped, for ideological reasons . . . as to how to conceptualize this science. A high-level conference was called to solve this problem. It concluded that statistics was an independent social science which studied social productive relations and therefore 'the use of the best mathematical methods . . . is neither shameful nor un-Marxist' " (Jessie Bernard, "Citizenship Bias in Scholarly and Scientific Work," *Alpha Kappa Deltan,* paper presented to Alpha Kappa Delta, University of Pittsburgh, February 18, 1959, 8–9; the Soviet scholar quoted was Ostrovitimov, 1955). At the Amsterdam meetings of the International Sociological Association—the first in which Soviet scholars participated—I watched the implacable and undeviating reply the Soviet participants made to Samuel Stouffer's questions about the methods they were using in their surveys of time-use in the Soviet Union: "The best." A few years later at Evian I watched the young Soviet men rushing madly from one mathematical session to another as though they just couldn't get enough of all the exciting new mathematically based research techniques.

25. The refugee scholars were notably reticent about discussing their experiences. I once attended a modest little party at the New York apartment of one of the stars, Paul Lazarsfeld. He was jovial, exciting; he made jokes about how hot Americans kept their apartments—but not a word about his experiences in Austria. Other refugee scholars I met later were equally silent. So, although we were beginning to learn something about Hitler and his followers, much of it from newsreels of marching storm troopers, most of the academic picture was blank.

26. Marianne Weber was allegedly one of those who chose "inner emigration."

27. Nor, unfortunately, did our fellow sociologists. "The absolute majority of early German sociologists were either helpless or susceptible towards Nazi ideology and its representatives. And this helplessness or susceptibility not only showed in their biographical fate but also on the level of their scholarly work." Even Jewish sociologists: Karl Mannheim, for example, who had, as a Jew, been obliged to leave Germany, when asked what he thought of Hitler, replied: "I like him." Not because of his policies, of course, which were wrong, but "because . . . he is an earnest, sincere man who is seeking nothing for himself, but who is wholeheartedly trying to build up a new Government. He is deeply sincere, all of one piece, and we admire his honesty and devotion." Alfred Vierkandt was also positive in his attitude toward Hitler. Tönnies was confused; Sombart pessimistic. Only the aging Franz Oppenheimer, though re-

signed, remained obstinately opposed to Hitler and his Nazis. "They cannot kill the spirit!" he cried defiantly. These remarks were made in interviews with an American sociologist, Earle Eubank, and reported by Dirk Käsler at the 1983 meetings of the American Sociological Association (109–13).

28. "It was not at all clear at first that the design of the Nazi government in 1933 was to force the emigration of Germany's Jews. The Civil Service Law of April 7 was couched in confusing terms, with qualifiers such as the cutoff date of September 30, when procedures were supposed to return to normal. This, coupled with the staggered manner in which the dismissals and forced leaves were announced, made effective protest nearly impossible. As was demonstrated in the case of the Göttingen physics and mathematics faculty, no clear focus for action could be decided upon. The academicians were also severely hampered by the superficial legality of the Nazi measures" (Beyerchen, 1981, 199).

29. Lest we feel complacent and assume a holier-than-thou attitude, it might be useful to remember that only thirty years ago a congressman was asking "how it happened that National Science Foundation money was being used to study integration [and] . . . was mollified only when he learned that the study he objected to . . . of integration in an oak forest community was a study in ecology" (Jessie Bernard, "Citizenship Bias in Scholarly and Scientific Work," 12). Or that the Reece Congressional Committee of the House forbade any federal funds from ever being used for the study of surrender (Tax-Exempt Foundations, Report of the Special Committee to Investigate Tax-Exempt Foundations and Comparable Organizations, 83d Cong., 2d sess., 1954).

30. In April 1945 the *Times* of London reported from Belsen, Dachau, Auschwitz scenes "beyond the imagination of mankind." The news of what had happened in those camps trickled into the West slowly after that. In June 1942 the gassing of Jews had been reported in the London *Daily Telegraph,* but because people remembered having been tricked by propaganda in World War I, they did not believe it. Not until the summer of 1945 were there fuller accounts of what had happened, now documented beyond the possibility of rejection.

31. I once offered the Library of Congress the cache of materials I had accumulated from this underground press, invaluable as documentary material for all the research that sooner or later would undoubtedly be done on the subject. There was no interest in these "ephemera."

32. I was much older than that baby-boom cohort of mothers. I was thirty-eight years old when my first child was born, forty-two when the second was born, and forty-seven when the last one was (by immaculate conception, I always add when I make this statement about the last child).

33. For example, when I was talking to a former president of the American Sociological Association about my book-in-progress on the female world, he had said, "You're all wrong," and proceeded to tell me about the female world. And when I laughingly asked wasn't it amusing that he was telling me about the female world, his reply was that he knew lots of women. In extenuation, I should add that he may have had one too many cocktails. Still, we are told, there is truth in wine.

34. I sometimes feel like the judge my father used to tell us about. In reply to

the husband in a case brought before him, he said: "You are right." In reply to the wife in the same case, he said also: "You are right." Or like the mother who gave her son two ties for his birthday. When he dropped by the next day to thank her wearing one of the ties, she asked: "So what's wrong with the other tie?" Selecting one line of thought does not imply that the other has no validity. I am grateful for the bon mot attributed to Emerson: A foolish consistency is the hobgoblin of little minds.

References

Bernard, Jessie. *American Family Behavior.* New York: Harper, 1942.

————. "Biculturality: A Study in Social Schizophrenia." In *Jews in a Gentile World,* edited by Isacque Graeber and Steuart Henderson Britt. New York: Macmillan, 1942.

————. "Can Science Transcend Culture?" *Scientific Monthly* 61 (October 1950): 268–73.

————. "Citizenship Bias in Scholarly and Scientific Work." *Alpha Kappa Deltan* (University of Pittsburgh), February 18, 1959, pp. 7–13.

————. *The Future of Marriage.* New York: World, 1972.

————. "The Power of Science and the Science of Power." *American Sociological Review* 14 (October 1949): 575–84.

————. "Reply to Lundberg's Comments." *American Sociological Review* 14 (December 1949): 798–801.

————. *Self-Portrait of a Family.* Boston: Beacon Press, 1978.

————. *The Sex Game.* Englewood Cliffs, N.J.: Prentice-Hall, 1968.

————. *Women and the Public Interest.* Chicago: Aldine, 1971.

————. *Women, Wives, Mothers.* Chicago: Aldine, 1975.

Bernard, Luther Lee, and Jessie Bernard. *Origins of American Sociology.* New York: Crowell, 1942.

Beyerchen, Alan D. *Scientists under Hitler.* New Haven: Yale University Press, 1981.

Caplow, Theodore, and Reece J. McGee. *The Academic Marketplace.* New York: Basic Books, 1958.

Christensen, Harold T., ed. *Handbook of Marriage and the Family.* Chicago: Rand McNally, 1964.

Hartmann, Edward George. *The Movement to Americanize the Immigrant.* New York: Columbia University Press, 1948.

Kephart, William M. *The Family, Society, and the Individual.* Boston: Houghton Mifflin, 1961.

Kundsin, Ruth B. *Women and Success: The Anatomy of Achievement.* New York: Morrow, 1974.

Lundberg, George. *Can Science Save Us?* New York: Longmans, Green, 1947.

————. "Comments on Jessie Bernard's 'The Power of Science.'" *American Sociological Review* 14 (December 1949): 796–98.

Rossi, Alice S., and Ann Calderwood, eds. *Women on the Move.* New York: Russell Sage Foundation, 1973.

CHAPTER FIFTEEN

Personal Reflections with a Sociological Eye

Cynthia Fuchs Epstein

Memories are selective, but so are our current visions of who we are and how we think others perceive us. The invitation to reveal a bit of the personal—the backdrop to our sociological work—is seductive, an excuse to reflect and make sense out of our lives. Of course, there is always the danger that one will not make sense but make nonsense (to paraphrase Clifford Geertz's evaluation of common sense). Nevertheless, our versions are probably as good as, and as true as, those of any other observer. For most of us, there will not be too much interest in the story of our lives anyway. But if we will not be noted individually, we might consider that our personal cases will add up to a data reservoir about the people who created the sociology of this period.

There is also the seduction of writing an essay that does not require extensive research and footnotes. A good friend, well known as a television personality who has written about her life experiences, quipped that she always writes about herself because she hates to do research. I do not hate to do research, but it is a joy to write from experience and without reference to the work of others.

Ten years ago I attempted some autobiographical writing for a small book that included the stories of six women who had made contributions to scholarship and the arts. That account forms the basis for parts of this essay and stands up to a decade of questioning what is true and what is illusion. But because I was somewhat more careful then about being personal, I thought I might expand a little here to include references to events that seemed unwise to mention in the past. My relationship with my parents, my husband, and others who were important to me is, of course, personal. But the events we shared, the choices we made, and the situations in which we found ourselves were not untypical; other women I know who went on to achieve some notice in academic life and other spheres of work had experiences that matched mine in some combination or another. In one way, then, this is meant as a personal memoir, and in another as an account of a woman coming of age personally and professionally in a remarkable time in our history. Scholars of my mother's age lived a different story, and the women students I meet today will live yet another. So what follows is a contribution to the record of that moment in between. I hope I have struck a proper balance between discretion and revelation in this essay.

For once, I can start at the beginning:

I was born at the Bronx Maternity Hospital on the Grand Concourse, a place I was told, also operated as an abortion center in the days when abortions were illegal, but routinely performed and seldom talked about. As the first child of a middle-class couple I was clearly a wanted child, and my early years were well documented by hundreds of photographs, notations of accomplishment, and the warm care of devoted household workers as well as my parents and maternal grandparents. Aside from being traumatized at age four by a mock initiation into Neptune's kingdom on crossing the equator with my parents en route to Argentina, where my father had a branch of his business, few memories stand out, and I gather all was well until my status as an only child was destroyed by the birth of my brother when I was seven years old. As the first boy in my father's family to carry the Fuchs name, he was doted on, to my considerable chagrin and unhappiness. I did not know what it meant to carry on a name, but I did know it was important, and I also learned that a boy was held in special regard. My mother observed then that I changed from a pleasant and "good" child into a moody, brooding, and at times selfish child. She pointed out that my brother was now the good one, exceptional in intellect as well as in character, and although I did not think much of her judgment, I was distressed to be no longer in favor. But coalitions were set in our family around this time over issues of good and bad, and if my mother was aligning with my brother (infant though he was), I aligned with my father, a clearly more interesting and loving person who encouraged my preference. My mother had made me understand that in her priority system love for husband came before love for children, a priority curious to me since I, as much a consumer of the common culture as anyone, believed in mother love as uncontested. Rather than experiencing the mother love that I knew to be normative, mine was to be unrequited until middle age. I have often wondered how much feelings of rejection by my mother affected me later in my relationships with men and in my distancing from a strictly conventional sex-role syndrome. Hindsight can foist causality on related experience. But if I felt somewhat unconventional in my pattern of life as a child, there were also forces that moved me onto a conventional path. In turning her back on the mythologies of motherhood, my mother was unconventional. She was also unconventional in the middle-class neighborhood in which I grew up because she was unconcerned about glamour and acquisitions, disdaining materialistic values and things in favor of moderation and limited acquisitions. As a result I had dreamed of material comfort and longed for the day when I could have the matching sweater sets and matching socks my classmates wore. Yet I also respected the priority my mother and father gave to intellectual values over material values, and they too played a part in my visions of the life I hoped to have.

In my family there was a general orientation toward service and doing good. Both parents were active members of charitable and political organizations. My father had been a socialist in his youth, became an active reform Democrat, and worked as a leader in the Jewish community to achieve statehood for Israel. My childhood world was sprinkled with activities tied to causes. My Jewish parents embodied the Protestant ethic. No money was spared for personal improvement, but little was spent on frivolity; hard work was prized. But my parents presented different perspectives on other pleasures. My mother seemed to deny the sexual component of life, whereas my father was a sensual man whom many women found attractive. I learned early in my teenage years that although my father's family was fiercely loyal to each other (and to their spouses), fidelity was not characteristic. Hence, as I grew up I developed an appreciation and tolerance for the complexity of loving.

I certainly had more dreams of loving than I did of intellectual achievement. As a girl I do not remember any fantasies of traveling to other countries and seeing my books on the shelves of scholars there and discussing my research with them, all recent experiences of mine. In fact I never imagined myself a writer of books at all. I kept my interests restricted to the political and the historical. Actually my fantasies ran mostly to achieving the heights of vicarious pleasures as a contemporary Madame de Staël. I imagined I could marry some articulate and poetic rich man and maintain a salon to which I would invite the brilliant minds of the era, providing good food and a good ear.

That was the dominant fantasy. Flights of fancy at various times revealed me as Wonder Woman (my comic-book hero) or an abandoned princess who had been left at the doorstep of my unappreciative parents. In fact my mother caught on to this last fantasy and taunted me for many years by calling me Cinderella, mocking my dream of being discovered as a true princess. My fantasies were all passive ones, appropriate to the sex-role designation of my generation: to be revealed, to be discovered, or to revel in the brilliance of others. I never imagined that by my own mind or hands I could achieve the exalted position to which I aspired, in spite of the fact that my father liberally bestowed on me books containing the biographies of great women, particularly great Jewish women: Deborah in the Bible; the poet Emma Lazarus, whose words are engraved on the Statue of Liberty; and the socialist Rosa Luxemburg. I suppose these had impact, however, because they exposed me to the idea that women could be doers and movers, although I was terribly insecure about my own competence to move or do anything.

Many people today insist that role models provide a framework that creates identification, and that early conditioning sets aspirations and motivation. I had some of those role models. One was an outstanding teacher in the third grade, a woman by the name of Ruth Berken, who until recently designed curricula for New York City public schools. Berken gave us research projects to do, visited our homes to learn about the environment from which we came, and argued that we stand straight and not depend on the artificial constraints of girdles and bras. She was the first teacher I had in an experimental program for intellectually gifted children (IGC). This was a rather exciting but also quite intimidating program in which one was immersed in a sea of precocity; large ideas were stuffed into small bodies. I suppose that what I came away with from this program was a set of intellectual standards and tastes, a real nose for the person who could generate and defend ideas best, and a good dose of humility. (I never had the experience that many of my colleagues in college or graduate school had of being at the top of their class. From third grade on, most of my contemporaries were intellectual strivers, and many were brilliant.) I, like many others in my classes (although I was sure it was only I), was made to realize that intellectual activity often did not provide closure and that there were a lot of smart people around who were always set to challenge. I ended up with a feeling of enormous insecurity along with strains of megalomania—an impossible combination that made me view the future with some trepidation. I never expected to achieve the kinds of success that Matina Horner tested for when she identified the syndrome she called fear of success, found in such endeavors as trying to become a doctor or a writer. But I did have a fear of failure, of not performing well in my studies or in other of my youthful activities such as ballet dancing, painting, or flute playing. That fear often stood in the way of putting myself in competitive situations or even striving hard. Not trying for first chair in the orchestra, for example, meant that I could not be turned down. The fear-of-failure part of this syndrome is probably not any more characteristic of women than it is of men, for I see it in certain of my male colleagues whose constant striving appears to be motivated not so much by a need to achieve more fame but to remain well regarded by their peers.

Perhaps Ruth Berken was a role model for me, as were my IGC classmates, many of whom have gone on to fame in the arts and sciences and world of letters. But they also seemed so impressive that I do not think I ever identified with them in any classic way. Rather, they made me afraid to fall behind. My mother, in truth or in the selective recall I offer in this essay, was not a positive role model in this strange process. She was a housewife who downgraded her own capabilities, whose own fears prevented her from pursuing her talents, and who because of her social and economic situation retreated into the worlds of domesticity and the local community. She was not forced to confront her own fears and lived with feelings of inadequacy—a classic female pattern. But her feeling of inadequacy also made her push the argument that women should become competent, not necessarily in an actual career but in a steady occupation just in case things should go wrong. I somehow got the message from my mother (a child of the Depression) that, as likely as not, things would go wrong, and therefore I came to believe it was important to have an occupation and not to depend on a husband, parents, or anyone else. So in a sense it was not positive identification that pressed me but negative role models and negative messages. They made me convinced in my later sociological thinking that perhaps motivation is created by a more complex web than we acknowledge, and that fears as well as rewards act to orient people to good things as well as bad.

I mention some of the various themes, strains, and contradictions in my early years because I am distressed at the somewhat linear view many psychologists have offered us of human development. My experiences were not consistent; my choices were not necessarily rational; unanticipated consequences flowed from chance events.

Later experiences were also certainly as important to me as those earlier orientations and fears. The choice of Antioch College turned out to be a good one, not only because I found a lot of intellectually kindred souls there but also because I became attached to a group of students in political science who were studying with Professor Heinz Eulau. Eulau frightened a lot of people because he was so demanding and uncompromising as a teacher, but I was used to being frightened, and it did not occur to me to buck authority, at least not the authority of a person I respected. I was exulted by this brilliant man who made each class an experiment and who assigned us weekly essays on our readings, including a wide range of thinkers such as George Herbert Mead, Robert K. Merton, Paul Kecskemeti, Harold Lasswell, Freud, Marx, and Darwin. Eulau had attracted a group of students who took pleasure in the constant intellectual interaction and interchange his classes offered and who with him explored theory to find new explanations for what caused the varieties and clusterings of human behavior. In fact, of that group of about ten or twelve, a good portion became professors in the social sciences with outstanding reputations. Others went on to become dynamic lawyers in public-interest law. Eulau was one of those facilitators of excellence Merton has written about.

It was also through Eulau that I was able to get a scholarship to the University of Chicago Law School—an abortive experience, as it turned out, since I found law to be incompatible with my humanistic-behavioral orientation and since my husband (whom I had married the summer before my senior year in college) and I both had unrealistic views of how we could manage on small savings and no income; by then he, a former newspaperman, had decided to go back to graduate school. My parents thought that as a married woman I ought to be cut off from financial help. I might note that I chose law school through no great motivation but because the scholarship was there, because I had not thought about graduate education in my field of political science, and because I did not know what I wanted to do or could do. I, like many of my sisters today, thought of law as a field of learning that turned one into a real professional, that is to say, a lawyer, a person with a marketable skill. I felt I could then make a living should I need to, reflecting back on my mother's suggestion that one should "know how to do something."

I carried the burden of guilt heavily on my shoulders as I left law school after only six months. I felt that I had let all women down by my decision. I cannot remember anymore why my husband and I were so discouraged, he in his field and I in mine. But I do know that there were not many channels of communication, support, or guidance available that we knew about. I was also uncomfortable being married. I was away from what I imagined to be a rich and interactive dormitory life, and I found marriage itself a constraining structure—different in feel from the surge of romantic passion that led me into it. The Chicago experience certainly raised my consciousness regarding information, how tracking is accomplished, what it means to be an insider and an outsider, and how people themselves come to make the self-exclusionary moves to water down their dreams and make unfulfilling compromises.

Tails between our legs, my husband and I both came back to New York, where we grew up, and took the kinds of jobs liberal-arts college graduates take. He, who aspired to become a reporter for the *New York Times*, got a job for the house organ of the taxicab industry. I found work as a secretary for Science Research Associates, a psychological testing firm, work made more boring than expected because my immediate supervisor was being cooled out by the organization. From there I worked at a series of jobs I held in organizations with social purpose. I spent three years as a writer and research assistant for the program director of Hadassah, the women's Zionist organization, which raised millions of dollars a year for hospitals and training programs. I learned a great deal about myth and reality there. The women at the top were high-powered executive types. They came in early in the morning and left late at night; they vied for power and control of the organization; they had strong ambitions not only for the organization but for themselves as well. Although they were described by the Census Bureau and themselves as housewives since they did not work for money, they were as involved and active as any IBM executive.

I suppose I had been asking questions about the place of women in society since childhood because my own searching led me to consider what being a woman meant in society and what options there were for a woman to develop as a person. The experience in Hadassah showed me clearly that while there were ongoing myths about women's nature and their abilities to control, dominate, and seek notice, women's performance simply did not match the myth.

During three years of working in this organization for low pay and with little autonomy I also went to the New School for Social Research at night for a master's degree in sociology. Afterward I decided to go to Columbia University for a Ph.D., encouraged by my most provocative teacher, Henry Lennard. His work on communication patterns and systemic analysis was the most exciting intellectual stimulation I had had since Antioch. I decided to go to Columbia after a lot of self-searching and guilt; I did not want to give up the autonomy of making money or to put a burden on my husband, who was also starting a new career. At that point I asked my parents for financial help, and they agreed.

I chose Columbia because it was the best school in New York. I did not know it had one of the finest sociology departments in the country. One of my first courses was with William J. Goode, who excited my imagination with his cross-national, cross-historical approach to family sociology and with his theoretical interpretation, which made sense of the diversity of practices people exhibited in this context. The chance to work for him came a bit later, and I helped do the research for books on changes in family structure and on a propositional inventory of the family.

From Robert K. Merton I became entranced by the ways in which role theory and systematic analysis opened explanation into other perplexing areas. I remember now thinking about the situation of women while making notes (which I later used in my book *Woman's Place*) as he discussed the articulation of roles, the problems of cross-cutting status sets, and sex-role stereotyping. I suppose that for years I carried in my head pieces of the book I was later to write, and I plugged the situation of women into whatever theoretical framework or methodology was offered as part of the Columbia curriculum. With each application I could see more.

I went to Columbia in 1960. I remained a student for a long time because I took on various teaching and research jobs in between and because I was afraid of taking my comprehensive exams. In the meantime I also had a baby, a consuming love affair (which I shall report on later in this essay), and four years of psychotherapy. In 1966 I was working on a dissertation about women lawyers—I had become interested in what happened to women in a male-dominated profession— when Betty Friedan started the National Organization for Women (NOW). Added to my other role obligations as teacher, student, research assistant, and mother, I also became an activist. I rode the bus to Albany with Friedan, Kate Millet, Ti-Grace Atkinson, and Flo Kennedy to picket the state legislature, and I wrote testimony to support new guidelines for the Equal Employment Opportunity Commission interpretation of the antidiscrimination laws.

My activism became intermittent after that. It soon became clear to me that my larger contribution would be on the scholarly side. But it has been through interchanges between the scholarly and activist worlds, as well as by keeping an eye on what has been happening to women's position, that I think my work has developed. I have translated my sociological work into social-policy directives, appeared before members of the United States Senate, and been on a committee advisory to the Council of Economic Advisors. I even managed to appeal for affirmative-action policy in the White House to President Ford. These excursions into the public realm gave me an appreciation for the impact of ideology on social action, and I noted how ideas competed for attention.

My own history as much as anything has made me dubious about the reasoning offered in recent times about why women have not gone far in careers. Of course I am generally wary about explanations that neglect discriminatory practices by gatekeepers and the institutionalized components of sexism. My own history indicated that with some help and luck, women could engage in work, social activism, and family life. I was one of a number of women who came of age in the 1950s and 1960s who managed to do a respectable amount of work while juggling not only family responsibilities but also other relationships and dealing with their emotional turmoil. Thus I, like many women graduate students I have known, became involved with one of my professors (who I shall now refer to as my friend since that is what he was and remains). Our relationship was for a time a synthesis of love and work and also of torment and guilt. We spent a lot of time together, and I spent a lot of time brooding; somehow time was found for all of this. I cannot say I was productive during this period—although he was very productive— but I certainly thought a great deal about sociological issues, and I learned a lot from him. He was a highflier in matters of mind and also in sports, arts, and food. He encouraged me to do more and suggested I could be more than I had ever expected. Of course there were other consequences of that association. Being in the shadow of an established person created many problems, as quite a few emerging professional women of my generation had good reason to know. There were many reasons why this relationship ended, and each of us remembers and explains it differently, although we both acknowledge the value it had.

I cannot say what it would have been like if we had made a life together. In retrospect, from the point of view of self-esteem and career, it was a good thing that we parted. Certainly I learned later how my private emotional attachment was seen by others as part of a more general pattern—the relationship between an older man and a younger woman, between a professor and a student. I do not mean to discredit the strength of the feelings that characterized such relationships by making a statistic of them and thereby depersonalizing them. Most were between people looking for intellectual as well as emotional excitement; many endured permanently. As for me, I believe separation enabled me to grow more professionally and develop an independent career, and it eliminated the question others might have had about whose mind it was that produced the work. The benefits of separation did not have to do with the attitude of my friend, who was always supportive of my work and generous with praise. It had to do with my own need to become independent and with the academic climate, which, I fear, still supposes that the contributions of younger women who associate with established men are usually reflections of the senior person's ideas.

When that relationship ended, my husband and I decided to try to work out a new life together, and we did so with new understanding and renewed love. He had always been a devoted partner, supportive of my work, and he continued to be so in his care for our child and as editor and intellectual companion. I suppose that I have come to believe that the combination of love and work is one of the most heady experiences possible, but I have come to accept the wisdom offered by my colleague Rose Laub Coser that in academia it is best accomplished with partners who are at the same tenure level.

The ways in which women are urged to look for men who are older and wiser than they are have become grist for my sociological analysis of the place of women in society. I became increasingly aware that the second ranking of women was not just an accident of fate, limited to the fact that many women had babies and thus were not available for other jobs, or that combining the jobs was too difficult; there seemed to be a systematic patterning to the ways in which women were suppressed. The mechanisms of domination that abounded in male-dominated occupations also worked in female-populated occupations. They were also operating in the family and in cultural life. Even in the microinteractions of everyday encounters that Erving Goffman and others have written about and that constitute one of the new and exciting subspecialties of sociology today, women faced controls that placed them, and kept them, in subordinate positions. Whether it was the insistence of the culture that ideally they be shorter, show less knowledge, and make less money than the men they chose to speak with or live with, or the argument that they were nobler, more tender, or more emotional than the men in their lives and therefore ought to segregate themselves from much of their daytime life, women were made agents in their own exclusion and domination. Women wanted the men in their work life or love life to be better than they were. They wanted, and they were instructed, to look up to them. Let me stress here that I am talking about not only early socialization experience but also the ongoing social process. Even in encounters with strangers women learned an etiquette of submissiveness and were subject to microcontrols of the lifted eyebrow and the put-down.

Why, I asked, was this true? I have decided that because women constitute the largest threat to male domination, intertwined as they are with the lives of men, gatekeepers of society invest much in keeping them down. In fact, as I learned through observing and studying the lives of women in the professions, the reinforcing or punishing experiences in adult life often act to change substantially the self-image and aspirations of women. I knew that the reinforcing events in my life had done more to change my own image of self and create aspiration than any amount of early socialization (although I did have some help in therapy). Among those events was an opportunity to teach at the college level early in my graduate-student career. Herbert Hyman, one of my professors at Columbia, offered to help me get a job at Finch College teaching cultural and physical anthropology, an assignment I took on with some bravado since I had little preparation in physical anthropology. Thus I had to immerse myself most intensively in the field to keep several steps ahead of my students. The experience was very successful: I brought excitement to the students over this new material I was only just learning myself and also discovered that I had the capacity to teach and influence students. I had never thought much about a career in college teaching, but the experience reinforced my sense of self and gave me direction. It seems odd now that what is commonplace to graduate students today should have been a revelation to me. I think we are all more aware of process now and stress the occupational facts of life to our students. The process was more haphazard then, and women students got less attention devoted to their career trajectories in these matters, although certainly many male students (I learned later) shared similar complaints.

The other major reinforcing event was the publication of my book *Woman's Place* in 1970. The book had a first life as a research report to the Institute of Life Insurance, which had given me a small grant to review literature on women in the professions, a virtually nonexistent topic in the 1960s. I presented a section of the report at a meeting of the American Sociological Association attended by Grant Barnes, then the social-science editor at the University of California Press. Barnes asked me about my work, and I sent him my report, never dreaming it could become a book. It was Barnes who redefined what I was doing, and his encouragement led me to revise my work, which was published just at the moment the women's movement seemed to be taking off. *Woman's Place* was the first sociology book analyzing women's exclusion from the male-dominated professions, and it was read widely. Many of the issues it raised became the agenda for other people's research as well, and it certainly became the base for my own further specialization in the realm of women and work—on black women, women in the legal profession, and the larger issues of the invidious distinctions created and maintained about men and women.

Although my work was programmatically about the issue of gender, I felt I was also forging some theoretical ground, first in applying Merton's framework on the dynamics of status sets in the analysis of women's place in society, and later in focusing on the impact of structure on creating differences in such attributes as capacity, aspiration, talent, and rank. The more research I did, the more I was finding that the sex differences identified by psychologists and sociologists could be explained by bias in method or perspective or by the revelations of research, which showed that more purported sex differences could be accounted for by differences in education or opportunity. My latest book, *Deceptive Distinctions: Sex, Gender and the Social Order* (1988), reviews and assesses some of my past work and that of others in identifying the skewed knowledge that dichotomous thinking both in the sciences and in the world of "common sense" has produced. Unlike some other feminist scholars, who claim that differences between the sexes exist but that women's perspective is distinct and contributes to a different and better understanding of the world, I believe such differences are few. Norms specify more humanitarian concerns for women, but there is no evidence that women are any more caring and noble than men. Women do benefit from having the sensitivity some outsiders and subordinates develop, but as I have stated in *Women in Law* (1981), it would be wrong to say that being humanitarian or alert to injustice is generically woman's work.

Women's work is, however, part of my work, and I believe myself to be enormously fortunate to have work that is intellectually gratifying as well as socially useful in revealing knowledge and debunking myths that limit people's lives. I have enjoyed teaching for this reason, as well as the opportunity to travel widely and meet hundreds of people interested in the work and the mission. Travel and its attendant notice have also made me a different person—stronger, more forceful, and always eager for new experience and opportunity. I am less easily satisfied now, more critical, but grateful for accomplishment and recognition. I am also more angry that work on women is seen as less global and less theoretical than work on other subjects. I have always considered my work theoretically interesting and indeed thought of my first book primarily as a work of theory that used the framework of status dynamics to explain exclusion of a status group from the high-prestige sectors of the professions. Later work focused on other aspects of status-set theory: for example, an article, "The Positive Effects of the Multiple Negative" (statuses) used black women as a case in point. Invariably, however, my work was seen for its substantive contributions to the analysis of women and not as an analysis of the stratification system, the dynamics of status acquisition, or the impact of structural variables in general on such characteristics as self-image, aspiration, and choice. In fact I believe the emphasis on gender that has come into focus in the last decade ought to have been on every sociologist's mind who is at all concerned with the social order. To that end, *Deceptive Distinctions* is a study in the sociology of knowledge, although no doubt it will be categorized as a book in women's studies. The intellectual ghettoization that relegates women as a subject matter to fields labeled *women's studies* (do we have *class studies?*) remains an intellectual disgrace. But the inattention to the theoretical dimensions of my work (because it was seen primarily as substantively interesting) helped me toward a better understanding of the political and ideological underpinning of the development of knowledge. In this too I am not alone: two major conferences on theory in sociology in 1986 and 1989 did not include any works on theory by scholars who have examined issues of gender.

In any event, these reflections are set down at what I consider to be a good time in my life. From 1981 to 1988 I had the opportunity to spend six years at the Russell Sage Foundation, a kind of miniature Institute for Advanced Study, where I wrote *Deceptive Distinctions* and began a new study of the workplace. I am based at the Graduate Center of the City University of New York, a bubbling intellectual center with a diverse student body. I am also in touch with many people in the publishing and writing world, partly through my husband, who has become a publisher, and partly through my own books and a large network of sociologists and feminist scholars.

Some of my satisfactions are quite conventional. I have a loving marriage and an interesting and attractive son who has grown to be an accomplished writer and poet and who has turned his considerable writing and technical skills to film making. In addition, I have many friends on whom I can depend for good discussion of intellectual matters, personal comfort, the exchange of warm hospitality with excellent food and wine, and the gift of optimism about human perfectibility.

That about sums up the pieces of life that come to mind at the moment and about which I can write at this time. It leaves out many of the warts in my soul, my behavior, yearnings, and strivings, and much of the minutiae of everyday life that fill most of my time but are not worth mentioning. It leaves out my life as a writer, a teacher, an active member in professional associations, a wife, a mother, and an administrator. There was a time when I poured out my soul in volumes of letters, in poetry, and in endless discussions about the meaning of it all with close friends. I have less time and patience for that now; I find it less interesting but also miss it. Drama in my personal life has caused me intense pleasure and pain, and although I am glad to be free of the pain, I am not content with the self that has become more careful and protective. Maturity has its advantages; it is helpful in producing more and better work, makes one feel wise, and is even amusing, but it precludes drama. I will try to settle for its benefits. Perhaps there is yet a new form of drama to be experienced around the corner.

CHAPTER SIXTEEN

Research on Relationships

Pepper Schwartz

There are different kinds of career patterns. Some involve a moment of pure chance, a choice made, a new path taken. Others are channeled from the beginning by a parent's ambition or a mentor's vision. Still others are ordained by necessity—a job is available, and the need to survive is paramount. My own history takes none of these routes.

My story—and my good fortune—is that my career, though not ordained or automatic and perhaps not even the best choice, was foreseeable from my earliest childhood interests and personality. In short, I have been studying intimate relationships all my life, but before it was a formal course of study it seemed just the stuff of life: being fascinated by my friends' and family's lives, being unduly intrigued with the topics of sex, love, and commitment, and being voyeuristic about the life-styles of others whether or not I felt I could, or should, share them. Even if I were to quit my work tomorrow, I would still chat with my friends about their relationships, endlessly analyze mine, and ponder what I consider to be the most important interpersonal questions that exist: what makes people bond together, what causes them to break apart, how do they create continuities in their lives, how do they operate in the face of unpredictability, sorrow, and loss, what makes them happy and fulfilled, and how does all this relate to their family of orientation, procreation, their gender, their sexuality, their life-style, and their life chances?

How early did these interests start? I will avoid loathsome psychoanalytic insights and begin with behavioral data. As a child I was gregarious with contemporaries and adults. I liked having knowledge because among my parents and their friends information was highly valued. In my family a child could not be too precocious, and I was determined to win my parents' approval by exhibiting intellectual ability. When I discovered that my parents found big words adorable, I became a veritable fountain of them. When I found I could use the same tricks with my friends and at school, I continued enhancing my vocabulary and academic achievements.

My parents were liberal, Jewish, upper middle-class people who wanted their children to have a social conscience, a work ethic, and high expectations for their own behavior. My mother was more intellectual than my father, and when she was younger, she was more antiestablishment than he. My father is more the day-to-day achiever who respects the recognition of others "of substance" and who thus insists on more worldly success than my mother finds necessary. My father demanded excellence (trying, for him, was not enough), and from my mother the message was that achievement in the world could be a shallow and unfulfilling thing. She insisted on a trained and critical mind. She had a no-holds-barred opinion of what is good and what is bad, and there was no favoritism in her judgment. On occasion, she refused to finish reading articles of mine that were not up to her standards or that she considered boring. She died in July 1988, and I lost my most treasured friend, critic, audience, and moral guide.

When I was growing up my parents kept a progressive library. My dad was born in 1903, and my mother in 1911, so *progressive* in this instance included new works of enlightened living by, among others, Havelock Ellis and Alfred Kinsey and associates. I poured over all of it. I loved the beautiful bindings, the discussion of intimate and secret stuff, and most of all the feeling that I was being trusted with adult material. That feeling intensified when I realized my friends did not have access to such treasures.

I also found out that my friends did not have access to my parents' freethinking. My mother, a serious student of art history and a bit of a collector, had a large drawing hung in our hallway of a sculptor's rendering of a woman naked from the waist up. It dominated the middle of a long stairway and was visible to anyone who entered the house from the front door. My mother loved the quality of the drawing; my friends fixed on the size of the subject's breasts. Both girlfriends and boyfriends found the picture endlessly entertaining. Amid the giggles I would announce in a serious tone that this drawing was *art* and that they should shape up. I found that this gave me great authority. I derived even more status from the sex books that my mom gave me when I was about ten. These might seem tame today—the usual egg-and-sperm chases and drawings of denuded vulvas and penises—but they were hot stuff to my peer group. I would hold educational sessions where these books were presented and explained.

Two incidents stand out in my memory. The first happened one afternoon when my girlfriend Sally came running over to my house in tears. In shame and fear she told me that her mother had caught her masturbating and had yelled at her that it was wrong and that she was going to go crazy. I was angry: I knew her mother had not read Ellis or Kinsey and that she was needlessly torturing my friend. I dragged out my scholarly sex tomes and showed her an alternate perspective. She was comforted—especially when I told her that my mom said it was okay as long as you did not do it in class.

The second incident was related to the first. I began to think there was a singular lack of sex information among my group, and sometime in my eleventh year I organized a sex information club. Each week about eight girls would meet in my knotty-pine basement and each time a new subject would be discussed. I remember one day we discussed sanitary belts and napkins and passed around products that my mother had provided. Another time we discussed french kissing, but we decided that it did not really happen because it was too yucky. The name of our group was the Change of Life Club, and though my mother tried to argue that this expression was usually applied to another phase of life, I resolutely maintained that our lives were changing and that the name fit. So we kept it.

And our lives *were* changing. The years between ten and eighteen contained the mundane things of life that create writers, feminists, and analysands. Although I was an excellent student, no one, least of all my demanding parents, took my aptitude for scholarship seriously, I suppose because I was other-directed and therefore inappropriate in their minds for a scholarly career. That honor was bestowed on my eldest brother Gary, who at sixteen entered the University of Chicago. My other brother also went to Chicago, but despite my high grades I seemed destined for a less lofty destination.

In high school I was, to put it in its most sympathetic light, possessed by my peer group, obsessed with my hormones, and seeking acceptance by everyone in every sphere of life. I worked like a steam engine to be all things to all people. I wore a lot of makeup, which disgusted my mother. I was definitely in heat, which worried and enraged my father. I became a cheerleader, and that revolted my brothers. Nonetheless, I also tried to please them all. I read voraciously for my mother, I held political office for my father, and I went to civil-rights demonstrations and meetings with my brother Herb. I tried to demonstrate to my family that I had a brain and a soul, even if the latter was hidden under a letter sweater. I lived in two worlds, and I found both entirely satisfactory in that I wanted to achieve in both, the contradictions be damned.

My eldest brother Gary, now a cultural anthropologist, probably understands this more today than he did at the time, for in recent years he has studied adolescent peer groups and the formation of adolescent identity. At the time, however, my mother and brothers saw me as somewhat aberrant. But I learned a lot about human relationships by trying to reconcile my various worlds.

I think that finally it was my sexuality, rather than my intellectual pursuits, that made me ditch most of my high-school compulsions. I wanted sexual independence—and respectability—which was basically impossible to achieve during that period in American history. I changed my reference groups. I switched from my social club to a nonequity theater group and became more interested in my English class than in the Girls' Athletic Association. I let my new theatrical friends become my peers. At sixteen I was rehearsing almost every night, doing shows on the weekends, staying up late, having a relationship with the tallest guy in my class (I was the shortest girl), and re-sorting my values. I was, however, still cocaptain of the cheerleading squad.

Cheerleading notwithstanding, the theater and my theater group in high school changed the way I looked at the world. *Front stage* and *back stage* were literal as well as analytically useful terms to me. I started to do some independent thinking about who I was and who I wanted to be. I did not come to any conclusions—they were several years away—but I knew I liked my motley world of actors, homosexual men, musical and literary types, and ambitious women.

Sometime in this period I decided I wanted to be either an actress, a writer, or a sociologist. I do not know how sociologist got in there; I do know, however, that it stayed because it survived a process of elimination.

I went to college at Washington University in St. Louis, which was my second choice after the University of Pennsylvania, which did not accept me. I applied to both because they were supposed to have excellent sociology departments. I remember my interview with the representative of the University of Pennsylvania. He was extremely wealthy, and he received me in the paneled study of his home on Lake Shore Drive along Chicago's gold coast. He radiated old money (to which new money has a profound attraction and repulsion), and I suddenly felt very Jewish, very nouveau riche, too made up, and generally unworthy. He evidently thought so too. And I felt discounted and shut out during the entire interview. I wanted to confront him or do something dramatic; but I did not, which I regret.

I went to Washington University and was placed in a variety of honors programs including those in English, history, and sociology. I tried out and acted in plays; I joined a sorority and eventually became its president; I ran for office on the student council and won. In other words, I repeated in most ways my high-school pattern: I was also a cheerleader.

But there was some change. Even though I knew my extracurricular activities encouraged my mother and brothers to think I might conform and follow a traditional route, to expect me to be rather ordinary (i.e., settle down with a doctor from Scarsdale and raise three lovely children), I began to be as ambitious for myself as fantasy would permit. This ambition helped me decide my future.

The first decision matured in my special English class. In high school I had taken an advanced-placement test, which if passed allowed the candidate to skip introductory courses in college. I had shocked my school (but myself only a little) by not only doing well on the test but getting one of the highest evaluations in the city of Chicago. In an inspired moment following a discussion with my English teacher, Mrs. Hurd, I had written the test essay on insight, using *Lord Jim* and *Oedipus Rex* as my material. When the evaluations were announced and I received special mention, there was quite a hubbub in my school because, given my bobbysoxer persona, I was not expected to achieve at that level. I remember that week of recognition vividly because it meant to me that I could be more complex than people perceived me to be and that I did not need everyone's ratification to have talent or get ahead.

At Washington University the test placed me in a class peopled by other achievers who were supposed to be gifted writers. There were eight of us; the professor bored us all into a stupor, and it was hard to keep my head off the desk. I got only one A on a paper the entire session. I decided I did not have the talent to be a writer.

I gave up on acting as well. I felt I didn't have the guts or requisite amount of narcissism to be successful. Everyone I knew who wanted to act was willing to kill for a part. I lacked, or was frightened by, that kind of ambition and also, upon reflection, I decided that living for applause was not going to help build character.

That left sociology and a new love, history. (I had correctly assessed that even modest writing skills would be adequate in those disciplines.) I loved almost every class I had in both subjects. I concentrated on medieval Japanese history and became—and have remained—fascinated with the politics and sociology of that period. I might be writing about samurai today if Helen Gouldner had not taken me under her wing.

Dr. Gouldner decided I was worth spending time on. She submitted a paper of mine (on my theater experiences) to Erving Goffman, who thrilled me by commenting on it favorably. She encouraged me to deliver a paper at an undergraduate sociology conference. She signed me up for a master class with her ex-husband Alvin Gouldner (I am not sure if they were divorced at the time), and soon, at her urging, I was interacting with graduate students and taking graduate classes. All this was in my freshman year. She helped me apply for (and win) a Woodrow Wilson Fellowship in my senior year. Her efforts are the real reason I am a sociologist by training as well as by inclination.

However, it was not clear at the time what my area of specialization would be. I took my Wilson Fellowship at Washington University because my boyfriend of four years was going to law school there, and I did a master's thesis on the socialization of law students. Since my father and one of my brothers were lawyers—and I thought I should consider law school—I decided to specialize in the sociology of law. After completing my M.A. and being released from Saint Louis at the end of my love affair, I applied to an East Coast graduate school with a good program in the sociology of law. It was important to me to go to an elite, eastern university I think because, obsessively, I was still smarting from the University of Pennsylvania interview.

I went to Yale University. That educational experience eclipsed all others and decided my future intellectual directions, but not because of the courses I took. Yale was virtually all male at the time; there were no undergraduate women and relatively few women graduate students or faculty. At first it was exhilarating to be one of the only women on the street. That experience became less sweet, however, when it became clear that a woman had to fight to be a first-class citizen of the university. While most of my own professors seemed unbiased, the rest of the university was solidly uninterested in women. There were numerous petty insults, like looking for a women's bathroom in Linsey Chittendon Hall and being told to go to some other building. A visiting woman professor, Jackie Wiseman, told me that the maids in the graduate hall in which she was staying would make male faculty beds but not hers.

Such incidents accumulated until ugly patterns of sexism became apparent and consciousness-raising. One incident was particularly shocking. I became an acquaintance of Elga Wasserman, who was appointed a sort of dean of women, although it was not called that. A distinguished chemist, and an elegant woman, she was kind to me and other women students but found our burgeoning feminism a bit overblown. She would listen to us complain about this or that insult while all the time giving us the feeling that she did not believe that it applied to her. She never doubted that she would be a full member of the Yale administrative elite—or so she thought at first.

Shortly after Elga began her job, she found out that the administration's meetings took place at Mory's, a drinking club that had been on the Yale campus for a long time and was a male-only retreat. A goodly amount of female outrage had been vented against the place, all of it to no avail. (Years later the club finally got nailed and had to admit women or lose its liquor license; but it did not accept women until its most sacred, and lucrative, function was endangered.) I do not know what Elga thought was going to happen, but I suppose she thought the administration was going to change the meeting place when she joined the staff. It did not. Instead she was asked to discreetly use the back steps to an upstairs room and help preserve the old traditions, despite the loss of dignity to herself. She did so for a time, but much as she wanted to be a good old boy, she could not keep humiliating herself. When she asked them not to continue putting her in this situation, they said the equivalent of "don't be a bitch," and she was left without further polite recourse. So she did what the rest of us were learning to do: she took impolite recourse. As a course of last resort, she wrote an open letter to the faculty telling them what was going on and asking their support. That was the end of Elga at Yale. I believe she went on to law school.

My postgraduate education in sexism was changing me and other women at Yale. Many of us had been successful in high school and at life by playing traditional roles well. We had learned to be pursued, have power in conventional ways, and shine in some great man's glory. I was never strong enough to totally reject that traditional route in high school or college. Until Yale, I had never understood the nexus between sex, sex-role, power, and privilege.

Yale taught me about systems, as well as values that are created by systems. I was not ready to give up all the accoutrements of peer certification—anyone who has tasted acceptance knows that you have to be extremely strong and self-confident to have had it, be willing to lose it, and really not give a damn about it—but I was beginning to understand what discrimination, crassness, and disregard could do and how they could be applied to a whole class of people. Because Yale was built for the privileged, or those who sought privilege, it had more than the usual population of men who had inherited sources of self-esteem by coming from wealthy or powerful families. The subtle (and unsubtle) intersections of class, sex, and status at Yale helped give me insight into the distinctions that were made between men and women.

Thus when my gender became a liability in terms of fair evaluation and equal opportunity, the allure of being a princess diminished, and the privileges of traditional feminity were no longer enough compensation. I do not think anyone ever entirely loses the desire to charm, using traditional gender skills to advantage; but when those traditions exclude some of the most important parts of identity—intelligence, ambition, honor, and dignity—the old bargains cannot be kept.

I remember a lunch where the caste implications of gender became clearer to me. At the time I was taking classes in the law school, partly because law interested me and partly because I thought the law school had the brightest students, and it was against those people that I wanted to be tested. God would strike me dead if I did not also admit that I thought it was the best place to find a worthy husband: I wanted to be free, but not forever.

I was sitting in the law-school lunchroom with some of the people I thought most challenging. They were having a debate—there were always debates—and I thought I had some sharp points to contribute. I made them, but no one seemed to notice. Each time, a few moments after I had spoken, a man at the table said the same thing, to everyone's admiration and applause. This happened about three or four times. I was crushed. Either I was not articulate about my opinions and had to relearn how to communicate, or my opinions were not worth hearing for some reason. Confused about what I had, or had not, said, I took a male friend aside and asked him if I had not said the same thing as others. I wondered if perhaps what I said sounded different from what they said. His answer both reassured and infuriated me. He said he had heard me make my points, but he thought he might have been the only one at the table who had. As far as he could tell, at that table, in that group of men, only men were certified as worth listening to. Certification also came from serving on the law review or as clerk to a Supreme

Court justice. He thought my points were correct and well made, but he did not think I was going to get much recognition from male law students and advised me to forget trying.

Reacting to major league dismissal and discounting, many of us women at Yale carried a chip on a shoulder and employed an attack-first strategy. This attitude was not the best way to win over the old guard, but we were so mad at them it was difficult to be politic. We annoyed a great many old blues, but we created a bond with one another. It was a time of sisterhood, not only at Yale but also across universities and across disciplines. Our new understanding of our experience prompted us to search for and support female friendship and colleagues, although I must admit we were elitist about which other women we sought out. (We were, after all, pretty snotty ourselves—we were not doing much organizing among women from Albertus Magnus, a local Catholic college—and it took a while longer for my friends and me to think about the women's movement in something more than self-interested, professional terms.)

I did make some of my closest friendships at that time. Participating in a social movement together certainly promoted emotional solidarity. The sociology women I grew close to during those years are still some of my dearest friends. Among many great friendships the closest was with Janet Lever.

I was drawn to Janet for a number of reasons, not least because she seemed to have an independence of spirit that exceeded my own. In addition, she was an excellent student, had better quantitative skills than I did (and was a generous and patient tutor), and shared some of my interests. We hung out a lot together—so much that people at Yale named us the Bobsey twins and continually called us by each other's names. We did not look alike, but at Yale, unlike almost any other place on the East Coast, two short, energetic, and irreverent Jewish girls were easily mistaken for each other.

The year 1969 found Janet and me challenged by our social life but not particularly by our academic curricula. We debated doing something on the side (opening an ice-cream shop was a serious contender), but a more academic pursuit caught our imagination. Yale's undergraduate college decided to go co-ed (five hundred missionaries were to be selected), and we thought studying the transition would be a great way of looking at the gender wars from above instead of from our position in the trenches. Yale was so consciously and unconsciously male that we felt that the first year of women on campus would provide a natural experiment since it would reveal male and female territories, show where gender traditions were most passionately conserved, and uncover what changes in intimacy and colleagueship might occur with gender integration.

For research purposes—and for fun—we entered Yale undergraduate life as participant observers. From this experience we produced a book, *Women at Yale,* and our first paper delivered at a national meeting, where Erving Goffman, the discussant (was this not fated?), took us apart. We also wrote our first journal article on courtship at mixers. It had the appropriately sophomoric title "Masculin et Féminine: Fear and Loathing on a College Campus."

We found studying undergraduate men and women unexpectedly unsettling and absorbing. We were not so far from our own under-graduate days that the research was without emotional impact. Fur-ther, it served to transfer some of our own need to know about gender, both politically and personally, into a framework where we could ap-ply sociological tools to the discovery process. We could go to a mixer, get involved in the choosing and rejecting sequence, feel it with all the immediacy and insecurity that the undergraduates did, yet still have enough distance to interview both the men and the women and see each perspective. By being slightly older—and not really in the under-graduate market—we could also take experimental license we could never have taken as real undergraduates, such as seeing what happened when a woman asked a man to dance or when some other norm was violated.

Another interest got professionalized through this project. As part of our involvement in the undergraduate experience we led discussion groups for Philip and Lorna Sarrel, who were starting up one of the first undergraduate sexuality courses in the country. They were counselors and researchers, and they wanted to know more about the students' needs and feelings. After reading the materials available at that time, I decided there was almost no good information about female sexuality and that the literature in general was opinionated rather than re-searched. Some books, like *Everything You Ever Wanted to Know About Sex but Were Afraid to Ask* (a best-seller then), struck me as so outrageous that I became zealously committed to producing alternative information and viewpoints. My first effort was a collaborative book with Philip Sarrel and the rest of the discussion group leaders called *Sex at Yale,* which later was taken over by a commercial publisher and republished as *A Student's Guide to Sex on Campus.*

Yale's greatest gift to me was an unstructured graduate program that gave me the time to focus my sociological interests. The school asked little more of me than to be smart and productive; it was an age of intellectual ambition rather than professional training. The conceit of the place was that the gifted would rise to the top, the disciplined would be productive and ultimately distinguished, and one should sample from campus life to be able to encourage the best in oneself and others. The program did not prepare me—or almost anyone else in my cohort—for a job. Although some people had mentors (I was not so lucky here; I had great friends among the faculty, but I did not replicate my undergraduate situation), few people were produced as so-and-so's student. It was a collectivity of individual accomplishment.

It was also a time of political awakening and individual conscience, of anti–Vietnam War activity and demands for social justice. New Haven has a large, poor black population, and town-and-gown problems, always present, increased in intensity when Bobby Seale was arrested and, as the Crosby, Stills, and Nash song immortalized, tied to a chair during his trial. Student and town activists called for "days of rage," and Abbie Hoffman and Jerry Rubin came to campus to demonstrate. Enormous numbers of Yale undergraduates and graduate students dropped whatever else was in our lives and attended meeting after meeting to address "the issues" and let out our adrenalin-enhanced emotions. Although then the protest seemed like a time-out from school, it was actually a graduate education in racism, sexism, and social movements. It remains one of the few times in my life where I was involved in trying to accomplish collective action within a truly diverse population. The war between the sexes, however, continued. Politically liberal men proved little more enlightened than the Yale old guard. Bringing coffee to the head of the Black Panthers had a lot in common with bringing coffee to a member of the Yale Corporation.

The Yale experience was, in equal parts, personally, politically, and intellectually challenging. By the end of my years there I had left the sociology of law and become committed to the study of gender, family, and sexuality. However, there was no one on the faculty seriously committed to those areas. I was pretty much on my own, though Stanton Wheeler, Burton Clark, and Louis Goodman were generous with time and suggestions. I more or less created myself.

I left Yale a year earlier than I should have because I became engaged to John Strait, a man I met in the law school. He was fighting for conscientious-objector status and had to do it from the West Coast (a long and interesting story—he won a 5–4 decision in the United States Supreme Court). Separated while I remained on the East Coast to write my first book with Janet, we got together for a few days to get married in Chicago and then went back to our separate coasts to our separate commitments the day after the wedding. He won a fellowship in poverty law, which sent him to Portland, and it was a year before I followed.

I arrived with my dissertation to finish and a severe sense of displacement. For the first time in my life I was on somebody else's turf. I was not there as Pepper Schwartz; I was there as John's wife. I did not enjoy being John's wife. I had no mission of my own, other than my dissertation, and my identity was obviously shakier than I thought it was. I snarled at folks when they introduced me as Mrs. Strait. I meant to keep my name, and my own life's trajectory, and I did not want to be second banana. I found a group of women who felt the same way and got involved in Portland's feminist and political scene. I was in no shape to keep a marriage together—or for that matter even start one. It was for both of us still a time of experimentation. We smashed a number of marital traditions. I wrote a few articles on alternative family structures. The marriage ended about two years later by a mutual understanding that we had never really begun it. We remain good friends to this day, probably because we chalk up the experience to the times and the obvious fact that neither of us was ready to make an emotional commitment or partnership.

After a year or so in Portland I applied for jobs. John loved the West and loathed the East, and I had become accustomed to both; so I applied almost entirely on the West Coast to keep some semblance of commitment to my relationship. It was a lush time in the job market, and my personal luck held up. Schools had just admitted that they had had no tenure-line women and decided they should listen to government admonitions about affirmative action. I received numerous job feelers, as did everyone in my cohort. Our group got paid for all the women who had been denied jobs before us.

I do not know if we were aware of the uniqueness of that period when we were going through it. I received an offer from the University of Washington in December 1971. I had never visited there and knew no one in the sociology department. All I knew was that the department was very quantitative and that my work up to that point was 99 percent qualitative. I thought myself an odd choice for them, but I visited Seattle, found it unexpectedly beautiful, and thought I would give living there a try. That's how privileged we were; we could not imagine a lack of opportunity; we had no reason to worry about money or life-style. It was a golden age.

I came to Washington during the summer, and a farewell luncheon for Otto Larsen was in progress. There was a certain amount of good-natured sexism going on (Otto was presented with a poster of a nude female torso as a going-away gift before he left for a three-year stint as executive officer of the American Sociological Association), but everyone was extremely nice to me, and I immediately hit it off with another assistant professor, Philip Blumstein. This association resulted in the most profound friendship, colleagueship, and partnership that I could ever have wished for. In the early years he was my guide to professional life. As our partnership matured, it resulted in more and more demanding research collaborations. It was, and is, one of the luckiest things that has ever happened to me. We have now been working together for more than fifteen years. Philip has given me a short course in quantitative sociology; and I reintroduced him to qualitative methods and encouraged his then dormant, but now very much alive, interest in gender, sexuality, and relationships. We have taken on challenges together that we might never have considered as independent researchers.

The association with Philip changed both our work. At the time we met, he was doing fairly orthodox experimental social psychology on personal accounts and identity formation. Although we have recently done a paper (with Peter Kollock) coding interactional data, I weaned him away from that tradition for a long time and got him engaged first in a small study of the transmission of affection and later in a somewhat larger interview study on the acquisition of sexual identity. As Philip got further and further away from his roots, he began to feel a need to return to experimental studies. But I intervened with an idea that kept us busy for the next decade studying relationships and gender by comparing heterosexual and homosexual couples. Philip was excited about the heuristic possibilities of the research design, and through our endless discussions (we normally spent full days together, parts of weekends, and occasionally vacations) helped develop it into a more sophisticated inquiry into the nature of marriage as an institution and the impact of gender on couple satisfaction, durability, and day-to-day life. He wanted to do the study "someday"; I wanted to do it right away and announced I was going ahead without him. About ten minutes later he came barging into my office and agitatedly declared that the study was too important for me to do without him, that I needed him, and that he was coming along. He was right on all counts, and I was delighted we were partners again. That was in 1975, and he and I and our students and colleagues are still writing up data gathered from that study.

Our research proposal was called "Role Differentiation in Conjugal and Quasi-Conjugal Dyads." The title was changed by the funding agency to "Family Role Differentiation" so as not to draw fire from an increasingly conservative Congress. At that time Senator William Proxmire was having fun denouncing various research projects, and some members of Congress were looking to scuttle projects they felt offended public morality. Still other politicians were generally opposed to anything that peered into the private and sacred spheres of family life. Since our study compared heterosexual and homosexual couples, funding organizations worried that we would attract such government opposition. In fact we did get denounced (on the floor of Congress by Jesse Helms) for studying homosexuality, but Proxmire never really did battle with us, perhaps because we organized strong support from the American Sociological Association, the National Science Foundation, and the two powerful senators from Washington at the time, Henry Jackson and Warren Magnuson.

We got through that period and entered on the most demanding regime I have ever experienced. To accomplish our research we had to create and run our own small survey research center. We were overwhelmed by the volume of responses to the study and by the size of the staff we had to assemble to handle the questionnaires and interviews. We had more than twelve thousand questionnaires come in over a period of several weeks, swamping the university mail service. We hired interviewers in other cities and traveled ourselves to ask people to participate. We elicited participation from organizations and special-interest groups, leafleted neighborhoods, went on television and radio, and utilized the national, local, and syndicated media to get people interested in cooperating with us. This last activity was a bit of an innovation in sociological research, and it not only drew the interest of our subjects but also attracted commercial publishers and book agents.

The entry of mass circulation publishing houses turned out to be very fortunate. We had drastically underestimated how expensive the research was going to be because we had underestimated how large a population we would need to get the diversity of cohabitors, gay men, lesbians, and married couples needed to complete the study design. By increasing our sample size we inflated other costs way beyond our original grant budget, and when publishers started inquiring about the possibility of a book written for a large lay audience—and dangled sizeable money up front—the idea of a new funding source became not only welcome but necessary. We had already reached the stage of using our salaries for expenses and building up a debt with the university.

The interest on the part of commercial publishers was another major event in my life. I had changed in the course of the research. It had become important to me to speak to both lay and academic audiences. Both Philip and I desired to write up the couples' study in a format and a prose style that was accessible to anyone with a high-school education. We wanted our work to be useful to both colleagues and our subjects. We were committed to a book that could be read both in a bedroom and a classroom.

We did not find out until we tried writing up our data how terribly difficult that task would be. Although our first book out of the project, *American Couples* (1983), did get noticed and utilized in both the trade-book and academic markets, it did not fit either one perfectly. On the one hand, mass-market reviewers found our book "readable" but still academic. The public, it seemed, was not comfortable with charts and footnotes. On the other hand, academic reviewers were distressed that certain conventions, such as an extensive literature review and page notes, were omitted. We engaged both the lay and professional reader— and pleased the majority of our reviewers—but did not fully meet each group's expectations.

When we decided to address a mass audience, we knew very little about the world of trade publishing. After some unsolicited calls from agents, we decided to get an agent to handle the transition from publisher's interest to publisher's contract. Most authors get an agent at a cocktail party, have one recommended by another author, or submit a proposal to an agent and are contacted by the agent if he or she thinks the project and the author(s) are worthy, or at least commercial. Philip and I were ignorant of the rules of the game, so we pursued a researcher's strategy. I got a list of ten "good agents" from Barbara Nellis, an editor friend at *Playboy*. We wrote them about our project and the kind of book we would like to write. Eight responded with interest, so when we were in New York to collect data, we also stopped in their offices and started interviewing them. This created a miniscandal in agent circles: competitive interviewing was simply not done. We did it anyhow and found many people who impressed us, but we ended up with someone not on our original list. Lynn Nesbit, one of the top agents in New York, heard about the project and tracked us down. We were too green to know how lucky we were to have her but fortunately not so dumb as to miss the opportunity. We met with her and signed with her on the spot.

Our agent held an auction to determine which publishing house would demonstrate its enthusiasm for our project by offering a substantial advance. (An auction, by the way, is not an ordinary way to sell a book; it is usually reserved for very famous authors or, as in our case, a situation where the agent or publicity has created a sense of urgent demand and competition for a book.) On the strength of two long outlines (two books were proposed), publishers offered us more money than purely academic books received. With the help of our agent we ended up with an excellent company (William Morrow) and a ferociously involved editor (Maria Guarnaschelli). Maria and the two of us embarked on a relationship that transcended the ordinary editorial relationship and more resembled the kind of intellectual intimacy, care, and friendship that the fabled Maxwell Perkins offered his authors.

Maria came to Seattle, lived with Philip and me for weeks at a time, once at a weekend farm my husband and I own, another time sharing our houses in the city. A driven and driving person, she would work us all day and then into the morning hours. She would not let us up from the table until we were reduced to pleading fatigue screaming in exasperation. She would question us about our assumptions and the assumptions of the discipline, our language, our analysis, and our organization. We would dissect a sentence for an hour, then come back and do it for two more hours. We learned an enormous amount from her.

In the meantime gossip made its way back to our profession, letting colleagues know that we had signed a lucrative commercial publishing contract. Collegial reaction ranged from being thrilled for us to mean-spirited envy and criticism. I knew we were in trouble when a close friend heard a rather prominent sociologist criticizing our book at an American Sociological Association meeting. She listened to his critique and then pointed out to him that the book was not yet written and had merely been sold as an outline. We gave up any hope of the book being received fairly by sociologists.

It turned out we were too pessimistic. Most of our colleagues were more gracious than the overheard critic. When the book came out, it garnered more approval and generosity than envy or dismissal. In fact, these days I periodically get phone calls from colleagues asking for the names of good agents.

I hope that more sociologists *will* write for the general public. And I hope they will bring back to the discipline the conventions of popular nonfiction. Trade publishers are loath to allow unclear technical language, and readability is among an editor's chief concerns. Most people who write for a lay audience clean up their style (as do, I think, most textbook writers), and it would be nice to see engaging prose filter into ethnographies, monographs, and, yes, even journal articles.

When a sociologist writes a book that aspires to interest a general audience, that person is reaching out to readers who are free to put down the book without even a twinge of conscience. I think solving the "free reader" problem is a good challenge for any writer. Even professional writing should woo and recommit the reader over the course of the book or article.

Obviously, the experience of writing *American Couples* has changed the way I feel about communicating research. I like cooperating with the media and talking to the public about what I think are compelling issues in family life and intimate relationships. I have developed some facility for interpreting my research interests in a format the media and audiences find accessible. As a result I find that I get asked by organizations like NBC or the *New York Times* to comment on everything, from demographic trends to why Ann Landers got letters from her women readers saying they preferred cuddling to sex.

Although some of this involvement with the media and general public merely provides entertainment, I have also found that there are times when a reasonably well-informed voice is a contribution. We sociologists relinquished social commentary almost entirely to the psychological professionals, who have had a field day attributing everything in society to states of mind and little to social forces. I think it is unconscionable for us to believe in our point of view and then fastidiously decline to present it to the public. Not that the public wants it right now: they have become addicted to psychological explanations of the most banal and simplistic sort. But I think they can be weaned if anyone wants to make the effort. I have found it rewarding to try, and I hope more colleagues will enter this arena.

To this end I have accepted such opportunities as serving on President Reagan's ad hoc advisory committee on the family and on the board of Jewish Family Services, and working with family-planning groups and gay-rights and women's groups. I regularly appear on national television shows and have had my own show on the local NBC affiliate, KING-TV. For the last two years I have done news analysis at least once a week for the Seattle CBS affiliate, KIRO-TV. My commentaries have covered such diverse topics as interpreting the appeal of Oliver North and trying to explain surveys on prochoice and antiabortion positions. From time to time I write articles on love, sex, marriage, or sex roles for magazines like *Ladies' Home Journal, New Woman,* or *Redbook.*

I know that mine is a strange career for a professor, but why should it be? Not all of us have either the ability or the desire to translate our work for more than one audience, but those of us who are attracted should be encouraged. Personally, I like a little creative schizophrenia. The danger, of course, is getting spread too thin and not doing the job right in any one area, and I admit to having succumbed to that pitfall on occasion. But more often having both academic and nonacademic goals just means working intensely on one project for a long time and then going on and working intensely on something different.

For me, this has been a fulfilling career pattern. I am happy with most of my choices. I listened to what I was writing about love and marriage and in 1982 got married again. My husband, Arthur Skolnik, and I had a commuting marriage for two years that was logistically difficult but necessary for us both to pursue our careers. Now we are back in the same city, exquisitely aware of what it takes to pull off an egalitarian dual-career marriage. We have two young children, Cooper and Ryder, and they have opened up a new set of preoccupations that are influencing my research interests. Not surprising, the book I am working on now, *A More Perfect Union,* is about egalitarian couples, how they handle everything from communication to child raising, and the benefits and costs to such couples' experiences. Between my friends, family, and general curiosity, I do not expect to run out of material in the foreseeable future.

PART V

The European Emigration

CHAPTER SEVENTEEN

Partisanship and Scholarship

Guenther Roth

I grew up in Nazi Germany in a hurry. War made me a political animal; liberation, an intellectual; emigration, a political sociologist. It is a truism that individuals react differently to the same events, even impressionable young people from the same social background. I lived through World War II more intensely and with greater awareness than most of my classmates, but with them I was part of the war's lucky generation. Not yet ten years old when the war began, most of us missed being pressed into military service in its last hours; hence we were not demographically decimated. More important, we were too young to have to choose between fighting for the Nazis or being persecuted by them. We could afford the luxury of not feeling "really" responsible for what "they" had done. But we were old enough to get a lifelong lesson. In our teens we were ready for the tremendous experience of intellectual liberation and political freedom, in a time that was also the formative period of the Federal Republic of Germany. Too young to actively rebuild German democracy and the German economy, we were prime beneficiaries of the reconstruction. We still studied under various kinds of material handicaps, but we entered professional life during the years of greatest economic prosperity and the best job opportunities. In the 1970s my political generation moved into positions of political influence and governmental responsibility in West Germany, just when the age of social reform came to an end and the world economy was shaken by the first oil crisis. I have remained a member of this generation as an outsider, an observer, and an occasional participant. I still maintain my friendships from classical school and from my short period of political activism in Germany in the early 1950s.

At some point not very clear to me formative experience turned into life pattern. The exciting things happened to me early, and I will focus my narrative on them. I will then attempt to reconstruct some of the (to me blurry) connections between my life and my work.

1931–1945

If my generation was lucky, I was particularly fortunate. I was born into an unusual family. I received an antifascist upbringing, an advantage that I tended to turn into self-righteousness later in my teens. By contrast, many families tried to shield their children from what was going on around them and exclude them from any political awareness and discussion.

I was born at the end of the Weimar Republic, in 1931, at the onset of the German depression, which had begun in earnest with the spectacular failure of the famed Darmstädter und National-Bank in my hometown, Darmstadt. To give birth my mother went back to her nearby native village, Wolfskehlen, where my great-grandmother, a midwife, delivered me. When the Nazis came to power two years later, my father retreated into free-lance journalism and photography. He had behind him a career as a parliamentary and wire-service stenographer and reporter at the constituent assembly of 1919, the Spa reparations conference of 1920, and the Reichstag. Subsequently he had been on the staff of a democratic newspaper. During the war he was to make sure that I would share his high regard for the men who had been statesmen and responsible political leaders, in contrast to the rulers of the day. Although reprimanded several times for politically questionable reporting, he could eke out a living by roaming the countryside, covering cattle and horse auctions and similarly mundane events. By declaring my mother typist and secretary of his news service—a mere letterhead enterprise—he succeeded in keeping her away first from political, then, during the war, from industrial, recruitment. My mother objected to the Nazis primarily for aesthetic and soundly ladylike reasons: Nazi speakers yelled too loudly and turned red in the face.

When the Nazis introduced military registration, my father was already relatively old—he was born in 1896—and received a low rating because he lacked prior military experience and could point to a history of psychosomatic and nervous ailments. In this manner he had survived

World War I, in which most of his classmates from classical school were killed in action. He taught me early that Langemarck, one of the great nationalist symbols of patriotic sacrifice, had been a crime; there, in Flanders, thousands of German student volunteers stormed to their death on November 11, 1914, four years before the great slaughter came to an end. My draft-dodging father proved that in the struggle for survival the fittest are most likely to get killed off. He never lifted a hammer or any other heavy object in his life, but he could take shorthand in four languages. In later years he reminded me very much of Siegfried Kracauer's self-portrait as a wartime survival artist, which had appeared anonymously in 1928, the same year as Erich Maria Remarque's *All Quiet on the Western Front.*[1]

My first political memory dates from November 9, 1938, known as Kristallnacht, when synagogues were burned down and Jewish shops vandalized. My parents woke me up and showed me the cloudy sky reddened by flames. Something was said about the horror of it, about the beginning of war. Six years later I watched my hometown being consumed by a fire storm under another red sky. When the second war, which my parents had expected as early as 1938, finally came, it strongly preoccupied my imagination. I can recall the streetlights going out—for many years, as it turned out—and the excitement of blacking out all light from the windows. Matters military fascinated me, but my father, a stern disciplinarian, refused to buy me military toys, although my friends had them in abundance. My gentle paternal grandmother bought me just a few, but it was a rule that I had to keep them in my room on pain of having them thrown at me if a tank dared advance into the living room.

I insisted on finding the newspaper at my bedside in the morning, but I needed my father to learn how to read it. When Denmark and Norway were attacked in April 1940, he called me into his study, showed me the headline, and asked me what it meant. It said something about the protection of neutrality. "It means," explained my father, "that we are invading and overrunning another little country." On June 22, 1941, my mother woke me up with the news of the German offensive against the Soviet Union: "Now Hitler will suffer the fate of Napoleon." When Hitler declared war on the United States in December in a long and rambling speech, my father exclaimed, "Now he has done everything to ruin himself." Other lessons remain in my memory. I remember vividly the day when a group of Jews were deported from our neighborhood. Police quickly cordoned off the area and stopped all traffic, shooing the pedestrians away. My father, who had noticed the commotion, fetched me and told me to observe the scene and "never forget how they treat human beings." I climbed up a tree to look over a high wall and watched old people being put in a covered truck.[2] Once when I walked to school in the morning darkness, I saw two armed Sicherheitsdienst-men (SD, i.e., security services) escorting a mother and two children.

Did I know what was going to happen to these people apart from their deportation to eastern "reservations" or "reservoirs," as the language sometimes expressed it with unconscious linguistic treachery? I knew the name of only one concentration camp, Dachau, about which anti-Nazi jokes circulated. I did not learn of Auschwitz, Bergen-Belsen, or Buchenwald until after the war, but I heard one of my political tutors tell about the SD's mass executions in Russia and about huge ditches being dug as graves. Truth remained a rumor since nothing could be verified in a totaliarian state that prosecuted people for spreading gossip when they spoke the truth. But since our little circle considered the Nazis capable of any crime, we tended to trust the very rumors that many people preferred to disbelieve.

I received much of my political education in the deep stone basement of the old villa from the 1870s that served as home for my family and two others. During more than one hundred nights, after air raid alarms woke us up and sent us down, I listened to the political conversations of my father and the two other men in the house, one a local businessman who happened to have an invaluable Swiss passport and brought reliable political news from abroad, the other a violinist in the opera orchestra who had joined the Nazi party early but turned against it when his Masonic lodge was outlawed. We were often joined by a former Schutzstaffel (SS) man who in the 1920s had had his skull cracked by a Hessian policeman in a street brawl but who had come to loathe the regime, which he did not survive. (He was killed in one of the air raids.) I read to them my fledgling attempts at anti-Nazi poetry until they made me promise not to write any more since it could endanger everybody in the house. How was such a house community possible under totalitarian conditions? In our case one important means of neighborhood surveillance had broken down. Our Nazi Blockwart, the party member appointed to watch out for anything suspicious in the neighborhood, was a very discreet janitor who combined deference to his "social betters" with simple human decency.

Another source of antifascist education was my experience in the Jungvolk, the compulsory drill and indoctrination organization for those between the ages of ten and fourteen. Twice a week after school we had to assemble at a public place or encampment. When I first reported to Fänlein 10/115 in 1941, it turned out that I was the only classical student in a tough working-class unit. As an only child from a middle-class family I was scared of the bullying teenage drill sergeants but perhaps even more of the physical prowess and violence of my peers. After about a year my quick physical maturation and growing self-confidence enabled me to hold my own in wrestling matches and to make friends with working-class children, whose parents had voted only eight years earlier for the Communist or Social Democratic party. At the same time there was much turnover among our "leaders," who volunteered for military service at the earliest possible moment and seemed in a hurry to get themselves killed. Former youth leaders who occasionally visited us during military leaves came away complaining that we were just a "herd of swine." We became ever more truculent and took to greeting one another with a defiant *Heil Moskau*. Nobody ever squealed.[3] For a time the police made a special effort to round up truants, but as the bombing raids multiplied and the Nazi regime attempted total mobilization after Stalingrad, there was increasing disarray and personnel shortage, and we managed to stay away more frequently until our local organization practically collapsed.

Much more important for my life than the Jungvolk was enrollment, in 1941, in classical school (*humanistisches Gymnasium*), the most prestigious of the secondary schools. Whether a person could someday attend university was decided at age ten, mostly by parents, but a pupil had to be competent enough to pass a fairly demanding examination. Only a small minority went to secondary school after due preparation, which often included private tutoring. The Nazis recruited their own future elite through a small number of boarding schools (*Napolas*). They disliked the classical schools and planned to abolish them after the war. Once I had passed the (to me frightening) admission test, my father assured me that henceforth he would no longer spank me since spanking was incompatible with a classical student's dignity. He also considered it appropriate to my new status to tell me that Christianity was a myth that need not be taken seriously. (Behind him were two generations of agnostic country schoolteachers and church organists.) The cessation of physical punishment was important since it eliminated my most basic fear of him. Instead of pushing me into early rebellion and toward the peer group camaraderie of the Nazi youth movement, as other stern fathers sometimes did unintentionally, he won me over to his view of the world without having to worry that I would report him. I suspect that my reliability was reinforced by another status factor. As an only child in the family and the house I was very adult-oriented and felt even more grown up when I was allowed to listen to serious talk about matters of state.

Our class quickly developed an esprit de corps. It was socially unacceptable to be an outspoken adherent of Nazism. Somehow the two or three self-declared Nazi enthusiasts flunked out soon. Had they been articulate Nazis because they were poor students, or was it the other way round? I have a hazy recollection that another status element may have been involved: these pupils came from lower middle-class families that identified with the regime but still considered classical school a social step upward—unattainable, as it turned out. Most of our teachers were committed to the embattled classical curriculum and tried to continue teaching us Caesar and Cicero in the vaults of our three-hundred-year-old school during air raid warning times. Some teachers taught beyond retirement age and were closer to the monarchist past than the present. Only the director was expected to be a Nazi, but some teachers were known to be true believers. Our art teacher, for instance, had no academic credentials and owed his job to his vociferously expressed party loyalty. We were at perpetual war with him, and he often screamed that we were "cultural Bolsheviks." Once we were kept for two periods after school and had to take turns reading aloud the account of Hitler's abortive march on the Feldherrnhalle in Munich on November 9, 1923, when he was fatefully spared by the police bullets—the most sacred event in Nazi mythology. That did nothing to win us over to the cause.

At that time I developed my first notions about the United States. Before the declaration of war Nazi propaganda had observed some limits, denouncing highly visible persons rather than the United States government. Fiorello La Guardia, the mayor of New York, was a favorite target. A famous photo of La Guardia leaning over the side of Roosevelt's car was evidence of how "the Jews" had the president's ear. I vaguely remember also a picture showing another political figure—perhaps New York governor Herbert Lehman—consorting with a stripteaser. After the declaration of war Nazi propaganda went into high gear and exposed American "cultural decadence." Film reels showed a black jazz band playing syncopated Schubert, boxing matches between big fat women and small thin men, and ladies wrestling in mud or on fish—all fascinating for an eleven- or twelve-year-old.

In 1943 I had my first visual contacts with the Americans, as the Flying Fortresses (B-17s) appeared in the daytime sky. Bombing by the Royal Air Force (RAF) had greatly increased during 1942, but the slow British Lancasters flew only at night and could only be heard, not seen. By 1942–43 many cities had been ravaged, but only 152 persons had been killed in my hometown. I had lived through four major nightime bombings, the last on September 23, 1943, which surprised me in bed. Christmas trees (marking flares) were already illuminating the city when I got up. The bombs came whistling, and their detonations were louder than usual, but I dared racing across the yard to get to a safer basement. Our house was lucky that night.

Relatively late, in May 1944, our school was finally moved into the countryside in a vain effort to get us out of bombing range.[4] I was sent to a very small village, which had no Nazi youth organization, to live with people I had never seen in my life. As the only classical student I immediately became the object of much taunting by the village youth as a city slicker, although relations improved as I worked with them during the potato harvest. The nine months on my own at age thirteen proved a very important step in my maturation and self-reliance. For about two years I was also free of the tutelage of my father, who in desperation had taken a job late in 1943 with an agricultural agency in another province, escaping by just a few hours the men who appeared at our doorstep to serve him a draft warrant and take him away on the spot.

During the night of September 11–12, 1944, from the safe distance of fifteen miles I watched my hometown being incinerated, knowing my mother to be in the inferno. Using a new fanning-out technique for creating a fire storm, the RAF carried out, according to its own claims, one of the war's most successful raids. About 240 Lancasters, with only two hundred blockbusters, five hundred other explosives, and about three hundred thousand incendiary devices, managed to kill more than twelve thousand people, about two-thirds of them women and children. Seventy thousand were left homeless, and 80 percent of the city was destroyed.[5] I made my way into the smoldering city past hundreds of bodies, among whom I discovered the parents of a classmate and some neighborhood children. At that moment the American air force appeared for a follow-through attack since most major factories, army barracks, and the railroad junction had escaped the RAF's fury. With the basements inaccessible, still burning and filled with thousands of suffocated and shrunken victims, there was nothing for me to do when the lead plane dropped its smoke signal but lie down in the rubble-strewn street among the living and the dead and hope to survive. The nearest bombs fell a few hundred feet away. A little later I was told by a survivor standing before the smoking ruins of my home that my mother belonged to the lucky half of my immediate neighborhood. She was alive. To this day I do not like to look at crowds of dozing sunbathers around swimming pools or on the greens of college campuses because they remind me of the bodies I saw that morning.

In 1983 my mother discovered letters I sent to her native village between the great raid and February 22, 1945. It proved an unexpected opportunity to check the accuracy of my fading memories against my sometimes guarded reporting at the time. I had forgotten how often I was cold, preoccupied with the food shortage and torn clothes, and plagued by colds, headaches, and stomach cramps. I had remembered correctly that in the village I lived in a room without heat or running water and that I cracked the frozen water in my washbowl with my fist in the morning before setting off in virgin snow to the railroad stop where I waited hours for a train with the windows blown out to take me to school. The dwindling number of teachers tried in vain to keep instruction going in cold school buildings. Teaching was more and more disrupted by a new scourge, American fighter-bombers, mostly Thunderbolts (P-47s) and Lightnings (P-38s), which bombed and strafed the countryside almost daily, leaving the cities to the big bombers. After a close hit near our school building we were scattered around town as soon as an air raid alarm sounded, but even more frequently the fighter planes appeared without any warning. With a friend I was assigned to a Protestant pastor who had been shell-shocked and buried alive in a bunker in World War I and whose face was distorted by involuntary grimaces when he preached. Discreetly absenting himself, he let me listen to the BBC in his study, after which I supplied my peers with the latest news. Many still considered a stalemate possible and questioned my conviction of the Nazi regime's impending doom. But to me the signs were obvious. On October 20, 1944, I reported to my mother, "All males between the ages of sixteen and sixty have been called up for the Volkssturm [people's army] in the village [ten exclamation marks]. . . . Our school director gave a speech in which he told us, 'We prefer to die for our beloved Führer than to become unfaithful to him.' The slogan of the new Hungarian government is, 'Destroy or be destroyed.' That shows clearly the way things are going." Carelessly I sometimes added the latest anti-Nazi joke.

Terrible moments were to come. I regularly informed my mother about the growing number of people and draft horses killed in the vicinity. Sometimes I was awakened by strafing planes; once broken windowpanes fell on my bed; another time I interrupted my letter writing to race to the bunker my foster family and I had dug in the garden and braced with old railroad ties. My freedom of movement came to depend exclusively on my bicycle since train travel had become too dangerous. How long would my often patched tires last? On January 15, 1945, several of my schoolmates were surprised in a train by P-38s, which machine-gunned them in the snowy fields that provided no cover. One died; several were seriously wounded, including the one whose dead parents I had found in my hometown. I grimly affirmed much of the violence as being necessary for the destruction of the Nazi regime, but I wanted to see my friends and myself spared. By now I was becoming anxious to be liberated by the Americans before they killed me in the daily chase. In August and early September 1944 I prematurely counted my liberation in weeks. Then came the disappointment of autumn, when Patton's Third Army ran out of gas and exhausted Eisenhower's blessing at the wide-open and undefended German border.[6] But Patton's hour (and mine) finally came. At 10 P.M., March 22, 1945, the Third Army bested Montgomery by crossing the Rhine at Oppenheim ahead of Montgomery's vast and cumbersome British operation further north. My mother and I were in my birthplace three miles east of the river, directly in the path of the Third Army. The village was supposed to be defended by two dozen overage policemen and a few dozen sixteen-year-old secondary-school students who served in the antiaircraft units. Some retreating students were later caught by the SS and hanged from roadside trees. The scattered remnants of the regular German army were sensible enough to flee. But the local authorities ordered all available hands to dig trenches, and that order should have included me, although I was barely fourteen. I did not care to be killed at the last moment and agreed with my mother that I should flee on my bicycle (she had none). I left at four on the morning of March 23, with exploding artillery shells coming closer and closer. Returning to my foster village, I was immediately taken to a military officer, who did not believe my report of the American crossing. But a few hours later all soldiers had fled. On March 25 I walked to my hosts' home from the house of the village schoolteacher, one of my father's reliable acquaintances, with whom I had discussed the American whereabouts. Spotter planes circled the village, and the hum of engines grew ever louder. The streets were deserted. Walking in the middle of the main street, I encountered the first tank of Patton's favorite division, the Fourth Armored, rambling over the top of the hill. The young gunner, his face covered with road dust, trained his machine gun on me but did not pull the trigger: I was liberated! That day has always appeared to me the most important of my life.

At the time my elation was ill received by my hosts. The husband yelled at me, "Here is one guy who can enjoy a moment like this!" Since the whole division had raced on, in true blitzkrieg style, without bothering to occupy the village, and German units might appear again, I did not feel safe. I packed a few of my belongings, got on my bicycle for one last trip, and set out for my native village, anxious to know whether my mother had survived. I made my way to a road crowded with thousands of GIs in their unending train of vehicles and, ignorant of curfew regulations, pedaled in the opposite direction from the American advance. The only other civilians were a few liberated foreign workers. Without being stopped once, I reached Wolfskehlen and found my grandfather's house half destroyed by tank shells but my mother alive and unhurt. It took several more weeks before we would know whether my father had outwitted the Nazi regime one last time and survived the dangerous moments of liberation. In the last weeks of the war he was sent to the western front with a rifle and a hand grenade, neither of which he could operate. When his incompetence was discovered, he was put in one of the safest of the Westwall bunkers to do paperwork, while outside most of his Volkssturm battalion was wiped out. In the last hours of the war my father was discharged at the testimony of a military doctor who complained that he was a nervous wreck who should never have been drafted.

1945–1953

Political liberation was an exhilarating experience. With much luck I had survived the Nazi regime during the years of its greatest power and in its period of disintegration. My personal feeling of liberation, however, met an ambiguous reality. In posters hung up in my native village General Eisenhower announced that he had come as a conqueror, not a liberator, and I too was treated accordingly. My maternal grandfather, a small building contractor, did not take the pronouncement too seriously. He had assured me during the war, "First the Americans will defeat us, then they will help us, just as after 1918." Actually what I lived through at first was a period of anarchy—another political lesson.

After totalitarianism and overregulation came the absence of any rule—*anarchism* in the literal sense of the Greek roots. No civil authority was left, and no police remained to back it up. Just before and after the occupation much looting went on, first by Germans, then by foreign workers. Several murders, which were never solved nor the perpetrators brought to justice, were committed locally. On top of this anarchic world an authoritarian military government was gradually established, beginning with strict curfew regulations and branching out into a thorough regulation of public and especially economic life. The military government was concerned primarily with public health, secondarily with a political purge, and lastly with food distribution.

Living conditions deteriorated in the spring of 1945. For the first time in my life I did not have a bed but slept for several weeks in a potato cellar infested with lice and worms. There was no running water, electricity, or gas. Fortunately there was an unpolluted well in the garden, from which I hauled buckets of water. I worked in the fields and at reconstruction and did my share of draft labor for the American army. Some of my grandfather's workers taught me the rudiments of masonry, plastering, carpentry, and roofing—still my favorite relaxation today. The reward for doing much repair work was getting a roof over the house and a bed in which I slept better than ever in my life before or after. For a while I seemed on my way to becoming a farmhand and construction worker, but my father's unannounced reappearance late in May changed all of that. He immediately made me take time to learn from him white-collar skills that might come in handy in the uncertain future—typing and the German shorthand he had helped standardize in the 1920s. He hired the widow of a U-boat captain to teach me what I wanted to acquire most—English. Soon I also began to write shorthand in English, which I still practice as a quaint skill today. At the time fraternization was still forbidden. In spite of this prohibition I felt awkward about my initial inability to communicate with my liberators and much better once I had mastered the rudimentary skills of explaining road directions to lost GIs. I never used my new language skills for the black-market transactions that soon became ubiquitous in violation of all political and economic regulations. A mixture of moralism and social incompetence held me back.

With the world opening wide before me, my father's employment by the military government was crucial for my intellectual liberation and incipient Americanization. As one of the few journalists who had not been a Nazi party member, he was hired by Radio Frankfurt, at first an

American agency, and also went to work for the *Frankfurter Rund-schau,* the second German newspaper to be licensed. Suddenly he had no illnesses anymore, and for twenty-five years he worked full-time, until he was seventy-five, without ever consulting a doctor. For me one benefit of my father's new career was permission to return as early as 1946 to Darmstadt, where our Swiss landlord had rebuilt our old home in record time amid all the ruins.[7] Another benefit was that over the next two to three years many newspapers and journals, which were published in rapidly increasing numbers in the four occupation zones, heaped up on my desk. To compensate for the book shortage of the time, I set up a meticulously kept archive, which by 1950 comprised more than ten thousand newspaper clippings on politics, economics, geography, history, philosophy, literature, theater, and the arts. (Ever since this excess I have been poor at keeping my files in order.) Not only did I read voraciously, I also tried not to miss any of the plays, operas, dance performances, exhibitions, and American, French, and English movies.[8] I shared these intellectual and aesthetic excitements with a small group of friends who were of great emotional and intellectual significance to me, in part because philosophy, literature, or the arts were their paramount concerns, whereas I tried to argue also for the importance of politics and society.

How did I discover sociology? It is not difficult to see that the profusion of interests just described—they existed side by side with the classical curriculum—made my friends and me a circle of teenage intellectuals. But my own turn to sociology, which none of my friends followed, needs a more specific explanation. To be sure, my father had taken a course with Franz Oppenheimer at the University of Frankfurt in the early 1920s and told me about him. As early as 1947, at age sixteen, I met Max Horkheimer on his first postwar trip to Germany. Speaking with a soft voice before a tiny adult-education class—an important vehicle of intellectual revival after the war—he impressed me much, but I do not remember a word of what he said. My interest in sociology was not awakened by being told about an academic discipline. Rather, it had to do with my political perceptions. It was my fervent conviction that democratic reconstruction required education to pay more attention to political, economic, and social issues. I was here echoing the American reeducation efforts directed toward changing the German national character through the democratic socialization of the young. It seems to me that I turned to sociology in large part as a protest against the classical curriculum with its emphasis not only on Greek and Latin but also on literature in general. As a student spokesman I took a hand in shaping the new and embattled civics course as well as geography, the only field in which economic issues could be given some attention. Thus I took a stand against the classical school's time-honored preoccupation with *Geisteswissenschaft* in favor of adding *Gesellschaftwissenschaft*.

Apart from the fledgling civics course, history was the curricular subject that lent itself best to the kind of exploration in which I was interested. During the war I had received my first A ever in this subject that had inevitably been the most nazified in our school. I had been fully aware of the propagandistic nature of the texts and had tried to counter them by studying my father's history books from his own schooldays. In the late 1940s I read my way through world history, beginning by memorizing Egyptian dynasties and parallel time tables. Leafing through my old papers, I see that I wrote a thirty-five-page typewritten essay, "On the Enlightenment of the Fifth and Sixth Century B.C.," using Greek sources. I also wrote the traditional composition on the causes of the decline of antiquity. In my last year in classical school, 1950–51, I dropped mathematics with the special permission of the ministry of education and chose history as a main field, producing a hundred-page senior thesis of sorts on a thousand years of Russian history. It was also my first sustained analysis of Leninism and Stalinism, reflecting my strong opposition to them. My eclectic view of Russian history was influenced by Arnold Toynbee's *Study of History* (1946), then much discussed in its abridgment. Beside it I read Oswald Spengler's *Decline of the West* (1918–22), Egon Friedell's *Cultural History of Modernity* (1930), and Hans Freyer's *World History of Europe* (1948).[9] My primary historical concern was, of course, the search for the causes of the German catastrophe, as the octogenarian Friedrich Meinecke called it in 1946 in his revisionist book on German history. In August 1949 I finished a long research paper on the rise and fall of Hitler and his Reich, the beginning of a project to write, in due course, my own book on Nazism. (I dropped the plan only many years later.)

In 1951, after ten years of classical school, which had been interrupted for about a year in the months before and after the end of the war in Europe, I graduated summa cum laude in a class of about two dozen students. I was still the most political among us and the only one clearly headed in the direction of the social sciences. Only I emigrated to the United States, probably an indication of how much more pro-American or Americanized I had been in my teens.[10]

When I went to the University of Frankfurt in the spring of 1951, I resolved not only to study sociology but also to become politically active. In fact my historical, sociological, and political interests were all bound up with one another in a tangle of scholarship and partisanship. I felt that ominous political developments were coming to a head. My antifascism had not ended in 1945. Since I did not have a father who had been a party member or was otherwise seriously compromised, as was true for some of my classmates, it was easy for me to advocate a far-reaching denazification in all major spheres of society. I did not understand that subjective aspect sufficiently at the time, but there was an objective situation: thousands of businessmen, judges, and other high-ranking civil servants, including professors and secondary-school teachers, crept back into their positions. Many vicious crimes went unpunished. It appeared to me that the Social Democrats did yeoman service in rebuilding the shattered communities physically and spiritually but that on the emergent federal level political and social restoration held sway. My political radicalism was a mixture of antifascism and socialism. But because of the cold war and especially the Communist suppression of the Social Democrats in Eastern Europe and East Germany, I never came close to becoming a true Marxist believer and never had to reconvert at a later time. My political concerns and probably also my agnostic Lutheranism made me oppose Konrad Adenauer, the first chancellor of the Federal Republic of Germany, who ruthlessly mobilized many nationalists of the 1920s and many Nazis of the 1930s for his paramount purpose, the establishment of a bourgeois Rhineland state in which the Catholic element would have not only numerical parity but also political dominance, a reversal of the Prussian and Protestant domination of the old Germany. I did not mind the separation from the Communist-controlled Prussian heartland, but I bitterly opposed Adenauer's resolve to rearm West Germany as the price for its protection by the Western powers and his blunt insistence that atomic weapons be stationed in the Federal Republic. (I remember the seventy-five-year-old patriarch in a peremptory tone informing a silent and stunned audience of fifteen thousand of his own followers in Darmstadt that there was no political alternative.) I feared, as I wrote in an essay on December 7, 1949, that "rearmament will ring the death knell for the young German democracy." Personally I found the idea of having to serve under officers from the Nazi Wehrmacht intolerable. In fact there was so much opposition among my contemporaries that in the mid-1950s Adenauer simply declared us the "white cohorts" and drafted instead younger men who barely remembered the war.

In Frankfurt I did the two things that made the most sense to me: I joined the Socialist Student Federation (SDS) because of my general sympathies for the Social Democrats and my specific interest in opposing rearmament; and I went to the Institute for Social Research, which Theodor Adorno, Max Horkheimer, and Friedrich Pollock had moved back to its original home in 1950 from Columbia University and California. Even though I was only a first-semester student, I dared to sign up for a seminar on planned and market economies with Pollock, who warned me that I would have to sink or swim. After I had handed in an essay on George Orwell's *1984*, Pollock asked me whether I had any experience in the Communist movement since I seemed to know what I was talking about. When I answered no, he offered me a job at the institute. Thus I became its youngest research assistant. For the next two years the institute was my workplace and intellectual home. At the time the Institute for Social Research fully deserved its name, although since the upheavals of the 1960s, which made the Frankfurt school of critical theory famous, it has not been much more than an empty shell. Most of my work at the institute involved its biggest project, a United States–financed inquiry into German postwar attitudes.[11] It was thematically, but not methodologically, related to *The Authoritarian Personality*, which Theodor Adorno, Else Frenkl-Brunswick, Daniel Levinson, and R. Nevitt Sanford had published in the United States in 1950 as part of Horkheimer's series "Studies in Prejudice."

In the early 1950s the University of Frankfurt did not yet have sociology or political-science curricula nor the bachelor's and master's degrees. There was no introductory sociology course, with the exception of Horkheimer's proseminar on basic sociological concepts. His idea of teaching that topic was to assign to me Georg Simmel's *Philosophy of Money* (1900). Very few students knew anything about critical theory, and even in the institute library the journal *Zeitschrift für Sozialforschung* from the years 1932 to 1942 was not in general circulation. Since the Nazi regime had disrupted the continuity of German social science, I had to go back to the sociology of the 1920s to pick up the strands. I read Hans Freyer's *Introduction to Sociology* (1931), Karl Mannheim's *Contemporary Tasks of Sociology* (1932), Karl Jasper's *Man in the Modern Age* (1931), and Max Scheler's *Bildung und Wissen* (1925). I also read Alfred Weber's *Farewell to European History* (1946) but not a line by his brother. The temperamental octogenarian from Heidelberg was a familiar political figure to me, thundering on the rostrum against the bureaucratic symbolism of the brand-new United

Nations office building on New York's East River and exchanging broadsides with the so-called architect of the German economic miracle, Ludwig Erhard.

Almost all my teachers were emigrants or well-known antifascists—not a typical situation at the German universities. Their small number was reinforced by a stream of American visitors, some emigrants too, some not. Thus I took a seminar, "Marriage in Law and in Reality," from Max Rheinstein and Everett C. Hughes from the law school and sociology department, respectively, of the University of Chicago. In 1952 I met Kurt H. Wolff, a refugee from my hometown, visiting at the institute. He was intensely interested in some of the same moral and political issues that had preoccupied me since the war.[12] Some of his closest family had been deported and murdered. He invited me to work with him at Ohio State University, in Columbus, for a year on a study of nationalist and Nazi attitudes and the rise and fall of denazification.

I desperately wanted to go to the United States to study. My motives were thoroughly mixed. Most basic was the excitement of the country to somebody who had grown up as I had. My life appeared incomplete without seeing the Empire State Building and the Golden Gate Bridge. (Most personal was a romantic attachment to a Viennese refugee.) The academic benefits of study in the United States appeared obvious. At the institute we read only English literature in the area of empirical social research, especially survey methods and social psychology. Adorno was eager for me to pick up more survey skills. But Horkheimer, distressed by the rise of McCarthyism, asked me skeptically, "Why do you want to go in this political situation?" The McCarran-Walter Act had just been passed and made entry more difficult: as chairman of the largest SDS club at a German university, I was no longer sure to be welcome.

Besides the pull of the country, there was also a push. My strenuous participation in the campaign against German rearmament was obviously doomed by 1953. From the right Adenauer moved ahead with his plans, with full American support; from the left the Communists did their usual best to infiltrate and undermine the peace movement of the early 1950s. My naive pro-Americanism during the early postwar period was badly shaken. I had lost many illusions about both countries but gained some political realism. Going to the United States, then, was a move away from political activism and toward the study of political reality.[13]

I believed that I was coming to the United States for a limited time and did not know that I was in fact emigrating. At least I came over the old way. The *Anna Salen,* a converted British aircraft carrier from the days of the convoys running the German gauntlet to Murmansk, was now an immigrant boat laden with thirteen hundred East Europeans and Germans, many with labor contracts. It was not some fancy Italian ship for Fulbright scholars, and commercial jet planes had not yet made the passenger ship obsolete. On September 22, 1953, I left Bremerhaven. The fall storms were terrible. Like almost everybody else, I was seasick. The ship's propellers often emerged out of the water, shaking the whole hull. Water swept through my cabin. After an eleven-day journey the *Anna Salen* safely reached her destination, Quebec; her sister ship was shortly to sink in a Pacific storm. On October 3, I crossed the border at Buffalo on my way to the heartland of America.

1953–1984

More than thirty years after arriving in this country I have been asked to write about my formative experiences and the direction of my work. I am very conscious of the anniversary and welcome the opportunity. For many years I had planned to put down my memories of the war and its aftermath. But each year I had forgotten a bit more and felt less inclination to write. Now that I have recalled some memories from my formative years in Europe, I would like to look back at my scholarly development, its genesis and setting. The danger here is not so much inaccuracy of fact and faulty memory as the temptation to read more sense and consistency into the accidents and vagaries of my career than are warranted. For a career, the opportunities and restraints are as important as the inclinations and aspirations.

The question about the impact of formative experiences requires that I characterize my work, if only in the most sketchy and superficial of terms. My kind of sociology has been historical and political. Substantively sociology has always meant for me the evolutionary and developmental theory of modern society; methodologically it has meant a set of generalizations embodying historical experience. I arrived in the United States with a conviction already formed that a science of society in the positivist (and Marxist *diamat*) sense of invariant laws is not possible, and if it were, it would not help us understand the distinctiveness of modern society. If I learned this from critical theory, it was also the main postulate of German *Historismus.* Thus I have advocated a historically oriented grasp of the nature of modern society. My work has been political not only because I have dealt with political phenomena but also because of its pedagogical animus. I have tried to help students understand the moral value and historical uniqueness of constitutional government, impersonal administration, and the imperatives of large-scale organization—what Benjamin Nelson came to call the social reality principle. Since dictatorships of various hues distort the historical truth and control the flow of information, I remain convinced that sociology has a moral obligation to assure its own preconditions.

I began my American journey with such views, which I sometimes expressed rather dogmatically, but I lacked solid historical knowledge and methodological comprehension. Working at Ohio State University on the history of American denazification gave me an opportunity to study seriously the decision-making processes in wartime and postwar Washington, clarify the distinction between a political purge and moral retribution, and assess the causes and consequences of the failure of denazification. The outcome was my first English monograph, which Kurt Wolff edited and rendered into intelligible English. In many respects a rough apprentice piece, it had something to offer as "an historical survey and appraisal" (its subtitle). At the same time my disciplinary training did not make much headway. In fact I was not studying for a degree and contemplating an American career. Since I had come on an exchange-visitor visa, not a student visa, I was required to have a research appointment at all times. I could not just study on some fellowship, as many foreign students did. This delayed my Americanization and socialization into the discipline of sociology. I missed out on the good and bad aspects of an American college education and graduate-school program, and did not acquire an M.A. Coursework remained secondary to research. Moreover, I was, in a manner of speaking, suspended between two worlds. I made a living looking backward to Europe rather than looking for America. Although I explored American everyday life with curiosity, including the new medium of television, and found the great distances and landmarks such as the Empire State Building stupendous, I perceived much of what I saw through a filter of political and intellectual abstractions, which came naturally to a young European, who took it for granted that the Midwest was a cultural wasteland. During the first year my mind also remained relatively closed to American intellectual influences. In fact, to Adorno's dismay, I spent much of my spare time not on learning survey techniques but on poring over issues of *Zeitschrift für Sozialforschung* from beginning to end and scrutinizing Herbert Marcuse's *Reason and Revolution* (1942) as well as Max Horkheimer's *Eclipse of Reason* (1947), two rarely read books.

At Ohio State nobody but Wolff understood anything about critical theory.

A year at the New School for Social Research in 1954–55 was not as much of a step backward as it appeared to some who worried that I was not having an "American" experience. It gave me a chance to meet a number of scholars who had been productive in the Weimar Republic; some had been politically active. It is true that I lived in the émigré community. But by learning more about the diversities of exiled German social science I gained a much-needed broader perspective. I argued with Alfred Schutz and Albert Salomon about the Frankfurt school, discussed denazification with Otto Kirchheimer, and met Herbert Marcuse again when he was writing *Eros and Civilization* (1955). My exaggerated views of the Frankfurt Institute and of critical theory were deflated, sometimes subtly, sometimes bluntly, by the redoubtable Siegfried Kracauer and the encyclopedic Arkadius Gurland, who had an inexhaustible store of information on revolutionaries and émigrés. From the American side the social psychologist Solomon Asch and the psychoanalyst Helen B. Lewis attacked the psychological and methodological assumptions of Adorno et al.'s *The Authoritarian Personality*, further increasing my doubts from having read, in Columbus, a critical volume about it.[14] I became increasingly disenchanted with the feasibility of using personality theory to explain political events and groped my way toward an institutional approach.

Thus I moved away from critical theory, which in those years had a heavy psychological bent. Moreover, I began to understand that holistic approaches—assertions about the totality of culture, civilization, or personality—could not be subject to empirical analysis and that the notion of a self-correcting, reflexive critical theory was a rhetoric that could give no practical political guidance. In this regard I was subject to an authentic American influence through the last major figure of pragmatism, Horace M. Kallen, who attacked the German philosophical tradition and championed a pragmatist, instead of a critical, integration of the social sciences.

I was ready to move on intellectually when Reinhard Bendix, with whose pamphlet "Social Science and the Distrust of Reason" (1951) I was familiar, invited me in the fall of 1955 to work full-time at the Institute of Industrial Relations at the University of California, Berkeley, for the Interuniversity Project on Labor and Economic Development. I was hired to work on labor problems in Imperial Germany. The simple fact of knowing German made me useful for such research in a situation in which most native graduate students merely went through the motions of learning a little French and German (before the pretense was abolished altogether). There was, however, a matching of opportunity and inclination of which probably neither Bendix nor I was fully aware. At the institute I could continue to combine history and sociology. From my preoccupation with Nazism and its aftermath I now moved further back into German history in search of the causes of "the German catastrophe." With a brief career in the German SDS behind me, I was especially interested in the failure of the German revolution of 1918–19 and the role played by the split Social Democratic labor movement. I had opinions, but little knowledge, about the labor movement in Imperial Germany. My only concrete relationship to it had been the (slightly ridiculous) moment at the founding of the Fifth Socialist International in Frankfurt, in 1951, when I held the funeral flag of Ferdinand Lassalle, the founder of the Social Democratic labor movement, behind the rostrum on which appeared socialist leaders from many countries. Skillful at discreet indirection, Bendix asked me essentially one big question, out of which *The Social Democrats in Imperial Germany* was to emerge (first in 1960 as a dissertation and then in 1963 as a book): "What was the meaning of the labor movement to the workers?" I buried myself in the splendid Berkeley library, trying to make myself spiritually at home in Imperial Germany. But that was only the historical side of the project, congenial to my political and cultural proclivities. The other side was sociological— American modernization theory, which postulated that economic progress in "newly developing" countries would favor democratic pluralism rather than Communist dictatorship. This thesis became the substantive core of the "newly developing" fields of political sociology and comparative politics, which Seymour Martin Lipset was spearheading at the institute.

But what were the lessons of the European experience? Bendix provided some major answers in *Work and Authority* (1956), which was also an early critique of modernization theory. I tried to supply a lesson from Imperial Germany. There the potential of industrialization for creating revolutionary conflict was contained by an authoritarian political system that permitted a hostile mass movement to exist legally but prevented it from gaining access to the power center. This historical conclusion could, however, also be couched in terms of a sociohistorical model, a sociological theory of negative integration, that was applicable to similar cases in other places at other times, for instance, the French and Italian Communist parties under parliamentary regimes. In a postscript, which Bendix suggested to me, I spelled out some of the personal lessons I drew:

> The facts of Nazism provide a powerful moral perspective for German history, but it is neither fair to past generations nor analytically adequate to view this history with the questionable wisdom of hindsight. When I began my research, my own perspective of the history of the German labor movement was strongly affected by German self-recrimination and conventional American perspectives. But gradually I came to change my views. I tried to arrive at a more balanced and detached view, influenced by the positivistic injunctions of an American graduate education and perhaps by the soothing atmosphere of the Pacific Coast, far removed from Germany in time and space. Looking over the completed study, I find myself more sympathetic to the right and the center of the Social Democratic movement than to the left. . . . I have endeavored to preserve a sense for the capacity of individuals and groups to change some parts of their lives as well as for the fateful persistence of social structures and the unpredictable uniqueness of historical events.[15]

By the time I reached this personal conclusion, I had given up my political ambitions in a faraway land and come to accept the role of the observer over that of the actor. I had become serious about the possibility of an American career. Yet writing a dissertation on Imperial Germany was then still unconventional in American sociology. Here I benefited from the intellectual climate of Berkeley. For many assistants at the Institute of Industrial Relations, then directed by Clark Kerr, the apprenticeship nature of research was more important than disciplinary study. We—Robert Alford, Bennett Berger, Robert Blauner, Amitai Etzioni, Juan Linz, Gayl Ness, Charles Perrow, and Arthur Stinchcombe— learned by looking over the shoulders of our masters. While I was a full-time researcher, I was also a part-time graduate student in the Department of Sociology, which Herbert Blumer was bent on making the best in the world, as he repeated at the beginning of each academic year. When I tried to take the qualifying examinations after only six months, I was flunked and sent back to read the seventy-five books—a totally eclectic list—that everybody had to read on pain of failing. Having to study books with a variety of different orientations that I had disdained or disregarded before broadened my horizon in a most salutary manner.

After 1960 I taught the new fields of industrial sociology and complex organization as well as the traditional subjects of sociological theory and social change, from which I branched out into political sociology and social and economic development, another set of new teaching fields. These subjects were inherently interdisciplinary, but I also taught in the formally interdisciplinary Social Science Integrated Course directed by Lewis Feuer at Berkeley (1958–60) and the Western civilization program directed by Benjamin Nelson in the earliest days of the Stony Brook campus of the State University of New York (1963–65). My background qualified me for such programs, but at the same time my inclinations held me back from becoming a mainline American social scientist. I did not turn myself into a survey researcher—the usual option at the time—or an organization theorist, another new and attractive possibility realized by several members of my American cohort. The gradual opening of American social science toward the world in the aftermath of World War II, an opening furthered by many émigré scholars, combined in the early 1960s with the stormy expansion of the universities and created considerable intellectual leeway for the pursuit of diverse interests. This latitude enabled me to move closer again to some of my intellectual roots and return to my old interests in world history in the guise of Weberian scholarship. I discovered Max Weber's work only at Berkeley, watching Reinhard Bendix compose his intellectual portrait and writing with him an essay on Weber's growing influence in the United States.[16] After Bendix had laid out the world-historical scope and the comparative logic of Weber's empirical studies, it became highly desirable to have *Economy and Society* (*Wirtschaft und Gesellschaft*) available in its totality to counteract the piecemeal and haphazard nature of the Weber reception. With the encouragement of Hans Zetterberg, I began to put together a variorum edition, not knowing that it would take six years even with the help of my Darmstadt classical schoolmate and New York City neighbor Claus Wittich. The complexity of translating and editing was wearisome, the tedium at times crushing, but both of us welcomed the chance to roam through world history in Weber's texts and our background reading and get away from the routines of economics and sociology.

Economy and Society appeared in 1968 at the height of the student rebellion, when Weber, of all people, was regarded as a patron saint of conformist American positivism and its vaunted value-neutrality. My past caught up with me at the Free University of Berlin in 1967–68 and in the civil-war days in Berkeley in 1969–70, where I held visiting appointments. With my memories of Nazi Germany, I could not sympathize with the moral outrage of a younger generation that equated the Federal Republic and the United States, two of the most viable constitutional democracies, with fascism, and Lyndon Johnson with Adolf Hitler.[17] With a generation of émigré scholars as my teachers, I knew what the dangers to scholarship would be if the university, a precarious institution at the best of times, were radically politicized. I was infuriated by the way German students singled out the few Jewish refugee scholars who had returned and were still teaching—Adorno, Ernst Fraenkel, Richard Loewenthal—as special targets of their "antiauthoritarian" and "antifascist" campaign. When the Bonn Bundestag debated the national emergency legislation that had become necessary because of a new treaty with the former occupation powers, student protest climaxed under the leadership of an SDS that was radically different from the SDS of my time. I simply could not forget my early Nazi memories, when I watched from close up as Rudi Dutschke waited for the most propitious moment to make his triumphant entry at a mass rally, which he then pushed into frenzy with a barrage of shouted slogans. At another occasion, when asked to "show my colors" as a university teacher, I professed my conviction, before hundreds of howling students, that the Federal Republic was the best and most democratic regime Germany had ever had and that it was the civic duty of the younger generation to accept its legitimacy. I ended up fleeing the Institute of Sociology, grabbing my American passport and my introduction to *Economy and Society,* never to return. In Berkeley I struggled to teach Weber's sociology of domination surrounded by strikers and demonstrators, sheriffs and national guardsmen. Both groups came close to shutting down the university not only physically but also intellectually. In a situation in which it was well-nigh impossible to go on teaching, I insisted that the university require and demand the separation of scholarship and partisanship. The sudden popularity of the Frankfurt school's critical theory appeared to me in some respects another eclipse of reason. The counterculture's drive to unite theory and practice, if not to replace the former by the latter and thought by emotion, negated the school's rationalist commitments and embittered the last days of Adorno and Horkheimer.

My political combativeness was reawakened by the challenge of a younger generation that knew nothing of war and fascism. My response took the form of a partisan defense of scholarship. Since the 1960s about half of my writings have addressed such topical themes as political critiques of Max Weber, his own generational rebellion and maturation, his relationship to contemporary Marxism, value neutrality in Germany and the United States, the counterculture's charismatic virtuosi and charismatic communities, and the relations between religion and revolutionary beliefs. The other half has dealt with core themes of sociology proper—rationalization and industrialization, authority and legitimation, personal and impersonal rulership, and the developmental history of the West in comparison with other parts of the world.

What can I say finally about the impact of formative experience on life patterns? Have I always been an exemplar of that hoary archetype of American sociology, the marginal man? To be sure, I was a political outsider in Nazi Germany, watching a tremendous catastrophe sweep over Europe. I found myself a political outsider in Adenauer's conservative republic. I was a foreign student in the United States, again a marginal person with little cultural preparation and no political rights. I finally became an American citizen and found a niche in the American academy but soon saw myself outnumbered in the campus rebellion. At the same time, however, I have never lacked the support of significant others, from the community in my wartime basement to our group in the classical school, from my German political friendships to the émigré scholars who were so generous to me, and from my Berkeley friendships to a network of cosmopolitans scattered around the world. In the end, of course, I cannot deny that culturally I have remained a hyphenated scholar, no matter how much I cringe at being sometimes labeled a German-American sociologist. The story I have told here may convince readers (and ultimately myself) that this is, after all, an accurate designation.

Looking back, I tend to believe that the most formative influence on my career has indeed been the stark lesson of my early years, the experience of the mortal dangers of political conflict. Hence my motivating conviction that power struggles must be contained by constitutional restraint, that universities must be institutionally protected to further rational comprehension and reasonable action, and that sociology must address the big political, cultural, and social issues of modernity.

Notes

1. See Siegfried Kracauer, *Ginster, von ihm selbst geschrieben* (1928; reprint, Frankfurt: Suhrkamp, 1963). The atmosphere of World War I in my immediate region is well captured in another famous antiwar novel, Ernst Glaeser's *Jahrgang 1902;* it too was published in 1928. Carl Zuckmayer, another local member of my parents' generation, wrote an autobiography that my mother declares accurately and vividly portrays the world of her own early memories: *A Part of Myself: Portrait of an Epoch* (New York: Helen and Kurt Wolff, 1970), trans. R. and C. Winston.

2. This seems to have been the last group deportation. On February 10, 1943, fifty-three persons were sent to Theresienstadt. They had been forced to

assemble in the former Rosenthal Clinic, which by then was called an old-age home. Afterwards persons from so-called mixed marriages were individually arrested under various pretexts and deported. Almost all perished. See Erckhardt Franz and Heinrich Pingel-Rollmann, "Hakenkreuz und Judenstern," in *Juden als Darmstädter Bürger,* ed. E. Franz (Darmstadt: Roether, 1984), pp. 185f.

3. In the summer of 1942, when the Nazi fortunes seemed to stand highest, a group of gold pheasants, as uniformed Nazi leaders were popularly called, inspected us and explained that the Führer had decided to turn us into military peasants (*Wehrbauern*) along the Urals so that we could defend Western civilization against the Asiatic hordes. Expecting the right answer, one functionary went down the line asking each of us for what we would volunteer. None of my peers, who were only two or three years away from finishing their eight-year schooling and beginning their apprenticeship, budged. They all insisted that they would become metal workers, mechanics, electricians, and so forth. I knew that I would spend many more years in school. I wanted to become an opera stage designer—I had rebuilt many stage designs I had seen in the theater—but I was more cowardly than my peers. So I answered that I did not know. After being harangued for being "dirty pigs," we were given two hours of penalty drill until our clothes were covered with dirt and soaked and we looked like the animals we were alleged to be.

4. Late in 1943 the Nazis decided to evacuate my school from Darmstadt and move us deep into Czechoslovakia, into the forests of the Beskids. The evacuation plan made us suspect that they were concerned less about nighttime attacks and direct hits on school buildings during the daytime than about isolating our school from our families and exposing us to more indoctrination. This threat led to the only semiorganized resistance during the war—families trying to protect their own. Although teachers warned my father that he was risking arrest, he called the Nazis' bluff by proving that contrary to their assertions the school could be moved to a nearby small town and the pupils boarded in private homes in the surrounding villages. His many connections from the pre-Nazi period with the rural hinterland served him well. After unsuccessfully sending youth leaders to our school and after an unprecedented parents' meeting with the highest Nazi official in town, the authorities yielded. This victory over the Nazis, whose curious legalism my father manipulated time and again, probably saved our school from being captured by the Russian army.

5. See "A Quiet Trip All Round: Darmstadt," chap. 13 in Max Hastings, *Bomber Command* (New York: Dial Press, 1979), pp. 303–26; "A Detailed Study of the Effects of Area Bombing on Darmstadt, Germany," *The United States Strategic Bombing Survey* 37 (January 1947); Klaus Schmidt, *Die Brandnacht* (Darmstadt: Reba, 1964); David J. Irving, *Und Deutschlands Städte starben nicht* (Zurich: Schweizer Druck- und Verlaghaus, 1964), pp. 266–78.

6. To this day I am studying the pros and cons of what many military experts still believe to have been an unimaginative and overly cautious strategy. See Russel F. Weighley, *Eisenhower's Lieutenants: The Campaign of France and Germany, 1944–1945* (Bloomington: Indiana University Press, 1981).

7. On the enormous reconstruction problems of Darmstadt, see the August 1946 report by an American journalist, "Ein Amerikaner in Darmstadt," *Heute* 3 (1945): 36–43. (*Heute,* modelled after *Life,* was the first magazine in the American occupation zone; it was published by the Information Control Division of the United States Army.) I described a night walk through the ruins of Darmstadt in an unpublished composition dated November 13, 1946, "After Sundown: A Walk Through the City."

8. The first German author to make a powerful impression on me was Heinrich Heine, for whom I had apparently been too young during the war. My father had kept his works in a closed bookcase, which he had made to order during the Nazi regime to hide his library from curious eyes. As early as 1946 (or 1947) I heard the first of the formerly outlawed modern music when the Darmstadt Summer Courses for New Music were organized to train musicians and composers; the courses soon became an international institution, for decades attracting many American musicians. The first abstract paintings I beheld were done by an American officer and shown in a half-ruined building. In 1947 I saw my first large art exhibition: riches from the Berlin Kaiser Friedrich Museum, which the American army had recovered from Thuringian salt mines and taken along with it after abandoning the area to Soviet control. The first American novel I read, still in translation, was Hemingway's *A Farewell to Arms,* which the Nazis had banned after 1933 (together with the works of Dos Passos and Upton Sinclair). It was printed on newsprint and looked like a newspaper. My first American movie was *Thirty Seconds over Tokyo.* In one sitting I devoured my first American play: my father brought home overnight a typewritten translated script of Thornton Wilder's *The Skin of Our Teeth,* which was being rehearsed for the reopening of the theater in Darmstadt.

9. Together with my father's Greek and Latin dictionaries, these history books were the only volumes of our family library that survived the war since I had taken them into the countryside. I still consult the dictionaries and find the textbooks remarkably balanced. See Friedreich Neubauer and Ferdinand Rösiger, *Lehrbuch der Geschichte für die höheren Lehranstalten in Südwestdeutschland,* vols. 4 and 5 (Halle: Buchhandlung des Waisenhauses, 1908).

10. In 1981, when we met for our thirtieth anniversary, the school opened its files. Ours were the only records saved because we were considered the most promising and successful group of the postwar period, together with the class just below us, to which my future Weber coeditor Claus Wittich belonged. It must have had to do with being at just the right impressionable age to draw maximum benefit from a bad war experience and the difficult postwar years, which nonetheless provided a liberating contrast. Eight of us ended up as professors, in archaeology, architecture, Catholic theology, electrical engineering, German literature, law, Romance literature, and sociology. The others are today corporate executives, judges, other high-ranking civil servants, journalists, physicians, engineers, and classics teachers. One became a Catholic priest—after the theologian our other convert in class—and one a member of Helmut Schmidt's federal cabinet in the 1970s. My closest friend, the one poet among us, dropped out. When the school files were opened for us, we discovered the predictions our teachers had made, including their evaluation of our "character," a category

later dropped in the course of the "democratization" that undermined our school in the 1960s. By and large our teachers had been accurate.

11. Out of a mountain of disparate materials and reports Friedrich Pollock finally pulled together the study under the title *Gruppenexperiment* (Frankfurt: Europäische Verlagsanstalt, 1955).

12. See the autobiographical statement "Wie ich zur Soziologie kam und wo ich bin: Ein Gespräch mit Kurt H. Wolff, aufgezeichnet von Nico Stehr," in *Soziologie in Deutschland und Österreich, 1918–1945,* ed. M. Rainer Lepsius (Opladen: Westdeutscher Verlag, 1981), pp. 324–46.

13. Shortly after my arrival in the United States I wrote in a research paper (still in German): "For young people like me the American turnabout in 1950 to rearm Germany was a bitter disappointment. The United States seemed to abandon the moral foundation on which it had fought the war and which had given it the moral justification for reconstructing Germany. My newly developed realism is not cynicism but has helped me to see matters in a less unrealistic, 'idealist' light" (my translation).

14. See Richard Christie and Marie Jahoda, *Studies in the Scope and Method of "The Authoritarian Personality"* (New York: Free Press, 1954); it includes the well-known methodological demolition by Herbert Hyman and Paul Sheatsley, and Edward Shils's vigorous political critique.

15. Guenther Roth, *The Social Democrats in Imperial Germany: A Study in Working-Class Isolation and National Integration* (Totowa, N.J.: Bedminster Press, 1963; reprint, New York: Arno Press, 1979), p. 325. Bendix agreed with Paul Lazarsfeld on the desirability of autobiographical statements for both author and profession. If the old German custom of appending a brief biography to the dissertation could be expanded to include some information about formative experiences and major changes of outlook, the cumulative evidence might be of service to sociologists of knowledge. Authors too might benefit from facing the question of the consistency and continuity of their own lives and work.

16. See Reinhard Bendix, *Max Weber: An Intellectual Portrait* (New York: Doubleday, 1960; reprint, Berkeley and Los Angeles: University of California Press, 1977); Guenther Roth and Reinhard Bendix, "Max Weber's Einfluss auf die amerikanische Soziologie, *Kölner Zeitschrift für Soziologie* 11 (1959): 38–53.

17. To be sure, I had learned enough from saturation bombing to understand that dropping more tonnage on the Vietnamese countryside than was delivered during all of World War II made no sense. I had also grown wary of American moralism, but I still did not dispute the right of the United States to try to stop communist expansion in the world—I had not only been liberated from Nazism but also saved from Soviet domination.

CHAPTER EIGHTEEN

From the Popocatepetl to the Limpopo

Pierre L. van den Berghe

This essay is an attempt at intellectual autobiography. Why did I become an academic and a social scientist? How has my thinking evolved, and in response to which events? How have my politics influenced my scholarship? In sociological jargon, the dependent variable is myself as a thinking animal; the independent variables can perhaps be broken down into two sets: general conditions of the social milieu and my place in it, and specific influences of individuals. I will interweave these two themes into a loose chronological account.

A confession of class origins is probably the first order of business in a sociological autobiography. They range, in my case, from rich peasants to the nobility, if I trace back four or more generations, but my grandparents and parents had comfortably settled into what might be called the intellectual and professional bourgeoisie. On my father's side all the males for three generations were physicians. My paternal grandfather was a general practitioner in the large provincial city of Ghent, Belgium, and married the rather homely daughter of a Flemish country doctor. He inherited his practice from his father, and thanks to the considerable amount of wealth brought by my grandmother's dowry and inheritance (she came from a rather rustic but rich peasant family with sizable land holdings), he enjoyed the comfortable life of a provincial bourgeois. After World War I the two horses, the carriages, and the coachmen were replaced by a custom-made Panhard automobile, but the live-in cook and maid, who had been with them for half a century, were permanent fixtures of the family scene, a provincial version of "Upstairs, Downstairs."

Staunchly conservative in politics, conventional in religion, puritanical in sex, and austere in life-style (except for culinary indulgence), my grandparents, Roman Catholics, were a living refutation of the Protestant ethic. From my paternal grandmother, a rather uncultured but strong-willed and highly intelligent woman, I learned the virtues of amoral familism. Fiercely defensive of her brood and her assets, she idolized my father in smotheringly Jewish mother–style, and she spoiled me shamelessly. From my grandfather I learned the meaning of fanatical zeal. He was a homeopath, and his medical sectarianism dominated his existence much more than his religion, which was a matter of social convention rather than conviction. The outside world to him was a vast conspiracy of allopaths against homeopathic physicians and pharmacists.

My father rebelled against his social milieu. He studied medicine to appease my grandfather but quickly turned to medical research (in tropical parasitology), moved to Brussels to escape the stifling adulation of his mother, and became a cosmopolite. He married a Frenchwoman, a somewhat eccentric choice from the perspective of his parents; went to the United States on a postdoctoral fellowship; did research in the then Belgian Congo (where I was born on January 30, 1933, the day the little Austrian lance corporal became Reich chancellor, an early lesson about the difference between correlation and causality); taught tropical medicine at Antwerp; founded and directed a research institute in the Congo; and retired as a gentleman farmer in Kenya. He was an egotistical and unstable person of many talents and great personal charm. I idolized him during my childhood, hated him during my adolescence, and ignored him in adulthood. His influence on me was considerable: I found his elitism, his contempt of authority and convention, his religious agnosticism, and his amiable cynicism engaging, although I resented his chaotic, undisciplined, self-indulgent life as a philandering husband and episodic father. My parents were divorced, after twenty years of marriage and five or six years of stormy conflict, when I was eighteen, my brother thirteen, and my sister six.

The maternal side of my family was anchored in Paris, where my grandfather, Maurice Caullery, an eminent biologist, taught at the Sorbonne and was president of the French Academy of Sciences as well as a fellow of the British Royal Society. He married a woman of striking beauty, great aristocratic pedigree, and artistic temperament but moderate intelligence. A more mismatched couple is difficult to conceive: she, the tall, slender, artistically sensitive, flighty, elegant socialite; he, the short, ill-dressed, curt, reclusive, absent-minded professor. They seemed to play in a respectable, high-society version of *The Blue Angel*. Henpecked at home, my grandfather withdrew into his scientific shell, taking refuge in his study, where a cloud of acrid smoke from Gauloise cigarettes kept my grandmother at bay. My grandmother exposed me to a strong dose of social snobbery and introduced me to a gallery of her colorful ancestors, including a cavalry general who took part in Napoleon III's Mexican misadventure in support of Maximilian, a bohemian painter who supported the 1871 Paris Commune (and was thus the red sheep in the family), and a pride of nine brothers who cracked the whip over their slaves in Haiti and were all killed the same day in the revolution of 1791.

My maternal grandfather, whom I am told I resemble in character, was a major influence. A stern, emotionally reticent and distant figure, he inspired instant respect in his intimates and sheer terror in his students. Impatient of anything but excellence, he exacted optimal performance (as, for instance, when he taught me to read Greek, expecting me by the end of summer vacation to translate Xenophon on sight). He punished shortcomings by disdainful withdrawal of interest in one's fate. All four of his children (my mother, her brother, and her two sisters) suffered from living in the shadow of his imposing intellect; but, perhaps sensing our affinities, he was fond of me in his gruff way, and I worshipped him. I particularly enjoyed his biting anticlericalism, a wonderful counterpoint to my Jesuit education, and his intellectual disdain for the merely rich and powerful. Few of his contemporaries found grace in his eyes. Most, including the leading political figures of the day, elicited his peremptory judgment, "*C'est un imbécile.*" The epitome of the rationalist, and a positivist in the grand nineteenth-century style, my grandfather initiated me into biology and taught me what science was all about. That this austere, shabby, physically unprepossessing, softspoken, unsociable, taciturn figure could so dominate his world by sheer strength of intellect was an early lesson in the superiority of mind over matter.

My mother (who is still alive) combined the physical beauty and artistic sensibilities of my grandmother and many of the moral qualities of my grandfather; I owe her much in the field of art appreciation (especially painting). What she also taught me was internal discipline.

My whole family expected me to excel, especially in school. But it was my mother who, by monitoring my homework, scrutinizing my report cards, supervising my reading, and taking me to museums actually saw to it that I did. My father and maternal grandfather, each in his own way, provided models; my mother gave me the drive.

In that endeavor she was firmly supported by the Jesuit fathers, who inflicted on me seven years of grueling intellectual discipline. Of my Jesuit secondary education I can only say that I hated almost every minute of it and that I shall be eternally grateful for the experience. Jesuits are famous for producing well-trained intellectual mavericks. The contradiction of the Jesuit system is that its casuistry encourages critical, disciplined thinking but that its theology expects blind faith. Like many, I took in the training and rejected its moral and religious content. By age twelve I was an atheist and a communist, having stumbled onto a secular theology similar in its dialectic to that of the good fathers. Two of my teachers were particularly influential, one a jovial, rotund bon vivant and superb pedagogue, Father Bribosia; the other a dry, austere martinet, but with a razor-sharp mind and a superlative *maître à penser,* Father De Wolf (I never knew their first names).

Three formative experiences in my upbringing remain to be mentioned because collectively they greatly influenced my choice of academic specialty. They are the so-called language problem of Belgium, World War II and life under Nazi occupation, and my colonial experience in the Congo. The Belgian language problem was my first exposure to ethnicity as well as class conflict; the two are intertwined in Belgium and were even more so in my youth than they are now. Inevitably French was our exclusive home language, first, because my mother was Parisian and did not speak a word of Dutch, and second, because my father, although raised in a Flemish city and entirely of Flemish descent, belonged to a bourgeois family that had become gallicized in the nineteenth century. Increasingly since the early nineteenth century the bourgeoisie of Flanders came to use French as a prestige language (much as the Russian aristocracy had before the Bolshevik revolution) and thus created a language barrier between itself and the lower classes. Language use thus became a marker of class snobbery and a continual source of conflict and humiliation. I learned early that language was not only a means of communication but also an idiom of exclusion and domination.

In Brussels that fact was not so obvious since French dominated the public life of the capital. Even there, however, there were French- and

Dutch-medium schools, which roughly corresponded to bourgeois and working-class schools. Even within the French-medium schools (which, naturally, I attended), it was clear that the best pupils also spoke the best French and the worst Dutch, so much so that having low marks in the compulsory Dutch course was a badge of high class status.

In a Flemish city like Ghent the invidiousness of language use was even more glaring. There every bourgeois household exhibited linguistic schizophrenia: French was spoken in the living room, Flemish in the kitchen—a vertical microcosm of the country at large. My grandparents, for example, were bilingual but never spoke Flemish with each other, with any member of the family, or with their class equals. Flemish was the language they spoke to menials—servants, tenant farmers, tradesmen, craftsmen, the vast assemblage they collectively called "*les gens du peuple.*" Since I belonged to the privileged group, I readily adopted the linguistic snobbery of the francophone, all the more so as these attitudes were strongly reinforced by those on the maternal side of my family, who indeed looked down on all Belgians as denizens of a *petit pays,* not of a *grande nation.* Flemish was considered an earthy, peasant dialect, well suited to the telling of scatological jokes (my grandmother's favorites, much as she was shocked by sexual jokes); but culture could only be carried through the vehicle of French.

World War II was perhaps my first lesson in cultural relativism. The ethnic table was turned on me. I was seven years old when "our war" first started, that is, when the Wehrmacht invaded the Low Countries and France on May 10, 1940. For me, the war began as a lark. Woken at 6 A.M. by the bombs of the Luftwaffe over Brussels, our family piled into our 1938 Chevrolet and headed south. We stopped at my grandparents' in Paris, then near Bordeaux, and finally had to turn back at the Spanish border, which we were unable to cross. The exodus, as we called it, meant school vacation two months ahead of schedule and a lot of excitement and adventure, like sleeping in barn lofts and playing paratrooper in vineyards.

Soon, however, our return to Brussels made it clear that we were a conquered people. That meant little to eat; a curfew; censored school books; newspapers full of lies; no gasoline (we kept our car hidden in our garage for fear it would be requisitioned); slow travel in overcrowded trains; an occasional bombing; and the presence of foreign troops, even in our homes. (We were forced to billet German officers, but I was strictly forbidden by my parents to fraternize with the enemy, despite an occasional tantalizing offer of chocolate from a homesick young father.) We were told that Paris, far from being the heart of Western civilization, was the rotten core of a decadent society, and that the Flemish, though one notch below the *Herrenvolk,* were far closer to the Aryan ideal than the effete Walloons or French.

We had several brushes with real physical danger, as when we sheltered a Hungarian Jewish colleague of my father; when my maternal grandfather was arrested and detained as a hostage, subject to execution in reprisal against resistance killings of Germans (the price of prominence); and when my father discovered that his laboratory in Antwerp had been converted by his assistant into an underground arsenal. The assistant, one of those psychopaths turned into heroes by the war, particularly relished telling me stories of his favorite wartime assignment— slitting the throats of prostitutes suspected of being Gestapo informers. I am sure that but for an accident of birth he would have worked just as enthusiastically for the other side.

Although my family was solidly anti-German and freely exchanged the latest anti-Nazi jokes, heroism was not in the family style. In fact it was regarded with some suspicion and distaste. The nearest thing to a hero my family produced was a third cousin who later volunteered in the Belgian paratrooper battalion during the Korean War and returned much decorated for bravery. He became a plantation overseer in the Congo, where he was tried for shooting workers in the legs with a .22-caliber rifle to encourage productivity; he briefly followed his true vocation when he rose to be chief of police for Moise Tshombe during the Katanga secession episode, meeting an untimely and undoubtedly disagreeable death at the hands of his Congolese captors. My almost exact contemporary, he was always presented to me as a negative role model, "un gosse qui a mal tourné parce que sa mère ne s'est pas assez occupée de lui" ("a kid who turned out badly because his mother neglected him").

That story brings me to my colonial experience in the then Belgian Congo. Although I was born there, I was brought to Europe as a ten-month-old infant, and I only returned in 1948, at age fifteen, to spend my last two years of high school. It is difficult to convey the excitement of an African adventure for an adolescent. Undoubtedly those two years were among the most formative of my life and played a determining role in my vocation as a social scientist. I was privileged, through my father's institute (IRSAC, Institut pour la Recherche Scientifique en Afrique Centrale), to see anthropologists like Jacques Maquet at work among the Tuzi of Rwanda, to follow ethologists on the tracks of mountain gorillas on the shores of Lake Kivu, to visit national parks a quarter century before the onslaught of mass tourism, to experience human cultural diversity in its most contrasting forms, and, especially, to be a participant observer in a colonial system of naked domination and exploitation, which was already doomed but did not yet know it. In 1950, just ten years before Zaire's independence, colonialism still seemed an unshakable system destined to last at least another century. The lessons of India, Indonesia, and Indochina had not even begun to sink in.

As I am trying to recapture my reactions to colonialism, I realize that colonial Congolese society was a considerable intellectual stimulant. Unlike many colonials, I was not taken in by the paternalistic ideology of the *mission civilisatrice,* nor did I share racial stereotypes of black inferiority. In the intellectual climate of IRSAC liberalism and cultural relativism were de rigueur and criticism of the colonial regime was a constant theme of conversation. That the regime rested on naked coercion was also glaringly obvious (this undoubtedly reinforced my anarchistic conviction that all governments were coercive). Blacks never seemed dumb or lazy to me. Indeed I was quick to observe how cunning they were in using the tactics of the weak (which were also the tactics I was using against teachers and other "hostile" adults and which I was later to use to good effect while a private in the army): passive resistance, evasion, sabotage, deception, malingering, deliberate misunderstandings, and the like. Colonialism (slavery, imprisonment, the military, and other social systems where the ideological veneer is thin) vividly exposes social structure and is thus an excellent training ground for social scientists. Tyrannical societies often produce first-class social scientists and social novelists: South Africa, Poland, and Russia come to mind.

At the same time as the sinews of Congolese society lay bare to my view, I was leading a comfortable and very pleasant existence based on unearned privilege. I would be less than candid if I said that it bothered me (as it would a decade later when I spent two years doing research on race relations in South Africa). If anything, I found racial prejudice an amusing form of mental aberration. I still remember how my brother came home from school one day having to copy a hundred times, as punishment for slackness, "If I have white skin, I must work, otherwise I am a white nigger." This motto reflected the mentality of the Catholic clergy, supposedly one of the liberal sectors of colonial opinion. (Naturally we attended a European school. There was a storm of protest when the Jesuits belatedly decided to start admitting "mulattoes" who had been legally recognized by their white fathers.)

After I finished high school in the Congo, my father thought it would be a good idea to send me to the United States for university studies, and he picked Stanford University. He also took the opportunity to dump my mother and sister in California in anticipation of divorce. Stanford in the early 1950s was not a major university; "the farm," as it was affectionately (not derisively) called, deserved its nickname. It was a dude ranch for the anti-intellectual brats of the West Coast plutocracy. After a Jesuit education Stanford was an academically undemanding Garden of Eden. I happily went horseback riding, swimming, and girl chasing (a result of my first unhindered access to the opposite sex after years in all-male schools) and breezed through a bachelor's degree in political science in two years, graduating in 1952.

For lack of better things to do, and to postpone my being drafted into the United States Army, I stayed at Stanford another year, receiving a master's degree in sociology. By that time I had decided that I wanted to become a social scientist. Political science (my first choice because I briefly thought of a diplomatic career) bored me, and I most enjoyed my sociology and anthropology courses, especially those of Richard La Piere and George Spindler. The joint Department of Sociology and Anthropology was minuscule (six or seven faculty members) and did not offer a serious graduate program, so my master's degree was another intellectual promenade, pleasant but unchallenging.

During my Stanford years, I spent a summer, in 1951, studying in Mexico City—the start of a lifelong love affair with Mexico. It was my first exposure to Latin America, and I immediately took to it as I never could to the United States. Mexico had the same wide open spaces that I had learned to appreciate in North America, but it also had a historical depth, cultural richness, and human density that I so badly missed in the United States. Most refreshingly, it seemed free of racial prejudices, which I found so suffocating in the United States. To be sure, Mexico was highly class-stratified, but in a way so similar to that which I had experienced in Europe that I felt culturally very much at home. In any case, I learned Spanish and equipped myself for later fieldwork in Latin America (Chiapas, Mexico, 1959; Guatemala, 1966; Peru, 1972–73).

With a worthless M.A. in my pocket and the United States and Belgian armies breathing down my neck (I was still a Belgian national, but as a permanent resident in the United States, Uncle Sam also considered me a prime candidate), I took a chance on starting a Ph.D. program at Harvard University. My luck soon ran out, but my one-year stint at Harvard was a revelation: I had my first exposure to a real university just as I was beginning to doubt any existed in the United States. In fact, with the arrogant self-confidence of youth, I did not bother to apply to another graduate school besides Harvard.

Harvard was great. I discovered on arrival that the guru of structual functionalism was away that year, but Gordon Allport, George Homans, Clyde Kluckhohn, Barrington Moore, Frederick Mosteller, Pitirim Sorokin, and Samuel Stouffer handsomely made up for Talcott Parsons's absence. I arrived during the formative period of the Department of Social Relations, or Soc Rel (and I was to finish my degree during its heyday in 1960). The holy trinity of Allport, Kluckhohn, and Parsons seemed to present a breathtaking synthesis of the social world, having grandly asserted the unity of psychology, sociology, and anthropology. La Piere had turned me against Freud and Durkheim (a lasting influence, I might add), and he had convinced me that social structures were nothing but people acting. I now found Homans reinforcing those views. As for the distinction between sociology and anthropology, it had never made sense to me. It seemed that the skin color of those studied did not justify the disciplinary boundary. Happily, I found everyone at Harvard in agreement on this point.

Although the holy trinity constituted the ruling triumvirate at Soc Rel, I was perhaps most attracted by the terrible three (my term): Homans, Moore, and Sorokin. Cranky, sarcastic, and arrogant, they terrorized most students, which left an empty niche to be filled. I found all three relatively approachable (after the initial protective rebuff) precisely because so few students dared come near them. Homans and Moore were both on my Ph.D. general examination committee, and most of my peers thought I was courting disaster. Indeed I was. Moore behaved true to form. He asked me in the oral exam to contrast industrial and preindustrial societies. I fell into the trap of answering in Parsonian platitudes unlikely to endear me to either Moore or Homans: on the spur of the moment the "pattern variables" seemed a convenient coat hanger for that kind of question. After an interminable five minutes or so, Moore interrupted with a devastating question: "But Mr. van den Berghe, what have you told me that I could not have found out by reading the *New York Times?*" It was Homans who came to my rescue. In his stentorian voice he interjected, "But Barrington, you haven't asked anything which could not be answered in those terms."

But I am running ahead of the story; Uncle Sam caught up with me long before I could take my generals. I was drafted in September 1954, after the Korean armistice but before the official end of hostilities, and spent two years in the Army Medical Corps, rising to the lofty rank of private first class. The move from a graduate dormitory at Harvard to a basic-training barrack at Fort Ord, California, was probably the most traumatic in my life. Yet it too was intellectually formative. Military life gave me a firsthand understanding of total institutions and, by extension, colonial systems, slavery, concentration camps, and other situations that were to exert a lifelong fascination on me.

I did not rebel against the military; I withdrew in amused cynicism, ridiculing and sabotaging the system and exercising my creativity by surreptitiously shirking my responsibilities without attracting punishment. I pursued my education by reading a substantial pocketbook library in latrines during extended coffee breaks and other disappearing acts. I successfully reduced an executive officer's authority by threatening to prefer charges of incompetence against him. (He had been responsible for burning six men on maneuvers, mistaking white phosphorus grenades for smoke grenades. They both came in olive-drab canisters, and he had not bothered to read the label.)

Above all, I became a barracks lawyer, mastering the Uniform Code of Military Justice, which I had discovered to be an intimidating weapon against illiterate noncommissioned officers and semiliterate officers. My worst punishment was one week's confinement to barracks, which I spent mostly listening to Mozart and Beethoven in the music room of the military hospital (the existence of which was only known to a half-dozen aficionados).

Luckily, after basic training among the rattlesnakes of California and Texas I was sent to defend the American empire on the Rhine. That assignment gave me the opportunity to renew contact with both the Belgian and the French sides of my family, and it was in Germany that I met my future wife, Irmgard Niehuis, in the dental chair of a military hospital where she was a dental assistant. To my father-in-law, a senior civil servant in Bad Kreuznach, I owe a keen appreciation of Rhine, Mosel, and Nahe wines; his job as head of the land-surveying office in the region gave him unmatched access to, and expertise in, the best vineyards. After a long military inquisition during which my fiancée was asked (supposedly for my protection) whether she had ever had venereal diseases or intended to emigrate to the United States to engage in prostitution, we were married by a Southern Baptist military chaplain in January 1956. That was also the period when I acquired United States citizenship, more as a matter of convenience than of conviction. My wife's nationality and her religion (Protestant) were matters of concern to some members of my family, but their misgivings were quickly allayed on acquaintance. Our differences in religious background were resolved through mutual agnosticism and indifference to religious matters, and we raised three sons, Eric (born in 1961), Oliver (born in 1962), and Marc (born in 1975) in a secular home, drawing eclectically from several religious traditions without affiliating with any. Nonetheless, my wife is not above reproaching me for my Jesuitical turn of mind whenever she loses an argument.

Released at last from the talons of the bald eagle, my wife and I spent an extraordinarily stimulating year in Paris (1956–57) courtesy of the GI bill. Our monthly stipend of $135 only sustained a Spartan standard of living, but the reduced-rate student restaurants, theaters, and concerts and the tuition-free university allowed a rich cultural and intellectual diet on a modest budget. That was the year I decided I would make Africa my main area of research, and Paris was a superb training ground. Georges Balandier, Paul Mercier, and Germaine Dieterlen were my main teachers in the African area. Roger Bastide initiated me to the African diaspora in Brazil; Claude Lévi-Strauss kindled my interest in the arcane field of kinship analysis; I listened to Raymond Aron talk about Weber, and Georges Gurvitch about Durkheim. Among my contemporaries and fellow students in and around the Sixth Section of the Ecole Pratique des Hautes Études, in the cavernous old Sorbonne building, were Claude Meillassoux and Rodolfo Stavenhagen.

The great political issues of the day were the war in Algeria and the Suez intervention, prompting routinized shouting matches around Saturday noon in the main courtyard of the Sorbonne. Rival student groups shouted at each other, "*Algérie française*" and "*Le fascisme ne passera pas.*" Dark blue trucks loaded with *gardes mobiles* stood by just outside but seldom had to intervene. It was then that I first became aware of the imminence and irreversibility of political change on the African continent and decided that I wanted to go back there soon. Both my political sympathies and my contacts were overwhelmingly with the left, at least on the issues of decolonization, but I also discovered in Paris that the right was not necessarily stupid (an impression readily gained from Republican politics in the United States).

The Parisian interlude was followed by reentry into the Department of Social Relations at Harvard, where I got my Ph.D. in January 1960. During those two and a half years I associated most closely with Gordon Allport and Talcott Parsons, who cochaired my dissertation committee. I was writing on South African race relations, and Allport was just back from South Africa with his student Thomas Pettigrew. He was thus a natural choice to chair my committee, and I have the fondest memory of his warm, avuncular interest in my budding career. He took great pains to expurgate my English prose of *which*es, and along with Bill Gum (at John Wiley, Basic Books, and later Elsevier) was the best editor I ever had.

My relationship with Parsons was more ambivalent. It was close, since I was both his research assistant and teaching assistant for two years, and he was quite pleasant with me, but I never felt at ease with his thinking. In fact the choice of South Africa as my dissertation topic quickly turned into a refutation of Parsonian consensus assumptions about the basis of social order. When I confronted him with the issue, his response was characteristically mild but unsatisfying. He suggested that either consensus was there but I had not looked for it deeply enough below all the surface noise, or perhaps South Africa was not really a society after all. It took me some five or six years to shed the Parsonian influence altogether. Eventually I came to resent the time spent trying to understand him when I belatedly discovered that the emperor had no clothes. But of course graduate students, even cheeky ones like me, dare not come to such conclusions.

In the summer of 1959 I got my feet wet doing anthropological fieldwork in Chiapas, Mexico, collaborating with Benjamin (Nick) Colby, the start of a long-standing friendship and a clear ethnographic vocation. Colby and I were in the first generation of students in the ongoing Harvard Chiapas Project directed by Evon Vogt, who was most helpful to me in the field. I also had the opportunity to establish contact with the Mexican school of anthropology, especially Gonzalo Aguirre Beltrán, Julio de la Fuente, and Alfonso Villa Rojas, and amicably to cross pens with my former Paris classmate Rodolfo Stavenhagen. At that time I looked at Chiapas as a training ground for the fieldwork I was planning in South Africa, but in the end I was to devote practically half of my research activities to Latin America.

A Ford Foundation Foreign Area Fellowship made it possible for my wife and me to go to South Africa in February 1960, and the next twenty-two months left an indelible imprint both intellectually and politically. My stay there coincided with the meteoric collapse of European colonialism in most of the rest of the continent and with an abortive revolution (Sharpeville and its aftermath) in South Africa itself: I had picked the right time to return to Africa. I also met more people of extraordinary stature and courage in South Africa than in any other period of my life, notably Albert Luthuli, Alan Paton, and among my university colleagues Leo and Hilda Kuper and Fatima Meer. I forged lasting friendships through my work in South Africa, especially with the Kupers and Hamish Dickie-Clark (then my colleagues at the University of Natal in Durban), Edna Bonacich (then Edna Miller, my first research assistant), and later Heribert Adam and Kogila Moodley (then a student of mine).

As a lecturer in the department headed by Leo Kuper at the University of Natal, I was both in one of the three main fermenting vats of South African social science and in the maelstrom of South African antiapartheid politics. I have related elsewhere my experiences there (in *Ethics, Politics and Social Research,* ed. Gideon Sjoberg [Cambridge, Mass.: Schenkman, 1967]) and need not repeat myself. If my South African stay left one indelible imprint, it is the firm conviction that any attention paid to race, whatever the stated intention, is noxious. This conviction later formed the basis of my vocal opposition to policies of race-based affirmative action in the United States and got me into considerable hot water. In South Africa, it was always touch and go whether I could finish my research before being expelled, but I finally left of my own accord in December 1961. Another event of my Durban stay was the birth of our eldest son, Eric, the first second-generation African in the family.

On the way back from South Africa we stopped over in Europe for six months, mostly in Paris. I renewed my 1956–57 contacts and taught at the Sorbonne. Our second son, Oliver, was born in Germany in 1962. The war in Algeria was now noisily winding down, and Paris was, as always, an exciting political and intellectual arena. Our stay was punctuated by OAS (Organisation de l'Armee Secrète, the underground of the right-wing French settlers in Algeria) plastic bombs, one within a hundred meters of my grandparents' flat.

The following three years marked our return to the United States and the start of my regular teaching career, first as an assistant professor at Wesleyan University (for a miserly annual salary of $7,200), then for two years at the State University of New York, Buffalo. At Wesleyan we found the combination of provincialism, mediocrity, and pretentiousness hard to take. Between the rowdiness of the fraternities, the chronic inebriation of the senior faculty, and the stench of the nearby rubber tire plant, we fled to Buffalo within a few months of arrival. Buffalo was not much of an improvement. The climate was rotten, the city grimy, and the university a shambles, but at least the salary was decent (twelve thousand dollars in 1963 went a long way). The State University of New York was then making its big push toward academic respectability, so the money spigots flowed generously. But the buildings of the old private university were bursting at the seams, the library kept books in crates for lack of shelf space, and the lectures were barely audible over the constant cacophony of the expanding university: bulldozers, pneumatic drills, and hammers successfully competed with professors. Politically those two years had their moments of excitement: the Kennedy assassination, the incipient protest against the Vietnam War, and, locally, opposition to a New York State loyalty oath.

When the University of Washington made me an offer in 1965, accepting was one of the easiest decisions of my life. Seattle, even on a drizzly winter day, as when I first saw it, beat Buffalo at its best, not to mention the blizzard I had just left. The university was distinguished in the life sciences and respectable in other fields; the sociology department was solid in a rather naively positivist, outhouse-empiricist way, but there was hope for it; the city, a bit like San Francisco but twenty years behind it, was trembling on the threshold of urbanity; the hinterland was gorgeous. That Seattle's attractive location would in later years cost me many thousands of dollars in rejected offers was far from my thoughts. Little did I know that at age thirty-two I had reached the apex of my purchasing power with a 1965 salary of fifteen thousand dollars!

No sooner had I arrived than the old guard of the department discovered in me more of a maverick and less of a positivist than they had bargained for. They tried to block my promotion to full professor two years later by claiming, with considerable justification, that I rejected the pretensions of sociology to being scientific and that I was really an anthropologist in sociological disguise. I counterattacked in the College Council, arguing that I was being subjected to a heresy trial, and won an unprecedented reversal of a departmental denial of promotion. From the late 1960s on, the department became more intellectually diverse and sophisticated, reaching its apogee in the early 1970s. In the late 1970s a succession of devastating budget cuts sent it, and indeed the entire university, into a tailspin, from which we are only now beginning to recover.

My tenure in Seattle was interrupted by several lengthy absences on overseas research. In 1966 I went to Guatemala to resume my collaboration with Nick Colby and to work among the Ixil, who have since been massacred in the thousands by the government and relocated in Vietnam-style "strategic hamlets." In 1967–68 the Rockefeller Foundation sent me to Kenya for a year to establish a sociology department at the University of Nairobi, and in 1968–69 I went to the University of Ibadan in Nigeria to develop a graduate program. Those were also the years when I had the satisfaction of seeing my sister Gwendoline turn into a professional anthropologist, first studying as an undergraduate at Berkeley and then continuing on to the Sorbonne for her doctorate.

Our second two-year stay in Africa was filled with excitement and proved a tremendous experience for our boys. Kenya, though officially at peace (except for frontier skirmishes with Somalis in the north), was in fact politically almost as oppressive as South Africa. Endowed with the kind of government Stanislav Andreski aptly called a kleptocracy, Kenya was a hotbed of conflicts, and the university was infested with police informers. I clashed with the principal and the authorities on several issues involving academic freedom and the intimidation of students, thereby making myself persona non grata with another African government. Nonetheless, extensive travel in Uganda (before it was gutted by Idi Amin), Tanzania, and Kenya, through the world's greatest game reserves and most spectacular scenery, made us forget the tensions of Nairobi.

Between Nairobi and Ibadan my wife and I took an extended anthropological excursion through Ethiopia (during the waning days of the Conquering Lion of Judah, Haile Selassie), India, Iran, and Lebanon. At least three of these societies have changed beyond recognition since, and hardly for the better. Ethiopia, even before the great famine of the 1970s and the ravages of war in the Ogaden and Erythrea, already qualified as one of the poorest, most depleted, most overpopulated countries in Africa, but its destitution barely affected its beauty. India, unlike Africa, exposed us to the problem, not of underdevelopment, but of overdevelopment: an overcrowded subcontinent whose resources had been depleted by five millennia of overexploitation under an advanced agrarian civilization. Nowhere else is the contrast between the splendor of the past and the squalor of the present so evident. Of all the African countries, Egypt and Ethiopia probably come the closest, but the sheer size and density of the Indian population magnify its problems and supply an even more nightmarish vision of the future of humanity.

Iran seemed oppressive enough in 1968, but, obviously, it had not yet reached bottom. As for Lebanon, it then seemed the model of consociational democracy; it was hailed as the Switzerland of the Middle East, the paradise of mercantile capitalism, the temple of religious tolerance! We had a most delightful week in Beirut, Baalbek, Tyre, and Sidon, another vacation taken just in time.

Our impending stay in Nigeria left us full of apprehension. It turned out that our fears were greatly exaggerated. Despite a raging civil war estimated to have killed between five hundred thousand and one million people, the Ibadan campus was an oasis of peace and intellectual freedom. I felt much more at ease in Yoruba culture than I had in East Africa. Nigerians were refreshingly free of racial consciousness and inferiority complexes vis-à-vis the outside world. There was almost no sign that they had ever been colonized, except for the social snobbery of the Western-educated elite. Most engaging, perhaps, was the sophistication of Nigerian political intrigues and the disarming charm and candor with which nepotism, favoritism, clientelism, and corruption suffused the social fabric. The whole society was a tissue of nepotism and amoral familism, stripped of hypocrisy and moralism, its structures laid bare by the transparency of its superstructures. In retrospect it was my Nigerian experience that later predisposed me to apply the sociobiological paradigm to human behavior. I always recall with amusement the clinching argument of Nigerians seeking to convince one of their truthfulness: "Why should I tell a lie?" by which they mean that in this particular instance they have no interest in deceiving.

The return to the United States brought, as usual, culture shock. Most disturbing was what I saw as a reversal of the integrationist strategies of the civil-rights movement and a revival of racial thinking and categorization first brought about by the black-power movement and further abetted by the institutional responses of affirmative action, quota systems, racial double standards, racial busing, and other forms of race-based, race-conscious discrimination. I opposed similar moves in the American Sociological Association and felt obliged to resign from some of its committees for the same reasons.

It was only a matter of time before the issue came to a head on my own campus. Double racial standards of admission at the University of Washington necessarily raised the problem of double standards of evaluation of students in classes. I refused to take a racial census of my classes, as the Black Studies Program demanded of me, and I refused to yield to intimidation on the issue of double standards of evaluation. The crisis was further complicated when I caught five black students in a crude attempt at tampering with a grade sheet. Groups of shouting, abusive students confronted me inside and outside my office, uttering verbal threats. A chorus of minority organizations, led by the vice presi-

dent for minority affairs (a retired army colonel without academic credentials hired to keep black students under control), demanded that I be
sacked as a racist. For a fortnight I made both local newspapers and at
least one of the three television news programs almost daily. With the
outstanding exception of my department chairman, Frank Miyamoto,
who courageously came to my defense, the university administration,
with characteristic cowardice and expediency, played possum. When I
tried to elicit from the provost a statement of university policy on the
fundamental issues of principle I was raising, he lamely replied that the
vice president of minority affairs and I were each entitled to our private
views as to whether racial discrimination should be entrenched in academic life.

A field trip to Peru (1972–73) under the auspices of the National
Institute of Mental Health soon delivered me from all that nonsense.
The exhilaration of eighteen months in one of the world's most spectacular areas (the Andes and the jungles of southern Peru and Bolivia) and
most fascinating situations of ethnic relations was a welcome change
from the dissipation of intellectual energy in sterile political fights. I am
frequently asked why I never did research in the United States. I suppose
it is because I suffer the anthropological malady diagnosed by Lévi-
Strauss in *Tristes tropiques:* I find it much more difficult to suspend
value judgments about the society in which I normally reside than I do
abroad. It takes physical and cultural distance to gain moral detachment
and political noncommitment. Relativism implies a solid measure of
indifference.

For all its beauty and fascination, I did not take to Peru as I did to
Mexico. I met stimulating colleagues like José Matos Mar, Fernando
Fuenzalida, and Jorge Flores Ochoa, and I made friends like Ben Orlove,
but I found Andean culture to be dour, hostile, and seemingly devoid of
joie de vivre. The music is hauntingly melodic but melancholy; even
during fiestas people are unsmiling; their sense of humor seems limited
to the misfortune of others; sexuality is repressed, and women under
their bulging multiple dresses exude the pungent sensuality of giant
peripatetic onions; even drunkenness seems to bring out depression
rather than release inhibitions. As Alfred Métraux had warned me ten
years earlier, "*Les Andes sont sinistres.*" I attributed his statement to his
own melancholy temperament (he took his own life soon afterward),
but my experience confirmed his judgment. In Brazil, especially in Rio
de Janeiro and even more so in Bahia, I encountered exuberant joy,
sensuality, and hedonism in a harmonious cultural blend of Latin Eu-

rope and West Africa. Lusotropicalism in all its flamboyant glory was a far cry from the *tristes tropiques* of the *sertao* described by Lévi-Strauss.

My return to Seattle marked rapid growth in a new interest, which had long been dormant but now would not leave me in peace. It simply had to be pursued. I am referring, of course, to what is now called *sociobiology*. There are few topics on which social scientists exhibit such a devastating blend of abysmal ignorance and unshakable irrationality. Not surprisingly, my alleged conversion had been variously seen as a profound departure from my previous work, a belated showing of my true reactionary colors, an act of treachery, or a case of creeping senility. Having experienced most of my colleagues' imperviousness to rational discourse on this score, I have few illusions that anything I say here will disabuse them. But the quixotic strain in my temperament impels me to try anyway.

For several years I had been reading extensively in ethology, especially primate and human ethology, and though I sensed much of interest there, I was also unsatisfied. Much of the work in human ethology was trivial: the underlying evolutionary thinking was sloppily group-selectionist; there seemed to be no overarching theoretical framework to a largely descriptive natural history; and cross-species comparisons were mainly piecemeal and at the level of loose analogies. At the same time it was becoming increasingly clear to me that the social-science orthodoxy of the past half century was now bankrupt and obsolete. The dogma that *Homo sapiens* was so unique an animal as to bear no comparison with other species; the continuous exclusion of human behavior from the process of evolution by natural selection; the treatment of human culture and social structure as phenomena entirely sui generis; causality defined in terms of an opposition of nature versus nurture, heredity versus the environment—all these notions seemed overdue for the intellectual junk heap. Too much evidence simply did not fit.

However, several approaches in the social sciences that had always made sense to me and that, together, exhausted social-science claims to at least quasi-scientific status all seemed to converge on a few simple assumptions about human behavior. Behaviorism, game theory, classical economics, Marxism, exchange theory, and rational-choice theory all appeared to be based on simple utilitarian, materialistic premises that humans were maximizers acting in seeming rationality in the pursuit of self-interest. These social-science models are in fact quite close to those used by population ecologists and other evolutionary biologists, and tantalizing vistas for the reincorporation of the social sciences into the mainstream of neo-Darwinian synthesis opened up. Indeed many of the glaring limitations in these fields seemed to disappear when problems were rethought in evolutionary terms. The charge of ahistoricism justifiably leveled at much would-be theoretical social science would lose its validity if the linkage with biology could be made. For example, classical behaviorism dealt with the ontogeny of behavior; it could only gain by linking up with the phylogenetic approach of ethology.

Edward Wilson's 1975 book *Sociobiology: The New Synthesis* suddenly seemed to point the way, not only to a brand of theoretical biology that revolutionized Lorenzian ethology, but also to a synthesis much more germane to a number of existing social-science traditions. I soon discovered that the pieces of the puzzle, which Wilson had conveniently assembled, had all been around for over a decade, in the works of Ernst Mayr, George Williams, William Hamilton, John Maynard-Smith, Richard Alexander, and others. Wilson was not so much the innovator as the synthesizer.

Why people keep wondering at how much I changed puzzles me; I see my interest in sociobiology as flowing logically from my lifelong insistence on the comparative approach. Much as I could never envisage a sociology that did not take in the entire range of human experience (and thus the field customarily reserved for anthropology), I now could not see why we should suspend our comparative perspective at the boundaries of our species. How can we define the parameters of human nature except by comparison with the nonhuman? Certainly we are unique, but we are not unique in being unique. Every species is unique and *evolved* its uniqueness in adaptation to its environment. Culture is the uniquely human way of adapting, but culture, too, evolved biologically. Culture does have some emergent properties, but it cannot be dissociated from biological evolution and continues to be intricately and integrally connected with it. The feedback loops are multiple and reciprocal. To determine the causal pathways and specify the proximate mechanisms that link genes, mind, and culture (to paraphrase Charles Lumsden and Edward O. Wilson) is the great intellectual challenge of late twentieth-century social science. The human mind is *not* a tabula rasa; it channels cultural development in recognizably human ways.

In 1976–77, I took the first sabbatical of my career, largely to retool as a sociobiologist studying humans. My previous junkets had found outside sponsors, but the halcyon days of academe were over. I collaborated with David Barash at the University of Washington, and met Richard Alexander, Richard Dawkins, William Hamilton, John Maynard-Smith,

Robert Trivers, Edward Wilson—indeed most of the leading lights in the field. I also took a fascinating trip to Israel, invited by the University of Haifa. There I renewed my friendship with Sammy Smooha, who proved a marvelous guide to an incredibly complex society, and met Joseph Shepher, who introduced me to his kibbutz and rekindled my long-standing interest in human incest avoidance.

Apart from my academic interest in race relations, Israel could not leave me unmoved. Old Jerusalem, that great rendezvous of monotheism, is perhaps the most gripping and haunting piece of real estate on earth, even for an agnostic like me. In 1976 there seemed to be a glimmer of hope that some solution to the regional conflict might be found, but rampant Israeli imperialism under Begin and the rape of Lebanon destroyed any prospects of peace. If the ultimate justification for the State of Israel is the Nazi Holocaust, as the Yad Vashem Memorial suggests, I always wondered why Israel was created at the expense of the Arabs. Would it not have made more sense to establish it in, say, East Prussia?

Meanwhile, back in Seattle another bit of excitement was awaiting me. In April 1978 I achieved instant world notoriety as the sociologist who spent one hundred thousand dollars to find his way to a brothel. Senator William Proxmire had awarded NIMH and me his monthly Golden Fleece Award, for extravagant government spending, allegedly for having wasted my Peruvian research money (ninety-seven thousand dollars of it) on interviewing twenty-one prostitutes in a Cuzco brothel. The story was of course a natural for the media, which got into the act with great alacrity, from the *Washington Post, Le Monde,* the *London Sunday Times,* and the *Wall Street Journal* to the *National Enquirer, Playboy, Penthouse,* and "The Dick Cavett Show." Friends started mailing me newspaper clippings from London, Paris, Djakarta, and Nairobi.

The sober truth of the matter was that my student and assistant, George Primov, had, with my knowledge and consent, independently conducted a little study of a brothel, on his own time, at the cost of perhaps fifty dollars of grant resources. The research was perfectly legitimate and related to the main project (ethnic and class relations in Cuzco). I felt I owed no one any apologies, and I counterattacked, calling Proxmire a clownish reincarnation of Senator Joseph McCarthy. In fact I felt flattered by the award. If an anti-intellectual politico like Proxmire found my research a waste of money, his attack must be a vindication of its merit. I soon discovered that I was indeed in distinguished company, including, amusingly, Edward O. Wilson. It also turned out that my colleagues Philip Blumstein and Pepper Schwartz were the first runners-up for the award, for the study published as *American Couples.*

The last few years have been a bit of an anticlimax, fortunately punctuated by several pleasant trips to Mexico, the Caribbean, Morocco, India, and Europe, a Fulbright lecture tour of Australia in 1982, visiting professorships in Strasbourg in 1983, Tübingen (1986), and Tel Aviv (1988), and a 1984–85 fellowship at the Center for Advanced Study in the Behavioral Sciences.

My unease with United States society has mounted, and the last few years of Reaganism (that coalition of millionaires, gun nuts, Bible Belt fundamentalists, and political idiots who vote against their interests) have only reinforced my distaste for the cult of mediocrity that suffuses American society, including, sadly, its system of education. The entire American educational system has been buffeted by successive waves of anti-intellectualism of the right and the left and has consequently spawned the first generation of functional illiterates ever produced by an advanced industrial society. The teaching profession, itself a bastion of mediocrity, has been in the forefront of this assault against intellectual quality and discipline.

The university has not been spared. In contrast to the British model of the university as an independent community of scholars ruled by a collective of professors and engaged in the diffusion and extension of knowledge, the American university is subservient to capitalist donors, football-crazed alumni, backwoods state legislators, Bible-brandishing synods, and missile-wielding warlords and run by supine, opportunistic administrators. Professors are tolerated court jesters, irrelevant eccentrics paid to keep the youth amused and off the streets and labor markets for a few years.

My intellectual elitism and political anarchism have won me few friends and allies on campus, and my peripheralness to sociology has scared away most graduate students. Not that I mind being an isolate, and my experience with the dozen students who have stuck with me to the doctorate has been most rewarding and broadening: they have ranged from historical macrosociologists to structural anthropologists and human sociobiologists. Most of my intellectual associates over the last ten years have come from outside of sociology—primarily anthropology but also psychology, zoology, history, and other fields.

In fact I have largely given up on sociology as a viable discipline. Fixated on methodology (and a very limiting brand of methodology at that), sociologists are increasingly bereft of substantive knowledge and have failed to produce a truly significant idea in the last fifty years. The golden age of sociology was during the first three decades of the century. Hiding its intellectual bankruptcy behind a shaky numerical façade, sociology has managed to get the worst of both C. P. Snow's two cultures: it is too philistine to qualify as a humanity and too antireductionist to become a science. Thus it richly deserves the low esteem in which it is held.

Indeed sociology seems to have missed every intellectually promising boat in the last half century. It lost its panhuman vision when it let anthropology preempt three-fourths of the world. It lost its historical vision when it turned its back on both evolutionism and "mere" historicism and became bad ethnography of contemporary industrial societies. It lost any chance of becoming a science when it rejected the relevance of biology and started treating human behavior as disembodied social structures and values. It retained the outward mark of a scientific discipline: quantification, or, better, as Sorokin put it, "quantophrenia." As with all disciplines in the process of becoming sterile scholastic traditions, sociology becomes increasingly ingrown. Henri Poincaré was indeed prophetic when, in 1909, he declared sociology the discipline most concerned with methodology and most bereft of substance.

CHAPTER NINETEEN

Relativism, Equality, and Popular Culture

Herbert J. Gans

To understand society, we study people's relationships, but we also study their lives. If we want to understand sociology's place in society, we must look at ourselves in the same way—and precisely because we are supposed to be detached social scientists. Sociologists are also people, and when we try to be value-free, knowledge about the values from which we are seeking to free ourselves becomes absolutely necessary.

Although I wish this were a volume of biographical studies, I suspect that no one is yet ready to pay for biographical research among sociologists; autobiographical accounts are therefore a useful precursor. Having myself been trained in the era of detached social science and impersonal scientists, I found it difficult at first to write about myself and could only begin by turning the assignment into a research project, a self-study. This essay attempts to determine how and why I got interested in the analysis of American popular culture and, since I am also a policy-oriented researcher, why I developed the cultural policies I have advocated. My data are largely based on recall, although having kept almost all my student term papers, I was able to refer to them, including a brief autobiographical report I had to write at age twenty, in 1947.

In my 1974 book *Popular Culture and High Culture* I argued that people's artistic and entertainment activities and preferences are sufficiently influenced by class that they can be analyzed as if they were aspects of class cultures, which I called taste cultures but which have long been known as brow levels in the vernacular. To this basically empirical theme I added a critical analysis that proposed that the expert practitioners of high culture seek to make the aesthetic standards of their own culture universal. In so doing, they condemn competing cultures, notably commercial popular culture, as emotionally and otherwise harmful and, without any convincing evidence, argue either that high culture is beneficial or popular culture dangerous. Moreover, they want people to convert to high-culture standards without supplying them with the income and educational prerequisites already obtained by the present high-culture audience.

My analysis reflected at least three value and policy positions—all of them essentially "populist." One is *cultural relativism,* that all taste cultures are equally valid as long as people choose the cultural activities and artifacts they think good. A second is *equality,* that all people are entitled to the same freedom of cultural choice. The third might be labeled *antiexpert,* insofar as I am critical of professionals and scholars who use their expertise—as well as their credibility and prestige as experts—in behalf of value judgments that overtly or covertly further their own interests. Although the book was published in 1974, I had prepared article-length versions earlier, and several of its basic ideas, including the ones summarized here, had already appeared in preliminary form in a paper written in 1950 for David Riesman's graduate seminar in popular culture at the University of Chicago. By focusing mainly, but not completely, on that paper, I can limit the length of this autobiographical account to my first twenty-three years.

I began my self-study with two hypotheses, which I will discuss further at the end of the essay. One is that having been born in Germany, my interest in American popular culture may have been in part a function of my own acculturation as a first-generation ethnic of Jewish origin; the other is that my espousal of cultural relativism and equality—as well as my interest in using social-science research for developing policy—was connected to changes and inconsistencies in class and status that came with my being an immigrant. I used these hypotheses mostly to help me structure my recall and to put boundaries on my self-study. This procedure can be questioned on methodological grounds, but autobiography cannot be science. I should add two other initial hypotheses: one, that more basic marginalities unrelated to ethnicity or class encouraged me to become an observer of society and a sociologist, and two, that being better at writing than talking about my ideas helped make me a writer of sociological studies. The latter two hypotheses are probably virtual axioms that are true for many sociologists, especially those who do qualitative analysis.

I

I was born in 1927 as the first child of a bourgeois Jewish family in Cologne, Germany. We were comfortable but not rich. My father ran a small family business that had been founded by his father, who had moved to the city from Herlinghausen, a Westphalian village, and from a centuries-old family cattle dealership. My mother came from a family of affluent small-town merchants and bankers in the Hanover area, though her father had been an eye doctor. Both my parents were *Gymnasium* graduates, and my mother had a year of junior college; my father had hoped to attend the university in Cologne but had to join the family firm instead. My mother's ancestors had broken with Orthodoxy earlier than my father's, but both my parents were nonreligious, acculturated, and unconnected to the formal and informal Jewish communities in Cologne.

My parents' social life was limited to a handful of relatives and family friends, and my own therefore almost entirely to their children. Athletically inept and shy, I soon found myself more comfortable with books than with these children or school friends. When I was old enough to read books, I spent a lot of spare time in my parents' library and now remember most vividly that I enjoyed reading both fiction and adventure (including James Fenimore Cooper, in German translation) and nonfiction (for example, books by archaeologists excavating in Egypt and especially the books of Sven Hedin, the first Westerner to explore Tibet). I think that by age nine or ten I wanted to be an explorer. I was too young for, and my parents were not much interested in, German high culture, and German popular culture was sparse. The creative output of the Weimar era was banned in 1933, and when German filmmakers began to make mostly Nazi propaganda films, we no longer went to the movies. Beyond that, I recall only the brothers Grimm and the "Max and Moritz" cartoons, which described how the minor mischiefs of young boys and girls inevitably ended in death, loss of limbs, or other forms of mutilation. Tibet was both less dangerous and more interesting.

By 1937 my parents had decided to leave Germany and applied for an American visa, but the number of applicants was huge and the quota small. Early in 1939 we therefore went to England, where my uncle and his mother had moved in the mid-1930s. Because one of my mother's aunts was a close friend of a high-ranking Sears Roebuck executive in Chicago, the latter gave us an affidavit, a crucial prerequisite to the visa, which enabled us to enter the United States, still visaless but under a special wartime exemption from the immigration law.[1] In September 1940 we arrived in Chicago, moving into a rooming house in Woodlawn, then a predominantly Irish low-rent area.

America was still in the throes of the Depression, and although our life in Nazi Germany and wartime England had already been austere, it now became even more so; my father worked as a Fuller Brush salesman, my mother as a domestic. Our downward mobility was surely harder on them than on me, although we were so happy to have escaped from Germany—even before we knew of the Holocaust—that our economic problems were bearable. Besides, the drive to regain bourgeois status began at once. I am not even sure that I even felt a decline in fortune. Compared to my mostly working-class fellow students, I was so well educated in English and already sufficiently interested in writing that a few weeks after I was enrolled in the eighth grade of the neighborhood school, I was made editor of the school newspaper.

My parents wanted nothing more to do with Germany or things German, and we spoke English at home. I knew precious little German culture anyway, but now I also discovered American popular culture. I still remember spending a lot of time in the basement of our rooming house reading a year's worth of Sunday *Chicago Tribune* comics in newspapers that had been stored there by a frugal landlady.

I must have been starved for adventurous and humorous popular culture because I also became a fan of radio serials like "Captain Midnight" and "Jack Armstrong" and of comedians like Jack Benny. When I had the money, I spent Saturdays at the local triple-feature movie theater, where I caught up on American Westerns. In addition I became a sports fan and especially admired athletes whose prowess was said to be based on brains, such as Chicago Bears quarterback Sid Luckman, and Ted Lyons, the aging knuckleball pitcher of the Chicago White Sox.

My unqualified enthusiasm for popular culture seems not to have lasted very long because in 1942, as a sophomore at Hyde Park High School, I was writing long essays, some of which were critical of the mass media. Later I submitted short features on the same theme to the high-school newspaper. I also wrote a couple of pretentious pieces urging my fellow students to enjoy the good music I was learning about in music appreciation class, by Tchaikovsky and Rimsky-Korsakov in particular. I was also still a sports fan, became sports editor of the high-school newspaper in my junior year, and contributed to a *Chicago Daily News* readers' column on the sports pages.

Meanwhile, both my parents had obtained easier, better-paying, and more secure jobs as their spoken English and the Chicago economy improved. We moved into our own apartment, first in a basement that flooded with every storm and then into a much better one in Southmoor, a small buffer area between poor Woodlawn and middle-class South Shore. And I gave up an afternoon newspaper route for a better job as a bookrunner in the University of Chicago library stacks.

Although I was as shy as ever, I was now on the margins of a clique, mostly the ambitious children of Jewish shopkeepers in the area. I paid little attention to my poor fellow students unless they were varsity athletes but was conscious of the affluent Jewish youngsters from Hyde Park and South Shore who dominated student life. While my clique wrote the school publications, the affluent students were active in fraternities and sororities, organizing Saturday-night dances for which they were able to hire nationally known bands. I imagine some of my cultural criticism was directed against them, although I do not remember any strong feelings of resentment.

In 1944, my senior year, I edited the high-school newspaper and began to think seriously about becoming a journalist, although my father thought I should play it safe and learn business skills and my mother was sure I would become a teacher. Lloyd Lewis, a *Daily News* editor, persuaded me to study liberal arts instead of journalism. Unable to afford Oberlin, then an "in" college for Chicagoans with writing ambitions, I applied to the University of Chicago. With the help of a half scholarship I had enough money the first year, which having begun in January I had to finish in record time because in August 1945 I was drafted. After fourteen months in the Army of the United States, first as a typist, then as an editor of an army base newspaper, I returned to the university in the fall of 1946. Thanks to the GI bill, some scholarship aid, and part-time work, I was able to stay until I received my M.A. in June 1950.

My socialization in the German and American class structures was accompanied by a very different set of experiences in the Jewish community. My parents had not wanted me to go to a Jewish school, but in 1933, when I started school, Nazi law required it, and I spent my first years in a secular Jewish public school. In 1937 my parents sent me to a strictly Orthodox *Gymnasium* because it taught English. This it did superbly, but I bitterly disliked the religious classes and teachers. However, in England I suddenly turned to prayer for a while, perhaps as a way of coping with *that* immigration. By the fall of 1939 World War II had begun, and all German-Jewish men, including my father, were interned by the British, who suspected that the Nazis had hidden spies among the refugees. Moreover, my fellow students could not distinguish between German Jews and Nazis, beating me up a couple of times. My religiosity ended after we arrived in America, but I was also back in a predominantly Jewish milieu, for Hyde Park High School was in effect another secular Jewish school.

In the summer of 1943, needing to earn some money, I went to a Jewish summer work camp which provided wartime "stoop labor" to Chicago-area truck farmers. There I met a young and immensely charismatic Jewish youth worker, Samuel Kaminker, who believed in reading Hebrew and American poetry rather than prayers at Sabbath services. I was sufficiently interested in his essentially nontheistic conception of Judaism, radical at the time, to take some courses later at the College of Jewish Studies, searching for what I described in my 1947 autobiographical paper as "a rational Jewish religion for myself."

Kaminker was also an admirer of the Israeli kibbutz, ran the camp on a modified kibbutz basis, and started me thinking about spending my life in an egalitarian community of farm workers in which no one had to struggle to make a living. That vision stayed with me for the rest of my student days, and just before I received my M.A. I joined a small group of budding sociologists who planned to go to Israel and carry out participant-observation research at a kibbutz—as a way, I think, of trying to see whether we wanted to become permanent members of a collective. Even so, my interest in equality extended beyond the kibbutz because, after reading R. H. Tawney in social-science courses and hearing him lecture at Chicago in 1948, I seriously considered studying with him at the London School of Economics. However, I never made it to Israel as a researcher or to London as a student.

II

My arrival at the University of Chicago in January 1945 produced a new set of marginalities, which had little to do with class, ethnicity, or religion but were more traumatic. One was the normal undergraduate experience of discovering my naïveté. Although I had been a top student at a top Chicago high school, where I had hung out with a quasi-intellectual clique, I was an utter provincial. My new fellow students were smarter and more sophisticated; many were combat veterans, four to five years older than I and many more years wiser in the ways of the world. I thought they were wiser in all respects, proper students with their own apartments, whereas I was socially immature, had to live at home and commute, and worked on the side to help pay the rent. Whatever inferiority feelings I had in high school were now magnified.

A second trauma was intellectual. In the 1940s the high-school curriculum did not include any social sciences or humanities, and even social studies had not yet been invented. There was only civics and American history, which was just more civics but about the past. All course materials at the university except in the natural sciences were brand new to me, and I had never even heard of Aristotle, Plato, Kant, Hume, or Karl Marx. Old assumptions and certainties were therefore shattered quickly and often.

A third and related trauma was political. Once the war veterans arrived, the campus was rife with political discussion and action, involving groups and ideas of which I had never heard. I was wooed by Socialists, Stalinists, Trotskyites, and others who stimulated my interest in politics but also overwhelmed me, so I joined nothing. By the 1948 presidential election I had begun to make up my mind, however, for I said no to the Progressive party and worked for Socialist party candidates Norman Thomas and Maynard Krueger.

The one early source of certainty at Chicago was my field of studies. Having spent the first college year in survey courses in the natural sciences, the humanities, philosophy, and the social sciences and having taken a graduate social-science course in my second year, I knew where I wanted to spend the three years of study toward the M.A. In my 1947 autobiographical term paper, written in the first semester of graduate school, I reported that I was majoring in social science "but confused by too many interests: writing, sociological research, teaching, educational administration, social work (youth groups) and . . . Jewish religion and community life."[2]

Sociology was already my favorite subject because it seemed closest to some of what I had already been writing about America and to the kind of feature journalism that interested me. It was also sometimes less abstract than the other social sciences. Although I did my share of reading—and even tried to write—abstract theory, I was always more comfortable with what later became known as grounded and middle-range theory, one reason to gravitate toward fieldwork. However, I also read some John Dewey and believed in the unity of the social sciences. In addition, I did not like some of the required first courses in sociology and therefore entered the divisional master's program in the social sciences, headed by Earl Johnson, a sociologist who advocated many of Dewey's values. Johnson's program gave me the chance to take graduate work in all the social sciences, which provided a fine background for my electives, almost all of which were in sociology.

Earl Johnson also taught that the social sciences existed to help improve society, and thus he supported and strengthened my predispositions toward what is today called social policy.[3] Still, those feelings were not strong enough to get in the way of what I was learning elsewhere about the virtues of detached research and how to do it. In any case, the relative ease with which I settled on my fields of interest reduced my earlier intellectual flounderings. Another source of reduced uncertainty was my discovery of cultural relativism. Because all beginning students in the social sciences were required to take two survey courses (which covered sociology, anthropology, social psychology, and "human development"), I heard lectures from all the Chicago social anthropologists and read the other major American and British ones. More important, I discovered Karl Mannheim's *Ideology and Utopia*, and was very excited by his concept of relationism as well as his emphasis on the idea that all knowledge was a function of the knower's perspective. Most of my papers that year were Mannheimian in one or another way, and his relationism provided a criterion by which to compare diverse ideas—or cultures—without having to choose between them. Later, when I began to do fieldwork in Park Forest, Illinois, Mannheim's notion of perspective proved useful, although I was surprised by how many perspectives toward the same event were possible even in a small, fairly homogeneous community. However, I also learned that for some issues, including high culture and popular culture, it is not always necessary to elevate one perspective above all others.

Two other authors helped me to develop my relationist position. One was W. Lloyd Warner, also one of my teachers, whose lectures and Yankee City books made the notion of class more meaningful to me at the time than readings in Marx, Weber, and even the Lynds. Warner also started me thinking about class and the mass media, and then about class culture, because of his lectures on what he called symbol systems. Since he taught that different classes looked at society from different perspectives, a culturally relativist approach to class made sense to me, although Warner himself clearly preferred the higher classes. The other author was Robert K. Merton, whose essay "Manifest and Latent Functions," which I first read in early 1950, made an enormous impression because, among other things, it enabled me to see that cultural patterns disliked by one group can be functional for another.[4]

My preoccupation with cultural relativism and relationism also helped, I now suspect, to nurture what I earlier called my antiexpert position. Although I was trying to become an expert myself and was spending most of my time listening to or reading experts, I had always disliked those whose expertise manifested itself in the exercise of absolute and autocratic authority. My early rebelliousness against Orthodox Jewish teachers in the Cologne *Gymnasium* was followed by similar reactions in Chicago to a number of rabbis I met during my activities in the organized Jewish community. As the editor of the school newspaper at Hyde Park High School, I had bitter but unsuccessful struggles with the supervising teacher and the principal, who censored every criticism of the school and the school system. Later I waged a less vocal campaign against Aristotle and Plato, who were the much-assigned experts in every college course at Chicago while Robert Maynard Hutchins was chancellor.[5]

In graduate courses at Chicago from 1947 to 1949 I studied other subjects as well. I learned to become a novice fieldworker in Everett Hughes's course, and took Louis Wirth's course on the sociology of knowledge only to discover that by then he was much less interested in teaching relationism than in improving race relations. I learned economic history—and I think a good deal of what is now called social history too—from Sylvia Thrupp, and was taught content analysis and communication theory by Barney Berelson and Douglas Waples. In fact I took as many communications courses as possible in the social sciences because, whenever possible, I was trying to connect sociology with communications and the mass media. In Avery Leiserson's course on public opinion and in other political-science courses I tried to figure out how the governed communicate with the governors, a subject that continues to fascinate me today but then helped lead to my M.A. thesis on political participation and to an interest in audience-feedback processes in mass-media organizations.[6] For Sylvia Thrupp I wrote a paper on the merchant writers of early seventeenth-century England, part of a larger and convoluted attempt to determine the functions of writers and symbol systems in social change. At one point I even studied the invention of the typewriter, and one of my early topics for the master's thesis was acculturation in the Yiddish theater.[7]

At that time I was not formally interested in popular culture—I am not sure I even knew the term. I tried to keep up with movies, best-selling books, and "Hit Parade" songs, but my interest was not scholarly and, besides, my own tastes were changing. I had been persuaded somehow that a successful graduate student had to be able to play tennis, which I could never master, and to appreciate chamber music, especially the Beethoven quartets, which was far easier for me and much more enjoyable. I also shifted from Hollywood movies to foreign "art" films and went to some of the Broadway plays that toured in Chicago.

If my interest in popular culture was latent, it quickly turned manifest in 1949, for two reasons. One was the appearance of an article in the February 1949 issue of *Harper's Magazine* by Russell Lynes, entitled "Highbrow, Lowbrow, Middlebrow,"a light but comprehensive survey of four "brow levels" and their cultural preferences and peccadilloes. Lynes described these levels with an implicit class terminology, although he was concurrently arguing that stratification by taste was replacing that based on wealth and education.[8] Lynes's analysis was often acute, but he was more interested in expressing his low opinion of all brow levels. However, the article crystallized a lot of disconnected thinking I had done about culture, class, and symbol systems, and I had no difficulty in jettisoning Lynes's tone and values and adapting the brow levels to Warnerian class culture.[9]

The other reason for thinking about popular culture was David Riesman's return to campus from Yale University, where he had been working on *The Lonely Crowd*. I had already corresponded with him about my plans for studying political participation for my M.A. thesis, and in the process he sent draft chapters of the book to me for comment, chapters which were filled with observations about popular culture. Dave was then, as now, one of the few professors I have ever met who treats students with intellectual respect, and once he arrived in Chicago, we engaged in frequent discussions about popular culture. Partly because he lacked time and, I think, inclination to keep up systematically with the mass media himself, he often interviewed his students about popular novels, movies, radio programs, and popular culture in general, and I learned an immense amount by keeping Dave *au courant*. His other important contribution was his insistence that studying popular culture was not only a legitimate but also a highly desirable scholarly endeavor. In those days American sociology was still close to its Germanic and American-Protestant origins, even at the University of Chicago, and popular culture was simply not a fit topic for study before Riesman returned from Yale.

One of Riesman's first graduate courses at Chicago was his seminar on popular culture. I took it in the spring of 1950, writing a paper called "The Metaphysics of Popular Culture." Of metaphysics there was nary a word, but in it I began to translate Lynes's approach into a more sociological one, developing the notion of leisure cultures and discussing how to assign people to them. I was apparently a total relativist then, for I suggested that the several cultures were functional for the creators and audiences in each and proposed the "complete equality [of cultures] from the point of view of social science research."

I also commented critically and at length about the different value judgments of some seminar members, who used the study of popular culture as a way of scorning disliked or less prestigious cultures and people. Above all I came out against an anonymous member of an unspecified elite I called the literary critic, who represented past aristocracies and the present humanities in advocating high culture and attacking popular culture. Although I observed that high culture was equivalent to the German *Kultur,* the literary critics I had in mind were writers like José Ortega y Gasset, Russell Kirk, and socialist Dwight Macdonald. I was then already bothered that some socialists were culturally as elitist as the conservatives—and later I said so in the second paper I ever published on popular culture.[10] My literary-critic figure was the autocratic expert who defended universal standards that fed particularist self-interests, resembling in some ways the high-school officials, rabbis, and student Stalinists I had encountered in earlier years.

III

The study design for my research on political participation called for a community with clearly visible boundaries, and Riesman suggested I speak with Martin Meyerson, a member of the University of Chicago's planning faculty, who was also involved, with his wife Margy, in community research related to the *Lonely Crowd* study. Meyerson told me about Park Forest, a new town south of Chicago, which proved a fine site for my thesis fieldwork. He also got me interested in urban sociology and city-planning issues. Although I still wanted to write, I had by then decided that I preferred writing as a sociologist to writing as a journalist. At that point I had neither the money nor the inclination to study for a Ph.D., however, and after I received my M.A. in June 1950 I worked first for Margy Meyerson and then for Martin, obtaining a marvelous basic education in city planning from them in the process.

By 1953 Martin Meyerson was teaching at the University of Pennsylvania, and he invited me to work on a study applying social-science ideas and analyses in planning and at the same time enroll for a Ph.D. in city planning.[11] Because of my interest in popular culture, my part of the research was a study of leisure behavior and recreation planning, which became my dissertation and in the process enabled me to keep my intellectual fingers involved in popular culture. In 1957, the summer after I finished my Ph.D. and before I took a job on the project studying the West End of Boston, I researched the popularity of American movies in Britain. This study turned into an opportunity to test empirically my ideas about popular culture and class. I discovered that British movies were then made by Oxbridge graduates mainly for the upper middle-class audience, and that the other 80 percent of the country's inhabitants, who were still working-class, went to imported American movies, which seemed virtually classless to them and in effect upheld many working-class values.[12]

In 1959, I began to develop the paper I had written for the Riesman seminar, and in the several longer versions that culminated in the 1974 book I began with a fuller historical critique in which the original literary critic was replaced by names both on the right and the left.[13] I also elaborated the idea of leisure cultures, later called taste cultures, and attempted to describe the cultural preferences and aesthetic standards shared by each culture. Moreover, I began to move from value judgments and general policy ideas to more concrete policy proposals, which I labeled subcultural programming and which essentially involved government aid to cultures that could not make it on their own in the marketplace, particularly those of the poor, folk, and ethnic and racial groups, but also high culture.

In the first longer version, written as I was studying the Levittowners and working on the first draft of *The Urban Villagers*, I drew on my fieldwork among working-class Italian-Americans to qualify my original relativism. Although I defended people's right to choose the culture they thought good, I also began to realize that being richer and better educated, upper middle-class people had a better life—and surely more cultural choice—than poor and working-class people. Consequently, I wrote diffidently that "it seems likely that the so-called 'higher' [leisure cultures] are, in the long run, more satisfying and desirable for their publics than the 'lower' ones for theirs."[14] I added emphatically, however, that the first step in readying people for the higher cultures had to be more income and education. My paper for the Riesman seminar had been apolitical, like its writer, but my stay in the West End had politicized me, first about urban renewal but then about other issues too.

By 1972, when I was writing *Popular Culture and High Culture,* I had played some minor roles in the War on Poverty, had written a good deal about poverty and antipoverty planning, and had just prepared for publication a collection of my essays about equality. As a result of the events of the 1960s and my own writing, I began to suggest that economic and political equality were far more important than culture, arguing that "a good life can be lived at all levels of taste and that overall taste level of a society is not as significant a criterion for the goodness of that society as the welfare of its members."[15] I was still being indirect and overly polite, but then as now, I think policies to reduce unemployment and poverty are absolutely essential, and until effective ones have been implemented, cultural policies are of minor importance.

Just as ideas and observations from my Boston and Levittown studies crept into the book on popular culture, themes from that work have also appeared in my other books. The literary experts whose judgments feathered their own nests I encountered again among the planners who decided that low-rent neighborhoods were harmful slums that needed to be torn down and replaced by middle-class housing, and among "poverticians" who decided that the poor suffered from a malady called the culture of poverty, which required behavioral therapies administered by other poverticians rather than jobs and income grants for the poor themselves.[16] I found another breed of the selfsame experts in my study of Levittown, for the critics who accused the Levittowners and other lower middle-class suburbanites of conformity, homogeneity, and various other alleged pathologies were blaming them for failing to support the higher taste cultures that were then exclusively urban.[17] The suburban critique also condemned the residential and other communal preferences of the lower taste cultures, once more using quasi-medical terms to legitimize the cultural attack. A somewhat later version of the same critique was employed against television entertainment, particularly violent programming, and although serious moral objections can be raised about television violence, I am not yet convinced by the now voluminous research literature that it is a significant cause of violence in the real world, even among children.[18]

Taste culture also plays a role in how people use the news media and what kind of news media and news they select as well as prefer, just as their position in American society influences the extent to which they find national news necessary or useful. I did not pursue this analysis in my book on the national news media because it was mainly a study of news organizations and because I could not find the audience data to back up my hunches. Even so, having retained my old interest in how the governed communicate with the governors, I devoted a chapter of the book to how national news organizations deal with audience feedback.[19]

The mostly indirect relationship of journalists to the news audience, and my fieldwork at the national news organizations, later made me start to think about how Americans connect themselves to their national society. That question then turned into a study of American individualism and society, on which I worked for several years until its completion in 1987 and publication in 1988. The study also tried to make explicit some populist ideas I had first begun to think about in graduate school, and to figure out whether a populist sociology is desirable and possible.[20] In my research I encountered latter-day versions of my 1950 literary critic because some current writers about individualism, for example those who charge young people with being a me-generation or diagnose them as suffering from narcissism, are offering new versions of some of the old charges of the high-culture critics.[21] These writers are unhappy with the "lower orders" for seeking the material comforts and self-realization that affluent income groups and the higher-taste cultures with which the critics are affiliated have already achieved. Once again, people are being attacked with medical terminology for not living like the critics or following their cultural prescriptions.

IV

In summary, I want to suggest which background and other factors seem to have influenced my work on popular culture and my advocacy of cultural relativism and equality. I began with two hypotheses, one relating to ethnicity and religion, the other to class, but both are limited in what they explain.

That I was born in Germany and am technically a first-generation ethnic undergoing acculturation and assimilation may help to explain why almost all my empirical work has been involved in trying to figure out what has been happening in America, and why I have done virtually no research in or about other societies. Perhaps being an immigrant encouraged my specific interest in American popular culture, but so did the sparsity and harshness of German popular culture for children, made sparser yet by my growing up under the Nazis. In fact I did not arrive in the United States with much of an old-country culture. German culture had no prescriptions or leads for being an adolescent, and there were few German or German-Jewish cultural patterns that my parents wanted me to retain. They did not always understand or like the American teenage ways I developed, but given our poverty, wartime conditions, and my shyness, I did not develop many. Further, we did not belong to an ethnic community that sought to uphold old-country ways; the small German-Jewish refugee community in Chicago interested neither my parents nor me. I think the only host society to which I ever wanted to acculturate and into which I wanted to assimilate was neither society nor host, but sociology—that is, what we still call *the discipline*. (This I think I have done, although only to the Everett Hughes–David Riesman branch of "Chicago Sociology." I continue to be a participant-observer and essayist in a discipline whose dominant research tradition is highly quantitative. Once more I am a member of a minority, albeit by choice.)

The critique of *Kultur* that was part of my earliest writing on popular culture was not a rejection of my German origins, for, as I noted earlier, the major targets of the critique were Wasps. Moreover, many of the leading figures in German high culture were themselves Jews, almost all of whom also became American immigrants.[22] Perhaps my unhappiness with autocratic authority and later with self-interested expertise was a reaction against Germany and my conventionally strict German upbringing. However, my identification of the literary critic as the enemy in my 1950 term paper may have been connected to the fact that when I was a graduate student the kind of sociological analysis in which I was most interested was being done by essayists, novelists, and scholars from literature and the humanities. They still dominated American intellectual life, saw no need for sociology, and did not want to lose their virtual monopoly on writing about America, particularly for the general reader. They also dominated the serious general magazines for which I most wanted to write. Coming from the humanities, they were expected to express feelings and judgments about society—and no one cared if these also served their own interests.

If ethnicity is a major variable in my background, religion is surely more important, for being a Jew and a Jewish refugee from Nazi Germany had to shape my ideas even if I was fortunate not to suffer personally in significant ways at the hands of the Nazis. Most of the relatives I lost in the Holocaust were old people I had never met or had met once as a small child, and by the time the full scope of the Holocaust began to be revealed, in the late 1940s, I was so American that I reacted no differently from most other American Jews at the time. My brief period of religiosity when I was about twelve years old may not have had an effect, but something kept me tied to, and in conflict with, the Jewish religious community all through my adolescence. I do not remember now what I was looking for in my rational Judaism, but perhaps it was a forerunner of my later interest in social policy and equality. For a while, and from a distance, the kibbutz may have been the manifestation of my rational religion, but I soon realized that what made me want to be a sociologist and writer would probably make me a poor *kibbutznik*. Further, I was too much of an American and too little a Zionist to want to live in Israel.

My involvement with Judaism as a religion was eventually sublimated and ended by research, for I think now that I undertook a study of the Jews of Park Forest in 1949 partly to demonstrate the obtuseness and shortsightedness of the Jewish experts who did not want to understand the Jews who moved to the suburbs, and who thought that sermons against acculturation and heavier doses of traditional Jewish education would bring back their own good old days.[23] However, the ingenious ways in which the young Jewish couples I studied in Park Forest, and later in Levittown, organized their communities *sans* experts were also fascinating to watch—and since the arguments about what was to be done were always held in public, fieldwork in the Jewish community was always far more lively than elsewhere.[24]

The roles that class and status changes and inconsistencies played in my early life and work are the most difficult to untangle. I would have to begin, of course, with my family's indirect tie to a high Sears Roebuck executive, without which there would have been no affidavit and no chance to come to America. I cannot imagine that I could have been an academic sociologist in England even if I had been pulled in the same career directions there. I suppose that coming to America without any money but with a good education, and arriving at a time when my own and my family's desire was to be upwardly mobile and pursue an American version of our past bourgeois life, evoked my interest in studying class, although I think Lloyd Warner's analyses of and anecdotes about Newburyport were also persuasive.

If my encounters with the American class and status hierarchies of the 1940s encouraged my endorsement of cultural relativism and my interest in equality, I cannot now picture the process by which that happened. Other advocates of cultural relativism and equality have been upwardly mobile, of course, but upwardly mobile people have also looked down on and oppressed poor people who were not mobile. My early interest in the kibbutz as a place where job security was guaranteed and materialism appeared to be absent may have been a response to my parents' initial occupational hardships and a just-reviving consumer culture in America that seemed strange to a European and wrong in wartime.

I do not remember feeling any kinship with, and sympathy for, the underdog in those early years, either among the poor whites of Wood-lawn who were our neighbors or among the much poorer blacks my father's employer was exploiting. Nor did the social science I learned at Chicago encourage such empathy, for it was largely apolitical and often indirectly supportive of the status quo. The realities of poverty and racial segregation really only hit home in the fall of 1957, when I began to live in the West End of Boston, met some of the poor residents of that working-class area, and saw how urban renewal would force additional West Enders into poverty or deprive them in other ways. I am still surprised, however, how unaware I remained earlier of the poor whites with whom I lived in Chicago's Woodlawn neighborhood, even as I was reading and admiring the egalitarian writings of R. H. Tawney and advocates of the kibbutz.

I imagine that my interest in equality and relativism was also a way of coming to terms with the feelings of marginality and inferiority that I experienced in high school and college and with the shyness that had already placed me on the social margins in Cologne. Surely yet other factors are relevant that a psychoanalyst can best fathom. I must add one more consideration: my two marriages have both been to women who were more emphatically and actively egalitarian than I. Since 1967 I have been married to Louise Gruner, a Legal Services lawyer who was helping poor people directly while I was lecturing and writing.[25]

Ultimately the personal needs and inclinations with which one enters a scholarly discipline are impulses that must be brought out and developed by the intellectual training one receives. Thus I must implicate and credit the people with whom I studied, especially at the universities of Chicago and Pennsylvania. The teachers (and authors) who are most responsible are mentioned by name in the text and notes of this essay, but many others are not named, some of them fellow students rather than faculty.[26] Then there are those people whom I did not even know but who helped to shape the intellectually and otherwise stimulating period from 1945 to 1950 at the University of Chicago. Surely I am also explained as a product of those particular 1940s.

Notes

1. Sears Roebuck had been built up by Julius Rosenwald, himself a German-Jewish immigrant in the nineteenth century, and the store was then still run mostly by Jews. Many years later we discovered that one of my mother's ancestors was a cousin of Rosenwald's.

2. The paper was written for an education course that some of my fellow sociology students and I took because it would make us eligible for high-school teaching later. I suspect that my interest in educational administration may have been included to impress the instructor, but I did not go back for the other required education courses. I suppose I would have liked to be a sociology professor even then, but such jobs were scarce, and I was not even in the department. I still do not understand my failure to make any practical occupational plans while in graduate school, but I do not recall any major anxiety about how I would earn a living after the M.A. However, the late 1940s were the start of the affluent society, even if it did not arrive for sociologists until much later.

3. Earl S. Johnson, *The Humanistic Teachings of Earl S. Johnson,* ed. John D. Hass (Boulder, Colo.: Westview Press, 1983). In addition, I was enrolled in an introductory graduate survey course entitled "The Scope and Methods of Social Sciences," which focused on "how the problem of a united, free, peaceful, prosperous world may be attacked by social science" ("Syllabus, The Scope and Methods of the Social Sciences," Division of the Social Sciences, University of Chicago, 1st ed. [October 1946], p. 11). My section of the course was led by Bert Hoselitz, but many other social scientists at the university lectured in the course.

4. I still remember virtually sneaking into the campus bookstore for my copy of Merton's *Social Theory and Social Structure* because the rivalry between the Columbia and Chicago sociology departments discouraged undue interest in Columbia authors.

5. During my undergraduate days I was on the staff of the college humor magazine and wrote a number of satirical pieces in which Plato and Aristotle were the villains. The only one I published reported the desertion of the university by its students after the chancellor banned bridge playing (of which I seem also to have disapproved) until researchers discovered that the game had been invented by a close friend of Aristotle; then the chancellor reversed his decision. "Hearts Were Trump When Aristotle Smiled," *Pulse Magazine,* April 1947, p. 17.

6. My interest in audience feedback mechanisms resulted in one of my first published papers, "The Creator-Audience Relationship in the Mass Media: An Analysis of Movie-Making," in *Mass Culture: The Popular Arts in America,* ed. Bernard Rosenberg and David M. White (Glencoe, Ill.: Free Press, 1957), pp. 315–24.

7. I had to drop this topic because I did not read or speak Yiddish and thus could not content-analyze the plays, but I later made and published studies of acculturation in the work of two popular American-Jewish comedians, Mickey Katz and Allan Sherman. My interest in sociological research in the Jewish

community was stimulated by a brilliant course that Erich Rosenthal, who later taught for three decades at Queens College in New York, gave at the College of Jewish Studies in 1947, using mainly novels because of the lack of sociological studies. In those days sociology was close to heresy at the college, and Rosenthal was able to give the course only once.

8. Lynes later reprinted the article as chapter 13 of *The Tastemakers* (New York: Harper, 1955).

9. In fact I did so virtually at once, in a term paper comparing the concepts of culture and *Kultur,* which I wrote in the spring of 1949 for Kurt Riezler, a visiting professor from the New School for Social Research.

10. Moreover, that paper was published in a socialist magazine and consisted largely of a critique of Harold Rosenberg, the art critic who was one of its major contributors. "Popular Culture and Its High Culture Critics," *Dissent* 5(1958): 185–87.

11. I also had an invitation from Robert K. Merton to study for my Ph.D. in sociology at Columbia University and a job offer from the Bureau of Applied Social Research, but it involved assisting Fred Ikle in a study of the evacuation of American cities in World War III. Partly because I had lived through the London blitz in 1940, it was not a subject I wanted to study.

12. I wrote a book-length monograph, which also dealt with the topics I had covered in my 1950 seminar paper, and later published an article, "Hollywood Films on British Screens: An Analysis of the Functions of Popular Culture Abroad," *Social Problems* 9 (1962): 324–28.

13. Herbert J. Gans, "The Social Structure of Popular Culture," unpublished paper, February 1959, p. 29. Later versions of the paper were "Pluralist Esthetics and Subcultural Programming: A Proposal for Cultural Democracy in the Mass Media," *Studies in Public Communication,* no. 3 (Summer 1961): 27–35; and "Popular Culture in America: Social Problem or Social Asset in a Pluralist Society," in *Social Problems: A Modern Approach,* ed. Howard S. Becker (New York: Wiley, 1966), pp. 549–620. A revised version, written for an abortive second edition of Howard Becker's text, is in *Literary Taste, Culture and Mass Communication,* ed. W. Phillips Davison, Rolf Meyersohn and Edward Shils (Teaneck, N.J.: Somerset House, 1972). An updated version of my book *Popular Culture and High Culture,* entitled "American Popular Culture and High Culture in a Changing Class Structure," appears in *Art, Ideology and Politics,* ed. Judith H. Balfe and Margaret Wyszomirski (New York: Praeger, 1985).

14. Gans, "Social Structure of Popular Culture," p. 29.

15. Gans, *Popular Culture and High Culture,* p. 130.

16. Herbert J. Gans, *The Urban Villagers,* updated and expanded ed. (New York: Free Press, 1982), pp. 283–88.

17. Here my conclusions agreed with those of the editor of this anthology. See Bennett M. Berger, *Working-Class Suburb* (Berkeley and Los Angeles: University of California Press, 1960).

18. This argument appears in my essay "The Audience for Television—and in Television Research," in *Television and Social Behavior,* ed. Stephen B. Withey and Ronald P. Abeles (Hillsdale, N.J.: Erlbaum, 1980), pp. 55–81.

19. Herbert J. Gans, *Deciding What's News: A Study of CBS Evening News, NBC Nightly News,* Newsweek, *and* Time, chap. 7 (New York: Pantheon Books, 1979).

20. The book is *Middle American Individualism: The Future of Liberal Democracy* (New York: Free Press, 1988). By the 1980s, populism had become a conservative term and for this reason and others, I went back to a concept I had learned from Martin Meyerson in the 1950s. It looks at people as users—of goods, services, ideas, policies, and the like, and I spent some pages of the book on the possibility of more user-oriented sociology.

21. One of those writers is Christopher Lasch, whose analysis I discuss in "Culture, Community, and Equality," *democracy* 2 (April 1982): 81–87.

22. Many of those immigrants were hostile to American popular culture, however, partly for class reasons but also because they felt that German popular culture had helped bring the Nazis to power and feared that the United States could become a fascist dictatorship.

23. That study also owed a considerable debt to W. Lloyd Warner and Leo Srole, *The Social Systems of American Ethnic Groups* (New York: Yale University Press, 1945). It is reported most fully in my "The Origin and Growth of a Jewish Community in the Suburbs: A Study of the Jews of Park Forest," in *The Jews: Social Patterns of an American Ethnic Group,* ed. Marshall Sklare (Glencoe, Ill.: Free Press, 1958), pp. 205–48.

24. My search for a rational religion ended more than thirty years ago, but occasionally the urge to do more empirical research in the Jewish community and to see whether the experts are still offering the same solutions has to be suppressed. For some observations of American Jewry not based on systematic research, see my "Symbolic Ethnicity: The Future of Ethnic Groups and Cultures," in *On the Making of Americans: Essays in Honor of David Riesman,* ed. Herbert J. Gans, Nathan Glazer, Joseph R. Gusfield, and Christopher Jencks (Philadelphia: University of Pennsylvania Press, 1979), pp. 193–220.

25. In 1987, my wife was elected to a judgeship in New York's Civil Court. During the latter half of the 1950s, I was married to Iris Lezak, an artist who had taken a vow of poverty.

26. Some other sociologists at the University of Chicago to whom I am indebted are two then junior professors: Reinhard Bendix, the first of my sociology teachers when I was an undergraduate, and Morris Janowitz, for whom I conducted some initial research as he was beginning his community newspaper study. I also benefited from teaching assistants and researchers associated with the Department of Sociology—and the names I now remember are Margaret Fallers, S. C. Gilfillan, Robert Johnson, and Harvey L. Smith—as well as from many professors in sociology and in other departments who are too numerous to mention.

CHAPTER TWENTY

How I Became an American Sociologist

Reinhard Bendix

. . . and how I came to write about it. There is an autobiographical side to the writing of autobiography. Sociologists, with their claim to detachment, ought to practice what they teach their students. The present essay originated in my two-year tour of duty as director of the Education Abroad Program (EAP) in Göttingen, West Germany, 1968–70. I had been teaching at the University of California, Berkeley, since 1947, and the director of the university's EAP approached me about the Göttingen position in 1967. At the time my children were eighteen, seventeen, and twelve, conditions in the Berkeley schools as well as at the university were unsettling, and the position was financially attractive: it seemed a welcome change of pace in my academic career.

My wife and I found ourselves in the role of surrogate parents to a good portion of the eighty or so students who attended the Göttingen program in each of the two years. Having to manage in a foreign language in the classroom and a new environment and being away from their real parents, often for the first time, many of these juniors welcomed a bit of parenting when it was done unobtrusively. They knew we were there and willing to help when they needed us. In each of the two years I organized an orientation meeting with all the students soon after their arrival, but on both occasions I used the opportunity to speak a bit about myself. I thought they had a right to know that I had been born and raised in Berlin, had emigrated to the United States because of the Nazi regime when I was twenty-two, in 1938, and had had my university education at the University of Chicago. My purpose was not only to show that I was open about myself and personally accessible. It was also to announce that I would organize a retreat during the year at which we would talk about the country in which they were about to spend their junior year. As it worked out, both retreats were attended by more than half the students (it was voluntary, of course, and free of charge). The program consisted of three speakers, a film on the Nazi period, and plenty of time for informal talk and recreation. At both retreats the Göttingen historian Rudolf von Thadden talked about German history, the Mannheim sociologist Rainer Lepsius talked about German society, and I elaborated on my personal experience not only in Germany but also as an emigrant to the United States. The three of us had the idea of putting out a small volume incorporating an expanded version of those talks. Nothing came of the plan, but in the course of our correspondence I began to put together an early version of this essay.

It did not stop there. Some two years later my two sons let me know that they wished I would tell them what had happened to me, particularly in the 1930s. Then, after our return to Berkeley, a student in an honors seminar said, "You know, we really don't know anything about you." She seemed to speak not only for herself. Years earlier I had often encouraged students to ask members of the faculty for their intellectual autobiography, and I had volunteered to meet with them for that purpose. Along the way I published a short "Memoir of My Father," which drew a heartening personal response from a number of colleagues whose judgment I valued. Eventually I wrote a full-scale biography of my father and an autobiographical sketch of my relations with him; both include intellectual portraits, such as I had written earlier about my teacher Louis Wirth and the sociological work of Max Weber. Intellectual biography has been one of my recurrent interests.

The reasons for that interest are rooted in my experience. My father, who had been a lawyer in Berlin until 1933, had written extensively about the personal side of judicial decision making, and he had influenced me in my early years. My own work had been shaped by my German background and emigration to the United States. In my relations with American students I had found that their best work depended on becoming absorbed in what they were doing. The first problem of teaching was somehow to make them feel that their particular subject really mattered to them. To acknowledge the "value relevance" of academic work actually helps to authenticate it and make it persuasive. The reflexive subjectivity of scholarly work has become a token of its objectivity in the eyes of many observers. But I have lingered over the preliminaries.

It is already more than fifty years since Hitler came to power in Germany. At the time I was seventeen. It always takes a little effort for me to realize that events of half a century ago mean nothing to the many students I have taught in the United States since 1943. My first students had been about eight years old when events occurred that had marked my life ten years earlier and have influenced my thinking ever since. That "recent" history of 1943 has now become "ancient" history for my students, though not for me.

My father was born in 1877 in a little village near Dortmund, part of the Ruhr district in Westphalia. His father had been the young Hebrew teacher of the Jewish children in that village. Earlier, Gumpert Bendix married my grandmother, who had had five children by a previous marriage; my father and his two sisters resulted from the new marriage. Soon the Hebrew teacher became an insurance agent to support his growing family, and in 1892 they moved to Berlin, then the capital of Imperial Germany. In the process my grandfather changed his Jewish name to Gustav, though he continued as an observant Jew and gave his children a Jewish education. In the case of my father that education did not have the desired effect. He was fifteen in 1892, and in the following years he came under the cosmopolitan influence of Berlin, which contrasted sharply with the village environment of his youth. He was especially attracted by the assimilated culture of many Berlin Jews. His main teacher in the Gymnasium (high school), though born of Jewish parents, had been baptized as a child, and his two best friends at school were Protestant, one of them the son of a Protestant minister. In the year my father graduated from the Gymnasium his mother died, and he wrote my grandfather that he would discontinue Jewish observances from then on. With his two school friends he began his university studies. Eventually he opened a law office in Berlin in 1907. Three years later he married my mother, who came from a middle-class Jewish family in Hamburg, had had a successful career as an actress, and seems to have been as detached from the Jewish tradition as my father wanted to be.

Later I came to see the large difference in outlook and temperament that bound my parents together but also divided them. After marriage my mother devoted all her artistic sensibility to raising my sister (born in 1913) and myself (born in 1916) and creating a beautiful home. Only my father put a limit on her efforts. From the beginning of his career, in addition to his law practice he devoted substantial time to the publication of legal writings. Personal inclination and this intellectual preoccupation made him easy-going and careless in his personal habits, a neverending source of irritation to my mother. However my parents coped with this difference, it made me side with my father when I became old enough to take an interest. What age is old enough? My father thought fifteen, and in 1931 he told me to start reading serious books. He was very nearsighted and liked to have books read to him. The first book he chose for me was Karl Mannheim's *Ideology and Utopia*. We did not make much progress, as I recall, but he had the patience to explain to me all those strange words. He was my university for some two years. Then Hitler changed our lives.

The Weimar Republic had a stormy history, which did not leave us children untouched. At thirteen I had had to ask my father which religious instruction I should take: the Weimar compromise among contending religions was to offer Protestant, Catholic, and Jewish instruction in the schools. He suggested that I try all three in succession, with the result that I remained uneducated in all three and acquired a youthful religious indifference. Some other influences were more positive. Discussions at the dinner table frequently concerned the political events of the day but also more theoretical questions since my father was an anti-Marxist Social Democrat who liked to challenge whatever abstract notions we picked up at school or from our peers. Even when we were unable to answer his questions (what is class? what do you mean by socialism?), they still helped to sensitize us toward the exploration of ideas; the political agitation of those years did so as well. After a quiet and sheltered youth, adolescence propelled me into social and political concerns, in part because the general agitation reached down into the high schools and in part because my father's preoccupations led me to imitate and challenge him. He was a militant humanitarian in his legal work, which to me meant instant identification with the weak and the afflicted. I understood from his psychological analysis of judicial decision making that ideas were important, as was the individual—an early form of the linkage that has led to these reflections.

Political agitation together with the importance of ideas led me straightaway to the study of Marxism. It seemed urgent to clarify theoretical questions because right action could follow only if the right answers were found. Some such notion was the kind of sediment that filtered down to us from the long tradition of theoretical Marxism cultivated by the Social Democratic party. This early intellectual excitation is also responsible for my lifelong interest in ideas. Given my secular upbringing, I had at most an indirect connection with Jewish traditions through the early experiences of my father, about which I knew nothing. That theoretical concern with Marxism had nothing to do with the labor movement I discovered rather quickly when for a short time I joined the Socialist Labor Youth (Sozialistische Arbeiterjugend) in 1932 and found myself out of place among my peers from working-class families.

Hitler's rise to power in 1933 changed this dabbling in theory and radicalism. In that year my father was disbarred by the Berlin Bar Association and arrested for the first time; I was dismissed by the Gymnasium for refusing to salute Hitler; former friends withdrew, and former clients tried to blackmail my father to get his fees back. Within three or four months the family was faced with the collapse of its accustomed way of life. The trauma of that experience was a major formative influence on me.

A mere enumeration of those formative experiences will have to do. I joined an illegal organization, Neu Beginnen, in which we tried to cope intellectually and politically with the phenomenon of fascism; hence my first political experience was in the underground. In 1934, out of school and with nothing to do, I pestered my father enough after his release from prison to find me an apprenticeship on an English farm, where I wanted to prove to myself that Jews could work with their hands, that Nazi propaganda about Jews as conniving bloodsuckers of honest working folk was a lie. If I had not been so ignorant about Jews or so unsure of myself, I might never have found out that I could do manual work, that I was not as inept as my father and yet not cut out to be a farmer. On returning to Germany because my father wanted to remain as a legal consultant (Nazis or no Nazis he was German, and members of minorities, he said, did not leave just because they were discriminated against) I worked for several years in a Jewish firm that exported textiles. My father was arrested again in 1935. During the next two years I studied on my own at night, reading philosophy and psychology, an isolated personal defense against the ever-more-threatening Nazi world around me. A full-time job; help around the house and, in his absence, with my father's dwindling affairs; study at night; and, also important, joining a Zionist youth group (Hashomer Hatzair) to find out for myself about Jews and Zionism, from which my parents had sheltered me carefully in the preceding years—after two years of this hectic life I was a nervous wreck at twenty-one. In 1937 we managed to get my father released from Dachau on the condition that my parents emigrate to a non-European country within two weeks. They went to Palestine because that was the only place to which we could get entry visas for them. In

1938 I emigrated to America, and a year later my sister followed. My father's long-distance contacts with former associates on our behalf were successful. All the relatives we left behind in Germany perished.

My parents were not Zionists and did not urge us to follow them to Palestine. Nevertheless, I might have gone there to assist them. But I had not become a Zionist either, and when friends of my father's obtained not only the needed affidavit for a United States visa but also a scholarship to the University of Chicago, no further decision was required. My father had induced academic interests in me strong enough that my nights were spent struggling with the writings of Kant, Marx, and Freud, so the opportunity to study free of other worries made emigration to America almost a foregone conclusion. Had I gone to Israel, I would have had no comparable opportunity and motivation.

Thus far I have said nothing about my childhood and adolescence, with the one exception of seeking some balance between the opposing tendencies of my parents. The trauma of the Hitler regime nearly obliterated my memory. I can recall many physical details of my childhood. My mother fussed over us and made us feel loved, and I have strong recollections about a little vacation home outside Berlin where we spent many summers. Of the class pictures I still have I can remember all the faces, but among some forty boys only a few names. I have not met a classmate of my youth since 1933. I enjoyed sports, especially track, and was fairly good at it. The friends I had at school (in the German system one stayed with the same group of students throughout Gymnasium) were not so close that I remember them as persons, but I was popular enough to be elected class representative. The only other thing worth mentioning is one basic fact. As a boy I had been rambunctious, but in adolescence I became very shy, especially with girls. As I grew up, romantic imaginings and sexual fantasies were strong in me, but self-doubt was stronger. My father was a physically impressive man, over six feet tall and heavyset with strong wrists and large, thick fingers. In comparison to him I was, and felt, puny. That feeling was reinforced by my tall sister, who was two-and-a-half years older; I remember quarrelling with her a lot. My self-doubt was physical: in my room I had a square coal stove made of tiles, and since I had no idea how broad my shoulders were, I remember leaning against that stove one summer day to measure myself, though that did not really help. My strong intellectual bent at a precocious age had much to do with trying to stand well in my father's eyes just because I could not match him physically, though he would have been the last person to notice that his stature by itself had a psychological effect on me. Eventually, though, I acquired a reputation in my family as the diplomat, which probably reflected my efforts to get around the poor self-image I had developed. It also had to do with my reactions against the exaggerated domesticity of my mother and the physical clumsiness of my father. I suspect my reluctance to take extreme positions was acquired at an early age.

I entered the University of Chicago as an aging freshman of twenty-two. Though the intimate intellectual contact with my father had lasted only two years, he had set my interests in motion. Probably his failing career, his imprisonment, and the family's misfortune even increased the importance intellectual pursuits acquired for me when I was working in Berlin and struggling to keep myself together emotionally in a rapidly deteriorating situation. Some account of these early autodidactic efforts seems necessary because I had become an academic before I became a freshman.

When my father was twenty, he not only discontinued Jewish observances but also made a formal declaration of his beliefs. That statement had been solicited by his principal teacher in the Gymnasium: in it my father declared his strong interest in critical self-examination and his belief in the personal values of people in all walks of life. These notions were a legacy of the German ideal of self-cultivation (*Bildung*) such that each individual might bring to fruition all the capacities within him or her. Unlike others, my father did not take a detached or ironic view of this ideal. His liberalism was bound up with a basic respect for, and interest in, the other person, whatever his or her station in life. Eventually this outlook had a major influence on his writings, in which he analyzed in ever-new ways how the formalities of the law and the personal disposition of the judges led to inadvertent abuses of the legal system to the detriment of the people coming before the courts. This approach was indebted to Marx's emphasis on the role power plays in every legal system and Nietzsche's emphasis on knowledge as a means to exert power rather than seek truth. Hence the reasons given for any action, including judicial decisions and the search for knowledge, tended to be rationalizations and needed to be uncovered as such. I suppose that this message got through to me even at fifteen or sixteen, though I was too young to take in the deep pessimism of the approach. What struck me more forcefully was my father's positive concern for the individual. After all, uncovering the truth behind every deception, including one's self-deceptions, was a passionate effort to give each his or her due and thus achieve truth and justice.

As a lawyer my father could use his analytical skills for the benefit of his clients, but that way was not open to me. I was not a lawyer, and conditions in Germany militated against an interest in law. Instead I sought peace of mind by means of study after my father was imprisoned for a second time. The kinds of questions that came to concern me in this private pursuit show some impatience with my father's ideas, however much I was influenced by them. His emphasis on human irrationality operated with a commonsense psychology that was probably sufficient for his purposes. But some reading of Freud revealed to me that simple words like *envy, hatred,* or *malice* were commonsense expressions that, like the phrase *irrational forces,* did not clarify matters. Further, in the society around me larger forces seemed to be at work under Hitler than could be comprehended by an analysis geared to legal disputes or psychotherapy. Such reflections brought me back to Marx and Mannheim and my father's skepticism toward the conditioning of ideas by class interest. That skepticism had made me cautious in ways he probably did not foresee. I wanted to understand what was meant by ideas or prejudices before I attempted to relate them to a person's position in society. Paradoxical as it may seem today, that is how I came to study for a year or so Kant's *Critique of Pure Reason,* by which I thought I could learn about ideas. I had no background for this task, and the lonely struggle with Kant's abstractions isolated me even more since contact with others obviously distracted me from what at the time seemed so important. After a while a philosopher gave a course on the book in classes arranged by the Judische Kulturbund in Berlin, and I discovered how little I had understood—a discouraging experience but oddly liberating as well. Gradually I had grown dissatisfied with mere categories of thought when I had set out to learn about interests and passions—the drives that presumably linked such terms as *group interest* and *social class* to the formulation of ideas.

My next step was to get at the connections between ideas and interests or emotional drives. That objective pointed toward readings in social psychology. I remember reading Charlotte Buhler's work on the life cycle and studies by a number of her students who examined the careers of people in different life situations. In that context I also discovered the work of Karl Buhler on the theory of language. The structure of language seemed especially important because language was a medium through which the conditions of life could have a formative influence on the individual. For the same reason I read books on child psychology as well as John Dewey's *Human Nature and Conduct.* This was my first

English book in philosophical social psychology, a field entirely new to me, but also a testing ground for my growing command of English. My readings gradually led me to the study of what is now called socialization. (Since World War II that word has become the German *Sozialisation*, which did not exist in the 1930s.) I can still remember the relief with which I turned from philosophical abstractions to these more empirical studies.

Today the atmosphere of my life in Berlin from 1933 to 1938 seems very remote. Poor memory and orderly exposition foreshorten the twists and turns of that experience. My preoccupations of that time owed a great deal to the cultured middle-class setting in which I had grown up, to the charged atmosphere of Weimar politics, and to my father's work, which led to the stimulation of ideas at an early age. I could not say, as my father did, that mere theory left me cold. After all, he built on his experience with specific disputes his critique of judicial decision making; in that way he satisfied himself that he contributed to the reconstruction of society. By contrast, I derived the impetus for learning from the Marxist belief that an accurate understanding of social forces would help bring about desired changes—one factor among many, and not the most important, but a factor nonetheless. By the 1930s little moral fervor was left in the Marxist tradition. As I watched my father, though, it was easy to see that ideas and passions were closely linked. But whereas his passion for justice imparted moral fervor to ideas, I tended to derive that fervor from the power attributed to ideas when access to ideas is the only thing left available. I knew that a gulf divided what was happening in the streets of Berlin (some of them only a few blocks from where I lived) and my struggles with ideas in my self-imposed studies. Hence my eager participation in Neu Beginnen, where we analyzed the prehistory and structure of fascism. Isolated as these illegal discussions were, I was left with the belief that a correct analysis of fascism could somehow be instrumental in defeating that political monster. For the time being I believed it because I wanted to believe it. But by then I had acquired the lasting interest in ideas with which I arrived in 1938 at the University of Chicago.

I turn now to my efforts at coping in 1939 and 1940 with the intellectual challenges in the Department of Sociology at Chicago. It did not take me long to find out that two schools of thought were in contention. One position was represented by Robert Park, a former student of Georg Simmel who early on had had a career as an investigative reporter. Beyond the Atlantic Simmel's sociology had become under

Park's leadership an empirical investigation of life histories, occupations and ways of life, and ethnic or residential neighborhoods. Titles like *The School Teacher, The Ghetto,* and *The Gold-Coast and the Slums* gave an impression of that literature. When I arrived in 1938, those interests of the 1920s were already abating. A second position was becoming dominant, consisting of demography and the study of public opinion with a heavy emphasis on research methods. Spokesmen claimed their respective positions to be scientific, but there was little agreement between them. The study of attitudes appeared to the first group as removed from experience with "real life" and hence of little sociological interest. Life histories and studies of subcultures appeared to the second group as sociological impressionism lacking in methodological rigor. This contrast points to the heart of the matter, though there were many qualifications in both camps.

The atmosphere created by this argument influenced me. Every investigation should follow the positivist program at least to some extent. What do I want to know? What kind of evidence is suitable to prove a point? How can it be assembled? Are there good reasons for assuming that certain facts can either prove or disprove the original contention? One will not find answers if one does not specify what one wants to know. In that way I felt receptive toward a positivist approach, unfamiliar as it was to me and contrary to the scholarly inclinations of my father. But my attitude was also influenced by contemporary political events. I am reporting on my first academic experience from 1938 to 1941. All my American teachers insisted on the strict separation between scholarship and partisanship. Their approach was bound to impress me, who had seen so much partisanship in the preceding years under the Nazis. To achieve dispassion and nonpartisanship meant a great deal to me, and so did the demand for reliable proof. After all, I had just come from a country in which racism had been broadcast with all the pretense of science and none of the substance.

Although answers are impossible as long as questions are unclear—a basic positivist claim I accepted—one had to know something of substance before one could pose clear and *interesting* questions. I was not convinced that the positivist approach gave attention to the preliminary inquiries that must precede questions that are worth asking, and I resisted the idea that such inquiries are not a part of science. Yet the positivists among my teachers restricted the realm of science to the logic of proof. By neglecting the "logic of discovery," which was not very logical really and could not be taught easily, they seemed to support the view that unproved, and ultimately unprovable, assertions had no place in science. That conclusion did not make sense if a science without presuppositions was a utopian idea. During my first years of study at Chicago I often heard social scientists mocked as people who knew more and more about less and less—a saying that had its reason in the emphasis on method at the expense of substance. It seemed to me at the time that the logic of discovery had to be brought into some appropriate relation to the logic of proof. In struggling with this question, I became preoccupied with the ideal of science as a problem in its own right.

Naturally students were affected by the arguments among the faculty, and I was no exception. Although we had to be familiar with both kinds of sociological study—the methodological and the contextual—we typically opted for one or the other in our dissertations. Yet what had this whole controversy to do with the main experience of my life? My family had been almost destroyed. I had been uprooted from the society into which I was born and wanted to understand the reasons for the German catastrophe that had led to our personal disaster. How could I make this large, amorphous concern researchable in the framework of American sociology as offered at the University of Chicago?

Eventually I was allowed to go ahead with a study of German sociology, even though it was hardly researchable in the terms then in vogue at Chicago. This decision speaks for the broadmindedness of my mentors, especially Louis Wirth, who sympathized with my moral and political concerns, as of course did others. But how was I to adhere to the requirements of empirical proof when my question was how to come to terms intellectually (and no doubt emotionally) with the reasons for the German catastrophe? The demand for rigor had to be balanced somehow against the interest in what is worth knowing and with what degree of accuracy. In the end I decided on a master's thesis that would examine historically this very question, namely, the social and scientific standing of a social science. What were the conditions under which scholars were permitted or encouraged to apply standards of scholarly investigation to the society that supported them to investigate it? I chose German sociology because that topic would also allow me to continue my inquiries into the German problem.

The title of my master's thesis was "The Rise and Acceptance of German Sociology" (1943); it was never published, so a brief description is in order. As an academic discipline sociology was older in the United States than in Germany. At the University of Chicago the department dated back to 1892, and the *American Journal of Sociology* was first published in 1895. By contrast, the first chairs of sociology at German universities were established in 1919. In America the field had developed out of a private and religious concern with social welfare. Many early American sociologists had begun their studies in theology and had subsequently turned to sociology as a properly academic approach to welfare. German sociology, however, had developed from the preoccupation of civil servants with welfare policies; a modern social-security system was developed in the 1880s under Bismarck. In this German tradition the monarch was responsible for the welfare of the population, hence the study of welfare measures was closely related to public administration and law. Accordingly, when German sociology was accepted academically, it was heavily influenced by ideas about the relation of state and society. The term *sociology* was used long before the discipline received academic recognition. Men like Ferdinand Tönnies, Max Weber, and Georg Simmel, who today are regarded as founders of the discipline, published much of their work before sociology was taught at the universities.

Actually I never got to the topic I had meant to study because documentation on the acceptance of sociology as an academic discipline was only available in German archives and inaccessible in wartime. But it is also true that I became preoccupied with the preliminaries of my inquiry. How had the study of society become a focus of academic interest in Germany? There had to be some agreement that sociology represented a legitimate field of research, and such agreement seemed to exist. In Wilhelmine Germany government officials, ministers of the church, and professors of law and political science (*Staatswissenschaft*) had made many detailed studies that were continued during the Weimar Republic. The publications of the Association for Social Policy (Verein für Sozialpolitik) testify to this public concern with social problems: some 180 volumes of research studies were published before the association was dissolved by the Nazis in 1933. The fact that much of the initiative for these studies originated with the government probably contributed to the controversy over sociology as an academic discipline. Why was it needed when studies of society were under way already? What was its academic rationale apart from the study of law and government? Conservatives suspected that under the guise of a newfangled discipline advocates of sociology wanted to introduce socialist ideas into the university curriculum. Thus arguments over the academic recognition of sociology turned into political arguments.

The very word *society,* or *gesellschaft,* was more controversial in Ger-

many than in the United States. The German word is not simply synony-
mous with an aggregate of social groups, as *society* tends to be in English.
Gesellschaft is often used to describe the grasping selfishness of the marketplace and the social isolation of the individual in a large city. By
contrast, the word *Staat* connotes not only government and authority but
also the moral values attributed to those in positions of public responsibility. The invidious contrast between a moral state and an immoral society
had many ramifications, which became the main theme of my master's
thesis. In any case, many prominent German scholars doubted that society could be studied dispassionately when the word itself could not be
used without arousing moral indignation. Implicitly I compared this approach with the American acceptance of sociology. The whole topic was
already far from my earlier interest in socialization.

In working on my thesis I learned a good bit of German intellectual
history, but I became increasingly unhappy with my own bookishness.
The United States joined the European war in December 1941, when I
was beginning my graduate work at Chicago. To retain a valid passport,
I had to submit it to the German embassy that had extended it, but only
after affixing a big red *J* for *Jew* in accordance with latest Nazi regulations. I remained a German citizen as long as my application for American citizenship was pending; hence I was also required by law to register
as an enemy alien after the United States entered the war against Germany. As a citizen I was in transit, stigmatized in one country and
distrusted in another.

My feelings were ambivalent in a different sense. While others went
to war against Germany or Japan, I sat on the sidelines, made thoroughly restless by my nonparticipation. I wanted to fight against Hitler.
Then in 1943 I was naturalized at the same time as I got my master's
degree in sociology. My exclusion from the draft ended, but I found
myself rejected on grounds of health. When it was clear that I would not
be drafted, I was offered an instructorship in the College at the University of Chicago, and I began work on my Ph.D. degree. It was back to
the books after all. My academic career in the United States was beginning in earnest now that I participated as a teacher of undergraduates in
the social-sciences survey course, which I had taken as a student only a
few years before.

However, the problem remained how I could make questions posed
by the contrast between Germany and the United States researchable in
the Chicago sense. I had escaped from the Holocaust, but millions of
others had perished—victims not only of personal tyranny but also of a

system organized for destruction. Perhaps if I examined that aspect of the German catastrophe, I would come closer to an understanding of its causes. Hundreds of thousands had done the bidding of one man's commands, millions had followed suit, and in the process they had created a bastion of barbarism in the center of Europe. In this setting, why had government officials become willing tools in the destruction of civilization? In the Germany I had known, especially through my father, officials had made a public display of their impartiality and legal rectitude. Yet under Hitler they had gone beyond mere compliance in their eagerness to follow the dictates of a criminal regime. By contrast, American civil servants at the federal level made few claims and were accorded little public recognition. But despite the tradition of the spoils system and the many loopholes of the civil service, those officials appeared on the whole to act responsibly under the law.

Again, the contrast was too diffuse to fit within the empirical framework required for a Ph.D. dissertation. Therefore I attempted to meet the demand for empirical verification at least halfway while still adhering to my own inclination to see the problem of bureaucracy in a larger context. By *larger context* I mean that exploratory effort that is somewhat like throwing a pebble into a pool of water to set ripples radiating out in all directions from the point of impact.

My intention in the dissertation, which was published several years later under the title *Higher Civil Servants in American Society* (1949), was to focus entirely on an American problem. But once more my initial impulse came from my continuing concern with Germany. In a study published in 1915, I found that more than 50 percent of Prussia's higher civil servants were themselves the sons of officials. As they grew up, unquestioning submission to higher commands must have been identified with the ideal of legality. If half of Prussia's officials had originated in families of civil servants, then such a milieu probably had a massive effect on the conduct of affairs. My father's lifelong experience with German officials and their subversion of the Weimar Republic helped to sustain these inferences.

The German example seemed to me to justify an inquiry into the social origins and careers of a sample of higher civil servants in America. Those officials were indeed distinct from their German counterparts. They came from all strata of the society except the lowest; few were children of civil servants. They had a wide range of educational experience in contrast with the emphasis on legal training in Germany. American federal administrators had often changed from private to public employment and back again. Moreover, within the civil service many of them had changed jobs from one agency to another rather than advancing through the ranks within the same agency. These external indicators showed marked occupational mobility and to that extent considerable independence within the hierarchy of government. In my oral dissertation defense my Chicago professors grilled me hard on the facts I had ascertained. They paid no attention to the more discursive, exploratory parts of my dissertation. By modern standards the study was not methodologically sophisticated. But I remember my caution concerning the inferences that could be drawn from the statistics I had gathered as well as my argument that more detailed and comprehensive data might not be worthwhile.

I had supplemented the data on civil-service careers by a broader discussion of administrative behavior. Two inferences emerged from that discussion. First, higher civil servants represented a highly educated group with professional degrees in some field. That information, supplemented by job histories and interviews, suggested that many of them did not consider their public service a lifetime commitment. By alternating between public and private employment and maintaining their professional interests, they showed a degree of independence, which could possibly be a foundation for noncompliance if necessary. With their experience in the private sector they had the possibility of an alternative career, which German civil servants typically did not have. Further, their professional commitment frequently led them to judge government work in terms of the competence with which it was performed and not only in terms of its legal attributes, as their German colleagues tended to do.

The second inference concerned the attitudes of American administrators toward the public. Testimony before congressional committees showed that in their view a government agency served the public directly and hence was entitled to inquire into what the people desired. Those administrators considered themselves part of the people they served rather than bearers of a higher status and authority. This interpretation of government agencies as representative institutions was strongly contested by congressmen who claimed the representative role for themselves as elected, rather than appointed, officials. Those were my observations on the bureaucratic culture pattern in the United States. They seemed to me at least as worthy of attention as the statistical data that could be gathered on career patterns. However uneasily the two parts of the dissertation held together, they reflected my adaptation to American thought as well as my continued preoccupation with German affairs.

Many American sociologists did not seem to be concerned with the intellectual implications of their own scientific, or rather scientistic, bent, although my teacher, Louis Wirth, used to say that any fact, no matter how firmly established on methodological ground, was controversial from someone's point of view. This saying may resemble the Marxist contention that in a class society everybody is partisan. But that was not Wirth's meaning. He wanted to characterize the disputed position of the social sciences. For my part I could not understand how someone could claim to be scientific and partisan at the same time. Yet the truth claims of classical Marxism were of just that kind: history is *only* a history of class struggles, and hence truth can only be a by-product of class interest. Wirth maintained instead that the social origin of a statement tells us nothing about its validity. In his course on the sociology of intellectual life he expounded the view that facts are established (or statements agreed on) by means of scholarly criteria that distinguish true from false statements. That is a logically circular statement: truth becomes the by-product of criteria worked out among scholars. But the circularity of a truth defined by the truth-confirming criteria of scholars is not self-defeating, for among themselves scholars rely on an ever-provisional process of truth finding, which is under constant scrutiny and can be corrected and improved. The fact is that scholars form groups of their own, dedicated to maintaining the impartiality of their work. That point, made by Karl Popper, does not fit in with Marxism, which regards all intellectuals as unwitting or conscious spokesmen of the classes arising from the organization of production, including the working class (whose truth, of course, is in the interests of all).

What were the intellectual antecedents of this controversy over the scientific status of sociological and historical inquiry? I had begun my serious reading in sociology with Karl Mannheim's book and was excited when I found the same ideas taken up in the seminal work of Hans Barth, *Wahrheit und Ideologie* (1945). (The book was published in an English translation, as *Truth and Ideology,* by the University of California Press in 1976.) Basing my arguments on Barth's work, I published an essay in 1951, *Social Science and the Distrust of Reason,* which became the first step of my subsequent contributions to American sociology. I found the other basis for these contributions in the work of Max Weber. The link between my 1951 essay and my subsequent work on Weber a. d comparative historical sociology is far from obvious, so this relation of ideas is worth spelling out as a basic aspect of my intellectual autobiography. Both Mannheim and Hans Barth refer to the fact that the development of modern science had been accompanied from its beginning by the analysis of error. Scholars make mistakes unwittingly and become entrapped in false judgments of their own devising. Further, both referred to Francis Bacon's typology of idols.

In *Novum Organum* (1625) Bacon pointed out that men are easily misled by wishful thinking, the influences of their education, the distortions arising from their use of words, and changing fashion in systems of thought. He called these four sources of error idols of the mind. This typology of error was to free science from the religious obscurantism of theologians. Bacon believed that God had endowed man with a mind capable of investigating nature. In the name of true faith he wrote against men of little faith, pleading for support from men of affairs.

A century and a half later science no longer needed a propagandist like Bacon; it had had its Sir Isaac Newton, who died in 1727. The great French *Encyclopédie* (twenty-eight volumes of text and illustrations in some editions) had been launched in 1751 to summarize and disseminate all human knowledge. But some obstacles to human advance remained, the church and its control over education foremost among them. Some French philosophers sought to emancipate education from the baleful influence of the church by developing a science of ideas, or *ideology*. They resolutely based their efforts on a physiological theory of perception that would enable them to remove prejudices from the human mind. Since Bacon's day the scene had shifted; not human error, but institutions interested in error, stood in the way of truth and reform.

By the middle of the nineteenth century the scene had shifted again. The advance of science aided by technology seemed to promise an era of plenty for all. Yet poverty prevailed among the many, while riches accumulated in the hands of the few. Neither the advance of science nor the struggle against institutional prejudice had been enough to put an end to the class struggles perpetuated by ideologies, which unwittingly served the interests of the ruling class. Those interests remained as the principal obstacles to human advance. In Marx's view only a revolution by the working classes of the world could destroy, once and for all, this last barrier against a society of plenty. Only then would truth prevail because ideologies would no longer be needed to help suppress the many in the interests of the few.

Nor did Marx have the last word. Nietzsche claimed that the whole quest for knowledge was an illusion pursued by men who needed it in their struggle for survival. In turn, Freud had examined the search for knowledge in terms of the unconscious drives sublimated by it, though he hoped for therapeutic effects from the often painful uncovering of those drives. *Social Science and the Distrust of Reason* traced these changing concerns with the sources of error from Bacon to Freud. It seemed that in this field the development of thought had consisted to a considerable extent in an increased understanding of human fallibility. And as new and more deep-seated sources of error were discovered, from Bacon's idols of the mind through prejudices and class interests to the struggle for survival and the hidden drives of the libido, the remedies needed to correct or prevent error became ever more drastic, from persuasion and educational reform to revolution and psychotherapy.

What can efforts to correct error and control bias accomplish in the face of this record? We can only believe, we cannot prove, that further reflections as well as improvements in methods can correct errors and bring the desired reduction of bias. This seems a reasonable faith to me because no one knows what cannot be known; but it remains an act of faith. At the time I pursued these questions, my concern with faith as the basis of a belief in reason and with the hazards of communication was not only theoretical. I well remembered the public burning of books the Nazis had staged at the beginning of their regime. In addition my father's books had been confiscated by the police after he had been ousted by the bar association and singled out as a recalcitrant opponent of the regime. In 1949, in an ironic twist of fortune, my own first book encountered a similar fate; *Higher Civil Servants in American Society* had been published by the University of Colorado Press that July. Perhaps a year after publication some inquiries made me aware that the book was already out of print. That seemed odd, and I asked some friends to inquire. They were told space had been needed for the secretaries to have their afternoon coffee. The press had written to some fifty authors on their list, offering them their own books for discount purchase; but only a few had replied, and subsequently the books had been burned. I had not been among those notified, and my book, which had just been published, had been destroyed along with the rest. The episode was a vivid reminder that books and communication are perishable, by negligence or inadvertence as well as by a policy of destruction. (The book was republished twenty-five years later by the Greenwood Press.)

Accordingly, the control of bias and of the hazards to which books and communication are exposed have a larger context, both past and present. Though I might be unable to cope with the social and political hazards, I had control over my own scholarly work. My conclusion was that along with the refinement of methods there should be (and I should practice) tolerance for more intuitive approaches to knowledge, which would fall short on verification but might more simply show the assets of experienced judgment. Perhaps there is such a thing as too much methodological concern with bias. "Any performance," Kenneth Burke wrote in 1936, "is discussable either from the standpoint of what it *attains* or what it *misses*. Comprehensiveness can be discussed as superficiality, intensiveness as stricture, tolerance as uncertainty—and the poor *pedestrian* abilities of a fish are clearly explainable in terms of his excellence as a *swimmer*. A way of seeing is also a way of not seeing" (*Permanence and Change* [New York: New Republic Press, 1936], p. 70). If we refuse all trust in a capacity for judgment, then we unwittingly undermine the basis of communication among scholars, which ultimately rests on an assumption of good will as well as on reasoning and demonstration. We make this assumption in the use of language itself. For science, like language, cannot prosper where we have grounds to believe that the other person is systematically engaged in the destruction of meaningful communication.

All this does not seem to have anything to do with political sociology and Max Weber, the two foci of my work since the late 1940s. But there is a close relation, and I would like to spell it out at this point, where the question of how I became an American sociologist verges on the question of what kinds of impulses I may have imparted to American sociology.

Trust in reasoned judgment as the shared value of communication and the pursuit of knowledge is the starting point to keep in mind. That trust is presupposed by any more specific purpose for which we seek knowledge. Without such trust institutions of learning are not viable. If that trust is unwarranted, then language, learning, and knowledge become impossible. In all of his work Weber was concerned with the chances of individualism and rational choice in a world (of power struggles, bureaucratic organizations, and capitalist enterprises) that militates against these chances. But as I look back, I am most impressed by his anti-utopian approach. It is best not to put a party label on this way of looking at the modern world and instead think of Weber's work in more abstract terms. Not the least of the many Weberian paradoxes seems to be that by his whole manner Weber resembled the Puritan divines or even the Old Testament prophets, who were surely utopians, whereas his work tends in an anti-utopian direction. I want to formulate this "message" of Weber's work as I came to perceive it in working my way through his writings.

The personal sense of one's own action is a force in society however it may be caused. Social scientists who neglect this part of the evidence abandon the legacies of the Enlightenment, as do those followers of Marx and Freud who fail to distinguish between caused and unavoidable behavior. Contemporary evidence as well as considerations of intellectual strategy support the old-fashioned view that studies of social determinants must not neglect individual differences. The numerous and often unknown dissenters in fascist Germany who defied that regime were such individualists. When writers and scientists in the Soviet Union prove themselves capable of challenging not only supreme power but also the apparent consensus of the entire population, it seems wrongheaded that some theorists in the West make social forces appear overwhelming. It seems just as wrongheaded for men and women of ideas to minimize the individual's capacity for innovation when a full acceptance of that view would destroy the importance these same men and women attribute to science. I could not be content with these contradictions or with a history of social theory that consists of mutually exclusive emphases on society and the individual, like a pendulum whose every swing in one direction necessitates an opposite swing of equal amplitude.

Ultimately these intellectual impulses led me to my interpretation of Weber's work. It seems to me that Weber promises an end to that swing of the pendulum. He offers an anti-utopian view of the social world that is nevertheless open to its possibilities of development. Karl Loewith put it admirably when he wrote some two generations ago, "Even the extreme casuistry of [Weber's] conceptual definitions in *Economy and Society* has not only the meaning to capture and determine reality in definitions, but, at the same time and above all, the opposite meaning of an open system of possibilities" ("Marx and Weber," in *Gesammelte Abhandlungen* [Stuttgart: W. Kohlhammer, 1968], p. 66). Weber's approach does not lead to a benign view of the human condition, nor does he have all the answers. But his definitions of human action encompass with equal emphasis our quest for subjective meaning and our compliance with the expectations of others. His definitions of class and status group do the same for our acquisitiveness and our quest for honor and power over others. His definitions of morality do the same for actions guided by a sense of responsibility for the outcome and those guided by a surpassing conviction that disregards all questions of consequences. Indeed his writings reveal polarities of this kind so repeatedly that I have come to think of them as the theoretical core of his work. This conceptual device is ancient and not confined to the Western tradition. But in Weber's hands it acquires two meanings that have been of special importance to me.

One of these meanings consists in a comparative historical perspective not only as a methodological device but also as a view of the individual and society. Every human achievement, every social fact or historical situation, allows a conceptual formulation only by emphasizing certain attributes while neglecting or excluding others. Hence every formulation bears within it the seeds of its own destruction—a phrase I borrow from Marx and apply at the conceptual level, a practice he would not have condoned. Accordingly, the study of the individual and society cannot rest content with the observation of any one set of facts without at least noting their cultural, chronological, and other limitations. Sooner or later such limitations will provoke contrary tendencies, what has been conceptually excluded will reassert itself, and new constellations will become the focus of attention.

What I have said here of conceptual formulations applies to intellectual positions more generally. I think Weber might have agreed, but I just do not know. Every intellectual position exacts a price that must be paid; for every insight gained certain other insights are foregone, left out, or underemphasized. Something like that is at work in Weber's casuistry, his anti-utopian position, and his use of comparative historical materials in preserving a sense of the indeterminacy of the human condition. (In other contexts I have called this indeterminacy the fallacy of retrospective determinism, which underscores that any outcome is caused but that we know the cause even approximately only by hindsight.) The price Weber paid for his indeterminacy—his openness to human possibilities revealed by his casuistry and by his comparative panorama of man in history—is that his scholarly work is a rather poor guide to positive ideals of political structure: note his emphasis that to him political questions are problems of institutional technique. Note also his comment that no sociological definition of the state can be substantive (he says the definition must be formulated in terms of administrative organization) because such a definition would imply specific policies, whereas history shows that states have pursued all kinds of policies, including the most contradictory ones.

But if Weber was a poor guide, then this limitation is also associated with one of his great strengths—the dialectic character of his types of domination, as of the paired concepts mentioned earlier. What has been said earlier is an interpretation of bureaucracy that shows how this concept can be specifically suited to the comparative studies that are central to Weber's work.

Weber points out that he has the specifically modern form of administration in mind. Consequently bureaucracy is initially limited to Western Europe and particularly to Prussia, all the more so as he understands this kind of administration as the executive organ of legal authority. The purpose of this historically limited concept is to contrast it with other forms of administration, such as Weber described in his analysis of Chinese bureaucracy. However, Weber's definition of bureaucracy appears in categorical form, which seems to suggest its general applicability. How can this general claim be reconciled with the historical limitation of the concept? I maintain that Weber's concept (the general claim) also contains a dialectical element (the historical dimension).

The well-known formulation seems to present bureaucracy as an "iron cage." Each administrative position is precisely circumscribed by its official duties, a position in a hierarchy, a salary fixed by contract, full-time employment, and so forth. All functions of bureaucratic work seem to be fixed, and yet Weber allows an element of uncertainty to enter into even this cage. That element is the technical qualification of the official. Technical and bureaucratic qualifications mean that one has to rely on the experience and good judgment of the qualified official— despite the many examinations and controls. The same is true of experts in any other context. The sense of specialized qualification lies in the expertise the layman can use to his benefit only through consultation or employment of a certified professional. Weber stresses the discrepancy between expert officials and political laymen. He also points out that technically qualified officials can make a secret out of their knowledge to avoid unpleasant or inappropriate controls. Technical qualification means not only technical know-how but also knowledge of official forms, procedures, appeal channels, and precedents—all things to which the official has ready access and which can easily degenerate into a special technique of bureaucratic abuse. Thus at the center of Weber's concept of bureaucracy lies an element of uncertainty, which lends itself to specific investigation, as that is the only way we can come to grips with the different meanings of the concept even *within* the European cultural sphere, let alone outside the Western orbit.

Having examined the dialectical use of a key concept in Weber's work, I want to comment on its anti-utopian orientation. Fascism and communism are two versions of the utopian mentality. However dissimilar in ideology, both assume that men and society are subject to total manipulation. If either racial identity or the organization of production is the ultimate determinant of history, then whoever controls those factors is capable of directing history. In both cases the consequences of utopia have been so abhorrent that I, for one, have come away with a fundamental distrust of utopianism. To my mind, Weber's conceptual polarities provide a block against utopian tendencies without downgrading the consideration of alternatives. Such considerations are essential, for this world is obviously not the best of all possible worlds, but neither is it the worst. Differences between democracy and a one-party dictatorship, between a technology used for benign or malignant ends, make a fundamental difference in our lives, even though many defects remain associated both with democracy and benign technology. But there is a genuine choice between a careful consideration of those differences, on one hand, and a summation of all real defects into one apocalyptic vision, on the other. Utopians set so high a goal for the future that nothing present is worth preserving, and it is this all-or-nothing posture that Weber's approach condemns as self-defeating. For if every human condition has limits and invites or provokes countervailing tendencies, then a utopian society is one with limits and hence without alternatives. Weber's whole work shows (though not in so many words) that a society without limits is not a possible human achievement, though he himself notes that aiming for the impossible is sometimes needed to achieve the possible. The point is that utopians militate against the possible by demanding the impossible as the only *rational* course in a totally *irrational* world. Weber's work means to me that it is more human and more predictable to continue to struggle with the imperfections of rationality, that this attitude keeps open more chances for individual choice compared with the prospects of unremitting manipulation. It is, for all that, a sober view of the human condition, one that anticipates adversity, and Weber would not have it otherwise. Sixty-five years after his death, who can honestly say that he was mistaken?

Yet in stating what Weber's work has meant to me and that it has been my inspiration for books like *Work and Authority in Industry* (1956), *Nation-Building and Citizenship* (1964), and *Kings or People* (1978), I have perhaps lost sight of my theme. For while I have traced how I became an American sociologist, I cannot be sure of how American a sociologist I have become. But then American sociology is a capacious mansion, and a hospitable one at that. In external terms my question does not make good sense. I have had a creative career at the universities of Chicago and California (not counting brief interludes elsewhere), and my published work has received its fair share of critical and appreciative appraisal. In earlier years I served on the Council of the American Sociological Association, was elected its vice president and then its president, and have served in various other capacities connected with the profession. Yet these are not the only terms in which that question can be asked, nor is it likely that I am a good judge in these matters. It would be inconsistent with the self-scrutiny I consider essential were I to omit the question, however vague and unanswerable it may be.

The year 1984 was not only the year of Orwell's famous book; it was also the three hundredth anniversary of the Mennonite emigration from Krefeld, Germany, to Pennsylvania. On that occasion I participated in three meetings devoted to a study of German emigration to North America. Even after a forty-five-year residence in this country of immigrants, I was (and am) still conscious in many ways of being an immigrant myself. When I began my studies at the University of Chicago, I was old enough to make use of what I found stimulating in the history of German thought, and although these interests have broadened in the interim, they have remained an active ingredient in my work. A whole industry of Weber interpreters has developed in the United States since I published my book on Weber more than twenty-five years ago; other German immigrants have taken a hand in making his oeuvre accessible to American readers after Frank Knight and Talcott Parsons did their pioneering work almost two generations ago. And there are now a good many American sociologists who have taken their inspiration from Weber's writings in one way or another. Perhaps I have helped alter the intellectual climate of sociology in this country, but that change might have come about in any case. The United States as a conscious world power is more hospitable to a comparative study of societies than the United States of the immediate post-Depression years when I arrived here. But whatever my contribution or influence may have been in the eyes of American scholars, the one thing I know is that European scholars look at my writings, including my book on Weber, as the work of an American sociologist. I am content to live with such ambiguities.

Index

Community Studies, Inc., 61
Comparative perspective, 428, 472
Computers, 345n.21
Comte, Auguste, xvi, 54
Conant, James B., 27
Concepts and Indices Project, 100, 101
Congress, U.S., 343n.5, 347n.29, 357, 376, 466
Connecticut, 17
Connecticut Yankee in King Arthur's Court (Twain), 24
Connolly, Janet, 182
Conrad, Joseph, 216
Conscience directed, vs. other directed, 59
"Consciousness-for-itself," 176
Constitution, U.S., 33–34, 47, 337
Consulting, 274–76
Contemporary Jewish Record, 198, 200, 208
Contemporary Social Problems (Merton & Nisbet), 84–85
Contemporary Sociology, xiv
Contemporary Tasks of Sociology (Mannheim), 397
Contextualization, 153, 158
Continuities in Social Research (Merton & Lazarsfeld), 90
Conversations with Eckermann (Goethe), 28
Cook County Jail, 225, 226, 227, 229
Cooley, Charles Horton, 6
Coolidge, Shepley, Bullfinch, and Abbott (architects), 29
Cooper, James Fenimore, 434
Cooperatives, 256–57
Cornell University, 168–84 passim
Coser, Lewis, 72n.36, 73n.40, 81, 112, 196
Coser, Rose Laub, 73n.40, 81, 112, 358
Costain, Thomas B., 216
Cottrell, Leonard, Jr., 64
Council for a Livable World, 71n.32
Council for Democracy, 48
Council of Economic Advisors, 357
Counterculture: Berger and, xiii–xiv, 162, 163; Roth and, 405. *See also* Hippies; Student movements
Courtship, 312, 372. *See also* Love affairs
Craig, Paul, 178
Crawford, David, 174
Crawford, Richard, 174
Creativity: Marx and, 270–71; Riesman's mother and, 24, 25
Cressey, Donald R., ix–x, xxiv, xxvi, 235–59
Cressey, Paul, 235

Criminology, 235, 236, 237, 240, 256, 258
Crimson, 26, 27, 29–30, 34
Critical theory, 397, 400–401, 405. *See also* Frankfurt school
Critique of Pure Reason (Kant), 459
Cuban missile crisis, 175
Cuddihy, John, xxiii
Culler, Jonathan, 188
Cultural anthropology, 10
Cultural History of Modernity (Friedell), 395
Culture-and-personality school, 207
Culture of Public Problems (Gusfield), 124, 125
Culture: Berger on, xiv–xv, xxi–xxiii, 162, 163; Gans and, xxi, xxv, 432–33, 434, 435, 439–42, 443, 444–46, 448, 450n.9, 451n.22; Gusfield on, 122; high, 432–33, 434, 442, 443–44, 446; Rosenblum and, 285–86, 293, 295, 296n.1; taste, xxi–xxiii, 432, 433, 441, 443, 444–45; van den Berghe and, 414, 416, 426. *See also* Biases; Counterculture; Popular culture, American; Relativism, cultural
Cunliffe, Marcus, 70n.25
Curtis, Richard, 149
Cutright, Philips, 226
Czechoslovakia, 180

Dahlberg, Frances, 177
Darkness at Noon (Koestler), 11
Darmstadt, Germany, xxvi, 384–90, 394, 408n.7
Dartmouth, 100
Darwin, Charles/Darwinism, 6, 172, 354, 428
Data analysis, 95–96, 146
Davis, Allison, 61, 220
Davis, Fred, 188
Davis, James A., 136–37, 146, 225
Davis, Kingsley: Berger and, 157; Coleman and, 77, 78–79, 80, 81; Gagnon and, 231; Wrong and, 15–16
Dawkins, Richard, 428
Death, 317, 319. *See also* Holocaust; War
Death of Nora Ryan (Farrell), 146
Debs, Eugene V., 6, 326
Decatur, Illinois, 88, 91
Deceptive Distinctions (Epstein), 360, 361
Decline of the West (Spengler), 25, 395
Deely, John, 188
Defamation law, 48–49
Defensiveness, xv

Compositor: Huron Valley Graphics
Text: 10/13 Sabon
Display: Sabon
Printer: Princeton Univ. Press/Printers
Binder: Princeton Univ. Press/Printers